MW01621246

The Gothic Stained Glass
OF REIMS CATHEDRAL

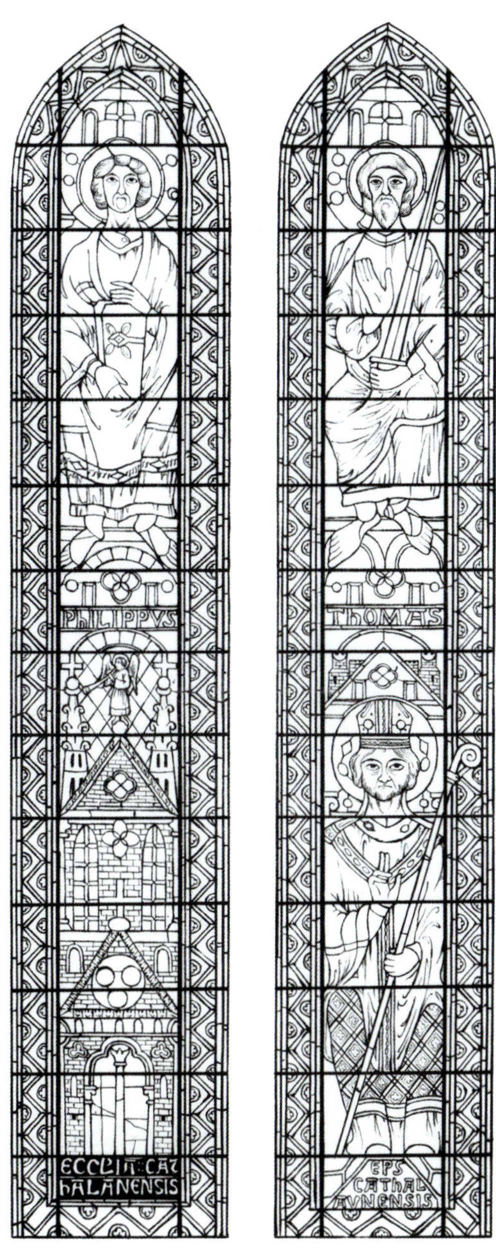

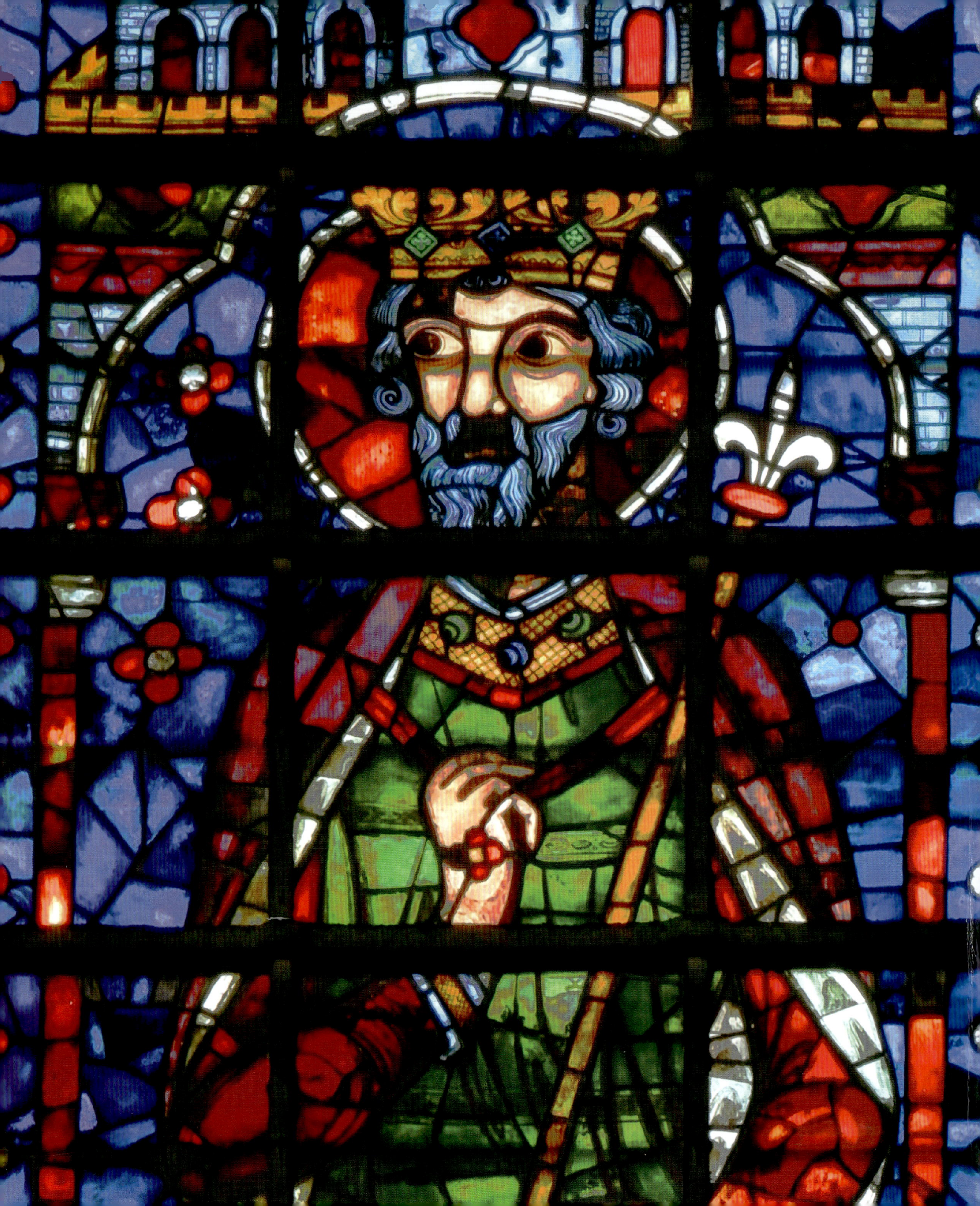

The Gothic Stained Glass
OF REIMS CATHEDRAL

MEREDITH PARSONS LILLICH

THE PENNSYLVANIA STATE UNIVERSITY PRESS
University Park, Pennsylvania

Frontispiece: King, originally in Bay 129, now in Bay 127, left lancet, lower row (photo: Painton Cowen).

Library of Congress Cataloging-in-Publication Data

Lillich, Meredith Parsons, 1932–
The Gothic Stained Glass of Reims Cathedral / Meredith Parsons Lillich.
p. cm.
Includes bibliographical references and index.
Summary: "Examines the stained-glass windows in the Gothic cathedral of Reims within the context of the evolution of the French monarchy and medieval art"—Provided by publisher.
ISBN 978-0-271-03777-6 (cloth : alk. paper)
1. Stained glass windows—France—Reims.
2. Glass painting and staining, Gothic—France—Reims.
3. Notre-Dame de Reims (Cathedral).
I. Title.

NK5349.R3L55 2011
748.50944′322—dc22
2010048476

Designed by Bessas & Ackerman, Guilford, CT
Printed in China by Everbest Printing Co., through Four Colour Imports, Louisville, KY
Published by The Pennsylvania State University Press, University Park, PA 16802-1003

The Pennsylvania State University Press is a member of the Association of American University Presses.

It is the policy of The Pennsylvania State University Press to use acid-free paper. Publications on uncoated stock satisfy the minimum requirements of American National Standard for Information Sciences—Permanence of Paper for Printed Library Material, ANSI Z39.48–1992.

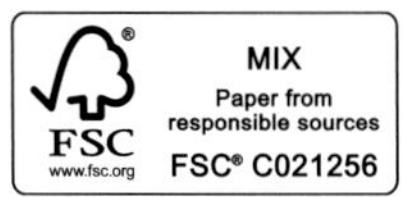

IN MEMORIAM

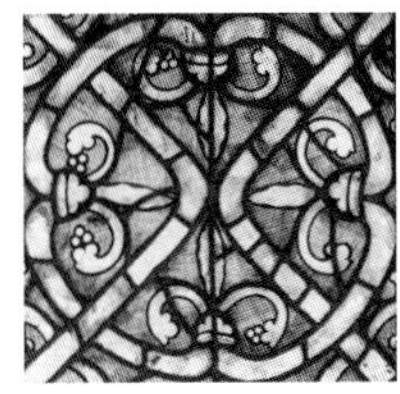

Senator J. William Fulbright
(1905–1995)

CONTENTS

List of Illustrations ix
Prolegomena xviii

CHAPTER I
Un Peu d'Histoire
1

CHAPTER 2
The Rosaces of the Chevet
17

CHAPTER 3
The Lancets of the Chevet
61

CHAPTER 4
The Transepts:
Grisailles, Roses, and *Belles Verrières*
105

CHAPTER 5
The Rosaces of the Nave
153

CHAPTER 6
The Lancets of the Nave
173

CHAPTER 7
The Glazing of the West Facade
211

Coda: *Comparanda*
237

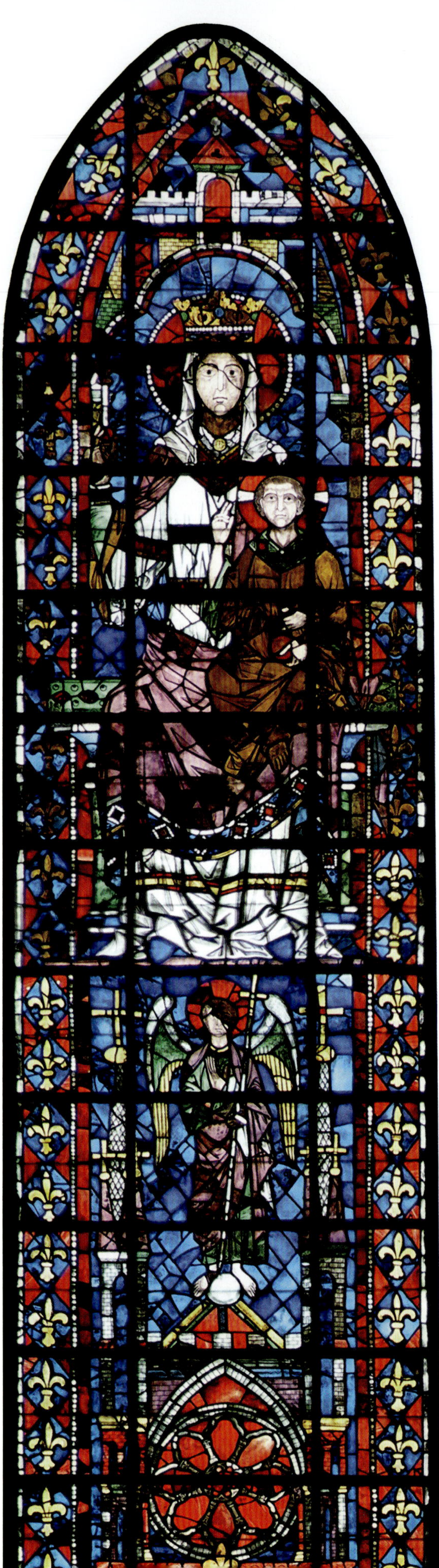

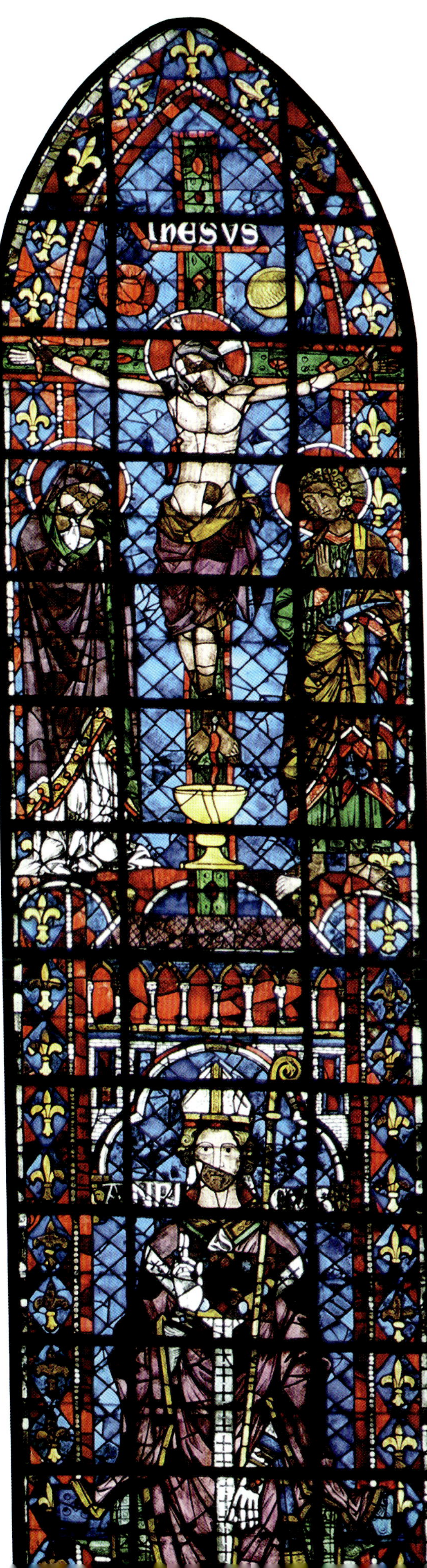

Appendix 1
Heresy in Champagne
241

Appendix 2
Genealogy of Archbishop
Henri de Braine
244

Appendix 3
Ogive Glass of Bays 100 Through 104
245

Appendix 4
The "Spanish Connection": Legends of the Apostle James, Translations by Pierre de Beauvais, and the Family of Archbishop Henri de Braine
247

Appendix 5
Pierre de Beauvais and the Bestiary
249

Appendix 6
King Solomon in Bed
(Song of Songs 3:7–8)
251

Appendix 7
Lectulus and *Ferculum*
(Song of Songs 3:7, 9)
260

Appendix 8
Two Seraphim Attributed to
Reims in U.S. Collections
263

Notes 265
Selected Bibliography 327
Index 331

Illustrations

1. Reims cathedral, view to east, showing the nave clerestories fully glazed. Postcard, before 1914.

2. Reims cathedral, view to west, showing the nave clerestories fully glazed. Postcard, before 1914.

3. Reims cathedral, the north nave: (left to right) Bays 135, 133, 131, 129 (after Kurmann, *La façade de la cathédrale de Reims*).

4. Reims cathedral, plan with Corpus Vitrearum bay numbers indicated (adapted after Kurmann, *La façade de la cathédrale de Reims*).

5. Reims cathedral, view to east, coronation of Louis XIV, 1654: [Jean] Le Paultre, *Seconde planche qui représente la grande cérémonie faite à l'autel, du sacre et du couronnement du Roy,* engraving, Reims, Bibl. mun., v II c GF 17 (photo: Reims, Bibliothèque municipale).

6. Reims cathedral, south flank, coronation of Louis XV, 1722: Antoine Danchet, *Le sacre de Louis XV, roy de France et de Navarre,* [Charles-Nicolas] Cochin [le père], engraving (photo: Bibliothèque nationale de France).

7. Bay 112, one of the grisailles colored with oil paints for the coronation of Charles X, 1825. Autochrome by Henri Deneux, 1915 (photo: Reims, Bibliothèque municipale, Fonds Deneux).

8. Clerestory of the hemicycle, 1840s: (left to right) Bays 103, 101, 100, 102, 104 (after Cahier and Martin, *Monographie de la cathédrale de Bourges*).

9. Clerestory of the straight chevet, 1840s: (left to right) Bays 107, 105, 106, 108 (after Cahier and Martin, *Monographie de la cathédrale de Bourges*).

10. Angel, left *écoinçon* of the west rose, detail (1881) (after Westlake, *A History of Design in Painted Glass*).

11. Ground pattern, Bay 122, left lancet (1881) (after Westlake, *A History of Design in Painted Glass*).

12. Medallion border, 1895 (after Olivier Merson, *Les vitraux*).

13. The Godhead with cruciferous halo, ogive over Bay 100: after a tracing by Paul Simon from the exterior, here reversed as it appears from the interior (after Simon, "Notes sur les vitraux").

14. Studio of Paul Simon during restoration of the west rose, 1910 (after Simon, *La grande rose*).

15. Tracings of thirteenth-century heads, Simon studio (after Orin E. Skinner, "Restoring the Stained Glass Treasures of Rheims Cathedral," *American Architect,* 1927).

16. Angel with the crown of thorns, detail from the lobe installed in Bay 127 after 1918. Tracing by Paul Simon from the exterior, here reversed as it appears from the interior (after Orin E. Skinner, "Restoring the Stained Glass Treasures of Rheims Cathedral," *American Architect,* 1927).

17. Reims, Porte de Mars, castle of Archbishop Henri de Braine (after Geruzez, *Description historique et statistique de la ville de Reims*).

18. Seating arrangement of the eleven suffragan bishops at provincial councils, established by Henri de Braine in 1231: [Jacques] Dassonneuille, engraving (after Marlot, taken from Geruzez, *Description historique et statistique de la ville de Reims*).

19. The north nave: (left to right) Bays 137, 135, 133, 131, 129, 127, etc. Photo by Abbé Remy Thinot before February 1915 showing initial war damage (after Maurice Landrieux, *The Cathedral of Reims: The Story of a German Crime*).

20. Ascension of Christ, Bay 39, rosace, central roundel (photo: Ministère de la Culture/Médiathèque du Patrimoine, Dist. RMN/Art Resource, N.Y.).

21. Architect, Bay 39, rosace, left lobe (photo: Ministère de la Culture/Médiathèque du Patrimoine, Dist. RMN/Art Resource, N.Y.).

22. Architect, Bay 39, rosace, left lobe: tracing by Paul Simon (after Louis Demaison, *La cathédrale de Reims,* 1913).

23. Heads in a panel of fragments collected during World War I, detail (photo: Isabella Stewart Gardner Museum, Boston).

24. Bay 100, rosace, the Passion (photo: Henri de Feraudy).

25. Flagellation, Bay 100, rosace, detail of bottom right lobe (photo: Lucien Mary).

26. Poitiers cathedral, bay 0, ca. 1165–70 (photo: Henri de Feraudy).

27. Chart of the chevet subjects, indicating the order of scenes in the lobes of the rosaces (measured drawings with kind permission of Jürgen Michler, after "Fenster- und Masswerksysteme in der nordfranzösischen Gotik des 13. Jahrhunderts," *Wallraf-Richartz Jahrbuch* 62 [2001]: 72, fig. 4).

28. Bay 101, ogive, Christ blessing (photo: Lucien Mary).

29. Bay 101, rosace, chart of scenes: Paul and James Major.

30. Bay 101, rosace, Paul and James Major (photo: Henri de Feraudy).

31. Paul preaching, Bay 101, rosace, detail of lower right lobe (photo: Lucien Mary).

32. Christ giving James Major a baton half stripped of bark: Le Mans cathedral, bay 111, detail, ca. 1254 (photo: Henri de Feraudy).

33. Bay 102, rosace, chart of scenes: Peter and Andrew.

34. Bay 102, rosace, Peter and Andrew (photo: Henri de Feraudy).

35. Crucifixion of Peter: Lyon cathedral, bay 7, detail of rosace, ca. 1190 (photo: Henri de Feraudy).

36. Andrew's hymn of praise to the cross, Bay 102, rosace, top right lobe (photo: Painton Cowen).

37. Crucifixion of Andrew: Lyon cathedral, bay 7, detail of rosace, ca. 1190.

38. Bay 104, rosace, chart of scenes: John the Evangelist and James the Less.

39. Bay 104, rosace, John the Evangelist and James the Less (photo: Henri de Feraudy).

40. John writing his Gospel, Bay 104, rosace, central roundel (1930) (photo: Henri Deneux; Ministère de la Culture/Médiathèque du Patrimoine/Dist. RMN/Art Resource, N.Y.).

41. John in the vat of boiling oil: Le Mans cathedral, bay 111, detail, ca. 1255–65 (photo: Henri de Feraudy).

42. John drinking from the poison cup, Bay 104, rosace, lower left lobe (1930) (photo: Henri Deneux; Ministère de la Culture/Médiathèque du Patrimoine/Dist. RMN/Art Resource, N.Y.).

43. John climbing into his tomb, Bay 104, rosace, top left lobe (1930) (photo: Henri Deneux; Ministère de la Culture/Médiathèque du Patrimoine/Dist. RMN/Art Resource, N.Y.).

44. John climbing into his tomb: Saint-Julien-du-Sault, bay 3, detail, ca. 1240–50 (photo: Henri de Feraudy).

45. James the Less, bishop of Jerusalem, and his cathedral facade, Bay 104, rosace, mid right lobe (1930) (photo: Henri Deneux; Ministère de la Culture/Médiathèque du Patrimoine/Dist. RMN/Art Resource, N.Y.).

46. James the Less preaching from the temple roof, Bay 104, rosace, lower right lobe (1930) (photo: Henri Deneux; Ministère de la Culture/Médiathèque du Patrimoine/Dist. RMN/Art Resource, N.Y.).

47. James the Less beaten with a fuller's club, Bay 104, rosace, top right lobe (1930) (photo: Henri Deneux; Ministère de la Culture/Médiathèque du Patrimoine/Dist. RMN/Art Resource, N.Y.).

48. Bay 103, rosace, chart of scenes: Thomas and Philip.

49. Bay 103, rosace, Thomas and Philip (photo: Henri de Feraudy).

50. The king and queen at the wedding feast, Bay 103, rosace, mid right lobe (photo: Lucien Mary).

51. Bay 103, rosace, showing Thomas's heavenly palace in the central roundel (before 1914) (after Cahier and Martin, *Monographie de la cathédrale de Bourges*).

52. Bay 106, rosace, chart of scenes: Bartholomew and Simon.

53. Bay 106, rosace, Bartholomew and Simon (photo: Henri de Feraudy).

54. The flaying of Bartholomew, Bay 106, rosace, central roundel (photo: Lucien Mary).

55. Simon destroys the idol of the sun, Bay 106, rosace, lower right lobe (photo: Lucien Mary).

56. Bay 105, rosace, chart of scenes: Matthew and Jude.

57. Bay 105, rosace, Matthew and Jude (photo: Henri de Feraudy).

58. The magicians Zaroës and Arfaxat send two dragons to attack a man, Bay 105, rosace, top right lobe (photo: Lucien Mary).

59. Matthew puts the dragons to sleep, Bay 105, rosace, mid right lobe (photo: Lucien Mary).

60. Simon and Jude before Varvardach, Jude addressing him, Bay 105, rosace, top left lobe (photo: Lucien Mary).

61. Bay 108, rosace, chart of scenes: Matthias.

62. Bay 108, rosace, Matthias (photo: Henri de Feraudy).

63. Bay 107, rosace, chart of scenes: Barnabas.

64. Bay 107, rosace, Barnabas (photo: Henri de Feraudy).

65. Bay 107, rosace, top right lobe and central lozenge. Tracings by Paul Simon from the exterior, here reversed as they appear from the interior (after Simon, "Notes sur les vitraux").

66. Barnabas and the old Cypriot widow, Bay 107, rosace, top left lobe (photo: Lucien Mary).

67. Barnabas seized by a Jew, Bay 107, rosace, lower left lobe (photo: Lucien Mary).

68. Lancets of the chevet, from the vaults (photo: Lucien Mary).

69. Bay 100 (photo: Henri de Feraudy).

70. Archbishop Henri de Braine, Bay 100, right lancet, lower row (photo: Henri de Feraudy).

71. "Facade" of Reims, Bay 100, left lancet, lower row (photo: Henri de Feraudy).

72. Angel on the Reims "facade" holding an archbishop's cross-staff, Bay 100, middle of the left lancet (photo: Henri de Feraudy).

73. Bay 101 (photo: Henri de Feraudy).

74. Paul, Bay 101, right lancet, top row. Autochrome by Henri Deneux, 1915 (photo: Reims, Bibliothèque municipale, Fonds Deneux).

75. Duck-monster, socle beneath the feet of James Major, Bay 101, left lancet, top row (photo: Henri de Feraudy).

76. Border of acanthus and quasi-naturalistic leaves, Bay 101 (1881) (after Westlake, *A History of Design in Painted Glass*).

77. James Major, Bay 101, left lancet, top row. Tracing by Paul Simon from the exterior, here reversed as it appears from the interior (after Orin E. Skinner, "Restoring the Stained Glass Treasures of Rheims Cathedral").

78. Paul, Bay 101, right lancet, top row. Tracing by Paul Simon (after Marcel Aubert, *Le vitrail en France*).

79. Bay 102 (photo: Henri de Feraudy).

80. Peter, Bay 102, left lancet, top row. Autochrome by Henri Deneux, 1915 (photo: Reims, Bibliothèque municipale, Fonds Deneux).

81. Bishop and "facade" of Soissons, Bay 102, lower row (photo: Henri de Feraudy).

82. Andrew, Bay 102, right lancet, top row. Tracing by Paul Simon from the exterior, here reversed as it appears from the interior (after Skinner, "Restoring the Stained Glass Treasures of Rheims Cathedral").

83. Bishop of Soissons, Bay 102, left lancet, lower row. Tracing by Paul Simon from the exterior, here reversed as it appears from the interior (after Simon, "Notes sur les vitraux").

84. Bay 103 (photo: Henri de Feraudy).

85. Bay 103, drawing by Ferdinand de Lasteyrie, ca. 1850 (after Lasteyrie, *Histoire de la peinture sur verre*).

86. Bay 104 (photo: Henri de Feraudy).

87. Angel blowing an oliphant on the "facade" of Beauvais, Bay 104, mid right lancet (photo: Lucien Mary).

88. The architect Jean d'Orbais, detail of the labyrinth of Reims: drawing by Jacques Cellier (after Robert Branner, "Jean d'Orbais and the Cathedral of Reims").

89. Enthroned figure on the "Saracen's Tomb," detail of the album of Villard d'Honnecourt (after Jean-Baptiste-Antoine Lassus, *Album de Villard de Honnecourt*).

90. Bay 105 (photo: Henri de Feraudy).

91. Telamon, Bay 105, mid left lancet (photo: Lucien Mary).

92. Border of abstract foliage, Bay 105 (1881) (after Westlake, *A History of Design in Painted Glass*).

93. Bay 106 (photo: Henri de Feraudy).

94. Telamon kings, Bay 106, mid left lancet (photo: Lucien Mary).

95. Bay 107 (photo: Henri de Feraudy).

96. Border of abstract foliage, Bay 107 (1881) (after Westlake, *A History of Design in Painted Glass*).

97. Bay 108 (photo: Henri de Feraudy).

98. Unidentified bishop, wearing archbishop's pallium! Bay 108, left lancet, lower row (photo: Lucien Mary).

99. Bay 109 (photo: Henri de Feraudy).

100. Bay 110 (photo: Henri de Feraudy).

101. Unidentified disciple, Bay 110, right lancet, top row. Autochrome by Henri Deneux, 1915 (photo: Reims, Bibliothèque municipale, Fonds Deneux).

102. View from the north to the south transept: (left to right) Bays 111, 110, and south rose (with twentieth-century glazing) (photo: J. Feuillie; Ministère de la Culture/Médiathèque du Patrimoine/Dist. RMN/Art Resource, N.Y.).

103. Chart of the grisailles in the eight transept bays, indicating whether their paired lancets contain the same or different patterns.

104. Grisaille patterns, drawings by Henri Deneux, 1925: Bay 114, lower right; Bay 117, left lancet, lower left; Bay 117, right lancet, top left; Bay 119, top right (photo: Ministère de la Culture/Médiathèque du Patrimoine/Dist. RMN/Art Resource, N.Y.).

105. Bay 112, detail (photo: Lucien Mary).

106. Bay 120, left lancet, detail (photo: Henri Deneux; Ministère de la Culture/Médiathèque du Patrimoine/Dist. RMN/Art Resource, N.Y.).

107. Bay 111, right lancet, detail, 1945 (photo: Ministère de la Culture/Médiathèque du Patrimoine/Dist. RMN/Art Resource, N.Y.).

108. Bay 113, left lancet, detail, 1945 (photo: Ministère de la Culture/Médiathèque du Patrimoine/Dist. RMN/Art Resource, N.Y.).

109. Bay 113, right lancet, detail, 1945 (photo: Ministère de la Culture/Médiathèque du Patrimoine/Dist. RMN/Art Resource, N.Y.).

110. Bay 120, right lancet, detail, 1945 (photo: Ministère de la Culture/Médiathèque du Patrimoine/Dist. RMN/Art Resource, N.Y.).

111. North rose (photo: Henri de Feraudy).

112. North rose, panel numbering, adapted from the system used by the atelier Simon.

113. North rose, present locations, since the 1872 restoration, of medieval panels; medallions created in 1872 are indicated by hatched lines.

114. North rose, reconstruction of the original panel locations, based on pre-1872 witnesses.

115. North rose: Creation of Eve (A-3); Expulsion from Paradise (originally C-3, now I-3). Lithograph of tracings by Paul Simon ca. 1875–86 (photo: Reims, Bibliothèque municipale, Fonds Jadart).

116. North rose, medallions with surrounding diaper ornament: above, A-9 (God as Logos); below, A-3 (scene garbled, cf. fig. 115) (after Victor Tourneur, *Histoire et description des vitraux*).

117. Genesis cycle in the archivolt framing the north rose, 1919 (photo: François Rothier; after Paul Vitry, *La cathédrale de Reims*).

118. North rose, upper left quadrant: L-3, K-9 and K-3, J-3 (photo: Jacques Philippot; Région Champagne-Ardenne).

119. Cain murdering Abel (north rose, G-3) (photo: Jacques Philippot; Région Champagne-Ardenne).

120. North rose: basic coloration of the diaper ornament, containing green cross.

121. The Creator surrounded by angels, the sun, and the moon (north rose, central rosette) (photo: Henri de Feraudy).

122. Adam digging (north rose, originally I-3, now E-3) (photo: Henri de Feraudy).

123. Sacrifice of Abel (north rose, H-3) (photo: Henri de Feraudy).

124. God cursing Cain (north rose, F-3) (photo: Henri de Feraudy).

125. Eve spinning with Cain in her lap (north rose, D-3) (photo: Henri de Feraudy).

126. Woman nursing infant, here identified as Eve nursing Abel (originally E-3, now in the ogive over the north rose) (photo: Lucien Mary).

127. North rose: caladrius and phoenix (originally J-9, now K-9); fish and eel (originally E-9, now H-9). Lithograph of tracings by Paul Simon ca. 1875–86 (photo: Reims, Bibliothèque municipale, Fonds Jadart).

128. Caladrius. Pierre de Beauvais's bestiary, long version (Paris, Arsenal 3516), fol. 199v (photo: Bibliothèque nationale de France).

129. Griffin (north rose, originally K-9, now J-9) (photo: Henri de Feraudy).

130. Caladrius and phoenix (north rose, originally J-9, now K-9) (photo: Henri de Feraudy).

131. Crane (north rose, originally I-9, now D-9) (photo: Henri de Feraudy).

132. Fish and eel (north rose, originally E-9, now H-9) (photo: Henri de Feraudy).

133. Ox and ass (north rose, originally F-9, now I-9) (photo: Henri de Feraudy).

134. Stag, dog, and wild goat (north rose, originally H-9, now E-9) (photo: Painton Cowen).

135. Bestiary creatures: griffin, caladrius, phoenix, crane, stag, wild goat. Pierre de Beauvais's bestiary, long version (Paris, Arsenal 3516). Drawings, ca. 1850 (after Charles Cahier and Arthur Martin, *Mélanges d'archéologie, d'histoire et de littérature,* vol. 2, 1851).

136. Temptation and Fall. "L'estoire d'Adan" (Paris, Arsenal 3516), fol. 4r (photo: Bibliothèque nationale de France).

137. Expulsion from Paradise. "L'estoire d'Adan" (Paris, Arsenal 3516), fol. 4v (photo: Bibliothèque nationale de France).

138. Adam digging and Eve spinning. "L'estoire d'Adan" (Paris, Arsenal 3516), fol. 5r (photo: Bibliothèque nationale de France).

139. Eve's maternity; Sacrifice of Cain and Abel. "L'estoire d'Adan" (Paris, Arsenal 3516), fol. 5r (photo: Bibliothèque nationale de France).

140. Cain murdering Abel; God cursing Cain. "L'estoire d'Adan" (Paris, Arsenal 3516), fol. 5v (photo: Bibliothèque nationale de France).

141. South rose (lost). Glazing of 1581 by Nicolas Dérodé; drawing by Ferdinand de Lasteyrie, ca. 1850 (after Lasteyrie, *Histoire de la peinture sur verre*).

142. Exterior of south rose: Ecclesia, Synagoga, eleven apostles, and Old Testament figures (archivolt above) (photo: Hirmer Fotoarchiv, Munich).

143. Châlons-en-Champagne, cathedral, north rose, ca. 1255–60 (photo: Jean Feuillie; Ministère de la Culture/Médiathèque du Patrimoine/Dist. RMN/Art Resource, N.Y.).

144. Châlons cathedral, north rose, chart of subjects (after Paul Lucot, *Les verrières de la cathédrale de Châlons, église Saint-Étienne,* 1907).

145. Reims cathedral, plan with reconstruction of the original project conserving Archbishop Samson's twelfth-century facade (after Kurmann, *La façade de la cathédrale de Reims*).

146. Bay 118 (1915) (photo: Henri Deneux; Ministère de la Culture/Médiathèque du Patrimoine/Dist. RMN/Art Resource, N.Y.).

147. Bay 118, left lancet: John the Baptist; an archbishop-saint here identified as St. Remi (photo: Stewart Henry Rosenberg).

148. Bay 118, right lancet: Virgin and Child; "facade" of Reims cathedral (photo: Stewart Henry Rosenberg).

149. St. Remi, Bay 118, left lancet, lower row. Autochrome by Henri Deneux, 1915 (photo: Reims, Bibliothèque municipale, Fonds Deneux).

150. "Facade" of Reims cathedral, Bay 118, right lancet, lower row. Autochrome by Henri Deneux, 1915 (photo: Reims, Bibliothèque municipale, Fonds Deneux).

151. John the Baptist, Bay 118, left lancet, top row, detail (photo: Stewart Henry Rosenberg).

152. Reims, abbey church of Saint-Remi, facade (photo: Stewart Henry Rosenberg).

153. Two possible reconstructions of the glazing of Archbishop Samson's facade, Reims cathedral, ca. 1220.

154. Second seal of the abbey of Saint-Remi, Reims, put into use in 1219. Document of Archives nationales,

Paris: Douët-d'Arcq, Supplément no. 2153 (photo: Atelier photographique des Archives nationales).

155. First seal of the Reims cathedral chapter, in use ca. 1155–60. Archives dépt. de la Marne, annexe Reims, 2 g 422 (pièce 7), 1192 (photo: Virginie Aréthens; Archives départementales de la Marne).

156. Second seal of the Reims cathedral chapter, in use ca. 1200. Document of Archives nationales, Paris: Douët-d'Arcq no. 7289, ca. 1220 (photo: Atelier photographique des Archives nationales).

157. Seal of officiality of Hugues de Bourgogne, grand archdeacon of Reims cathedral, 1218–25. Archives dépt. de la Marne, annexe Reims, 56 H 175 (pièce 1), 1221 (photo: Virginie Aréthens; Archives départementales de la Marne).

158. Seal of the Reims cathedral chapter, *sede vacante,* probably in use in 1202. Document of Archives nationales, Paris: Douët-d'Arcq no. 7012, 1244 (photo: Atelier photographique des Archives nationales).

159. Bay 121, rosace: King Solomon in Bed. Autochrome by Henri Deneux, 1915 (photo: Reims, Bibliothèque municipale, Fonds Deneux).

160. Reims cathedral, plan of the nave (adapted after Kurmann, *La façade de la cathédrale de Reims*).

161. Chart of the rosaces, nave clerestory.

162. Bay 122, rosace (photo: Reims, Bibliothèque municipale, Fonds Deneux).

163. Bay 123, rosace: nimbed, enthroned bishop; censing angels (photo: Stewart Henry Rosenberg).

164. Bay 124, rosace: the Judgment of Solomon. Autochrome by Henri Deneux, 1915 (photo: Reims, Bibliothèque municipale, Fonds Deneux).

165. Bay 125, rosace: enthroned bishop; four angels with candles and two with censers (photo: Stewart Henry Rosenberg).

166. Bay 126, rosace: the Last Judgment, Christ showing his wounds, four angels with oliphants, two with symbols of the Passion (photo: Stewart Henry Rosenberg).

167. Bay 127, rosace: Christ vested, enthroned, pointing up and down (that is, establishing the Church); Peter with keys and cross-staff (top right); angels, two of them vested as deacons (photo: Stewart Henry Rosenberg).

168. Bay 128, rosace: Virgin and Child, four angels with censers, two with candles (photo: Stewart Henry Rosenberg).

169. The Ordo of 1250 (Paris, BnF, lat. 1246), fol. 26r, detail. The peers of France hold the crown over the king's head; the king, surrounded by the peers, receives the kiss of the bareheaded archbishop (photo: Bibliothèque nationale de France).

170. Reconstruction of Solomon's bed from Hincmar's poem *In ferculum Salomonis* (after Burkhard Taeger, *Zahlensymbolik bei Hraban, bei Hincmar—und im "Heliand"? Studien zur Zahlensymbolik im Frühmittelalter*).

171. Coronation Book of Charles V, 1365 (London, Brit. Lib., Cotton Tiberius B.VIII), fol. 44v, detail. King Charles in the archbishop's palace, roused by the bishops of Laon and Beauvais (photo: The British Library Board).

172. Nimbed, enthroned bishop, Bay 123, rosace, central roundel, detail (photo: Lucien Mary).

173. Enthroned bishop, Bay 122, rosace, mid right lobe, detail (photo: Lucien Mary).

174. Christ showing his wounds, Bay 126, rosace, central roundel, detail (photo: Lucien Mary).

175. Christ establishing the Church, Bay 127, rosace, central roundel, detail (photo: Lucien Mary).

176. Bay 125 (photo: Henri de Feraudy).

177. Bay 125, montage of war damage, after 1918 (photo: Henri Deneux; Ministère de la Culture/Médiathèque du Patrimoine/Dist. RMN/Art Resource, N.Y.).

178. Bay 122: the archbishop-saints Donatianus and Viventius (photo: Henri de Feraudy).

179. Archbishop Donatianus. Bay 122, left lancet, lower row. Tracing by Paul Simon from the exterior, here reversed as it appears from the interior (after Simon, "Notes sur les vitraux").

180. Archbishop Viventius. Bay 122, right lancet, lower row (photo: Henri de Feraudy).

181. Bay 124: Archbishops Baruc and Barucius (photo: Henri de Feraudy).

182. Archbishop Baruc. Bay 124, left lancet, lower row. Autochrome by Henri Deneux, 1915 (photo: Reims, Bibliothèque municipale, Fonds Deneux).

183. Archbishop Barucius. Bay 124, right lancet, lower row (photo: Henri de Feraudy).

184. Bay 126: Archbishops Barnabas and Bennadius (photo: Henri de Feraudy).

185. Archbishop Barnabas. Bay 126, left lancet, lower row (photo: Henri de Feraudy).

186. King with bare sword. Bay 122, left lancet, top row (photo: Henri de Feraudy).

187. King on high-backed throne with animal heads at the sides. Bay 124, right lancet, top row (photo: Henri de Feraudy).

188. Bay 128: Karolvs (photo: Henri de Feraudy).

189. Bay 128, montage of war damage, after 1918 (photo: Henri Deneux; Ministère de la Culture/Médiathèque du Patrimoine/Dist. RMN/Art Resource, N.Y.).

190. Karolvs. Bay 128, right lancet, top row. Autochrome by Henri Deneux, 1915 (photo: Reims, Bibliothèque municipale, Fonds Deneux).

191. St. Remi, detail, mid–twelfth century. Reims, Saint-Remi, bay NtIIb (photo: Lucien Mary).

192. Bay 121 (photo: Henri de Feraudy).

193. King. Bay 121, left lancet, top row. Tracing by Paul Simon from the exterior, here reversed as it appears from the interior (after Simon, "Notes sur les vitraux").

194. Bay 123 (photo: Henri de Feraudy).

195. Archbishop. Bay 123, lower row (1881) (after Westlake, *A History of Design in Painted Glass*).

196. King. Bay 125, right lancet, top row. Autochrome by Henri Deneux, 1915 (photo: Reims, Bibliothèque municipale, Fonds Deneux).

197. Lion(?), socle beneath the feet of a king. Bay 121, right lancet, top row (photo: Painton Cowen).

198. Man, socle beneath the feet of an archbishop. Bay 123, right lancet, lower row (photo: Painton Cowen).

199. Reims cathedral, plan, after Jacques Cellier, 1583–87.

200. Bay 127. The two lower figures salvaged from Bays 129 and 130 (otherwise lost) (photo: Henri de Feraudy).

201. Bay 127 (1915). Autochrome by Henri Deneux (?), obtained from Lucien Mary.

202. Bay 129 (before 1914), now lost. Photo by François Rothier (after Arthur J. de Havilland Bushnell, *Storied Windows*).

203. King. Originally in Bay 129, right lancet, top row, replaced in Bay 127, left lancet, lower row. Watercolor by Paul Simon, before 1893, 15.7 × 9.6 cm, *Fragment d'un des quatre personnages de la sixième fenêtre, grande nef nord,* Reims, Bibl. mun., XV II a 27-BMR 14-036 (photo: Reims, Bibliothèque municipale).

204. King. Originally in Bay 129 and now in Bay 127, left lancet, lower row (photo: Henri de Feraudy).

205. Archbishop. Originally in Bay 130 and now in Bay 127, right lancet, lower row (photo: Henri de Feraudy).

206. Chart of the directions in which the nave figures face (those omitted cannot be established).

207. Chart of archbishops who do not bless (all others do, as far as can be established).

208. Chart of thrones.

209. Chart of archbishops wearing rationals and of archbishops holding cross-staffs (all others have croziers, as far as can be established).

210. Chart of figures with haloes and of figures waving.

211. Bay 131 (lost). Rosace has Virgin and Child; six censing angels. In the lancets, kings finger their mantle straps; nimbed archbishops hold closed books. Drawing by Leblan, before 1858 (photo: Reims, Bibliothèque municipale).

212. King, waving; archbishop, frontal, nimbed in red. Bay 132 (lost), left lancet, top row. Autochrome by Henri Deneux, 1915 (photo: Reims, Bibliothèque municipale, Fonds Deneux).

213. Border of fleurs-de-lis, Bay 132 (after Louis Ottin, *Le vitrail: Son histoire, ses manifestations à travers les âges et les peuples,* 1896).

214. King, waving. Bay 133 (lost), right lancet, top row. Autochrome by Henri Deneux, 1915 (photo: Reims, Bibliothèque municipale, Fonds Deneux).

215. Archbishop, blessing. Bay 133 (lost), left lancet, lower row. Autochrome by Henri Deneux, 1915 (photo: Reims, Bibliothèque municipale, Fonds Deneux).

216. Bay 134 (lost), 1915 (photo: Lucien Mary).

217. Archbishop, waving. Bay 134 (lost), right lancet, lower row. Autochrome by Henri Deneux, 1915 (photo: Reims, Bibliothèque municipale, Fonds Deneux).

218. Border of quasi-naturalistic leaves and berries, Bay 134 (after Louis Ottin, *Le vitrail: Son histoire, ses manifestations à travers les âges et les peuples*).

219. King, waving. Bay 135 (lost), left lancet, top row. Autochrome by Henri Deneux, 1915 (photo: Reims, Bibliothèque municipale, Fonds Deneux).

220. Archbishop, blessing. Bay 135 (lost). Tracing by Paul Simon, before 1911 (after Simon, "Notes sur les vitraux").

221. Border of lozenges, Bay 137 or 138? (before 1881) (after Westlake, *A History of Design in Painted Glass*).

222. Reims cathedral, interior of the west facade, 1845 (after Charles Nodier and Isidore Taylor, *Voyages pittoresques et romantiques dans l'ancienne France, Champagne*).

223. West facade, portals, 1654, engraving by Androuet du Cerceau, detail, Paris, BnF, Est., VA 51 (15) 1 fol-H134406 (photo: Bibliothèque nationale de France).

224. West facade, tympanum of the north portal, 1625: *Le somptueux frontispice de l'église Notre Dame de Reims, ville du Sacre,* engraving by Nicolas de Son, detail, Reims, Bibl. mun., x II a 15-BMR 9-323 (photo: Reims, Bibliothèque municipale).

225. West facade, tympanum of the central portal, 1625, showing the original glazing of the small rose: *Le somptueux frontispice de l'église Notre Dame de Reims, ville du Sacre,* engraving by Nicolas de Son, detail, Reims, Bibl. mun., x II a 15-BMR 9-323 (photo: Reims, Bibliothèque municipale).

226. West facade gallery, watercolors by Henri Deneux, 1914: (left to right) king and archbishop; aristocratic youth and archbishop; king and archbishop; aristocratic youth and archbishop; king. *Les vitraux de la cathédrale Notre Dame de Reims: Galerie du revers de la façade occidentale,* Reims, Bibl. mun., Fonds Deneux, L066–L070 (photo: Reims, Bibliothèque municipale).

227. King, west facade gallery, central lancet, detail (photo: Painton Cowen).

228. Aristocratic youth, west facade gallery, right side, detail (1881) (after Westlake, *A History of Design in Painted Glass*).

229. Grisaille (lost) of naturalistic foliage within fleurs-de-lis borders, probably from the western nave aisles, 1895 (after Olivier Merson, *Les vitraux*).

230. Bay 39, debris of grisaille and Castille borders, probably from Bays 139–40 (photo: author).

231. West rose (photo: Henri de Feraudy).

232. West rose, lower left quadrant (photo: Henri de Feraudy).

233. West rose, detail, 1857 (after Victor Tourneur, *Histoire et description des vitraux*).

234. West rose, detail, 1858 (after Jules Gailhabaud, *L'architecture du ve au xviie siècle*).

235. West rose, detail, 1895 (after Olivier Merson, *Les vitraux*).

236. Chart of the west rose, by Paul Simon (after Simon, *La grande rose*).

237. West rose. Amateur photo taken several hours after the 1886 hailstorm (after Paul Simon, *La grande rose*).

238. West rose and gallery, and Bay 139. Photo by Jacques Doucet, before 1914 (after Étienne Moreau-Nélaton, *La cathédrale de Reims*).

239. West rose and gallery, and Bay 139. Photo by Abbé Remy Thinot, before February 1915 (after Maurice Landrieux, *The Cathedral of Reims: The Story of a German Crime*).

240. Virgin of the Assumption, west rose, central medallion. Photo by François Rothier, before 1914 (after Louis Bréhier, *La cathédrale de Reims: Une oeuvre française*).

241. Christ in heaven holding the Virgin's soul, ogive over the west rose. Tracing made by Pierre Simon in 1853 (after Paul Simon, *La grande rose*).

242. West rose, tracings made in situ between 1875 and 1886: central medallion, 3A, 9A, 2D, 12D (after Paul Simon, *La grande rose*).

243. West rose, tracings made in situ between 1875 and 1886: 6A, 2B, 8B, 4C, 8C (after Paul Simon, *La grande rose*).

244. West rose, tracings made in situ between 1875 and 1886: left corner medallion, 6B, 10B, 11B, 12B (after Paul Simon, *La grande rose*).

245. Seraph (11C), west rose, tracing made in situ between 1875 and 1886 (after Paul Simon, *La grande rose*).

246. Seraph (7B), largely an early restoration, west rose, tracing made after the 1886 hailstorm (after Paul Simon, *La grande rose*).

247. West rose, tracings made after the 1886 hailstorm: 1A, 1B, 2C, 2D, 3C, 3D, 4B, 4D, 6C (after Paul Simon, *La grande rose*).

248. West rose, watercolors by Henri Deneux showing medallions 1A and 12A, 1914. *Les vitraux de la cathédrale Notre Dame de Reims,* Reims, Bibl. mun., Fonds Deneux, L072–L073 (photo: Reims, Bibliothèque municipale).

249. West rose, watercolors by Paul Simon of restored panels ca. 1910: 8B, 8C, 10D, and examples of both lancet grounds (after Simon, *La grande rose*).

250. West rose, watercolors by Paul Simon of restored panels ca. 1910: 2B, 4C, 5C, 10B, left corner medallion (after Simon, *La grande rose*).

251. Sculptures from the facade of the House of the Musicians, rue de Tambour, Reims, now in the Musée de Saint-Remi (after Aymar Verdier and François Cattois, *Architecture civile et domestique*).

252. Royal musicians, Reims cathedral, west facade, central portal (after Louis Bréhier, *La cathédrale de Reims: Une oeuvre française*).

253. Chart of the angels in the west rose, in Simon's reconstruction, 1909.

254. Strasbourg cathedral, reconstruction of glazing in the Romanesque nave, detail (after Fridtjof Zschokke, *Die romanischen Glasgemälde des Strassburger Münsters*).

255. King Solomon in Bed. Herrad of Landsberg, *Hortus Deliciarum,* fol. 204v, ca. 1175–85 (destroyed). Tracing copy made by Auguste de Bastard d'Estaing ca. 1840 (Paris, BnF, Est. Ad 144a Fol, pl. 85a, 1 [detail]) (after Sirarpie Der Nersessian, "Le lit de Salomon").

256. King Solomon in Bed. Homilies on the Virgin, by the monk Jacobus of Kokkinobaphos, Constantinople, ca. 1130 (Paris, BnF, gr. 1208), fol. 109v (after Sirarpie Der Nersessian, "Le lit de Salomon").

257. King Solomon in Bed. Moralized Bible, ca. 1235–45 (Paris, BnF, lat. 11560), fol. 77v, detail (after Alexandre de Laborde, *La Bible moralisée conservée à Oxford, Paris et Londres*).

258. Westminster, Painted Chamber. Conjectural view of the bed enclosure of the king's chamber, showing murals of the Coronation of St. Edward and one of the Guardians of Solomon's bed, ca. 1263–72 (after Paul Binski, *The Painted Chamber at Westminster*).

259. King Solomon in Bed. *Canticum canticorum* block book, ca. 1465 (Munich, Bayerische Staatsbibliothek, Xylograph 32), fol. 15v (after Adrien Jean Joseph Delen and M. Meertens, eds., *Canticum canticorum*).

Prolegomena

When Gioachino Rossini premiered his opera giocosa *Il viaggio a Reims* on June 19, 1825, King Charles X—for whom he had composed it—had been anointed and crowned for exactly three weeks. Charles's *sacre* in the Gothic cathedral of Reims was the final coronation seen there in a long series begun, as was the structure, in the thirteenth century. The interior of 1825 remained scarcely altered until the First World War (see figs. 1–2). And following the extensive repairs necessitated by that war, visitors still acclaim Reims cathedral's dazzling combination of lucidity, opulence, and grandeur.

The visitor to Reims first responds to the soaring height, what Whitney Stoddard called "the bigness of scale."[1] Reims is taller—and narrower—than Chartres. The breathtaking verticality is held in repose by the horizontal accents of the sculpted capitals and the triforium, as well as by the insistent linear grid of colonnettes and stringcourses (fig. 3). Regularity and consistency in the detailing impart clarity, elegance, and rhythm to the dynamic vertical thrust. The traceried windows are the most original element in this impressive interior. Two rows of windows, the aisle bays below and the clerestories above, all but eliminate wall surface. Each of these arched wall openings has tracery dividing it into paired lancets surmounted by a six-lobed rosette, the interstices between these elements also pierced for glazing. The repetitive doublet-and-rose design binds floor to high vault, while the enhanced dimensions of the clerestories—around fourteen meters tall[2]—contribute lightness to the rising space. This is a book about what other contributions these windows make.

Only the high windows are studiable. Well before 1825—by the mid–eighteenth century—the aisle bays had been stripped of their glazing, and no description exists of their subjects or even of formats. That is, we do not know whether the lower windows contained medallions, resembling Chartres or Bourges, or if any of them held grisailles combined with larger figures, as in the axial chapel of Auxerre.[3] Until 1914 the clerestories and the great rose windows survived in some form or reconstruction, and observers made notes and drawings of them. The glass that survived the war, and what was remade thereafter, benefited from the cataloging project of the French Corpus Vitrearum, published in Recensement IV in 1992.[4] The Recensement's very useful bay-numbering system has been adopted in this book (see fig. 4).

The heavy international publicity attendant upon the extensive restorations of the 1920s–30s discouraged scholarly interest in the stained glass of Reims. The brief overview provided in Hans Reinhardt's monograph of 1963 (see my bibliography), based though it was upon the repaired glazing, long remained unchallenged. The government archives left by Henri Deneux, architect of the repairs, have gradually become more accessible. In 1988—fifty years after the completion of his work—an appreciation was mounted in the form of an exhibition at Reims accompanied by a publication, *Rebâtir Reims: La collection photographique Henri Deneux 1870/1938,* edited by Isabelle Balsamo et al. And in 1995 one of Deneux's descendants donated to the Bibliothèque municipale de Reims a precious collection of fifty autochrome photographs detailing the windows, made following the initial bombardments of 1914. As Sylvie Balcon-Berry has made clear, these pioneer color images—while not all sharp or legible—nonetheless allow us to establish the precision and accuracy of the postwar restorations.[5] They are particularly valuable for the nave, where repairs were abandoned for the twelve bays most severely ruined (Bays 130 through 141). Only the clerestories in the four easternmost nave bays now contain stained glass; the blankglazing filling the remainder is a stark reminder of what has been lost.

The accuracy of the restorations was possible because the glazier Jacques Simon had at his disposal the collection of full-scale tracings and drawings assembled over decades by his grandfather Pierre and his father Paul Simon, previously in charge of the cathedral glass. Begun in 1848, these *frottis* were made directly from the surface of the glass. Paul Simon published several in 1911 (see my bibliography); a few more exist in copies in the Bibliothèque municipale de Reims.[6] These fragile and unwieldy documents have remained in private ownership. Their preservation has long been a concern, and they are finally being photographed.[7] Once they are preserved, inventoried, and digitalized, a volume on Reims cathedral under the auspices of the French Corpus Vitrearum should then be possible.

This book has a different purpose, sustained by the resources noted above as well as by careful reassessment of the evidence left by nineteenth-century witnesses. The subject programs of the Reims glass are the primary focus here, and they are considerably more complex and sophisticated than has been recognized. Their careful investigation is coordinated with current scholarship in the liturgy, historical documentation, physical environment of the cathedral close, archeology, and recent dendrochronology, with the goal of advancing our understanding of this great enterprise: the who, when, why, and how of it.

Chapter 1 provides an entry to these perspectives. Because the cathedral's subject programs are set forth in the rosaces crowning the lancets, chapter 2 discusses the iconographic importance and uniqueness of the apostles cycles in the chevet rosaces. They are the most complete ensemble since the mosaics of San Marco and emphasize the themes of Faith and Charity opposing Heresy and Avarice. Chapter 3 follows with the iconography and sequential production of the chevet lancets, the arguments based on program, timing of patronage, and style. The circle of archbishop and suffragan bishops in these lancets proclaims the themes of apostolic succession and the power of Ecclesia to combat the sins of disbelief and disobedience. Chapter 4 opens with the glazing of the transepts in grisaille, framing the high altar there. The north rose presents themes concerning the sinfulness of rebellion against God (and the clergy), while the lost south rose countered with the ultimate triumph of Ecclesia (and the clergy) at the end of time. This chapter concludes with an investigation of the images later inserted into the transept grisailles of Bay 118. I hypothesize that they are remnants of glazing added to the Romanesque west facade about 1220 and then redeployed to Bay 118 above the repositioned baptismal font when the nave was extended and a new facade designed.

Chapter 5 investigates the iconography of the nave rosaces, based on the ritual of the coronation ceremony and various writings of the influential Carolingian archbishop Hincmar. Chapter 6 continues the examination of the nave bays and the theme of the distinctive power of Reims to anoint and crown the French kings, articulated by Hincmar. The nave program initially was planned to reach the Romanesque facade (see figs. 3, 160, 161); study of the later, western nave extension is challenging in the absence of remade designs there. Chapter 7 discusses the glazing of the west rose, integrating the coronation of the Virgin with French coronation ceremonials. The lancets beneath the rose, dated around 1290, project a (royal) layperson's donation. Such lay patronage is otherwise unknown among extant windows. And a coda briefly undertakes a comparison of the Reims glazing with that of monuments of comparable stature.

The chronology I provide is, if anything, straightforward and moves from east to west:

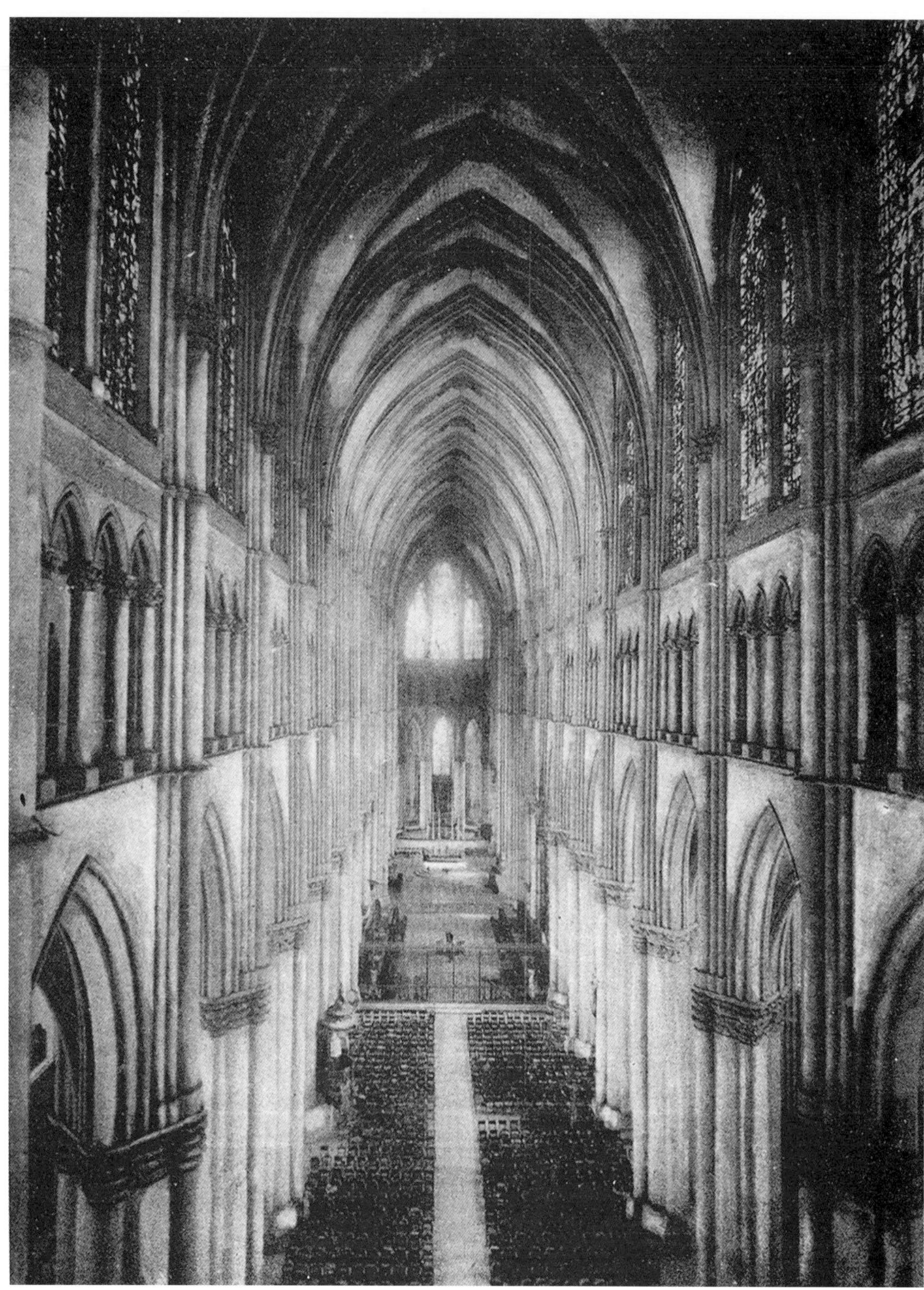

FIG. 1 Reims cathedral, view to east, showing the nave clerestories fully glazed. Postcard, before 1914.

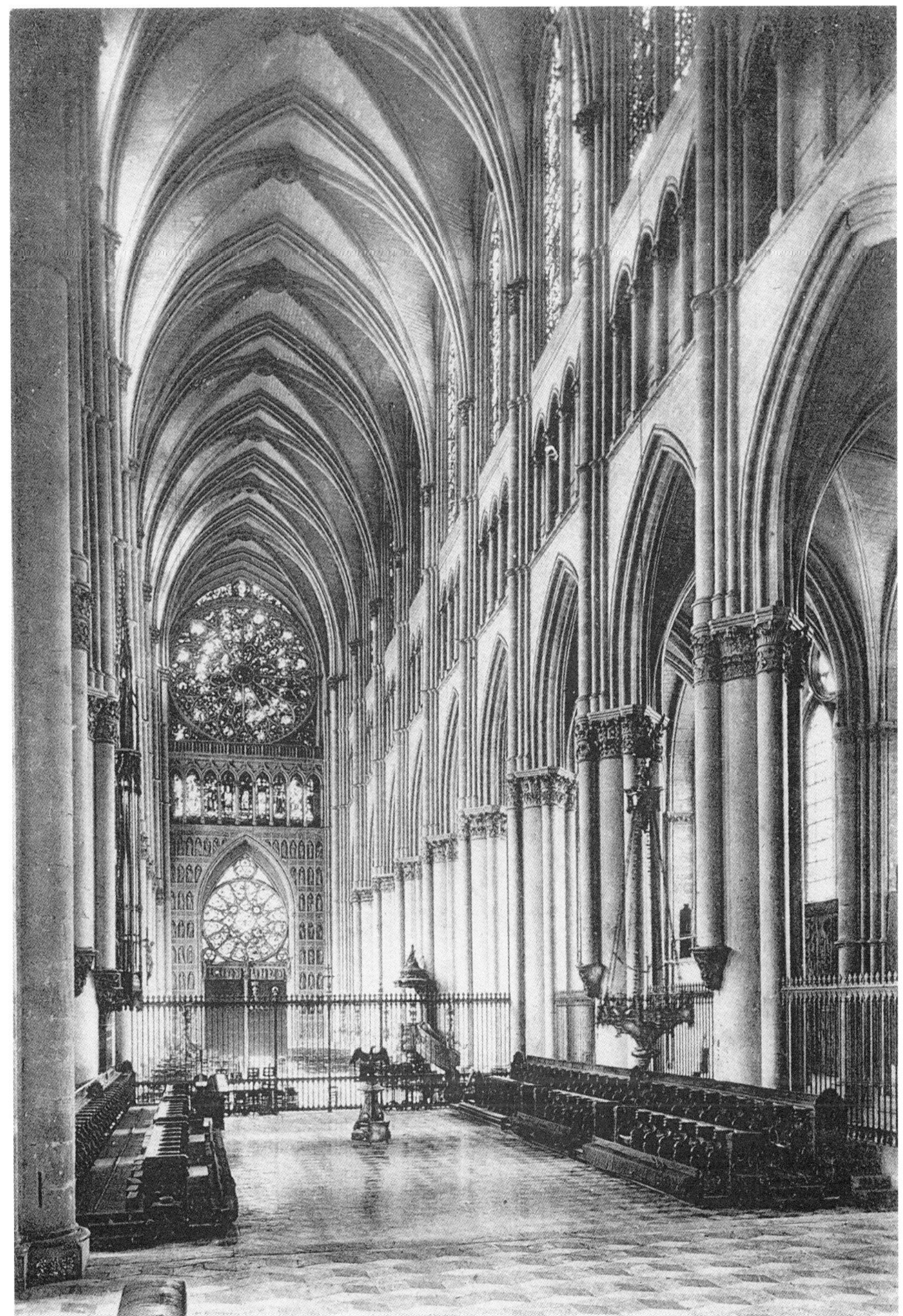

FIG. 2 Reims cathedral, view to west, showing the nave clerestories fully glazed. Postcard, before 1914.

- *Belles verrières* (now in Bay 118): ca. 1220
- Bay 100: 1227–30
- Bays 101 and 102: 1231–33
- Bays 103 and 104 (and irons of Bay 106 rosace?): 1233–34
- Hiatus in the work (canons in exile): November 1234–January 1237
- Bays 105 and 106: 1237–mid-1238
- Bay 108: mid-1238–mid-1240
- Bay 107: after July 1240
- Bays 109 and 110 (and some transept grisailles?): July 1240–September 1241
- North and south roses: ca. 1241–45
- Bays 121 through 126: ca. 1245–55
- Bays 127 through 130: ca. 1255–70
- Bays 131 through 140: ca. 1275–85
- West facade gallery: ca. 1290
- West rose: 1290s

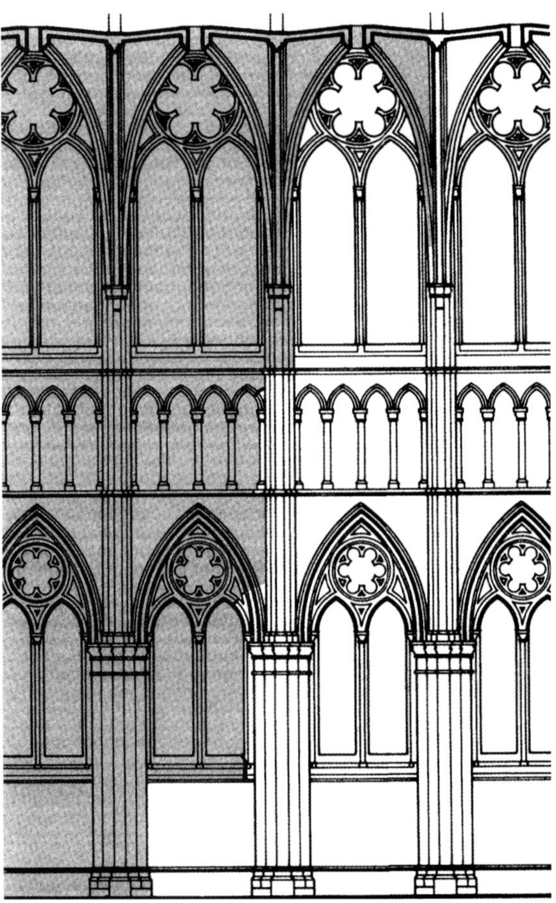

FIG. 3 Reims cathedral, the north nave: (left to right) Bays 135, 133, 131, 129. The gray area shows the nave extension, indicated by the so-called *coupure Tourneur* (after Kurmann, *La façade de la cathédrale de Reims*).

These dates were not dictated by any of the timetables proposed for the structure or the sculptural programs, though I have noted those hypotheses where they coincide. Reims has been called "une vraie forteresse du gothique *classique conservé*."[8] Its glazing, extending throughout most of the thirteenth century, seems to affirm this judgment—no band windows, no heraldry, no soaring canopies. But conservatism implies tradition, "the disposition and tendency to preserve what is established; opposition to change" (*Webster's*). It is hardly the appropriate term for stained-glass programs that have few *comparanda* either before or after.

A fellowship from the John Simon Guggenheim Foundation made it possible for me to write this book. Research began in 1990, though I collected materials even earlier. Since then a sea of friends, strangers, and partners in crime have come to my aid. It was also in 1990 that I purchased my favorite guidebook, in a café across from the cathedral: *À la découverte des secrets de Reims,* authored by the ten-to-eleven-year-old students of the École primaire Mazarin. Their interview with Madame la Cathédrale includes the question, "Avez-vous quelque chose de coloré pour faire plus gai?" to which she replies: "Entrez, venez voir mes vêtements bordés de rubis, d'émeraudes, de saphirs, de diamants qui m'illuminent et que les hommes ont appelé des vitraux." Venez, entrez . . .

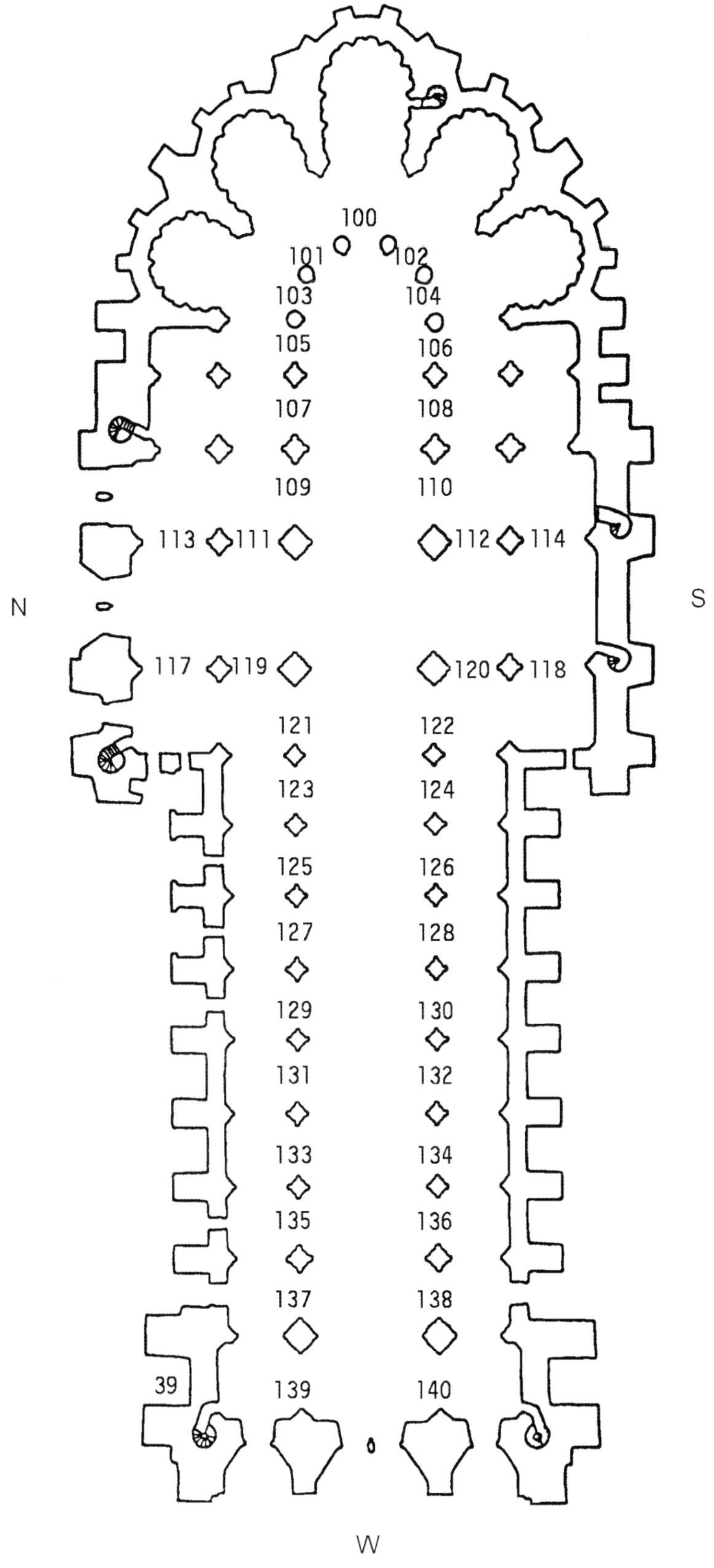

FIG. 4 Reims cathedral, plan with Corpus Vitrearum bay numbers indicated (adapted after Kurmann, *La façade de la cathédrale de Reims*).

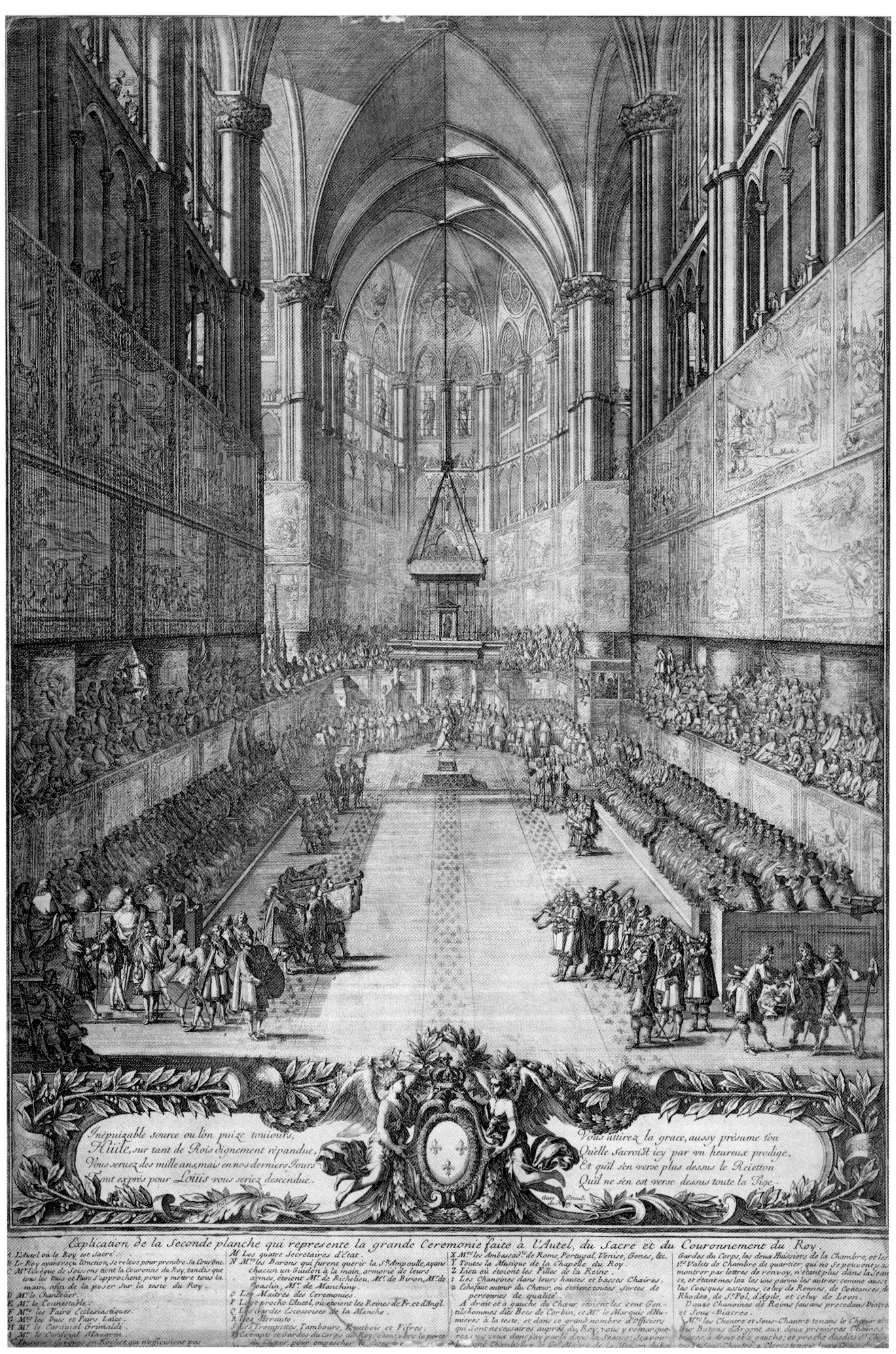

FIG. 5 Reims cathedral, view to east, coronation of Louis XIV, 1654: [Jean] Le Paultre, *Seconde planche qui représente la grande cérémonie faite à l'autel, du sacre et du couronnement du Roy*, engraving, Reims, Bibl. mun., V, II c GF 17.

CHAPTER I

UN PEU D'HISTOIRE

Medieval voices tell us that the cathedral of Reims burned on May 6, 1210. Exactly one year later the foundations of a new chevet were sufficiently complete for the ceremonial laying of a cornerstone of the new walls. In July of 1221 the axial radiating chapel of this new chevet was put into service. On September 7, 1241, the chapter of seventy-two canons took possession of "their new choir," often believed to be the three easternmost nave bays, where their stalls were ultimately located. And the new Gothic facade was begun following the clearing of houses on the site around 1252.[1] This deceptively straightforward east–west trajectory has been interpreted, through analysis of the structure itself, in almost as many ways as there have been architectural historians interested in the question. But recent scholarship is revisiting and reinterpreting these oft-repeated data. And dendrochronological evidence now suggests that construction had begun before the fire, perhaps as early as 1207.[2] Add to this the profusion, confusion, and infinite variety of the renowned sculpture of Reims, and the destruction of evidence in the tragic bombardments of World War I. Reims is a puzzle with many pieces missing.

As is the norm with thirteenth-century documentation, stained glass is nowhere mentioned. The windows first received a nod in a short paragraph by Dom Guillaume Marlot (1596–1667).[3] In the following century—the Age of Enlightenment—systematic removal of all the lower glazing (aisles and chapels) enlightened the interior that Marlot had so briefly noted. In spite of this huge loss, in the nineteenth century the remaining stained glass of Reims rivaled that of its sister cathedrals in fame, and the careful descriptions and drawings by a cloud of witnesses provide much of the backbone to the present study. The earliest images of the windows appear in the commemorative engravings issued upon the coronations of Louis XIV, in 1654, and Louis XV, in 1722 (see figs. 5, 6). The clerestory glass is rendered with fantasy—or not at all—and tapestries hide the rest. The coronations took their toll. These engravings bear witness to the practice of removing the lowest clerestory panels to allow a view of the ceremony to brave observers occupying the outside ledge.[4] Inevitably some of these lower panels were damaged or lost. For the final coronation, in 1825, many of the grisaille bays were covered with patterns in oil paint (fig. 7), not removed until a century later.

The first attempts to record the stained glass accurately are the drawings of the chevet clerestory published by Charles Cahier and Arthur Martin in the 1840s (figs. 8–9). Visiting glaziers in the next decades sketched details of interest, including

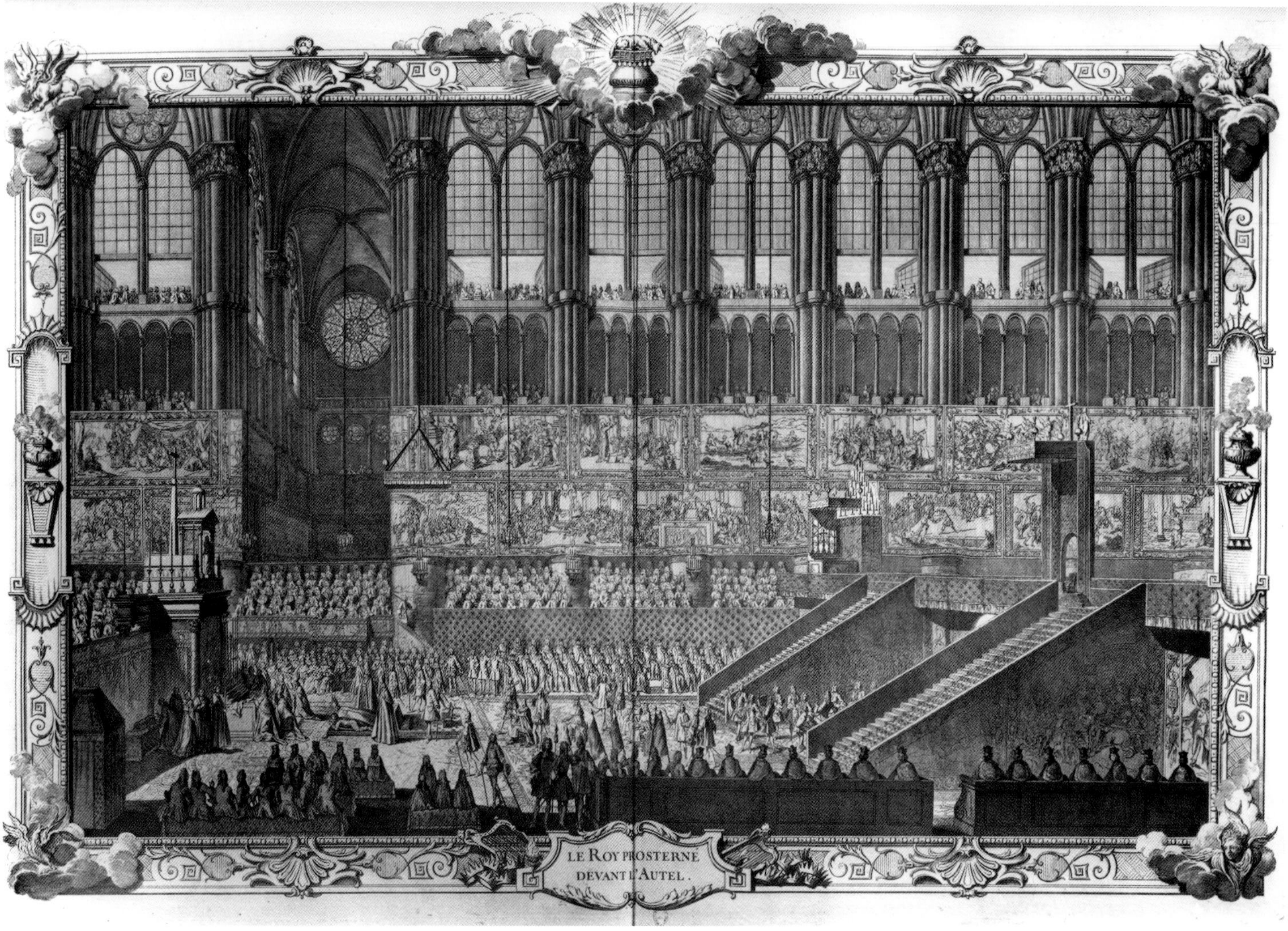

FIG. 6 Reims cathedral, south flank, coronation of Louis XV, 1722. The artist has "replaced" the Gothic windows with the large clear rectangular glazing featured in the Versailles chapel consecrated 1710: Antoine Danchet, *Le sacre de Louis XV, roy de France et de Navarre,* [Charles-Nicolas] Cochin [le père], engraving.

ornament and grisailles (figs. 10–12). Pierre Simon, of the Simon atelier whose family had cared for the cathedral windows for generations, began in 1848 to record the designs in tracings made directly on the glass and then worked up into watercolor drawings made to scale; his son Paul continued this practice, often from ladders in situ (e.g., fig. 13). This invaluable treasure made possible Paul's painstaking restoration of the west rose in 1910 (fig. 14) and enabled his son Jacques to achieve the massive restorations following the tragic losses of 1914–18. American glaziers visiting his atelier have published a few of his cartoons (figs. 15–16).[5] And finally, photography. A few precious photos of prewar date survive, and Henri Deneux, the architect in charge of the postwar work, used photography extensively. Besides the collection taken for or by him in the government's Archives photographiques, the serendipitous donation ca. 1995 to the Bibliothèque municipale of Reims of a group of photographs made by Henri Deneux at the very beginning of the First World War—in color!—constitutes an incomplete but precious addition to, and confirmation of, the nineteenth-century record.[6]

The losses of World War I were extensive and ill-reported, as were the careful reconstructions of many of the damaged windows in the decades

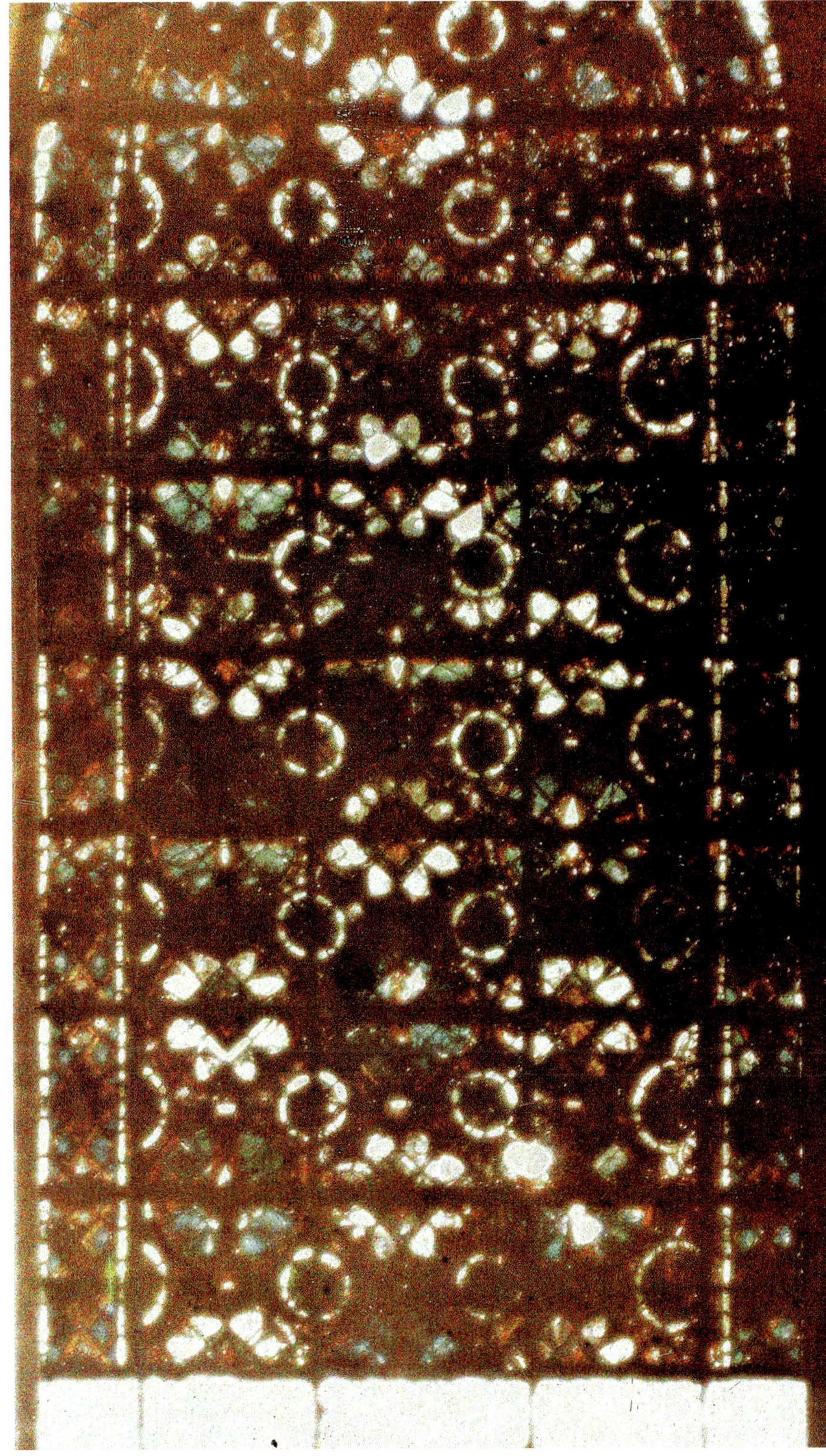

FIG. 7 Bay 112, one of the grisailles colored with oil paints for the coronation of Charles X, 1825; the bottom row of panels had been removed previously and lost. Autochrome by Henri Deneux, 1915.

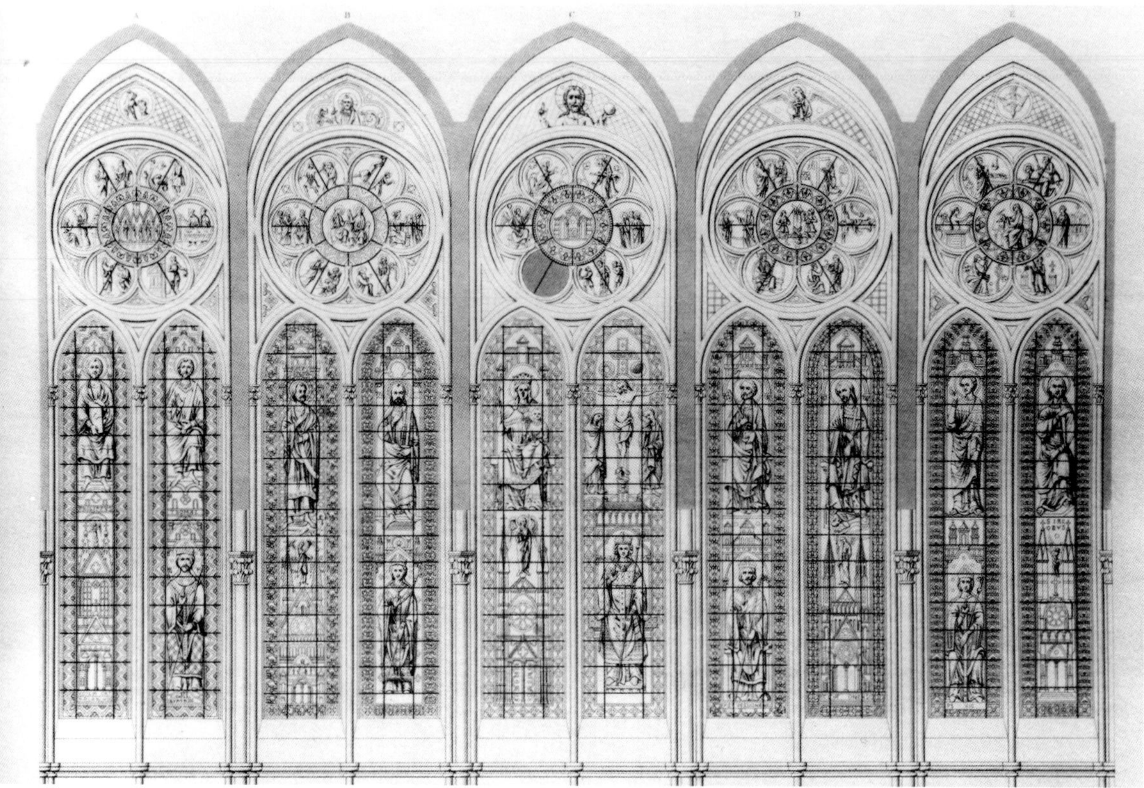

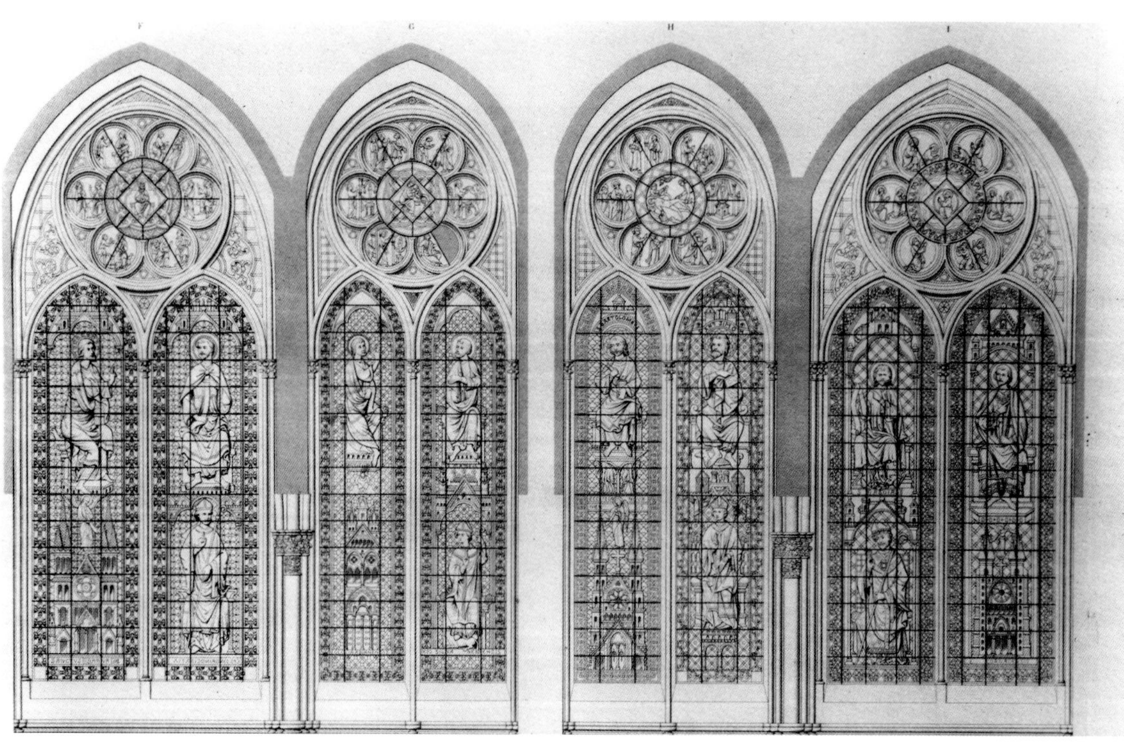

FIG. 8 Clerestory of the hemicycle, 1840s: (left to right) Bays 103, 101, 100, 102, 104 (after Cahier and Martin, *Monographie de la cathédrale de Bourges*).

FIG. 9 Clerestory of the straight chevet, 1840s: (left to right) Bays 107, 105, 106, 108 (after Cahier and Martin, *Monographie de la cathédrale de Bourges*).

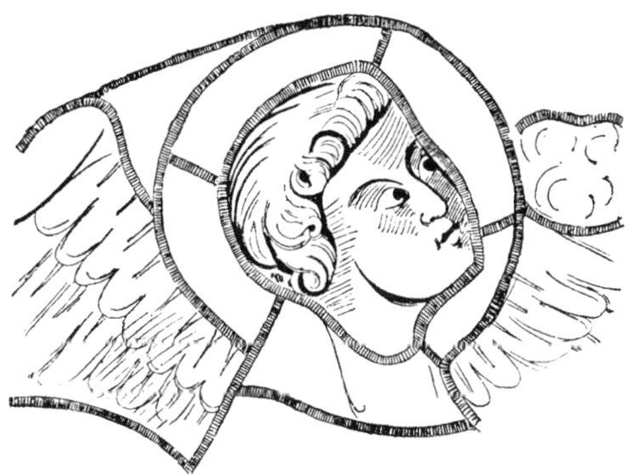

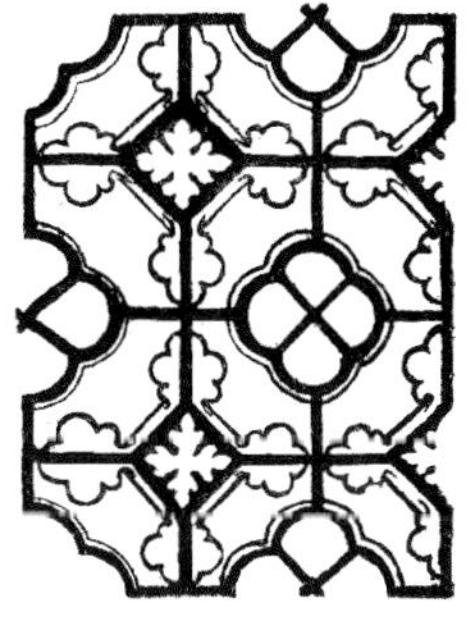

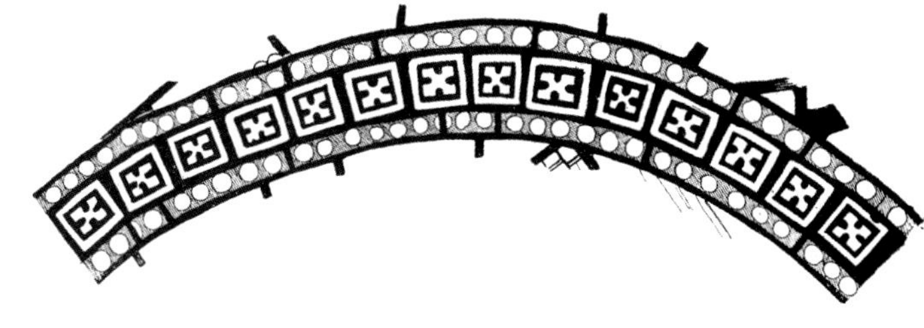

FIG. 10 Angel, left *écoinçon* of the west rose, detail (1881) (after Westlake, *A History of Design in Painted Glass*).

FIG. 11 Ground pattern, Bay 122, left lancet (1881) (after Westlake, *A History of Design in Painted Glass*).

FIG. 12 Medallion border, 1895 (after Olivier Merson, *Les vitraux*).

thereafter by Jacques Simon. Scholarship of the last generation, with some justification, was suspicious of the results.[7] It is not too much of an exaggeration to say that the windows of Reims have been ignored by specialists and that recent accounts have been content to adopt the untested hypotheses proposed by Hans Reinhardt in 1963.[8] He made them—it must be emphasized here—on the basis of the postwar reconstructions.

As a result, style is not a reliable basis for the study of these windows, generally speaking. On the bright side of the coin, the careful twentieth-century reconstructions of many of the present windows were based on the authentic records referred to above. Thus iconography *can* be scrutinized. And as Kurt Weitzmann has said, "The iconographic study of . . . any classical or medieval work of art of great complexity is not only indispensable but has to *precede* stylistic analysis" (his emphasis).[9] While the general subjects of the lancet figures of Reims have been recorded, the iconography of the rosaces above them—surprisingly—has received no scholarly attention at all and provides another mainstay of this investigation.

A third perspective on artistic creation is of course history, the circumstances of the conception of a work of art, the goals and methods of its

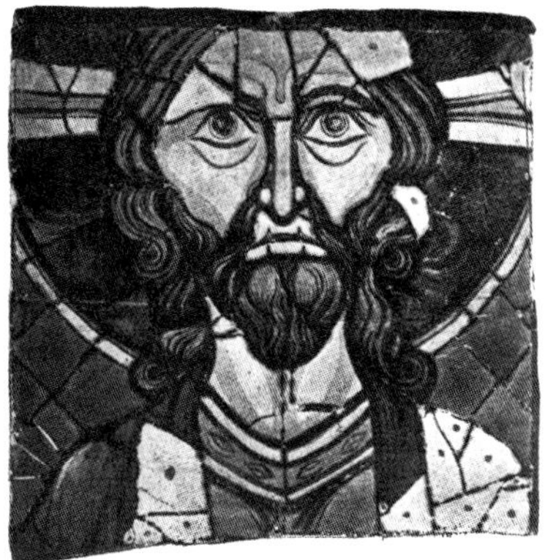

FIG. 13 The Godhead with cruciferous halo, ogive over Bay 100: after a tracing by Paul Simon from the exterior, here reversed as it appears from the interior (after Simon, "Notes sur les vitraux").

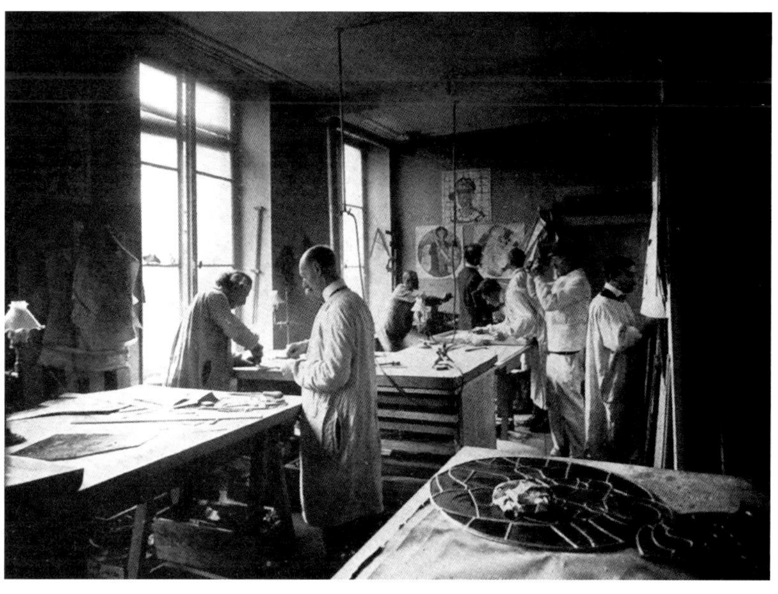

FIG. 14 Studio of Paul Simon during restoration of the west rose, 1910 (after Simon, *La grande rose*).

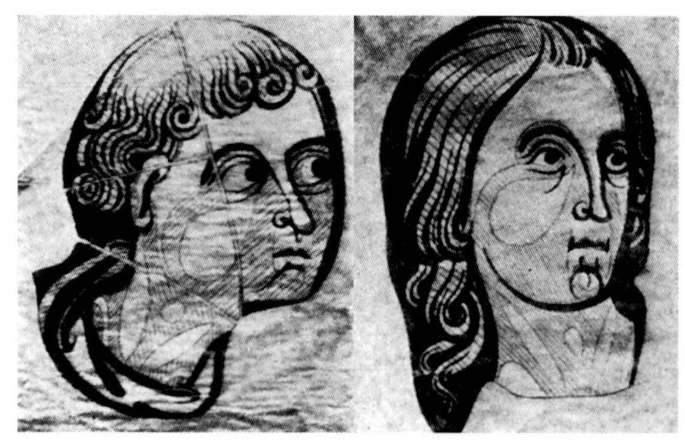

FIG. 15 Tracings of thirteenth-century heads, Simon studio (after Orin E. Skinner, "Restoring the Stained Glass Treasures of Rheims Cathedral," *American Architect*, 1927).

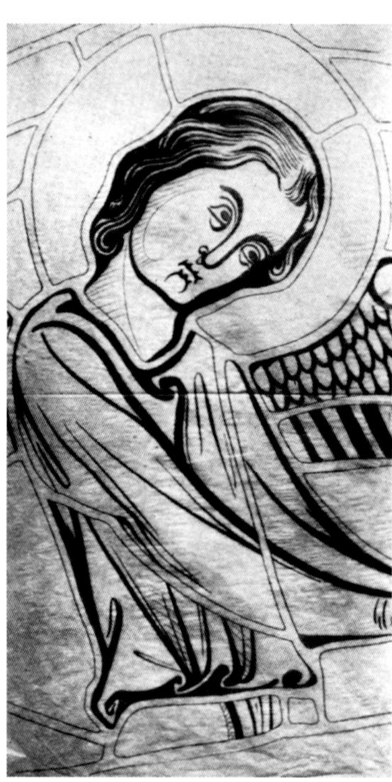

FIG. 16 Angel with the crown of thorns, detail from the lobe installed in Bay 127 after 1918; original location unknown. Tracing by Paul Simon from the exterior, here reversed as it appears from the interior (after Orin E. Skinner, "Restoring the Stained Glass Treasures of Rheims Cathedral," *American Architect*, 1927).

patrons, and so forth. The turbulent civic life and strife in Reims during the initial period of cathedral construction have received the attention of scholars without achieving consensus. It has even been said that the building shows no evidence of the turmoil. It is in the themes chosen for stained glass (even more than sculpture) that the tensions, hopes, and fears of such times may be revealed. For that reason this chapter will outline the history of the civic struggle in Reims before and during the period the Gothic cathedral was going up. As John Gage has observed, "Although historiography inevitably works backwards from the present to the past, history as it is experienced does not. And it is one of the tasks of the historian to reconstitute the original order of events."[10]

Remembrance of Things Past: The Question of Spolia

The cathedral that suffered the fire in the early thirteenth century was a composite structure much like Abbot Suger's Saint-Denis. To a Carolingian nave had been added, to the east, a choir with ambulatory and radiating chapels, while extensions at the west ended in a twin-towered facade, replacing an earlier tower-porch. Archbishop Samson (r. 1140–60), who had attended the consecration of Suger's chevet in 1144, is credited with these additions. Recent excavations have revealed still more about these previous constructions, the western parts of which may have remained in liturgical use during much of the building of the present Gothic structure.[11] Almost nothing is known of the twelfth-century decoration of Samson's cathedral. However, it inspired a similar rebuilding—at both ends—of the *rémois* abbey of Saint-Remi ca. 1165–1205. Anne Prache and Madeline Caviness have provided much information about Saint-Remi, and at least fragments of the evidence survive there.[12] It has been customary to consider Saint-Remi as an important model for the stained glass of the Gothic cathedral of Reims. I would like the reader to consider, on the other hand, the date and impetus for the abbey's east- and west-end construction and to entertain the possibility that Samson's cathedral—partially damaged in the fire and under reconstruction—was more likely the ur-source for both the abbey church and for various design solutions in the spectacular building that replaced Samson's structure.

It has been generally recognized that the glazing of Reims differs from that of its sister cathedrals in being intensely site-specific, dominated by images of its suffragans and of French kings crowned there. Two coronations had been held at Reims in the eleventh century, those of Henri I, in 1027, and Philippe I, in 1059. While Louis VI was crowned elsewhere, his sons Philippe (in 1129) and Louis VII (in 1131) had their coronations at Reims, instigating a long tradition lasting until 1825. Around the mid–twelfth century that tradition was not, however, ironclad, and it was, moreover, under attack from Saint-Denis, where the kings were buried and where their regalia were housed.[13] Little can be assumed about the decoration of Samson's cathedral, but under those circumstances its message was probably similar in basic ways to that of the Gothic glazing program under study here. The famous enthroned king in the south nave inscribed with the name Karolvs (figs. 188–90) is, I believe, a fragment recycled from Samson's program. Arguments for this, as for subsequent hypotheses mentioned here, are laid out in the chapters devoted to that glazing. Unfortunately, Karolvs is now a postwar construct, and the physical evidence for this hypothesis is gone.

While Karolvs has not been recognized previously as a reused figure, four images inserted into Bay 118, the south-transept window to the right of the rose, have been universally acknowledged as such. Salvaged glass of this kind is sometimes referred to in the literature as spolia. A more appropriate term might be *belles verrières,* the description used already in the Gothic era to denote precious glass images that had been saved and reused.[14] The transept group contains an enthroned Virgin and Child, an enthroned archbishop-saint, a standing John the Baptist, and an image of the cathedral "facade" (figs. 146–48). Although the glazier Paul Simon believed these images to have come from the previous cathedral,[15] most now assume, following Reinhardt's monograph of 1963, that they are the initial glazing of the axial clerestory of the present building, replaced by the autocratic archbishop Henri de Braine (r. 1227–40) with stained glass containing his own named image (fig. 69). This theory does not stand up to close scrutiny. These four panels are reused but not from the Gothic cathedral's axial window. On December 24, 1218, Archbishop Aubry de Humbert died, in Pavia, on his way home from crusade. Imposed by the pope after a series of contested elections, he had been more often absent from Reims than not, and the canons foresaw a repeated situation *sede vacante*.[16] The reign of King Philippe Auguste was then approaching the length of his predecessors' rules, and he had a mature son, Louis VIII—proven warrior and father—whose coronation could be anticipated. The nave of the ancient cathedral was still in liturgical use while only the ambulatory and chapels of the new chevet were nearing completion. Peter Kurmann has proposed a campaign of decoration of Samson's cathedral facade with sculptures, those later recycled as jamb statues on the far right of the later Gothic facade.[17] I believe that the four stained-glass images now in the south transept formed an extension of that embellishment of the twelfth-century facade, in anticipation of the coronation of Louis VIII. There are several compelling reasons to date this glazing project to 1219–20, when there was no archbishop in power and thus a genuine danger that a coronation might be held elsewhere.

Several other "problem areas" of the Reims glazing have accrued "solutions" achieving nearly the status of myth. One is Reinhardt's hypothesis of a "first choir program" that was abandoned and partially recycled into the present glazing there. Another is the group of six named archbishops—all of noteworthy obscurity—in the three southeastern bays of the nave (figs. 178, 181, 184). Their names, which have been taken to establish that the prelates and monarchs of the nave represent specific historical individuals, are almost certainly of sixteenth-century fabrication, as are the images of the prelates they name. And finally there is the gallery below the great west rose window (fig. 226), whose lancets have routinely been identified as depicting somebody's coronation—Clovis, St. Louis, the dauphin and Jeanne d'Arc?—or perhaps simply the Embodiment of French Kingship. It does not, however, depict a coronation per se; for one thing, there is no crown. History informs solutions to these puzzlements, the evidence for which I offer the reader, in the chapters to follow, with the adage, "Truth can be stranger than fiction."

Civic Strife, Heresy, and Usury

The desire of the Reims bourgeois to establish a commune, and the opposition to it by the Church, date to 1139, the year before Archbishop Samson was consecrated. In the same year the citizens' "rebellion" was first connected with the taint of heresy (a subject to be investigated below and in appendix 1). During Samson's reign (1140–60) there were frequent incidents, and in 1147 some violence. The winter of 1166–67 saw an insurrection against the next archbishop, Henri de France (r. 1162–75), brother of the king. Archbishop Guillaume aux Blanches-Mains (1176–1202), a peacemaker who wished to avoid such civic distress, in 1182 issued a charter known as the *Willelmine.* It loosened the reins somewhat but did not establish the hoped-for commune, and the problem continued to fester.[18] The problem—and the desire of the bourgeois to run their own city—again came to a head during the period of Gothic construction with which this book is initially concerned, under the reign of the high-handed and detested Henri de Braine. By that time the issue of heresy had moved center stage.

One of the first events of the brief reign of the imposed archbishop Guy Paré (1204–6) had been his attendance at the burning of heretics at Braine, just west of Reims. Archbishop Aubry de Humbert (1207–18), who followed him and was likewise imposed by the pope, fought alongside Simon de Montfort in the Albigensian crusade, attended Lateran Council IV, where heresy was a major theme, and joined the Fifth Crusade, dying on his return through Italy. Next, Archbishop Guillaume de Joinville (1219–26) fought with Louis VIII in his campaign against heretics at Avignon and died of dysentery two days before the king did. The next archbishop, Henri de Braine (1227–40)—whose named image appears in the cathedral's axial clerestory, Bay 100—was similarly motivated. His uncle and mentor, Philippe de Dreux, bishop of Beauvais, had been a famous, or infamous, warrior who had participated vigorously in several crusades to the Holy Land and two against the Albigensian heretics.[19] Henri's election as archbishop was a personal triumph as well as vindication for his uncle, whose reputation for bellicosity had denied him the post in 1202. The conflicts between Henri de Braine and the bourgeois of his city have been rehearsed numerous times in art-historical literature.[20] Since these events are so basic to an understanding of the glazing of the chevet and transepts, they will be outlined here in a time line as uncontroversial as I can make it.

Archbishop Henri de Braine was a great-grandson of a king of France, a fact that saturated his worldview. His archconservative and arbitrary manner fanned the anticlerical mood of his city and made for an extremely turbulent reign. From very early in his pontificate he was in conflict with the young Louis IX, his kinsman, over the preservation of ecclesiastical privileges in his archdiocese. At the same time, his relations with the citizenry of Reims deteriorated rapidly. The city's rich bourgeois, whose wealth was chiefly derived from the textile trade in fine linens and serge, had—as outlined above—for nearly a century been trying to escape their feudal yoke. Over the course of this conflict the citizens' frustration had occasionally turned to violence, and the Church's response to excommunication. But in the 1230s the situation was becoming sinister. Among the lucrative business activities of the merchants was moneylending to other communes, and when in 1234 the archbishop canceled one of their deals on the grounds of usury and moved his law courts into a fortified castle at the Porte de Mars (fig. 17), tensions increased dramatically.

Chronicles report that numerous bourgeois in Reims had been labeled as usurers and had begun to fear the Church's persecution.[21] In 1230 both the pope and the king had issued attacks on usury. Sermons of the papal legate Jacques de Vitry maintained that the usurious practices of the bourgeois made them particularly susceptible to heresy. In 1231 the noose began to tighten in the archdiocese of Reims itself, when Henri de Braine called a council of his suffragan bishops to authorize the pursuit of usurers by methods comparable to those used for heretics—that is, by denying them legal counsel and the right to know their accusers. Finally, in 1233 the infamous papal inquisitor Robert le Bougre (a Dominican and converted heretic) arrived in the province. Matthew Paris comments about this notorious inquisitor that he tended to confound heretics and usurers.[22] And in 1235 he burned them in groups of thirty, in towns as close to Reims as Châlons-en-Champagne. In May of 1239 he burned 183 people at Mont-Aimé, forty-five kilometers south of Reims. The threat was real and the rich cloth merchants of Reims had good reason to fear.[23]

The bourgeois of Reims responded to the threat with panic and anticlerical fury, in a campaign of physical harassment of the cathedral's canons in the public streets. As a result the canons fled into exile in November 1234, placing the city under interdict. During the exile, which lasted until January 1237—over two years—the merchants turned their frustration and alarm against the archbishop. In his absence they attacked his law court at the Mars Gate, where heresy trials took place. The violence involved street barricades, war machines, stone missiles robbed from the cathedral's workshops, numerous casualties, and finally a murder: the death of the archbishop's marshal. During these troubles the archbishop called his suffragan bishops to eight provincial councils, an unprecedented number, five in 1233 and three more in 1235, trying to muster support for his excommunication of the region as well as his pleas to the king to come to his aid. Louis IX refused support and stalled long enough to force the case into the jurisdiction of the royal courts. After he settled the conflict by arbitration, in 1236, extracting monetary compensation and humiliating public penance from the citizens responsible,[24] the calm lasted no more than two years. In 1238 the citizens refused to pay the third and last annual settlement to the archbishop, revolted again, and hired archers; the archbishop confronted his subjects with armed militia. Before the year's end, however, he was again forced to flee, and the town was once more placed under interdict. The imbroglio ended only with Henri de Braine's death in exile in July 1240.

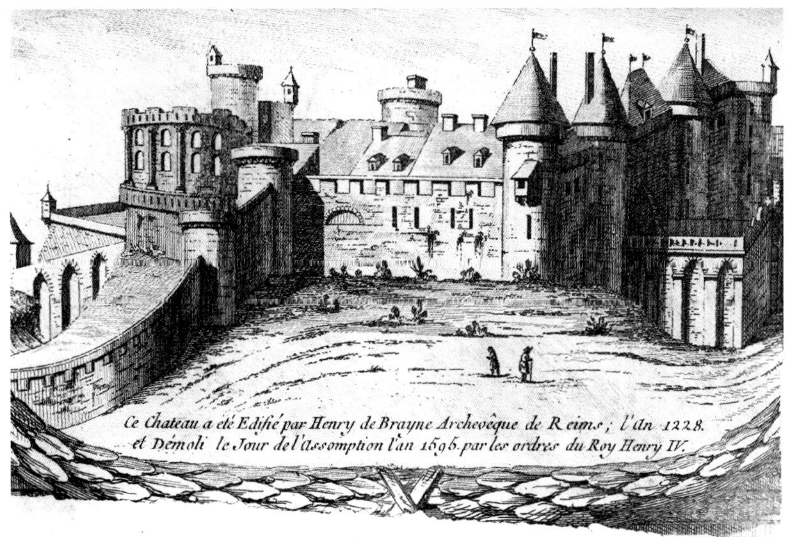

FIG. 17 Reims, Porte de Mars, castle of Archbishop Henri de Braine (after Geruzez, *Description historique et statistique de la ville de Reims*).

The conflict between bourgeois and canons was, in effect, a separate matter, although this only became apparent over time. Certainly, the experience of physical harassment and twenty-six months' exile deeply affected the chapter, but their return in January 1237 was triumphant. It has not been generally recognized that the canons remained in Reims when the archbishop was forced to flee the second time. Following his death they and the townsmen hastened to come to a settlement and a lift of excommunication. Historically, the cathedral chapter and archbishop had fought. The oath taken by a prospective canon stressed the loyalty expected of him toward the chapter and the church, including the assurance that he would not reveal the secrets of the chapter. As Anne Robertson has noted about the oath, "Significantly . . . one person whom the canon does not have to obey is the archbishop, who is never mentioned."[25] During Henri de Braine's second and final exile, the canons lay low, holding Mass during the interdict for themselves, their families, and their retainers, in the chapel of Saint-Michel on the north side of their cloister.[26] The archbishop's efforts to pressure them to discontinue services only succeeded within days of his death.[27]

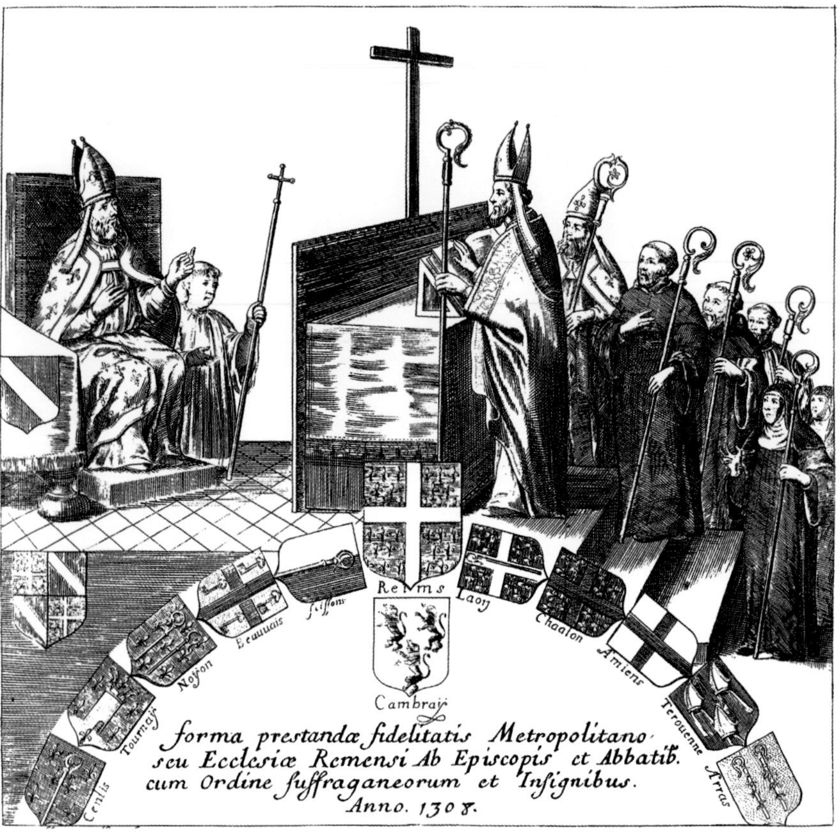

FIG. 18 Seating arrangement of the eleven suffragan bishops at provincial councils, established by Henri de Braine in 1231: [Jacques] Dassonneuille, engraving (after Marlot, taken from Geruzez, *Description historique et statistique de la ville de Reims*).

The implications of this saga are clear. Archbishop Henri de Braine came from an aristocratic family notable, even by the standards of its time, for its stained-glass donations. The glazing of the church at Braine, where he was born, has been published by Madeline Caviness; his brother was Pierre Mauclerc, donor of the south-transept rose window of Chartres; Henri himself is recorded as having donated a window with his image to Saint-Nicaise; and I have identified another such image given to the cathedral of Châlons-en-Champagne.[28] Henri de Braine's successful gamble for the archbishopric in 1227—no doubt in his eyes a family triumph vindicating the rejection of his uncle and mentor for the post in 1202—is the most likely impetus for his gift of Bay 100 (fig. 69). Its inscribed images of himself in full regalia next to his cathedral proclaim that triumph. The window is executed in an advanced Parisian style and is a unicum in Reims, without stylistic precedent or successor. The archbishop was a busy man during his first years in office, deep in intrigue involving family as well as matters of state. A date for Bay 100 before or around 1230 is most likely.

The unusually innovative chevet glazing program, employing different, possibly local glaziers, probably commenced in the early 1230s, from 1231 to 1234. The concept was, without much doubt, again the archbishop's. In 1231 he held the provincial council of his suffragans at which he established the seating arrangement mirrored in the chevet glass (fig. 18). As mentioned above, in 1233 and 1235 he held a total of eight such councils. In early 1234 he accused his bourgeois of usury/heresy, and by the end of that year his chapter had fled their attackers and the town was under interdict. Work on the cathedral would have ceased during the more-than-two-year exile. The break is, in my opinion, clearly apparent between the hemicycle bays 101 through 104 and those to the west of them.

Upon the canons' return in 1237 the glazing program seems to have fallen into their hands. This was appropriate. It was normal for a cathedral chapter to be in charge of cathedral building projects, and by the end of 1238 Henri de Braine had lost his pocket civil war with his townsmen and fled for the last time. The town remained under interdict until he died, in mid-1240, but the canons remained in residence. Clearly no obvious construction work could be carried out under such circumstances, but a number of chaplaincies were established in the radiating chapels of the closed cathedral during these years.[29] It is not impossible that the chapter identified a few craftsmen to work quietly and store glass panels as they were completed. Such a procedure would explain a few visual anomalies in the westernmost straight bays of the choir. Until the archbishop died, however, his glazing program (the images of his suffragans and their cathedrals, in apostolic succession from Christ's apostles) was—grosso modo—carried out, since who could predict when circumstances would bring him back?

Following the demise of Henri de Braine in 1240 the canons were in no hurry to elect a

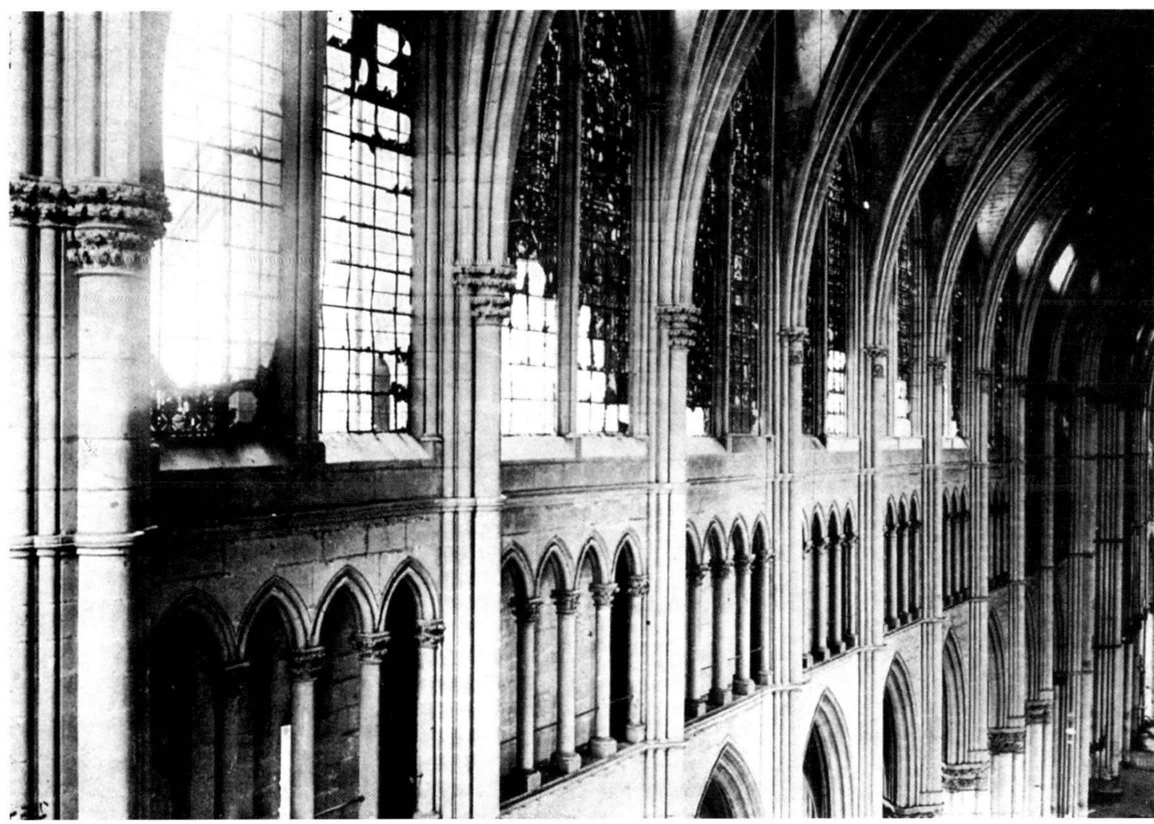

FIG. 19 The north nave: (left to right) Bays 137, 135, 133, 131, 129, 127, etc. Photo by Abbé Remy Thinot before February 1915 showing initial war damage (after Maurice Landrieux, *The Cathedral of Reims: The Story of a German Crime*).

successor, and when they had not done so by 1245, the pope imposed the aged and pious Juhel de Mathefelon.[30] During this breathing space the north rose, and no doubt the lost south rose, were accomplished. The former, rising above the canons' entrance to their cloister, celebrates their triumph over the persecutions of the bourgeois in a masterly glazing program unique among Gothic rose windows. These transept projects were probably complete when a quest for building funds was sent out in 1246.[31]

Dates from the Nave Glazing

The next large glazing project was the eastern nave, up to Samson's twelfth-century facade (fig. 160). The chevet is the domain of Ecclesia, and its program presents her irresistible authority—and specifically that of Ecclesia Remensis—through direct succession from the apostles of Christ down to the suffragan bishops of Henri de Braine. The eastern nave, location of the canons' stalls, was to be the site of the coronation ceremony. Thus the unique power of Ecclesia Remensis to anoint and crown kings is appropriately the theme of the nave.

Study of the nave windows is restricted by the massive losses of World War I (fig. 19); only the first four easternmost bays, north and south, were reconstructed (Bays 121 through 128). Nineteenth-century descriptions and drawings as well as some recently available photographs by Henri Deneux, before the damage and in color, allow some judgments to be made in spite of the great destruction. The program of the nave was based on the chapter's careful research into two sources and probably occupied the late 1240s, perhaps after Louis IX took the crusaders' cross in December 1244. One source was the extensive body of writings of that famous kingmaker, the Carolingian archbishop Hincmar. The other was the so-called

Ordo of 1250. The latter is a compilation that could not be used for an actual ceremony but seems to represent research on how the ceremony had been and should be run. Saints of Châlons, in the litany of this collection of coronation procedures, suggest that it was assembled before 1240, since canons of Châlons cathedral were Henri de Braine's most loyal supporters. A single "fair copy" (Paris, BnF, lat. 1246) was then produced,[32] probably in Paris during the 1240s—and possibly intended for the eventual instruction of the young sons of Louis IX, who left on crusade in 1248. The Ordo of 1250 would thus be contemporary with the conception of the nave glazing program, and as regional a product as Archbishop Hincmar's texts.

Architectural historians have come to no consensus about the progress and dating of the nave construction. Evidence gleaned from the glazing is offered here for what it may contribute to the discussion. The nave glazing unquestionably postdates that of the chevet. With money tight and the king and barons away *outre-mer,* progress of the nave windows was no doubt slow and sporadic. The canons' stalls were to occupy the first three eastern nave bays; the fourth bay contained the choir screen and various attached altars; and the fifth bay provided the first clear space in the nave for the laity. Early observers noted that the nave clerestories were in two styles, the earlier group extending to this bay (from Bay 121 through 130). This fifth bay was also the location of the so-called *rouelle* of St. Nicaise, a marble slab surrounded by a wrought-iron fence and lit by a chandelier, marking the spot of his martyrdom (see fig. 199); the *rouelle* was the first station of processions leaving the canons' choir. This fifth bay also contained the Porte du Cerf, an entrance from the public area of the archbishop's compound to the south. Serendipitously, a prewar photograph exists of the glass made for the clerestory facing this entrance (Bay 129, fig. 202), and two of the eight large figures of Bays 129 and 130 (one king and one archbishop, figs. 204–5) survive, salvaged from the war debris and now installed in Bay 127. It is thus safe to make the judgment that the glass at this location of the nave was spectacular, unusual in quality, style, and subject, the obvious focal point of the program.

The reason for such display at this spot is most probably anticipation of the coronation of Philippe le Hardi, commencing at least from the time when the ailing Louis IX made the universally unpopular decision to return to the Holy Land on crusade. He did this in 1267. Even more likely is that the possibility of a coronation loomed in the minds of the chapter during the three-year *sede vacante* between the death of Archbishop Thomas de Beaumetz, in February 1263, and the pope's imposition of Jean de Courtenay, in July of 1266.[33] By the late 1260s Samson's facade had probably been razed, and the western nave area would have presented a visitor with a noisy and messy construction site. With no archbishop in office a coronation might be held elsewhere. If these arguments sound familiar, it is because they are the same motivations that, I believe, instigated the glazing of Samson's facade in 1219–20 (see above and chapter 4). In any event, Louis IX took the Crusaders' cross in 1267, left in 1270, and died the same year—as did Archbishop Jean de Courtenay, who accompanied him—and the king's son Philippe III was crowned in 1271, in Reims cathedral. In short, the glazing of the five easternmost nave bays, those in the "early style," was in my opinion complete by that date, though perhaps just barely.

The extension of the nave beyond Samson's facade and the replacement of the latter with the present masterful structure may have been discussed in the 1230s, as many scholars believe, but the project was only undertaken later. How much later depends upon interpretation of a *vidimus* document of 1252 concerning houses that stood on the site.[34] Either they were still there, or they had already been demolished and the *vidimus* was made for subsequent litigation. The earliest that real work could have been under way is assumed to be the 1250s, and that work was considerable. The dating of the clerestory glass of Bays 129 and 130 to the late 1260s folds into this sequence perfectly and presumes some kind of temporary closure between the eastern nave—in use—and the active building site beyond.

The "second style" of nave glazing, from Bay 131 westward, is now completely destroyed. The subject program of the rosaces of these windows, as reported in the nineteenth century, was casual and haphazard, in stark contrast to the complex research evidenced in the eastern nave. Topics from the eastern-nave program were simply repeated as needed to fill the new western bays. A few of Deneux's autochrome photos (e.g., figs. 214–15) as well as early descriptions indicate that the glass was lighter and brighter, made of larger pieces, the ornament and painting "simpler," all traits typical around 1280 and beyond.[35] The final western bays at the facade towers received grisailles. These windows also included borders of fleurs-de-lis and the castles of Castille, providing a neat terminus ad quem: ca. 1285. In that year, the seventeen-year-old Philippe IV was crowned following the unexpected death of his father, and the "Spanish tilt" became a political dead letter. That construction and glazing had reached the Gothic facade by 1285 is confirmed by the chapter's establishment of professional singers as well as resident choirboys in that year, to enhance the quality of performance of the divine liturgy.[36]

The glazing of the three layers of the facade was planned to form another focal point of the interior (fig. 222). The unique and spectacular sculptural component of the facade verso in itself proves this point. The riveting microcosm/macrocosm design of the two roses dominates the western vista even more than the same play of form at different scales focuses the view to the east. Thus the loss of the facade's three glazed tympana, removed in the eighteenth century, is much to be regretted. Old drawings establish that the tympana over the flanking doors, in the aisles, were glazed in grisaille, while the small rose of the central door contained medallions probably surrounding a central standing figure of the Virgin and Child (see figs. 223–25). Her ultimate triumph in heaven occupies the large rose window (fig. 231), the iconography of which is more unconventional than has previously been recognized. Again, the long shadow of the Carolingian archbishop Hincmar falls on this program. The rose's angel-musicians have not previously been acknowledged as one of the earliest—and unquestionably the most dazzling of the earliest—examples of this new theme.

The gallery below the rose (fig. 226) is in very poor condition and has been assumed to present some sort of coronation, either of a specific monarch or generically. Careful examination does not support this standard identification. What is more surprising, it provides a date and a probable donor, in a cathedral where identifiable donors are rare. The date—ca. 1290—is based on several arguments. One concerns the ornament containing castles on nonheraldic blue grounds, found in a few of the gallery lancets (figs. 226C, 227). With the advent of Philippe le Bel in 1285 and the demise of the monarchy's interest in Spain, as mentioned above, the heraldic motifs of the castles of Castille remained in glaziers' repertoire for a few years, but by the 1290s, if they appear at all, they adopt nonheraldic color. Another argument derives from the gallery's bizarre and stilted lineup of figures: four archbishops, two crowned kings, two aristocratic youths, and a central uncrowned figure in a dark blue robe covered with enormous fleurs-de-lis, presenting a bare sword. This disparate group is so bizarre and atypical of the thoughtful and careful research and thematic bent of the glazing programs of the rest of the cathedral that the will of a powerful donor is implied. The only likely one is Philippe le Bel himself, in the period around 1290–92, when his beloved queen donated heraldic glass to Saint-Nicaise in Reims.[37] I am aware of the audacity of this conclusion, but, well, there it is. All the evidence leads there.

The Missing Link: *Le Rez-de-Chaussée*

The time line sketched in this chapter is, it must be remembered, incomplete. The entire sequence of glazing in the chapels and aisles—that is, all the glass on the ground floor—was removed around the second quarter of the eighteenth century,

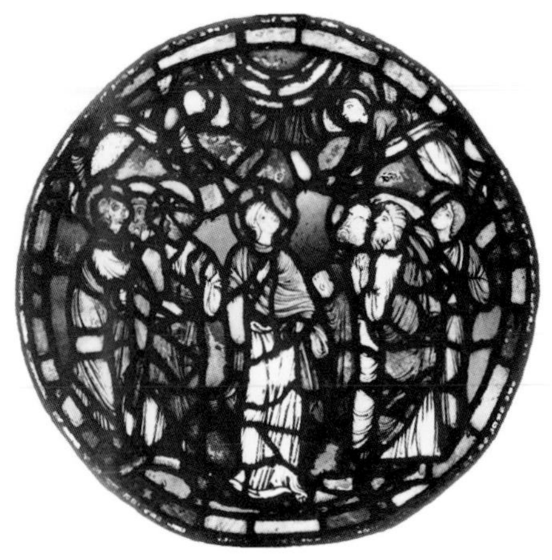

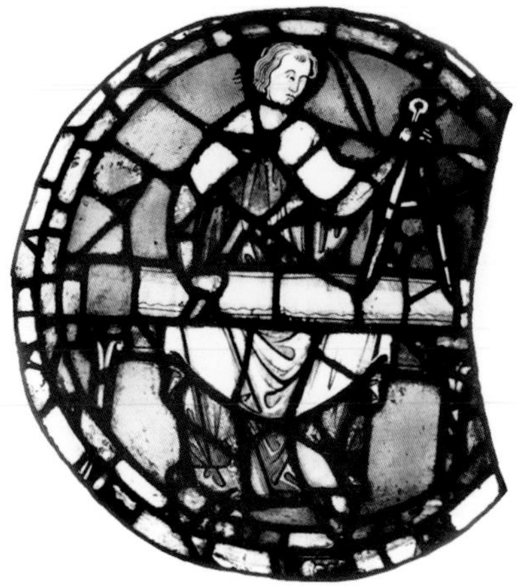

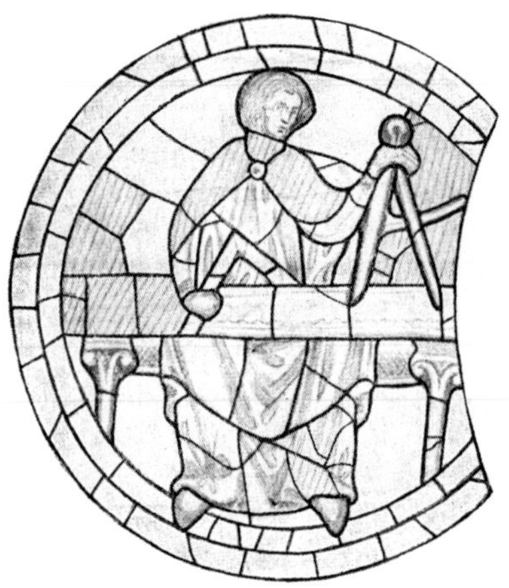

FIG. 20 Ascension of Christ, Bay 39, rosace, central roundel.

FIG. 21 Architect, Bay 39, rosace, left lobe.

FIG. 22 Architect, Bay 39, rosace, left lobe: tracing by Paul Simon (after Louis Demaison, *La cathédrale de Reims*, 1913).

chiefly financed by the canon Jean Godinot.[38] Grisaille (fig. 229) filled some of the nave bays,[39] but it is not even known if the colored windows were all medallions or included large figures. As Patrick Demouy wryly observes, "Nul n'a songé à les décrire."[40] At present only the rosace of Bay 39, at the west entrance to the north aisle, contains spoliate panels from this destruction. Baron François de Guilhermy, the most reliable witness among nineteenth-century observers, records there, as now, Christ's Ascension (fig. 20), angels, various unidentified seated and standing figures, and the famous image of an architect at his work-table holding L-square and compass (figs. 21, 22).[41] Since the lower windows are smaller than the clerestories, these spolia in Bay 39 assuredly came from various aisle bays. Sylvie Balcon-Berry has identified two styles in these fragments; the greater number, including the Ascension roundel, date ca. 1210–20 and undoubtedly came from the choir, while a few others, like the architect, are later.[42]

The latter panel has been recognized as unique, and perhaps it is not so surprising to find him in a cathedral that once had a famous labyrinth with four of its architects pictured (see, e.g., fig. 88). It has not, however, been recognized that the Ascension is an interesting image for its stylistic date. Only Christ's lower body is shown. This form of the subject, while typical of Anglo-Saxon art from the late tenth century on, does not become common in French art until the Gothic period.[43] The Reims image is among the earliest. Closest in date is the Leber Psalter (Rouen, MS 3016, between 1218 and 1228), folio 218v; then come the Psalter of Saint Louis and Blanche de Castille (Paris, Arsenal, MS 1186, ca. 1223–26), folio 27v, and the Jully Psalter (Lyon, MS 539, after 1228–ca. 1250), folio 245v.[44] Might the Reims panel have been inspired by a Psalter?

In addition to these panels reset in Bay 39, Balcon has published a number of small-scale heads surviving from the lost lower windows: a group of fifteen in the Palais du Tau museum and others installed in the atelier of Benoît Marq, a descendant of the Simon glaziers who cared for the cathedral glass for many generations.[45] The heads preserved in the Palais du Tau were perhaps returned by citizens who had picked them up during the war years, in response to Henri Deneux's subsequent call for restitution. But if they came from the lower windows, as seems likely, their whereabouts in the nearly two centuries since their original removal from there remains totally conjectural. Five heads were found loose in identifying envelopes, while the remaining ten had been composed into two "collector's panels," five heads in each one. To these can now be added two heads in another such collector's panel, hanging in the Chinese Loggia of the Gardner Museum in Boston. The fragments composing this panel were

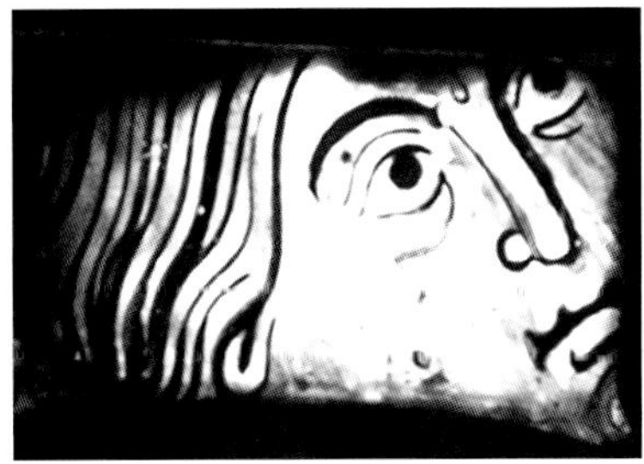
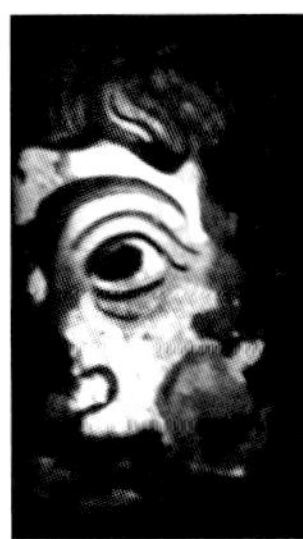

FIG. 23 Heads in a panel of fragments collected during World War I, detail. Acquired in 1920 by the Isabella Stewart Gardner Museum, Boston.

presented to Mrs. Gardner by an American ambulance driver on his return in 1919 and first published in the American Corpus Vitrearum's Checklist I in 1985 (fig. 23).[46] Unfortunately, two handsome seraphim now in American collections and attributed to the great rose window of the facade cannot come from Reims (see appendix 8).

Thus the time line of this chapter extends to the present. The chapters that follow offer arguments and evidence for the preceding judgments. The extraordinary richness of the Reims sculpture, in both its visual and thematic dimensions, has long been appreciated. It is the very specificity and uniqueness of the sculptural programs that contribute to the difficulties in their interpretation and analysis. The same observations apply equally well to the incredible creativity and opulence of the stained glass, both in style and iconography. Almost no decorative patterns were repeated, and few cartoons reused (*pace* what has sometimes been asserted); borders do not shrink in width, as in so much of the glazing appearing after the Sainte-Chapelle. The subject programs go far beyond the norm for Gothic cathedral glazing, composed as it normally is of saints, apostles, prophets, donors, and Christological and Marian images. The careful research behind the Reims programs presupposes educated and highly motivated canons as the iconographers.

It is admittedly hard to reconcile this artistic splendor with the documented civil strife raging during much of the creative period that produced these windows. Furthermore, when the artists were working, their number seems to have been great. In spite of Reinhardt's valiant attempts, it is rare to find an identifiable hand in more than, say, the figures of one bay (and not always that). The assessment of style in the chevet windows of Reims, in particular, and consequent judgments about dating and chronology have been beset by the general assumptions, now questioned, concerning drapery styles: the change in the second quarter of the thirteenth century from antiquizing, "wet," or "soft" fabric represented in a linear manner (*plí mouillé*) to presumably Parisian, heavier textile indicated by sparer line, "broken folds" (*plí cassée*), the *"style dur."* Increasingly, scholars are recognizing that these modes of drapery representation in art coexisted for a period of time.[47] This now frees us from applying lock-step a scholarly chronology and "evolution" of style onto the images—in a sense forcing the art we see into its procrustean bed. For a monument like Reims it liberates us to take a fresh look at all the evidence.

Complicating close examination of these creations is, of course, the heavy restoration. There is very little that is pure antiquizing ("soft"), just as there is also little that is typically *"dur"* in the Parisian manner. The majority of draperies contain some spoon-folds, J-hooks, long Vs, sometimes with shading, sometimes not. Both Paul Simon, restorer in the late nineteenth century, and his son Jacques, who reconstructed the glazing after 1920, commanded a neo-Gothic painting style in this idiom. The tracings that were the basis of restorations establish the outlines, but any comparison of a tracing with its surviving panel serves to make one extremely wary of "stylistic analysis as usual" (see figs. 21, 22). On the other hand, these precious tracings have preserved many details of a unique and highly nuanced iconography. In the end let us be grateful for what evidence we have of this matchless and unique artistic creation.

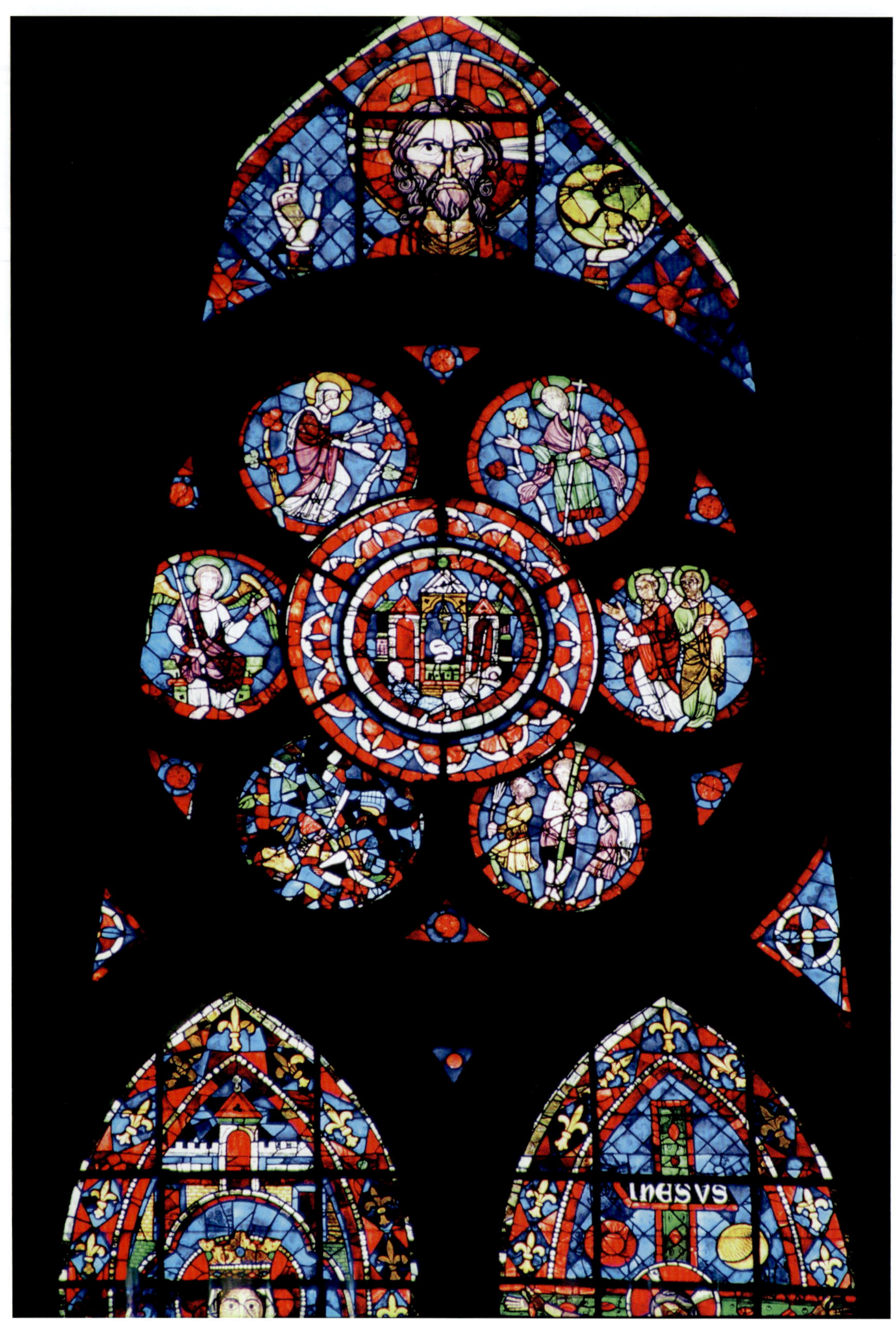

FIG. 24 Bay 100, rosace, the Passion.

CHAPTER 2

THE ROSACES OF THE CHEVET

What could justify an entire detailed chapter devoted to the tracery lights over the clerestory windows of the chevet, preceding discussion of those lancets themselves? Reasons for this scrutiny are not difficult to provide. First, aside from the two engravings published in the 1840s in the Cahier-Martin volumes on Bourges (figs. 8–9), these rosaces have not been illustrated in print or discussed in scholarly venues.[1] Moreover, the scenes of the apostles' lives in these rosaces have not been correctly identified in numerous cases, and they have never been the object of serious investigation. Victor Tourneur and Charles Cerf in the nineteenth century attempted some identifications, by no means all correct; Reinhardt's single page listing the subjects is crammed with errors, which have been propagated not only in numerous guidebooks but in recent scholarly literature.[2] Earlier twentieth-century French scholars knew of the rosaces—for example, Yves Delaporte, Émile Mâle, and Louis Réau—but their references are often less than accurate.[3] Unquestionably the most basic reason to introduce the chevet's program with the rosaces is because they establish that program—its *raison d'être*—and lay it out in greatest detail.

The careful study of the chevet rosaces provides a number of surprises. For a start, the concept of a complete series of lives of the apostles—not just their deaths as grouped in martyrologies, or isolated narratives devoted to a major player like Peter or John—is almost a "first" in medieval art. Only the cycle of apostles' lives in the mosaics of San Marco in Venice precedes the Reims rosaces (Bays 101 through 106). Reims has no direct connection to San Marco and varies from the mosaics considerably. Thus the question of sources for the program assumes importance. Many Reims scenes are drawn from apocryphal legend, and just as fascinating is the selection made from these stories for each apostle. These choices are often surprising, opting for unusual events and rejecting more popular scenes.

In addition, the scenes are much more regularly placed and organized than Reinhardt imagined; in fact, they are in near perfect order. Each rosace contains six lobes, the three on each side devoted to the apostle whose image appears in the lancet directly below. The rosace's central light is accorded to the apostle considered more important in each lancet, not always the one of greater prestige. Even more impressive as evidence for the complexity and sophistication of the planning, the order of each apostle's three scenes was carefully controlled to connect them in an asterisk-shaped network, to be discussed below (see fig. 27). The purpose of such an intricate pattern was to underline the group character and status, the unity as well as the diversity, of the Twelve. This enhanced the main theme of the chevet—the apostolic succession. Indeed, the rosaces provide much information about the large questions of the chevet glazing: dating, artists, changes in campaign, programmer(s) and their sources, agenda, and so forth. The unusual selection of scenes at Reims is site-specific and only appropriate to the urban situation during a brief period in the 1230s. Thus the tracery rosaces offer an extremely rich field of study for the understanding of the cathedral, its history, and its ornament.

The six-lobed tracery roses of Reims cathedral are called, in recent French terminology, *roses du tympan* to distinguish them (about a meter and a half in diameter) from the great rose windows of the facades. They are referred to here by the English term "rosaces." Six- or eight-lobed rosaces can be found in the clerestories of Chartres and Bourges and make up the north rose window (ca. 1175–80) of Laon, a suffragan diocese of Reims. Such rosettes have a long history in Christian and even pre-Christian art. In Christian usage the rosette was a stellar and then an apotropaic sign. As Walter Horn states,

> The motif . . . became so closely associated with the cross of Christ as to be practically interchangeable with it. The symbol placed its bearers under the stellar protection of Christ, and through a vernacular vulgarization of its original meaning eventually assumed the role of a charm against lightning and fire, or against disease affecting the health of livestock. The symbol appears frequently in monastic medieval tithe barns, and survives to this very day in the repertoire of decorative motifs, which are locally referred to as "hex-signs," on numerous barns in the state of Pennsylvania, in the United States of America.[4]

It is probable that, as with other religious symbolism, some meaning still hung on in Romanesque usage, but by the thirteenth century the design had become more simply an ornament considered traditional and appropriate for a church. In short, in the Gothic period it was used as a pattern not simply because masons could produce it with a compass, though I am not suggesting that the Reims rosaces were intended to forestall lightning!

Preamble

A brief summary of the chevet program, described in detail in the following chapter, is useful here. The apostles occupy an upper row in the lancets, flanking the axial bay, which depicts the traditional subjects of the Virgin and Child and the Crucifixion. The series of apostles zigzags across the chevet in the order of the Canon of the Mass, beginning on the south in Bay 102, and the Twelve are supplemented by anonymous "apostles" to complete the chevet bays. This part of the program is pro forma, one might say. So too are the elements of the Trinity located in the ogive lights of Bays 100 through 104 (see appendix 3). The lower row of images, on the other hand, is unique. In Bay 100, the axial bay, is the donor of that bay, Archbishop Henri de Braine, paired in the doublet-and-rose window with the "facade" of his see, Reims cathedral. Flanking him are his suffragan bishops, again zigzagging across the chevet in the hierarchy he established for their seating at provincial councils in 1231 (see fig. 18). Each bishop, like him, is paired with the "facade" of his cathedral.

That is the horizontal lineup. The vertical connections thus established directly relate the college of apostles above to the suffragan bishops below, again highlighting the theme of apostolic succession. In the rosaces we can expect to see the apostles, as the first bishops of the Church, appearing in activities appropriate to "the threefold office of the bishop: to act as priest, to teach [i.e., preach], and to rule. . . . Christ had given to them the rights and duties exercised later on by the bishops, their successors."[5] The apostles were empowered by Christ to remit sins (Luke 24:47; John 20:23), and "the power given to them has been transmitted to the bishops . . . but it is the Lord who forgives the sins"; again, "Christ sets the example for suffering and martyrdom. . . . He accords remission of sins, giving power to the Apostles and through them to the bishops."[6] Thus is it appropriate that the rosace of the axial bay depicts the Passion of Christ.

Bay 100: Christ's Passion

Above the lancets of Bay 100, depicting the Virgin and Child and the Crucifixion (fig. 69), the rosace embellishes the theme of the Passion (fig. 24). In ascending order, the rosace presents, first, in the bottom right lobe (the left lobe being lost), the Flagellation, which preceded the Crucifixion; next, across the middle lights of the rosace, the Resurrection in the form of the Marys at the Tomb; and finally, in the two lobes at the top, Christ's appearance to the Magdalene, the *Noli me tangere*. This ascending order of scenes is of course appropriate to the subject matter. The rosace design of Bay 100 is, one could say, horizontal, with the scenes grouped in three layers from bottom to top. This horizontal arrangement is also followed in the rosaces of Bays 101 and 102, discussed below, though not in all the remainder of the chevet.

The lobe at the bottom left of the Bay 100 rosace was lost at some unknown time before the 1840s, when the Cahier-Martin engraving indicates it as missing (fig. 8). Scenes paired with the Flagellation (bottom right lobe, fig. 24) in stained glass contemporary with Reims are various. At Troyes (bay 200, ca. 1235–40) is the Crowning with Thorns, while at Sens, a suffragan of Reims (bay 100, ca. 1240), the paired scene is Christ Carrying the Cross.[7] The Flagellation scene appears in the symmetrical arrangement, already found in the ninth century, that was standard for Gothic France.[8] The left executioner and Christ bound to the central column, at Reims (fig. 25), are similar to those at Saint-Julien-du-Sault (bay 0, ca. 1235–40), while the right executioner resembles the figure at Sens (bay 100).[9] The Reims artist has oriented the focus of the Flagellation scene slightly to the left to make a visual connection—which we unfortunately cannot appreciate—with the lost lobe to the left. Such connections can be seen as

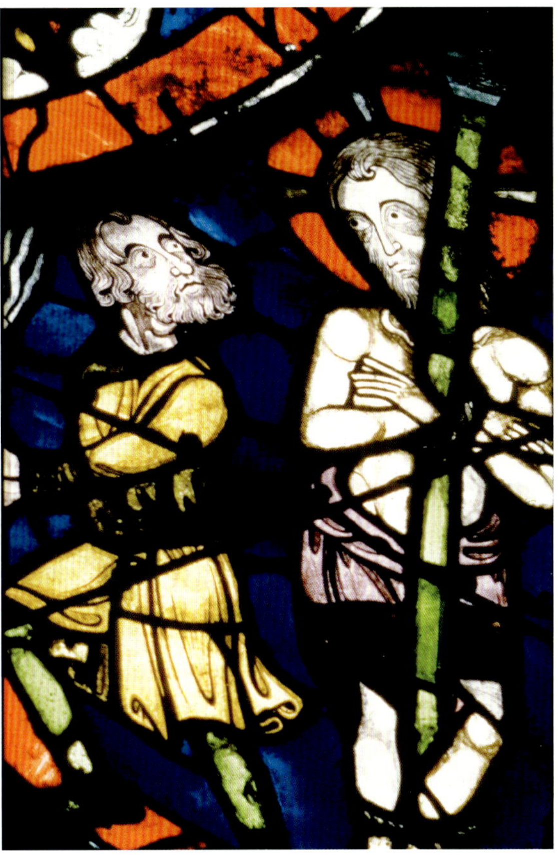

FIG. 25 Flagellation, Bay 100, rosace, detail of bottom right lobe.

well in the two lobes at the top, depicting the *Noli me tangere*. The latter scene also appears in the traditional and standard Gothic format. As earlier at Chartres (bay 46, ca. 1205–15) and later at the Sainte-Chapelle (axial bay H, ca. 1245), Christ, fully clothed, holds a cross-staff, while the Magdalene reaches out, crouching slightly.[10]

The sequence of the Marys at the Tomb, presented across in the three middle lights of the rosace, is a late example of the scene. By the mid-thirteenth century it was largely replaced in France by Christ Leaving the Tomb, a scene already found in two windows at Bourges (bays 3 and 6, ca. 1210–15).[11] Reims joins other late examples: Saint-Julien-du-Sault (bay 0, ca. 1235–40), Troyes (bay 200, ca. 1235–40), Lyon (the south rose, ca. 1235–40), Sens (bay 100, ca. 1240), the Sainte-Chapelle (axial bay H, ca. 1245). Even later examples are found at Tours cathedral (bay 2, from Saint-Julien de Tours, ca. 1250; bay 200, ca. 1257–70); and at Saint-Gengoult, Toul (bay 0, ca. 1255–61), and nearby at Ménillot (bay 0, after 1263), both in Lorraine.[12]

Unlike Reims, however, all these thirteenth-century examples show the scene compressed so that the angel sits on the sarcophagus and the three Marys stand beside it. The Reims rosace displays the scene in full Romanesque splendor. Indeed, it is remarkable how close the Reims depiction is to the same subject in Poitiers cathedral (bay 0, ca. 1165–70; fig. 26): the angel seated to the left, the three women approaching at the right, and in the center a building with two towers flanking a central trilobed arch from which hangs a lamp, sleeping guards placed below and to the sides.[13] At Poitiers the shroud is piled on the centrally located sarcophagus, with four holes on the front face, while the Reims sarcophagus is decorated with three niches and two circles. Of the several theories that have been suggested for these "holes" in the sarcophagus, the most logical seems to me the one suggested by William Forsyth. "The Emperor Constantine Porphyrogenitos had covered the rock (bench on which Christ's body lay) within the Holy Sepulchre with a marble facing to protect it, and the Russian pilgrim Daniel thus describes, in 1106–7, the three holes through the marble: 'And now this holy bench is covered with marble plaques and one has cut in the side three little round windows and by these windows one sees this holy stone.'"[14] The appearance of the Reims sequence of the Marys at the Tomb and its close resemblance to Poitiers suggest that it replicates the scene as it appeared in twelfth-century glass of the previous Reims chevet, built by Archbishop Samson (r. 1140–60). Such glazing would have been lost in the cathedral fire, traditionally dated May 6, 1210, but possibly several years earlier.[15] A similar argument is made in chapter 3 concerning the Crucifixion below the rosace of Bay 100. A good example of such replication would be the axial clerestory of La Trinité, Vendôme. Louis Grodecki argued convincingly that its graceful Trinity of ca. 1280 reproduces the theme's earlier Gnadenstuhl design from a lost Romanesque image in the same axial location.[16]

The color of the Bay 100 rosace reflects that used in the lancets below. The palette is focused strongly on blue and red with main accents in white and purple-brown and smaller areas of gold and green. Although the axial bay has sometimes been dated as late as the 1240s, my argument (presented in chapter 3)—that it was a donation of Henri de Braine to celebrate his consecration as archbishop in 1227—provides some support for the theory that parts of it reproduce elements of the Romanesque glazing lost in the fire. That glass would not have remained in the canons' collective memory forever; less than twenty years later, perhaps it might.

Scholars now believe, and I concur, that the suffragan bishops flanking Bay 100 (in Bays 101 through 108) were arranged in the hierarchical seating established by the archbishop for provincial councils in 1231 (see fig. 18). In other words, if Bay 100 commemorates Henri de Braine's consecration as archbishop in 1227 and the remainder of the chevet program replicates a seating plan after 1231, that program was not necessarily conceived with Bay 100. Certainly none of the other bays is by the same artist (as analyzed in chapter 3). Since the rosaces of most of the chevet bays coordinate closely in style with their lancets, the investigation of their iconographic program, which follows below, represents planning, study, and achievement starting after 1231. And as we shall see, the rosaces are a remarkable achievement.

Apostles' Lives

The number and names of the apostles appear in the Gospels, and a few of their evangelizing activities are recounted in the New Testament book of Acts. The early Church invented fabulous tales to flesh out this bare history, tales now most accessible to us in the late-thirteenth-century compilation—and bestseller—known as the Golden Legend.[17] Before the thirteenth century—with the exception of stars like St. Peter or John the Evangelist—the apostles most commonly appear in art as a group, with little to distinguish

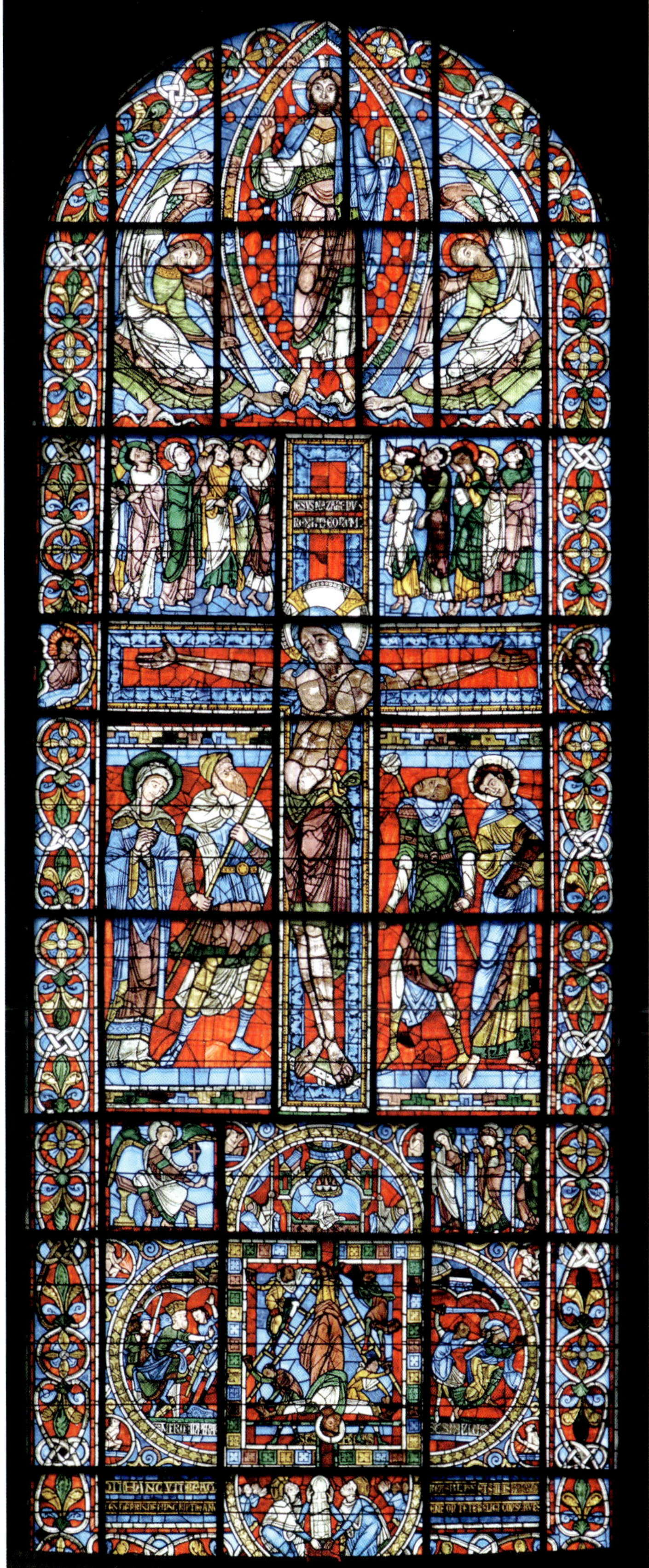

FIG. 26 Poitiers cathedral, bay 0, ca. 1165–70.

one from another except perhaps a name inscription. It may come as a surprise to the reader—it certainly did to me—that before the Reims rosaces of the 1230s, there is only one full series of apostles' lives known in monumental art.[18] That one example is San Marco in Venice, where selected scenes from the lives of all the Twelve were included around 1200 in the mosaics below the western Pentecost dome. While two or three scenes there are devoted to each apostle, as in the Reims rosaces, the choice of stories and their visualization are not particularly close. Otto Demus states that the study of the San Marco series is "especially difficult because of the small number of preserved cycles of the theme [of the apostles' vitae]," noting that there exists so far no comprehensive study of it.[19]

In manuscripts such as lectionaries and passionals containing the legends of the apostles to be read on their feast days, a few twelfth-century examples include illustrations for those texts. Examples include the Stuttgart Passional and Regensburg Martyrology (in which John and Philip are omitted, since they were not martyred).[20] Such manuscripts concentrate on the apostles' martyrdoms, a saint's feast day being the day of his death. The Reims rosaces avoid martyrdoms; this is increasingly so in the later bays. In only two of the six "apostles rosaces" is the central light devoted to a martyrdom. One is the very traditional and well-established scene of the upside-down crucifixion of St. Peter (Bay 102, in the hemicycle); the other is the skinning of Bartholomew (Bay 106, the earliest window of the straight chevet), a very special and interesting case reflecting the canons' research on the glazing program, discussed below.[21] The early rosaces, that is, those in the hemicycle, contain martyrdoms in the lobes: of Paul and James Major in Bay 101, probably the first bay to be made, ca. 1231, and of Peter and Andrew in Bay 102, probably the next.[22] In the lobes of the later rosaces (including 107 and 108, devoted to Matthias and Barnabas), violent death is increasingly and studiously avoided. Its omission is all the more surprising since, for these lesser-known saints, the only event in their lives that had any visual tradition was their martyrdom. One conclusion can be drawn so far, and that is that the Reims rosaces were not, as a group, modeled after some illustrated manuscript martyrology.

Previous to Reims some of the more important apostles had been the subjects of extensive narrative cycles in glass, most significantly at Chartres, where bays are devoted to the lives of Paul, Andrew, James Major, John, Thomas, and Simon and Jude together.[23] Such medallion windows contain numerous individual scenes, sometimes over two dozen, and often include extensive martyrdom sequences. At Reims, in contrast, each rosace contains only three or four scenes for each apostle. Thus the choice of these scenes required great selectivity, unlike elaborate medallion windows such as those of Chartres and Bourges. The six rosaces of the Reims chevet that are devoted to the Twelve, extended by Matthias and Barnabas, were without much doubt planned as a group as an important element in the chevet program of 1231. The apostles appear in the order of the Canon of the Mass: Peter, Paul, Andrew, James Major, John, Thomas, James the Less, Philip, Bartholomew, Matthew, Simon, and Jude.[24] They alternate across the chevet according to what might be called Gothic protocol; that is, they start with Peter in the position of primacy and zigzag back and forth across the chevet, concluding with Jude. The order of scenes in the lobes of the Twelve reads bottom–top–middle in the first bay (102, Peter and Andrew) as well as in Bay 105 (Matthew and Jude), which form the beginning and end of the series (see fig. 27). Next, the scenes in Bays 104 (John and James the Less) and 103 (Thomas and Philip) read middle–bottom–top. And finally, Bays 101 (Paul and James Major) and 106 (the lobes of Bartholomew) read from bottom to middle to top. Thus the ordering of scenes in the lobes creates a very subtle network that binds the Twelve together as a distinct group, at once establishing their hierarchy of importance while proclaiming their corporate identity as apostles of Christ. And since Simon's narrative, in Bay 106, at

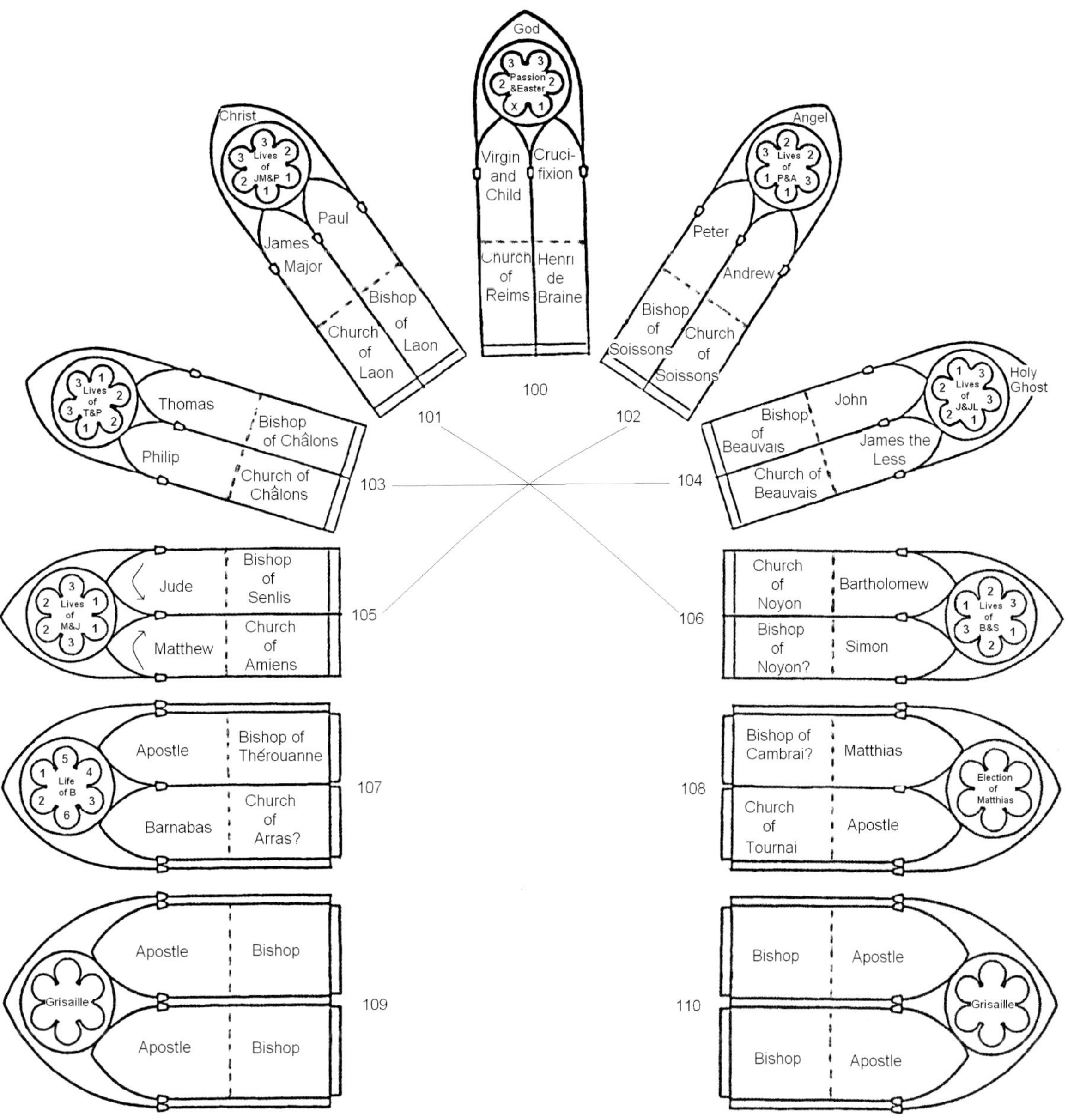

the very end of this series, breaks with this pattern, we have a clue to a significant break in the glazing program. I argue below that this hiatus was the canons' exile from November 1234 to January 1237.

The Pseudo-Abdias

While the San Marco mosaic cycle and the Reims rosaces certainly have no direct connection, it is worth considering the similarity of the artistic challenge. Both are full cycles of the lives of the Twelve, for which there were no precedents in art. In both the apostles appear in the same sequence; in both they were arranged, within a distinctive and imposing monumental space, in a coherent group and also in hierarchic order. In Venice the series begins (Peter) and ends (Jude) on the outermost, that is, the north and south, aisle walls

FIG. 27 Chart of the chevet rosaces indicating the order of scenes in the lobes (measured drawings with kind permission of Jürgen Michler, after "Fenster- und Masswerksysteme in der nordfranzösischen Gotik des 13. Jahrhunderts," *Wallraf-Richartz Jahrbuch* 62 [2001]: 72, fig. 4).

of the nave, dominated by the Pentecost dome.[25] In both Venice and Reims the choice of scenes was severely limited to around three per apostle. Demus concluded that the mosaics' ultimate textual source was not Byzantine but a Western, Latin collection of apocryphal lives of the apostles known as the Pseudo-Abdias.[26]

It seems a reasonable hypothesis that the same collection, well known and widely distributed in the West, may have been mined for the program at Reims. While the selection of scenes at Reims often differs from that at San Marco, the extensive narratives of the Pseudo-Abdias—much longer than in other such collections—provide ample choice; the themes preferred at Reims and the reasons for their selection are addressed below. And there was a copy of the Pseudo-Abdias in Reims in the thirteenth century in the extensive library of the Benedictine abbey of Saint-Thierry. The manuscript survives and is now Paris, Bibliothèque nationale de France, lat. 5563.[27] Lest such a hypothesis seem far-fetched, one should consider that the Saint-Thierry library was the most extensive in the region around Reims and that the unusual iconographic programs of the cathedral's rosaces, both chevet and nave, provide evidence for the use of other Saint-Thierry manuscripts.[28]

The development of stories of the apostles is complicated, and so I will only sketch it here. The five oldest apocryphal acts of apostles—those for Peter, Paul, Andrew, John, and Thomas—were separate works composed during the second to third centuries.[29] The Manichaeans adopted them, grouped them together, and substituted them for the canonical Acts; thus they were condemned as heretical works by the Roman Church in the mid-fifth century. The popularity of these wonder stories among orthodox Christians, however, gave rise to several "scrubbed" compilations of the apostles' acts during the next century in the West, which have come to be known as the Pseudo-Melito and the Pseudo-Abdias.[30] While both include all twelve apostles and both were largely based on the same sources, they differ in their approach as well as occasionally in the episodes included. The Pseudo-Melito was probably composed in Rome ca. 450–500. The author is a rigid theologian who eliminates everything morally questionable or theologically suspect; he intends to produce a strictly orthodox work. In contrast, the Pseudo-Abdias was compiled in Gaul, probably in the circle of Gregory of Tours, in the late sixth century. The author is a raconteur, not particularly concerned about orthodoxy, who adapts and embroiders in order to enrich the apostles' fame with stories of their miracles, producing a clear and accessible work for a popular audience. As Eric Junod and Jean-Daniel Kaestli sum up the difference between this work and the Pseudo-Melito: "Quand il est choqué par le texte de sa source, il recourt à la plume plutôt qu'au ciseau."[31]

The orthodox Pseudo-Melito enjoyed greater diffusion throughout the Western Church—ten times as many manuscripts surviving—while the Pseudo-Abdias was only known in France and southern Germany. The Pseudo-Abdias, however, includes more stories. In the chapter on John, for example, the Pseudo-Abdias recounts the story of the trial with boiling oil, which is found in the rosace of Bay 104, while the Pseudo-Melito does not.[32] Although, according to Junod and Kaestli, the Golden Legend was primarily based on the Pseudo-Melito, Émile Mâle recognized the Pseudo-Abdias as a source for French medieval art.[33] It contains eleven books or chapters, one each devoted to the story of an apostle, with Simon and Jude grouped together.[34] As such, it would provide a very handy reference for an iconographer seeking themes to illustrate from the apostles' lives.

The apostles' legends in the Pseudo-Abdias are quite lengthy, and the question remains: what governed the selection of only three (or four) scenes for each saint in the rosaces? As mentioned above, only in the first two bays to be undertaken (Bays 101 and 102) are martyrdoms regularly included.[35] Three themes are stressed. The first theme is perhaps surprising, since it is not particularly dramatic—it is preaching. However, the preaching of the apostles was at the command of Christ himself, and preaching was one of the important duties of bishops. This theme underlines the apostolic succession of Reims's suffragan bishops and the source of their authority, which was being seriously challenged by the townsmen in the 1230s.[36] A second important theme in the rosaces is the confrontation of the apostles with secular antagonists at all levels, from kings down to ordinary citizens and servants. The archbishop's difficulties with Louis IX, as well as the townsmen's physical attacks on the canons, no doubt energized this theme. And the third theme is that of the apostles' triumphs over idols. This motif is not as strange as it might appear once one realizes that (as outlined in chapter 1 and appendix 1) the Inquisition was increasing its activity in the region in the 1230s and was beginning to equate, and punish equally, heresy (i.e., worship of idols, disbelief) and usury. These three themes are in many cases by no means the most significant incidents in a given apostle's legend, which highlights their selection for the rosaces.

The following study of the rosaces takes them up in what I argue is their chronological order. The rosace of Bay 100, described above, along with its lancets, in my opinion dates ca. 1227–30 as a celebration of Henri de Braine's consecration as archbishop. After ca. 1231—and the establishment by the archbishop of the seating arrangement for the suffragan bishops—follow the next bays, 101 and 102. Bays 103 and 104, and some work on 106, were completed before the canons were forced into exile on November 9, 1234. Upon their return in triumph on January 2, 1237, work continued on Bays 106, 105, 107, and 108. But with Henri de Braine's confrontation with the town growing increasingly violent, the town once again placed under interdict, the doors of the cathedral locked, and the archbishop in exile in late 1238, this final work was sporadic and the glass may have been stored, rather than installed, as it was made. Following the death of Henri de Braine, still in exile on July 6, 1240, this glass could be installed, and Bays 109 and 110 and possibly some of the transept grisailles were produced before the inauguration of the canons' choir on September 7, 1241.

Rosace of Bay 101: Paul and James Major

Bay 101 offers several hints that it was the first of the chevet series to be undertaken following, by a few years at most, the gift of Bay 100 by Henri de Braine to commemorate his election in 1227. One could affirm, in addition, that the rosace (figs. 29, 30) and lancets of Bay 101 (fig. 73) are very close in style; the palette in both uses a lucid medium blue that appears nowhere else in the chevet, and the drapery painting in both is accomplished with thick, short, jagged strokes. The ogive of Christ blessing (fig. 28), on the other hand, resembles the lancets of Bays 103 and 104 (see appendix 3).

The order of scenes in the lobes of the 101 rosace is bottom, middle, top, the same as the rosace of Bay 100 (see fig. 27). The designer has copied the Bay 100 rosace in using a similar horizontal arrangement of scenes in the lobes, here linking the two apostles by pairing very similar events in their lives in the left and right lobes. At the bottom the first lobes for both Paul and James show them preaching, while the second and third lobes depict their conflicts with secular tyrants. Paul appears in fetters before Nero, while James, with a rope around his neck, is dragged before

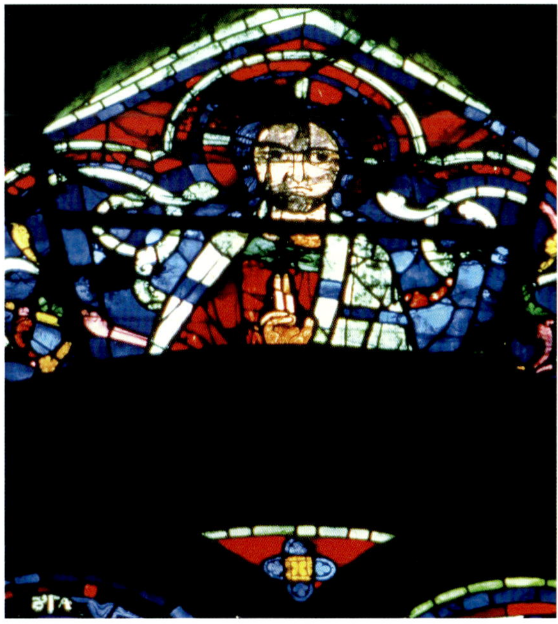

FIG. 28 Bay 101, ogive, Christ blessing.

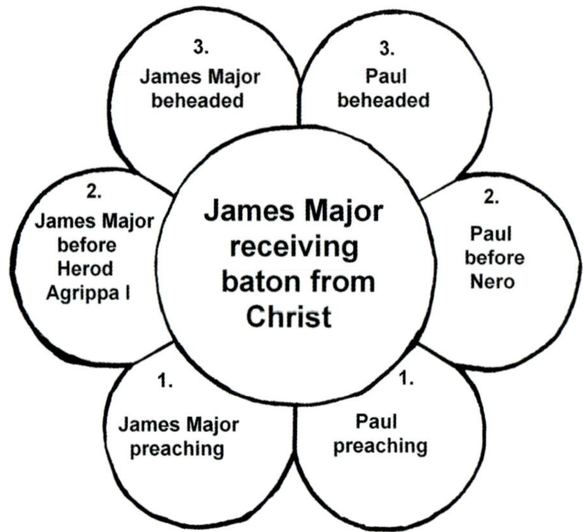

FIG. 29 Bay 101, rosace, chart of scenes: Paul and James Major.

FIG. 30 Bay 101, rosace, Paul and James Major.

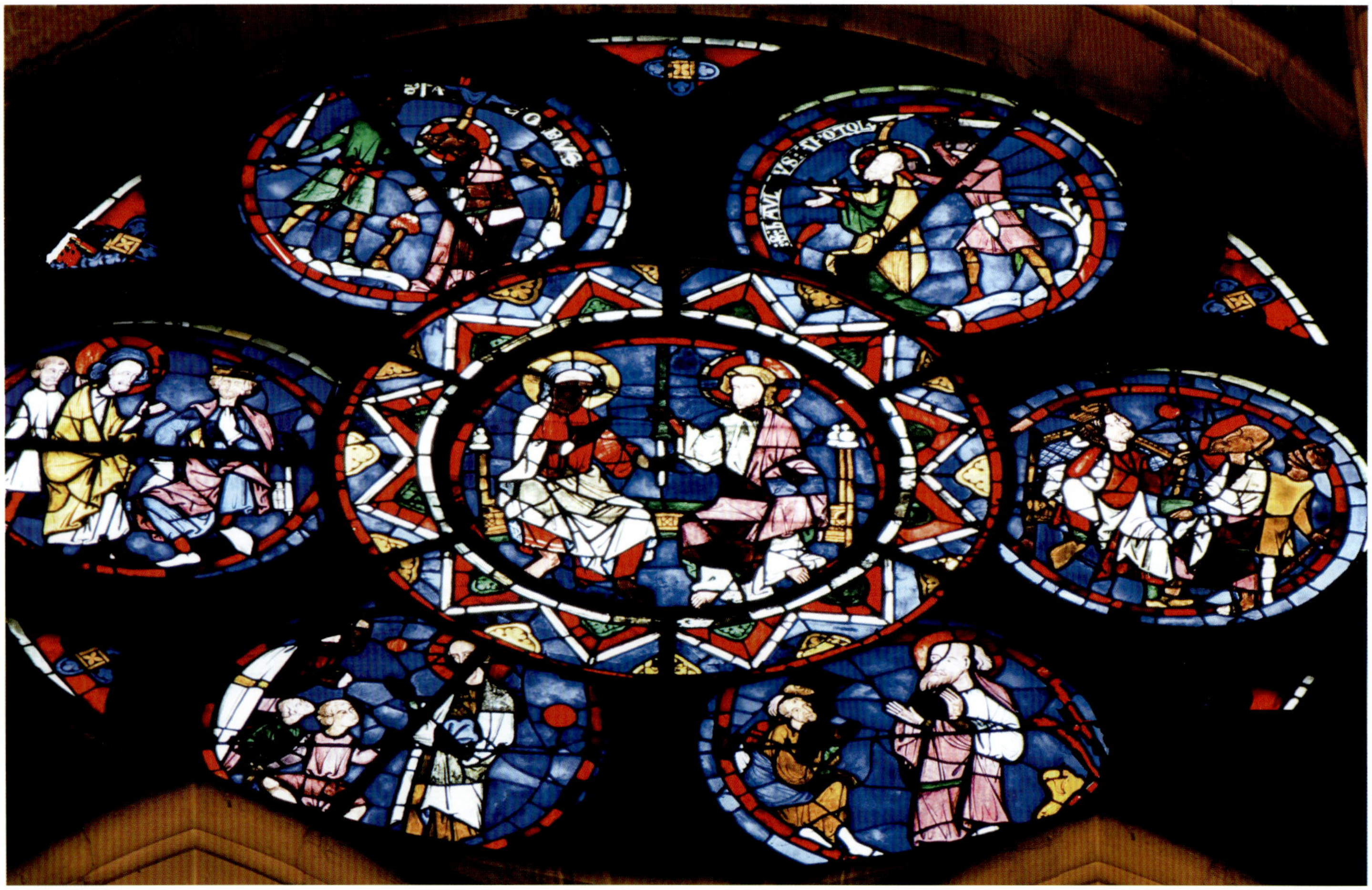

Herod Agrippa. In each case the tyrant orders the saint's beheading, shown in the paired lobes at the top. Each upper lobe includes an inscription naming the apostle, to help those with eagle vision identify figures that are more than 120 feet above them. Once these panels were installed, the uselessness of these name inscriptions was surely obvious, and they were never repeated. This is one clue that Bay 101 started off the chevet series of apostles and suffragans.[37]

In his three lobes on the right of the rosace, Paul is typically bald (fig. 31). He is described as "a man small of stature, with a bald head," in *The Acts of Paul and Thecla* 3.3, part of the Early Christian *Acts of Paul* that was written ca. 185–95 C.E. and later condemned by the Church. Since Paul died ca. 67 C.E. and this description may not be historically accurate, it has been explained by János Bollók as an example of the ancient pseudo-science of physiognomy.[38] Paul appears in art with a bald pate before the fifth century, an early example being the scene of Paul's arrest carved into the famous sarcophagus of Junius Bassus (d. 359) in the Vatican Grottoes.[39] It was traditional in Western art long before the Gothic age.

Omitted are the colorful Pauline episodes of Damascus, Melita, and so forth. Rather, the first lobe introduces Paul preaching to a group of four, presumably in Rome. His universal reputation as a missionary preacher made such scenes constant in art, and another was later included in the facade sculpture of Reims. In stained glass that dates before Reims, the medallion window in Rouen cathedral (bay 14, ca. 1220–30) could be mentioned, containing four scenes of Paul preaching.[40] The Pseudo-Abdias (chaps. 1–6) generally follows the text of the book of Acts, which concludes with Paul preaching in Rome; to this biblical account it appends a coda (chaps. 7–8), drawn from an apocryphal source, on his final confrontation there with Nero.[41] In the middle lobe of the Reims rosace Paul, holding a book, is led before Nero by a guard brandishing a rope.

The top lobe shows the beheading, Paul kneeling and the executioner standing behind him,

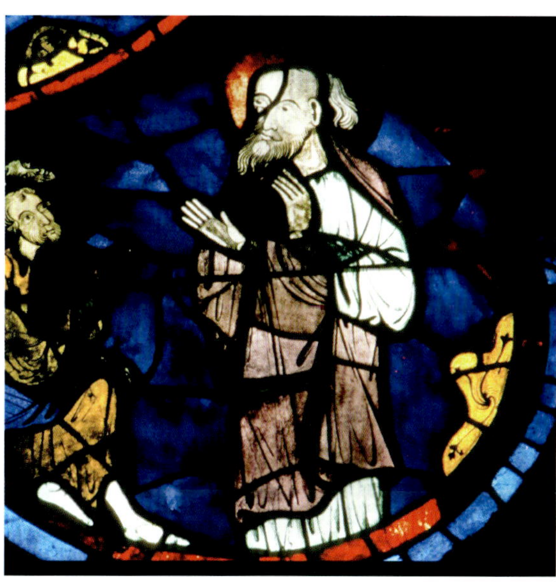

FIG. 31 Paul preaching, Bay 101, rosace, detail of lower right lobe.

raising his sword with one hand and grasping the saint's hair with the other. Paul is still alive, and there is no blindfold or other reference to the popular story of Plautilla and her veil—which is not included in the Pseudo-Abdias. The source of the blindfolded version is a text known as the Pseudo-Linus, and the story appears in windows at Poitiers (bay 0, ca. 1165–70), Chartres (bay 4, ca. 1210–25), and Rouen (bay 14, ca. 1220–30).[42] Luba Eleen states that liturgical manuscripts depict Paul's beheading with a great deal more gore, while biblical illuminations maintain the rather restrained format of Reims.[43] Her observation underscores the conclusion reached earlier, that lectionaries and martyrologies were not the models for the Reims rosaces.

The three lobes on the left, devoted to James Major, mimic the Pauline scenes in visual arrangement as well as theme: from bottom to top, preaching, confrontation with secular authority, and beheading. The tyrant in the middle lobe is Herod Agrippa I, who, according to the biblical book of Acts 12:1–2, ordered James's execution in Jerusalem in 44 C.E., making him the first apostle to be martyred.[44] The Pseudo-Abdias mentions, among many much more entertaining episodes, James's successful preaching career, the scribe

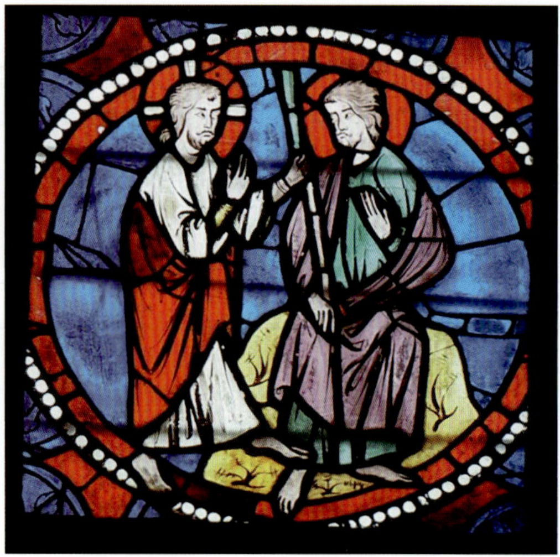

FIG. 32 Christ giving James Major a baton half stripped of bark: Le Mans cathedral, bay 111, detail, ca. 1254.

Josais dragging him before Herod by a rope around his neck, and his beheading.[45] The rope is visible in the middle lobe with a modern lens but, like the name inscriptions, certainly cannot be seen from the floor. These scenes are also embedded in a number of medallion windows throughout the thirteenth century both before and after Reims.[46] In conclusion, the lobes of the Reims rosace are traditional and pro forma in their iconography.

The horizontal layering of the Bay 101 rosace is more sophisticated than that of Bay 100 (the sequence of the Marys at the Tomb) or Bay 102 (the crucifixions of Peter and Andrew). In Bay 101 the horizontal row presents two holy figures enthroned majestically in the central roundel, dignified and serene in their power. Flanking them are the lobes with the two tyrants (Nero and Herod Agrippa), similarly enthroned but sprawling and twitching, undignified, unsettled. Their confusion and mental distress are a sensitive artist's judgment on their sinful actions.

The literature on Reims, however, has completely mistaken the identity of the two majestic figures—and for that matter their actions—in the central roundel scene (fig. 30). In the nineteenth century Cerf called the roundel "Christ giving St. Paul a scepter"; Reinhardt said it was "Paul offering his sword to Christ"; and the French Corpus Vitrearum labeled it "Peter offering his sword to Christ."[47] The figure on the right, with the cruciferous halo, is indeed Christ. However, the figure enthroned next to him is neither Peter nor Paul, and the object is not a scepter or sword. The scene depicts Christ enthroned next to James Major, giving him a rod or staff, green on top and white below. While this scene has not (yet) been found in any vita of James, it is not unknown in thirteenth-century French art, though not always recognized. Examples in stained glass before Reims include Chartres bay 5 and lost bay 111; contemporary with Reims, Troyes bay 211 (ca. 1228–35); and later, Le Mans bay 111 (ca. 1254, fig. 32), Tours bay 210 (ca. 1260–70), and Saint-Urbain de Troyes bay 103 (ca. 1270).[48] The figures sometimes sit, sometimes stand, and occasionally are accompanied by an angel.

The scene has been identified by Humbert Jacomet from a scathing comment in the sermon *Veneranda Dies* found in book 1, xvii, of the *Codex Calixtinus* in Santiago de Compostela.[49] Among folk fables stigmatized by the preacher is the belief that Christ appeared to St. James with a branch half-stripped of its bark, saying that all who prayed in his sanctuary would be cleansed of their sin as the staff was cleaned; pilgrims thus imagined that it sufficed to invoke the saint to be instantly sin-free. Jacomet concludes that the branch merged in art with a pilgrim's baton, and this seems to be occurring at Reims. James's baton was a relic at Santiago, enclosed in a silver case that pilgrims were allowed to touch. The baton in the Reims rosace is green and white, as appropriate to the half-stripped branch, but has a knob on it resembling those of the batons held by James on the trumeau of Santiago's Portico de la Gloria (1183) and by the possibly twelfth-century figure of James on the high altar there.[50]

The Troyes cathedral glass, roughly contemporary with that of Reims, includes James's familiar shells set into the background. The Reims image, however, is even more noteworthy for a different, significant detail. Unlike any of the other examples mentioned above, James wears a striking, medium blue head covering (fig. 30), a very precocious version of the apostle's typical pilgrim hat that was later to become standard for his image. It encircles his head like a second halo and seems to have a flap to cover his neck. The original section of the clear blue glass, at the right, is decorated with a patterned band of x's (xxxxxxxxxxx); the replaced part at the left, as well as the blue hat James wears when confronting Herod in the middle left lobe, have been misinterpreted in modern glass as "blue hair."[51] This pilgrim hat serves, like Paul's bald head, to identify the apostle James. I have found no other example in any medium earlier than the 1260s: for example, at Amiens, on the lintel of the Saint-Honoré portal (south transept, 1259–69), and the stained-glass panel probably from the Château de Rouen (Musée nationale du Moyen Âge, Paris, ca. 1260s).[52]

James was first connected with Spain in the seventh century; thus the Pseudo-Abdias account, which was compiled earlier, contains no mention of Spain. Therefore the question of why the Reims rosace features this scene—explored below and in appendix 4—is potentially significant. The earliest text connecting James with Spain in any way is the *Breviarium Apostolorum,* a very brief descriptive list of the apostles written during the seventh century (thus after the Pseudo-Abdias) and copied in Paris by ca. 750. The complete entry on James Major is as follows: "James, whose name should be interpreted as the one who follows, the son of Zebedee, the brother of John, preached in Spain and in the western regions; Struck with a sword, he died, under Herod, and was buried in Achaian Marmarica on July 25."[53] The legend was continually enlarged and embroidered, notably after the tenth century, when the cult of James in Spain began to take on broader European dimensions.[54] Between 1139 and 1173 such texts and stories were incorporated into the Santiago texts known as the *Codex Calixtinus* and the *Historia Compostellana,* and "depuis lors, la tradition peut être considérée comme fixée."[55] Included were the legend of translation of James's body from Jerusalem to Spain, many miraculous events thereafter, various apocryphal papal letters as "proof," the Pseudo-Turpin legend of Charlemagne, and so forth.

The Reims image—Christ giving a half-stripped staff to St. James, who wears a precocious pilgrim hat—is a very surprising scene to find as the central subject in a rosace that dates to the early 1230s. It is particularly surprising since the normal order followed at Reims, in all other bays, allots the central roundel to the more important of the two apostles in that window; in Bay 101 the higher honor should certainly be accorded to Paul. The figure of James in the lancet below is also unusual. He is standing, and is the only apostle to be vested as a priest (fig. 73). Why is James so important? How to explain the special Spanish tinge to James's rosace at Reims, where the saint does not seem to have been celebrated more than his apostolic condition would dictate in any Christian church?[56] A hypothesis can be made that the donor of Bay 101, installed around 1231, was Archbishop Henri de Braine.

Although the archbishop had never been to Santiago, so far as we know, his cultured, aristocratic family did have such connections—including an unusual and potentially significant literary one. Henri de Braine's uncle and mentor, Philippe de Dreux (bishop of Beauvais, 1180–1217), had made a pilgrimage there in 1182.[57] Among other things, Philippe was a collector of a notable library, which at his death in 1217 he willed to his nephew Henri, then in his first job as treasurer of Beauvais cathedral. There are several reasons why this library may have included a manuscript, perhaps in French, concerning St. James and based on the *Codex Calixtinus* (which surfaced in Santiago ca. 1173) or the *Historia Compostellana* (ca. 1140). The final contributor to the latter work was a canon of Santiago named Girardus, who was a Frenchman from Beauvais. In 1212 the writer Pierre de Beauvais, whose career was in the service of Bishop Philippe, put into the vernacular the *Translatio* and *Miraculi Sancti Jacobi* for "Countess Yolande," possibly Bishop Philippe's sister-in-law and Henri de Braine's mother. Earlier Pierre had also written a French version of the Pseudo-Turpin; these texts form books II–IV of the *Codex Calixtinus* and are also incorporated into the *Compostellana.* In other words, while no physical

FIG. 33 Bay 102, rosace, chart of scenes: Peter and Andrew.

FIG. 34 Bay 102, rosace, Peter and Andrew.

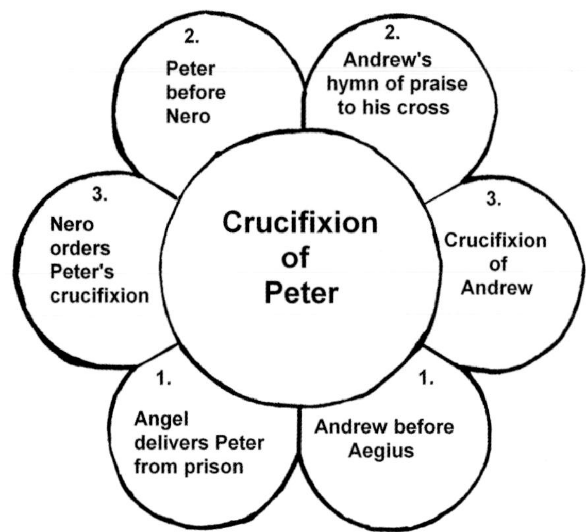

or documentary evidence exists except the strange importance and Spanish iconography of St. James in Bay 101, it is a reasonable theory that Henri de Braine was interested in the apostle. He may have owned a manuscript from Compostela or one in the vernacular, made for his family by Pierre de Beauvais, concerning Spanish material about St. James Major.[58]

The Rosace of Bay 102: Peter and Andrew

Bay 102 probably followed Bay 101 closely in time, early in the chevet campaign begun ca. 1231. It is by a different artist, who attempts to correct the perceived flaws of Bay 101 in legibility. The design is cleansed of superfluous ornament and focused in palette, particularly by the choice of green to tie the design together. The rosace resembles the lancets below in this palette as well as in a beautifully shaded drapery painting found nowhere else in the hemicycle, while copying the format of horizontal rows of scenes of both Bays 100 and 101. One hint that this artist has a different background is his use, in four of the six lobes, of an inner red circle in the blue ground behind the figures. This is a trait associated particularly with glass at Laon,[59] one that recurs at Reims later in the mediocre rosace of Bay 108 and then in the definitely not mediocre north-transept rose.

The order of scenes in the lobes is bottom, top, middle (see figs. 33, 34). The three lobes on the left and the central roundel are devoted to Peter.[60] The bottom lobe illustrates Peter's delivery by an angel from the prison of Herod Agrippa I in 43 C.E., one of the rare rosace scenes to be found in the Bible (Acts 12:1–11).[61] This story was commemorated by the feast of Peter in Chains on August 1 as early as the fourth century, also read on June 29 (feast of Peter and Paul), and referred to in the Requiem Mass; it is also related in the Pseudo-Abdias.[62] The Reims lobe adopts the most standard medieval format, with Peter in three-quarter pose, chains on his ankles, and the angel gesturing with raised hand. It was interpreted early as the soul's liberation in death, and by the twelfth century as the triumph of the Church (or the pope) over secular foes, among which events was the Spanish Reconquista.[63] At Reims, in a window of the early 1230s associated with Archbishop Henri de Braine, the choice of this scene—over popular miracles like Simon Magus, for example—might reflect his troubles with Louis IX or the "Spanish connection" in Bay 101, discussed above. It is impossible to say.

Peter's second lobe (top left) depicts his confrontation with a crowned, enthroned ruler, and the third (middle) shows the same ruler pointing to the crucifixion of Peter in the rosace's central roundel. The ruler is not Herod Agrippa I, as in the first lobe, but Nero, so named in the Pseudo-Abdias and as commonly identified by the medieval period.[64] The most common format for Peter's crucifixion in French medieval art was for the saint to be clothed and flanked by executioners, as at Reims. Most early sources, including the Pseudo-Abdias, do not specify how he was attached to the cross. Tertullian (ca. 155–222 C.E.) states that Peter was tied; only the Pseudo-Marcellus specifies that Peter was nailed.[65] While the tied version is standard in sculpture of Gothic France, in stained glass both traditions existed. St. Peter is nailed to the cross in western French glass from the

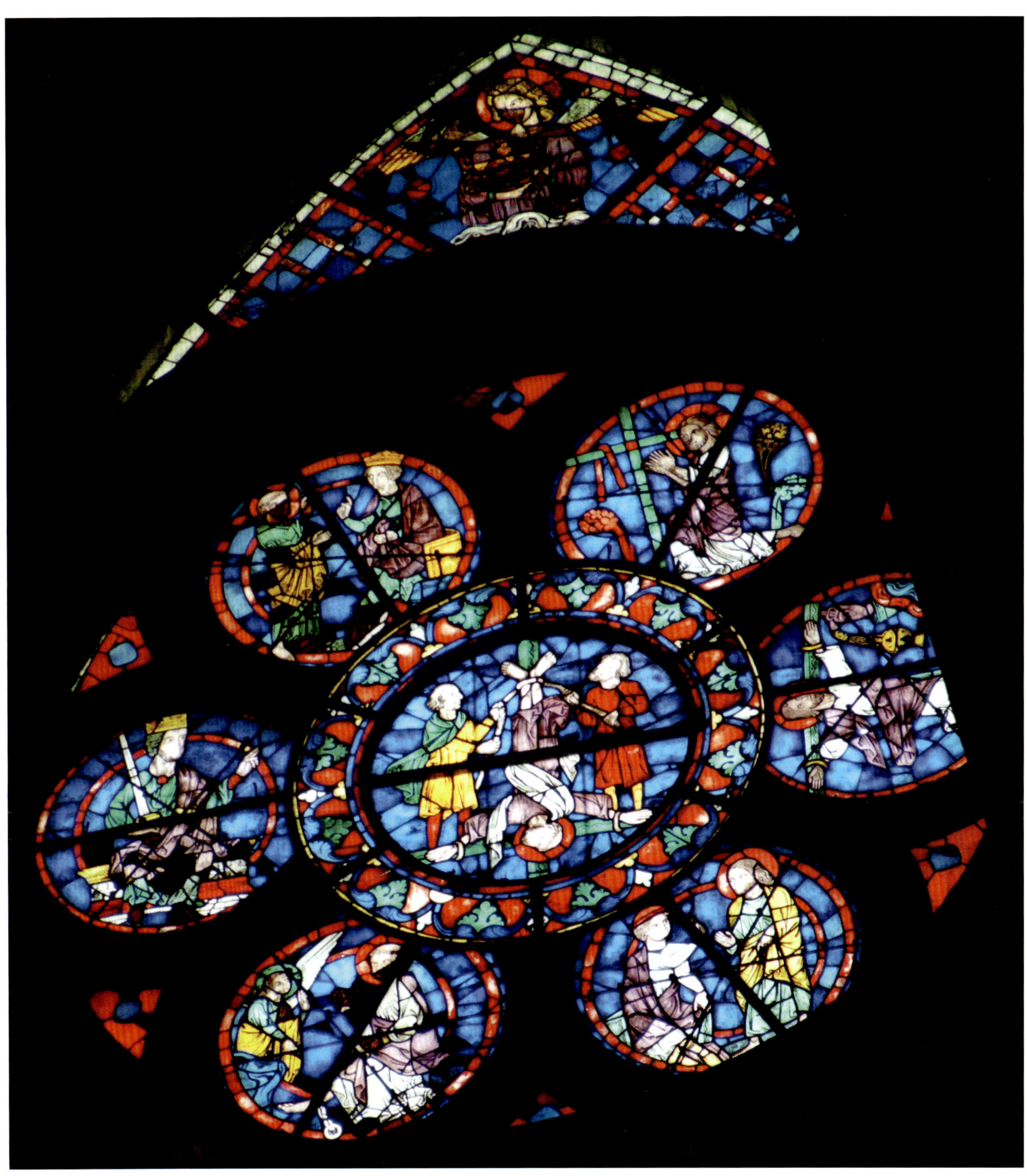

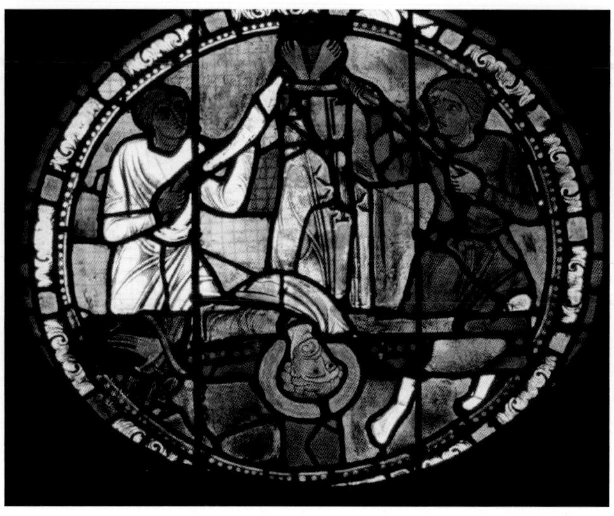

FIG. 35 Crucifixion of Peter: Lyon cathedral, bay 7, detail of rosace, ca. 1190.

mid–twelfth century (Poitiers) to the end of the thirteenth century (Saint-Père de Chartres).[66]

The Reims rosace, on the other hand, conforms closely to the type of tied crucifixion that was preferred in eastern French glass during the earlier period. It is particularly close to a roundel at Lyon cathedral now set into the rosace of bay 7 (ca. 1190, fig. 35); other examples are in the cathedrals of Clermont-Ferrand (ca. 1180–1200), Troyes (ambulatory bay 14, ca. 1200), and Bourges (ca. 1210–15).[67] It is noteworthy that Reims adheres so closely to this earlier tradition, since eastern French windows immediately following Reims depict St. Peter nailed to his cross: Troyes clerestory bay 204 (ca. 1235–40) and Auxerre bay 7 (ca. 1250).[68] Even more noteworthy are the scenes not depicted at Reims: there are no appearances of Peter with Christ, none of Peter's miracles canonical or apocryphal, not even the very popular legend of Peter's contest with the magician Simon Magus.[69] What are stressed at Reims are Peter's conflicts with various secular authorities, depicted first through his angelic delivery from Herod's prison and then his persecution by the tyrant Nero. The three lobes devoted to Andrew, on the right side of the rosace, continue in the same vein (fig. 33).

The first of Andrew's lobes (bottom right) shows the saint standing before Aegius, proconsul of Patras, who orders him into prison and later to his death. Again, the apostle's fabulous adventures are completely omitted. This confrontation scene appears in stained glass at Chartres (bay 2, ca. 1210–25) and Auxerre (bay 13, ca. 1235–45), though both include an armed guard as supernumerary.[70] The reduction to essentials at Reims is typical of the strong focus of the artist, who is not interested in storytelling or ornament but concentrates on composing readable icons that focus and transmit the themes of the program. Lobe two (top right) illustrates the saint's prayer of adoration addressed to his cross of martyrdom, delivered immediately before his crucifixion. This prayer, famous in the Middle Ages and available in numerous excerpted forms, is the most celebrated part of the ancient *Acts of Andrew*.[71] Kneeling before the cross, the apostle prays: "Greetings, O cross! Greetings indeed! I know well that, though you have been weary for a long time, planted and awaiting me, now at last you can rest. I come to you, whom I have known. I recognize your mystery, why you were planted. So then, cross that is pure, radiant, full of life and light, receive me, I who have been weary for so long."[72] Andrew's hymn of praise, not illustrated before the mid–twelfth century, seems to have become more popular around the time of the Reims rosace. Examples can be cited in glass at Angers (bay 119, lost, ca. 1220) and, nearly contemporary with Reims, at Notre-Dame de Dijon (bay 15, ca. 1230–35) and Troyes cathedral (bay 11, ca. 1235–45).[73]

Reims differs from them in several ways. Unlike the windows cited above, no executioners or witnesses are included. The image is reduced to the kneeling, praying Andrew, the cross, and several "artichoke trees" to set the scene outdoors.[74] Unique, moreover, is the red object hanging from the cross arm (fig. 36), a detail not mentioned in the legend and not found elsewhere in art. It could possibly derive from a misunderstanding of the phylactery that infrequently accompanies the scene.[75] In the context in which it appears at Reims, the object resembles a priest's stole, a vestment priests and higher clergy wear when celebrating Mass. Its red color is said to have been designated by Innocent III

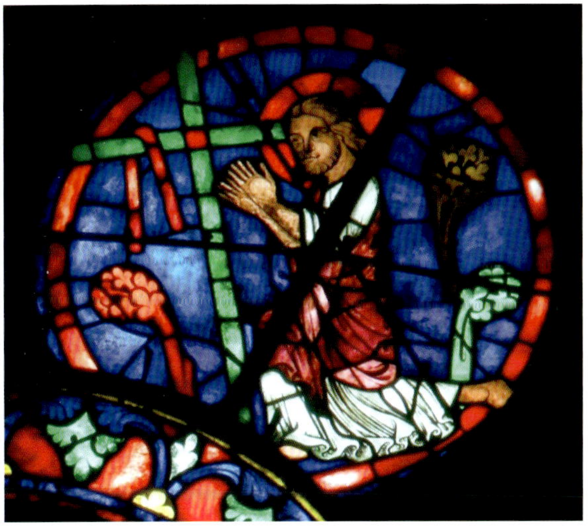

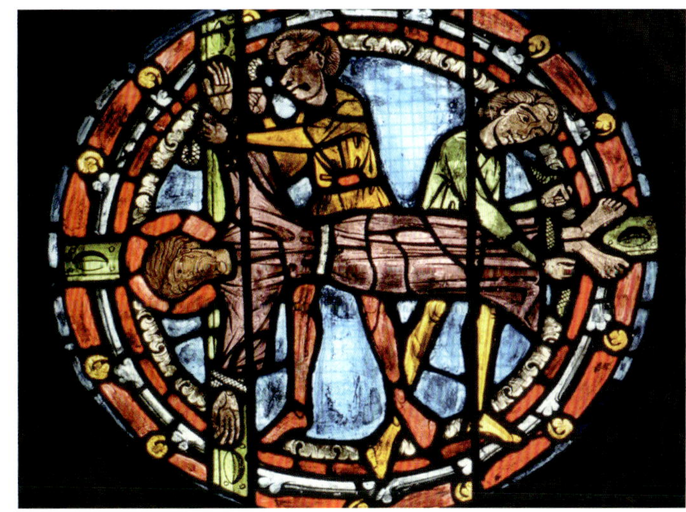

FIG. 36 Andrew's hymn of praise to the cross, Bay 102, rosace, top right lobe.

FIG. 37 Crucifixion of Andrew: Lyon cathedral, bay 7, detail of rosace, ca. 1190.

for apostles and martyrs and for Whitsuntide.[76] The appropriateness of such a banner, signifying at once apostle, priest, and Whitsun—that is, Pentecost and the gift of the Holy Spirit, which first empowered the apostles—is obvious. It is a visual icon distilling the basic theme of the Reims chevet program: the apostolic succession.

This reduction to essentials for clear legibility also marks the image of Andrew's crucifixion, in the third lobe (middle right). The apostle is tied to a horizontal cross and censed by a divine hand; nothing else invades the scene. Andrew's horizontal cross is common in French Gothic glass, though in medieval art his cross could be upright, sometimes upside-down like Peter's, diagonal, or occasionally saltire, a type that only later became standard. Much ink has been spilled over the introduction of the X cross; however, the Autun Troper (Paris, Arsenal, MS 1169, 1005–24 C.E.) folio 15r, has now been removed from consideration as the oldest example, since it depicts not St. Andrew but St. Vincent.[77] The upright cross is probably the oldest type. It is not infrequent in twelfth-century art, and among earlier examples is folio 215r from a Reims manuscript, the Lectionary of Manasses de Châtillon (Reims, Bibl. mun., MS 295, before 1096 C.E.).[78] Manasses had this large-size manuscript made and gave it, among others, to the cathedral chapter while he was provost and treasurer (from 1076 to 1096); he became archbishop of Reims in 1096. This provides more evidence that, as concluded earlier, the Reims rosaces were not based on a lectionary or passional.

The horizontal cross, found in the Reims rosace, does not appear until the end of the twelfth century. Denoël suggests that its origins were in oral tradition, first recorded in Jean Beleth's *Summa* (ca. 1160–64), and cites the earliest example as folio 208v of the Pamplona Bible (Amiens, Bibl. mun., lat. 108, ca. 1200).[79] An example in stained glass at Lyon cathedral (fig. 37), a fragment of the late twelfth century reused in the rosace of bay 7, may be even earlier. Horizontal crosses are fairly common in French thirteenth-century windows.[80] The difference at Reims is the extreme focus of the scene, eliminating all but the apostle, the cross, and God's censing hand.

Since Andrew's third lobe adjoins the central roundel of the rosace, the crucifixions of the brothers Peter and Andrew are closely connected visually. Both are tied to the cross. They are depicted in the same scale and are dressed in the same colors. The scenes read horizontally across left to right. The choice of a horizontal cross for Andrew and the elimination of onlookers of any kind aids in this composition and in addition provides immediate legibility and identification of the two saints, even to observers on the floor of the choir. The artist wished to improve on Bay 101 without violating the unity of the hemicycle group, and he has succeeded.

The Rosaces of Bays 103 and 104

Bays 103 and 104 complete the hemicycle glazing, and their rosaces were probably designed—though perhaps not completely executed—by a new and exciting artist. While clarity and legibility are no less important to him than to, for example, the designer of the Bay 102 rosace, his art is much more dramatic. The bodies are larger in scale, more massive, and draped in swathes of so-called wet drapery, an antiquizing style suggesting a comparison with the earliest Gothic sculpture of the cathedral. However, his figures have none of the classical serenity associated with that style, and the faces are particularly distinctive. The artist's hallmark—found in both lancets and rosaces—is hugely enlarged eyes, set within heavy facial shadowing, and ears that are placed too low.[81]

Because the roundel of the Bay 103 rosace has been lost, it is preferable to discuss first the rosace of Bay 104. The artist's dynamism can be appreciated even in the relationship of the central roundel to the surrounding lobes, making the loss of the Bay 103 roundel all the more unfortunate. Gone is the horizontal layering of scenes in rows, the approach to rosace design found in all the bays so far (100, 101, and 102). The designer of 104 (and, if we had it all, 103) orients his scenes on diagonals, basing the rosace design on that of, say, a star or an asterisk. It is yet another aspect of his dynamism.

The Rosace of Bay 104: John the Evangelist

The order of scenes in the lobes is middle, bottom, top (figs. 38, 39). The lobes on the left present John the Evangelist in the most consistently illustrated scenes of his legend, which was enormously popular during the Gothic period: the boiling oil, the poisoned cup, and John climbing into his tomb. All three episodes occur in the Pseudo-Abdias and in this order.[82] These three scenes occur at the very beginning and at the end of the Pseudo-Abdias text, while numerous colorful tales in between are ignored at Reims. As I have noted in previous rosaces, the chosen scenes emphasize themes that form the leitmotifs of the Reims chevet program: not only the apostolic succession but more generally the clergy's difficulties with secular authority figures and, in this case at least, the saint's ultimate triumph over all adversity. To emphasize the contemporary relevance, John is tonsured throughout—as were the medieval clergy. The canons of Reims had their tonsures shaved for seven annual feasts—Christmas, Easter, Pentecost, the Assumption, the Nativity of the Virgin, the Purification, and the Dedication of the Church.[83] This detail of the tonsure, as well as aspects of the Bay 103 rosace, probably reflects the waning of the archbishop's involvement in the glazing project after Bays 100 through 102. Starting in 1233 his struggles with the king (as outlined in chapter 1) heated up rapidly. From this time onward, the chapter seems to have been the controlling body in the chevet's glazing program.

The three scenes in the left lobes are common in narrative accounts of John,[84] who was a very popular saint in the Gothic period, and they also could serve to represent the whole. Suzanne Lewis has noted that the three illuminated initials provided for the three Epistles of John in an East Anglian Bible of ca. 1240–50—nearly contemporary with the Reims rosace—show these three episodes. And in glass one could mention another near-contemporary example, the huge medallions of clerestory bay 202 at Troyes cathedral (ca. 1235–40).[85]

There is, however, an important difference in the Reims rosace. The central roundel (fig. 40) shows John writing at his desk, but unlike Troyes and nearly all the examples invoked above, he is not on Patmos and not penning the Apocalypse. There is no water, there are no churches of Asia; John, accompanied by his eagle, appears as author of his Gospel.[86] The omission of Patmos from the rosace might seem surprising, given the appearance of the apocalyptic angels on the roofs of the suffragans' cathedral "facades" in the chevet lancets below

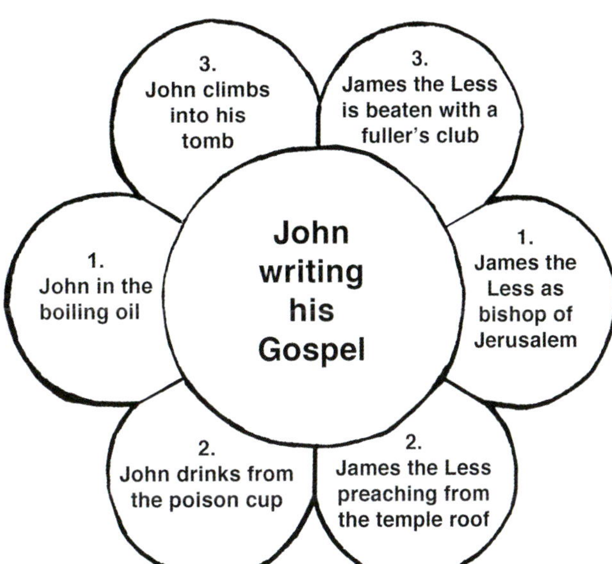

FIG. 38 Bay 104, rosace, chart of scenes: John the Evangelist and James the Less.

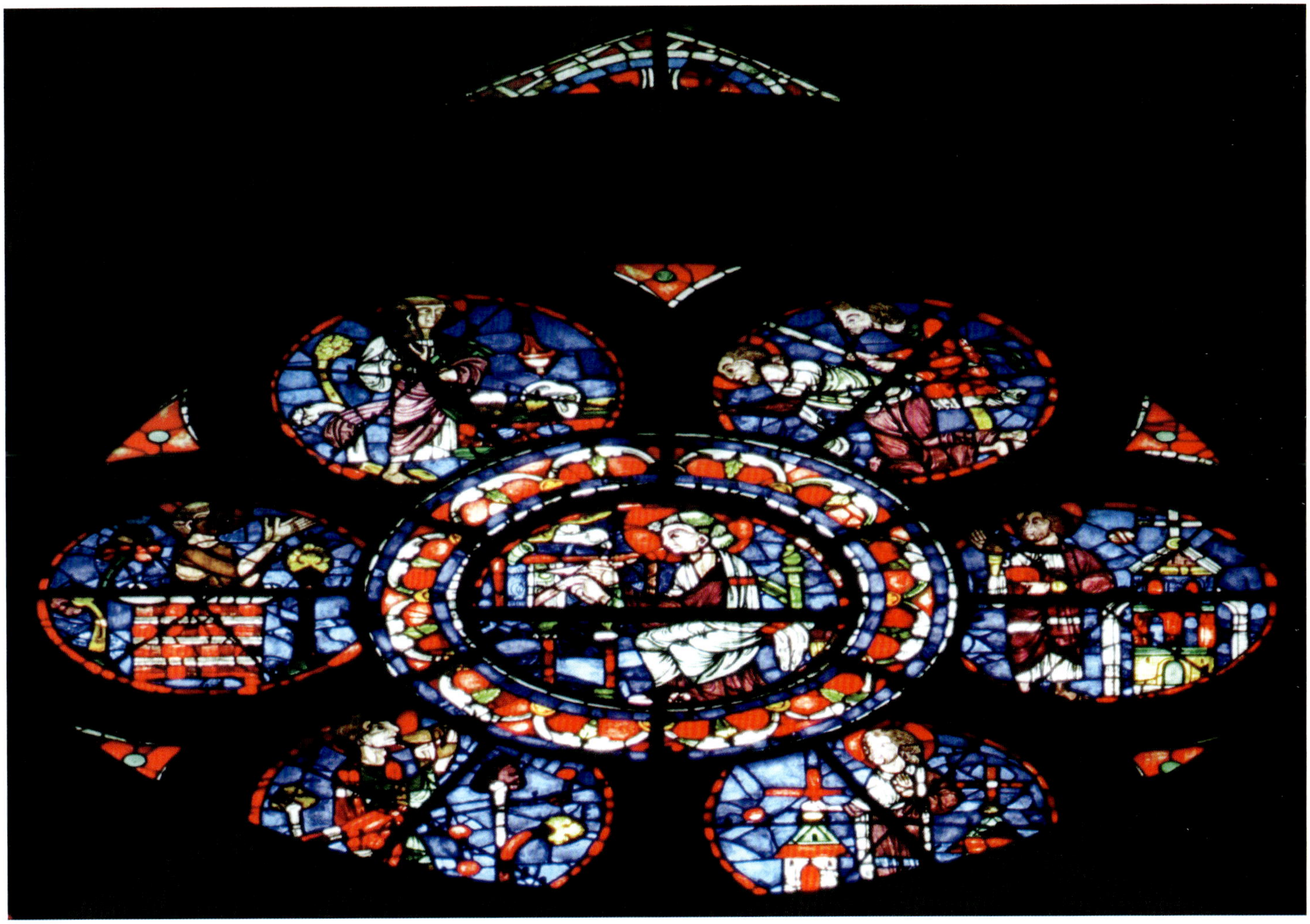

FIG. 39 Bay 104, rosace, John the Evangelist and James the Less.

FIG. 40 John writing his Gospel, Bay 104, rosace, central roundel (1930).

FIG. 41 John in the vat of boiling oil: Le Mans cathedral, bay 111, detail, ca. 1255–65.

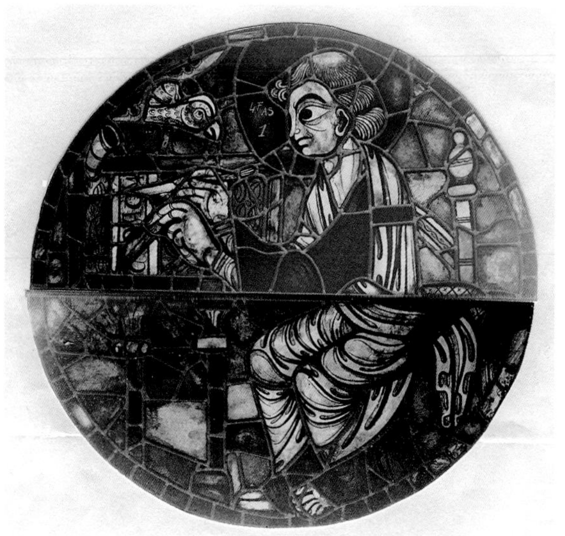

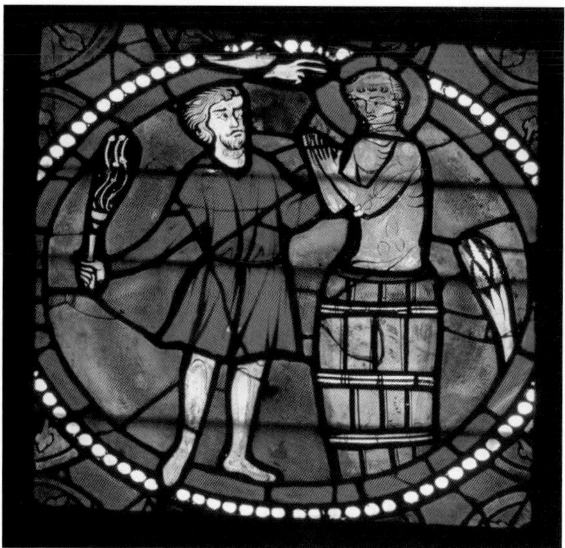

(discussed in chapter 3). Matthew, in the rosace of Bay 105, also appears in an author portrait, as in Gospel manuscripts. Again the emphasis is on the apostles' authority in Christ. It is perhaps unnecessary to point out here that several early manuscripts containing Evangelist portraits survive from the medieval libraries of Reims; also, Michael Cothren has noted a distinct tradition of author portraits of John in thirteenth-century Bibles.[87] Models would not have been hard to find.

Another difference: John is alone in his lobes at Reims. In the first lobe (middle left) he prays, nude and immersed in the vat of boiling oil. The Pseudo-Abdias sets the scene in Ephesus.[88] Although Tertullian (ca. 155–222 C.E.) votes for Rome, the legend was not current in that city until perhaps the early sixth century, date of the first church of San Giovanni a Porta Latina. Pseudo-Melito, who probably wrote in Rome at that time, omits the story altogether. He either did not know it or was suspicious of its authenticity. Pseudo-Abdias, who wrote in Gaul, would not have had such scruples, but perhaps Ephesus was given in his source. In the Reims lobe, John's tub is horizontally striped, and no fire appears beneath it. Such striped tubs are not rare; in glass, one could mention Sens (bay 1, ca. 1180), Saint-Julien-du-Sault (bay 3, ca. 1240–50), and Le Mans (bay 111, ca. 1255–65, fig. 41). The scene is rare, however, without executioners, tyrant, or witnesses—the focus strictly on John.[89] The Reims artist prefers this intense, antinarrative focus.

John's second lobe (bottom left, fig. 42) presents the story of the poison cup. Aristodemus, high priest of the temple of Diana at Ephesus, had challenged the apostle to drink it to prove the power of the Christian God. But as in the other lobes of Reims 104, there are no supernumeraries. John drinks alone. Not only is he tonsured but he drinks from a chalice, which he holds by the knop, rather than the usual large bowl.[90] Again the stress is on the "priestliness" of the apostle and thus his relevance to the contemporary ecclesiastical trials at Reims. By around 1233, when Bays 103 and 104 were probably undertaken, the cathedral canons had twice had to resort to interdict to rebuff bourgeois attack, and worse was to come. As for the archbishop, 1233 was the year that his confrontation with his monarch came to a boil. John's triumphs over his antagonists would provide welcome reassurance.

In the third lobe (top left, fig. 43), John climbs into his tomb. The scene is reduced to bare essentials, and again John is alone: no blinding light, no manna from heaven, no altar, no witnesses, angels, and so forth. Gothic art normally shows John inside

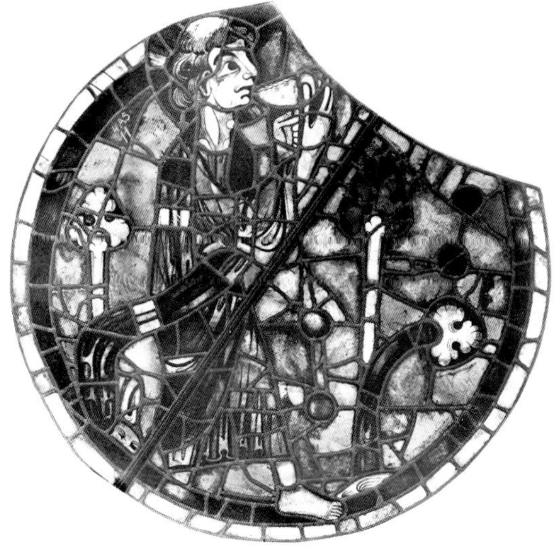

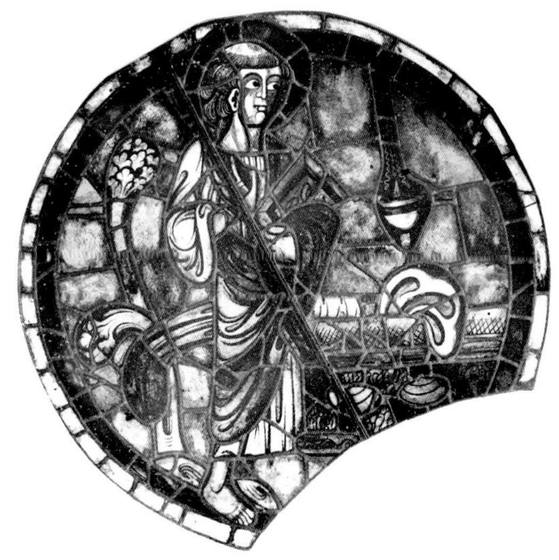

FIG. 42 John drinking from the poison cup, Bay 104, rosace, lower left lobe (1930).

FIG. 43 John climbing into his tomb, Bay 104, rosace, top left lobe (1930).

FIG. 44 John climbing into his tomb: Saint-Julien-du-Sault, bay 3, detail, ca. 1240–50.

the tomb, seated, lying down, or sometimes standing.[91] Reims depicts him—tonsured, holding a book—standing on one leg, with the other already flung over the sarcophagus. Only bay 3 at Saint-Julien-du-Sault in Burgundy (fig. 44), slightly later than Reims, shows John in this pose. But at Saint-Julien, a censing angel stands behind him, and Christ himself waves John on. Colette Manhès-Deremble, who adds that the scene of John climbing into his tomb also appeared in a twelfth-century lectionary lost in 1944 (Chartres MS 500), calls John's pose "un peu provocante."[92] What the posture achieves is to move the story from passive to active voice. It presents John as a man of action, powerful, here finally triumphant over the petty adversaries of the past.

The Rosace of Bay 104: James the Less

James the Less shares the rosace with John. Unlike John, Peter, Andrew, and so forth, this James was not well represented in Gothic art. No windows or

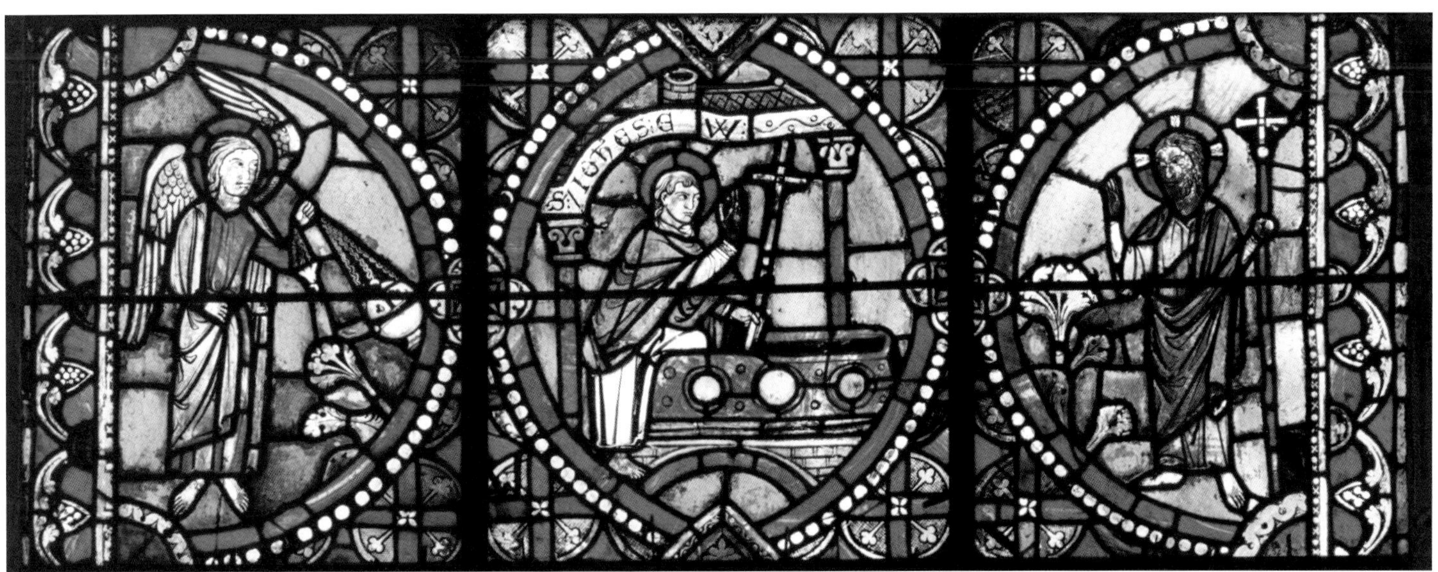

FIG. 45 James the Less, bishop of Jerusalem, and his cathedral facade, Bay 104, rosace, mid right lobe (1930).

FIG. 46 James the Less preaching from the temple roof, Bay 104, rosace, lower right lobe (1930).

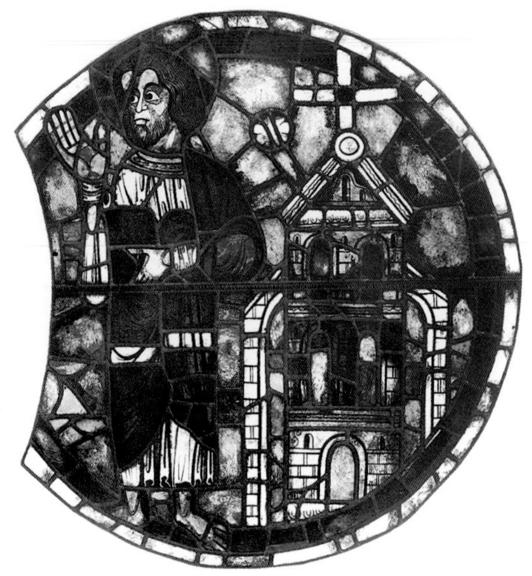

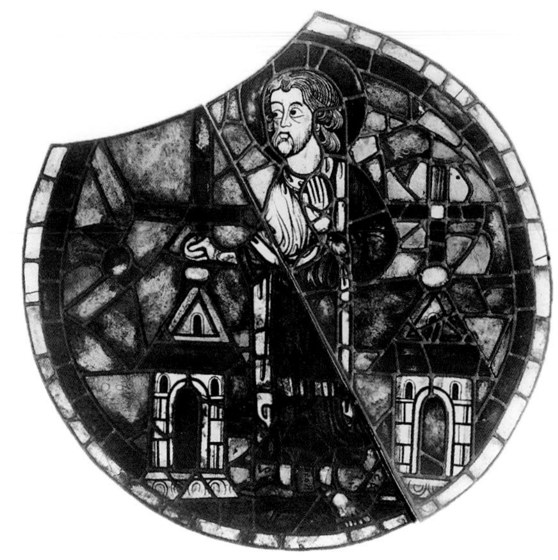

sculpture cycles were devoted to him, and only a few twelfth-century manuscripts (as well as the Stavelot Altar, ca. 1150) illustrate events of his martyrdom, as does the mosaic in San Marco, Venice, ca. 1200.[93] The Pseudo-Abdias (bk. 6, chaps. 1–6) presents James the Less largely based on the New Testament plus an account of his martyrdom available in Eusebius's *Church History* of ca. 325 C.E.[94] While James is described in the Bible—in Acts 15 and also Acts 21:18—as leader of the church in Jerusalem, Pseudo-Abdias goes further and identifies him as the bishop there, serving in the Temple of Solomon. This conceit is also found at San Marco, where the temple resembles the Dome of the Rock, and in the Regensburg Martyrology (ca. 1180), where James wears a bishop's vestments and miter and holds a crozier.[95]

That provided the link the Reims designer needed to conceive several remarkable images. Just as the rosace emphasizes John's priestliness with a tonsure, so too it stresses James's "bishophood." Lobe one (middle right, fig. 45) shows James standing next to his cathedral "facade," a minuscule version of the large-scale suffragan bishop of Beauvais paired with his cathedral in the lancets below (fig. 86). James's elegant striped vestments resemble those on the holy men in the lancets, and his tiny cathedral facade is not only topped by a cross, as is Beauvais cathedral below, but it also sports flying buttresses!

In lobe two (bottom right, fig. 46) James gestures, preaching, flanked by two cross-topped towers. He is in fact on the roof of a facade closely resembling the larger Beauvais "facade" in the lower lancet. The episode recounts how the Jewish leaders took James to the roof of the temple to address the Passover crowds, to tell them that Jesus was not the Messiah. James of course preached the opposite and very successfully, and the Jews threw him off the roof. The San Marco mosaics and a number of twelfth-century representations show James falling headfirst.[96] The unique version at Reims chooses the previous moment, when James's eloquent preaching has won the day. As noted earlier, one of the distinguishing activities of a bishop was preaching. This rosace would have been particularly meaningful to Archbishop Henri de Braine, who had begun his church career at Beauvais cathedral when his uncle and mentor, Philippe de Dreux, was bishop there (see the discussion of Bay 104 in chapter 3, and appendix 4).

In lobe three (top right, fig. 47) James is attacked by one of the Jewish mob, who threatens him with a fuller's club. Although the ultimate

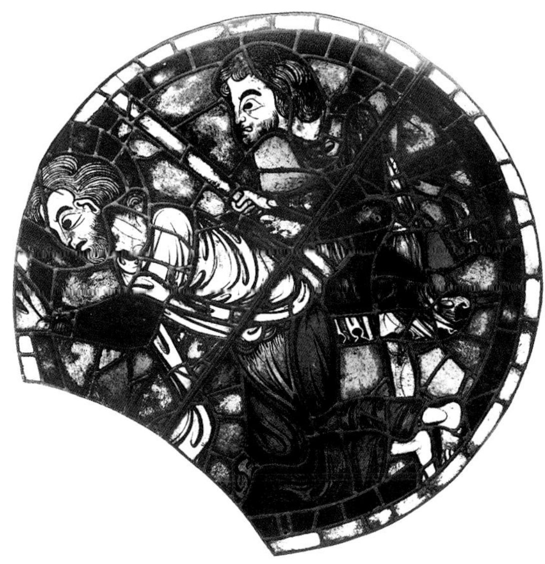

FIG. 47 James the Less beaten with a fuller's club, Bay 104, rosace, top right lobe (1930).

result will be martyrdom, James appears here very much alive. The topic of physical attacks on the clergy by mobs of Reims citizenry (as outlined in chapter 1) is unquestionably foremost here.

The drama and expressionism in the art of this glazier have been mentioned earlier. His methods of organizing and focusing the design of the rosace also differ from the laterally balanced approach of Bays 101 and 102. He reduces the scenes to a single figure if at all possible; only the assault on James requires an attacker. The strong orientation of all these figures is toward the central roundel, the figures in the upper and lower lobes being positioned diagonally; indeed, the scenes in the lobes seem to radiate out from it. The artist uses the same colors, white and brown, for his saints throughout, excepting only John with the poison cup (lower left). He wears red and green to correlate with James's attacker (upper right), creating a strong diagonal axis. A comparable diagonal is achieved by the colors (red, green, white) of the architectural elements in the scene of John climbing into the tomb (top left) and that of James preaching from the roof (bottom right). Other axes are achieved by compositional devices such as the striped vat opposite James's striped vestment, its blocky shape recalling the blocklike cathedral "facade" next to James. These axes organize and interconnect the rosace as a star—or more precisely an asterisk—pattern that is much more dynamic than the quietly balanced and stable compositions of the previous bays.

The Rosace of Bay 103: Thomas

The loss of the central roundel—now a meaningless invention installed after World War I—complicates analysis of the artist's compositional devices in the rosace of Bay 103 (figs. 48, 49).[97] It seems clear, however, that the fabulous, not to say incredible, adventures associated with the apostles Thomas and Philip presented a challenge, one that was not taken up but avoided. All three lobes on the right, devoted to Thomas, concern the same story drawn from the Pseudo-Abdias, book 9, chapter 3, though Thomas's full narrative there occupies twenty-five chapters in all. And the Pseudo-Abdias itself is a great simplification of the original *Acts of Thomas,* the only one of the five Early Christian apocryphal acts to survive in its entirety. Condemned by Augustine and others as heretical, this prolix text eventually reached the sixth-century Latin version of the Pseudo-Abdias not only purged of questionable matter but continually excerpted and cut in order to reduce its length and verbosity.[98] Narrative medallion windows at Bourges (bay 16, ca. 1210–15), Chartres (bay 23, ca. 1220–30), and Tours (bay 213, ca. 1270) all include the story shown at Reims, but amid a fair number of the many Thomas legends.[99]

Like the attack on James the Less by the fuller in Bay 104, the story here tells of the physical abuse of an apostle by a commoner. The reason why this particular story was featured at Reims is not obscure. The concentration on this story, spread over all three of Thomas's lobes, is a strong indication of the central importance of its message there. But the tale here, unlike that depicted in Bay 104, ends in sweet, oh-so-sweet vengeance. Thomas, sent to India by Christ, makes a stop in a city where wedding festivities for the king's daughter are in progress. Enjoined to attend,

FIG. 48 Bay 103, rosace, chart of scenes: Thomas and Philip.

FIG. 49 Bay 103, rosace, Thomas and Philip.

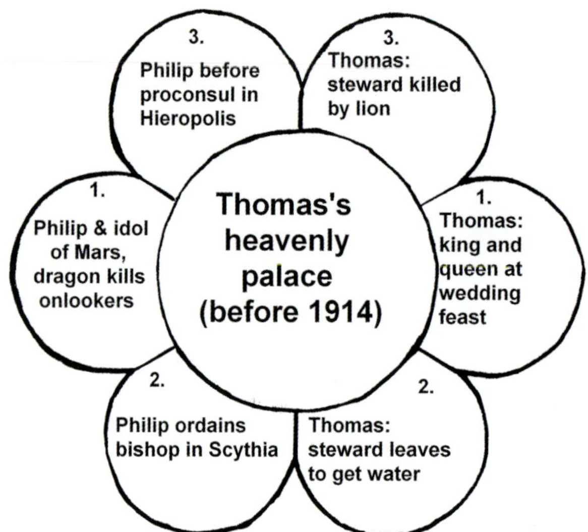

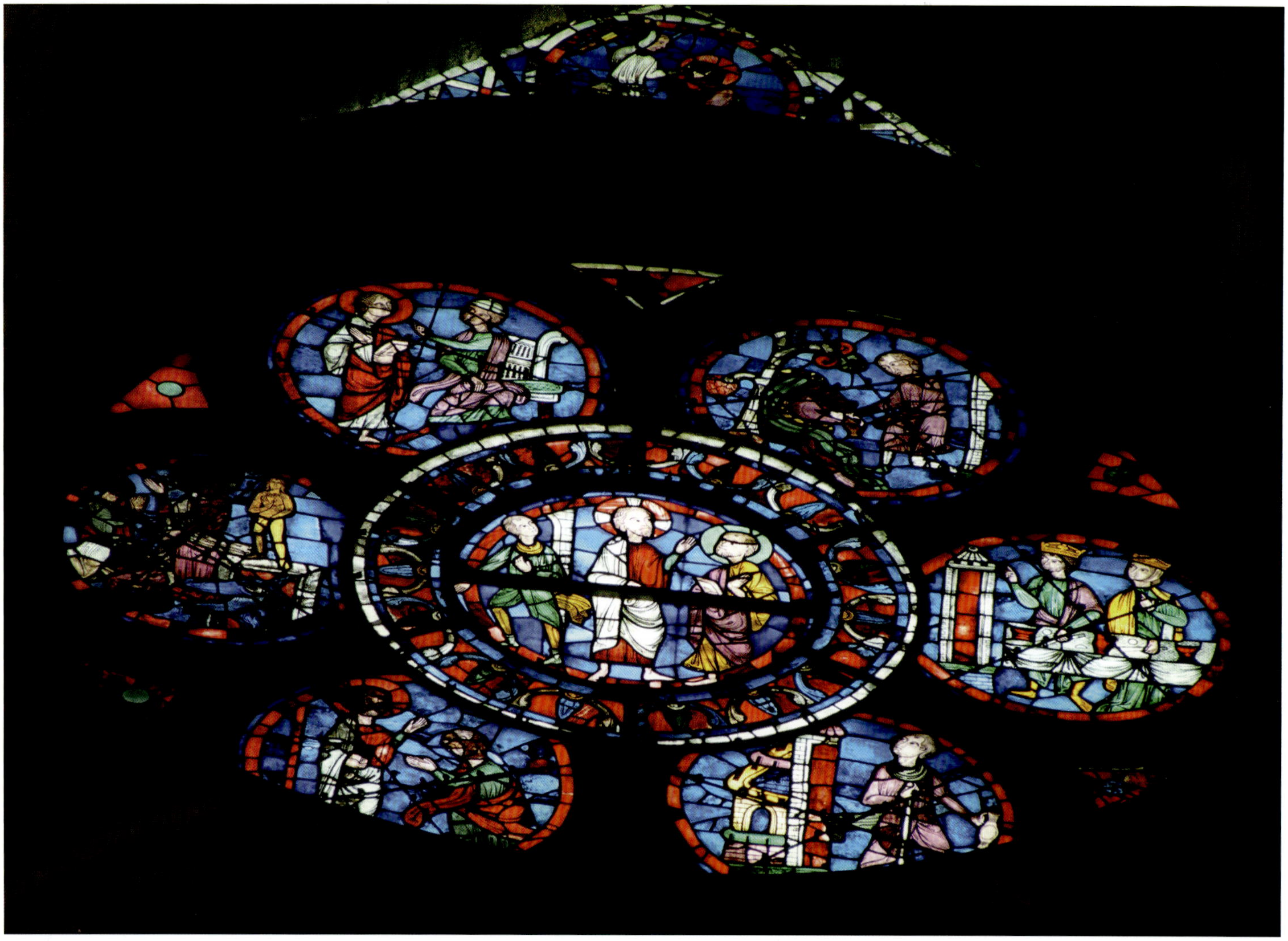

Thomas does so, but, as a Jew, his foreign behavior causes the king's steward to deliver him an angry slap.[100] Thomas responds that before he will leave the table, the hand that struck him will itself be struck down. And lo! it comes to pass. The steward leaves the palace to get more water at the fountain, where he is killed by a lion, and a passing dog snatches his severed hand and brings it to the banquet table.

As in the rosace of John and James the Less (Bay 104), the lobes of Thomas reduce the story, to the extent possible, to a series of signs. The order of scenes in the lobes is middle, bottom, top. The first lobe (middle right, fig. 50) shows the king and queen at table. The banquet table appears often in medieval art, in the three medallion windows mentioned earlier as well as in two examples roughly contemporary with Reims: bay 0 at Sens (ca. 1230s) and the tympanum of the north-transept portal at Semur-en-Auxois (ca. 1240–50).[101] All show a number of guests at table, sometimes a great crowd, Thomas, the steward slapping him, the Jewish flute-girl, and occasionally—telescoping the story—a dog with a human hand in its mouth. At Reims, however, the actual slap is entirely omitted, unless it occupied the lost central roundel. The evidence, discussed below, suggests that that was not the case. Rather, the second lobe (bottom right) shows a lone figure, the steward, leaving the palace with a jug to get water, and in the third lobe (top right) he has reached the fountain, where a lion mauls him. While the lion attack appears in the three medallion windows mentioned earlier (Bourges, Chartres, and Tours), the image of the steward leaving the palace to get water is not found elsewhere. It is unique to Reims. In other words, not only do Thomas's lobes treat only one story, they elaborate it more than any other example. What narrative purpose is served by omitting the slap but at the same time drawing out the story with the view of the steward leaving for water? Very simply, it distills the message down to the evilness of his action and the unavoidable punishment it incurs. The rosace is not cluttered with picturesque detail: no flute-girl, no dog carrying a severed human hand. It invokes a physical affront on a man of the Church and the price to be paid for it—not in a narrative but as a succession of signs.

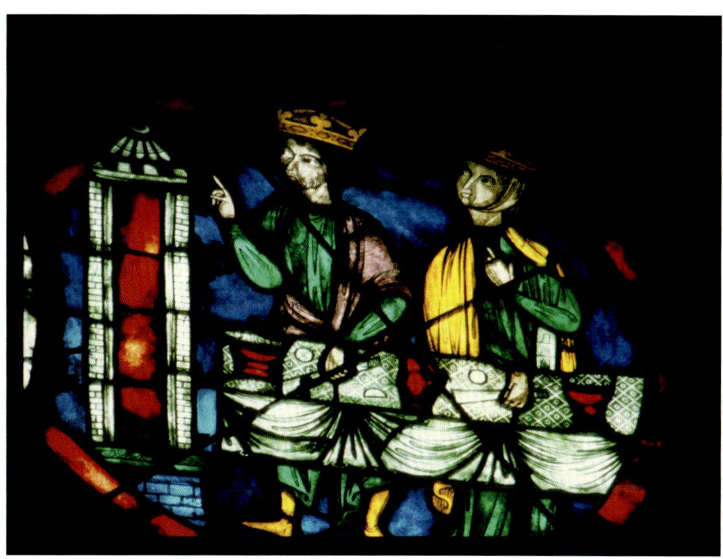

FIG. 50 The king and queen at the wedding feast, Bay 103, rosace, mid right lobe.

Why the actual slap was, most probably, omitted is a more complex question, with an answer that must remain circumstantial and hypothetical. The story of Thomas at the wedding banquet was well known, so depiction of the slap was not absolutely necessary. By leaving it out one could avoid offending clergy who might have been aware that many Church Fathers, chief among them St. Augustine, were troubled by the story's message of vengeance. Augustine mentions the story three times, and each time he identifies the fable as part of the Manichaean apocryphal books and emphasizes that it is not part of the Catholic canon; hence one does not have to believe it.[102] And of course, omitting the slap universalizes the message. Ultimately the story that so embarrassed Augustine was a great comfort to the beset clergy of Reims around 1233–34.

The central roundel replaced after the First World War is known from nineteenth-century witnesses (fig. 51).[103] It depicted the heavenly palace built by Thomas through his charity, as outlined in the Pseudo-Abdias, book 9, chapters 5–6: Thomas has continued to India, to the court

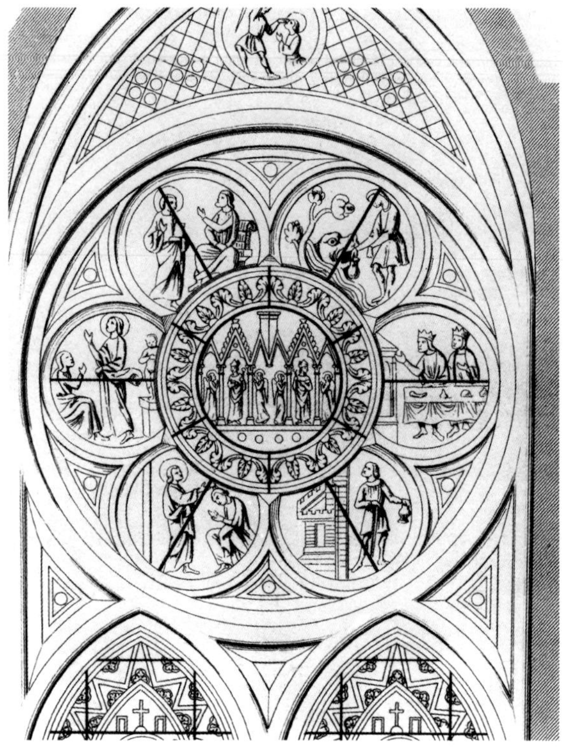

FIG. 51 Bay 103, rosace, showing Thomas's heavenly palace in the central roundel (before 1914) (after Cahier and Martin, *Monographie de la cathédrale de Bourges*).

of King Gundaphorus, for whom he had made the journey to build him a palace.[104] The king gave Thomas money for construction and departed on a journey. Thomas gave the money to the poor. When the king returned and learned of it, he imprisoned the apostle. But then the king's brother died; while in heaven he was shown the palace that Thomas had built there with Gundaphorus's charities, and he was allowed to return to earth to try to buy it for himself. The king declined to sell, and both brothers were baptized. The heavenly palace appears in Chartres, in the Semur tympanum, and later on the facade of Poitiers.[105] The theme of the heavenly-palace story is of course charity, and the opposite of that virtue is the vice of avarice, or greed. Greed—the greed, in the view of the Church, of usurers—was one of the main points of conflict in the city of Reims during the years the hemicycle windows were made. Fear of the Inquisition (outlined in chapter 1) was increasing in the years from 1230 onward and came to a head in Reims in attacks of the bourgeois on the clergy that culminated in the canons' flight in late 1234. There is good reason to associate these events with the program of Bay 103.

The lost roundel of Bay 103 was described in 1861 by Charles Cerf exactly as pictured in figure 51: "Dans le médaillon central, apparaît un temple orné de deux vastes portiques; sur le seuil sont placés les deux apôtres [Thomas and Philip?], vêtus de chasuble."[106] They also have bishops' miters and croziers and are flanked by angels. Such details are not part of the story, but they do make good use of the opportunity to glorify the two apostles of the bay and to identify them clearly with the suffragan bishops throughout the chevet. Again, apostolic succession.

Stylistic features suggest that this lost roundel was a later insertion into the rosace. The form of the gables of the heavenly palace, decorated with crockets on the exterior and a trefoil arch on the interior, would be more appropriate to the end of the thirteenth century or later. If the roundel glass was of a slightly later date, that might explain its replacement in modern times: if destroyed in World War I, one could argue that it suffered more severe damage than its surrounding lobes because its glass was thinner; if it survived the war and was replaced during the Simon restoration, then he removed it because he could see that it was not part of the original glazing (e.g., if it was silver stained, a technique not yet in use in the 1230s). In the latter case, the panel may survive somewhere.[107] If the panel known in the nineteenth century was, indeed, a work of ca. 1300 or later, I believe that it copied the original scene fairly closely. In any event, the original message clearly was retained.

The Rosace of Bay 103: Philip

In the three lobes on the left, devoted to Philip, the programmer faced a situation totally different from that concerning Thomas, much more like that pertaining to James the Less (Bay 104), with whom Philip shares his feast day, May 1.[108] There are no French Gothic artworks devoted to his life, and book 10 (Philip) of the Pseudo-Abdias is even shorter than the section on James, having only three chapters. Largely based on Eusebius, the Pseudo-Abdias states that Philip died of old age rather than martyrdom. Thus he was often omitted from passional manuscripts, for example, the Regensburg Martyrology (ca. 1180).[109] However, traces of the Greek version of Philip's legend—in which he is crucified and stoned—appear very early in the West. The Golden Legend reports this version based, as it says, on Isidore of Seville (d. 636). Isidore's work, *Liber de ortu et obitu patriarchaeum* (chap. 50.2), is a very brief account of each apostle; a similarly brief Western listing, the *Breviarium Apostolorum,* first appeared in the mid–eighth century. Both state that Philip was crucified but not that he was upside-down, as the Greek text specifies. Hence Western objects, for example, the Stavelot Altar (ca. 1150), occasionally show Philip on an upright cross.[110]

This brief excursus on Byzantine influence in Western apocrypha has no obvious application to Reims, of course, where Philip's death does not appear in any guise. However, several details of the Philip lobes are difficult to explain without the possibility of an ultimately Greek source. In Byzantium Philip is beardless. At San Marco, where he dies peacefully at age eighty-two in the Western manner, he is also beardless, an obvious merging of traditions.[111] At Reims, in the first lobe (middle left) he appears to have a short pointed beard, though the glass is so darkened that it is impossible to be sure; in the second lobe (bottom left) he has a slight youthful fringe of hair around his chin, though the face is a shattered repair and the glass at the chin appears to be a restoration; and in the final, top lobe he is beardless (fig. 49), his chin line more clearly a restoration. How much confidence one can place in the restorations, based on the full-scale tracings made by the Simons before 1914, is impossible to say. What one can say is that in the cathedral's massive and richly decorated *legendarium* (Reims MS 1403, dated before 1096), Philip is most definitely bearded.[112] This would appear to be one more piece of evidence, if one is needed, that the lives of the apostles in the Reims rosaces were not based upon such a book.

The first lobe (middle left) illustrates Philip's only miracle (Pseudo-Abdias, bk. 10, chap. 2), a story shown at San Marco as well as earlier in the Stuttgart Passional (ca. 1120).[113] The Scythians want the apostle to sacrifice to an idol of Mars. A dragon emerges from its pedestal and poisons the bystanders with its foul breath. Philip urges them to replace the idol with a cross, orders the dragon to leave, and resuscitates its victims. In a crowded scene the lobe depicts the nude golden idol and the blue dragon, on the right, and Philip, standing in the middle, gesturing to the victims, bunched to the left.

This episode is the first to introduce a new theme in the Reims program, that of the apostles' triumphs over idols. The subject has more contemporary relevance than one might suspect. The reference is to the vice of idolatry, considered at the time the opposite of faith. Michael Camille notes that the classical statue standing on a base is the most common type of idol shown in medieval art. His example, from the Moralized Bible (Paris, BnF, lat. 11560) showing the abominations witnessed by Ezekiel (8:16–17), makes clear the relevance to the time in which the Moralized Bibles and the Reims rosaces were produced. Ezekiel's sun worshippers, who point to a naked golden idol, are described in the Moralized Bible text as *heretici.*[114] Philip's achievement in overturning the statue of Mars undoubtedly appealed to the Reims programmer all the more since the Pseudo-Abdias (bk. 10, chap. 3) credits the apostle also with eliminating a heresy that declared Christ not to have been human or born of a virgin. That was a key tenet of contemporary Catharism—the heresy that had set in motion the Albigensian crusade in thirteenth-century France.[115] With the Inquisition closing in on Reims in the 1230s, it was a topic uppermost in everyone's mind.

In lobe two (bottom left) Philip stands before a doorway and gestures to a single figure who kneels before him in prayer. He is, most probably, ordaining him as bishop. The Pseudo-Abdias (bk. 10, chap. 3) states that Philip preached to the Scythians for twenty years, ordained priests, deacons, and a bishop, and constructed many churches, before he moved on to Hieropolis. Emphasizing the apostle's action in ordaining a bishop underlines once again the apostolic succession of the Church's suffragan bishops shown in the lancets below. Lobe three (top left) is even more generic, showing Philip before an enthroned proconsul. While Pseudo-Abdias mentions no specific antagonist, the crucifixion noted by Isidore and the Golden Legend certainly indicates that there was one. In the Greek text he is named Tyrannographos, proconsul of Hieropolis.[116] Whether or not his name was known at Reims, the scene provides yet another example of the apostles' confrontations with secular authorities, one of the rosaces' constant themes.

The three lobes for Philip present all the symptoms that art historians have considered to reveal a medieval artist dealing with a new and unfamiliar story, one for which he had no visual tradition. Adaptation of existing models to the task would normally be his first choice. The generic scenes in lobes two and three are difficult to specify precisely because they have been so adapted. In cases where no usable model could be found—such as Philip's triumph over the idol of Mars—the new composition probably would exhibit, as it does at Reims, some clumsiness or insecurity. This would disappear as successive artists reworked and refined the image. The dramatic bent of the glazier of Bays 103 and 104 emerges chiefly in the size and focus of his figures' eyes and in his "monsters"—Thomas's vengeful lion and Philip's Mars dragon.

The less familiar apostles presented a different sort of challenge from that of the major saints such as Peter or John the Evangelist. With no strong visual traditions to draw on, artists had to invent compositions for stories that were probably related to them orally. Increasingly, then, the identifications of these images will be problematic here. The Reims program, however, did not require simple narration of the saint's life (as, e.g., in a window lighting a saint's altar) or a forceful reminder of his martyrdom (as in a manuscript passional). Paramount were the ideological themes of the chevet clerestory glass—its message. And this message was unique to Reims: preaching and its apostolic authority, charity (against avarice, usury), and opposition to "idolatry" (heresy). Usury and heresy at that time were closely associated in ecclesiastical opinion. The lesser-known apostles' lives discussed below reveal the increasing concentration on these themes, as the civic situation lunged from crisis to crisis in 1234 to the archbishop's death, in 1240.

The Rosace of Bay 106: Bartholomew and Simon

The bays discussed above complete the Reims hemicycle. In all their rosaces, the central ironwork presents the glazier with a larger roundel, and this is also true of Bay 106. In Bay 105 opposite it, however, and in the remaining chevet bays with colored glass, the ironwork creates a small lozenge as the center of the rosace, with more space for borders and ornament surrounding it. Another hint that a change occurred in working campaigns at this point is the order of scenes in Bay 106 (fig. 52). While the sequence of Bartholomew's three lobes, on the left (bottom, middle, top), conforms to the grand plan of the chevet—the asterisk pattern tying together the Twelve in a comprehensive network (fig. 27)—Simon's lobes, on the right, do not. They run from top to bottom. This order, while straightforward enough, conforms to none of the other chevet rosaces and thus seems to indicate a breakdown in the tightly controlled iconographic plan. The evidence suggests that the longest break in normality at the cathedral—the canons' exile from November 1234 to January 1237—occurred at this point (see chapter 3).

The three left lobes, devoted to Bartholomew, present first (bottom) the apostle curing a madman, then (middle) Bartholomew contacted by agents of King Polymius seeking a similar cure for his daughter, also mad, and finally (top) Bartholomew rejecting the grateful king's gifts of treasure, gems, and rich clothing. The apostle maintained that he wanted nothing earthly but only to convert the king to the faith. These stories

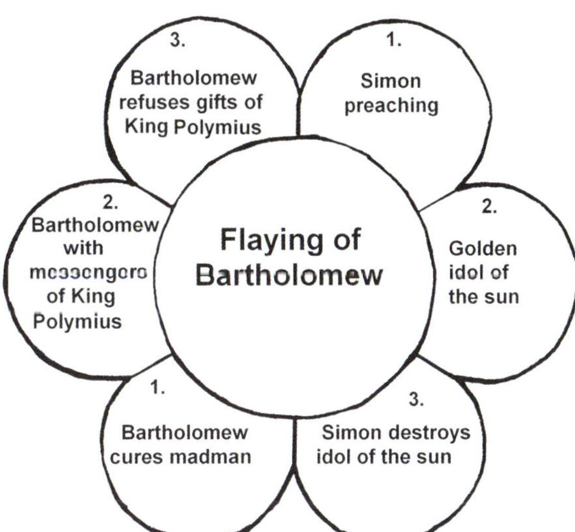

FIG. 52 Bay 106, rosace, chart of scenes: Bartholomew and Simon.

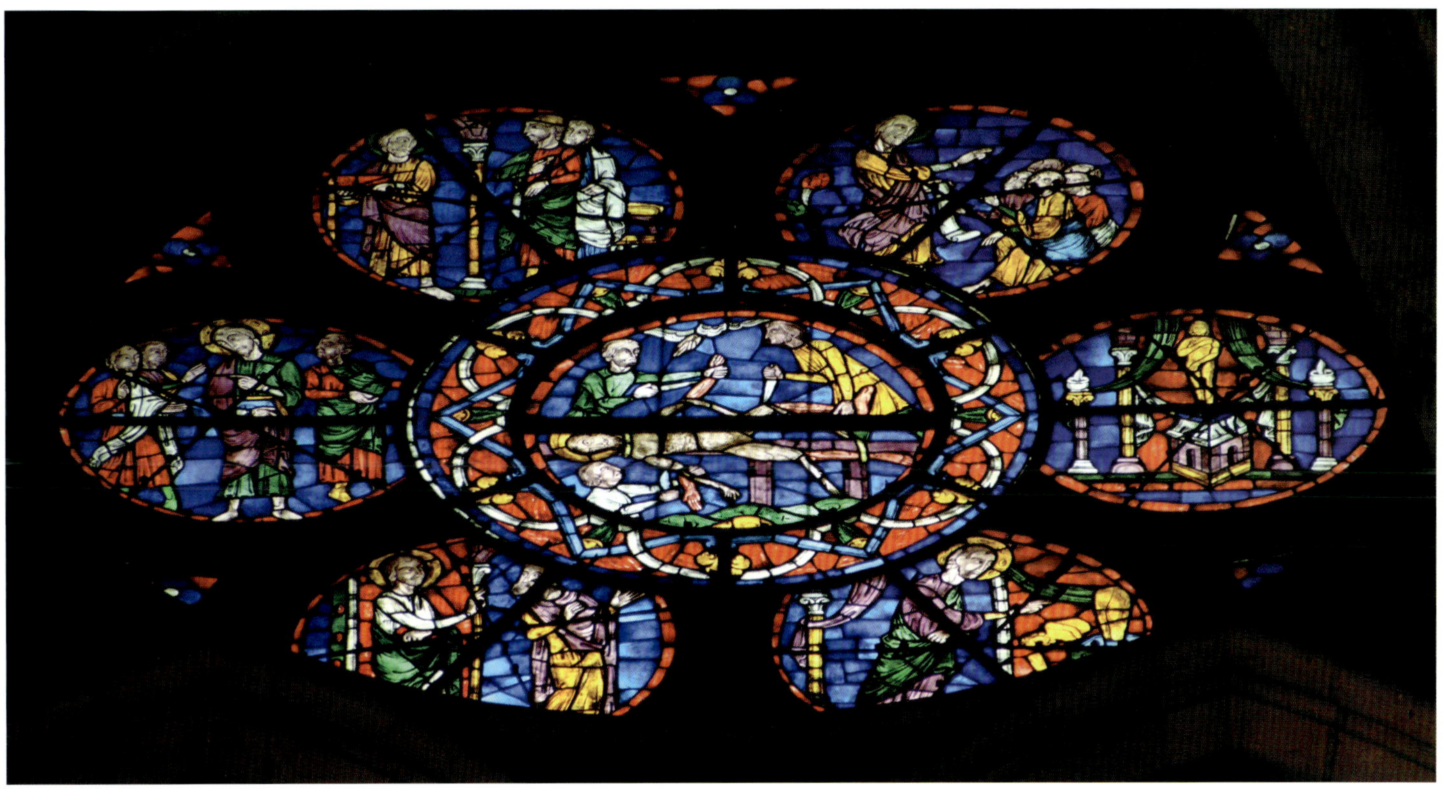

FIG. 53 Bay 106, rosace, Bartholomew and Simon.

come from the Pseudo-Abdias, book 8, chapters 3–4.[117] Clearly the theme is charity, the rejection of avarice or greed, and as mentioned earlier, avarice was associated with usury and persecuted identically with heresy in the 1230s. The sin of avarice is one of the main threads running through the fabric of the chevet program.

Two stained-glass cycles of Bartholomew can be compared to these scenes, though neither is earlier than Reims: those from the Dominican church in Strasbourg (ca. 1254–60) and the nave of San Francesco, Assisi (ca. 1275–1300). Eighteen medallions of the Dominican window are now installed in Strasbourg cathedral. Victor Beyer uses the Golden Legend to identify them. Among the numerous episodes, Bartholomew cures a madwoman and appears before the king, as at Reims.[118] The Assisi cycle is closer to the one at Reims in that it has only five scenes and they are placed above a large figure of the saint. Bartholomew heals a madman; two messengers invite him to the king's palace; he cures the king's daughter; the king offers gifts.[119] The final scene depicts Bartholomew's martyrdom by beating, following the Pseudo-Abdias, chapter 9.

The central roundel of Reims Bay 106 (fig. 54) depicts not the beating but the flaying of Bartholomew, which is not in the Pseudo-Abdias. This creative martyrdom, standard in Greek texts, was known early in the West via Isidore's *De ortu* and the *Breviarium Apostolorum* and later via the Golden Legend, where Voragine identifies his source as St. Theodore the Studite.[120] Here is a likely explanation for why it was adopted at Reims. The life of Bartholomew written in Greek by St. Theodore (d. 826), a theologian in Constantinople, was translated into Latin in Rome by Anastasius the Librarian ca. 850–78.[121] The Reims programmer, if he worked at the library of Saint-Thierry, as I have suggested, would have found there not only the Pseudo-Abdias manuscript now in Paris but also richly abundant textual material on Bartholomew. The apostle was the patron of that abbey, and their rich library owned at least two copies of the Anastasius translation of his life: Vatican, Reg. lat. 466 (eleventh century), and Reims, Bibl. mun., MS 1407 (eleventh century).[122] Both are lavishly decorated. Moreover, the section on Bartholomew (fols. 96v–103v) in the Saint-Thierry manuscript of the Pseudo-Abdias (Paris, BnF, lat. 5563) is crowded with corrections and marginal notes; the Bartholomew entry is the only one so annotated.[123] Anyone using that manuscript would have been made aware of the flaying martyrdom found in the abbey's precious manuscripts of the life of Bartholomew composed by St. Theodore and translated by Anastasius.

Demus states that the scene of the flaying of Bartholomew first appears in art in the twelfth century.[124] The knife as his attribute, one of the earliest to be firmly established in Gothic art, appeared on the saint's jamb statue on the Last Judgment portal of the Chartres south transept (ca. 1210–15; it is now broken off). It appears in sculpture at Reims, approximately contemporary with the Bay 106 rosace, held by the Bartholomew jamb statue in the north-transept Judgment portal as well as by the large figure of the saint in the Bay 106 lancet beneath the rosace.[125] The flaying scene is variable at this date. The saint is sometimes seated, sometimes half-reclining on the ground. In the Reims roundel he is nude and lies horizontally on a table, surrounded by executioners working at his various limbs with knives. This posture, which appears before Reims only in two isolated manuscripts of ca. 1200, remains just one of many.[126]

The scenes in the three lobes on the right of the rosace, devoted to the apostle Simon, begin with a generic preaching scene at the top, then a depiction of the golden idol in its temple (middle), followed by Simon's destruction of that idol (bottom lobe, fig. 55). As mentioned earlier, Simon's lobes do not follow the correct order established for the chevet rosaces (fig. 27). There can be no doubt, however, as to their order, since the preaching scene must precede those concerning the idol. The apostle's destruction of the idol precipitated Simon's martyrdom—which is omitted, as is increasingly the case at Reims. The flaying of Bartholomew and the crucifixion of Peter, in Bay 102, are the only

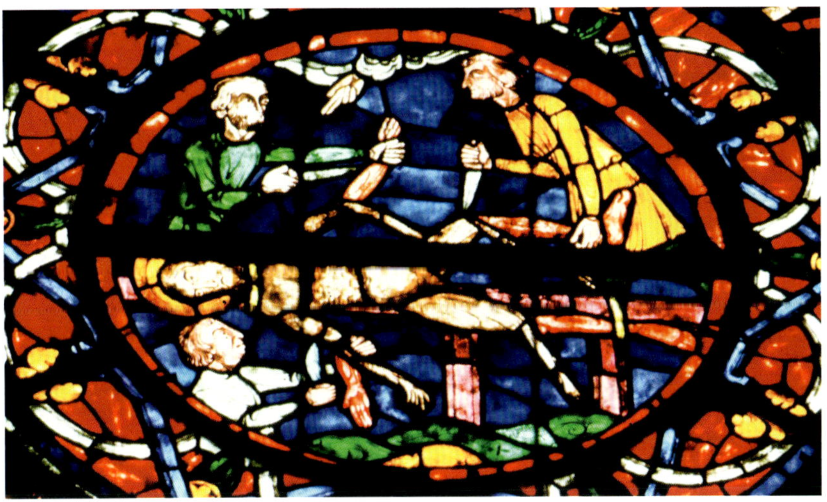

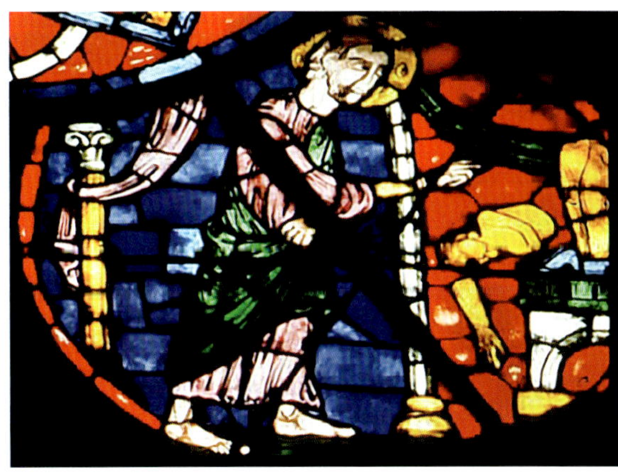

FIG. 54 The flaying of Bartholomew, Bay 106, rosace, central roundel.

FIG. 55 Simon destroys the idol of the sun, Bay 106, rosace, lower right lobe.

martyrdoms featured in the rosaces' central lights. The several themes I have noted in the chevet program are more central to its message, and several of those are repeated in Simon's lobes of Bay 105: preaching (as the identifying activity of apostles and bishops) and the defeat of idolatry/heresy (confounded with usury).

Simon and Jude are the inseparable twins of apostolic legend, sharing the same feast day (October 28) and treated together in the Pseudo-Abdias (bk. 6, chaps. 7–23).[127] Their legend is rare in art. At San Marco their scenes are practically mirror images; they share an elaborate medallion window at Chartres (bay 1, ca. 1220–25).[128] The program at Reims, however, stresses—to the extent possible—their individuality. The Twelve in the chevet appear following the order of the Canon of the Mass but in what might be called "Gothic order," that is, in a hierarchy zigzagging back and forth across the choir from east to west. This places Simon on the south (Bay 106) and Jude on the opposite side of the chevet, on the north (Bay 105), where each is paired with a different apostle. Simon appears as a preacher, based on the Pseudo-Abdias account emphasizing his successes in that role. The episode in which Simon destroys the golden idol (chaps. 21–22) also shows Simon acting alone. According to the story, Jude destroys the idol of the moon in a temple next door, not illustrated.

As with the pagan idol featured in Philip's rosace (Bay 103), the programmer seized upon the story of the sun god's statue through a careful reading of the Pseudo-Abdias. Although Simon destroys the golden statue immediately preceding his martyrdom at the end of the story (chap. 22), the account of Simon and Jude begins (chap. 7) with a lengthy exposition of their antagonists Zaroës and Arfaxat, two evil magicians. The doctrine of these sorcerers is spelled out in elaborate detail. They not only blaspheme the creating God of the Old Testament and declare the sun and moon divinities to be worshiped, they espouse a Manichaean dualism that specifically rejects, according to Pseudo-Abdias, the idea that Christ had a human nature. He merely appeared to be human, but was not really a man, not born of a virgin, did not really suffer, was not actually buried, and did not rise from the dead. Thus, as with Philip, the reverberations at Reims unquestionably arose from the heresy of the contemporary Cathars. Their doctrine could hardly have been put more precisely.

The Rosace of Bay 105: Matthew and Jude

As noted above, the ironwork of the rosaces of 105 and 106 (figs. 53, 57) marks a break in design, from Bays 100 through 104 (larger roundel) to 107 and 108 (smaller central lozenge). Bay 106 has a roundel in the center; Bay 105 has the smaller lozenge irons. Both rosaces, however, share a similar palette, painting style, and design approach, and these differ noticeably from the lancets below them in both bays. The palette of the rosaces of Bays 105 and 106 is one of cheerful primary colors, used in large areas that enhance legibility. It is closest to that of Bays 101 and 102 but emphasizes red and eliminates secondary color accents. While the scenes of 105 and 106 can be complex, the figures are set clearly against plain red or blue grounds, and supernumeraries are omitted. In both, antiquizing drapery employing flying folds and fine line hugs the body contour and outlines the hip; the figures are smaller in scale, however, than those of Bays 103 and 104, also garbed in "wet drapery."

The asterisk-type design of Bays 103 and 104, based on strong diagonals in the lobes, is gone, and so too is the approach of lobes reading in horizontal rows, related symmetrically (Bays 101 and 102). The lobes' design, particularly in Bay 106, provides no strong visual connection to its central roundel, but the network of connections and use of color areas in the grounds of the lobes "spin" the rosace. In Bay 105, this function is achieved by the ornament of the central area, which frames the small lozenge with an undulating quatrefoil that "points" to the various lobes. In both, the designer has adapted the figures to the curved shapes of the lobes to a greater degree than in the previous rosaces. It seems a reasonable conclusion that the ironwork of Bay 106 was made before the canons' flight (November 1234), but work on the rosaces was only taken up again after their twenty-six-month exile (January 1237).

In the ornament of the Bay 105 rosace (fig. 57) are small fleurs-de-lis. By 1237 these were more likely a respectful bow from the chapter to Louis IX for his support in arranging their triumphant return from exile than an emblem of the royal ancestry of Henri de Braine, as in Bays 100 and 101. Whereas the rosaces of the previous campaign are closely allied to the lancets below them in all aspects of style, this is not true of Bays 105 and 106. The lancets (discussed in the next chapter) are not by the same artists, nor are they closely related to any of the previous lancets. It would seem that, following the city's long excommunication, the cathedral chapter needed time to attract craftsmen and to find funds to pay them. The archbishop, who in his struggle with the king had called three more provincial councils during the canons' exile in 1235, was by 1238 embroiled in a more immediate civil war with his townspeople. His interest in the cathedral project seems to have evaporated, and from 1237 on the program of the Reims chevet clerestories seems to have become the chapter's province.

The three lobes on the right side of the Bay 105 rosace (fig. 56) present the apostle Matthew, introduced in the smaller central lozenge in his traditional Evangelist portrait writing his Gospel, as is John in Bay 104. At present the large apostles in the lancets below are switched, that is, installed in the wrong lancets. Matthew is now on the left and Jude on the right, with their backs turned to each other in an obviously nonmedieval arrangement. The mistake is recent, from the postwar installation. The saints appear correctly (Matthew right, Jude left, as in the rosace above them) in the nineteenth-century drawing published by Cahier and Martin (fig. 9).

While Matthew's Evangelist portrait recalls that of John, the artists differ completely. The artist of Bay 105 is a miniaturist with a flair for narrative but commands none of the expressionist power of John's artist. A curtain indicates that Matthew writes inside a study, but, unlike John's portrait, no Evangelist symbol (angel or winged man) is included. Matthew's central space is more compressed, while John's eagle no doubt was needed to distinguish the scene from the more expected one of John writing the Apocalypse on Patmos. The depiction of both John and Matthew as Gospel writers underlines the apostles' authority in Christ, ultimate source of power of the apostolic succession. Among countless examples of Matthew's Evangelist portrait in medieval manuscripts is a miniature in a Carolingian Gospel surviving from the library of Saint-Thierry, near Reims (Reims MS

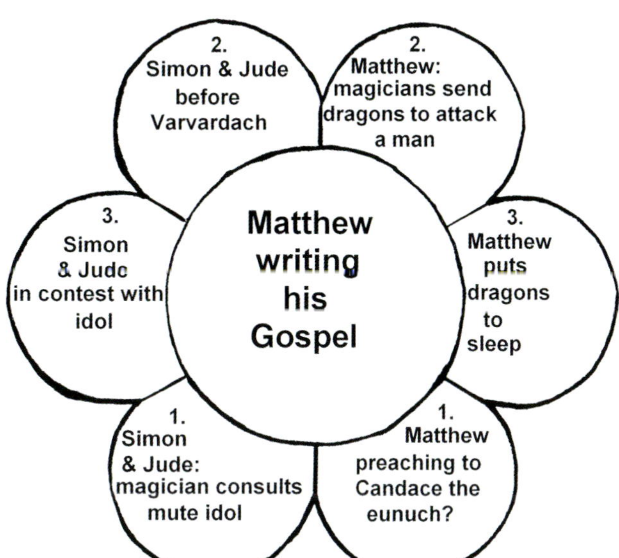

FIG. 56 Bay 105, rosace, chart of scenes: Matthew and Jude.

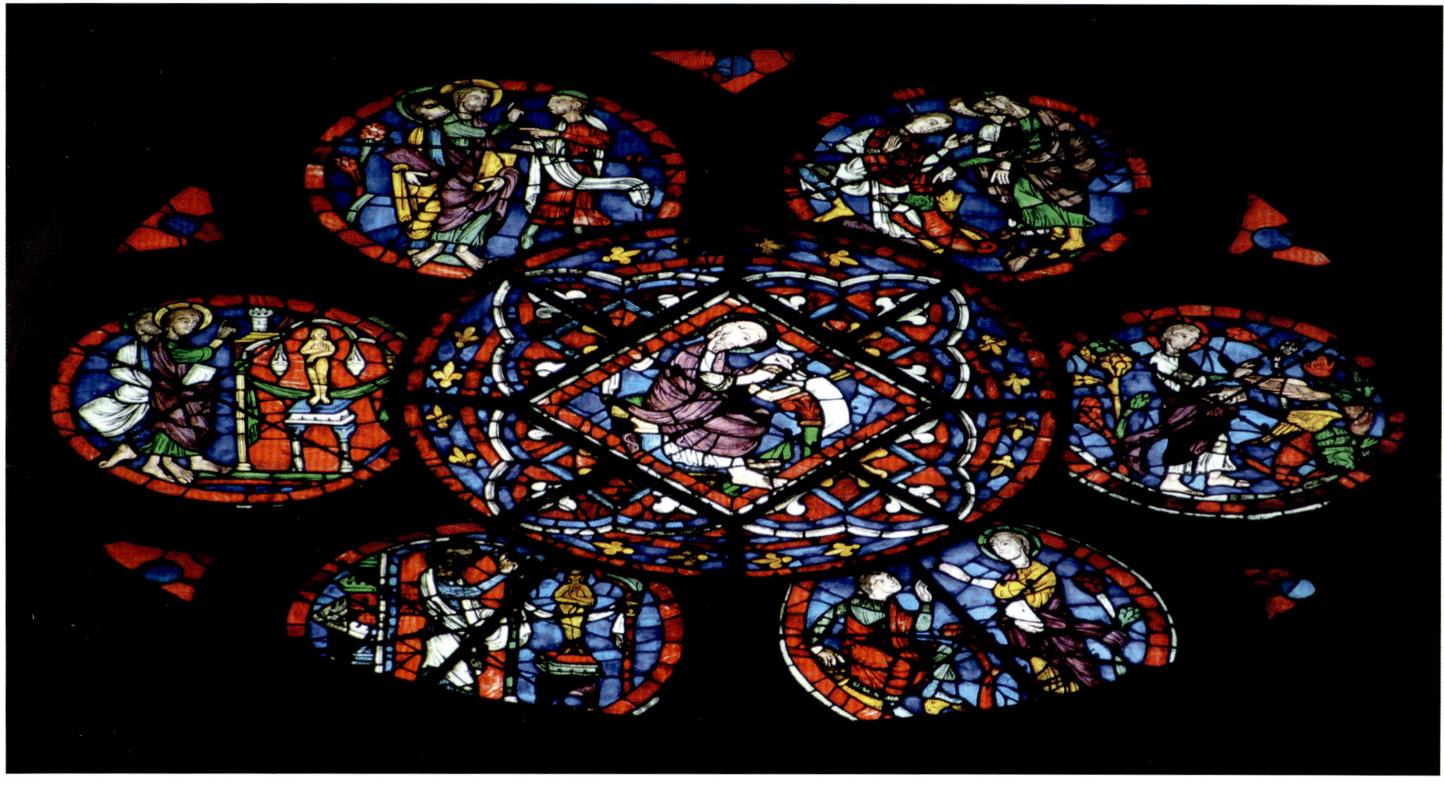

FIG. 57 Bay 105, rosace, Matthew and Jude.

7, fol. 21r).[129] While this Gospel is a manuscript that would have had great prestige and interest for the Reims programmer, since it was associated with the famous archbishop Hincmar (r. 845–82 C.E.), the Matthew portrait includes the angel Evangelist symbol and is not particularly close to that in the rosace of Bay 105.[130] Closer to the Reims lozenge and similar in simplicity, omitting the angel, is a contemporary example found on folio 1 of Arras MS 779, a glossed Gospel.[131]

Matthew cycles are rare in medieval art, and none are helpful in identifying the three Reims lobes. The sources for these few examples—as for Reims—are no doubt textual, that is, the legend as found in the Pseudo-Abdias and then in the Golden Legend.[132] There is no visual tradition in the arts. Cycles preceding Reims include those of the Nazareth capital (six scenes, ca. 1150–87), the Regensburg Martyrology (Munich, Clm 13074, fols. 90r–v, six scenes, ca. 1175), the seven scenes inserted as stopgaps in the south rose of Notre-Dame, Paris (ca. 1180), and the mosaics of San Marco (two scenes, ca. 1200); following Reims are examples in the stained glass at Assisi, bay II (five scenes, ca. 1275–1300) and Saint-Ouen de Rouen, bays 25, 27, and 29 (six scenes, ca. 1320–30).[133] Missing from Reims is the apostle's martyrdom, an omission common in the rosaces for all but the most firmly established visualizations; also missing is a thirteenth-century favorite, the scene of the biblical episode of the Calling of St. Matthew.[134]

The order of scenes in the Bay 105 rosace is bottom, top, middle (figs. 27, 56). The identification of Matthew's introductory scene (bottom right) is tentative because the right half was lost by the nineteenth century (see fig. 9) and now contains a modern design. The original, left half of the lobe shows a beardless gesturing figure semi-reclining out of doors, as indicated by vegetation beneath his left foot and a tree to the right. Beneath his right hand is what appears to be a curved sword. He is not lying on a bed, nor is his gesturing hand being pulled by Matthew, as in the scene of the apostle resuscitating Euphranor, son of King Egippus, a scene found in some medieval cycles (Pseudo-Abdias, bk. 7, chap. 6).[135] He is most probably the queen's eunuch Candace, a closet Christian who befriends Matthew upon his arrival in Ethiopia and questions him about the faith, receiving in response a lengthy sermon from the apostle concerning Babel and Pentecost (Pseudo-Abdias, bk. 7, chap. 2). Pentecost (Acts 2:2–4)—arguably the initiatory moment of apostolic succession, when the Twelve were empowered by the touch of the Holy Spirit to preach and to heal—would be a most appropriate theme in the Reims chevet program.[136] Again the programmer's close familiarity with the Pseudo-Abdias text has dictated his selection of the scene.

The second (top right) and third (middle) lobes present Matthew's triumph over the magicians Zaroës and Arfaxat and their two dragons (Pseudo-Abdias, bk. 7, chap. 3). In the top scene (fig. 58), the sorcerers appear to the right, the one in front pointing to command the dragons, who pursue a victim escaping to the left. According to the legend, Matthew first puts the dragons to sleep and then commands them in the name of the Holy Spirit to leave peaceably, hurting no one. The Reims rosace is unusual in expanding the story while omitting numerous others. Several Matthew cycles include the magicians and their dragons, though none shows them in actual attack, as at Reims; and several examples indicate Matthew putting the dragons to sleep. The closest comparison is the stopgap in the south rose of Notre-Dame, Paris, in which a seated Matthew blesses two dragons whose heads begin to droop; accompanying the scene is the inscription "DRACONES . . . DORMIERVUNT."[137] Reims shows Matthew standing left and the dragons not dozing but beginning to come to life; the green dragon head below has its eyes closed, while the red dragon head above appears to be electrified by Matthew's blessing hand (fig. 59). Thus the emphasis shifts from the oddity of sleeping dragons to the story's finale—Matthew's sermon, preached before a large crowd, in which he rouses the dragons and commands them in the name of the Holy Spirit to depart. The power of his preaching is the message.

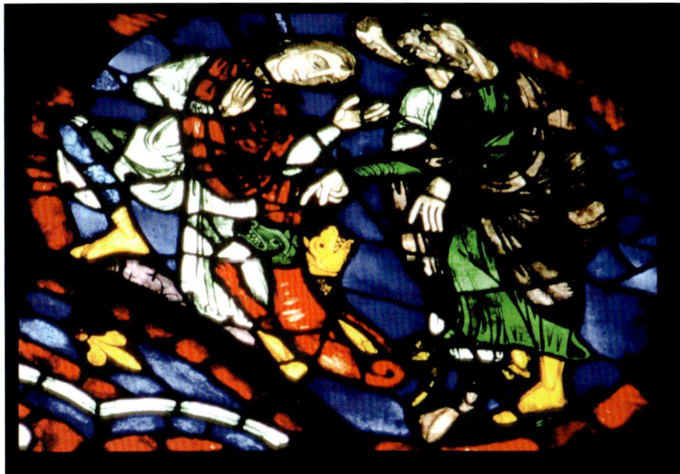

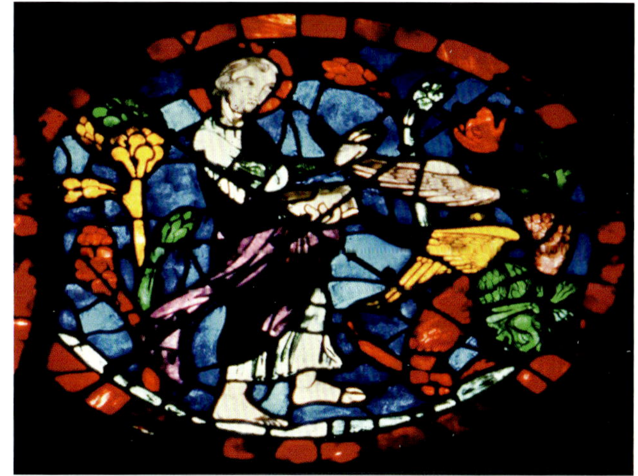

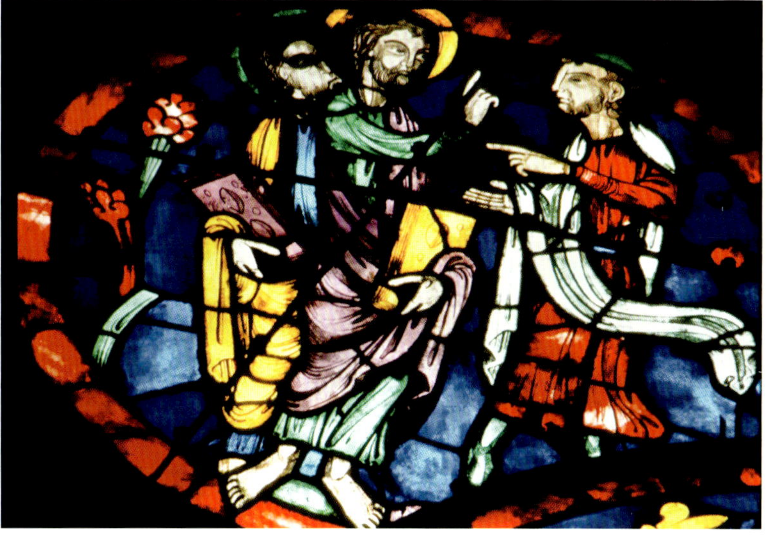

The Reims programmer has taken a legend that even in the thirteenth century may have provoked smiles—eunuchs, magicians, dragons put to sleep—and extracted themes emphasizing the gift to the apostles of the Holy Spirit and their success in invoking it in their preaching, central themes in the chevet program.

The left lobes, originally above the large lancet figure of Jude, present an episode from the Pseudo-Abdias account of Simon and Jude (bk. 6, chaps. 7–23) earlier than that presented in Simon's lobes in Bay 106. Unlike Simon's scenes, selected to show Simon acting alone, the two apostles appear together here, reflecting Jude's extremely minor role in the entire legend.[138] The story, occupying all three lobes on the left, in fact may have been selected because it is the only event in the entire Pseudo-Abdias account where Jude delivers a speech on his own (bk. 6, chap. 8).

The tale describes how Simon and Jude encounter Varvardach, general of Xerxes' army. The general, preparing for war, consults his oracles daily, but upon the arrival of the apostles his sources turn mute. His divines consult an idol in a nearby town, which tells them that the newly arrived apostles are so powerful that no oracles in their vicinity dare to speak. This is pictured in the first lobe (bottom left), where a figure addresses a statue, which raises its hand in response. Varvardach, upon learning this, sends for the apostles and expresses interest in their teaching but states that presently he is occupied with preparation for battle. It is at this moment that Jude speaks directly to him, declaring that their message, if he would agree to hear it beforehand, might give him victory. The second lobe (top left, fig. 60) shows this exchange between the general and Jude; Simon, who also speaks, is here tucked behind him. The apostles then propose a sort of contest, between their prophecy of the outcome of the coming conflict and that of the general's gods, whom the apostles offer to empower to speak as usual (bk. 6, chap. 9). In the final lobe (middle), they authorize the idol to speak and by

FIG. 58 The magicians Zaroës and Arfaxat send two dragons to attack a man, Bay 105, rosace, top right lobe.

FIG. 59 Matthew puts the dragons to sleep, Bay 105, rosace, mid right lobe.

FIG. 60 Simon and Jude before Varvardach, Jude addressing him, Bay 105, rosace, top left lobe.

doing so make possible the contest and ensure its successful outcome.

Missing here are the deeper references to heresy or to the apostles' own empowerment by the Holy Spirit to confront it, themes that enrich the confrontations of Philip (Bay 103) and of Simon (Bay 106) with pagan statues. The message is more naive, a simple story of the apostles' triumph. Varvardach is a willing convert who rewards Simon and Jude handsomely with gold and fine clothes. That idea, much like the story of Thomas's revenge in Bay 103, may have appealed to the canons following their long exile.

The Rosace of Bay 108: Matthias

The rosaces of the twelve apostles occupy Bays 101 through 106, commencing to the right of the axial bay and proceeding according to the order of the Canon of the Mass, zigzagging across the choir. Two apostles share each bay, the zigzag sequence dictating that the two in each rosace not be consecutive in the Canon. The chevet provides four more great doublet-and-rose bays, 107 through 110. The rosaces of the eastern pair (107 and 108) are each assigned to a single figure: Matthias and Barnabas, saints occasionally included in apostle groups in Gothic art. I have suggested that the hiatus in work on the cathedral during the chapter's twenty-six-month flight surfaces in the glazing between Bays 103/104 and Bays 105/106, and more evidence—concerning their lancets—is presented for this hypothesis in the following chapter. Resumption of work on Bays 105 and 106 may have taken time to get moving and probably occupied the (relatively) peaceful period in Reims following the canons' triumphant return in January 1237. The peace was brief. By mid-1238 Archbishop Henri de Braine was again at loggerheads with his citizenry; by the fall he had brought in an army; before the end of the year he had had to flee, placing the town yet again under interdict; and in July 1240 he died while still in exile. The chapter was not concerned in this imbroglio and stayed put, albeit saying their offices in a closed cathedral or their cloister chapel. It is in this tense situation, I believe, that Bays 107 and 108 were produced. The patchwork of styles found in Bays 105 and 106, where the rosaces do not match the lancets below them, grows more exaggerated in Bays 107 and 108, although the glazing continues to follow, more or less, the grand chevet plan. As long as the archbishop's return was anticipated, the canons would not risk dropping his program.

Matthias and Barnabas were late additions to the Canon, probably made by Gregory the Great (d. 604).[139] The Pseudo-Abdias, composed in the late 500s, does not include either of them. Matthias—though not Barnabas—appears following the Twelve in what E. A. Lowe considered the oldest example of the *Breviarium Apostolorum,* in a French manuscript of the mid–eighth century (Paris, BnF, lat. 7193, fols. 55r–56r).[140] The group to which Lowe assigned these leaves on paleographic grounds includes Reims MS 8, manuscript fragments bearing an ex libris and anathema added when they entered the library of Saint-Thierry in the twelfth century.[141] By the thirteenth century the cathedral celebrated the feasts of Matthias and Barnabas, but with somewhat less pomp than those of the Twelve: using five candles before the altar as opposed to nine.[142]

While fabulous legends of Matthias—notably accompanying Andrew in the land of the cannibals—were common in many languages, they do not seem to have enjoyed popularity in the Latin West.[143] The Golden Legend, for example, devotes over half its Matthias entry to Judas Iscariot and to the biblical account of the election to replace him with Matthias; appended is a short and bland vita of Matthias from Trier, which like Rome claimed his body, ending with a short reference to the fabulous legend without specifically mentioning cannibalism.[144] The Reims programmer opts for discretion and devotes the entire rosace to the election of Matthias in Acts 1:23–26. Matthias kneels in prayer in the central lozenge; the eleven apostles do the same in the six lobes (figs. 61, 62). The rosace simply establishes Matthias's legitimacy as an apostle.

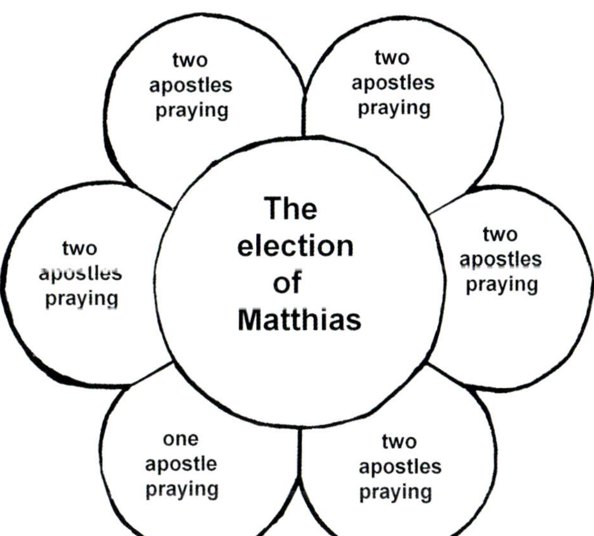

FIG. 61 Bay 108, rosace, chart of scenes: Matthias.

FIG. 62 Bay 108, rosace, Matthias.

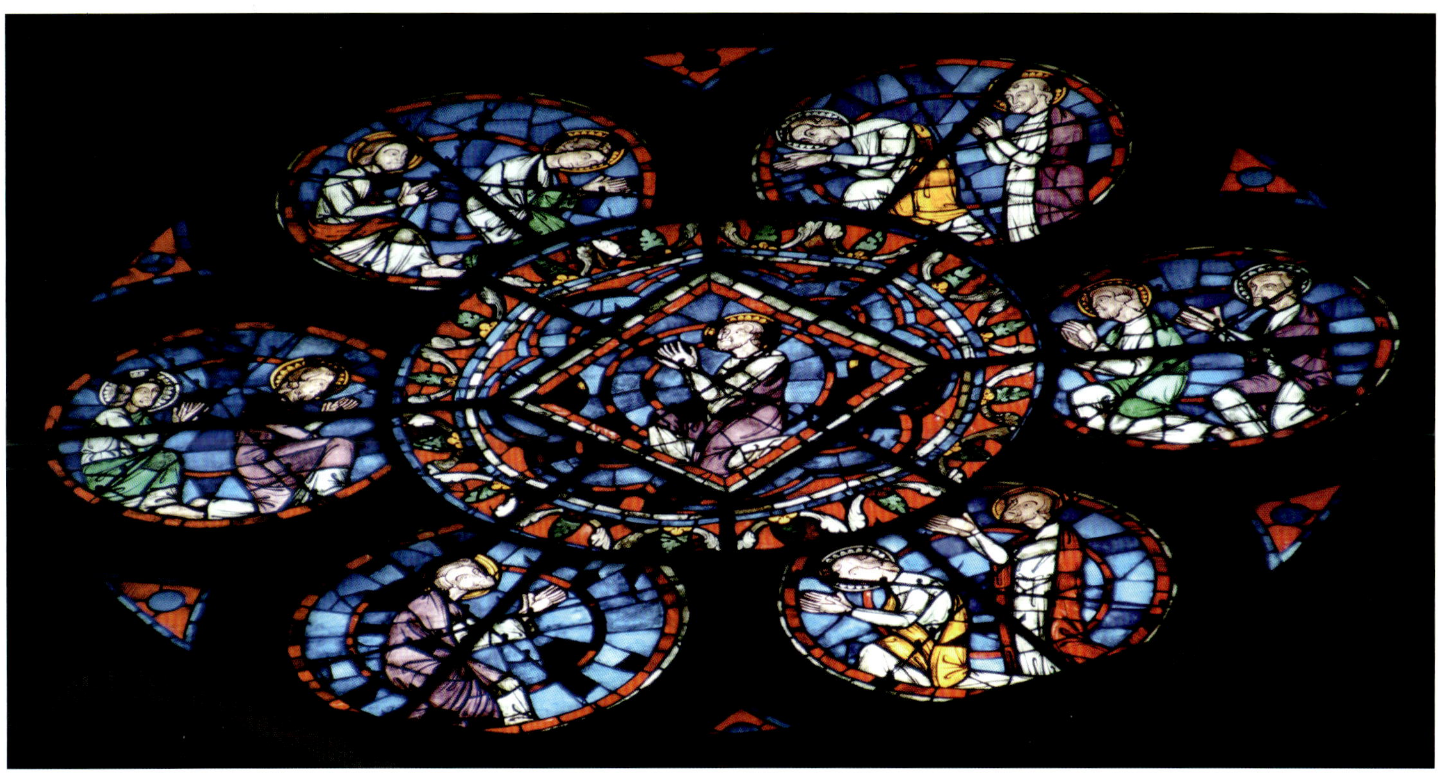

Matthias's election, illustrated in Eastern twelfth-century manuscripts, is rarer in Western art.[145] Noteworthy at Reims is what is omitted. The glazing makes no reference at all to the apostles' casting of lots (Acts 1:26). That biblical reference had long been an embarrassment to the Church. The Golden Legend chews over the matter at some length, providing the justifications of Jerome and Bede as well as the view of Pseudo-Dionysius the Areopagite, that it was only a metaphor for divine choice.[146] Dice appear in the scene in several twelfth-century manuscripts. The *Hortus Deliciarum* (fol. 180v) showed the apostles seated, one of them holding a footed dish with three dice in it, while in the Zweifalten Martyrology (fol. 25r, ca. 1160) two apostles are shown on their knees while a standing St. Peter throws three dice. One might also note a fourteenth-century manuscript of the Golden Legend in San Marino, California (Huntington, H M 3027, fol. 35v), which depicts the apostles standing, flanking two of their number who are seated at a game board with three dice on it![147]

But not at Reims. A few years after Reims, the cathedral of Châlons, a suffragan of Reims and situated nearby, installed two stained-glass cycles of standing apostles (ca. 1255–70) in which Matthias holds as his attribute the vase or jug used for the casting of lots.[148] The reticence of the Reims programmer in ducking the touchy subject underlines his characterization as a sophisticated and erudite scholar. Might he have been educated in Paris, where the Pseudo-Dionysius was still taught as an authority in the first quarter of the thirteenth century?[149]

The rosace of Bay 108 is not of the highest quality. It exhibits study of the earlier rosaces: copying the border of 103 exactly and the red concentric circles in the ground from Bay 102, in a palette like Bay 100 (blue, red, white, murrey), with drapery painting in thick line (reduced to a formula) from the type in 101, and the "asterisk" focus of the lobes on the center as in Bay 104. Color is used to try to break up a balanced but monotonous overall composition. In a chevet filled with treasures, the rosace is a surprise and a disappointment. At least the glazier does not appear to have been given other work.

The Rosace of Bay 107: Barnabas

The rosace of Bay 107, on the opposite side of the chevet, on the other hand, is the product of a stunning and gifted artist (figs. 63, 64). He is also a maverick at Reims. His scenes have a red ground, unlike all other rosaces. This red field sets off an unusual palette of blue, medium green, and white. The figures are larger, with small heads and massive bodies. Their actions display a veiled dynamism, and their confrontations are marked by an immediacy and focus that energize the whole. The figures in the lobes are reduced in almost every case to a pair, who interact with intensity. At the same time, their size dominates the space. The lobes are oriented toward the center, as in a number of previous bays, but the figures are adapted to the curved space, and their postures create a closure that gives the rosace design a strongly centripetal force. The faces are heavily painted with sensitive shading; the drapery is beautifully rendered with elaborate and varied line. This is the artist who uses sticklighting in the ornament; as noted in chapter 3, this technique appears in the lancets below only in the panels of the angel on the roof of the "facade." While the proportions of the lancet figures resemble those of the rosace—small, elegant heads set on massive, powerful bodies—the palette in the lancets is unfocused and the ornament fussy, a totally different artistic language. The glazier of the rosace stands out from the pack.

It is a tempting game to try to pair some of these later artists with those of the earlier bays and to speculate on the possible growth of their art during the several-year hiatus in the Reims shop, when they must have worked elsewhere. Scholars have made similar assumptions about the masons who were building the transept roses, and of course some sculptors.[150] While the glazier of the Bay 107 rose seems related to the expressionist of Bay 104 (similar eye shading, massive bodies, diagonally

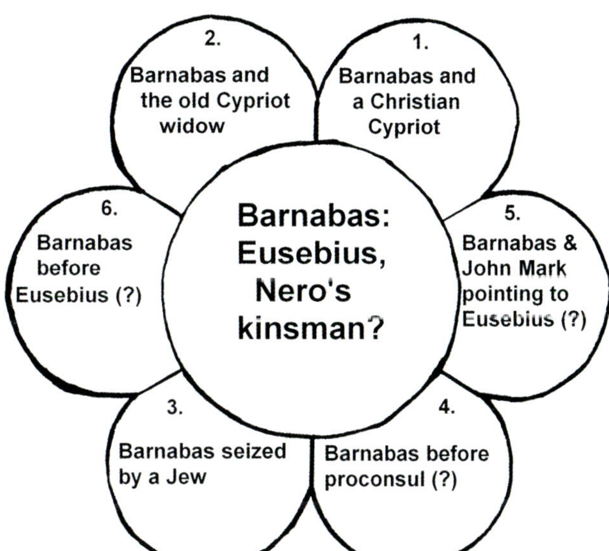

FIG. 63 Bay 107, rosace, chart of scenes: Barnabas.

FIG. 64 Bay 107, rosace, Barnabas.

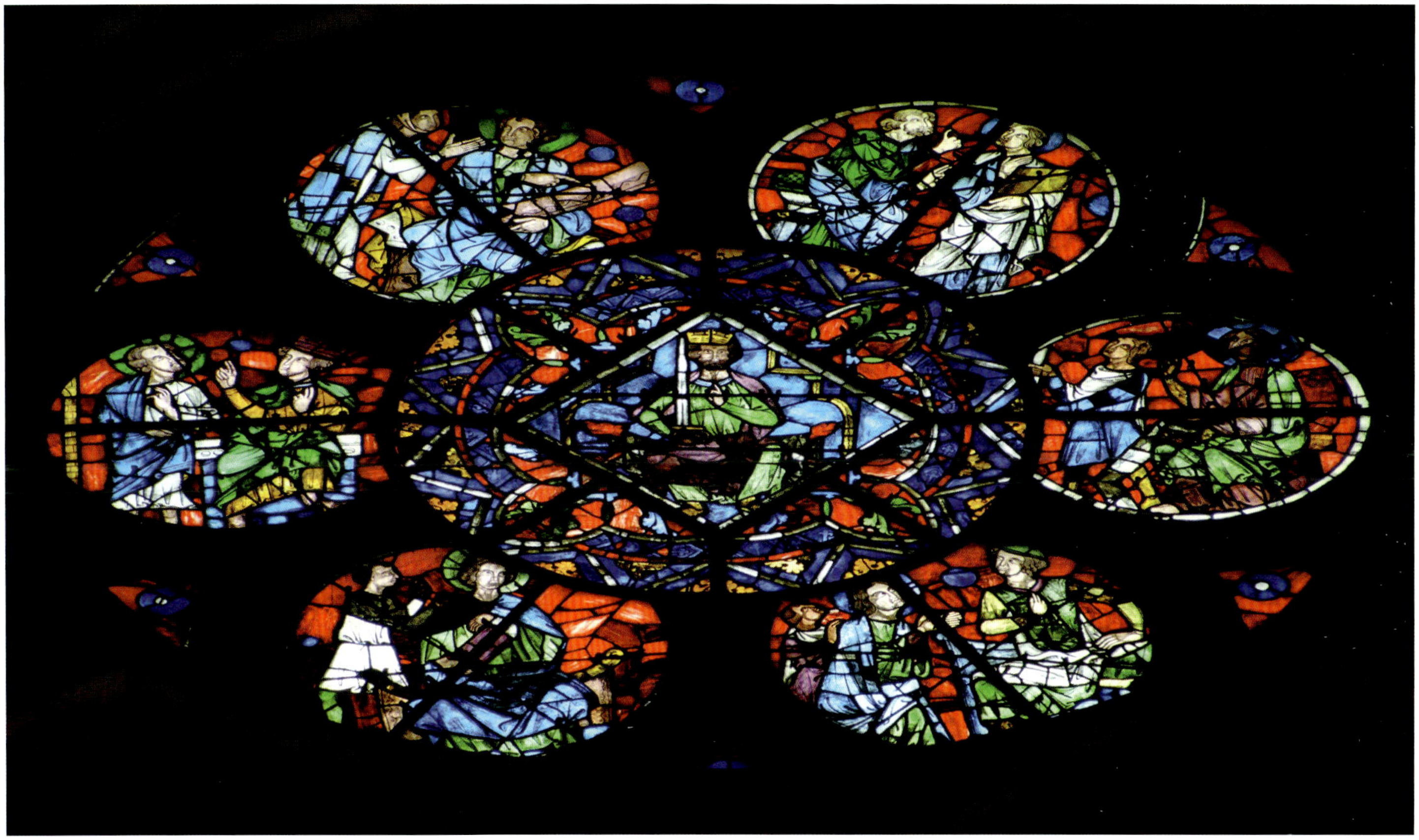

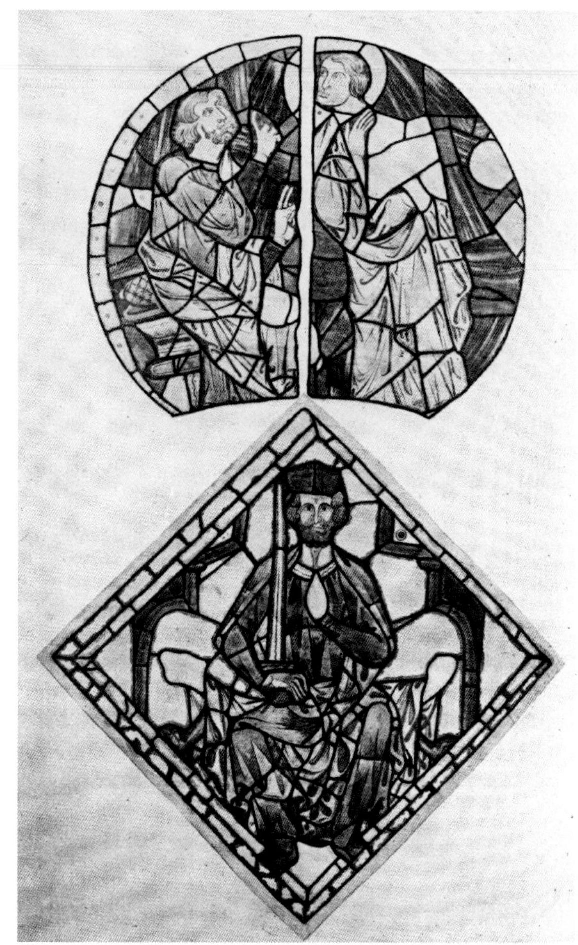

FIG. 65 Bay 107, rosace, top right lobe and central lozenge. Tracings by Paul Simon from the exterior, here reversed as they appear from the interior (after Simon, "Notes sur les vitraux").

organized rosace design), he is much closer to the calm and collected designer of Bay 102 in his preference for green to tie together his design, and in his handsome, nuanced drapery shading. In the end one must give up the game and take each creation for itself. Only Bays 103 and 104 and, later, the rosaces of 105 and 106 form clear visual pairs, but they tell us no real secrets.

The Bible twice refers to Barnabas traveling with Paul as "apostles" (Acts 14:4 and 13). He was probably added to the Canon of the Mass by Gregory the Great and is first listed in the martyrology of Bede (d. 735).[151] The legend of Barnabas's life after separating from Paul and going to Cyprus, like Matthias's vita, is not part of the Pseudo-Abdias. It is called the Pseudo-Marcus because the author purports to be the saint's companion John Mark. It was composed in Greek around 500 C.E. and appeared in Latin translation a century or so later.[152] His figure occasionally appears in apostle groups of the thirteenth century, but scenes of his legend are extremely rare in art until a century later. The rosace at Reims is thus, once again, unique.

Barnabas's martyrdom by fire is included in the twelfth-century Stuttgart Passional but is omitted as usual at Reims. The late-twelfth-century Regensburg Martyrology precedes the martyrdom with scenes of Barnabas preaching and healing, which he does by touching the sick with his copy of the Gospel of Matthew. Contemporary with Reims, Barnabas is shown preaching to three figures in a Psalter/Hours for the use of Soissons.[153] None of this helps to identify the Reims lobes. Subjects can be suggested by reference to the Pseudo-Marcus legend, which, however, only circulated in the West in highly excerpted forms.[154] The fiery death and burial common to them and to martyrologies are ignored at Reims, or perhaps "edited out" and replaced by a distinctly bowdlerized finale. Without knowing the programmer's precise source, one can only guess how much of this rewriting was his.

The order of lobes is most probably in horizontal rows: the top two, the bottom two, and finally the middle row of lobes flanking the central lozenge. Unfortunately, the first lobe (top right, fig. 65) makes a problematic beginning. Barnabas, beardless as he is throughout, stands to the right and clutches a large book—no doubt his precious copy of the Gospel of Matthew. To the left a seated, bareheaded, bearded man talks in an animated way and gestures toward him. This man seems to point up with his right hand and makes what resembles a blessing gesture, but with his left.[155] Here Barnabas is listening, not preaching, and the meaning of the speaker's gestures is puzzling. The artist of this rosace has painted many extraordinary hands, and indeed no specific meaning may be intended. Barnabas was received on Cyprus by a succession of Christian hosts, named Euphenus, Timon, Heracleius (whom he ordained bishop of Cyprus), and Aristoclianus. Thus, precise identification of this scene seems impossible.[156]

With lobe two (top left, fig. 66) we are on firmer ground. Barnabas is seated to the right, pointing to his volume of Matthew's Gospel (which is even larger than before and could possibly be an encased scroll). To the left is a supplicant woman wearing a jeweled mantle, hairnet, and a cap with barbette (chin strap) that was popular with elderly ladies of rank. She is undoubtedly the unnamed eighty-year-old Christian widow who later provides hospitality to the saint.[157]

The bottom lobes (left to right) present the story of the Jews' seizure and binding of Barnabas with a rope in order to deliver him to Hypatius, governor of Salamis. The left lobe shows the saint seated, holding his precious book, while a Jew to the left holds a cord behind his neck (fig. 67). In the lobe to the right the Jew pushes Barnabas before the enthroned Hypatius. This is the point at which the recasting of the story begins. According to the legend, while the Jews intended to take Barnabas before the governor they did not actually do so, but burned him instead. They had changed their plans upon learning of the pending arrival of "a pious Jebusite" named Eusebius, a powerful kinsman of the emperor Nero, whom they feared would free the saint.[158]

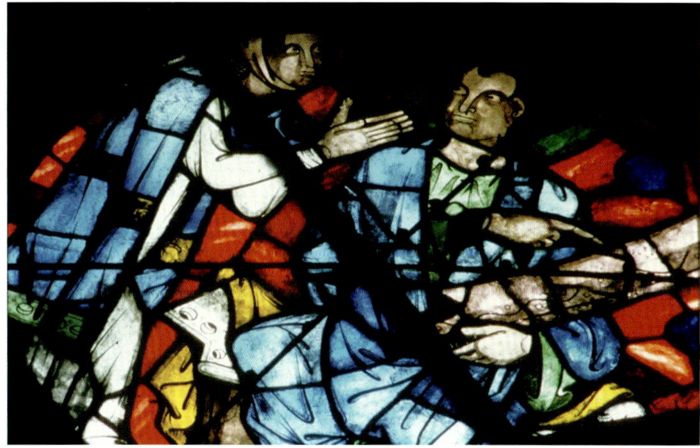

FIG. 66 Barnabas and the old Cypriot widow, Bay 107, rosace, top left lobe.

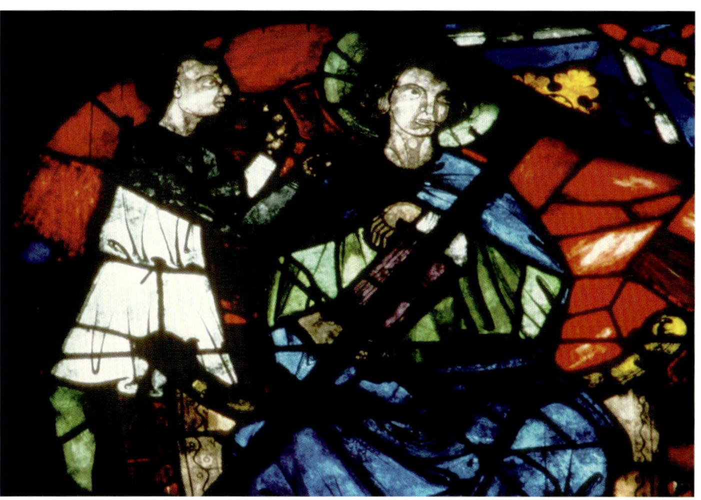

FIG. 67 Barnabas seized by a Jew, Bay 107, rosace, lower left lobe.

The central lozenge of the rosace depicts a crowned enthroned ruler who can only be Nero's kinsman (figs. 64, 65). No other crowned ruler appears in the legend. The light green color, facial shading, and elaborate drapery painting of this figure are repeated in the lobes of the rosace, so he is not a stopgap foreign to the group. In the middle lobe immediately to the right of this enthroned figure, a seated Barnabas unrolls his scroll and gestures in teaching, while his young companion—presumably John Mark, declared companion and author of the Pseudo-Marcus legend—points to the crowned Eusebius in the central lozenge. The final lobe, to the middle left, shows the same monarch gesturing in blessing (!) to Barnabas standing before him. The rosace thus has a happy ending, though according to the Pseudo-Marcus legend Barnabas was not actually brought before the governor or saved by Nero's kinsman. Not only does the rosace rewrite the finale as might Hollywood, it ignores the legend's most remarkable episode, a religious rite involving a race between naked men and women. In that tale an incensed Barnabas destroys their pagan temple and many of them with it.[159]

If the programmer did intentionally bowdlerize the story, why?[160] To return to the themes prominent throughout the Reims rosaces, preaching is certainly underlined by the saint's manner and gestures in several lobes (upper left, middle right). The theme of confrontation with secular antagonists is clearly addressed in the two bottom lobes, where a Jew seizes the saint and pushes him before the governor. The crowned monarch in the lozenge, in a distinctly positive role, however, adds a new theme to the rosaces. In the coronation cathedral such an image could not but invoke the king of France, Louis IX.

Thus it can be suggested that this final rosette was only composed following the death of Archbishop Henri de Braine, on July 6, 1240. The archbishop's relations with the Capetian monarch, his younger kinsman, had never been cordial and at times had approached genuine hostility. Henri de Braine, along with his infamous brother Pierre Mauclerc, had supported the rebellious barons against the regent Queen Blanche in 1229–30. In 1233, even before Louis had reached his majority, royal intervention between the commune and the bishop of Beauvais had drawn the archbishop into strong support of the latter, his suffragan, including a brief attempt to excommunicate the province. Louis did not forget this when, in November 1234, the canons of Reims were forced to flee the violent rebellion on their own doorstep. Nor did the king in spring 1235, when those burghers attacked the archbishop's new tribunal at the Porte de Mars, where heresy trials were held, and Henri de Braine asked his monarch for assistance. After repeated vain requests, the archbishop attempted to put under interdict that part of the royal domain that lay within the archdiocese. Louis bided his time until January 1236, when he succeeded in moving the issue into his royal courts. When the town again erupted in fall 1238 and the archbishop's party had to flee, Henri did not bother to ask again for the king's assistance but brought in his own army. In the end he was forced into a second exile and little over a year later died there.[161]

The relationship between the archbishop and the chapter throughout the turbulent 1230s was also troubled more often than not, and the canons unquestionably had a rather more sympathetic view of the French king. His court's ruling had allowed them to return in triumph over the antagonistic burghers in January 1237. During the archbishop's final flight and interdict they remained *chez eux,* their cathedral closed, celebrating their offices in their cloister chapel of Saint-Michel until almost the very day of his death.[162] Their reconciliation with the townsmen after his demise was swift and again, certainly in their own eyes, triumphant. By mid-1240 crusading was in the air, and the crown of thorns had arrived in the king's palace in Paris. The canons' view of the crowned monarch who was Louis IX was probably not so very different from the glazier's depiction of the beneficent enthroned king in the central lozenge of the Barnabas rosace of Bay 107. Would they have dared put up such an image while Henri de Braine might still return to his palace in Reims? The obvious negative answer to that question provides a date following his death for the rosace and then for the greater break in the last two bays, 109 and 110, where with the introduction of grisaille the archbishop's elaborate program for the chevet is abandoned.

The Canons' Program?

The archbishop's program for the chevet, which is most obvious in the eastern bays of the hemicycle, displays the power of the Church and its ministers, and specifically the power of Ecclesia Remensis and hers. Henri de Braine's attention was, however, directed elsewhere after the beginning of the program, and in any event the details of glazing, like all projects concerning the cathedral fabric, would have been in the hands of the chapter. I have suggested that it involved research into the lives of the apostles as found in the Pseudo-Abdias, a copy of which survives from the famed *rémois* library of Saint-Thierry nearby. The canons' program, as it takes over from the archbishop's, strongly emphasizes the themes of faith and charity, two of the Church's three great "theological virtues." The opposite of faith, as then codified, was idolatry—that is, disbelief, heresy. And the vice opposed to charity is avarice, miserliness, or—in the climate of the 1230s in France—usury. The use of various writings, famous and obscure, of the Carolingian archbishop Hincmar, which I have proposed for the nave program and then for the great west rose, suggests a similar scenario for the canons' choir program. Hincmar's most frequently copied work was *De cavendis vitiis et virtutibus exercendis,* a treatise on virtues and vices written at the request of Charles the Bald. In this work *avaritia* is declared to be the root of all evil and "idolorum servitus" (the service of idols).[163] The surest way to avoid the consequences of vice: penitence and the Eucharist. As Hincmar's most popular work, with thirty-nine copies known from the ninth through the sixteenth centuries, *De cavendis* was surely available and familiar to the programmers of Reims, and it is hard to conceive of a more pertinent message. But there we must leave it.

Of course the rosaces tell only part of the story. While it is to a degree artificial to study them in isolation in this chapter, the goal has been to establish and clarify their rich, complex, and hitherto unexplored evidence. The rosaces set the program, in exquisite detail. The following chapter, treating the lancets associated with them, takes up more broadly the themes, observations, arguments, and questions that have been outlined here.

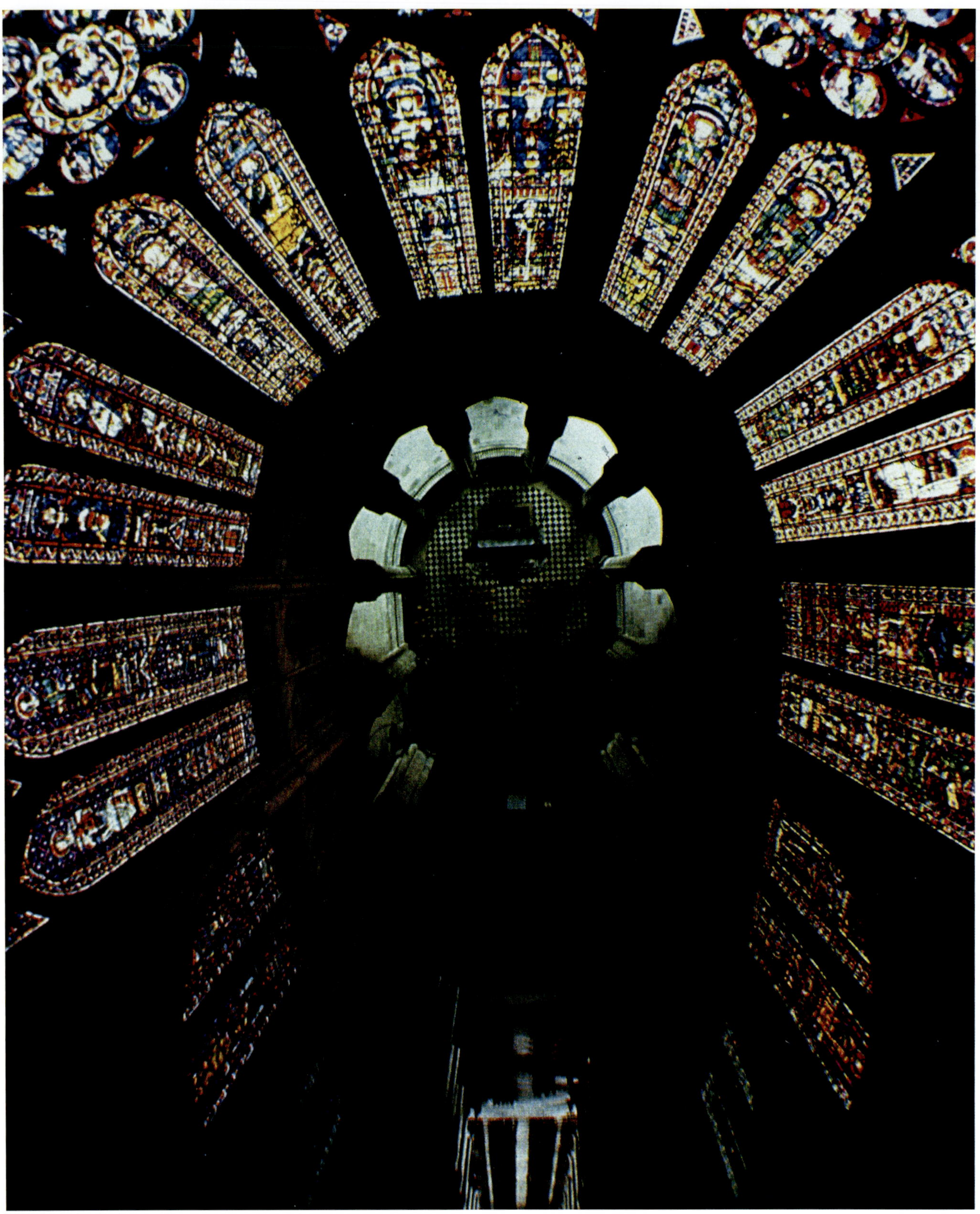

FIG. 68 Lancets of the chevet, from the vaults.

CHAPTER 3

THE LANCETS OF THE CHEVET

It would be an understatement to say that architectural historians have not agreed on the chronology of construction of Reims cathedral. The issue is of some importance here, affecting the dating of the clerestory and vaults of the chevet (fig. 68). Henri Deneux, the architect in charge of restoration following World War I, observed a change in the curve of the choir vaults at about a third of their height and calculated that the originally planned height had been raised by 1.7 meters (5 ft. 7 in.).[1] In 1983 Jean Bony noted that the elevation drawn by Villard de Honnecourt shows the earlier proportion, and further commented:

> Since the clerestory windows were built from the start to the greater height, it [the raising in vault height] must have taken place at a fairly early state in the construction of the upper stories, probably no later than the mid-1220s and certainly well before the interruption in operations due to civil strife in the city between 1233 and 1236; after which it took only five years to complete the whole eastern ensemble of choir and transept, which was put into service in 1241.[2]

A document published by Jean-Pierre Ravaux establishes that the choir's axial chapel, and thus the ambulatory and perhaps other chapels, were in use in 1221. For just a sampling of opinions: Ravaux (1979) dated the clerestory and high vaults above this ambulatory ca. 1231–33; Dieter Kimpel and Robert Suckale (1990) moved the termination date back to ca. 1231 and added much of the nave; and Peter Kurmann (1987) preferred a date for construction of the choir up to the vault departures after 1233 but for the high vaults after 1241.[3] In light of such divergent perspectives, how should a glass study proceed? The only course open is to record one's observations and hypotheses in the hope that they will contribute to the argument.

The analysis of the choir rosaces in chapter 2 seeks to address such issues as their careful and studied iconography, their groupings according to patterns of ironwork and the artists' approaches to the design of narratives in a six-lobed field, and their similarities or dissimilarities in decorative motifs, palette, and painting style. These judgments will now be put at the service of the larger questions concerning the chevet, such as the iconographic program of the clerestories (and its disintegration as the glazing neared completion), those who may have been in charge of which decisions, and *au fond* when and why these windows were planned, designed, and made. Vital to this discussion is my first observation, that in almost every case the rosace is closely related to the lancets beneath it. While the medium of stained glass allows for nearly anything to be added, subtracted, or otherwise altered, absolutely no evidence suggests that the choir lancets were patched to raise their height.[4] To put it another way, the present lancet glass was not made for the original proportions Deneux believed were intended for the choir vaulting. Thus the question of the construction of those clerestories, or at least the dating of the decision to raise the vaults (and to construct the clerestories to the new height), takes on importance.[5]

The chevet windows were restored—and in some cases re-created—after the First World War on the basis of tracings *grandeur nature* that had been made previously by the Simons, whose atelier had been in charge of the cathedral's stained glass for generations. According to Sylvie Balcon, the most severely damaged bays were 105 and 109, while 107 fared well since it had been partly dismounted for restoration in the war years.[6] The Deneux autochrome photographs, which were made around 1915 and became accessible for study in 1995, include thirteen details of the chevet, far from complete coverage and not always sharp or readable, but precious evidence in several cases.[7] In the end it must be admitted that while the general patterns, decorative designs, and color are generally trustworthy on the basis of the Simon tracings, conclusions about the painting style—which may be modern even in parts of the least damaged bays—often must remain tentative.

The only scholar to attempt to categorize all eleven chevet bays by style was Hans Reinhardt in 1963, and unfortunately his four ateliers do not hold up to scrutiny, as has been noted numerous times. His observations were of course made from the restored windows that we see now. Nonetheless, some of his judgments have enjoyed a remarkably long life. Chief among them has been the belief that the four glass images now recycled in the south transept (Bay 118, figs. 146–48) were made for the chevet's axial bay, where they would have formed the core of a hypothesized earlier choir program.[8] In chapter 4, I have assembled evidence to counter this assertion, beginning with Reinhardt's own puzzlement over the large size of these *belles verrières*. They could only have been accommodated in the axial bay if they had had no borders, an unthinkable state of affairs in a French Gothic cathedral of the stature of Reims. Rather, I have argued, the reused images probably were made for the other end of the church—Archbishop Samson's twelfth-century facade—about the year 1220, when Reims was *sede vacante*, the reigning Philip Augustus was aging, the postfire Gothic construction had only achieved a new ambulatory and some chapels, and the possibility that the next coronation might be held elsewhere was looming.

The Alleged First Choir Program

The four *belles verrières* of Bay 118 are here mentioned because they feature in several unwarranted theories concerning the chevet glazing. Put succinctly: if these recycled images never graced the chevet, where does that leave the other choir figures that have been proposed, with them, for a hypothesized original choir program? Before taking up that question, let us examine several recent scholars' theories concerning the makeup of a "first choir program" grouped around the spolia now in Bay 118. The Kurmanns have suggested that three of the images (Virgin and Child, "facade" of Reims, and the haloed archbishop) would have been accompanied in Bay 100 by a seated apostle, probably Peter (now in Bay 102).[9] In my view such a program would be unprecedented in the axial bay of a cathedral, particularly one dedicated to the Virgin, as Reims is; it would only be conceivable were the building dedicated to Peter.[10] Moreover, the figure of Peter (Bay 102, fig. 79) is in a style totally different from that of the *belles verrières* of Bay 118 (fig. 147–48).[11] And another apostle is even less likely than Peter in the axial bay.

A more extended hypothesis has been floated by Balcon to include the fourth spolium: the standing turned figure of John the Baptist (fig. 147).[12] In this scenario, he and John the Evangelist (Bay 104, fig. 86), who also stands and turns, would flank the axial bay, the Baptist leading a file of prophets on the north and the Evangelist heading the apostles on the south. The lower row would contain bishops and archbishops of Reims (now in Bays 103 and 104 and presumably 109 and 110). Too great suspension of disbelief is required to entertain this theory. The Baptist and the Evangelist show unrelated conventions in pose, proportions, and painting of faces, feet, and draperies. Since no prophets now exist in the Reims chevet windows, drastic remaking would be required of the now barefoot, bareheaded, and haloed apostles of Bays 109 and 110, all but one of whom carry books. Only ten apostles could be accommodated in the south side of the chevet. The fact that John the Evangelist stands and gestures is not unique among the present choir apostles. Many of them gesture or point, and James Major (Bay 101, fig. 73) also stands and is indeed even more unique as the only apostle garbed in chasuble, dalmatic, and alb.[13]

Such imaginative theories were spawned by Reinhardt's declaration of an original choir program centered around the recycled images now in Bay 118.[14] My solution for these *belles verrières* (see chapter 4) dates them to 1219–20, relieves us of the obligation to hunt for remnants of a "first choir program," and allows a fresh look at the surviving evidence in the chevet.

A word could be said about the scholarly tradition linking the glazing of the cathedral with that of Saint-Remi (ca. 1165–1205). Both clerestory programs consist of two rows of equally large figures, among them (in various locations) archbishops of Reims, apostles, and kings, surrounding the Virgin and Child and the Crucifixion. Madeline Caviness has reconstructed the glazing of Soissons, a suffragan cathedral of Reims, along similar lines and dated it 1201–23.[15] Another of Reims's suffragan cathedrals, Châlons, has a clerestory program (ca. 1230–36) including prophets, as at Saint-Remi and Soissons, and local saints as well.[16] In short, since Reims's chevet and facade constructed by Archbishop Samson (r. 1140–60) preceded—and are considered the model for—those areas of Saint-Remi, it seems likely that the abbey's glazing takes its cue from the twelfth-century cathedral. Samson's chevet was destroyed by fire around 1210, and its glass is unlikely to have survived. At least parts of the cathedral's Carolingian nave, however, were probably in liturgical use—possibly for at least twenty or more years after the fire, during which time the coronations of two kings took place (1223 and 1226). Indeed, the old nave had hosted the previous coronation, that of Philippe Auguste, in 1179.

Archbishop Henri de Braine (r. April 18, 1227–July 6, 1240), whose inscribed image appears in Bay 100 (fig. 70), was of Capetian lineage and never for one moment forgot it.[17] He was born ca. 1197 in his family's château at Braine, less than forty kilometers from Reims. His ecclesiastical career began at Beauvais, a suffragan cathedral of Reims, where he served as treasurer under his uncle and mentor, Bishop Philippe de Dreux (d. 1217). Uncle Philippe's candidacy for archbishop of Reims in 1202, supported by Philip Augustus, had failed because his reputation as a warrior preceded him; Henri's great-uncle Henri de France, brother of King Louis VII, had previously reigned as archbishop from 1162 to 1175. In December 1225 Henri de Braine became grand archdeacon of Reims, in which office he participated in the 1226 coronation of the twelve-year-old Louis IX—with whom he shared a great-grandfather, Louis VI. Following the death on February 18, 1226 (n.s.), of the bishop of Châlons, another suffragan cathedral of Reims, Henri de Braine was elected their bishop. He had not yet been consecrated in November when Archbishop Guillaume de Joinville died unexpectedly of dysentery, as did Louis VIII, with whom he was joined on the Albigensian crusade. Henri de Braine quickly renounced the Châlons bishopric and in February 1227 was elected archbishop, though only after the canons' first choice had declined the office. Bay 100 (fig. 69) is his song of triumph, probably conceived soon after his election and executed before ca. 1230.[18]

Stained glass was a medium that Henri de Braine would have thought of. His brother Pierre Mauclerc and family appear below the south rose of Chartres, "portraits" that I believe are likely to date from 1227–28.[19] Henri himself gave a window

FIG. 69 Bay 100.

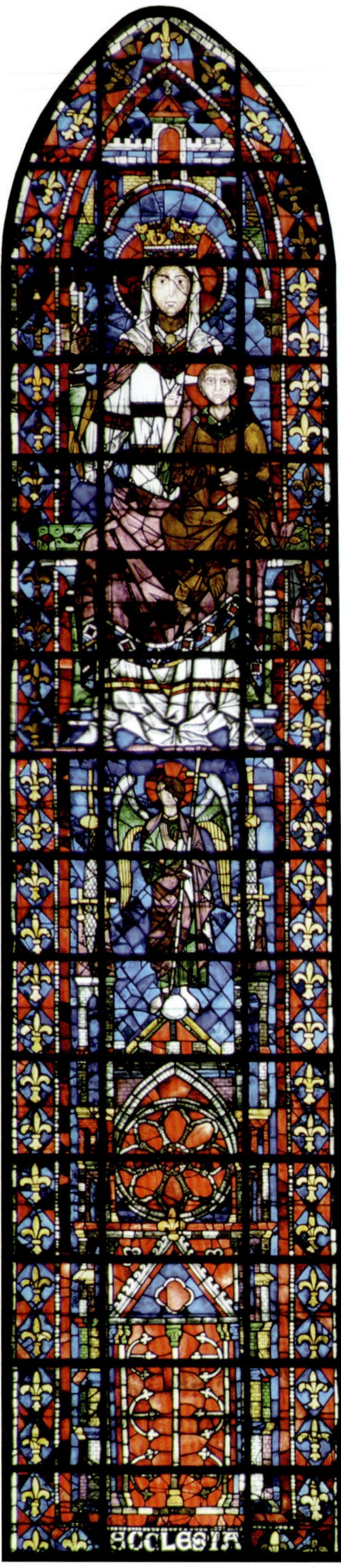

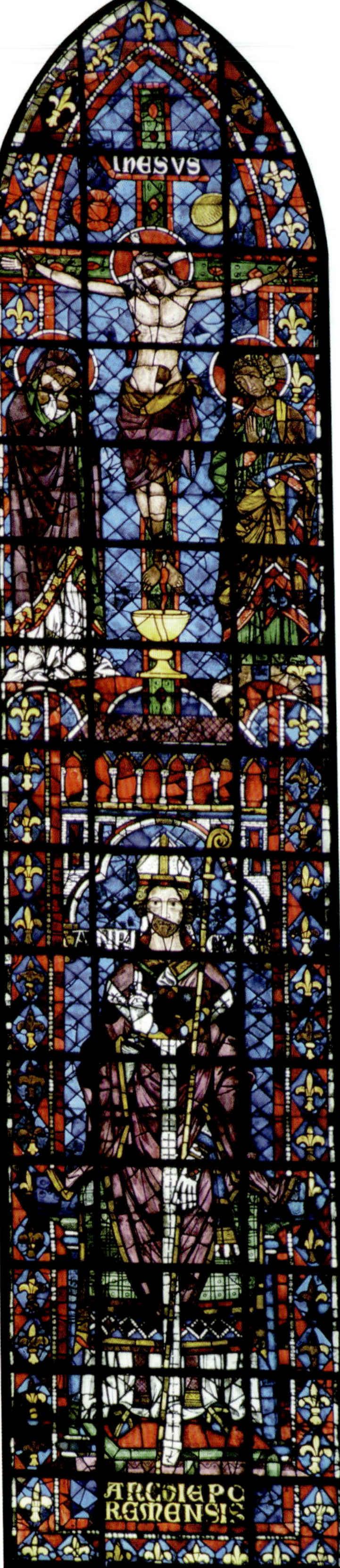

with his image for the nave clerestory of Saint-Nicaise in Reims, where he had laid the foundation stone; its inscription is reported to have included the date 1229.[20] I have identified another window containing Henri de Braine's image that I believe he donated to Châlons cathedral when the Gothic chevet was first in liturgical use, ca. 1237.[21] Caviness has estimated that the church of Saint-Yved at Braine, where Henri was born, was largely finished and glazed by 1204—when its chief patron and his grandmother Agnes de Braine died—and that the church was definitely complete by 1208.[22] Henri de Braine during that period was at the impressionable age of seven to eleven years.

Bay 100, with his image in it, is a unicum in the Reims choir—there is nothing like it.[23] The figures have a markedly courtly proportion and elegance, though without surviving large-scale glass from Paris in these years such a judgment remains tentative. The small heads, somber blue/red palette (with white and purple-brown color blocks), and the broken-fold silhouettes of the figures have little to do with large-scale programs in and near Champagne: Saint-Remi, Orbais, Soissons, Châlons, and so forth. Bay 100, moreover, is an intentional and carefully studied citation of the *belles verrières* now in Bay 118 (figs. 147–48). I have argued (see chapter 4) that they were located at the other end of the cathedral, in Archbishop Samson's mid-twelfth-century facade, at the time when Henri de Braine came to office. Here is a list of similarities:

- large red haloes with white pearled border;
- elongated proportions with oval heads, long thin noses, similarly drawn mouths and chins;
- both John the Evangelist, at the Crucifixion in Bay 100, and John the Baptist, among the spolia, wear somber green robes under golden yellow mantles;
- both "facades" have a portal with trumeau, under a pierced gable framed in crockets, and a rose window under a pointed and pierced ogive, crenellations, and a roof gable;[24]
- both Virgins wear tall crowns and white veils, a white robe and purple-brown mantle, and blue shoes; even the horizontal band on the lower skirt is the same (gold flanked in red fillets); the same jeweled design decorates their thrones.

The differences that are observable between the Virgins (see figs. 69 and 148) can be explained by comparison with two Marian seals of the cathedral (figs. 155, 156). The recycled Virgin now in Bay 118 copies the first Marian seal of ca. 1150–60 (in use 1192) in wearing a mantle resembling a chasuble falling in a V-fold between the knees, her right hand lowered to hold the long stalk of a lily, and the Child is frontal; however, she is crowned as on the second seal of ca. 1200 (in use until ca. 1350, fig. 156). The Virgin in Bay 100, like the second Marian seal, wears a crown and a mantle that falls back over the shoulders and is pulled up across the legs, and her right arm, bent up at the elbow, grasps a short-stemmed lily-scepter. Her frontal Child, however, follows the first seal as well as the image in Bay 118.[25]

The glass likeness of Henri de Braine in Bay 100 (fig. 70) has the same oval face, long nose, and round chin as the recycled bishop-saint in Bay 118 (whom I identify as St. Remi, fig. 147), and in each figure both the pupil and iris of the eyes are indicated. The differences between the two figures have more to do with Henri's self-aggrandizement. Unlike the saint, he wears gloves and rational—the twelve-jeweled pectoral worn by *rémois* archbishops on solemn feast days. His throne is not the foldstool that St. Remi sits on, but the archbishop's throne located directly below Bay 100, which was known as *la chaire de saint Remy*.[26] His archbishop's pallium is so long that it trails on the ground. His colors repeat those of the Virgin and Crucifixion above him, and the same orphrey pattern decorates his dalmatic and the Virgin's mantle. Even though a throne is indicated, the figure's extreme elongation has been compared to his standing image on his archbishop's seal.[27] Henri held office in Reims cathedral by 1226, before becoming archbishop, and undoubtedly knew that the stained glass in Samson's facade that he was emulating, made ca. 1220, had been modeled on seals (see chapter 4). Finally, the fleurs-de-lis border of Bay 100 is the only one in the chevet. Henri's seal has six fleurs-de-lis in the ground and another on the counterseal. They refer, of course, to his Capetian lineage, as does the fleurs-de-lis border around his older brother Mauclerc's image below the Chartres south rose—which is lacking around the images of his wife or children there.[28]

As has often been noted, the Crucifixion of Bay 100 does not relate to the Bay 118 *belles verrières,* while its chalice, below the cross, has been considered a copy of that detail in the axial bay of the tribune at Saint-Remi (ca. 1180–85).[29] But instead of copying Saint-Remi, is it not possible that the cathedral's Crucifixion—as well as Saint-Remi's—recalls the axial image that glazed Archbishop Samson's cathedral chevet and was probably lost ca. 1210 in the fire? The Crucifixion is, one might say, pro forma for an axial bay. An example nearly contemporary with Samson's chevet survives in Poitiers cathedral (ca. 1165–70, fig. 26), a broad lancet including near the bottom the Three Marys at the Tomb.[30] The latter scene appears in very similar form in the rosace of Reims Bay 100. It is the traditional older visualization of Christ's Resurrection, replaced in the thirteenth century by Christ Rising from the Tomb—for example, twice at Bourges (bays 3 and 6, ca. 1210–15).[31] It must be admitted that this does not constitute proof of an earlier model for the Bay 100 rosace, since the scene of the Marys at the Tomb lasts on in the axial clerestory of Troyes (ca. 1235–40) and even later in the vicinity of Toul in Lorraine.[32]

Other axial Crucifixions include that in the clerestory of the suffragan cathedral of Châlons (ca. 1230–36), as well as an earlier one there (before 1147), which, I have argued, was in the axial bay of the Romanesque apse and then installed in the same location in the Gothic apse from the 1230s and remained there until at least 1680.[33] Later than Reims, Troyes (ca. 1235–40) and Auxerre (late 1240s) have Crucifixions in the axial clerestory, as does Reims's suffragan cathedral of Beauvais (ca. 1260–65). The Beauvais Crucifixion includes the chalice.[34] Henri de Braine's Bay 100 may include a chalice in imitation of the one in the Saint-Remi tribune, but it most probably has a Crucifixion because it replaces a lost twelfth-century window of the Crucifixion in Samson's chevet.

It is likely that this unique window, Bay 100, was Henri's initial gift, made between April 1227, when he was consecrated as archbishop, and 1231. The commission, to celebrate his new office, could have occupied a few years for completion, and the artist was almost certainly not parochial. In December of 1228 Henri had the first of several run-ins with his canons, a dispute that went to arbitration.[35] In the next few years Henri de Braine was otherwise occupied with family matters, one might say, but matters that touched the highest levels of state. In the several months between his election and consecration as archbishop (February/March 1227), he and his eldest brother, Count Robert III de Dreux, were in the west country negotiating a peace treaty, on behalf of Queen Blanche, with the rebellious barons led by their brother Pierre Mauclerc. The agreement stipulated that Mauclerc's daughter Yolande would marry Louis IX's brother Jean d'Anjou, then aged eight, when he reached fourteen; in the meantime Yolande was to be in the custody of five nobles, two of whom were her uncles Henri de Braine and Robert de Dreux.[36] In 1229–30, on the other hand, Henri de Braine supported Mauclerc's partisans clandestinely, supplying them with provisions when they invaded Champagne.[37] Then again—in June 1231—Henri de Braine was in Brittany as one of the ambassadors for Queen Blanche who negotiated a three-year truce with Mauclerc. In July of that year the thirty-year-old poet Count Thibaud de Champagne became a widower, and Henri and his brother Robert hatched a plot secretly to marry their young niece and ward Yolande to him! The scheme was thwarted by royal messengers only at the eleventh hour.[38]

Finally, in August 1231, Henri held what may have been his first provincial council of the eleven suffragan bishops of his archdiocese. It was at this council that he introduced the seated arrangement of the suffragans (fig. 18) that we see mirrored in the Reims chevet windows.[39]

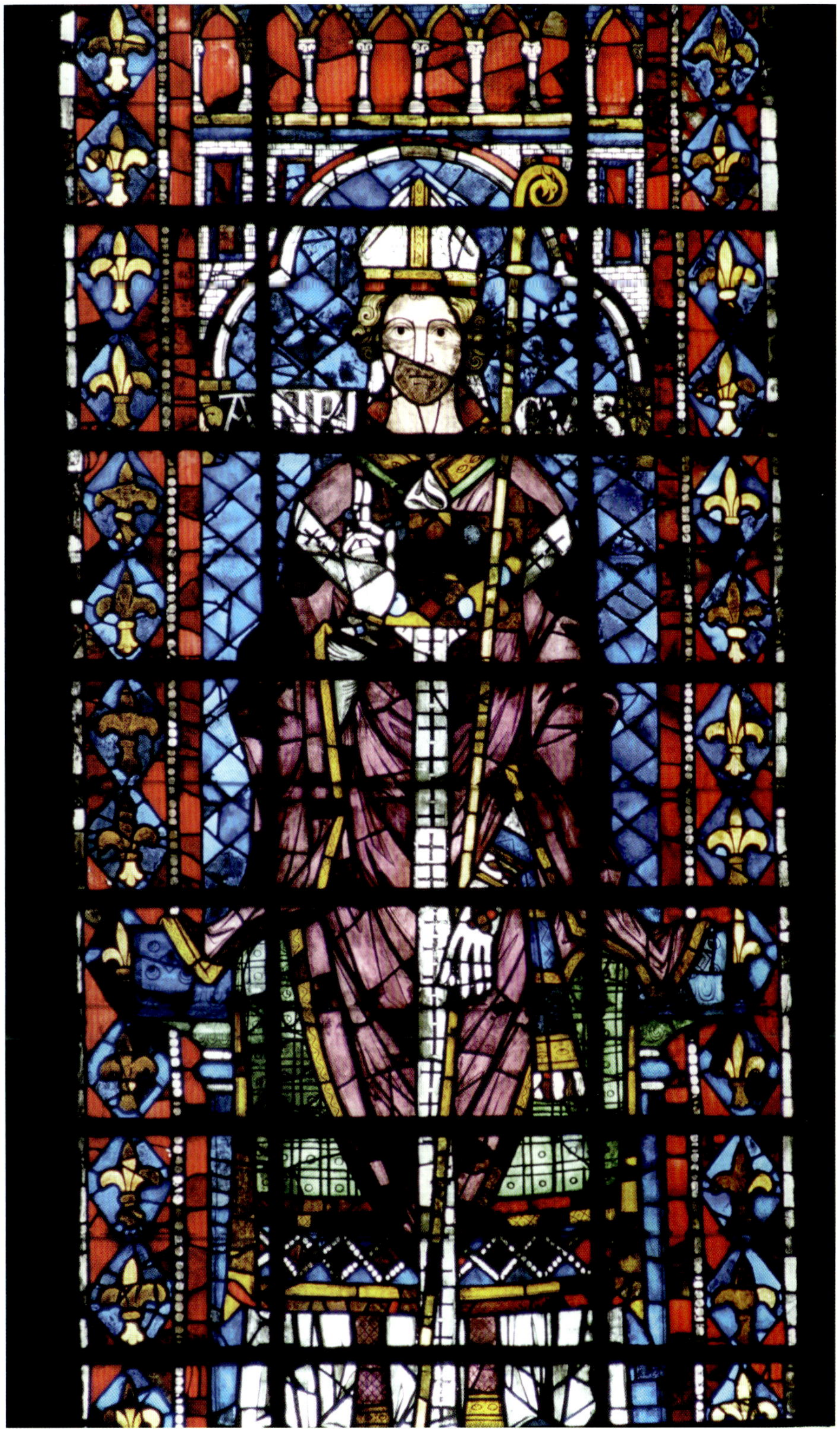

FIG. 70 Archbishop Henri de Braine, Bay 100, right lancet, lower row.

Henri de Braine's Intended Choir Program

The glazing program planned for the ten remaining clerestories (Bays 101 through 110)—the chevet windows flanking the archbishop's axial bay—depicts his suffragan bishops seated in the protocol he instituted for provincial councils in 1231 (fig. 27). Each bishop is accompanied by the "facade" of his cathedral, as is Henri de Braine in Bay 100. The upper row of figures, flanking Bay 100's images of the Virgin and Child and Crucifixion, depicts the apostles, in the protocol established by the Canon of the Mass. The rosace over each bay presents stories of the two apostles in the lancets below. The elements of this program are clear, becoming somewhat jumbled only at the western end of the chevet. Implications of this deterioration are investigated below.

Parts of the program—the upper row of apostles flanking the Virgin and Crucifixion—followed traditional formulas for chevet glazing. The lower row of bishops and their cathedral "facades," on the other hand, are unique to Reims. Their horizontal lineup supports the cumulative power of the archdiocese, while their vertical connection to the apostles above them stresses the theme known as apostolic succession:[40] the direct, unbroken line of descent of authority from the apostles, passed by the laying on of hands at a bishop's ordination. Thus it is appropriate that the bishops appear in the seating arrangement that Henri de Braine had established in 1231 for provincial councils, where decisions were taken affecting pastoral care—indeed, the very lives—of the faithful.

The counterpoint of this network of themes could be fitted into the ten available chevet bays only approximately. The apostles appear as they are found in the Canon of the Mass in twelfth-century *rémois* manuscripts: Peter, Paul, Andrew, James Major, John, Thomas, James the Less, Philip, Bartholomew, Matthew, Simon, and Judas Thaddeus.[41] They are placed in what might be called Gothic protocol, beginning next to the axial Christ and zigzagging back and forth across the choir. Thus Peter and Andrew share Bay 102; Paul and James Major occupy Bay 101; and so forth (see fig. 27).[42] Normally the place of greatest honor is at Christ's right hand (i.e., dexter). At Reims, however, Peter—chief of the Twelve—is on Christ's left (sinister), that is, on the south side of the chevet. In the lower row, the suffragan bishops' seating arrangement has the same reversal. Several scholars note this inversion without explanation, but in fact there is a simple one.[43] In Reims the archbishop's palace is on the south, as was the medieval archbishop's entrance to the sanctuary. In cathedrals where this was the case, such as Notre-Dame in Paris, Bourges, and Châlons-en-Champagne, the bishop's entrance and throne—and thus the position of primacy—was on the south.[44]

The twelve apostles, paired in each doublet window, fill only six of the ten chevet bays available. They were augmented with Matthias, the elected replacement for Judas Iscariot (Bay 108), and Barnabas, Paul's sometime companion who occasionally is accorded apostolic status. Accompanying each of these two is a nameless apostle, often suggested to be Mark and Luke.[45] Four more nameless apostles, barefoot and nimbed, occupy the final chevet bays, 109 and 110. I do not believe that Mark, Luke, or indeed any other names were ever intended for these anonymous disciples. Great care was taken to identify the Twelve plus Matthias and Barnabas, all of whom have inscriptions except Peter (holding a key), Andrew (with a cross), and John (beardless and clearly identified by his "author portrait" in the rosace above him). Unlike the rosaces of the Twelve, each of which assigns three of its six lobes to the life of the apostle directly below, the rosaces over Matthias (108) and Barnabas (107) devote all six lobes to those saints, which strongly emphasizes the anonymity of their barefoot companions. In stained-glass cycles of Gothic France into the early fourteenth century, a degree of fluidity existed concerning the number, and even the identities, of the apostles.[46] While at Reims the identities are clear for those in rank, the remainder filling out the chevet program were intended from the beginning to support—but not to dilute—the grand theme, that of the apostolic succession.

A short excursus on the state of development of attributes held by the apostles will support a generally early dating for the Reims chevet glazing. While Émile Mâle's pioneer list is incomplete and not entirely accurate, it does offer a basic framework for charting the rise and elaboration of attributes during the thirteenth century.[47] I have suggested that this phenomenon is tied to the greater individualization and need for personal identification that comes with urban, as opposed to rural or feudal, society; a similar development in heraldry and eventually in surnames can be charted during the same period. At Reims the attributes appear in a fairly undeveloped state: Peter's key, Paul's sword, Andrew's Latin cross, and Bartholomew's knife (figs. 73, 79, 93). All other apostles have books or open scrolls, except Thomas (Bay 103, fig. 84), who has a sword but in a very few years will usually be easy to identify by an architect's compass or calipers. And since Thomas's rosace presented the palace he built in heaven (fig. 51), his lack of a precise architect's attribute is all the more significant. The date I have proposed for the establishment of the Reims choir program, ca. 1231, is supported by such a detail.[48]

It seems clear that generic apostles of some sort, filling out the final chevet bays, were intended from the start—simply because they would be needed. Below them were to be the eleven suffragan bishops of the archdiocese. Each bishop was to be paired with his cathedral's "facade," developing the charming conceit of Henri de Braine's Bay 100 (fig. 71), which in turn drew from the glazing made in ca. 1219–20, as I believe, for Samson's twelfth-century facade (fig. 148). The series of stained-glass "facades" forms a visual pun on the concept, substance, and power of Ecclesia, which is the grand message of the chevet. For all eleven suffragans to be included in the ten bays of the chevet, the entire chevet would be included in the program and, even so, two of the less important dioceses would have to double up.[49] The program as it was carried out, and now survives, includes three such doubled-up bays (105, 107, and 108). However, the idea of doubling up was already present in the program planning from its inception.

Inscriptions identify most of the bishops and their "facades" in Bays 101 through 108. On the basis of nineteenth-century witnesses, only the bishops of Bay 106 and 108 were nameless, while all the "facades" could be accounted for.[50] Of the eleven suffragan dioceses, inscriptions refer to all but Arras and Cambrai, those at the "end of the table" in provincial councils (see fig. 18). What emerges is that the intended program of ca. 1231 begins to break down following the completion of the hemicycle glazing (Bays 101 through 104), and we shall see below that a sea change in style occurs at exactly the same juncture. The bishop of Senlis shares Bay 105 with the "facade" of Amiens (fig. 90).[51] In Bay 106 (fig. 93) the bishop is anonymous and occupies the wrong lancet; in all other bays the bishop appears in the lancet closest to the axial bay (left on the south, right on the north). This is also the bay where the sophisticated interlaced ordering of narrative scenes in the rosaces disappears (see fig. 27).[52] In Bay 107 (fig. 95) the inscription for Barnabas, who appears in the top row of the left lancet, is located at the bottom of that lancet, below the "facade." The "facade" itself is apparently unidentified. Guilhermy reads the bishop's inscription as "eps et morense civita"; Cerf gives it as "Episco. Morinen. civita"; Tourneur reports "Ecclesia Morinensis," the letters *bouleversé;* and the Cahier-Martin engraving shows eighteen letters, many of them reversed or upside-down (see fig. 9).[53] If the transcription in the engraving is correct, the glazier was an illiterate either working without oversight or paying limited attention to his instructions![54] Such anomalies are addressed below and searched for hints of the original program, of what happened to it—and why.

The "Facades"

Besides Henri de Braine's "facade" of Reims in Bay 100 (fig. 71), the chevet contains eight more, seven of them named. Since the mid-nineteenth-century

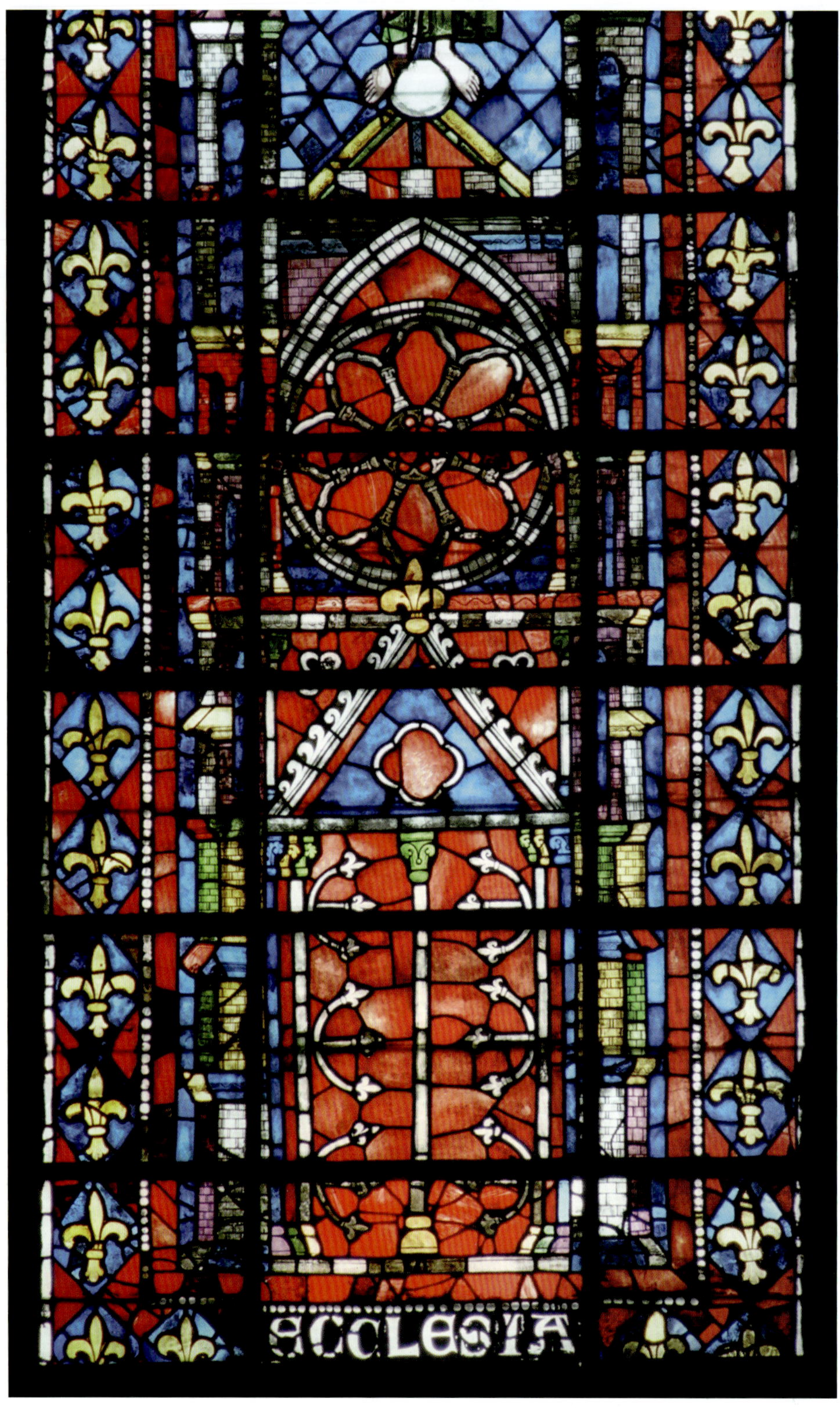

FIG. 71 "Facade" of Reims, Bay 100, left lancet, lower row

observations of Charles Cerf, it has been believed that they bear little resemblance to the actual diocesan cathedrals in question, and since the pioneering study by Eva Frodl-Kraft, it has been accepted that they combine various architectural elements (portals, towers, rose windows, gables, etc.) to produce an idea—indeed eight ideas—of a Gothic cathedral.[55] Scholars of the Middle Ages are accustomed to the minimal degree of similitude required for a medieval "copy," for example, of the Holy Sepulchre or Charlemagne's chapel at Aachen. The term "facade" is itself suspect, as Stephen Murray has noted: "The word 'facade,' although convenient for the modern student of the cathedral, would not have come to the lips of a thirteenth-century person, who would probably have referred to the western frontispiece as the 'towers and portals.'"[56] Indeed, not many of the suffragan cathedrals actually had Gothic facades by the 1230s. Of the cathedrals named in the Reims images, Laon's facade was finished by ca. 1200; the three portals of Soissons date ca. 1220 but the rose level and towers are much later; the dating of Amiens, controversial, is pushed back by Murray to ca. 1225 for the lowest part of the facade, but ca. 1243 for the rose level, and even later for the parts above; the facade of Noyon, with porch, probably a rose, arcade above that, and towers, was complete by 1235.[57] Beauvais never got a Gothic facade, nor did Châlons or Tournai.[58]

Frodl-Kraft suggested that "Soissons" (fig. 81) represented an actual facade, not of Soissons, however, but of Laon.[59] Recently, architectural historians have been taking a closer look at this question. In a tour de force study, Kurmann collects and expands these observations, turning the nineteenth-century judgment of Cerf on its head.[60] The portal zone of "Laon" (Bay 101, fig. 73), according to Frodl-Kraft, reflects the south-transept porch of Chartres. However, the large gargoyles, and the overlapping of the towers and central bay above the rose, come from Laon itself; so does the rose, though this is not the one from the west facade but the earlier rose window in the north transept.[61] Again, while Frodl-Kraft saw elements of "Tournai" (Bay 108, fig. 97) in the pre-restoration facade of Saint-Remi in Reims, the many small openings in the towers recall the transept towers of Tournai itself.[62]

"Amiens" (Bay 105, fig. 90) contains doublet-and-quatrefoil openings like those in the actual cathedral's gallery over the portals, and the pinnacles of the "facade" cite those separating the gables at the same level.[63] The two hanging lamps within the portal of "Noyon" (Bay 106, fig. 93) might identify that area as the deep porch of the cathedral, and Kurmann suggests that the three gables might reflect the way the porch was actually constructed.[64] The plain massive wall and untraceried windows of "Châlons" (Bay 103, fig. 84) probably refer to the now lost twelfth-century facade, while the two spires emerging behind it correspond to the north and south transept towers.[65] And Kurmann has brilliantly observed that "Beauvais" (Bay 104, fig. 86) depicts a part of that cathedral in existence before 1232: the tripartite facades of the eastern aisles of the transepts.[66]

The existence of a constellation of architectural drawings for the cathedral of Reims, at a time when hardly any survive, has occupied historians of architecture for many years. The most famous are those forming the extensive series in the Villard de Honnecourt manuscript (Paris, BnF, fr. 19093).[67] It is presumed that Villard copied drawings in the Reims *chantier,* as James Ackerman has argued, concluding: "Further evidence that Reims was an incubator for the maturation of architectural drawing and that Villard would have had models is provided by the survival of two project drawings for the Cathedral facade on sheets that have been called 'The Reims palimpsest.'"[68] These are considered the oldest surviving geometrical drawings, made with rule and compass. They are orthogonal drawings, that is, every part is projected onto a single plane, which is the only way that a drawing can be made to scale. And engraved into the triforium walls of the Reims transept are working drawings made to full scale.[69] While Kurmann believes that at least one and possibly both of the facade elevations on the Reims palimpsest were for microarchitecture (e.g., reliquaries in precious metal), he stresses that the actual parchment on which they were drawn was reused by one of the cathedral canons, Alanus de Rosceio. It is another reminder that the chapter of canons was in charge of the cathedral's architects, sculptors, glaziers, and goldsmiths.[70]

The charming stained-glass "facades," completely unique in their medium, form yet another block of evidence for the hypothesis that the Reims *chantier* possessed a collection of orthogonal drawings at a precocious moment in architectural history. The two "facades" of Reims itself—Henri de Braine's Bay 100 (fig. 71), which I have dated ca. 1227–30, and the spolium of ca. 1219–20 (fig. 148) upon which it was based—include numerous *rémois* details. Frodl-Kraft has discussed their roses, each set within a pointed arch in the manner of the Reims roses, as well as the portals, above all of which are glazed areas in the tympana as eventually built on the new west facade, and she concludes that the glaziers had access to masons' designs.[71] The rose tracery in the Bay 100 "facade" is more modern than the earlier one in Bay 118. Kurmann has noted that the spires of "Reims" (Bay 100, fig. 72), surrounded at each base by four cones, replicate the crowning designs of the cathedral's buttresses and are also used for three more "facades" (Bays 106, 107, 108, figs. 93, 95, 97). Villard's drawing of these buttresses (fol. 32v) indicates passages in these cones.[72]

The observation that the rose windows of the two Reims "facades" indicate a chronological development can be carried much further. The pointed arch framing each allows a pierced ogive light above the rose. The recycled "facade" of ca. 1219–20 (now in Bay 118, fig. 148) resembles the Reims transept roses as built, resting on a solid masonry wall, while the Reims "facade" in Bay 100 (fig. 71) also shows pierced corner lights flanking the rose, as were later built in the two west facade roses, small and large. The traceries of these two "Reims facades" provide another kind of evidence. Neither image offers any indication of the kind of regional centripetal tracery for which Reims is noted. The colonnettes in a centripetal rose have their capitals close to the center rather than out toward the rose's circumference.[73] The tracery of the reused Reims "facade" (118) has a rosette design that would only be found on much smaller constructions, even microarchitecture; the Bay 100 Reims "facade" has a wheel window with centrifugal spokes, a standard twelfth-century design. The observation that the two other "facades" with centrifugal wheel windows—"Beauvais" (Bay 104, fig. 86) and "Noyon" (106, fig. 93)—most probably replicate actual windows in those monuments makes the two "Reims facades" all the more puzzling in this regard. It is a puzzle that is quickly solved. The wheel windows at Beauvais and Noyon, upon which their stained-glass facsimiles at Reims were modeled, were not major facade roses but small, minor lights elsewhere on the monument.[74]

The evidence of the Bay 100 Reims "facade" (fig. 71) thus suggests that the distinctive centripetal tracery of the Reims transept rose windows (and later the west tympanum) was a design idea not yet born ca. 1227, when I believe Henri de Braine commissioned his axial window. It does not follow that the transepts could not have been built then, as tracery infill might be delayed in installation (just as the back triforium wall could exist for a period without the colonnettes making up its inner face and thus could be used for engraved scale drawings).[75] On the other hand, the centripetal rose design associated with Reims was known around 1234. A copy of it by Reims masons exists in the small church of Notre-Dame in Cluny. That church had suffered a fire in 1233 and was in reconstruction when, on November 9, 1234, the canons of Reims were forced by civic unrest into exile, putting the town under interdict and almost surely bringing to an abrupt halt the cathedral construction.[76] In other words, we can date the tracery design of the Reims transept roses between about 1228 and 1234.[77]

In fact, this dating can be narrowed further, to ca. 1231–34. The tracery pattern of the Reims transept rose windows is best understood as an improved version of the Laon west rose, ca. 1190–1200, copied in the Laon east rose, ca. 1215–20.[78] But neither the "facade" of Laon (Bay 101, fig. 73) nor that of Soissons (Bay 102, fig. 81)—the latter considered since Frodl-Kraft to present the facade of Laon—contains a centripetal rose of the Laon type.[79] Bays 101 and 102 probably initiated the choir glazing program as it was developed ca. 1231, when the seating plan of the suffragan bishops, which it mirrors, was established by Henri de Braine. Thus one could surmise that around ca. 1231 the question of the Reims transept tracery pattern had not yet risen to the top of the pile on the architect's agenda, but the renewal of the glazing of the choir clerestories was again under way and at full steam.

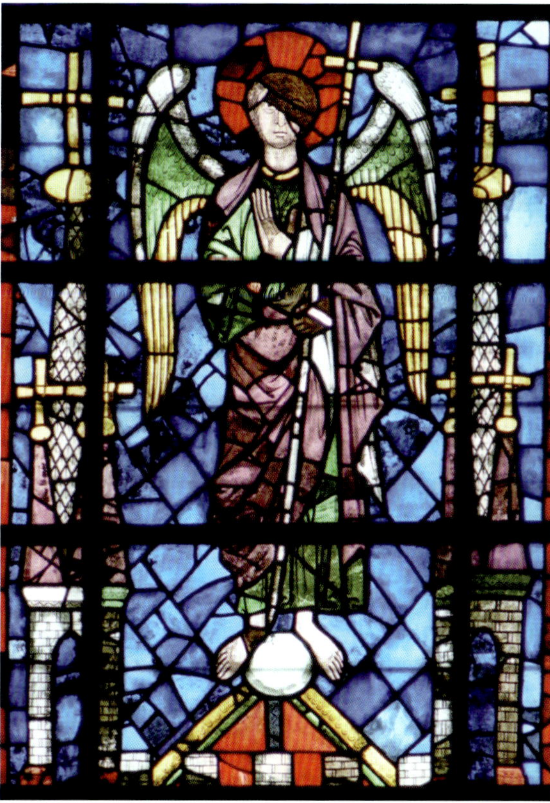

FIG. 72 Angel on the Reims "facade" holding an archbishop's cross-staff, Bay 100, middle of the left lancet.

The Angels on the Roof

Reims is known as the "cathedral of the angels," primarily for the series of gigantic angels crowning the buttresses. Villard de Honnecourt's elevation drawing, folio 31v, shows them, at least at the idea stage.[80] The angel on the Reims "facade" of Henri de Braine in Bay 100 (fig. 72) may reflect this idea. This angel holds one of the archbishop's insignia, his cross-staff.[81] This cross is never held by the archbishop himself, always by an attendant. Like Henri's pallium and rational, it shouts his rank. In other words, at the time of commission of Bay 100, around 1227, the angel on the roof need not have had any particular apocalyptic significance.

When the choir program was resumed around 1231, the archbishop's angel may have triggered the introduction of the theme of the seven churches of Asia (Apoc. 1:4, 11, 20; 2; and 3).[82] Angels often sit or stand on the roofs of these churches in illustrated Apocalypse manuscripts, as noted by Kurmann.[83] Yves Christe has observed that in commentaries by Cassiodorus and Rupert of Deutz, as well as the *Glossa Ordinaria,* the angels of the seven churches are their bishops.[84] Given that the choir program of ca. 1231 presents the suffragan bishops and their churches, the idea to place angels on the buildings may indicate a programmer—one of the canons?—of university education. That is certainly the conclusion reached in studying the rosaces (chapter 2) as well.

Of the eight "facades" flanking Bay 100 in the chevet, one of them ("Amiens," Bay 105, fig. 90) has no angel.[85] While scholars have puzzled over this omission, I believe the programmer may have intended it. For an apocalyptic reference, seven angels on seven churches were enough. Reinhardt's belief that the angels of "Châlons" (Bay 103, fig. 84) and "Beauvais" (104, fig. 87) were added has already been questioned by Frodl-Kraft, for whom the inserted angels would be those of "Châlons" and the unidentified "facade" in Bay 107 (fig. 95).[86] In fact none of the angels need to have been added—or all of them could be. In the medium of stained glass, in which nearly anything can be altered, this is not a particularly helpful line of inquiry to pursue. The angel of "Châlons" (103) is by far the tiniest, both "Beauvais" (104) and "Tournai"(108, fig. 97) have very small angels, and these bays fall at the beginning and very near the end of the chevet glazing.

But there is more. Six of the angels blow trumpets, while the angel on "Soissons" (Bay 102, fig. 81), chief of the suffragan dioceses, holds a rolled scroll and points a finger in a gesture of admonishment.[87] The trumpets introduce an entirely new apocalyptic reference—to the seven avenging angels (Apoc. 8, 9, and 11 passim). Parisian exegetes such as Robert of Saint-Victor and Peter the Chanter, as well as the *Glossa Ordinaria,* saw in the seven trumpeting angels an image of the preaching of the Church in present time.[88] The sermon is not gentle. At the sound of the first six trumpets come hail, blood, fire, shipwreck, poisoned water, darkness, giant locusts, plague. . . . We have here another possible reason why "Amiens" has no angel, and why the "Soissons" angel holds a scroll of prophecy, admonishing. Six trumpeting angels are enough. The seventh trumpet (Apoc. 11:15–19) "is a prelude to the end of time" that will announce the Four Last Things: Death, Judgment, Heaven, and Hell.[89] While the messages of the six occur within time, that of the seventh trumpet remains in the future of mankind.[90] It is worth recalling that preaching is a constant theme in the chevet bays (see chapter 2), and therein lies the connection between the angels on the roof and the apostles and suffragan bishops who surround them.

William Clark has pointed out that the theme of the constellation of archbishop and eleven suffragans underlies the early group of eleven processional angels and Christ, the large statues embedded in the exterior chapel walls by 1221.[91] The diocesan "facades" paired with the suffragan bishops, as noted above, develop the idea from the "facade" of Bay 100 and ultimately from its model, the spolium "facade" originally installed in Samson's west facade around 1219–20. Thus the chevet's glazing program of ca. 1231 elaborated on two cycles of artworks made and installed around 1220 at either end of the cathedral. One could note further that the elaboration on those themes was pursued with great thought and study, as is evident in the apostles' narratives in the rosaces, the "facades" themselves, as well as the angels on their roofs. Although the program was not fully realized as intended, it is nonetheless recognizable, remarkable, and—as many have stated—unique.

The Choir Program as We Have It

What happened to this elaborate intended program, then, 'twixt cup and lip? Several breaks are evident. The most obvious is the introduction of grisaille in the final two bays, 109 and 110. The program of ca. 1231 was without doubt intended to be fully colored, with two rows, apostles above suffragans, filling the chevet. The grisaille/color combination found in Bays 109 and 110 (figs. 99, 100)—a central column of color surrounded by grisaille—was a format that only emerged around 1240, notably in the axial chapel and choir clerestories of Auxerre cathedral.[92] The use of grisaille indicates a final break in the planned program, as has occasionally been suggested. Moreover, the grisailles match in style those filling the transept clerestories, a glazing campaign following the death of Henri de Braine, in mid-1240 (discussed in chapter 4).

An earlier break of this kind—that is, in formal design—has not drawn previous comment. It is in the design of the ironwork of the rosaces. The bays in the hemicycle (100 through 104) have large roundels, surrounded by borders, in the centers of their rosaces, as does Bay 106 (e.g., figs. 34, 39, 53), while Bays 105 and 107 (adjacent to each other), as well as 108 opposite, have smaller central lozenges enclosed in more elaborate framing (figs. 57, 62, 64). However, the design and color of the glass in Bays 105 and 106 is clearly of a piece in spite of the differences in ironwork. In other words: the ironwork of the 106 rosace aligns with the first group in the hemicycle, while its glass goes with the second group, in the straight bays of the chevet. This observation coordinates with the great sea change to be observed in the style—that is, the general mood, what one might call the ductus—of the chevet lancets, a break that occurs between the hemicycle bays (100 through 104) and the remainder. I believe that this major break in approach must indicate a cessation of the glaziers' work for some time. The documented chronology of the cathedral indicates only one such hiatus, when the canons were forced into exile on November 9, 1234, putting the town under interdict, and only returning twenty-six months later, on January 2, 1237.[93]

Reinhardt put hemicycle bays 103 and 104 into his "first atelier," which he associated with the *belles verrières* now in Bay 118 and believed to be remnants of an abandoned "first program" for the chevet. His theory, while still in vogue, does not survive close examination.[94] Very little in the four reused images of ca. 1219–20 (figs. 147–48)—including color, proportions, conventions of facial and drapery painting, even mood—can be related to Bays 103 and 104 (figs. 84, 86). Frontality and the absence of leading around the eyes do not make an atelier.

The suffragan bishops of Bays 101 through 104 (figs. 73, 81, 84, 86) are rigid, frontal icons, images not of real people but of hieratic offices, pronouncements of weighty and ancient authority. They are abstractions, unmoving, unreal, untouchable, menacing. Even the apostles above them are less frightening and more relaxed: James Major (Bay 101, left) and John (104, left) stand and gesture (figs. 73, 86), turning toward the altar, as do Peter and Andrew (102, fig. 79), while Paul (101, right) and Thomas (103, right) are seated casually with one knee raised (figs. 73, 84). The grim aspect of the bishops perfectly coordinates with the message of the trumpeting angels with their brimstone and stinging locusts. Where could this somber rigidity have come from? The spoliate figures of ca. 1219–20 (the Virgin and haloed archbishop, figs. 147–48) are frontal, yes, but charming in detail and cheerful in color. Similarly, the congregation of late-twelfth-century archbishops in the chevet of Saint-Remi look almost jovial by comparison.[95] To find a comparable degree of detachment and abstraction, one must go as far back as the earliest figures at Saint-Remi, for example, St. Remigius (fig. 191), probably dated to the mid–twelfth century.[96]

Thus comes to mind whatever lost glazing may have adorned Archbishop Samson's cathedral, dated around 1160 and surviving in part until at least the early 1220s and perhaps until 1241.[97] One thinks also of the Romanesque program of Strasbourg's Carolingian nave (fig. 254), as reconstructed by Fridtjof Zschokke, dating perhaps between 1150 and 1176.[98] The rigid bishops of Reims Bays 101 though 104 cannot be from Samson's cathedral, however.[99] They coordinate in every way—color, facial features, painting style, ornament, and so forth—with the apostles above them as well as with the rosaces at the tops of their bays. If there is a connection with the past, these ferocious bishops are copies, one might say "citations," of such earlier glazing. The stiff frontality of Henri de Braine (Bay 100), and for that matter of the *belles verrières* of ca. 1219–20 (Bay 118), may be translations from the same source.

Bay 101: Paul, James Major, Laon Bishop and "Facade"

Bays 101 through 104 are, in my opinion, contemporary designs by at least three artists, dating between late 1231—when the archbishop established the suffragans' seating pattern—and the canons' exile in November 1234. I am emboldened to argue this judgment by Michael Cothren's masterful analysis of the three bays of the Beauvais axial chapel, which are disparate in subject matter, in painting style, indeed in almost every way, yet convincingly argued by Cothren to be a unified and contemporary ensemble.[100] Reims Bay 101 (figs. 73–76) probably preceded the others, if only slightly, by several lines of reasoning. It is the only one of the group to follow Bay 100 in displaying fleurs-de-lis, which may suggest that Henri de Braine was still actively promoting the glazing program.[101] Fleurs-de-lis are scattered in the ground surrounding the bishop of Laon, and also at the tops of both lancets.

Another reason is that several design decisions taken in Bay 101 were evidently judged unsatisfactory once the window was installed and were never

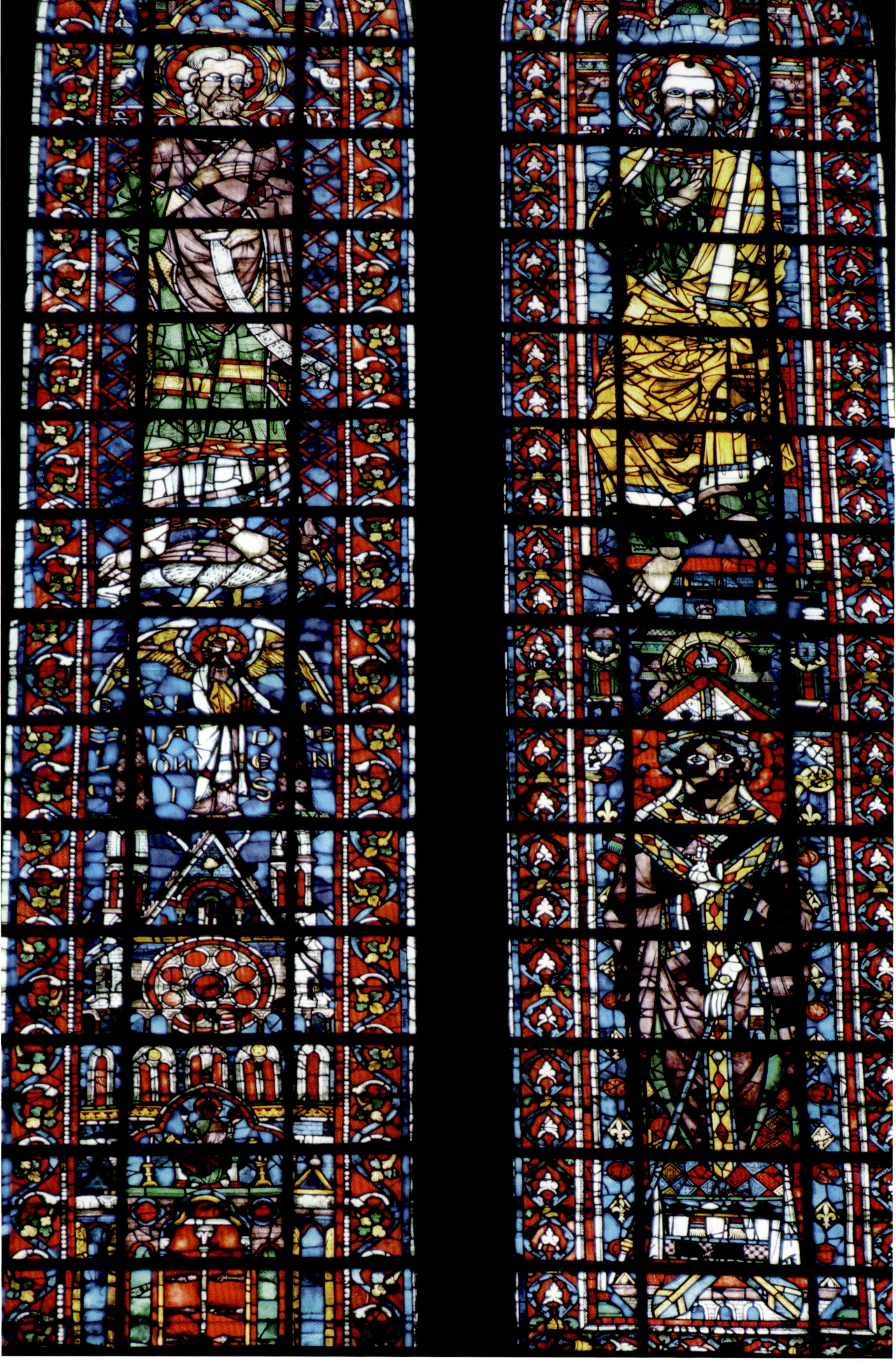

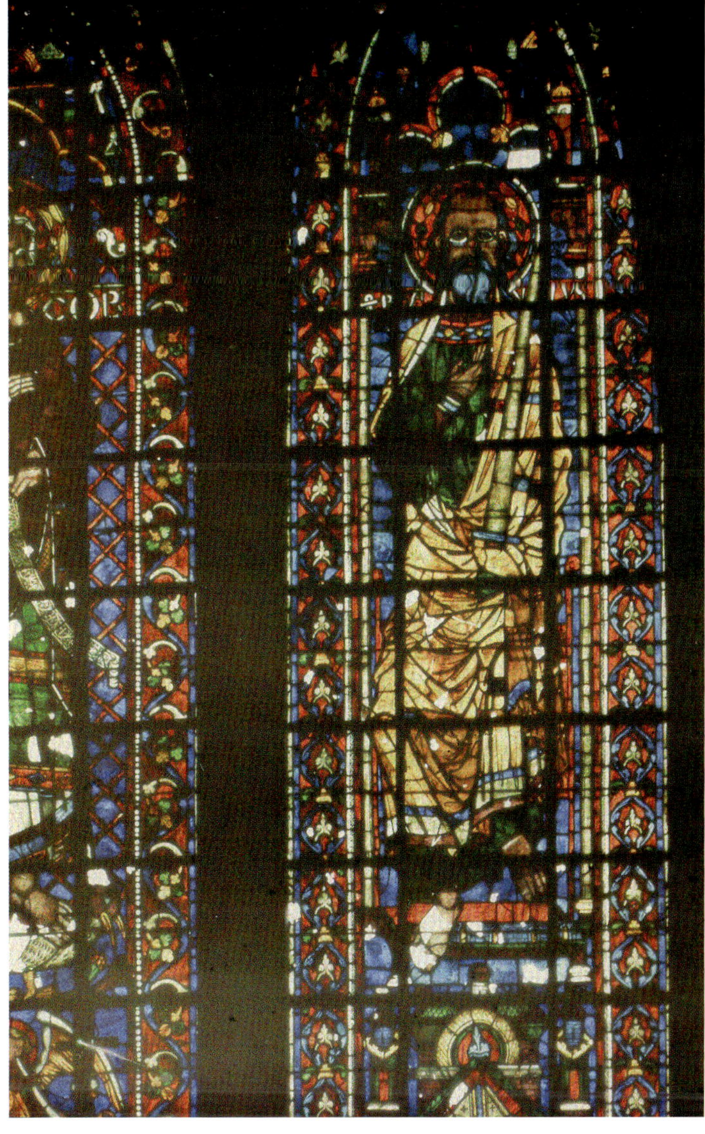

Opposite
FIG. 73 Bay 101.

FIG. 74 Paul, Bay 101, right lancet, top row. Autochrome by Henri Deneux, 1915.

FIG. 75 Duck-monster, socle beneath the feet of James Major, Bay 101, left lancet, top row.

FIG. 76 Border of acanthus and quasi-naturalistic leaves, Bay 101 (1881) (after Westlake, *A History of Design in Painted Glass*).

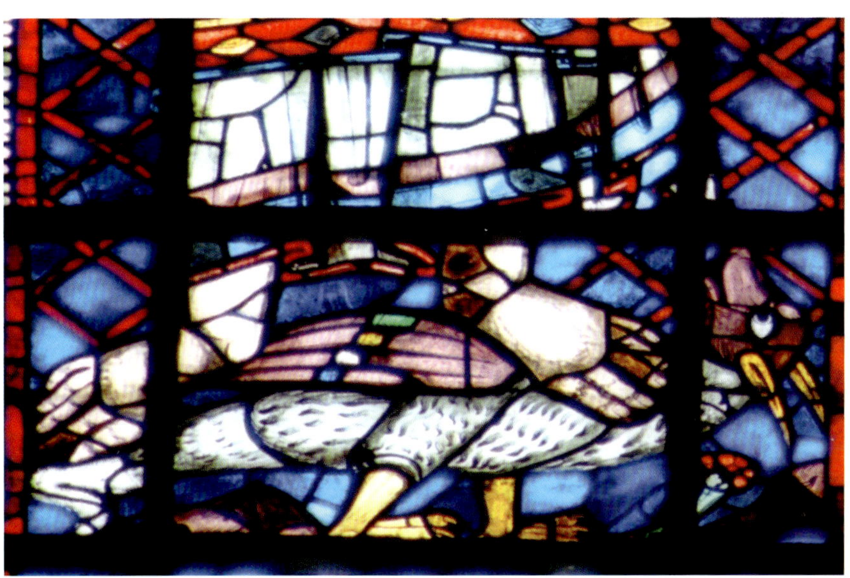

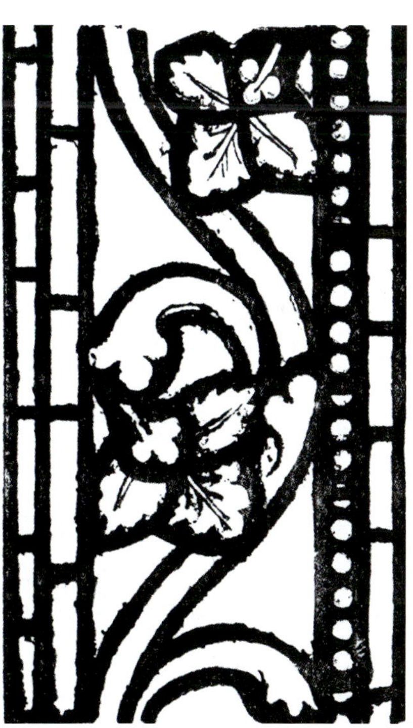

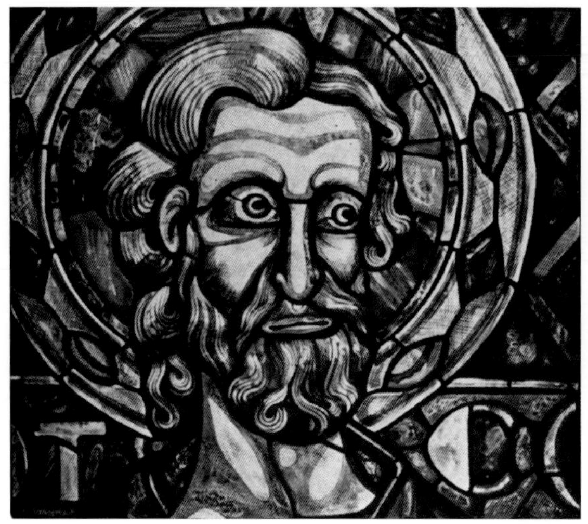

FIG. 77 James Major, Bay 101, left lancet, top row. Tracing by Paul Simon from the exterior, here reversed as it appears from the interior (after Orin E. Skinner, "Restoring the Stained Glass Treasures of Rheims Cathedral").

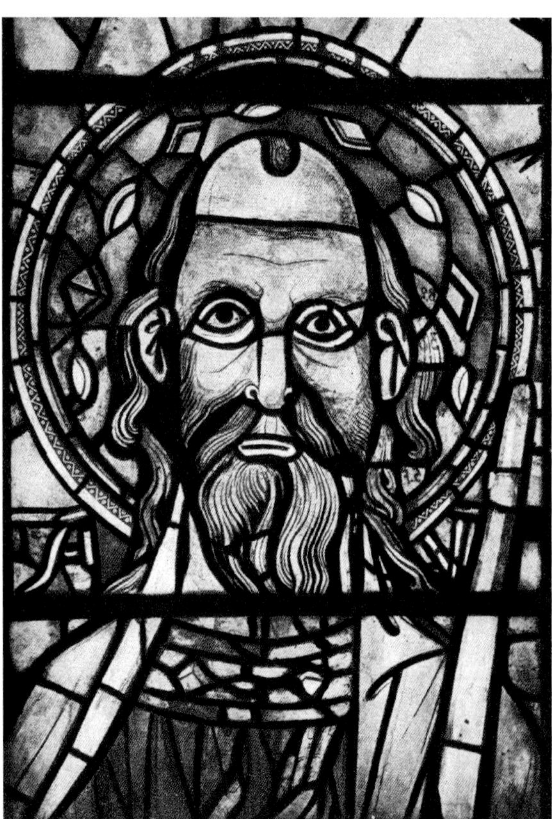

FIG. 78 Paul, Bay 101, right lancet, top row. Tracing by Paul Simon (after Marcel Aubert, *Le vitrail en France*).

used again.[102] One is the use of inscriptions in the rosace. There are two of them, "S'IA COBVS" in the top left lobe and ":S:bAVL VS:APOTOLV" in the top right lobe (fig. 30), and of course they require a high-powered modern lens to be legible. The Laon "facade" has tiny gargoyles spewing rainwater[103] and colored sculpture on the tympanum, details that likewise cannot be seen and do not appear again in the chevet series of "facades." Another failed experiment was the treatment of the eyes. Like the eyes in Bays 102 and 106, those in Bay 101 (figs. 73–74, 77–78) are leaded in the familiar "eyeglasses" manner found in large-scale Gothic figures. Chartres has examples predating those at Reims; Strasbourg has figures dating before and after Reims, while those of Beauvais date ca. 1255–65.[104] However, as Lewis Day commented in 1909 about Reims Bay 101, "[T]he iris of the eye was not represented simply by a blot of paint but was itself glazed in blue. The effect of this might have been happier if the lines of the painting generally had been more nearly of the same strength as the leads. As it is they are not strong enough to support them: the great white eyes start out of the picture and spoil it. They have a way of glaring at you fixedly; they look, in fact, more like huge goggles than live eyes."[105] A century later than Day, we might say that these strange leaded irises give the figures the eerie aspect of robotic aliens. After Bay 101 the technique was never repeated.

The designer of Bay 101 could be dubbed The Decorator, an artist who prefers a broad and unfocused palette and variety rather than conformity in ornament, pose, ground patterns, halo decoration, and so forth. He is the only glazier who uses several shades of blue, including a clear lucid medium blue; it is found in the rosace, the bishop's hair, Paul's beard, and in smaller amounts throughout. He is the only glazier to scatter the letters of the inscription identifying the "facade" across the ground above it, like so many starry constellations.[106] His drapery painting (see fig. 74) is spare and consists of short, angular, thick strokes, in both the rosace and the lancets.[107]

Each of the three large figures is treated differently. The bishop is an icon; St. Paul is a monumental masterpiece—note the raised knee and turned hand. He links the other two, frontal like the bishop but relaxed and approachable like St. James Major. The artist has singled out James, in a number of ways. He, rather than Paul, appears in the central roundel of the rosace above. Bay 101 is the only one in which the central roundel was not accorded to the apostle of higher "rank" in the Canon of the Mass. The large-scale figure of James is standing, as is John the Evangelist (who was his brother) in Bay 104; beneath James's feet is a "socle" like Andrew's in Bay 102. James's "socle" (fig. 75) has the wings and feet of a duck but a dragon's tail, and its head closely resembles the sharp-eared dog heads on many of the gargoyles on the cathedral as well as on the gargoyles on the Reims "facade" of ca. 1219, which this artist seems to have carefully studied.[108] It is not a duck but a playful monster. Finally, James (fig. 73) is the only apostle who wears priestly vestments: alb, dalmatic, and chasuble.[109]

Why is James Major, who ranks below Paul in the hierarchy of apostles, accorded these distinctions? Two responses can be suggested. First, the only choir chapel dedicated to an apostle, and the first of the Gothic cathedral to be opened to the cult, in 1221, was the axial chapel dedicated to St. James.[110] The axial chapel of course is below the archbishop's axial bay, 100, but Bay 101 would be the next closest available window. A second reason for James's importance might be personal interest on the part of Henri de Braine.

The rosace of Bay 101 also contains several details of Santiago-based iconography that are extremely precocious for northern France.[111] Henri de Braine's uncle and mentor, Philippe de Dreux (bishop of Beauvais, 1180–1217), had made the Santiago pilgrimage in 1182. He was a book collector of note, and upon his death his library came to Henri. Since the final author of the *Historia Compostellana* (ca. 1140), Girardus, had been a canon of Santiago who came originally from Beauvais, the book may have had a special interest to Philippe. Moreover, in lifelong service to Philippe was the recognized author Pierre de Beauvais, who (in 1212 in the city of Beauvais, as he tells us) translated from Latin to French an account of the translation and miracles of St. James for the "Countess Yolande." It is likely that she can be identified as Bishop Philippe's sister-in-law and Henri de Braine's mother. Pierre de Beauvais had previously written a French version of the Pseudo-Turpin, and these stories form books II–IV of the *Codex Calixtinus* and are also included in the *Compostellana*.[112] A reasonable, albeit circumstantial, argument can be made that Archbishop Henri de Braine had a personal and family interest in, as well as some knowledge of, the Santiago cult.

Bay 102: Peter, Andrew, Soissons Bishop and "Facade"

Bay 102 (fig. 79) is the product of a totally different artist, though certainly close in time. To start with the similarities, the rosaces of the axial bay, 100, and both 101 and 102 (figs. 24, 30, 34) are designed, one might say, horizontally, with strong visual connections across the top two lobes, across the middle lobes and the roundel between them, and across the two lobes at the bottom. The rosaces of Bays 103 and 104, both possibly designed by a third artist, follow a different visual pattern (to be discussed below). Another similarity of Bays 101 and 102 is that in each the outermost apostle (James in 101, Andrew in 102) stands on a "socle": similar winged monsters with different feet but the same sharp-eared dog face (figs. 75, 79). Andrew's monster has two-toed paws (see also fig. 81, top right). The borders of both bays have abstract foliate patterns, and in both bays each lancet has a different border design. In both bays the bishops are rigidly frontal, while the apostles take varied, more relaxed poses. Bay 102 adopts the "eyeglasses" leading of Bay 101 but paints the irises of the eyes in the more traditional and acceptable manner (figs. 82–83).

The artist of Bay 102 simplifies, focuses, and unifies. While the palettes are similar, he prefers

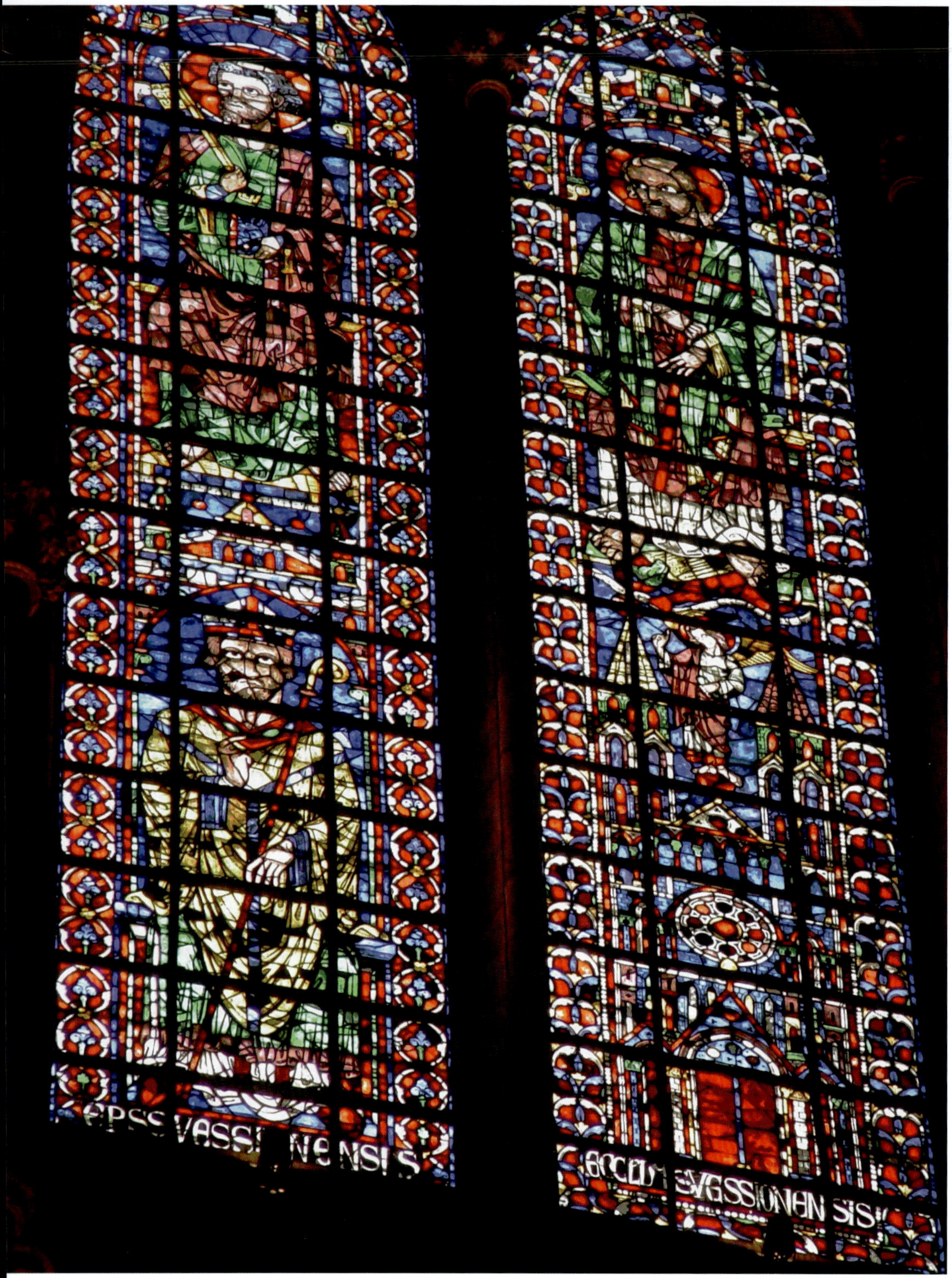

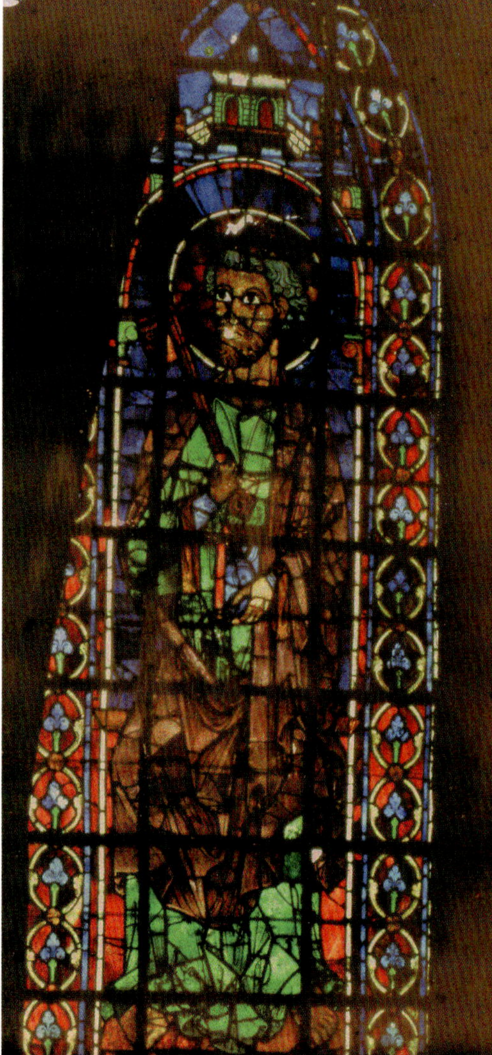

FIG. 79 Bay 102.

FIG. 80 Peter, Bay 102, left lancet, top row. Autochrome by Henri Deneux, 1915.

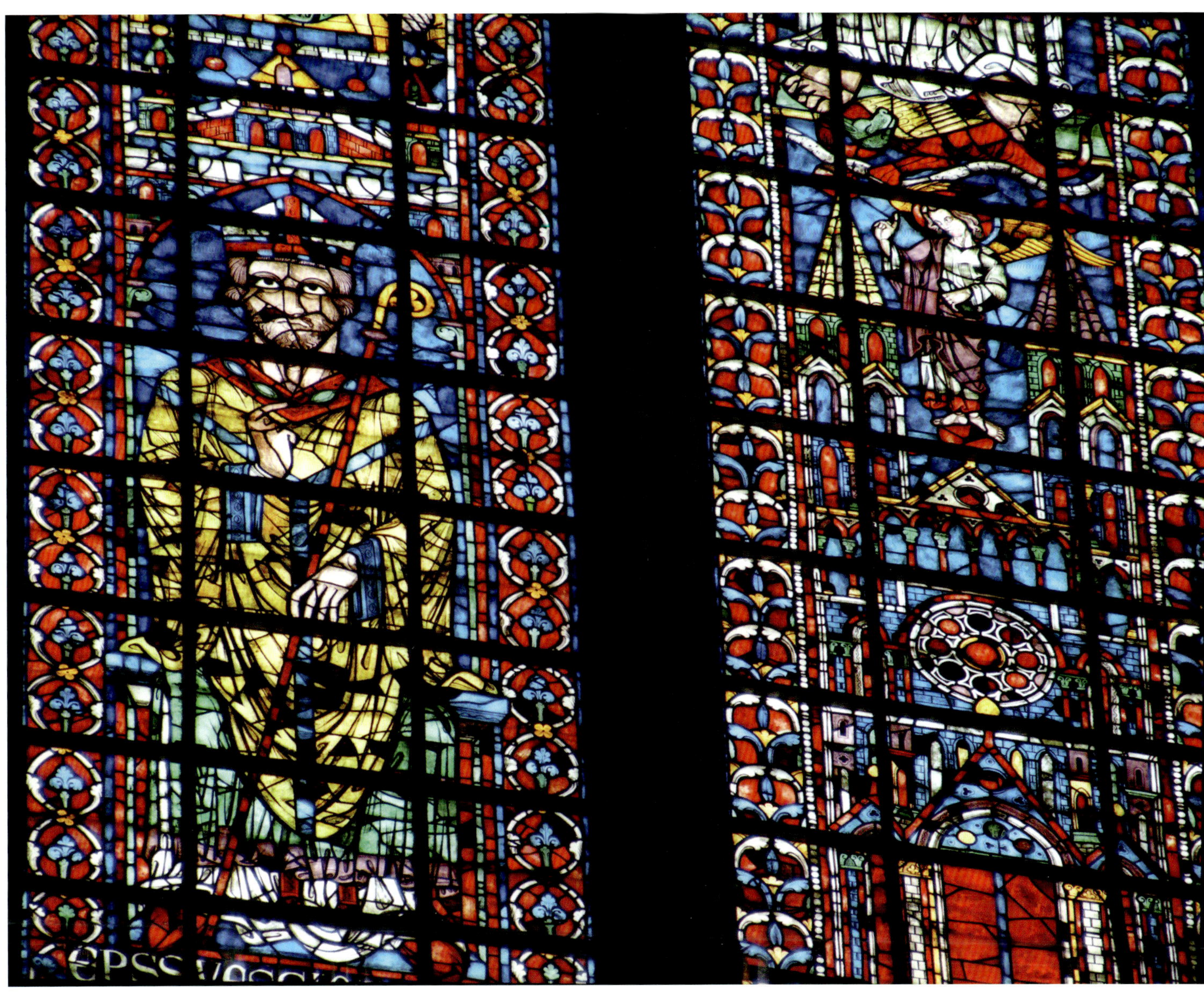

FIG. 81 Bishop and "facade" of Soissons, Bay 102, lower row.

large unbroken areas of a single color rather than lots of unrelated ornament. He uses a medium green in abundance to tie his designs together.[113] He makes connections to the axial bay, 100, in a number of ways: all his grounds are blue; his haloes are red with a white border (cf. the adjoining Crucifixion); his two apostles face the same way, toward Bay 100. The most striking feature of his art is what might be called his "handwriting," by which I mean the beautiful shaded folds in his drapery painting, not found elsewhere in the hemicycle. This shaded drapery—and the unusual prominence of green—appear throughout the rosace and can be verified as authentic since they are noticeable in a Deneux autochrome of 1915, of Peter (see fig. 80).[114]

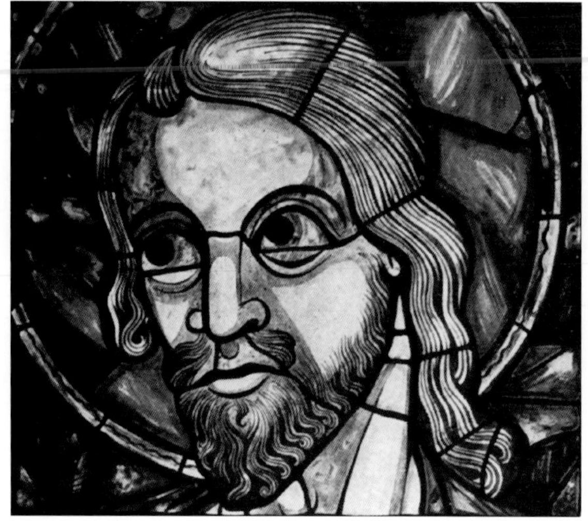

FIG. 82 Andrew, Bay 102, right lancet, top row. Tracing by Paul Simon from the exterior, here reversed as it appears from the interior (after Skinner, "Restoring the Stained Glass Treasures of Rheims Cathedral").

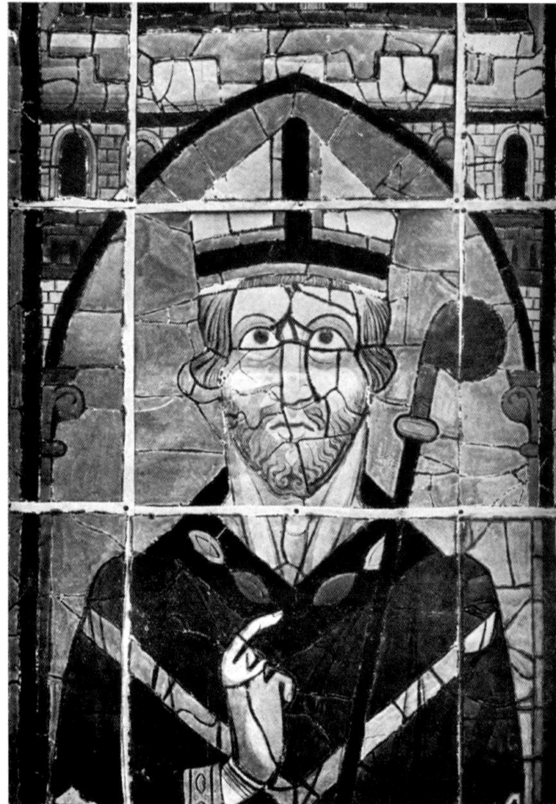

FIG. 83 Bishop of Soissons, Bay 102, left lancet, lower row. Tracing by Paul Simon from the exterior, here reversed as it appears from the interior (after Simon, "Notes sur les vitraux").

Bay 103: Thomas, Philip, Châlons Bishop and "Facade"; and Bay 104: John, James the Less, Beauvais Bishop and "Facade"

Bays 103 and 104 complete the hemicycle group and introduce a new artist—or perhaps a new designer with assistant(s). The similarities to Bays 101 and 102 indicate that this artist, whose training and artistic personality individualize him, studied the other windows closely. He uses the same border design for both lancets of a bay, unlike 101 and 102 but like the axial bay, 100, and these border designs are sharply angular, altogether different from the curvilinear foliate patterns of the previous bays.[115] Moreover, the border of 103 (figs. 84, 85) is an exact copy of the roundel border in the Bay 101 rosace (fig. 30). The face of Christ in the ogive of 101 (fig. 28) resembles the faces in 103 and 104 (see appendix 3). Could this new artist have been an apprentice when Bay 101 was undertaken? If so, he was a talented and free spirit even then. His rosaces (103 and 104, figs. 39, 49) are not designed in horizontal rows, as are those of the first three bays (100 through 102); rather, they are oriented with the foci of the lobe designs strongly directed toward the central roundel in what might be termed an asterisk format. Like the zigzag borders, these diagonals energize the compositions and introduce a degree of visual excitement that characterizes this artist as dynamic. The drapery painting is much more agitated and closer to antiquizing "wet drapery" than to the late, simplified versions of spoon- and V-folds used by the other artists. Perhaps not so surprising at Reims as it might be elsewhere, his drapery style may reflect this artist's close study of the cathedral's early sculptures.

The two bays are not at all of a piece, however, as they have oftentimes been treated. The similarities suggest that the variation between parts of Bays 103 and 104 is probably the result of execution of the designs by several artists. The most effective of them go farther in the direction of expressionism. Bay 103 has a cool, quiet, red/blue/purple-brown palette in the lancets as well as in the lobes of the rosace (the roundel is lost) (figs. 49, 84). The heavily decorated haloes resemble those

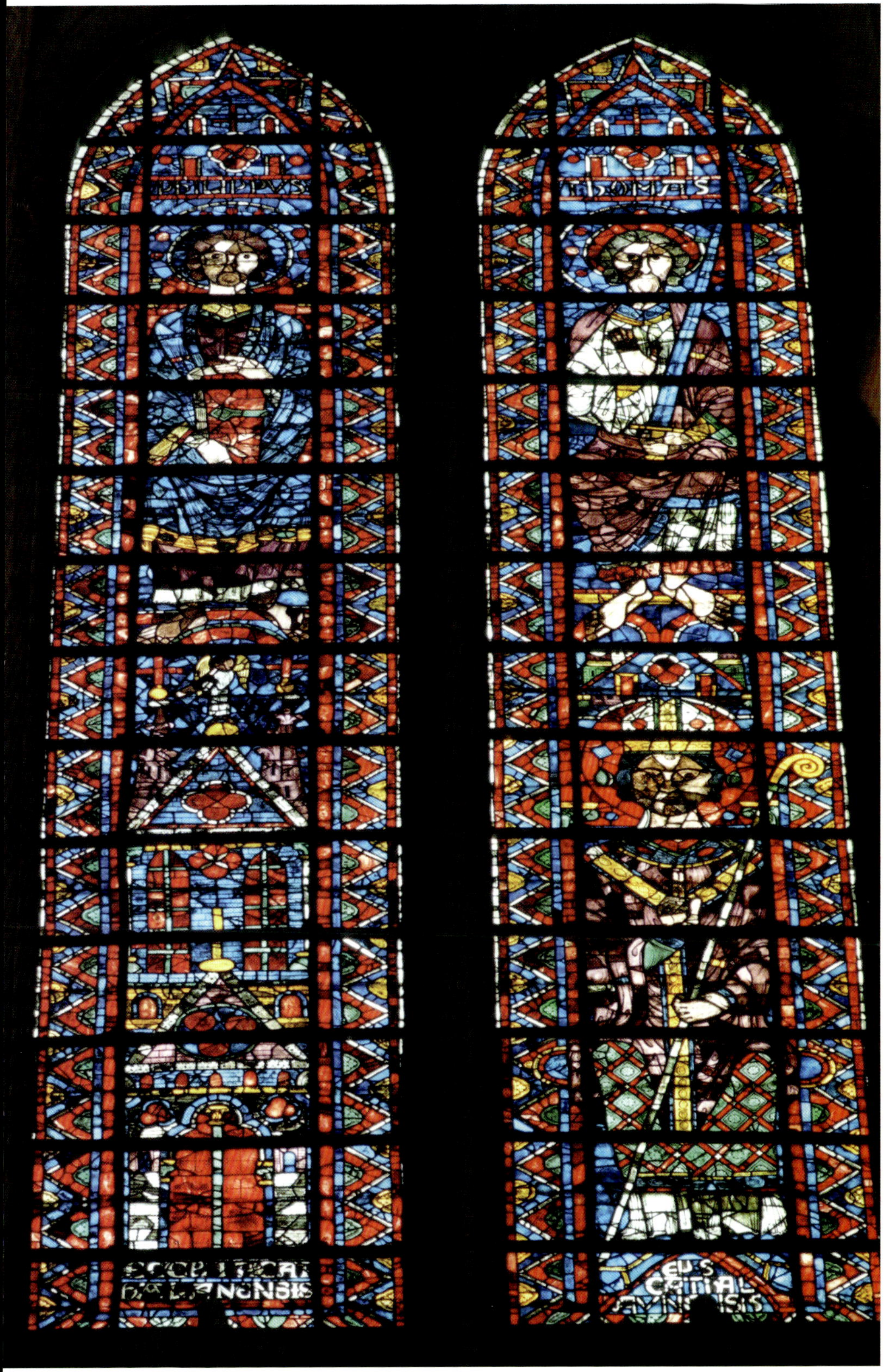

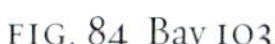

FIG. 84 Bay 103.

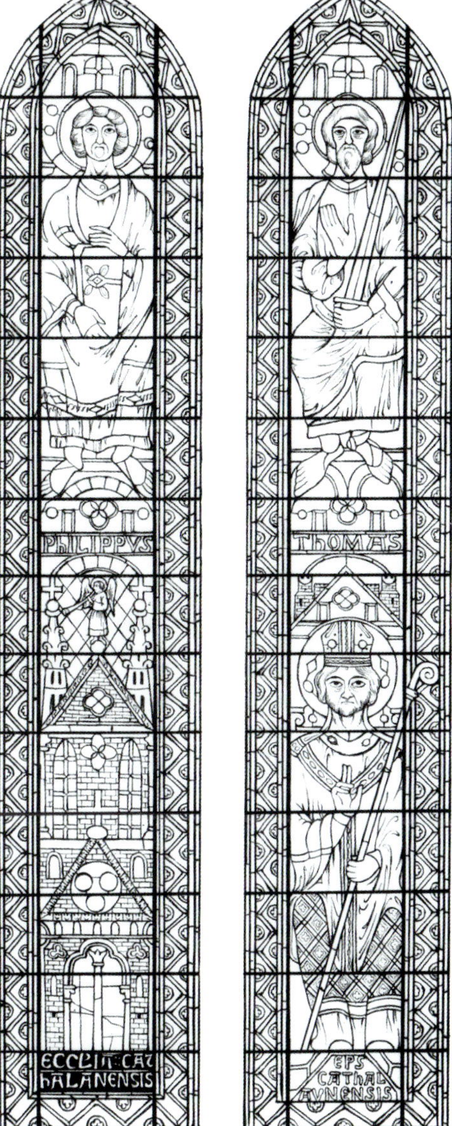

FIG. 85 Bay 103, drawing by Ferdinand de Lasteyrie, ca. 1850 (after Lasteyrie, *Histoire de la peinture sur verre*).

of Bay 101. While the eyes of all figures (including those in the rosaces) are huge, with great black irises floating hypnotically in the whites, they are shaped differently in some figures. The figures in Bay 104 (fig. 86), including the rosace, have low-placed ears and a straight base line on the eyes; the large figures in Bay 103 have almond-shaped eyes.[116] Many faces have prominent, elaborate shading, great black smears around the eyes giving the figures the appearance of so many professional footballers. Among these figures are the standing St. John and some in both rosaces. The power of these figures derives from the fixed-focus staring eyes coupled with the compression of figural mass within the borders, more pronounced in Bay 103 than 104. Like Wiligelmo's prophets on the jambs of Modena's west portal,[117] these (mostly) frontal figures appear to have been wedged and shoe-horned into their spaces, injecting—like the rosaces' asterisk formatting—a palpable visual tension. Particularly in Bay 103, almost no room is left over for ground color or for the figures' silhouettes. This compacting is also evident in the "facades" of both bays and seems to be the designer's choice.

In Bay 104 (figs. 86, 87) the palette is lighter, more varied, with lots of white accents. The drapery includes numerous horizontal color bands. A few of these can be found in Bays 100 and 101 but never lavished to such an extent. Bay 104's plain blue grounds and red haloes, bordered in a white fillet, refer to Bays 102, 100, and perhaps to the latter's source in the recycled images of ca. 1219–20 in Bay 118. Just as in Bay 101 (fig. 73), the bishop in 104 is rigidly frontal, the apostle above right (James the Less) is frontal but with more casually arranged legs, and the other apostle (John) stands, turns toward the axial bay, and gestures. This too seems a deliberate reference.

John is a figure with personality, and his vitality is even more pronounced in the rosace, which is a masterpiece. The electricity in the roundel's "Evangelist portrait" of John writing his Gospel[118] (fig. 40) makes one wonder if the artist might even have seen Evangelist portraits in one of the famous *rémois* Carolingian manuscripts such as the Ebbo Gospels.[119] Equally impressive is the skill with which the designer has tied the rosace to the lancets visually. In the right lobes of the rosace, presenting the story of James the Less, one finds the charming fancy of the small-scale James shown as bishop of Jerusalem standing with his tiny "facade" (fig. 45). This tiny figure binds the ensemble together. He wears the same colors as the large St. James directly below him; he postures and gestures like St. John in the left lancet; and he and his "facade" recall the bishop and "facade" of Beauvais at the base of the window (fig. 86).

Like the large-scale figure of James Major in Bay 101, the standing figure of John in Bay 104 is unusual and poses questions. These two apostles were brothers. John is unquestionably by the same artist who produced the masterful rosace above him. He is strongly oriented toward the axial bay and makes an unusual gesture, his hand supinated, with the thumb touching the ring finger (fig. 86). I can suggest two possible reasons why John is emphasized in these ways, but I cannot support either one with solid evidence. First, John's Gospel was written in Greek. His gesture bears some resemblance to the Greek gesture of benediction as described by the Byzantine "Guide to Painting" (twelfth century with later additions):

> When you represent the hand in blessing do not join the three fingers together; but cross the thumb by the fourth finger, so that the second, named the index, remaining upright, and the third being slightly bent, they may both form the name of Jesus (IHCOYC) IC. Indeed, the second, remaining open, indicates an I (*ióta*), and the third, when curved, forms a C (*sigma*). The thumb is placed across the fourth finger; the fifth is also a little bent, so as to indicate the word (XPICTOC), XC; for the junction of the thumb and the fourth finger forms a X (*chí*), and the little finger by its curvatures forms a C (*sigma*). These two letters are the abridgment of Christos. So, by the divine providence of the Creator, the fingers of a man's hand, whether they be long or short, are so

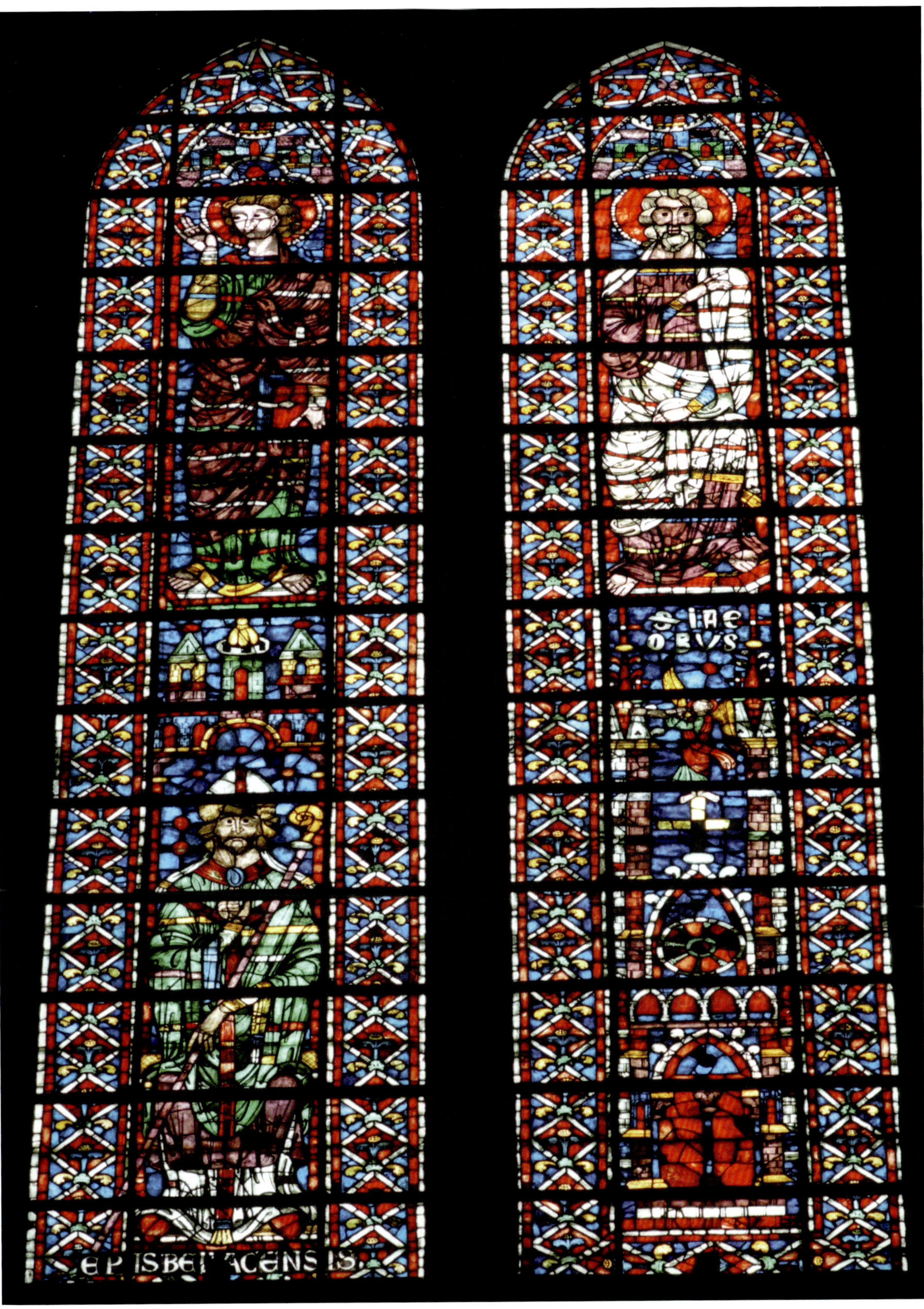

FIG. 86 Bay 104.

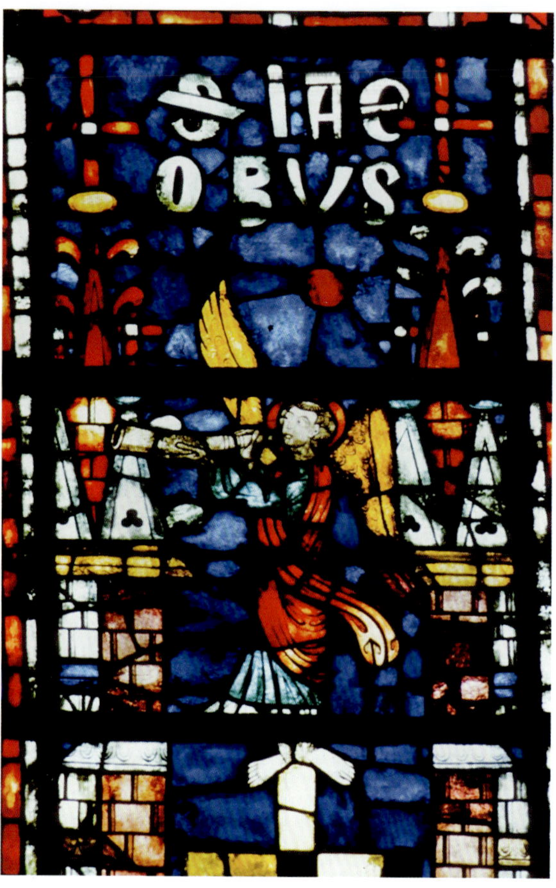

FIG. 87 Angel blowing an oliphant on the "facade" of Beauvais, Bay 104, mid right lancet.

> placed that it is possible for them to figure the name of Christ.[120]

John's gesture only approximates this, three of his fingers being straight. If a Greek benediction was intended, it may have been recalled by a Westerner who was unfamiliar with the symbolism. My second hypothesis refers again to James Major in Bay 101. One reason suggested above for the unusual James (vested and standing, fig. 73) invoked an architectural reference, to the first chapel of the new cathedral to be opened to the cult, in 1221. Might St. John have been singled out in a similar fashion as the name-saint of the new cathedral's first architect, probably Jean d'Orbais?[121]

The idea is not as absurd as it might at first appear. The lower windows contained an architect's "portrait," now preserved with other fragments in the north nave aisle (Bay 39, fig. 21) and probably originally from one of the rosaces of the aisle bays.[122] According to Robert Branner, the image of the architect Jean d'Orbais in the Reims labyrinth showed him designing the choir hemicycle (fig. 88), in which Bay 104 is located.[123] While name-saints are more frequent later in the thirteenth century, several examples can be found at Chartres.[124] According to Colette Manhès-Deremble, the patron of the Chartres masons was John the Evangelist.[125] The strange gesture made by St. John in Bay 104 may provide the key. He touches his right thumb and ring finger together. While something like a Greek benediction, as noted above, the gesture differs completely from the numerous Latin blessing gestures made by bishops throughout the cathedral windows. It is not among the hand gestures in medieval art studied by François Garnier; nor is it found among the many hand gestures forming the ancient and medieval systems of finger reckoning, where the number eight somewhat resembles a blessing gesture but must be made with the left hand.[126]

John's hand position does, however, resemble the right-hand gesture of the enthroned figure in Villard de Honnecourt's puzzling drawing of the "Saracen's Tomb" (fol. 6r, fig. 89). Recently it has been argued that Villard's drawing represents the masonic tracing board presented to a freemason at his initiation. The enthroned "Saracen" figure would be the master mason.[127] Without opening this Pandora's box any further, perhaps one might acknowledge St. John's unusual gesture as signifying knowledge and authority.

Bays 103 and 104 formed the core of Reinhardt's "first atelier," which he believed to be remnants of a "first choir program" that included the spoliate glass now in Bay 118. If one now accepts that—by his own measurements—the Bay 118 images are too large to have fit the axial bay, the necessity for a "first choir program" evaporates. What features of Bays 103 and 104, then, allowed Reinhardt's hypothesis such a long life?[128] In their amorphous charm and appeal and in details such as palette and facial painting, the spoliate panels of ca. 1219–20 speak in a totally different accent from the ferocious energy of Bays 103 and 104. The basis for Reinhardt's claim would seem to boil down to rigid frontality, greatly enlarged eyes, bodies that are thickset (*trapus*), and heads that are powerful (*fortes*). Reinhardt does not specifically mention drapery, though he connects his "first atelier" with the earliest *rémois* sculptures, which presumably would involve not only body type but linear, antiquizing "wet drapery."

So is it possible, as I believe, to date the initial choir bay, Bay 100 of Henri de Braine, between 1227 and 1230, and the glass of Bays 103 and 104 after 1231 and close to 1233? It seems to me that there can be no problem in dating the antiquizing detail of Bays 103 and 104 to that time. The famous Visitation jamb statues on the facade have been dated to the 1230s.[129] More challenging is the placement of the archbishop's Bay 100 around or before 1230, since it is so totally foreign to the Reims glazing and no large-scale figural glass survives from Paris in those years. Comparing the immense Reims clerestory bays—some ten meters high—to Parisian manuscript figures is an exercise in apples and oranges. What can be agreed as similar are the red/blue palette, the elongated lean proportions (one hesitates to say courtly), the small elegant heads, and the looped drapery.[130] It may not be possible to identify Henri de Braine's glazier as Parisian, but he certainly was not local. The idea that both "soft" (linear, *plí mouillé*) and "hard" (blocklike, *plí cassé*) styles of drapery existed throughout the 1230s is finding increasing scholarly support and, where a different artistic venue is likely, perhaps can rest its case there.

As we have seen, elements in Bay 101 indicate that the archbishop was involved in the glazing project in the early 1230s, and there are numerous reasons why he might have had a special interest in Bays 103 and 104. These windows are devoted to his suffragans Châlons and Beauvais. His uncle and mentor, Philippe de Dreux, had been bishop of Beauvais for thirty-seven years, and Henri had held his first ecclesiastical office there. The apostle Philip (Bay 103) was his uncle's name-saint. In 1233 the archbishop was engaged in a fierce struggle with his

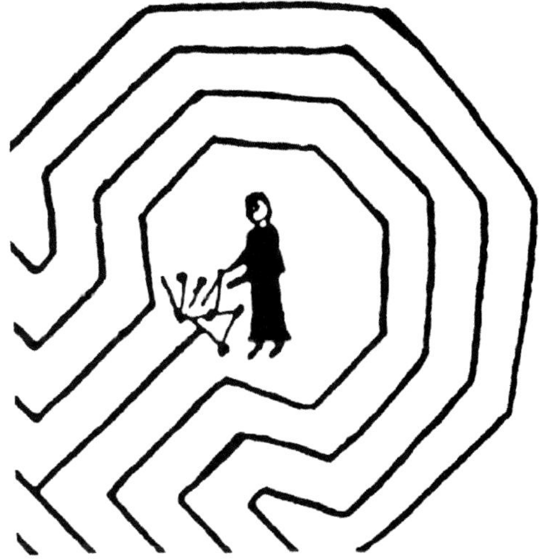

FIG. 88 The architect Jean d'Orbais, detail of the labyrinth of Reims: drawing by Jacques Cellier (after Robert Branner, "Jean d'Orbais and the Cathedral of Reims").

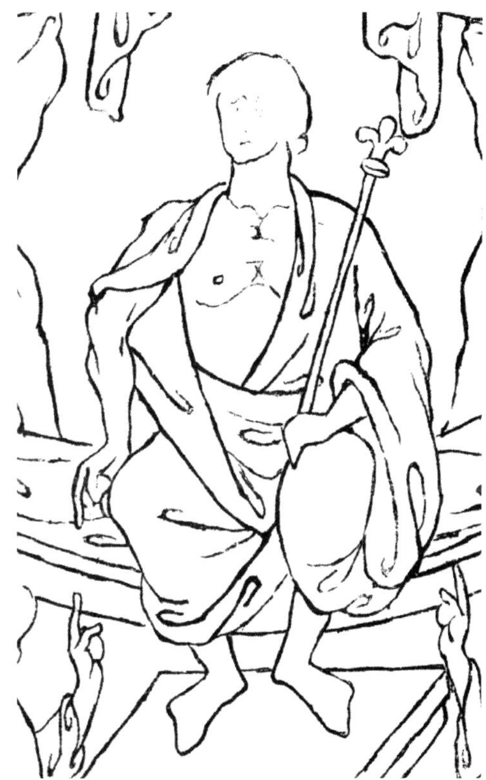

FIG. 89 Enthroned figure on the "Saracen's Tomb," detail of the album of Villard d'Honnecourt (after Jean-Baptiste-Antoine Lassus, *Album de Villard de Honnecourt*).

monarch, who was still a minor, over the latter's treatment of Henri's suffragan, the bishop of Beauvais.[131] Henri de Braine called his bishops to the extraordinary number of five provincial councils during the year 1233 to deal with this matter; at the third council (spring, at Senlis) they authorized the bishop of Beauvais to put his diocese under interdict, and at the council in late November (at Saint-Quentin) the archbishop tried to excommunicate the entire province.

As for Châlons, Henri de Braine had been elected bishop of Châlons in 1226, renouncing that office before his consecration when the demise of the Reims archbishop later that year opened up a better possibility.[132] The bishop and officers of Châlons, of all his suffragans, seem to have remained loyal and obedient to Henri. Their cathedral, rebuilt in the early 1230s, contained a window donated by the archbishop.[133] The panel has an image of St. Stephen, to whom Châlons is dedicated, and a kneeling portrait of the archbishop presenting the saint with a tiny window, and the dark washes of shading around the eyes of these figures identify the glazier as someone who had worked on Bays 103 and 104 of Reims. At that moment, 1235–36, Reims was under interdict, the canons were in exile, and work surely had been halted at the archepiscopal cathedral.

Finally, since the rosaces of Bays 103 and 104 match the lancets below them so closely in color and in facial and drapery conventions, the apostles as well as the bishop of Beauvais, if they had been reused from a "first choir program," would have had to occupy the same relative positions. Without exception among the twelve apostles in the chevet, each rosace contains three lobes on the left dedicated to the apostle in the left lancet below, as well as three on the right for the right-hand apostle. This has not been noted before because the scenes in the lobes have not previously been accurately identified. As for the Beauvais bishop: the right three lobes of the rosace of Bay 104 (James the Less) show him as bishop of Jerusalem with his cathedral "facade," just like the bishop of Beauvais in the lancet below. There is no evidence of alteration in the glazing—with one possible exception. The ornaments and leading in the ground surrounding the head of the bishop of Châlons (Bay 103, fig. 85) form what might be seen as a "ghost halo."[134] It might be evidence of reworking. Or it might be accidental effect. It could just as easily be taken as another "thank-you" from the archbishop for his stalwart support from that cathedral[135]—one more sign of arrogance on the part of that most imperious of prelates, Henri de Braine.

The Straight Bays of the Chevet (Bays 105 Through 110): An Introduction

Moving from the hemicycle to the straight bays of the chevet, we present our passports, have them stamped, and cross into a different land. We move, in a manner of speaking, from a totalitarian state to a constitutional jurisdiction (well, canons vote!). While my metaphor is grossly exaggerated—and the previous section has devoted some attention to the differences between hemicycle bays, as the following text will continue to do for the remainder—the similarities within each group are more compelling than the differences. The insistent frontality and severity of the hemicycle bishops make the greatest contrast with those to come, who turn, glance, point, cross their legs, and so forth. The liveliness and immediacy of both the apostles and bishops in the straight bays appear to derive from the earlier glazing traditions studied by Caviness, such as Saint-Remi, Braine, and Soissons,[136] rather than from the Reims hemicycle adjoining them. This seems to me to indicate a hiatus, most reasonably the twenty-six months that the canons of Reims spent in exile: November 9, 1234, to January 2, 1237. The weighty shadow of the imperious archbishop of the hemicycle vanishes, and the remainder of the choir glazing seems to reflect a series of the canons' decisions as the situation in Reims evolved from their return in triumph in 1237 to September 7, 1241, when they first occupied "their new choir."[137]

It seems almost too neat that the hemicycle glazing should have been completed just as the canons were being forced into exile. Ravaux comments on a similar phenomenon in his dating of an architectural campaign, the completion of which coincided with the civic insurrection that drove the canons away:

> A convenient accident, one will say. However, this accident is less extraordinary than it might at first appear. Indeed, the revolt occurred at the end of the year. Now the study of medieval monument construction shows that they did not build any which way; a program was settled on for each year and worked at accordingly; moreover, each program sought, as far as possible, to complete a coherent ensemble. In other words, let us say, if the insurrection would have occurred a year later, it would have coincided with the completion of another part of the building: the vaulting of the choir, the triforium of the transept, etc.[138]

I do not quote Ravaux with the goal of adopting his architectural chronology; rather, I wish to underline the way that glaziers may have worked. In fact we know very little about what they did during the winter. The masons' activity would have slowed down or gone indoors—due to lack of light, heat, safe exterior working conditions, and so forth—and while windows can be begun once funding, subject matter, and the masons' templates are available, it is unlikely that glass panels would have been installed during the severest winter conditions. It is a subject that we actually know little about and for which we have minimal evidence for conjecture.

The concerns of the archbishop and of the chapter, as well as their relationship with each other, took different paths from 1234 to the death of Henri de Braine in mid-1240 (see chapter 1). While the canons were in exile in 1235–36 in several of the archbishop's châteaux, the bourgeois attacked his law court, probably in May 1236, murdering his marshal, and eventually the king stepped in to bring them to justice, in January 1236. The townsmen paid Henri de Braine the first two of three years' reparations, due each October, but in 1238 produced violence rather than money. The canons had returned just over a year and a half earlier. The archbishop invaded his own town with armed men but was forced into exile in late 1238 and died there on July 6, 1240. When Henri de Braine fled, putting the town yet again under interdict, the canons locked the doors of their cathedral and recited their daily office in their cloister chapel.[139] Upon the archbishop's death they again made peace with the townsmen as quickly as possible, hurried to finish work on their new "choir," and in just over a year opened it to the cult on September 7, 1241.

As discussed in chapter 1, the growing contagion between 1230 and 1240 was the king's and pope's increasing campaigns against heresy and the inquisitors' developing tendency to treat usurers as heretics. Particularly after public mass burnings in 1235 as close to Reims as Châlons, the panic of the rich *rémois* bourgeois grew, since they were actively engaged in large-scale municipal moneylending.[140] Thus, when the canons continued the glazing program upon their triumphant return in 1237, the new themes to appear were violence suffered by men of Christ (apostles, canons) and their triumph over heresy (disbelief, idolatry, usury).

The time line sketched above indicates that even after the chapter's return from exile in January 1237, efforts to complete the chevet glazing program would have been sporadic at best. Assembling (or reassembling) craftsmen would have taken a little time, and just how much of a workforce could be kept busy under conditions of street violence and interdict is unclear. It is my belief that the chevet glazing was in place for the inaugural ceremony in September 1241. I base this opinion upon indications of haste and confusion in the terminal bays of the choir as well as iconography reflective of the canons' mood in the final rosaces and then most definitely in the north rose, the next project to be undertaken. As much as I have argued elsewhere that grisaille in mid-thirteenth-century France was not simply an economic measure, its repeating patterns are certainly faster to produce and can be done by less skilled craftsmen. Among the reasons for the grisailles in Bays 109 and 110 of the chevet and throughout the transepts, speed was probably one of them. It certainly did not hurt, however, that grisaille in the 1240s was theologically and aesthetically *le dernier cri* in Paris.[141]

Bay 106: Bartholomew, Simon, Noyon Bishop and "Facade"; and Bay 105: Matthew, Jude, Senlis Bishop, Amiens "Facade"

I indicated earlier that the irons for the Bay 106 rosace conform to the center-roundel design of the hemicycle (Bays 100 through 104), while the remainder of the figural rosaces (Bays 105, 107, and 108) have ironwork centering on a smaller lozenge (cf. fig. 57 to fig. 53). The glass in the Bay 106 rosace, and the six lobes of the rosace in Bay 105, are close in palette, design approach, and painting style. As they both differ notably from their lancets below, one might assume that Bay 106, with the older type of ironwork, was initiated before the canons fled. The rosaces occupy the tops of their bays, and in glazing installation (as in painting your bedroom wall) it is advantageous to start at the top. Again, we have no information about medieval glaziers' practice, only the evidence of what we see. Thus, the change in ironwork between 106 and 105 suggests that the work hiatus occurred there and that the glazing of both rosaces was the first, limited project of 1237.

The asterisk format of the Bays 103 and 104 rosaces is gone, and the palette is completely different, a cheerful combination of primary red, blue, and yellow. The themes in the rosaces now reflect more clearly the canons' preoccupations than those of Henri de Braine. In the hemicycle, the rosaces present the apostles and bishops in the relationship of apostolic succession, as preachers and as combating (and usually succumbing to) secular power. In the bays of the straight chevet, the physical attacks that drove the canons into exile appear to have made the concept of martyrdom less attractive. This absence of martyrdom images is particularly noteworthy for the lesser-known apostles, for whom the only available images would have been in illustrated martyrologies.[142] With the Inquisition raging around Reims, the theme of the Church's triumph over disbelief (= usury) became a shield with which the canons could assert their untouchability.

The archbishop's elaborate program for the chevet clerestories begins to break down in Bays 105 and 106. The intricate ordering of scenes in the rosaces (fig. 27), uniting the Twelve as a group, is abandoned in the final three lobes in the Bay 106 rosace (those of Simon, on the right). In the same bay (fig. 93) the bishop of Noyon is the only suffragan who does not occupy the "inner" lancet—that is, the closest to the axial bay, left on the south and right on the north. He and his "facade" are switched in position. As designs they could not simply have been installed in the wrong places; the ground and canopy of the Noyon bishop go with Simon above him, and Simon is in the correct location according to the Canon of the Mass. These are errors at the design level.

Bay 105 (figs. 90–92) is the first bay where the "facade" (Amiens) and the bishop (Senlis), both labeled, do not form a pair. Amiens is in the correct position. However, the bishop of Senlis faces left, the only suffragan to turn away from the axial bay, suggesting strongly that he was intended for the south side of the choir. According to the suffragans' seating arrangement at provincial councils (fig. 18), as adopted—flipped—in the Reims glass, Senlis does belong on the other (south) side and near the end, perhaps Bay 110. This is another error at the design level. The elaborate ground pattern throughout Bay 105 precludes a simple miscalculation or error in installment. Do these anomalies indicate that interest in the archbishop's chevet program had flagged, that perhaps it was no longer at hand for reference, or simply that nobody was "minding the store"?

The lancets of Bays 106 and 105 (figs. 93 and 90) have a number of features in common, though they also have numerous differences in detail such as halo decoration, eye leading, painting of facial features, palette, and figural proportion.[143] The

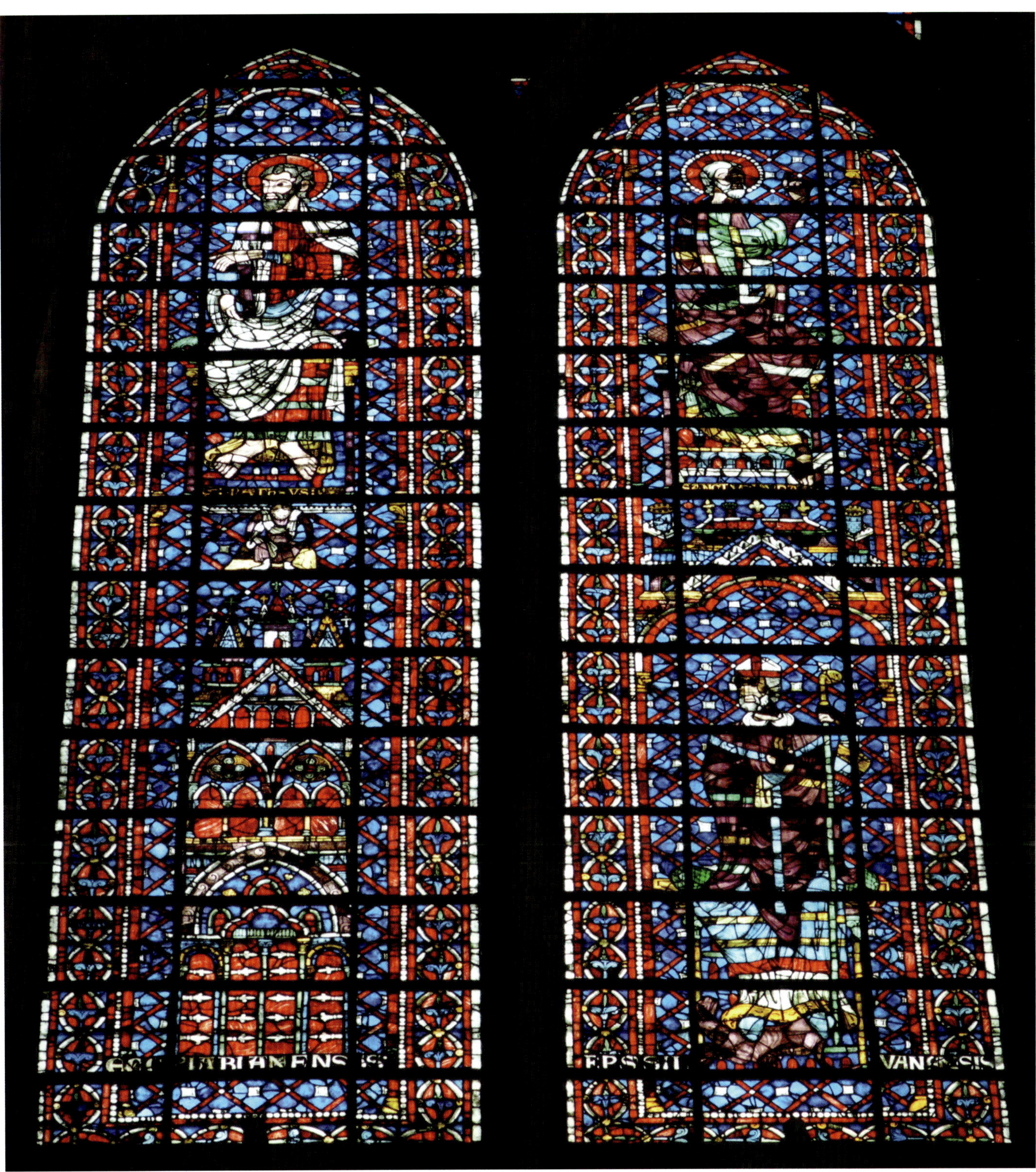

FIG. 90 Bay 105.

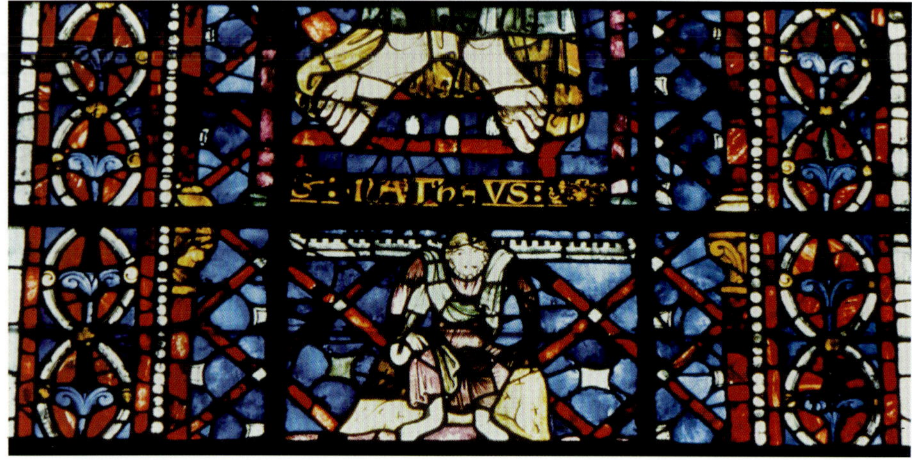

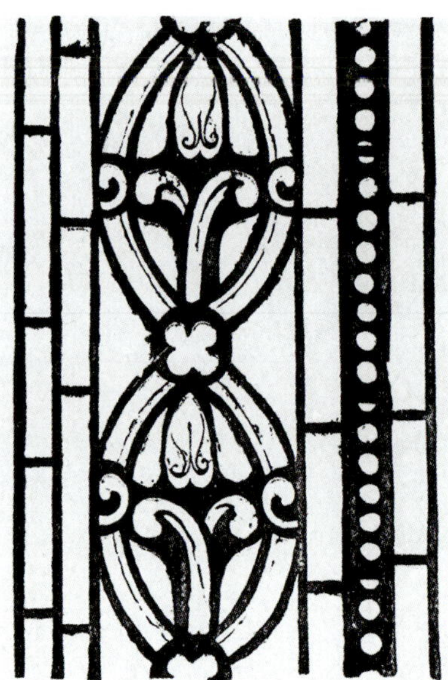

FIG. 91 Telamon, Bay 105, mid left lancet.

FIG. 92 Border of abstract foliage, Bay 105 (1881) (after Westlake, *A History of Design in Painted Glass*).

Opposite
FIG. 93 Bay 106.

similarities suggest that the designer of these lancets could have been the glazier of Bay 101, whom I nicknamed The Decorator, or perhaps someone who trained under him. Both bays have "socles" under a number of their figures, as in Bays 101 and 102. The closest to the earlier ones is the duck-winged gargoyle with pointed ears and a curly tail, beneath Simon (106), which resembles the monsters under James Major (101) and Andrew (102) (figs. 75, 79). In Bay 105 the bishop of Senlis stands on a "socle" that is a sort of lion, tan with pronounced rib cage and haunches. Below Matthew in the same bay is a small seated telamon (fig. 91). Most unusual of all is Bartholomew's "socle" in Bay 106 (fig. 94): two telamons who are crowned kings leaning on crutches and bare to the knees.[144] A message there! It is so much the archbishop's mind-set rather than that of the canons that one might consider it another reason to identify this designer with The Decorator, who had worked for Henri de Braine in Bay 101.

Like the lancets of Bay 101, those of Bay 106 are jammed with disparate ornament in a varied and unfocused palette (figs. 73, 93). The artist prefers a different border design in each lancet, varied and highly ornamented grounds, and large jeweled haloes in contrasting colors. As in Bay 101, drapery is painted in short, heavy, angular J-hooks, straight-line mouths are leaded in, and the eyes have "eyeglasses" leading—though the weird leaded irises of Bay 101 are not repeated. If it is not the same artist over half a decade later, the two bays are clearly speaking the same artistic language.

Bay 105 (fig. 90) is more difficult to assess, because Balcon has established that it was severely damaged in World War I and is now largely a modern re-creation based upon tracings made before 1914 by the Simon studio.[145] The palette is more somber than in Bay 106 and the ground and border designs simpler. The heads are small, the eyes painted on the face without leading. I mentioned above that the Bay 106 rosace and the lobes of the rosace of Bay 105 match in their bright primary colors and in their antiquizing drapery marked by flying folds and drawn taut around the hip and calf. They are certainly the products of an artist different from the one who produced the lancets below. However, the central lozenge of the Bay 105 rosace (Matthew writing his Gospel, fig. 57) employs the somber palette of the lancets below. Its ornament includes fleurs-de-lis, and three more of them decorate the castle above the Senlis bishop (fig. 90). By 1237 and under the canons' jurisdiction, fleurs-de-lis would more probably have been a salute to Louis IX than an obeisance to their quarrelsome archbishop (unlike

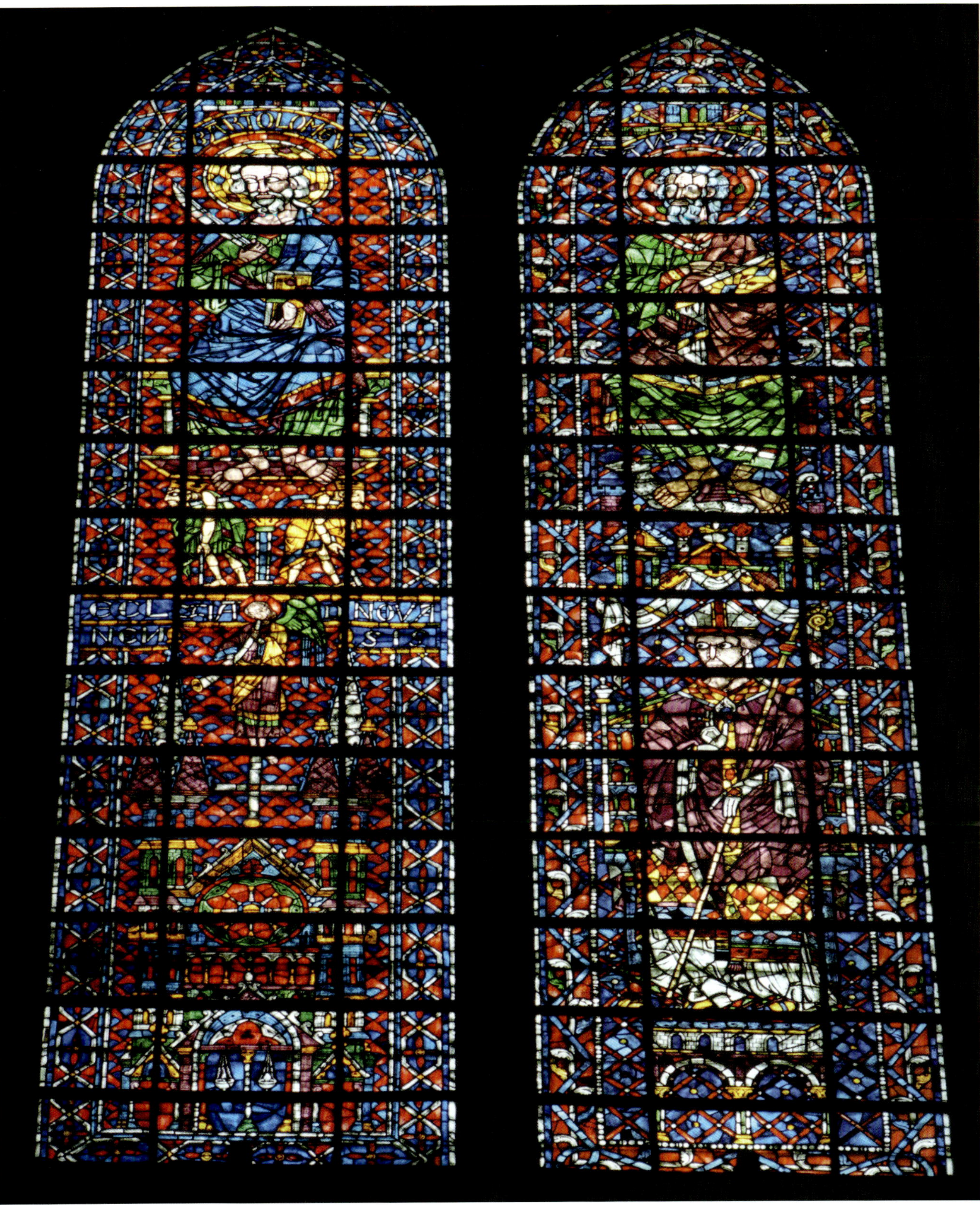

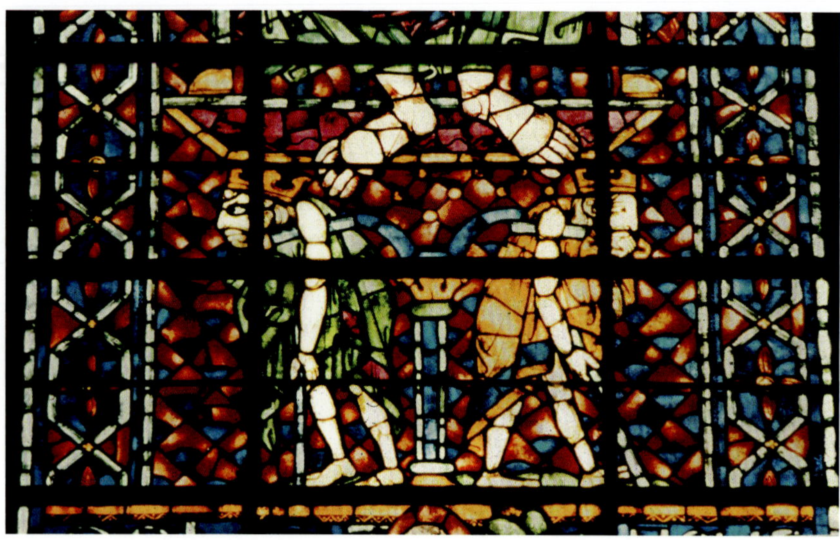

FIG. 94 Telamon kings, Bay 106, mid left lancet.

the fleurs-de-lis of Bays 100 and 101 earlier). The details of Bay 105 suggest that the artist studied the chevet bays already in place. The border design of the lancets (fig. 92) is like that of Bay 102's left lancet, and the haloes in these bays are similarly colored, red inside white fillets, though those of Bay 105 are smaller in scale. The 105 draperies include horizontal color bands in all three large figures, the bands somewhat wider than those in earlier windows such as Bay 104. Whether this is because they were re-created in modern times from tracings is difficult to say. The modern installation switched the positions of Matthew and Jude. Nineteenth-century observers (fig. 9) indicate that they faced each other, pointing and debating, Jude seated casually with crossed legs. The apostles of Bay 107 do likewise.

All in all, Bays 106 and 105 were most probably contemporary productions by several artists during the relative calm of the working seasons of 1237 and 1238. Whether they were actually installed at that time or stored for safekeeping is not possible to guess. In October of that year the rich townsmen refused their annual payment to the archbishop and attacked his agents and court; he answered them with armed men, but by the end of the year he had had to flee, the churches had been closed, the bourgeois had once again been excommunicated, and their eighty hired archers were patrolling the public streets.[146]

Bay 108: Matthias, Apostle with Palm, Unidentified Bishop, Tournai "Facade"; and Bay 107: Barnabas, Apostle with Scroll, Thérouanne Bishop, Unidentified "Facade"

The last two colored bays are works of a mood with Bays 106 and 105, highly ornamented, the figures marked by immediacy, interaction, and casual poses (figs. 95, 97). The original chevet program of the archbishop has incorporated all twelve apostles at this point, and the identifications by inscription of Matthias and Barnabas—each with some biblical claim to be included—may have been planned from the start. The anonymous apostles accompanying them, one pointing to a palm (Bay 108) and the other to an open scroll (107), are generic figures. Although frequently labeled by scholars as Mark and Luke—indeed, both names have been applied to both figures in the literature up to the present[147]—there is no indication that these identifications were intended. Moreover, if these Evangelists had been intended, their identities could have been established easily by providing their attributes, Mark's lion and Luke's ox, for which a long iconographic tradition existed by the thirteenth century. Even more obviously generic are the four disciples located in Bays 109 and 110 (figs. 99–100), whose anonymity is, most likely, intentional. It might be pointed out at this point that the archbishop's final absence allowed the chapter at least some degree of freedom in completing the chevet glazing. Reims had seventy-two canons, "a number chosen to reflect the size of the band of disciples that Christ sent out into the world to preach."[148] The finishing touches to the glazing program increasingly reflect the hopes and fears of the chapter, its struggles and triumphs real or perceived, in short, its self-identity.

To return to Bays 107 and 108, while there are minor anomalies as in Bays 106 and 105, the

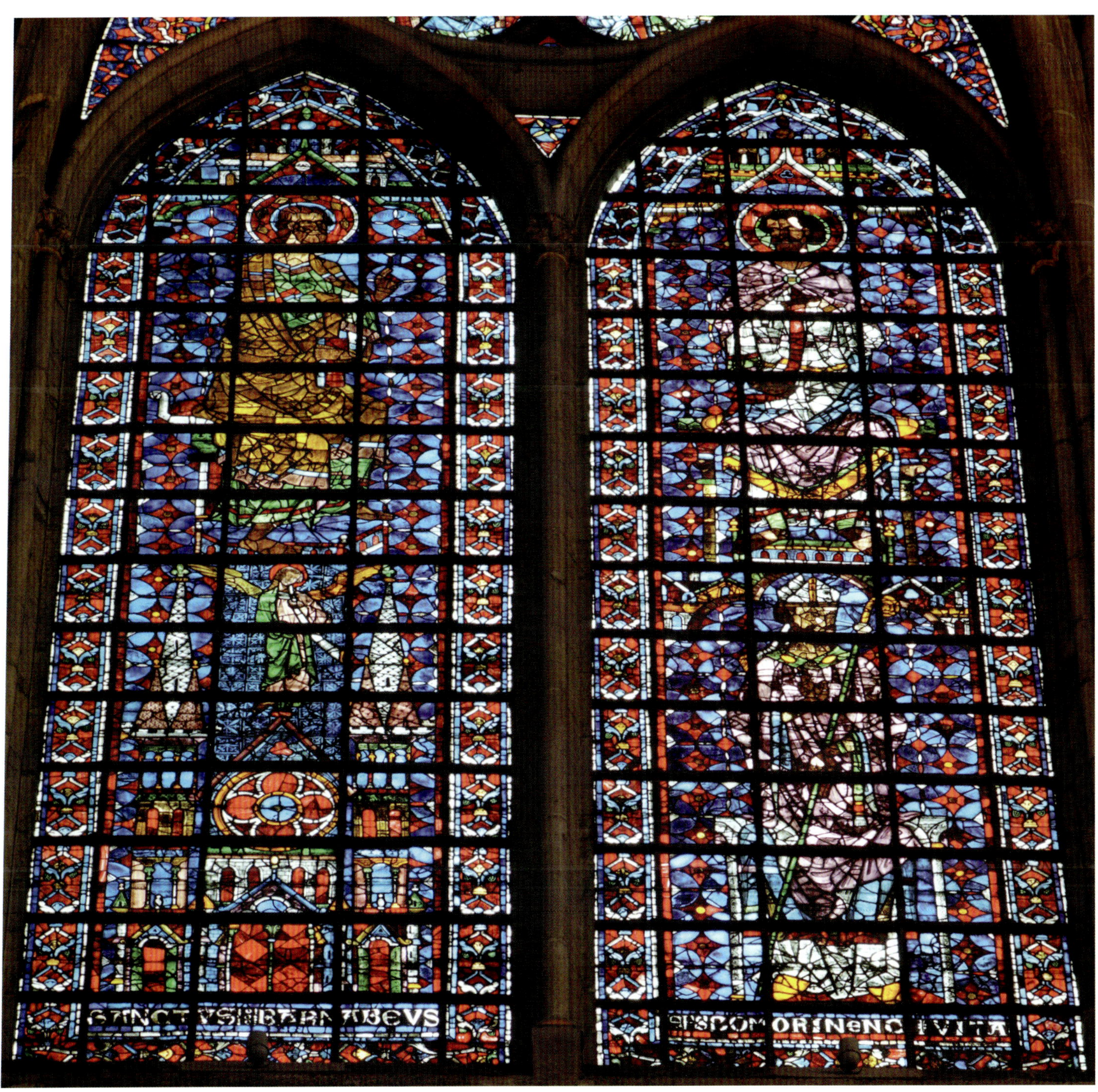

FIG. 95 Bay 107.

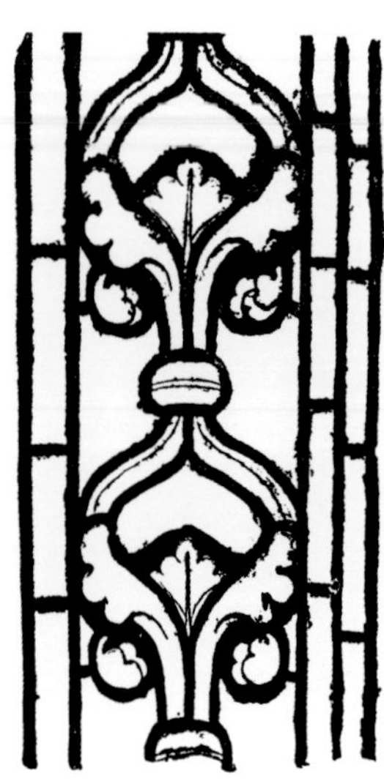

FIG. 96 Border of abstract foliage, Bay 107 (1881) (after Westlake, *A History of Design in Painted Glass*).

named bishop of Thérouanne (Bay 107) and the "facade" of Tournai (108) are in the correct locations, and the unlabeled "facade" and bishop accompanying them were surely intended to pair with them as in the hemicycle bays. Noyon's bishop (106), also unlabeled, is in the correct bay as well. The grand plan is still in evidence. It seems most likely that Bays 108 and 107 were created in 1239 and early 1240, as workmen could be found. The glass panels produced may have been stored as they were completed, for future installation, the church being closed and the canons no doubt careful to avoid trouble. The assumption would have been that sooner or later the local situation would return to normal, the archbishop would return, and work on the cathedral would proceed. It is not likely that the canons would have dared to radically alter—as they eventually did in Bays 109 and 110—Henri de Braine's chevet program while he was alive and there was the expectation that he would return to residence in his city.

Abundant visual evidence suggests that the work was piecemeal. Neither of the rosaces of Bays 108 and 107 (figs. 62, 64) relates in style to the lancets below it, or to each other, or indeed to any other bay. The rosace with the election of Matthias (108) is a routine production in both style and iconography, the drapery painted with spare, short, thick strokes; it is not a particularly skillful or interesting ensemble. The glazier uses the red background circles associated with the Laon east rose, which are found previously in the Reims rosace of Peter and Andrew (Bay 102, fig. 34) and which appear later in many of the medallions of the Reims north rose and the nave rosaces. The single noteworthy detail of the Matthias rosace of Bay 108 is the fancy pearled decoration on the apostles' haloes, not found elsewhere in the cathedral. It has an Alsatian look.[149]

The lancets in the straight chevet bays are much wider than those in the hemicycle (see figs. 8, 9, and 27).[150] The increased ornament in these designs seems to have been adopted in order to keep figures at more or less the same scale as in the hemicycle and to keep the factorization of color to the observer's eye roughly comparable. The differences in shop practice in the straight bays, however, are enough to seal the judgment that each pair of lancets was painted by a different artist. I refer to such elements as the painting (and leading) of eyes and other facial features, the drapery, the palette, amount and type of ornament, and so forth. The designs of both 107 and 108, however, indicate study of the earlier hemicycle glass.

The haloes of Bay 108 (fig. 97)—red with a white edge—can be found in Bays 100, 102, 104, and 105 (where they are much smaller). The figures of 108 have heavy, dark shading around the eyes, something like that in Bays 103 and 104. Indeed Reinhardt grouped Matthias and the apostle with the palm (both in Bay 108) with his first group (Bays 103 and 104), which he considered to be recycled from a "first choir program." His criteria are difficult to understand, much less to agree with. Aside from the black smearing around the eyes, nothing in Bay 108 relates to the compacted, hypnotic power of Bays 103 and 104.[151] Some of the "quotations" of detail from earlier windows are sporadic; that is, they are found in only one figure or one glass panel of Bay 108. One might conclude that the panels were made piecemeal and/or, once produced, were stored and not available for reference as the window was completed. An example is the apostle with palm, who is the only figure in Bay 108 to have the horizontal color bands in his drapery that one finds in Bays 104, 105, and 107. The latticework ground pattern in Bay 108 also has this erratic quality. The red-and-blue lozenge network is limited to the area within the figures' canopies in the left lancet and even more restricted in the right, where it is found only around the apostle's head. A simpler latticework ground occurs in the left lancet of Bay 101, and a more elaborate one in Bay 105 and the right lancet of 106, and each of these grounds is maintained throughout its lancet.

Certainly the most surprising and puzzling detail in Bay 108 is in the vestments of the unidentified bishop. This extremely handsome figure (fig. 98) wears a pallium, which is among the insignia

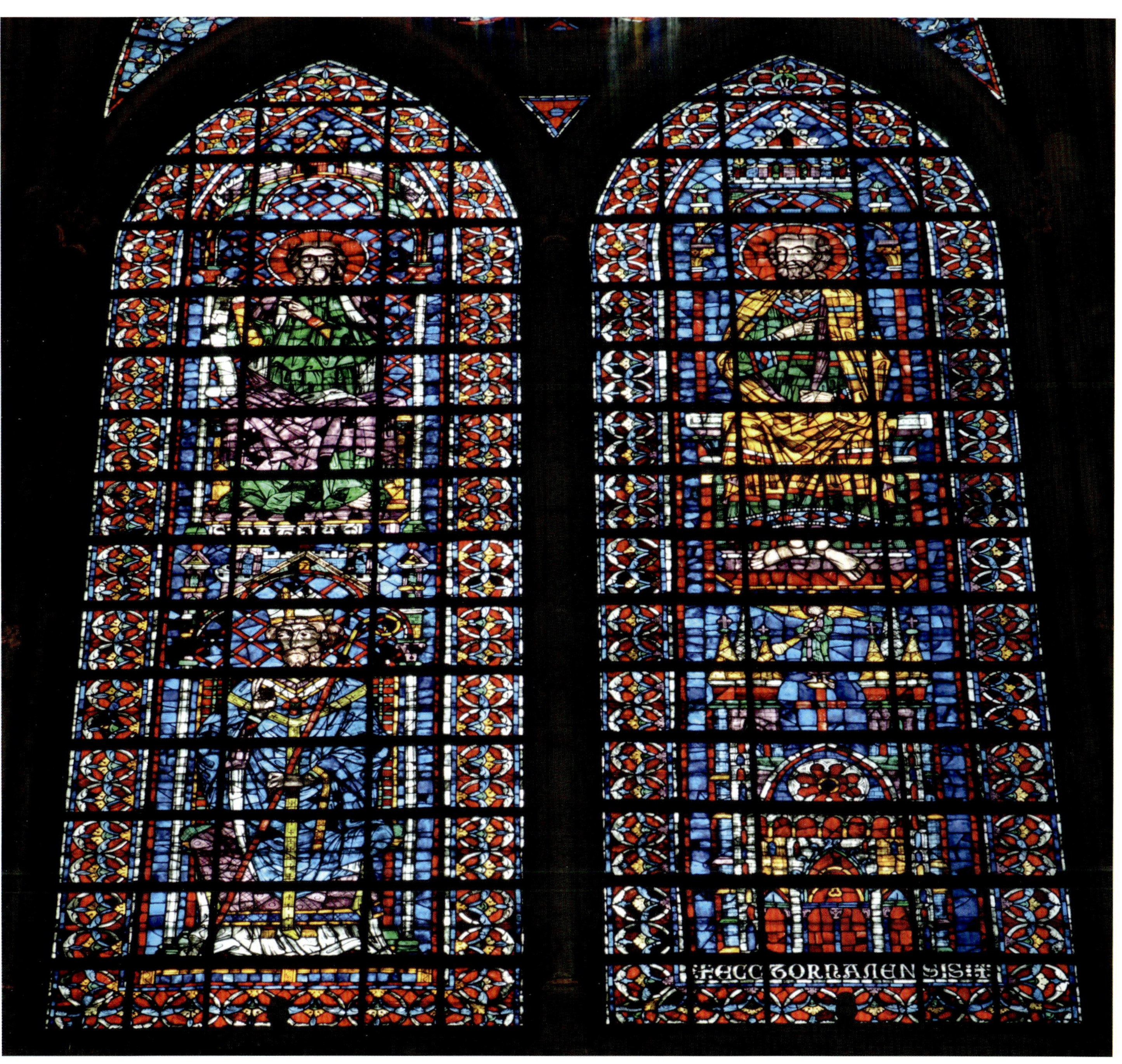

FIG. 97 Bay 108.

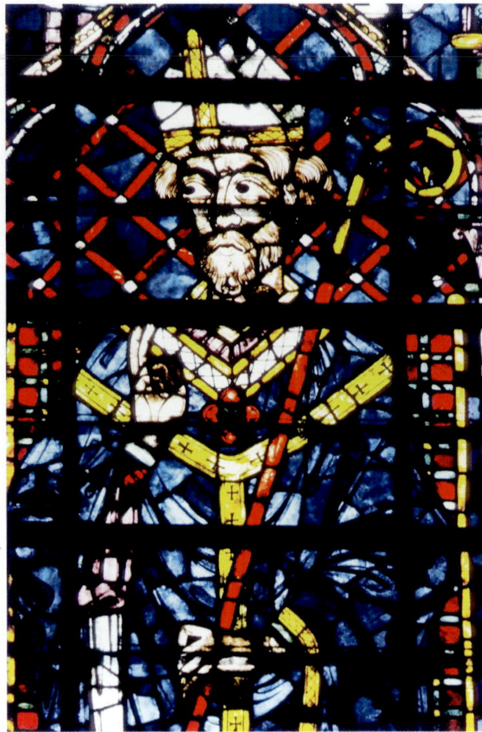

FIG. 98 Unidentified bishop, wearing archbishop's pallium! Bay 108, left lancet, lower row.

appropriate only to archbishops. This cannot have been intended! No one has ever suggested that this alert, beautifully painted bishop could have been recycled from some series of archbishops elsewhere.[152] Did the glazier "quote" the image of Henri de Braine in Bay 100 without knowledge of vestments, or of the chevet program?

The lancets of Bay 107 (figs. 95, 96), like the other straight chevet clerestories, have heavy ornamentation and figures turned casually in interacting poses.[153] Barnabas (top left) is seated sideways and gestures to his companion, like Jude in Bay 106. However, the figures in Bay 107 are noticeably larger. The drapery of all three includes horizontal color bands, as in Bays 104 and 105, and the elaborate jeweled haloes are "quotations" from Bays 101, 103, and 106. One anomaly is the misplacement of Barnabas's inscription band, incongruously located at the very bottom of his lancet, beneath the otherwise unlabeled "facade."

On the other hand, the rosace of Bay 107 (fig. 64) breaks the mold. It totally differs from all the others, not least in palette. The grounds are red, unlike any other rosace. Set on this vivid ground is a focused palette of blue, medium green, and white. The order of scenes in the lobes is top-bottom-middle, again a sequence not found elsewhere in the choir (fig. 27). The figures, large in scale, have the mass and power of the antique, facial painting is full of nuanced shading, and drapery painting is exquisite, marked by broken silhouettes and handsome shaded folds. While each of these characteristics can be found in other rosaces, together they signify a new arrival—of the greatest skill—in the glazing workshop. He was probably a late arrival. One of the features of the ornament in his startling rosace is a pattern painted in stick-work; that is, the design is picked out (removed) from a black-painted ground with a stick such as the end of a brush. Stickwork is not a technique that is suitable for viewing from the ground floor of a structure the scale of Reims. Though it was also used in the pearled haloes of the lesser-quality rosace of Bay 108 (fig. 62),[154] stickwork appears nowhere else in the chevet—except in a small area of this same window. Around the angel on the roof of the "facade" (fig. 95), the ground is decorated with a stickwork pattern not found elsewhere in the lancets.

This anomaly prompted the judgment by Frodl-Kraft that the angel of Bay 107 was an insertion.[155] I argued earlier that the angels on the roofs are as planned. So is there another possible explanation for this minimal appearance of a stickwork ground? I have suggested that these last colored bays were made piecemeal during 1239–40, a time of interdict, the churches closed, the citizens ruling the town, and the canons keeping a low profile. The glass was probably produced more or less as glaziers could be found, their work put into safe storage for future installation as soon as they completed it. The stickwork ground area behind the angel forms the link, in the lancet, between the apostle above and the "facade" below and may have been left until those images had been made. And the totally different rosace is likely also to be a very late project, by an artist unfamiliar with the details of the program of the ensemble.

These final colored bays were not produced cheaply, hastily, or by cutting corners in any way. They are creations indicative of study, care, and taste. Individual elements are masterpieces, such as the bishop of Bay 108 and the strange, handsome rosace of Bay 107. There was no reason to rush. The archbishop was still in exile though very much alive, and the town was still excommunicate.

Sede Vacante

According to the chevet's grand plan, Bay 109 was most probably to be dedicated to Arras and 110 to be shared by Cambrai, the only suffragan not in France, and Senlis, the tiniest suffragan diocese.[156] But Henri de Braine died, still in exile, on July 6, 1240. The chapter made its peace with the towns-men as rapidly as possible—by August 15—and hastened to resume construction so that part of their spectacular Gothic cathedral could be opened to the faithful. They achieved this goal in little over a year, inaugurating "their choir" on September 7, 1241.[157] I suggest that the glazing work involved in this spurt of activity comprised the installation of glass panels made and stored in the previous year(s) of interdict as well as glass for Bays 109 and 110 (figs. 99–100) and very probably some of the grisailles in the transept clerestories. The four grisaille designs of Bays 109 and 110 are identical in type and style to the extensive series in the transepts (discussed in chapter 4). The stalls of "their choir," in 1241, may have been in a temporary location in the transept crossing.[158]

Some of the information in print concerning Bays 109 and 110 is erroneous and should be corrected before any assessment here. The French Corpus Vitrearum's Recensement IV states that Bay 110 has two bishops, while Bay 109 has two archbishops.[159] In fact all four are bishops. None wears the pallium or bears any other insignia appropriate only to an archbishop, such as rational or cross-staff. The same source reports that the bishops of Bay 110 are identical and the "archbish-ops" of 109 likewise. Actually, the reuse of the same cartoon—which could be done only while the full-scale design was still available on the white-washed glazing table—is more subtle.[160] The right bishop of Bay 109 and the left bishop of 110 are made from the same cartoon, while the right apostle of 109 and the left one in 110 used the same cartoon but "flipped"; that is, both were cut on the same table, though one was painted on the opposite side of the glass, so the resulting figure is reversed. The four other figures in these bays may be adaptations of the same designs in the shop's pattern book (a topic to be addressed below), but they are not made from the same full-scale car-toons. This implies that a certain amount of finesse was exercised in these final bays, as does the fact that each lancet has a different grisaille pattern.

Balcon has established that Bay 109 was destroyed in the 1914–18 war and is now a modern re-creation based on the Simon tracings.It was remade in 1931.[161] At present the irises of the eyes are noticeably larger in the re-created Bay 109 than in Bay 110, including those of the figures made from the same cartoons.[162] This could be accounted for by the following hypothesis. The theory of a "first choir program" found in Rein-hardt's monograph of 1963 is likely to have been discussed much earlier in the *chantier* of the cathedral's postwar restorer, Henri Deneux (d. 1969). Reinhardt states that his book was con-ceived in 1927; Deneux was in charge of the reconstruction of the cathedral from 1919 until his retirement in December of 1939.[163] From 1922 to 1933 Deneux conducted archeological excavations in the building, and "Reinhardt spent many years in the dig and claim[ed] to be Deneux's heir, with access to all his material."[164] Reinhardt's "first atelier" is based on the spolia of Bay 118 (restored ca. 1930) and Bays 103 and 104 (restored in 1925). These bays are notable for enlarged eyes, and in the re-creation of Bay 109 (in 1931) the eyes may have been enlarged based on this theory of a recycled "first choir program."

It is a fair question, then, to ask, In what way(s) do Bays 109 and 110 (figs. 99–100) resemble Bays 103 and 104 (figs. 84, 86) and the spolia in Bay 118 (figs. 147–48)? In fact, not many—or at least not in

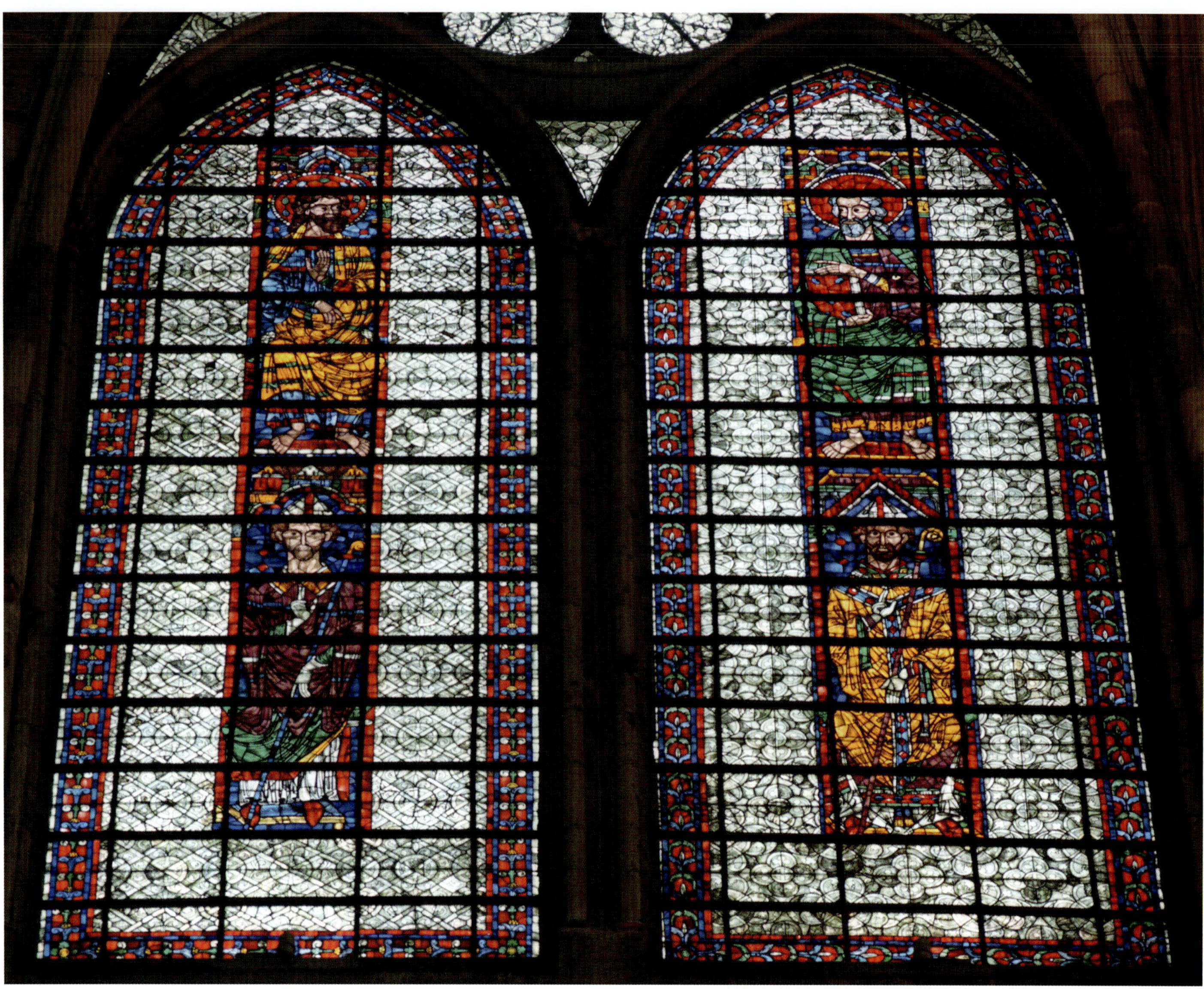

FIG. 99 Bay 109.

design details other than those that recur throughout the chevet bays. Reinhardt's criteria for his "first atelier" have already been criticized because none appears in all the bays he groups in this atelier and none distinguishes these bays as a group from the others.[165] So I have compiled the following list of details found in Bays 109 and 110:

- Haloes: two red haloes bordered by white fillets (also found in the Bay 118 spolia and in Bays 100, 102, 104, 105, 108); one jeweled halo, also found in 101, 103, 106, 107.
- Horizontal color bands in draperies: a few in all bays except Bay 102; prevalent in 104, 105, 107.
- Facial leading: the leaded-in mouth appears in 101, 106, 107, but is not used in Bays 103 and 104 or the Bay 118 spolia; the leading across the eyebrows and down one side of the nose is fairly common, especially in Bays 102 and 108, but is not found in 103 and 104.
- Drapery painting in Bay 110 (109 is modern): the heavy spoon-fold painting in the right apostle's blue mantle resembles that in the re-created Bay 109 but is not found in the prewar Deneux

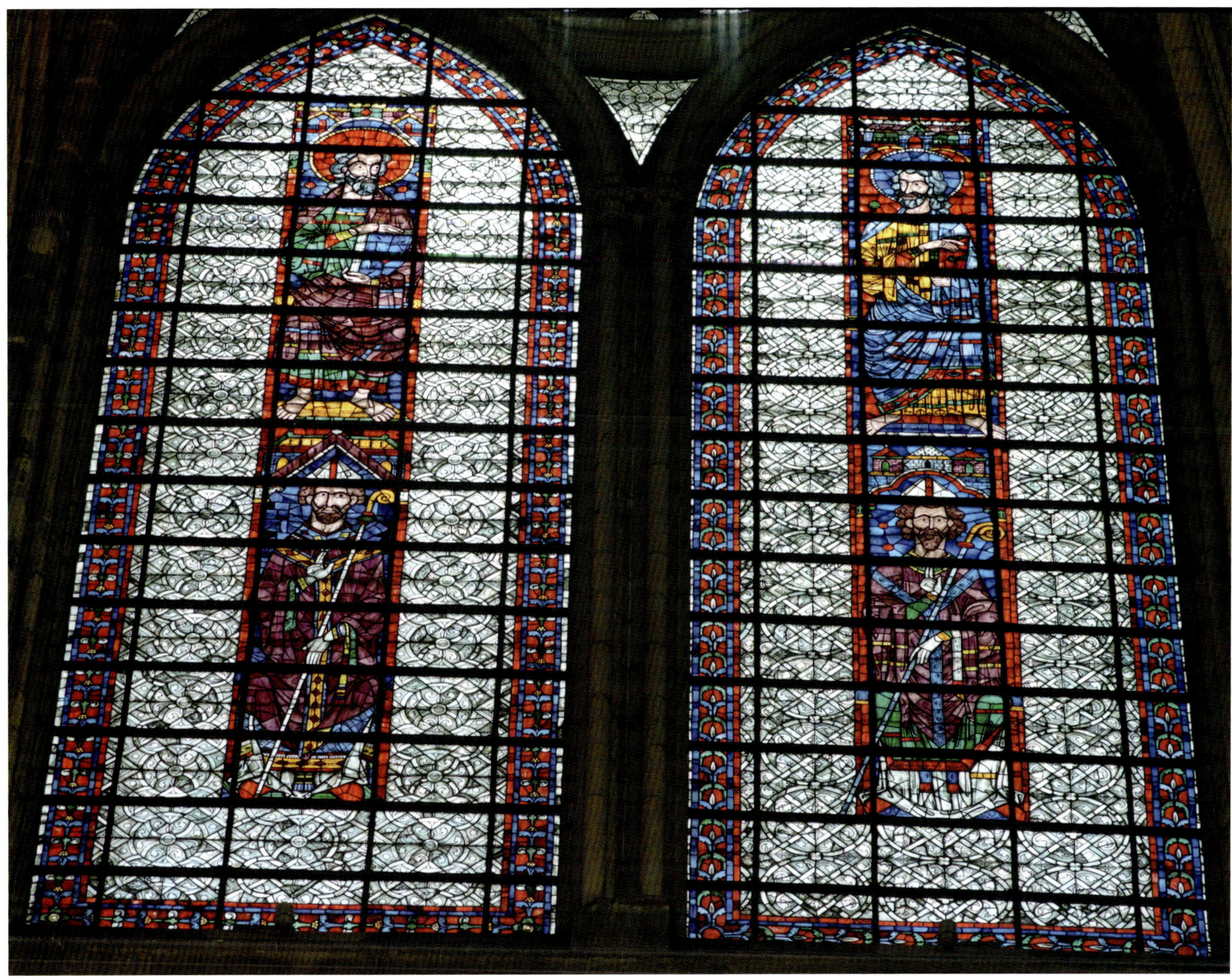

FIG. 100 Bay 110.

autochrome photos (fig. 101) or for that matter in the other figures in Bay 110.

Indeed, Bays 109 and 110 look "older" because the bishops are rigidly frontal while those in the adjoining bays 105 to 108 are turned and more relaxed, and because the apostles facing each other in 109 and 110 are near mirror images. Although combinations of frontal and three-quarter figures appear earlier at Saint-Remi, Braine, and Soissons,[166] frontal figures also occur in ensembles in the 1240s and later. Examples include figures of the 1240s at Auxerre, of the 1250s at Saint-Quentin, and of 1269 at Amiens.[167]

It should not surprise the reader by now that I do not see why the four figures of Bays 109 and 110 need have been recycled from some previous ensemble, a "first choir program" of some sort.[168] What I see is simpler craft procedures to finish the chevet glazing under pressure of time. The border designs, identical in the two bays, are simplified and use a reduced palette. The grisaille framing, a Parisian innovation that was adopted at Auxerre contemporary with Reims, is faster to produce

FIG. 101 Unidentified disciple, Bay 110, right lancet, top row. Autochrome by Henri Deneux, 1915.

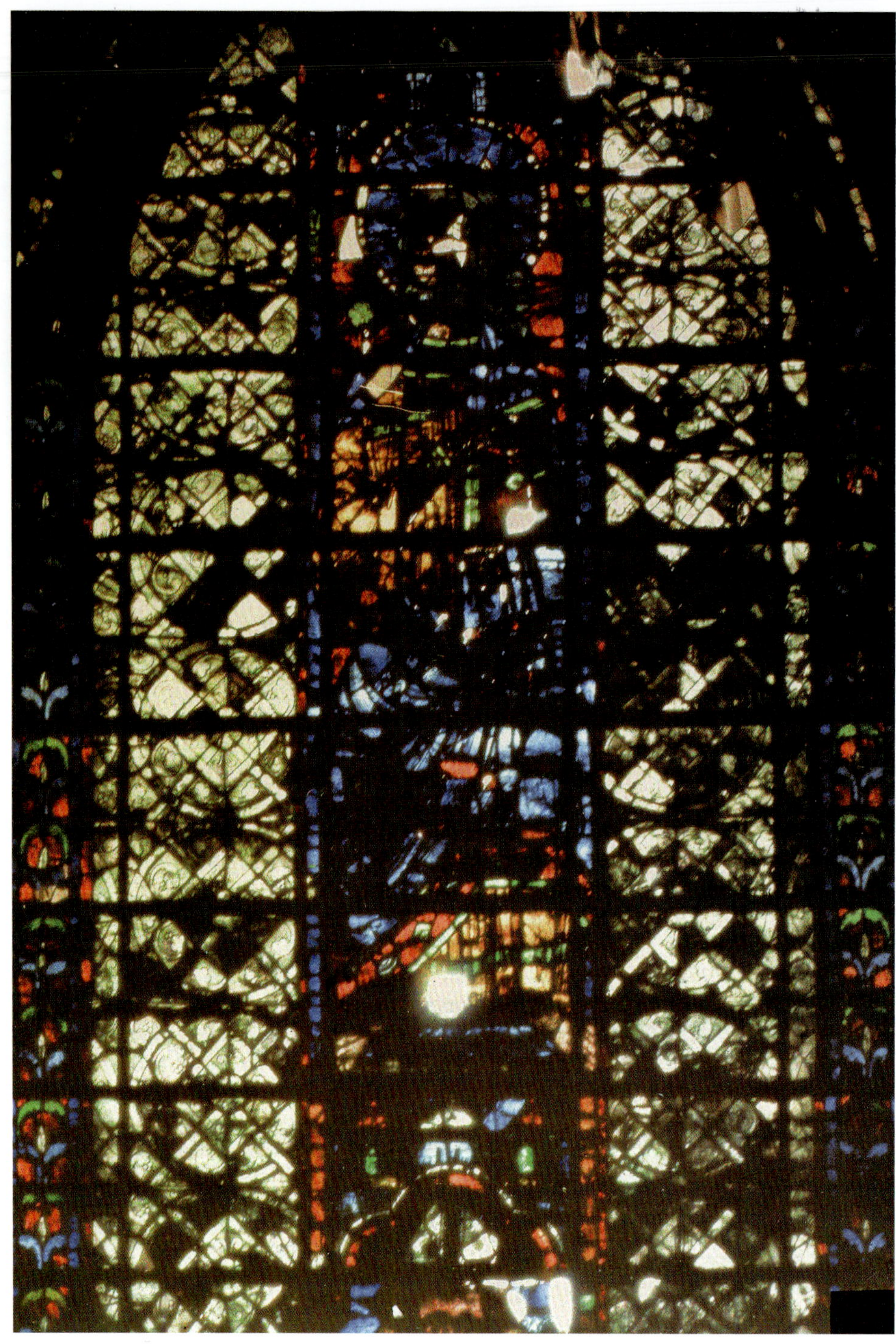

than figural imagery.[169] The elimination of "facades" and inscriptions would also save some time. In short: the grand chevet plan was abandoned upon the death of Henri de Braine. The chevet now illogically displays twelve bishops to represent his eleven suffragans.

The reuse of full-scale cartoons for the apostles of Bays 109 and 110 is a procedure that had never been followed in the Reims shop before.[170] It is easy to understand why not. In a program that was built on repetition—of apostles, bishops, "facades"—figures were sometimes created from the same shop pattern sheets or model books,[171] but care was always taken to inject variety. Frodl-Kraft's illustrations are very useful in investigating this question at Reims. She groups Paul (Bay 101), Bartholomew (106), and the anonymous apostle with palm (108) as what might be three different artists' variants made from the same shop pattern. Another of her groups is James the Less (104), Matthew (105), and the right apostle of Bay 110.[172] Significantly, this Bay 110 apostle is not one of the two in Bays 109 and 110 made from the same full-scale cartoon, discussed above.

Postscript

The grand chevet program at Reims is unique in medieval glazing. When one considers how potentially static and uninteresting such a program might be, composed of lineups of apostles, bishops, and churches, the spectacular richness and infinite variety of the visual banquet that is the Reims chevet are compelling. Unity is achieved by the use of a reasonably limited color range, while variety is the result of infinite care taken to enrich and alter designs, even when based on the same model. The whole has the impact of a great symphony orchestra in full flight. The remarkable inventiveness in the designs of the unique "facades" has been delineated by Frodl-Kraft and Kurmann, among others. One can also appreciate the individuality and characterization of so many apostles, both named and supernumeraries. And the episcopate of bishops is as varied as no doubt it was at one of the suffragans' provincial councils—the young and the senile, the crafty and the ingenuous, the religious zealots and the simply ambitious.

The chapter of canons, as I see it, was in charge of the execution of the archbishop's complex and interwoven glazing program probably from their triumphant return from exile in January 1237, and certainly from the time of Henri de Braine's exile in late 1238. Once he died, they abandoned his program and pushed to completion the glazing of the choir and probably some of the transept grisailles in order to open the new Gothic construction to liturgical use in September 1241. The canons managed very well without an archbishop and indeed did not elect another until the pope finally imposed the seasoned veteran Juhel de Mathefelon on them in March 1245.[173] During those years the chapter glazed the surviving north rose and no doubt the lost south rose. That is the story of chapter 4.

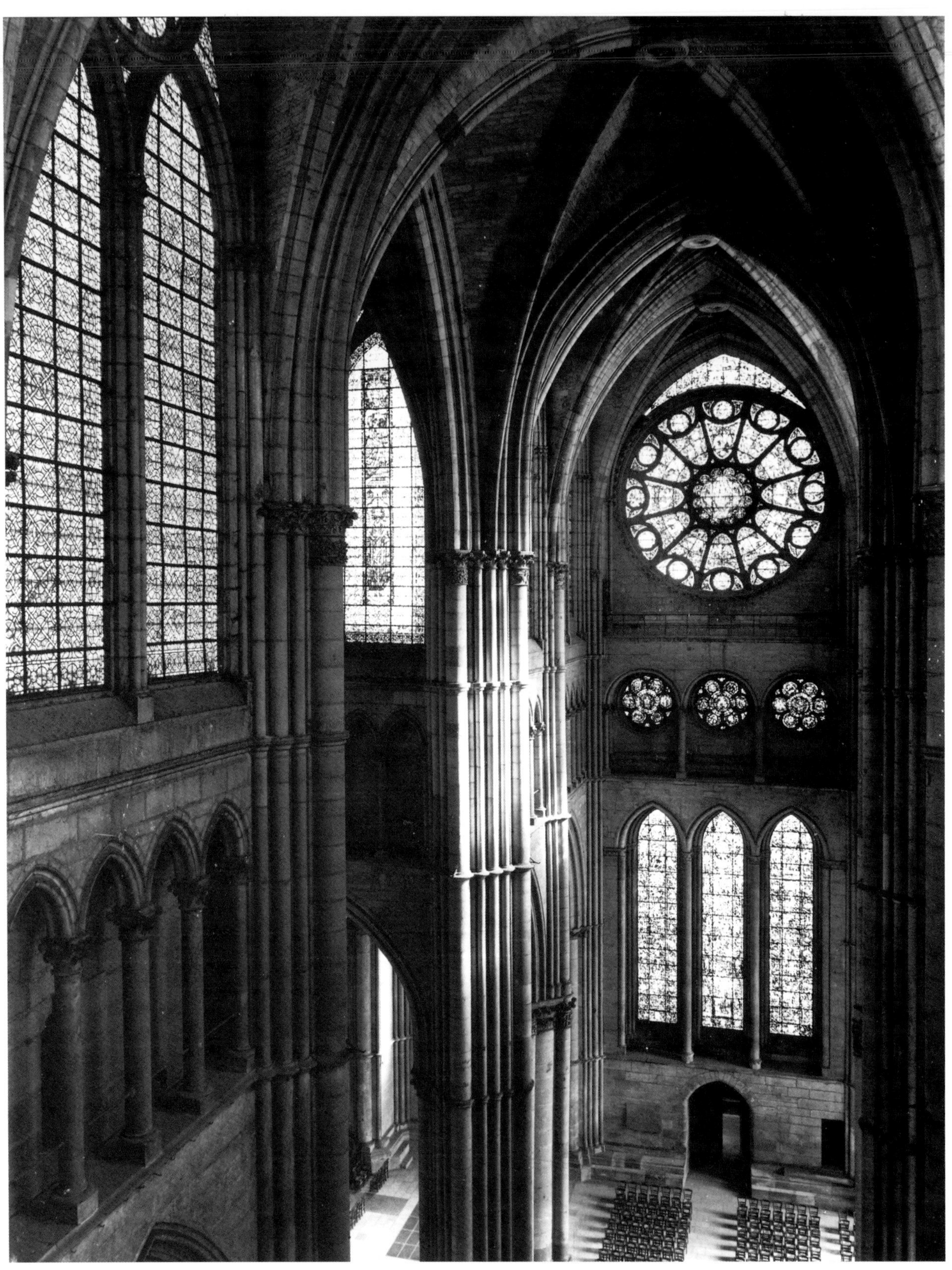

FIG. 102 View from the north to the south transept: (left to right)
Bays III, 110, and south rose (with twentieth-century glazing).

CHAPTER 4

THE TRANSEPTS

Grisailles, Roses, and *Belles Verrières*

The grisailles and roses of the transepts provide a unique setting for the high altar in the crossing, which emphasizes, with great success, the "specialness" of this focal point of the church. That emphasis is much more evident to someone within the transept area than to an observer situated along the axis of the nave and chevet. In other words, the unity and variety that are both hallmarks of Gothic creation at Reims are at play in the transept. The separate treatment of this area successfully highlights its importance—and not only for coronations—but is not allowed to interfere with the strong repetitive rhythms that give the architecture its grand sweep.

The strength and excitement of the dominating frame provided by paired transept roses was an effect already in place at Chartres and later pursued at Notre-Dame in Paris and any number of *rayonnant* Gothic churches to follow. In these churches the high altar was located beyond, to the east. At Reims the grisaille framework polarizes and intensifies the effect of the roses while also of course providing the altar, in the crossing, with much greater lighting. Another goal sometimes suggested is economy, but a close examination of these grisaille clerestories dispels that myth. While no color at all is introduced, thus enhancing the lighting to the full, no shortcuts were taken in making these grisaille designs as rich and handsome as the glaziers' invention could accomplish.

The glazing mode using grisailles to flank a focal colored accent zone, such as an apse or in this case a transept facade, is a format I have called "summer-and-winter." It was a new fashion around 1240 and occurs regionally in and near Champagne as well as in the Parisian area. I have argued that such grisaille experiments originated in Paris, fundamentally motivated by the theological battle between Pseudo-Dionysius and Augustine that came to a head at the university at that time.[1] Among early examples are the Lady Chapel of Saint-Germain-des-Prés (1245–early 1250s) and the choir clerestories of the cathedrals of Sens (ca. 1240–50) and Châlons-en-Champagne (begun ca. 1236–early 1250s).[2] Reims is a precocious example of the new format. At Reims the adoption of grisaille was probably accomplished quickly, upon the death of Henri de Braine in June 1240, by canons familiar with Paris, its monuments, its university, and its theological turmoil. And grisaille certainly served another useful purpose for them, in highlighting and setting off the area of the high altar where the coronation took place.

The Eight Grisaille Clerestories

In chapter 3, I argued that one of the reasons for the introduction of grisaille in Bays 109 and 110, at

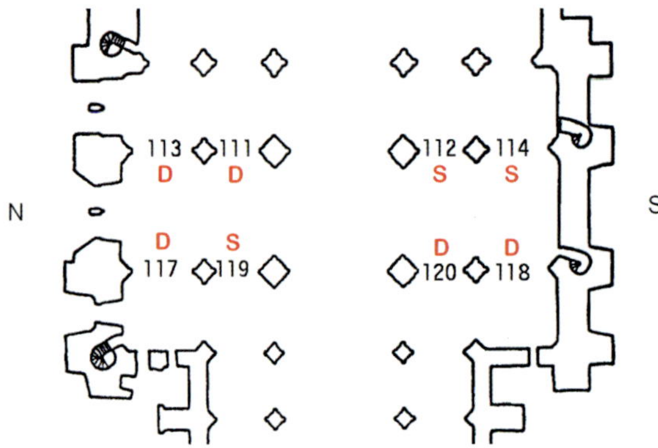

FIG. 103 Chart of the grisailles in the eight transept bays, indicating whether their paired lancets contain the same (S) or different (D) patterns.

the crossing, was speed—but not speed at any cost. Each lancet of those two doublet bays has a different grisaille design (figs. 99–100). The transition from the heavily color-saturated chevet to the area of the high altar in the crossing also benefits from the transition provided in those two final choir bays (see fig. 102), a subtlety that is perhaps too easily overlooked.[3] This implies that the decision to use a "summer-and-winter" glazing format in the transepts was made at the same time, that is, immediately upon the death of the troublesome archbishop in 1240. Some of the transept grisailles may have been pushed to completion before the grand opening of the new building in September 1241, though a careful study of the grisaille designs exposes no stylistic break at all.

Of the eight transept clerestories, each one a doublet as are all bays in the cathedral, five have a different grisaille pattern in each lancet (fig. 103),[4] as do choir Bays 109 and 110, mentioned above. The location of these five is random and impossible to connect with any proposed building sequence yet suggested by architectural historians. Since the outermost bays of each transept (113, 114, 117, 118) are wider than those bays at the crossing, the designs are not all readily interchangeable.[5] Finally, the patterns in the bays having the same design in both lancets are by no means, it must be emphasized, simpler or more routine than the others; indeed, they are as rich and complex as any. An example is Bay 114 (fig. 104, lower right), the pattern of which requires six panels to complete, as does that of the right lancet of Bay 120 (fig. 110). Given this richness and complexity, one is obliged to admit that the transept grisailles are a lavish collection of ornament made basically for the purpose of lighting—since no color is introduced anywhere—but in the same handsomely creative style and at the same moment.

The characteristics of this style are found not much later than ca. 1240.[6] The grounds are crosshatched. The strapwork fillets are occasionally leaded on both sides (figs. 107–10), which is rare after ca. 1240; the foliage consists of abstract palmettes but also incorporates occasional berries as well as stylized leaf and decorative motifs, again supporting the early dating (figs. 107, 110). The foliage generally grows both up and down in mirror image, with no rising vertical elements (except in borders, where vertically repeated motifs are standard from the beginning of the thirteenth century). Only the left lancet of Bay 117 (fig. 104, lower left) has vertically undulating strapwork and palmettes growing only upward, characteristics one associates with the future of grisaille development. Most important, there is little focus on the ironwork *panneautage;* that is, there is little emphasis on a central accent in each glass panel and no sense, as yet, that the panel design was a module to be repeated. On the contrary, the grisaille patterns—networks of strapwork and acanthus—seem to spread across the irons of the entire lancet surface like a carpet, a perfect example of Viollet-le-Duc's "tapisserie translucide qui ne préoccupe pas"[7] (figs. 105, 106). Finally, the total absence of any features associated with the development of grisaille from the mid-century onward supports a dating of all the Reims transept grisailles very close to 1240.

The early 1240s provided a much needed period of calm and healing for both the cathedral chapter and the city. Manufacture of the transept grisailles, once their design had been decided, could be left to the craftsmen involved, and the programs of the two great roses certainly provided the main object of the canons' attention in the embellishment of the new structure. They remained without an

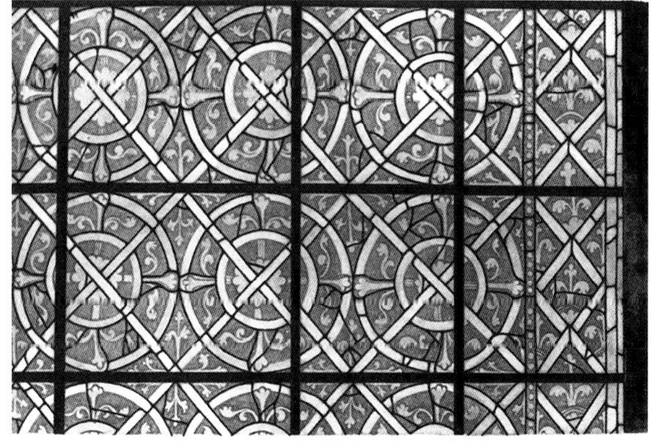

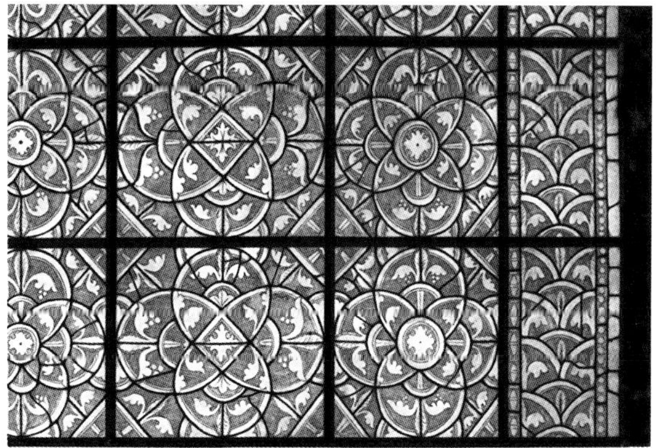

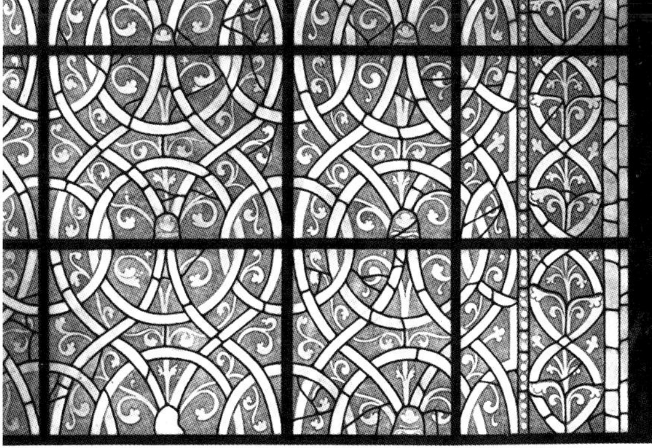

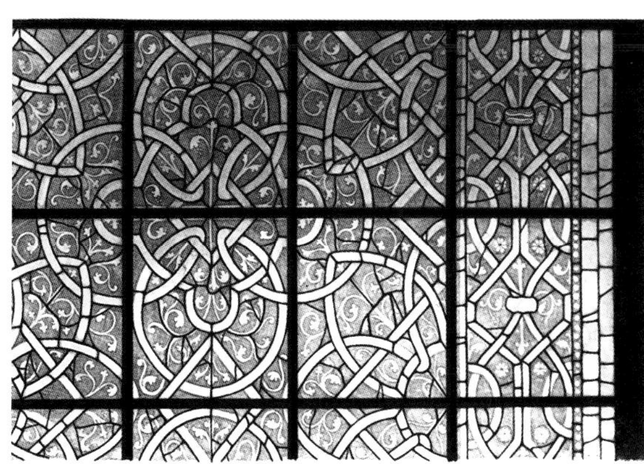

FIG. 104 Grisaille patterns, drawings by Henri Deneux, 1923. Bay 114, lower right; Bay 117, left lancet, lower left; Bay 117, right lancet, top left; Bay 119, top right.

archbishop until the pope nominated the aging Juhel de Mathefelon in March of 1245. Although his initial actions threatened to reopen the old urban wounds,[8] the Seventh Crusade provided a distraction. Louis IX had taken the cross in December of 1244, and the aged archbishop did likewise but apparently was too infirm to depart with the crusaders in 1247 and died in December 1250.[9] The transept roses are the canons' story. The loss of the south rose in 1580 hampers full appreciation of their program; so too does the drastic rearrangement of the north rose in 1872 by the restorer Oudinot. Study of the evidence for both north and south roses, nonetheless, points to a theologically sophisticated and complete statement of nothing less than the totality of God's creation and establishment of his Church on earth, from Genesis through the Second Coming.

The North Rose: Prolegomena

The Gothic rose window of the north transept of Reims cathedral (fig. 111) has been described as "a huge jewel suspended in the air, and sparkling with silver and ruby and sapphire."[10] Like a number of other north roses (e.g., those of Chartres and Paris), it is devoted to Old Testament themes. At Chartres and Paris, prophets and patriarchs surround the Virgin; at Reims, although the cathedral is dedicated to the Virgin (as are Chartres and Paris), the north rose presents the beginnings of time, the Creation, as recounted in the first four chapters of Genesis. The stories of Adam and Eve and of Cain and Abel, presenting the Fall of Man, appear more commonly in Gothic glass in conjunction with the parable of the Good Samaritan (lancets at Sens, Chartres, and Bourges), while

FIG. 105 Bay 112, detail.

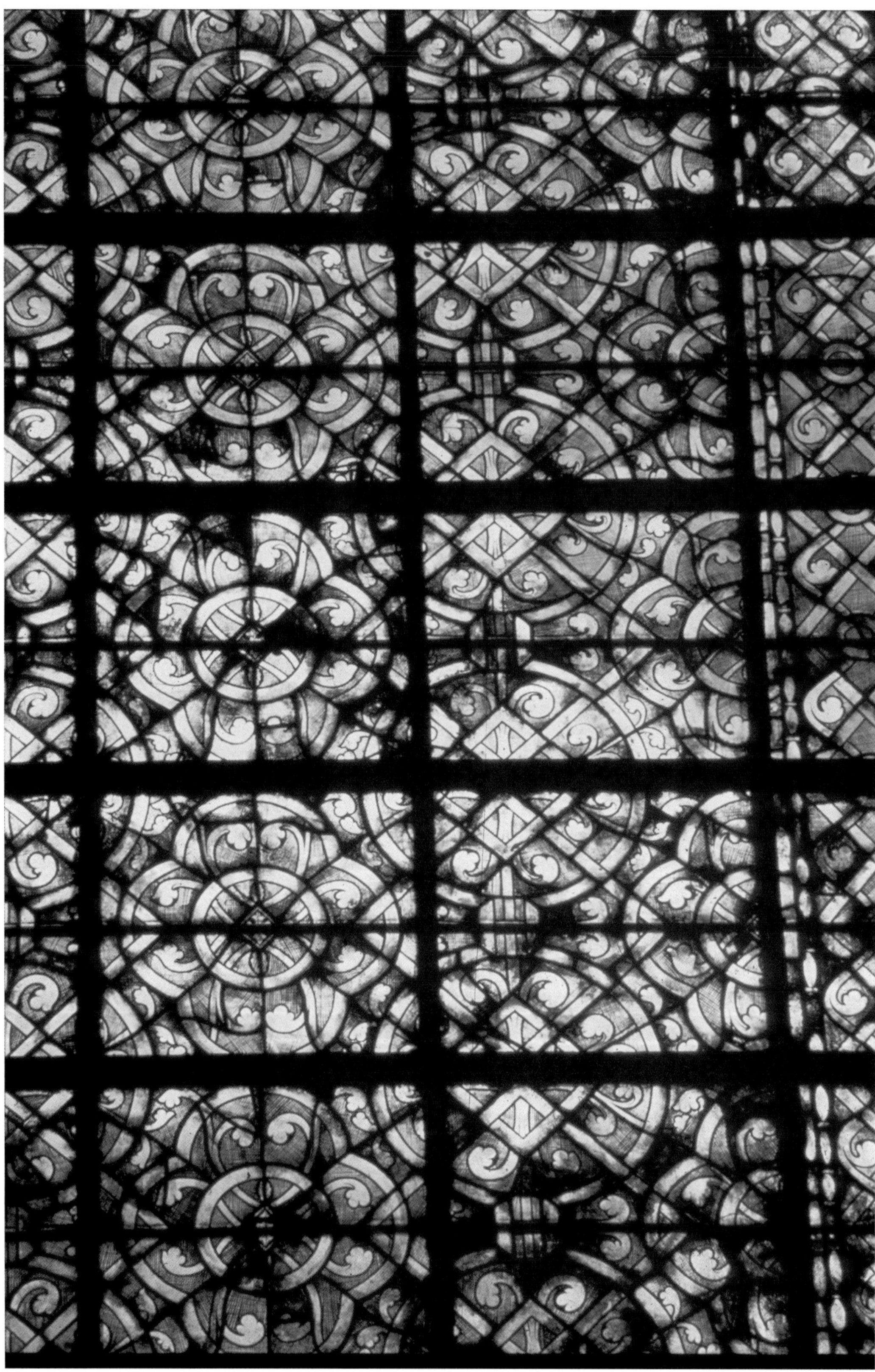

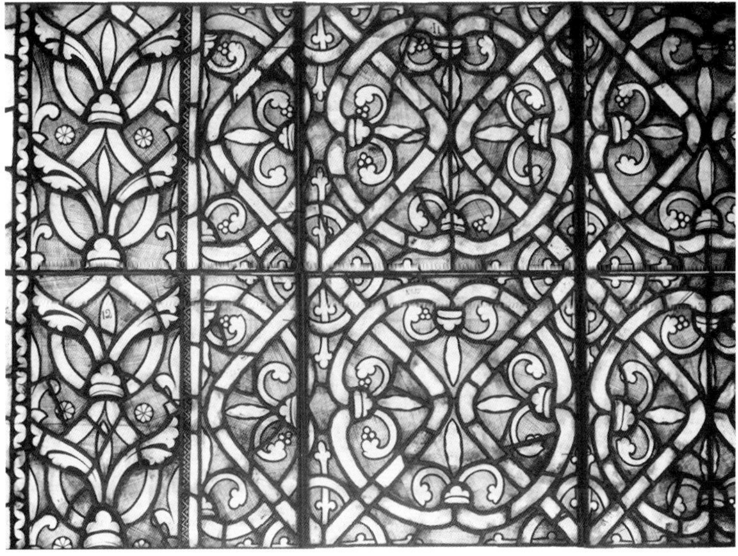

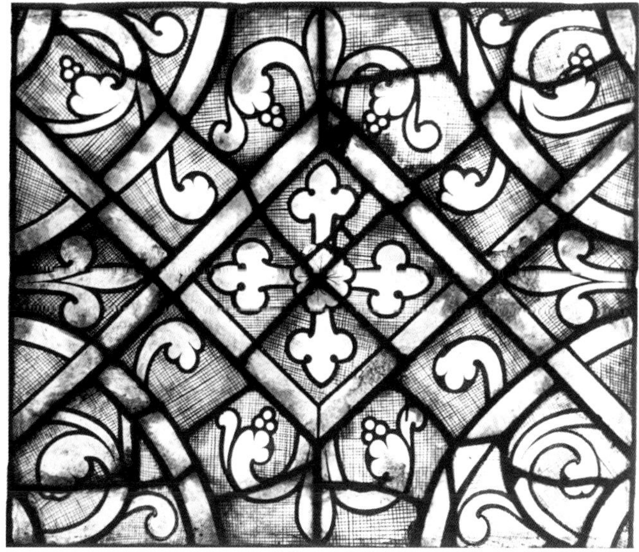

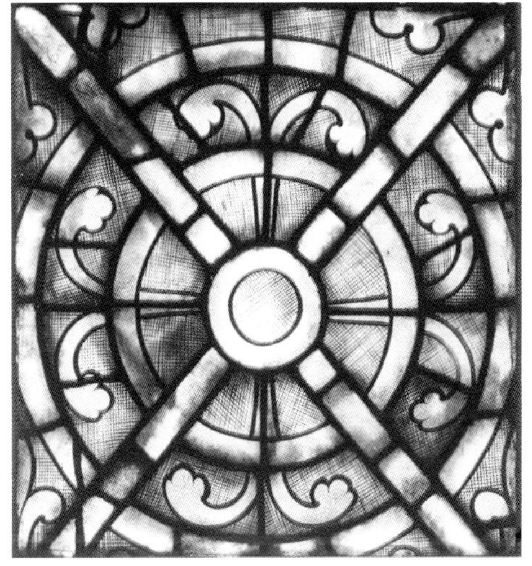

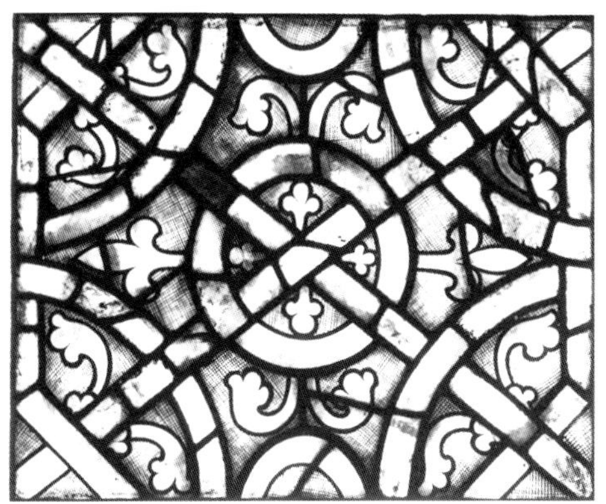

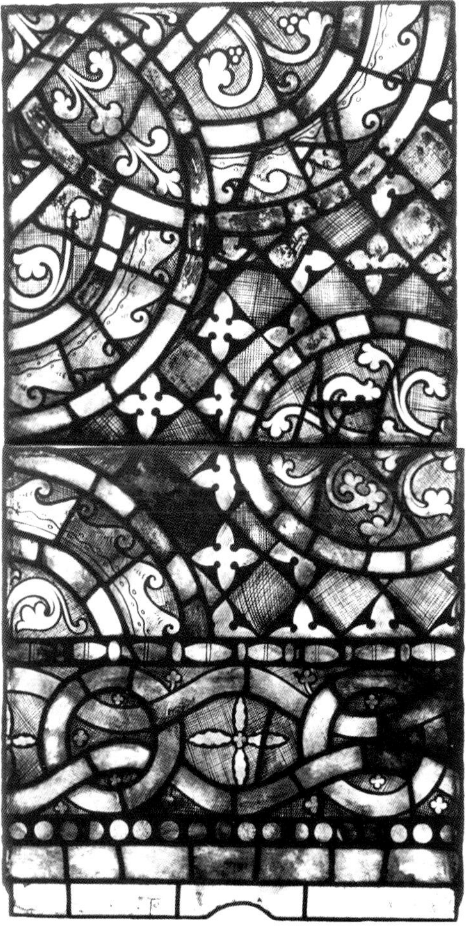

FIG. 106 Bay 120, left lancet, detail.

FIG. 107 Bay 111, right lancet, detail, 1945.

FIG. 108 Bay 113, left lancet, detail, 1945.

FIG. 109 Bay 113, right lancet, detail, 1945.

FIG. 110 Bay 120, right lancet, detail, 1945.

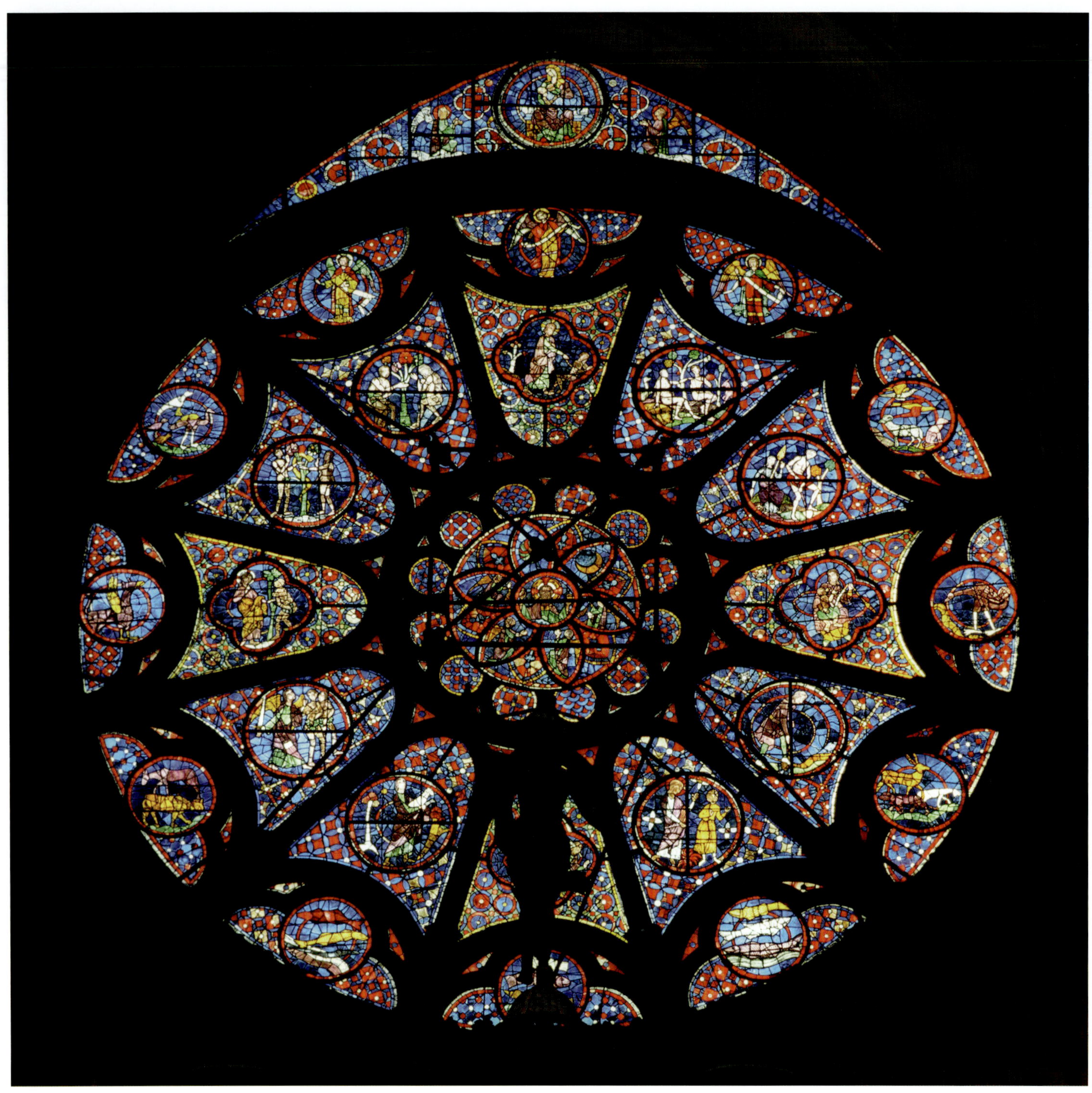

FIG. 111 North rose.

in the south rose of Lyon one finds the cycle of the "two Adams," that is, the Fall of Man and his Redemption, offered by Christ.[11] The Reims rose is unique. This study seeks to comprehend and explain that uniqueness.

It is assumed that the north rose of Reims made a pair with the rose window facing it in the south transept, which lost its stained glass and tracery in a windstorm (1580) and received replacements the following year.[12] The general themes of both transept roses appear on the exterior sculpture that frames them. On the north are large figures of Adam and Eve below an archivolt presenting the narrative of Creation through the descendants of Cain; on the south the statues of Ecclesia and Synagoga appear below the apostles and various Old Testament worthies, including Moses and Job. That is, the north presents the created world *ante legem,* and the south continues with *sub lege* and *sub gratia.*[13] Thus, in the grand glazing scheme of Reims, where the chevet presents the power of Ecclesia Remensis and the nave is devoted to the power she bestows on the anointed kings of France, the transept—site of the anointing and coronation of the king by the archbishop—presents the created world from its beginning to its dramatic finale.

The north rose survives to our day in modified form. Six medallions (fig. 112: A-9, B-9, C-9, F-9, B-3, C-3) are totally nineteenth-century designs, and only about a third of the remaining glass is medieval. Five restorations are noted: an undocumented restoration of 1600–1650, possibly following a fire in the organ below the rose; 1739–43, following a storm; 1872, following another storm, a complete and drastic revision by Oudinot under the direction of Viollet-le-Duc; 1930, repairing World War I damage; and 1980, cleaning and minor restoration.[14] Although a number of unrelated stopgaps were used to patch damage in the early period, only the restoration of 1872 involved the rearrangement of scenes and the invention of new medallions (fig. 113). It is the state of the rose as it had survived up to 1872 (fig. 114) that is most important for our understanding of the original program, and fortunately there are several nineteenth-century witnesses, whose observations will be the basis for the present discussion.

Before 1872 the rose is described as beautiful and medieval in appearance, though damaged:

> The ensemble of this composition certainly belongs to the thirteenth century. One finds in it the color of that epoch, the translucency without transparence, the naive design, the character of its style and disposition. Unfortunately, nearly all the subjects are mutilated; one hardly finds two or three complete. The holes caused by the fall of thirteenth-century glass have almost all been filled by fragments of sixteenth-century borders, easily recognizable by their paleness and their design.[15]

In addition to published nineteenth-century descriptions and the always valuable manuscript notes of Baron François de Guilhermy, a series of tracings and drawings made during the 1872 restoration by the glazier Pierre Simon (figs. 115, 127) aids in establishing the location and appearance of scenes in the rose before that date. This material, along with his notes, is still in the possession of the Simon-Marq atelier in Reims. The north-rose tracings have been catalogued in a thesis by Nathalie Frachon.[16]

My reconstruction (fig. 114) is based on these sources and will be used as the basis for discussion of the medieval iconographic scheme. The presumptions in this approach are that restorations before the nineteenth century patched or replaced lost areas but did not move things wholesale unnecessarily and that by the eighteenth century such patching had to be accomplished by recycling extraneous (medieval or Renaissance) glass, since colored glass was no longer being made. It is of course not impossible that panels were accidentally interchanged when they were reinstalled, but I argue that the evidence for such relocation before 1872 is slight and that my proposed reconstruction does indeed reflect an iconographic program that has all the hallmarks of sophisticated Gothic thought.

FIG. 112 North rose, panel numbering, adapted from the system used by the atelier Simon.

FIG. 113 North rose, present locations, since the 1872 restoration, of medieval panels; medallions created in 1872 are indicated by hatched lines.

FIG. 114 North rose, reconstruction of the original panel locations, based on pre-1872 witnesses.

FIG. 115 North rose: Creation of Eve (A-3); Expulsion from Paradise (originally C-3, now I-3). Lithograph of tracings made after restoration by Paul Simon, ca. 1875–86.

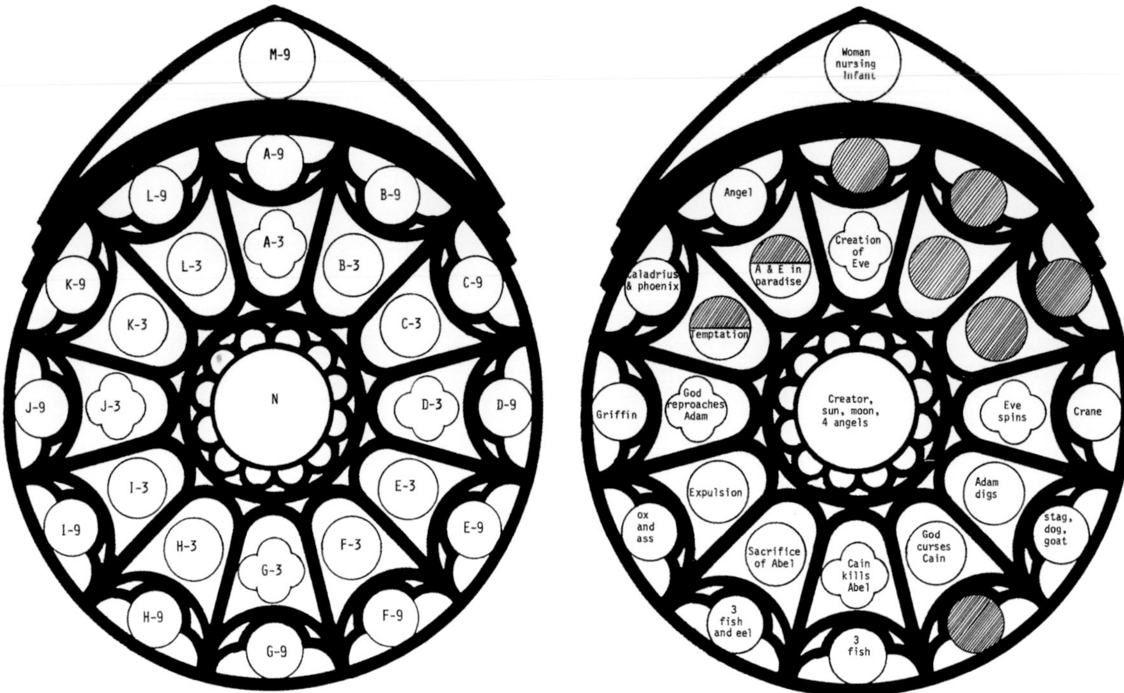

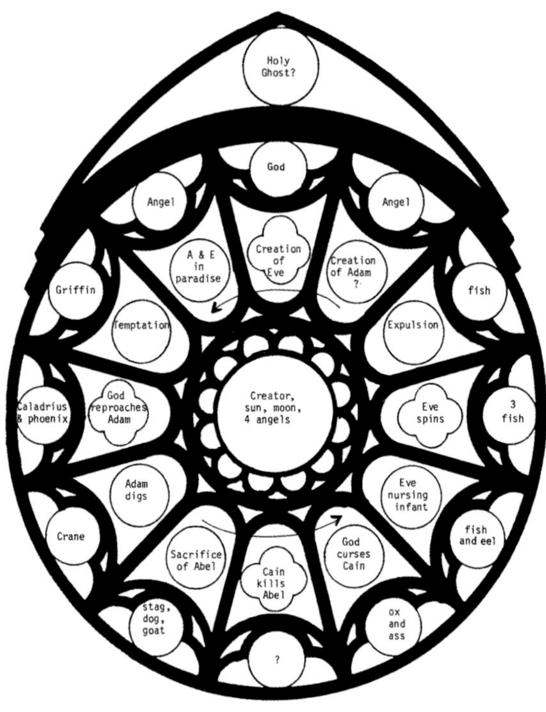

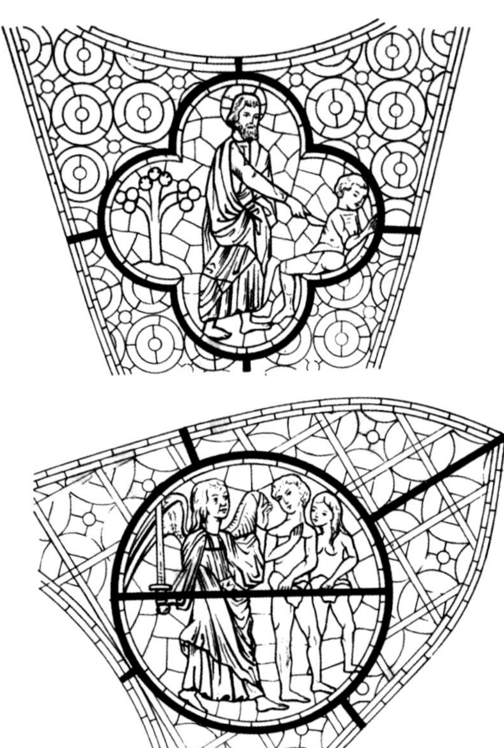

The North Rose: The Subjects and Their Original Placement

The subjects of the north rose as they are now and as established by Oudinot in the 1872 restoration appear in figure 113. A reconstruction of their locations before 1872 is presented in figure 114, based on nineteenth-century descriptions and images.[17] The subjects will be listed here briefly and discussed more fully below. The central rosette depicts the Creator holding the orb of the world, surrounded by angels and the sun and moon (fig. 121).[18] The primary circle of twelve medallions contains stories of Adam and Eve (above) and Cain and Abel (below). In the outermost circle of medallions are birds, fish, and animals, beneath two angels flanking a second image of the Creator (the latter shown in nineteenth-century illustrations—for example, the upper medallion of fig. 116).[19]

The most cursory perusal of these subjects reveals that they do not portray Genesis per se but an unusual selection of themes drawn from it. The sun and moon (central rosette) were created on the fourth day (Gen. 1:16–19). The fifth day (Gen. 1:20–23) produced the birds and fishes; on the sixth day (Gen. 1:24–31) God created the animals and then Adam and Eve, whose story continues in the rose, with that of their children Cain and Abel, to Genesis 4:15 (God cursing Cain).[20] The selection of Genesis subjects in the rose, moreover, in no way conforms to the Genesis subjects of the exterior sculpture ornamenting the voussoirs framing the same window.

The subjects of the sculpture are as follows:[21] Large figures of Adam and Eve, clothed and holding respectively, as attributes, the apple and the serpent, flank the bottom of the rose. Above them the archivolt enclosing the rose contains eleven scenes on each side, the narrative reading fairly directly from bottom to top on the left and then bottom to top on the right (excepting only Tubalcain among Cain's descendants at the apex of the arch). (See fig. 117.)

God's work on the first days of Creation is omitted altogether. Rather, the sculpture presents

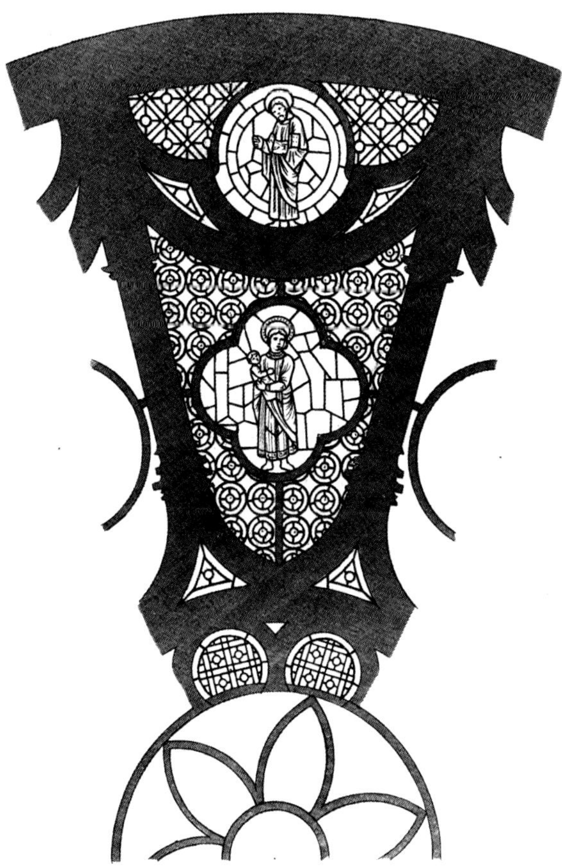

FIG. 116 North rose, medallions with surrounding diaper ornament: above, A-9 (God as Logos), below, A-3 (scene garbled, cf. fig. 115) (after Victor Tourneur, *Histoire et description des vitraux*).

the origins of mankind, through the establishment of trades by Cain's descendants. The cramped space available in the archivolt is most suitable to isolated figures, and many details are omitted, while other scenes are spread over several voussoirs. The most significant difference from the subjects of the rose's stained glass is the emphasis in its sculptural frame on the descendants of Cain, who comprise six of the twenty-two units.[22] The theme of the *artes mechanicae* is unexpected in Gothic France. Its most famous appearance is later, in the reliefs at the base of Giotto's Tower (the Florentine campanile), underlining its ultimately positive and civic nature.[23] At Reims the narrative's rising motion is appropriate to a genealogical tree such as the Tree of Jesse. This genealogical emphasis is totally absent from the stained glass of the rose, where, on the other hand, half of all the

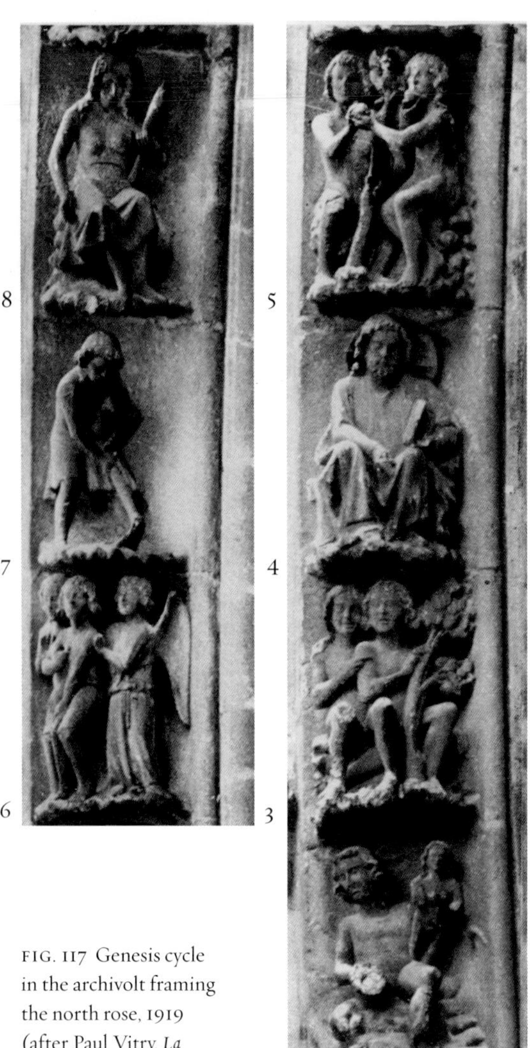

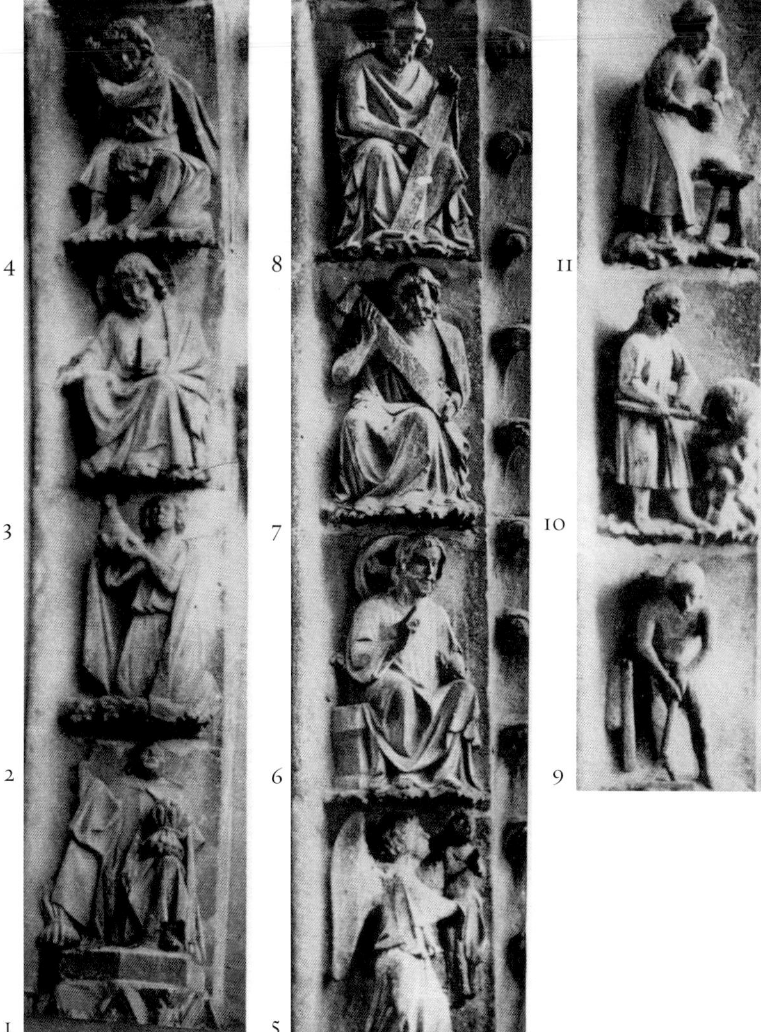

FIG. 117 Genesis cycle in the archivolt framing the north rose, 1919 (after Paul Vitry, *La cathédrale de Reims*).

LEFT
(scenes in italics not pictured)

11. *Tubalcain at the forge*
10. *Cain tilling earth*
9. *Abel as herdsman*
8. Eve spinning
7. Adam digging
6. Expulsion from Eden
5. Temptation and Fall
4. God enthroned, above
3. Adam and Eve seated in Eden
2. Creation of Eve (as bust rising from Adam's side)
1. *Adam (alone)*

RIGHT

11. Working potter?
10. Baker baking bread, oven
9. Figure raking wheat
8. Prophet (Enoch?)
7. Prophet (Lamech?)
6. God accepts Abel's soul
5. Angel receives Abel's soul
4. Cain murders Abel
3. God accepts Abel's sacrifice
2. Sacrifice of Abel
1. Sacrifice of Cain

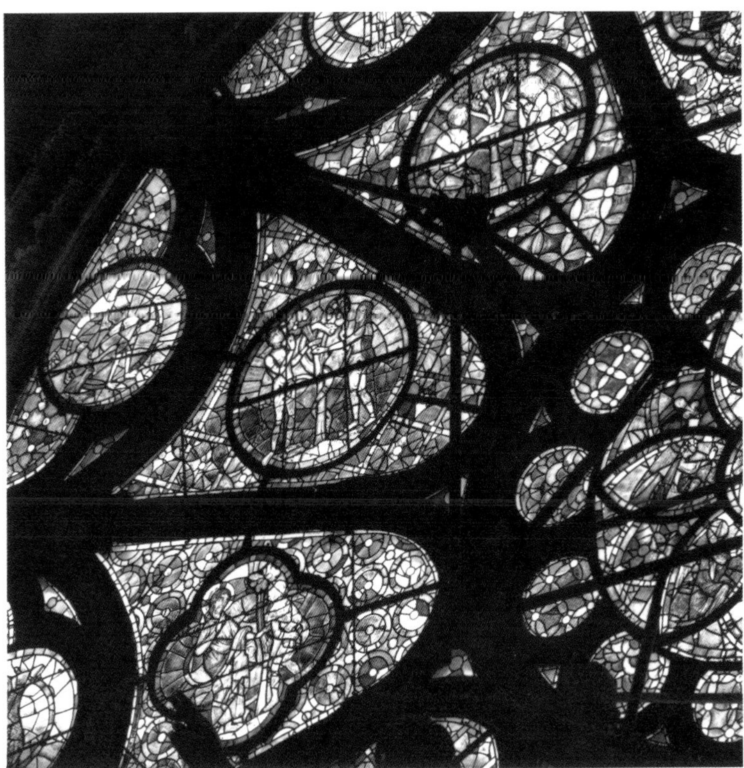

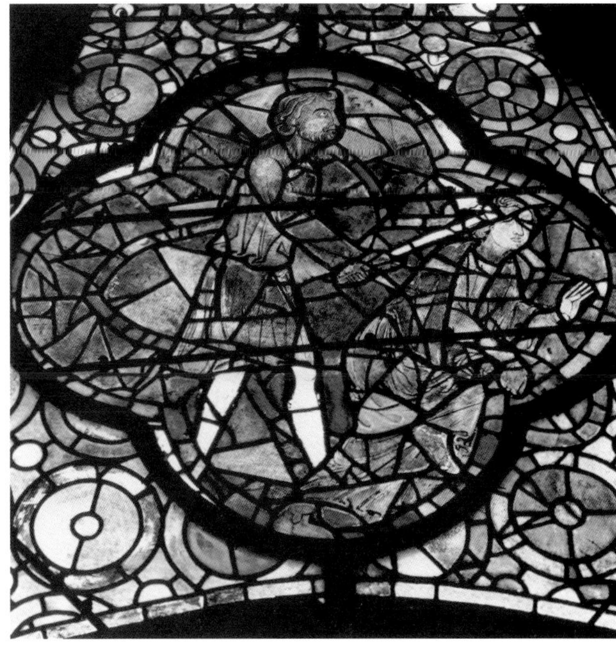

FIG. 118 North rose, upper left quadrant: L-3, K-9 and K-3, J-3. The upper halves of L-3 and K-3 are modern.

FIG. 119 Cain murdering Abel (north rose, G-3).

medallions are devoted to God's earlier creation: the creatures of the earth and sea (Gen. 1:20–25).

That is not the only difference between the sculpture and the glass. Besides details included or omitted, the chief dissimilarity is that the stained glass scenes are arranged from the top down (fig. 114). The motion downward emphasizes sin: the Fall of Man, culminating in the first murder, in the rose's bottommost medallion (fig. 119: G-3). Since the sculpture undoubtedly predates the glazing, perhaps only by a few years, the difference in storytelling is significant and will be addressed in the conclusion of this investigation.

To return to the arrangement of stained-glass subjects before 1872, the ornament, which has not changed significantly, offers useful clues to the rose's design and message (figs. 118, 120). The twelve lobes of the central rosette contain two simple patterns of diaper ornament in alternation, based on red and blue. The medallions of the outermost ring (creatures of the earth) are all circular in shape, and the diaper ornament in which they are set similarly alternates two designs of red and blue. Thus the ornament connects these medallions horizontally, left–right, while their subjects appear according to the progression of Genesis (figs. 114, 120): the creating God flanked by angels at the top (L-9, A-9, B-9), the fish and birds created on the fifth day (Gen. 1:20–23) in the middle on both sides, and the animals of the sixth day (Gen. 1:24–25) below (H-9, G-9, F-9). The effect is appropriately one of order within diversity.

The inner circle of medallions also alternates patterns of ornament across the rose, left–right. However, a cross is overlaid on this circle of scenes (fig. 120). The medallions at the four "cardinal points" are not circles but quatrefoils, and their diaper fields are composed of the only ornament of the entire rose that is based on green (all other patterns being combinations of red and blue). The scenes thus highlighted in the four points of the green and verdant cross can be assumed to have greater significance, and they do (fig. 114): the upper quatrefoil, God creating Eve (fig. 115, A-3);[24]

FIG. 120 North rose: basic coloration of the diaper ornament, containing green cross.

FIG. 121 The Creator surrounded by angels, the sun, and the moon (north rose, central rosette).

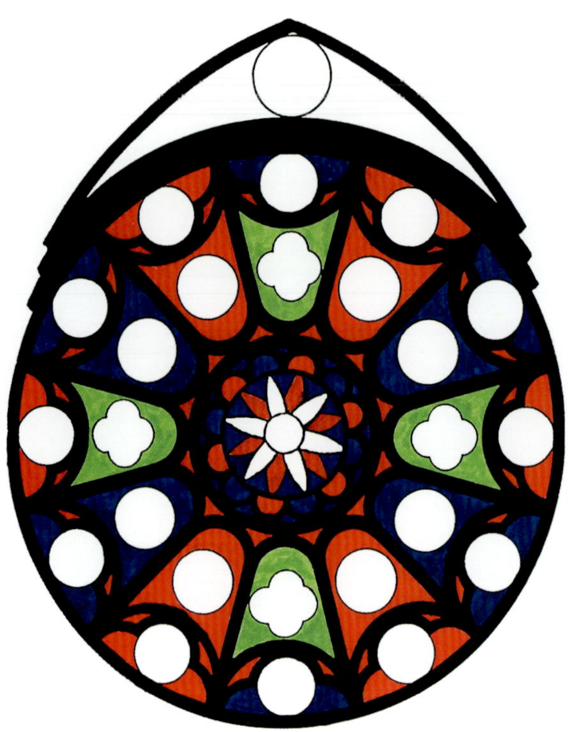

the left quatrefoil, God admonishing Adam after the Fall (fig. 118, J-3); the right quatrefoil, Eve spinning with Cain on her lap (fig. 125, D-3); and in the lower quatrefoil, the first murder (fig. 119, G-3). Adam gets off with a lecture, while the emphasis clearly is on the willfulness and disobedience of Eve and Cain, that is, on their state of sin.

This analysis of the subjects' locations before 1872 indicates that the rose did not have a stable equilibrium but rather a rocking sequence of narrative motion, indicated by the arrows in figure 114. Damage has rendered the story line of the top three scenes conjectural (as will be discussed below); however, the direction of action in the bottom three medallions is clear. It is counterclockwise: H-3 (Abel's offering, Gen. 4:4, fig. 123); G-3 (Cain murders Abel, Gen. 4:8, fig. 119); and F-3 (God curses Cain, Gen. 4:9–15, fig. 124).[25] This spinning motion probably was present as well in the three upper medallions, of which B-3 was totally lost before 1872, as was the upper half of L-3 (fig. 118). The lost scene of B-3 was most likely the

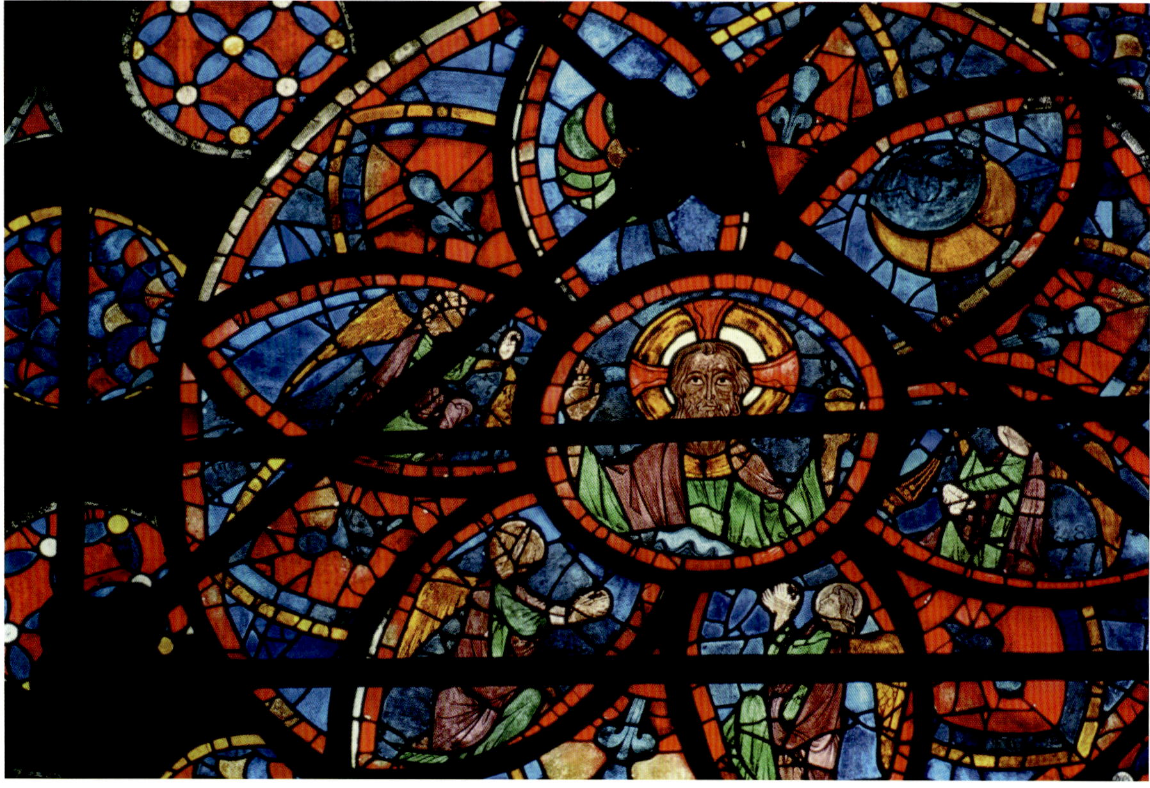

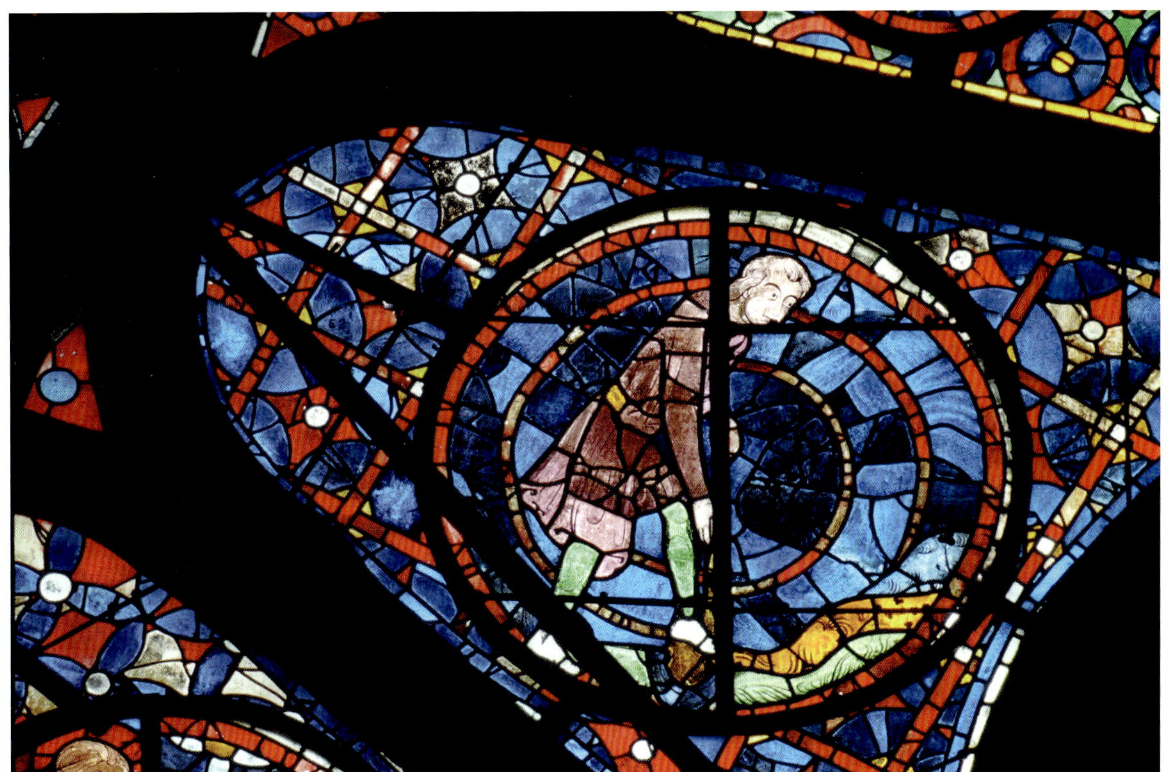

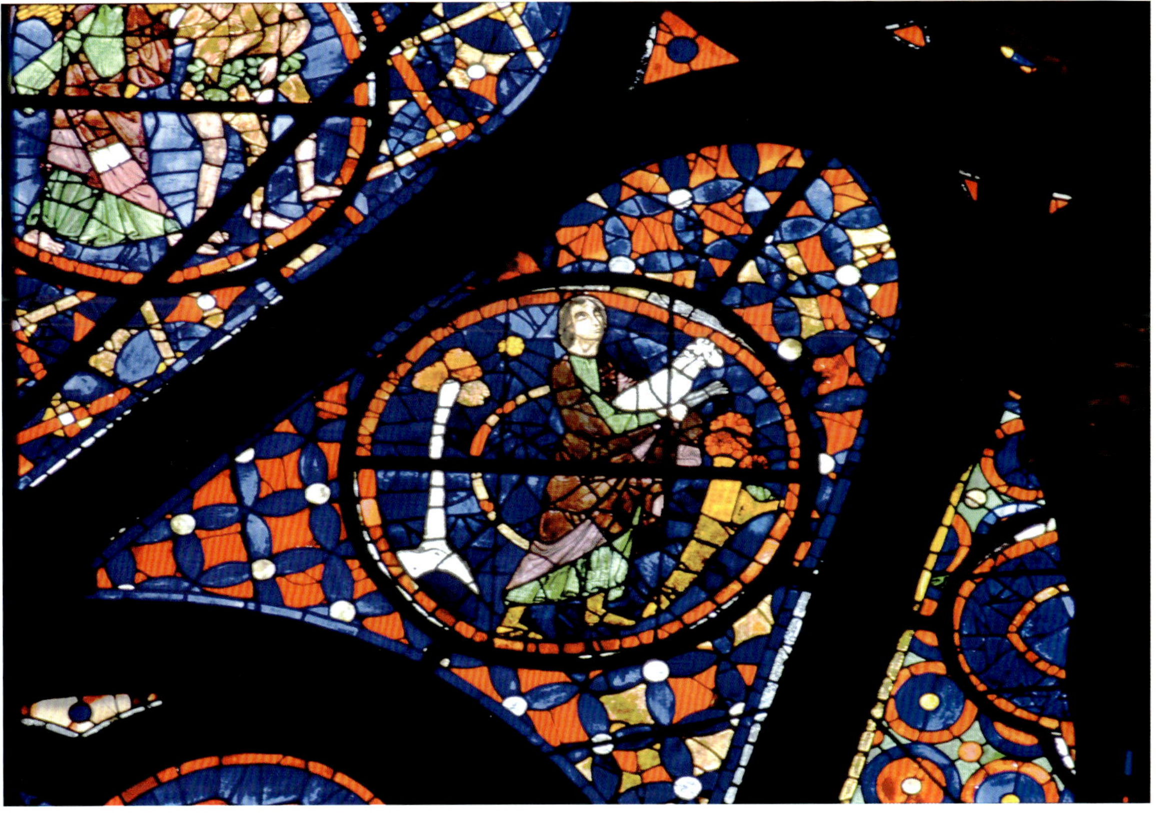

FIG. 122 Adam digging (north rose, originally I-3, now E-3).

FIG. 123 Sacrifice of Abel (north rose, H-3).

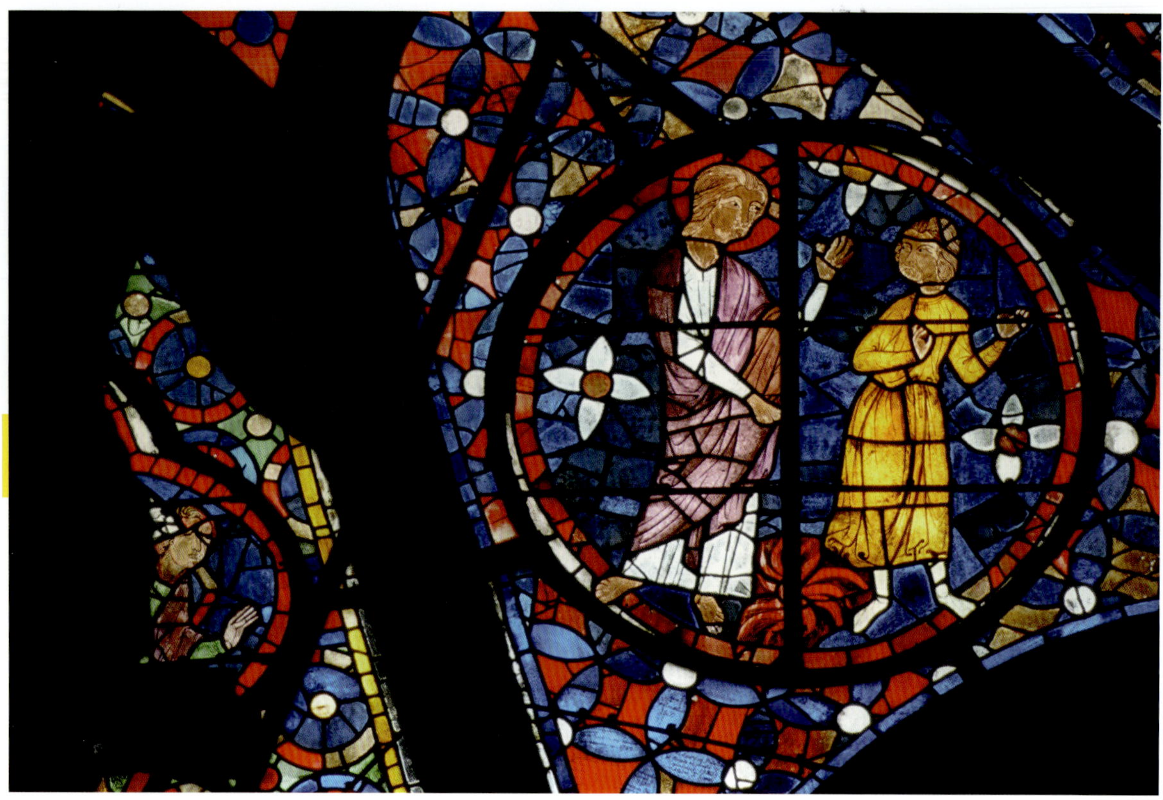

FIG. 124 God cursing Cain (north rose, F-3); both heads are original.

creation of Adam (Gen. 1:26), which immediately follows the creation of animals depicted in the outer circle of medallions and thus begins the story of mankind. The creation of Eve in A-3 follows counterclockwise, and then L-3, Adam and Eve sitting in paradise, in the order of appearance of these themes in the exterior sculpture.[26]

If a spinning movement governed the top three and the bottom three scenes, the two groups of three scenes making up the sides of the ring interrupt this motion. The left group—thus on the right hand of God (in the rose's center)—consists of K-3 (Temptation and Fall, Gen. 3:1–6); J-3 (God reproaching Adam, who cowers before him, Gen. 3:9–12, fig. 118, bottom); and I-3 (Adam digging, Gen. 3:17–19, fig. 122).[27] Thus this left trio of scenes originally presented the downward saga of Adam.

Eve's punishment was relegated to the three medallions on the right—in the less important position, at God's left hand. In C-3 was the Expulsion from Paradise (Gen. 3:24, fig. 115);[28] below it, D-3 depicts Eve seated, spinning, with a very large child squirming in her lap and attempting to nurse (fig. 125); and before 1872, E-3 contained a second seated woman nursing a younger child held horizontally like an infant (Gen. 4:1–2, fig. 126). The latter panel was removed in 1872 and installed in the ogive above the rose, between two flanking (and partly original) angels. Thus installed, it has commonly been labeled as depicting the Virgin nursing the Christchild, an identification that I believe is highly unlikely (and will oppose in arguments below). Nineteenth-century witnesses described the two women and children then in D-3 and E-3 as Eve shown twice, nursing *ses enfants,* and Étienne Povillon-Piérard in 1823 identified them as Cain and Abel, which I will argue is correct.[29]

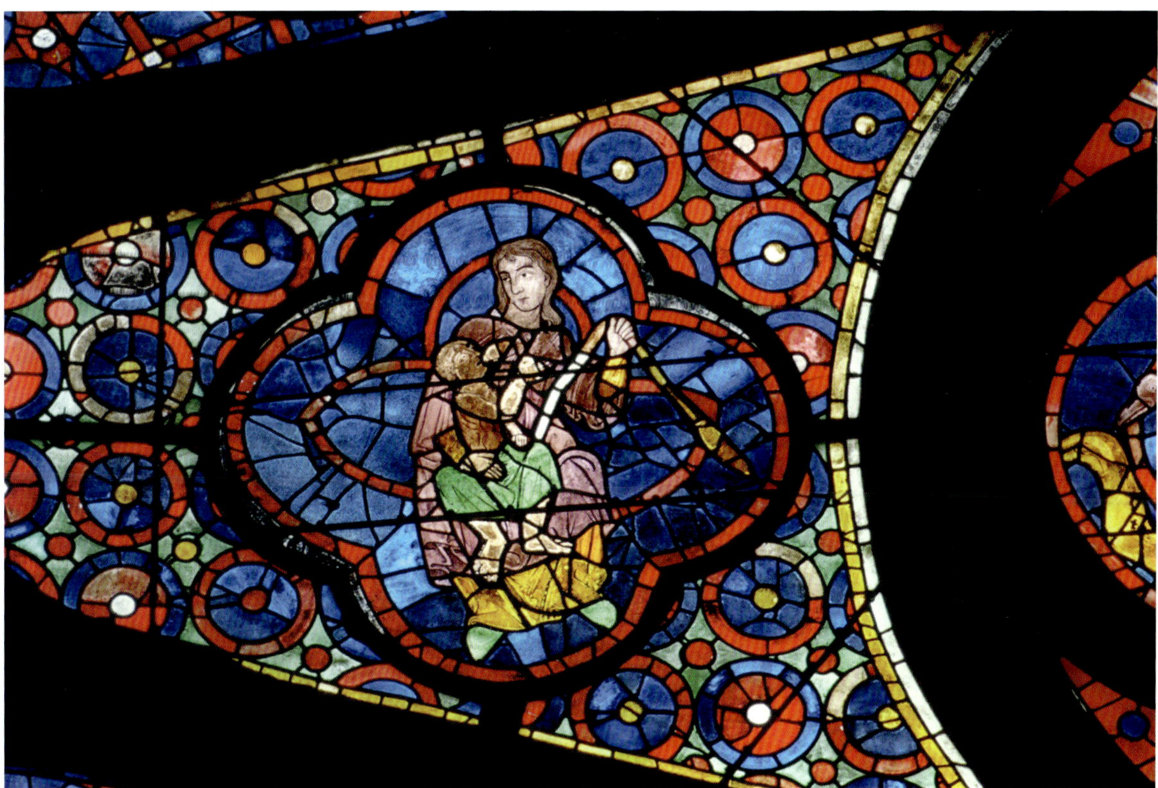

FIG. 125 Eve spinning with Cain in her lap (north rose, D-3).

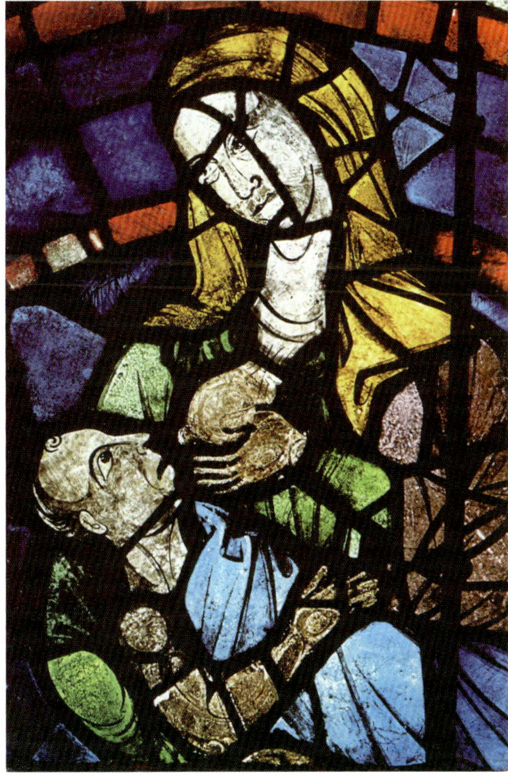

FIG. 126 Woman nursing infant, here identified as Eve nursing Abel (originally E-3, now in the ogive over the north rose).

The North Rose: Eve, Her Punishment, and the Color Yellow

The repetition of Eve in two medallions is not so surprising as one might think. What they depict, sequentially, are Eve spinning (D-3, fig. 125) and Eve's maternity (E-3, fig. 126), the two traditional "labors" that are paired with Adam's toil (digging) throughout the course of Christian art. At Auxerre cathedral, coeval with Reims and likewise in eastern France, two separate (now fragmentary) Genesis cycles in the windows of the choir aisle depict, in one case, Eve spinning and, in the other, Eve seated, holding two children.[30] Genesis 3:16–17 is the basis of Eve's maternity as toil. But Eve spinning, which may have its roots in Jewish legend, appears in art from the Early Christian period and becomes standard by the twelfth century.[31] Often she combines the two "labors," spinning and simultaneously holding or even nursing a child or children. Twelfth-century examples include relief sculpture at San Zeno, Verona, and Ferrara, as well as an image in the third English copy of the Utrecht Psalter (Paris, BnF, lat. 8846, fol. 1r).[32] This combination is increasingly common in late medieval art.

A few Gothic examples present the two distinct scenes together, one of Eve spinning and the other of Eve carrying or nursing children, and that, I propose, is what existed at Reims. One of the Moralized Bibles (Vienna, ÖNB, cod. 2554, fol. 2v, ca. 1215–30), shows, compacted within a single medallion, Eve and Adam with children to the left and, on the right, Eve spinning and Adam digging. Two separate scenes (Eve spinning and Eve's maternity) appear in the French manuscript Paris, Arsenal 3516 (figs. 138–39, to be discussed below); see also the elaborate Genesis cycles of Tours cathedral (choir windows, bay 207), Rouen cathedral (medallions of the Portail des libraires) and, in the mid–fourteenth century, Saint-Thiébaut, Thann, in Alsace (voussoirs of the portal).[33] The Genesis cycles at Tours, Rouen, and Thann are particularly extended and include rare apocryphal details that scholars have related ultimately to Jewish lore repeated in the *Book of Adam and Eve.* Linda Papanicolaou has suggested as the proximate source the Paris schoolmasters, notably Peter Comestor.[34] The Reims north rose is not such an elaborate cycle, but the point to be made here is that the themes and motifs were widespread and generally available to educated churchmen in Gothic France.

A close examination of the two Reims medallions depicting seated nursing women reinforces my identification of them both as Eve. In D-3 (Eve spinning, fig. 125), she wears a yellow robe with purple-brown mantle and green shoes; the huge child sitting in her lap wears green. The child's head is original, but Eve's was lost by the time the 1872 rubbing was made,[35] and thus it is impossible to know whether or not she was originally veiled; the large statue of the clothed Eve flanking the exterior of the rose wears a veil revealing her hair.[36] The nursing woman in the medallion from E-3 (fig. 126), now located in the ogive directly above the rose) wears a green robe with purple-brown mantle, red shoes, and a yellow veil. Her head is largely original and shows no indication that it ever was haloed or crowned. The nursing infant wears blue. His head is the restorer Oudinot's replacement, a copy of one in place that was either corroded and becoming opaque, or broken with a mending lead through it. But the replaced head by Oudinot—who had the damaged original before him—could not possibly represent the Christ-child, and moreover has no halo. While it has been argued that this woman is enthroned and thus must be the Virgin, the cushions and upper parts of the "throne" are replacements of ca. 1600 (according to Frachon's restoration diagram), and only the lower areas of tawny glass with a vegetal pattern are original.[37] The vegetal design compares with the same area flanking the legs of the nursing Eve in the Hildesheim doors, dated 1007–15, an image in the Carolingian Bible tradition.[38]

While color symbolism in the Middle Ages was far from an exact science, one might point out, without pushing it too far, that an unnimbed, uncrowned Virgin wearing a yellow veil, without blue or white on her person anywhere, is unlikely. Blue was her traditional color. Abel, the infant I believe to be represented in E-3, is in blue, and Abel was a type of Christ (as will be discussed below). The choice of yellow for Eve's robe in D-3 (fig. 125) and for the head-veil in E-3 (fig. 126) is particularly meaningful. The negative connotations of yellow have been summed up usefully by George Ferguson: "Yellow is sometimes used to suggest infernal light, degradation, jealousy, treason, and deceit. Thus, the traitor Judas is frequently painted in a garment of dingy yellow. In the Middle Ages heretics were obliged to wear yellow. In periods of plague, yellow crosses were used to identify contagious areas, and this use led to the custom of using yellow to indicate contagion."[39] According to Michel Pastoureau, the devaluation of yellow is notable from the thirteenth century on.[40] Ruth Mellinkoff has commented at length on the association of yellow with treachery, avarice, lust, and the unbelief of heretics and Jews. By the thirteenth century yellow had become the standard color for the badges that penitents and Jews were forced to wear, and the pictorial tradition of robing Judas in yellow emerges in that century, whereas prostitutes had been linked with the color yellow since ancient times. Among Mellinkoff's plethora of examples is a sermon by Berthold of Regensburg (third quarter of the thirteenth century) "in which he berated women for their extravagant dress and pointed out that none were supposed to wear yellow headbands or veils except Jewesses, prostitutes, and concubines."[41]

In the north rose of Reims, all figures of Cain (the murder of Abel; God cursing Cain, fig. 124) wear the same yellow. The medieval glazier who made those figures of Cain and who robed the figure of Eve spinning in yellow (D-3, fig. 125) would not have adorned the Virgin with a yellow head-veil. The woman in E-3 (fig. 126), I submit, was Eve, nursing Abel.

As a final argument, a nursing Virgin would be unexpected in French art as early as ca. 1240, when the north rose was conceived. Only one example (in which the Child actually feeds) is known to me, a twelfth-century stone relief from the altar of the abbey of Saint-Laurent, Liège, and it depicts both the Virgin and the Child nimbed, as expected. The theme of *Maria lactans* first becomes common in Western art in trecento Italy.[42] French scholars describe as "la Vierge allaitant le Christ" several Gothic images that, however, actually show Mary baring a breast (to the viewer) and holding a seated Child, who blesses (and does not nurse): Chenu (Sarthe), stained glass now at Rivenhall (Essex), England, ca. 1170; Chartres, bay 138, ca. 1205–15; Chartres, bay 30, ca. 1215–20; Pontigné (Maine-et-Loire), fresco, ca. 1220.[43] In such examples, both figures are nimbed and the Virgin is crowned, while the blessing Child usually holds a scroll or book. The Reims woman and nursing child are totally different from this group.

The placement since 1872 of the medallion of the seated woman nursing a child (E-3, fig. 126) in the ogive above the rose, where it is flanked by partially original angels, commonly has been accepted as appropriate for a cathedral dedicated to Notre Dame, as is Reims. However, this false Marian emphasis skews our understanding of the rose's original meaning no less than the wholesale relocation of other medallions in 1872. There is little focus on Mary—or on female saints or Old Testament heroines—in the choir, transept, or nave of Reims, either in sculpture or glass, and the Virgin's place was established only in the later development of the west facade. The pre-1872 north rose partook of this misogyny. The Eve-Mary theme did not occur in the rose, and no hint there of the Virgin interrupted the general disparagement of Eve and her rebelliousness and disobedience.

The North Rose: What Originally Filled the Ogive Above the Rose?

The flanking angels of the upper ogive, which are in part authentic, must have adored a sacred image of some kind originally.[44] If not the Virgin, then what? The creating God in the rose's central rosette (N, fig. 121), likewise adored by angels and holding the orb of the world and blessing, has a cruciferous halo in reference to the eternal composition of the triune Godhead of Christian belief. In Christian art a cruciferous halo frequently is given to the Creator. The uppermost figure of the rose itself (A-9) is also adored by angels (L-9 and B-9) and depicted, according to nineteenth-century illustrations (fig. 116), a figure of God holding a book.[45] This would be the Logos, or second person of the Trinity (John 1:1–14). The Trinity may have been completed in the ogive directly above these two images by a third manifestation of the triune God, perhaps the dove of the Holy Spirit. In an analogous manner, in the rose of the Reims west facade the upper ogive scene (Christ with the soul of the Virgin in heaven) completes the theme of the central medallion (the Virgin's Assumption).[46] In the chevet clerestories, the ogive lights over three of the five hemicycle bays contain similar images (see appendix 3): in the axial window, Bay

100, a bust of Christ, holding the orb of the world and blessing, with cruciferous halo; in Bay 101, another bust of Christ, blessing, with cruciferous halo; and in Bay 104, the dove of the Holy Ghost.[47]

In the Creation cycle of the north rose the Trinity would be on solid theological ground. Adelheid Heimann has commented on the insistence in Western Christianity, from the Council of Nicea (325 C.E.) through the Middle Ages, on a trinitarian Creator. While the pictorial tradition is inconsistent, she notes that on the Chartres north porch God is accompanied by a second figure (the Logos?) on the fifth day (when the birds and fishes were created), and on the Portail des libraires at Rouen the three divine persons appear on the sixth day to collaborate in the creation of man.[48] The creatures of the fifth and sixth days, of course, dominate the Reims north rose.

The North Rose: Types of Christ and Types of Sinners

The placement of scenes of Adam and Abel down the left, "honorable" side of the rose (fig. 112: J-3, I-3, H-3), and those of Eve and Cain along the right and at the bottom (D-3, E-3, F-3, G-3), reveals the tenor of the rose's message. Both Adam and Abel were types of Christ. The connection of Adam with Christ, the new sinless Adam, is based on St. Paul's letters to the Romans (5:12–14) and to the Corinthians (1 Cor. 15:22, 45). It appears in Augustine and other Fathers of the Church; medieval texts are numerous.[49] St. Paul also compares Abel to Christ (Heb. 12:24; cf. 11:4), and elsewhere in the New Testament, Abel is a symbol of good, and Cain of evil: Matthew 23:35, Jude 11, 1 John 3:12. Medieval texts maintain the comparison of Abel to Christ.[50]

Cain, along with Judas, was the most despised of mankind from the time of the early Church Fathers. By the thirteenth century he had come to signify a good deal more. In manuscripts of the *Somme le roi* his murder of Abel is the image illustrating felony. Mellinkoff has demonstrated that Cain had been understood for a long time as a symbol of the Jews, as well as heretics. Pearl Braude has confirmed that in France by the twelfth century Cain was the quintessential heretic, with special reference to the textile trade, as well as to those who revolted against paying tithes.[51] The Jews, in Gothic France, were associated in the minds of all with usury and were routinely grouped with heretics.[52] These three labels—murderer, heretic, usurer—had reverberated in the city of Reims throughout the 1230s, notably in relation to the wealthy merchants in the important cloth trade there (as discussed in the previous chapters and appendix 1).[53]

In sum, in the north rose Eve's appearances make no reference to her prefiguration of the Virgin. The message of the rose is otherwise: God's power and humankind's disobedience, rebellion, and sin. An examination of the outer ring of birds, fish, and animals further embroiders on these themes.

The North Rose: Birds, Fishes, Animals

The outer circle of medallions presents the creatures with which God filled the earth on the fifth and sixth days. Oudinot in 1872 created four new panels (fig. 113: A-9, B-9, C-9, F-9) and heavily retouched and rearranged almost all the others (see, e.g., fig. 127). As with the cycles of Adam and Eve and of Cain and Abel, my comments here are based on the pre-1872 locations (fig. 114). Like the inner medallions, those containing the creatures of the earth were originally arranged in trios at the top, bottom, and sides of the rose, and in a similar hierarchy. The uppermost three (fig. 112: L-9, A-9, B-9) presented the Creator, probably holding a book as the Logos (fig. 116), flanked by angels, of which the one in L-9 is partially original.[54]

The group of three medallions running down the left side of the rose, at the right hand of God (fig. 112: K-9 to I-9), presented birds—or at least winged creatures, since the first of them (originally K-9, now moved to J-9) was a winged hybrid, the griffin. The fifth day of Creation (Gen. 1:20–23) was completed by the trio of medallions running down the right side of the rose, depicting the creatures that swim in the seas (C-9 to E-9). Finally, the medallions at the bottom of the rose contained animals (F-9 to H-9), God's creation on the sixth day, preceding that of Adam (Gen. 1:24–25).

Working with the pre-1872 arrangement (fig. 114), it is clear that the creatures selected for depiction all have symbolic significance, a dimension that has not been identified previously. The creatures and their symbolism draw heavily on medieval bestiary manuscripts, both text and illustration. Though founded on ancient lore, the illustrated bestiary became particularly popular in the period from about 1180 to around 1260. It seems to have been used first in monasteries and "as an instructional tool for those who were not functionally literate."[55] The creatures of the north rose—and their meanings—would also have been familiar to its medieval audience from sermons incorporating moral-ethical lessons about God's creatures. While a particular manuscript source for Reims cannot be identified, I hypothesize below that it may have been a luxury volume in French, including a bestiary, originally in the possession of the archbishop Henri de Braine (see appendix 5).

The trio of winged creatures occupying positions of highest status (i.e., on the left, at God's right hand) commenced with a winged quadruped, the griffin (fig. 129: K-9, now in J-9). The only hybrid in the rose, the griffin combines the body of a lion with the wings and mask of an eagle. Similar griffins appear in the bestiaries (fig. 135A) and elsewhere in medieval arts. Griffins were noteworthy for their awesome power and ferocity and often were depicted attacking something (horse, boar, man, etc.).[56] King of beasts and king of birds, both the lion and the eagle were likened to Christ in their royal grandeur and were associated particularly with the Resurrection in medieval commentary, while the griffin's binary nature made it a perfect symbol of Christ. Scholars have traced the theme, which appears in Dante (*Purgatorio*, canto XXIX), to Isidore of Seville (*Etymologies*, XII); in art, griffins were associated with Christ as early as the fourth century—for example, on the Good Shepherd sarcophagus (Rome, Lateran Museums).[57] The griffin's ferocity, however, provides an emphasis on divine retribution. That emphasis is particularly pertinent to the rose's message condemning heresy, disobedience, and sin (to be discussed below).

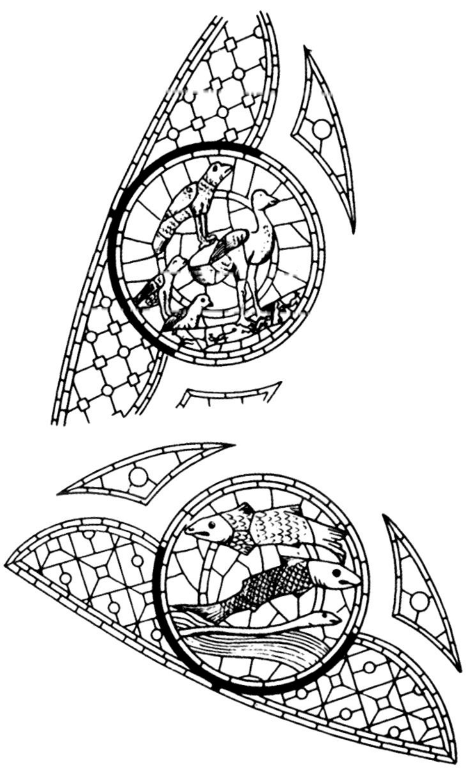

FIG. 127 North rose: caladrius and phoenix (originally J-9, now K-9); fish and eel (originally E-9, now H-9). Lithograph of tracings made after restoration by Paul Simon, ca. 1875–86. The two small birds are by Oudinot, 1872.

Following the griffin was a medallion in J-9 (now moved to K-9; see figs. 127, top, and 130) depicting a caladrius and a long-legged bird resembling a heron.[58] The caladrius (*charadrius*), a completely white bird, is described in ancient *Physiologus* texts and many medieval bestiaries (fig. 128). It is shown, labeled, in Lyon cathedral, in stained glass of 1215–20 based on a sermon by Honorius Augustodunensis taken from the bestiaries.

> There is a bird called *charadrius,* which is able to divine whether a sick person will escape death. It is placed near the sick person; if he is to die, the bird turns its head away; if he will live, the bird fixes its gaze on him and absorbs the malady into its open beak. It flies away at once into the rays of the sun, and the sickness it has absorbed oozes from it like

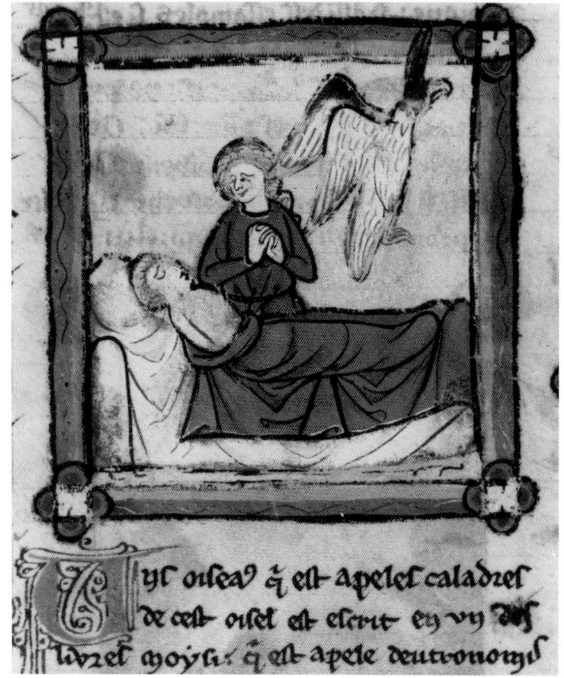

FIG. 128 Caladrius. Pierre de Beauvais's bestiary, long version (Paris, Arsenal 3516), fol. 199v.

> sweat. And the sick man is healed. The white *charadrius* is Christ born of a virgin. He came to the sick, when his Father sent him to save mankind. He turned his head away from the Jews and left them in death, but he looked toward us and carried our sickness onto the cross.[59]

Like the griffin, the caladrius represents the power of Christ, in this case the power to save and to condemn.

Accompanying the white caladrius (in addition to the two small birds added in 1872) is a long-legged, long-necked bird resembling a heron or stork (fig. 130). The coloring, however, suggests neither of these birds. While medieval bestiaries can show considerable confusion in their depiction and nomenclature, a very useful comparison is provided by a mid-thirteenth-century miniature that depicts, among other named birds, a heron (*ardea*), stork (*cyconia*), and crane (*grus*): Cambridge, University Library, Mm.v.31, folio 140r (*Apocalypse Commentary* of Friar Alexander, ca. 1250).[60] The zoologist Brunsdon Yapp has observed that herons are rare in bestiaries and that in nature the heron has "no striking colour-pattern, and is often impossible to identify in manuscripts except as an indeterminate bird that is neither a crane [larger with a bustle] nor a stork [white body, broad black edging on the wing, red bill and legs]."[61] Medieval bestiaries typically depict the heron's natural bluish gray, with lighter tones of the same on the stomach and head.

The Reims bird in figure 130 is soft purple[62] with yellow wings and white feet. I suggest that it is intended to be a phoenix, a mythological bird that has often been identified as the purple heron (*ardea purpurea*) and whose name was explained "because of its reddish purple colour (*phoeniceus*)."[63] Since no one had ever seen a phoenix, medieval illustrations of it vary considerably in shape; often the phoenix resembles an eagle, swan, or even a crow, and sometimes it has a peacock's crest (fig. 135C). Most texts, ancient and medieval, avoid the issue by omitting a description and refer to the phoenix simply as a "bird." In many medieval images the color is a pinkish brown or brown.[64] The pale purple and yellow coloration of the bird at Reims derives from a tradition as old as the fourth-century poem by Lactantius, *De Ave Phoenice,* where an extended description of the phoenix, a cross between peacock and pheasant, includes the following details: "Her color is like that of the tender pomegranate seeds. . . . Her tail is . . . marked by metallic yellow, on which a scarlet mixture blushes."[65] The purple-yellow color combination survives in Brunetto Latini (d. 1295), *Li livres dou tresor:* "The feathers around its neck are shiny like fine Arabian gold, but below that as far as its tail it is purple in color, and its tail is pink."[66] While I have not found a phoenix depicted with as long legs as those of the Reims bird, it is clearly a "purple heron," and there was a tradition, recorded in the twelfth-century Vienna *Physiologus,* that the phoenix was "tall in stature."[67]

The phoenix was from earliest Christian times a symbol of the Resurrection, since this mythological creature periodically burned itself up and rose from the ashes.[68] The association of the phoenix with the caladrius in the same medallion at Reims would be particularly apt, as they were symbols respectively of Christ's Resurrection and of his Ascension (the caladrius absorbs the sick person's disease and flies to the sun).

The third medallion devoted to winged creatures in the north rose (fig. 131: originally I-9, now moved to D-9) depicts a crane (*grue*). This Reims bird is identified as an ibis or an ostrich in numerous publications, but it does not resemble either of those birds in medieval manuscripts.[69] It has the characteristic "bustle" and is without much doubt a crane (cf. fig. 135D). The *grue* (crane) is noted for vigilance, loyalty, and good works and likened to "those who by righteous living form within themselves the teachings of Scripture," such as the priest whose good example and sermons "demonstrate to his followers the path of good behavior."[70] Its location in the rose, as the lowest of the winged creatures, placed it below the more exalted symbols of Christ, and appropriately the griffin, caladrius, and phoenix face in toward the Creator, while the crane is turned left, out toward the world. Moreover, in its original location (I-9) the crane adjoined the goat, dog, and stag in H-9, the symbolism of which similarly emphasized the Church's care of souls (as will be discussed below).

But before the animals were created, there were the fish. The trio of winged creatures described above, originally in K-9, J-9, and I-9, was balanced by three medallions of sea creatures on the right side of the rose. Surviving are a panel of three fish (D-9, now moved to G-9) and a panel of an eel and two fish (figs. 127, bottom, and 132: E-9, now in H-9).[71] While fish are not allotted much attention in bestiaries, the twelfth-century Cambridge manuscript says of their virtues, "Fish do not seek to live without Water. . . . It is their nature that, if separated from the sea, they die immediately."[72] This observation suggests the theme of baptism, for as the fish cannot live except in water, the true Christian cannot live save through the waters of baptism.[73] The original location of the fish is significant, adjoining the three scenes emphasizing Eve's punishment: Expulsion from Paradise (C-3), Eve spinning (D-3), Eve's maternity (E-3). Fish were believed to propagate chastely, without semen: "An antiseptic birthing process [eggs laid in water] provides additional grounds for a positive moral view of fish, probably because it contrasts with the bloody, painful method suffered by Eve and all of her female descendants as punishment befitting the Transgression."[74] Also noteworthy is the original location of the eel in E-9, lowest of the three fish medallions, where it adjoined E-3, which I have identified as Eve nursing Abel. The Cambridge bestiary notes that *Enguillae* (eels) are similar to snakes,[75] suggesting an additional reference, to Genesis 3:15: "I will put enmities between thee [the serpent] and the woman . . . ; she shall crush thy head, and thou shalt lie in wait for her heel." Furthermore, in the panel of three fish (originally at D-9), the central fish is much larger and swims in the opposite direction from the other two. The Cambridge bestiary recounts that great fish eat smaller ones, an idea seized upon in the Moralized Bibles, where the former—the great fish—signify usurers: "Li gros poisson senefie les gros usuriers qui mainiuent les petiz, ce sunt la pouvre gent"; "Magni pisces significant magnos feneratores per quos minimi pauperes devorantur."[76] And usury, as noted in the chevet program and elsewhere (see below), was in the eyes of the Church one of the main sins of the rich citizenry of Reims.

Finally, the animals. Of the trio of animal medallions originally at the bottom of the rose, two survive: a medallion of a stag, dog, and goat (fig. 134: originally H-9, now moved to E-9),[77] and that of an ox and ass (fig. 133: originally F-9, now I-9). Since antiquity the stag was described as an enemy to serpents (fig. 135E); thus it can serve as a symbol of Christ, enemy of the devil.[78] In many bestiaries the stag is equated with good Christians, devoted to the holy Church. The stag swallows the snake (sin), which poisons him, but he runs straight for the fountain (Christ, Ps. 41:2) and drinks deep to be saved; and he casts off his antlers (pride) completely.[79] If the stag is equated with the good Christian, the dog (*canis*) in the bestiary is a

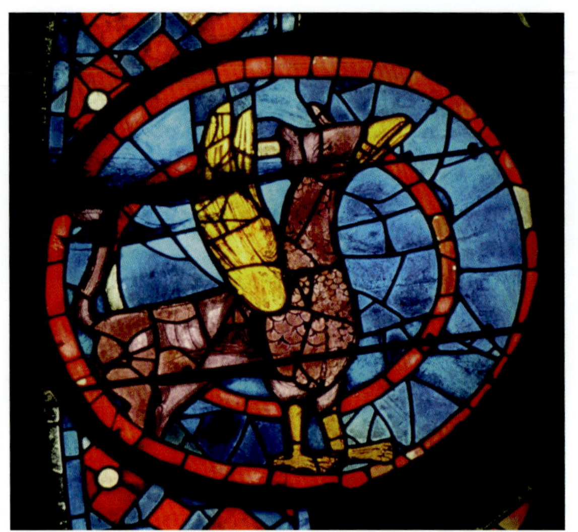

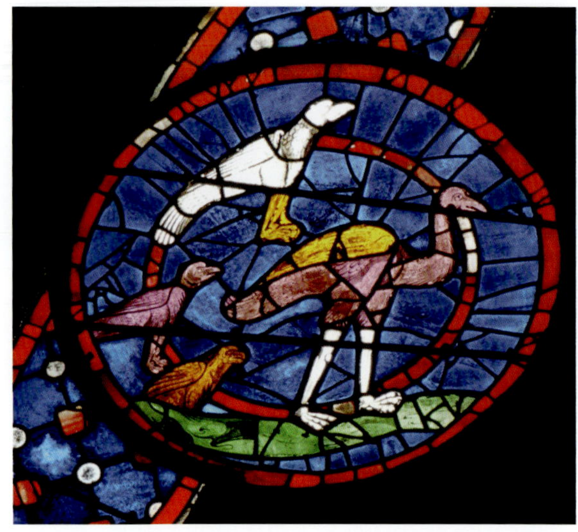

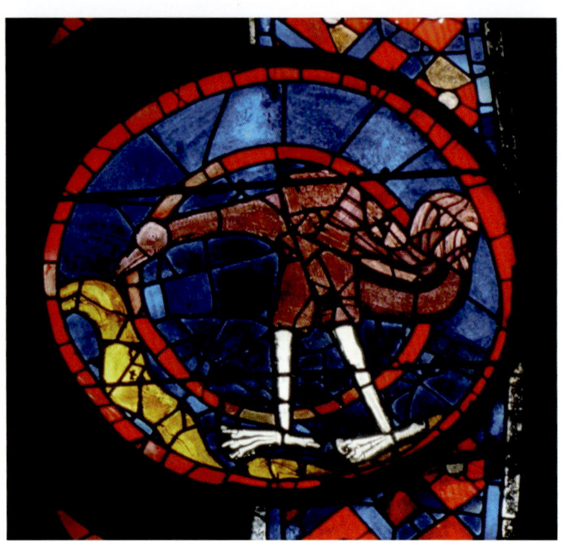

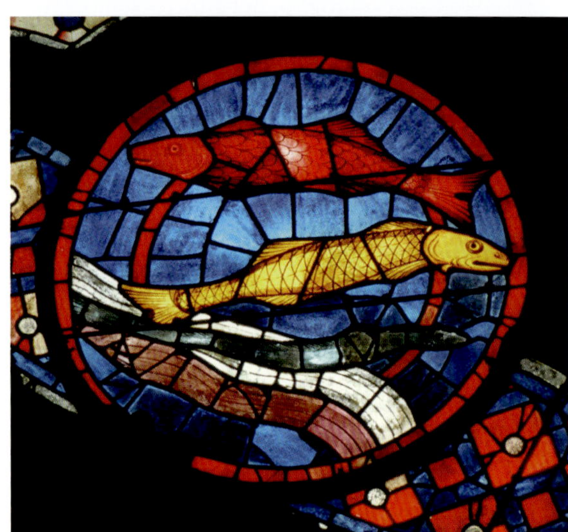

FIG. 129 Griffin (north rose, originally K-9, now J-9).

FIG. 130 Caladrius and phoenix (north rose, originally J-9, now K-9).

FIG. 131 Crane (north rose, originally I-9, now D-9).

FIG. 132 Fish and eel (north rose, originally E-9, now H-9).

creature of watchfulness and fidelity, that is, the priest: "Priests are like watchdogs. They always drive away the wiles of the trespassing Devil with admonishments—and by doing the right thing—lest he should steal away the treasury of God, i.e., the souls of Christians. The tongue of a dog cures a wound by licking it. This is because the wounds of sinners are cleansed, when they are laid bare in confession, by the penance imposed by the Priest."[80] If the stag symbolizes the Christian faithful, and the dog the priest, the inclusion of the goat with them in the same medallion seems, at first, surprising. Goats are associated with the damned of the Last Judgment and have a bad reputation generally. The bestiary, however, distinguishes between the domestic goat (*hircus,* he-goat) and the wild goat (*caper* or *dorcon,* fig. 135F).[81] The description of the *caper* usually follows directly after that of the stag. Terence H. White's translation of the Cambridge bestiary states:

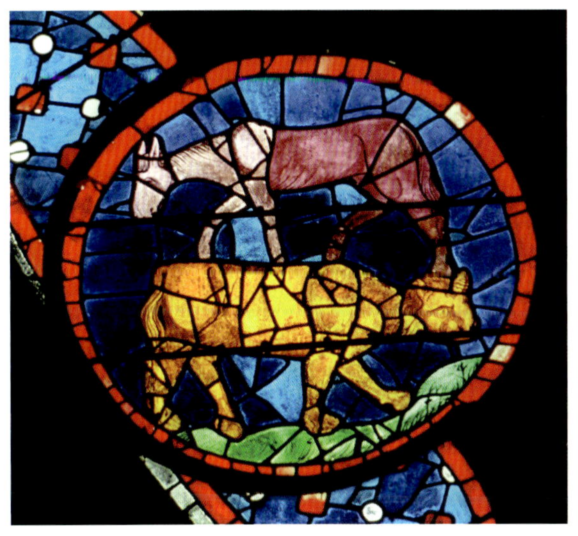

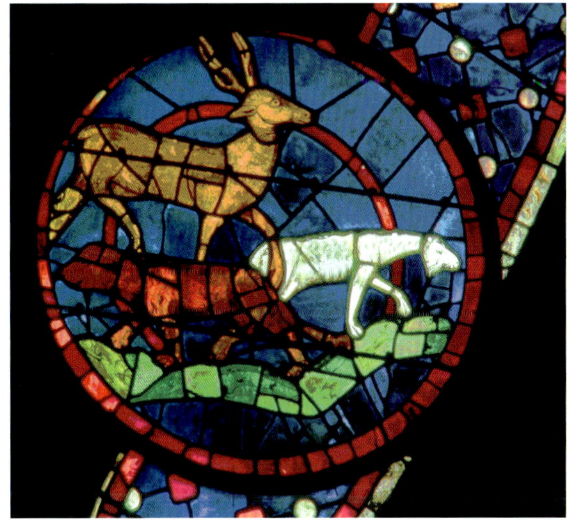

FIG. 133 Ox and ass (north rose, originally F-9, now I-9).

FIG. 134 Stag, dog, and wild goat (north rose, originally H-9, now E-9).

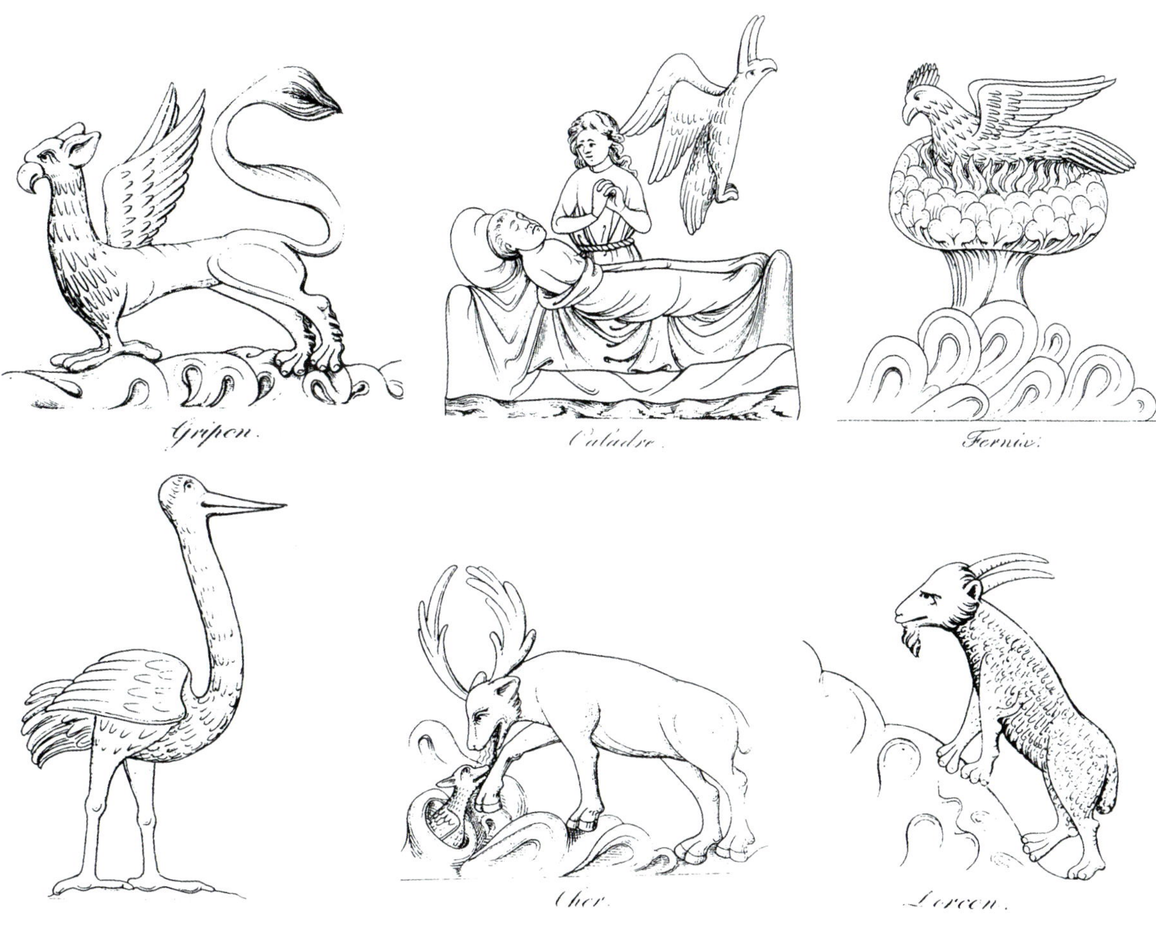

FIG. 135 Bestiary creatures: (A) griffin, (B) caladrius, (C) phoenix, (D) crane, (E) stag, (F) wild goat. Pierre de Beauvais's bestiary, long version (Paris, Arsenal 3516). Drawings, ca. 1850 (after Charles Cahier and Arthur Martin, *Mélanges d'archéologie, d'histoire et de littérature*, vol. 2, 1851).

> Caper the Goat is an animal who . . . strives to attain the mountain crags. . . . These linger on the highest mountains and can recognize approaching people from far away, distinguishing the wayfarer from the sportsman. Thus Our Lord Jesus Christ is partial to high mountains, i.e. to Prophets and Apostles. . . . Our Lord is pastured in the Church—you see, the good works of Christians are food for him. . . . Because the sharpness of a goat's eyes is very acute, and they see everything and know men from afar, this symbolizes Our Lord, who is the Lord God of all knowing. . . . [W]hen the High God looks down to the humble and gazes upon the haughty from afar—he who created all things and founded and knows absolutely anything which arises in our hearts—then indeed that Holy Goat [!] does recognize the approaching sportsman from afar.[82]

The medallion of the stag, dog, and goat (fig. 134) was located in H-9, adjacent to the scene of Abel's offering to God, and appropriately it presented themes of the faithful, their priests of the Church, and the "Holy Goat" himself.

The final medallion (I-9, originally F-9) depicted the ox and ass (fig. 133). The main reference is undoubtedly to their presence at the Nativity, where these humble creatures recognized the newborn Jesus as the Son of God, fulfilling Isaiah 1:3: "the ox knoweth his owner and the ass his master's crib." The long-suffering patience, humbleness, and usefulness of these work-animals are paramount in bestiary commentary. An extended discussion of their symbolism can be found in a luxurious bestiary in Oxford (Bodleian, MS Bodley 764, ca. 1240–60): "Oxen in scripture can mean many things," among them "the strength and labours of the preachers, the humility of the Israelites."[83] Although the ass, like the goat, could carry positive or negative connotations,

> in spiritual terms the ass, being a brutish and lecherous creature, signifies the pagan people over whom the Lord was thought worthy to preside when He entered Jerusalem, making them subject to Him, and leading them to the heavenly country. . . . So the pagans whom the Lord ransomed with the price of His blood were beforehand like brutish and lecherous animals, ignorant of reason. Now indeed they have become strong, subjecting the hidden things of the mind to our Saviour, and by setting their neck under the Redeemer's dominion, they bear the yoke of the teaching of the Gospel. They are made to bring tribute, offering to Christ their King the good works of faith and gifts of good things.[84]

The reference to tribute, offerings, and gifts to Christ underlines yet another aspect of the symbolism of Cain, false tithing (to be discussed below). The original location of the medallion of the ox and ass (fig. 133), on the lower right side of the rose, was immediately adjacent to the final scene of the Genesis narrative in which God curses Cain (F-3, fig. 124). Their humility contrasts with Cain's pride, their enduring submission with his arrogant rebellion. That is the key to the message of the north rose of Reims.

The Message of the North Rose in Context

In sum, the drastic 1872 relocations of scenes in the north rose garbled the original iconographic program and, with the relocation of the panel I have identified as Eve nursing Abel (E-3, fig. 126) to the ogive crowning the rose, introduced a false Marian cast to that program. The main themes, as originally stated by the selection of scenes and their careful arrangement and juxtaposition, were (a) the awesome power of the Creator and (b) the culpability of humankind in the grievous saga of disobedience, rebellion, and sin. As noted above, this presentation of the Genesis story differs markedly from the sculptural cycle ornamenting the exterior of the same rose. The latter is a more positive presentation of the story of the origins of mankind, underlining the progeny of Adam and Eve and their development of crafts, mechanical arts, and occupations common to us all, especially pertinent in a civic context. Between the creation of the rose's sculptural rim and its stained glass, there is a shift in focus.

What might be responsible for this shift? Although neither the sculpture nor glass is dated in documents, we can reasonably suppose that the former preceded the latter; the architectural framework of the north-transept facade must have been in place and the tracery of the rose designed in order to provide the measurements needed for making the stained glass. Although a date in the 1240s or early 1250s has been proposed for the upper level of the north facade by Kurmann, Kimpel and Suckale have argued for its completion before the interruption of construction during the period of civic strife in Reims ca. 1233–38.[85] They argue that, during the period between those dates, the cathedral masons would have moved elsewhere to find work and would have produced during that time a small version of the Reims north rose (and many other architectural and sculptural details of *rémois* imprint) in the parish church of Notre-Dame, Cluny, which was rebuilt after a fire in 1233.[86] The early date seems reasonable, since the Reims north rose is set firmly in a solid masonry wall and within a heavily sculpted relieving arch, as previously were the west and east roses of the cathedral of Laon, suffragan of Reims. I have argued elsewhere that the early date also accords well with the general development of centripetal rose tracery in Gothic architecture.[87] The sculpture surrounding the Reims north rose has been dated before 1241 by Willibald Sauerländer on stylistic grounds.[88]

The stained glass of the rose may or may not have been installed for the ceremony of September 7, 1241, when the canons took possession of "their new choir." It seems more reasonable to hypothesize that, following Henri de Braine's demise in mid-1240, their attention and that of whatever craftsmen they could find would have been directed to completing the chevet glazing and at least some of the transept grisailles for that occasion. Although scholars have theorized that "their new choir" refers to the present location of the stalls in the three eastern bays of the nave, the glass in those bays is clearly later. On balance, the north rose—and the lost south rose to follow—were most likely projects of the early 1240s. Between 1241 and 1245 the canons would have had the time—not to mention freedom from a difficult archbishop's interference—to conceive and see to execution the complicated and sophisticated iconographic program that forms the subject of this chapter. In any case the north rose's Genesis program, so markedly different from that of its sculptural surround, clearly reflects a reinterpretation, a new mood following the period of strife of the 1230s. Disobedience, rebellion, and the need for repentance were the message of those years.

The civic unrest in Reims during the 1230s (outlined in chapter 1) provided a main theme for the chevet glazing during that decade (as discussed in chapters 2–3). The merchants of Reims achieved their wealth in the production of linen textiles, and among their lucrative business ventures was moneylending to other communes. The conflation of usury with heresy and the increasing persecution of both can be traced from 1230. By the mid-1230s, the infamous inquisitor Robert le Bougre had burned groups as close to Reims as Châlons-en-Champagne, and the bourgeois uprising in Reims had sent the canons and archbishop into exile. Three years of stiff fines were imposed by the king in 1236, followed by public penance upon the canons' return from exile in 1237. In 1238 the merchants refused to make the final payment owed to the archbishop; his resort to armed force sparked the civic violence that concluded with his renewed exile and excommunication of the city. This time the canons remained there, behind locked doors. The themes of the north rose—disobedience, rebellion, and sin—suggest that it represents the mood of the cathedral chapter following the second reconciliation, on August 15, 1240. Quickly following Henri de Braine's death, in June the chapter and bourgeois made peace, the ringleaders of the opposition to the archbishop underwent ceremonial public flogging, and the excommunication was lifted by the canons, acting *sede vacante*. The final payment of the fine, however, had not been paid, and it still remained unpaid when in 1245 the pope imposed the next archbishop, Juhel de Mathefelon. This explains the emphasis on Cain in the rose.

Pearl Braude's study of the sacrifice of Cain and Abel has established that Cain was connected with the Jews as early as St. Ambrose, and with heresy by Prudentius. Evasion of the tithe was later added to these evils. By the twelfth century, "Cain's offering came to symbolize not only the heretic but an evil-minded and niggardly attitude towards the Church which resulted in falsifying the amount due [in tithing]."[89] By the time Jewish moneylending was coming under violent attack in the thirteenth century, the conflation of heresy, miserliness, and usury was complete. Moreover, in the mid–twelfth century heresy had become associated specifically with weavers and cloth merchants. St. Bernard, in Sermon 65 on the Song of Songs, specifies *textores* and *textrices*.[90] To the canons of Reims, Cain would have seemed the obvious symbol of the *rémois* insurgents: wealthy cloth merchants, active in moneylending, who defied the Church and refused to pay their fines.

The sculptural program of the exterior archivolts of the north rose (fig. 117) undoubtedly was established, and work at least begun, before the exile of the canons in late 1234. Its positive civic message reflects the aspirations of the urban community with no hint as yet of the impending storm. Upon the canons' return, in early 1237, when fines and public penance were first extracted from the humbled insurgents, whatever program had been intended for the stained glass of the north rose may have been reconsidered. The murder of the archbishop's marshal had occurred in 1235, the burghers' refusal to pay the final installment of the imposed fine in the autumn of 1238, and the archbishop's subsequent second flight later that year. The program of the rose's glass—with its heavy emphasis on God's omnipotence and mankind's disobedience, rebellion, and sin, culminating in the first murder—might have been rethought as early as 1239, while the town was still under interdict. Conditions under excommunication, however, would suggest that it was not yet installed at the moment the ringleaders were ritually flogged on the cathedral *parvis* (August 15, 1240), and probably not yet completed in the hasty work undertaken to open the new church construction to the cult on September 7, 1241. It seems reasonable, however, to date the installation of the north-rose glazing well before the third payment on the fine was finally extracted from the merchants by the new archbishop, with the pope's backing, in 1245.[91]

The North-Rose Program and the Idea of a Bestiary

This dating, before 1245, is supported by the unusual combination of Genesis scenes and beasts found in the rose. The bestiary featured in the north rose is unique in cathedral glazing. Bestiaries generally have been associated with monastic, not cathedral, usage. While all the creatures of the north rose appear in the most extended of the so-called Second-Family Latin texts, such books remained monastic, and "there is strong circumstantial evidence of a lack of interest in Bestiaries in secular cathedrals in general. No surviving Bestiary can be localized to such a foundation."[92] God's creation of animals and birds, moreover, is conspicuously absent from the sculpted Genesis cycle framing the rose's exterior, discussed earlier. Thus it is a legitimate question to ponder what sort of stimulus might have spurred a bestiary theme in the new program of the rose glazing ca. 1240.

I suggest that a luxury manuscript owned by Archbishop Henri de Braine became available to the cathedral chapter upon his death and that it contained an illustrated copy of the French bestiary composed by Pierre de Beauvais and dedicated to his patron, the prelate's uncle and mentor, Bishop Philippe of Beauvais (see appendix 5). The uncle's extensive library had been left by testament to Henri. The dedication of Pierre's bestiary to Bishop Philippe is preserved in many exemplars of the work, while another is dedicated to Philippe's brother—and Archbishop Henri's father—Count Robert II de Dreux, suggesting that copies may have been made for various members of the family. Pierre de Beauvais composed for Count Robert another work, his *Mappemonde,* and in 1212 he wrote *La translation et miracles de saint Jacques* by order of Robert's countess—and Archbishop Henri's mother—Yolande de Coucy (see appendix 4). It is not an unreasonable hypothesis that the archbishop owned a copy of Pierre de Beauvais's *Bestiaire* and that upon his death, unexpected and in exile, his books could have become available to the canons, who were then in residence in Reims.

What makes this hypothesis worth arguing is the close visual similarity of the Genesis medallions in the Reims north rose to the Genesis illustrations found in a manuscript that also contains the earliest surviving exemplar of the "long version" of Pierre's *Bestiaire* (Paris, Arsenal 3516). As discussed in appendix 5, several important links are missing in this chain of connections. Pierre's *Bestiaire* exists in a "short version" (dated before 1217) and a "long version" (now dated after 1246), the precise relationship of which remains a matter of conjecture.

Thus the visual conformity of the Genesis cycles in the Reims north rose and in Arsenal 3516, while puzzling, is potentially significant. As Patricia Stirnemann has put it, "Textual historians are interested in retrieving the purest possible text, in tracing textual transmission, and in editing library inventories; the visual historian has ways, as yet not fully appreciated, of contributing to the history of text, to the history of libraries, and indeed, to history. . . . In some cases, the art historian can provide relationships for later manuscripts that will bear on the history of transmission."[93] In that spirit I offer the following observations.

The Genesis miniatures in Arsenal 3516 illustrate "l'estoire d'Adan" (fols. 4r–6v), part of the *Bible anonyme,* a twelfth-century work by an unnamed monk of Saint-Denis—the abbey where Pierre de Beauvais tells us that he often did research. The conjunction of the bestiary and Genesis story is explained by Ron Baxter's study of the ways the bestiary evolved from the *Physiologus* in the twelfth century. One development was the rearrangement of chapters "in increasingly legible orders to users familiar with the Genesis myth."[94] Baxter also notes that the *Physiologus* was a treatise on virtue and vice, that heresy was "the vice *par excellence,*" and that "the issue of heresy is explicitly . . . and implicitly [addressed in many chapters] . . . which combine the rehearsal of issues of dogma with exhortations to remain in the Catholic and Apostolic church."[95] In other words, canons educated in the early thirteenth century would, it seems likely, quickly connect a bestiary manuscript with both Genesis and heresy, the two themes that are paramount and tightly intertwined in the north-rose program of Reims.

Pierre's bestiary contains neither the ox and ass nor fish (found in the north rose), while the "short version" available to Archbishop Henri also omits the griffin and crane.[96] These inconsistencies constitute not as much of a difficulty as it might seem. It is the concept of the bestiary that has been adopted in the rose—that is, the use of God's creation of beasts, birds, and so forth, in Genesis for moralizing purposes. The precise examples would have been familiar to any educated person of the time, from Isidore's *Etymologies,* Pliny the Elder's *Historia naturalis,* Ambroise's *Hexameron,* not to forget the Bible. Willene Clark's authoritative study of these sources underlines the point that many of them were basic school texts.[97]

The following list of similarities between the Genesis scenes in the north rose and the illuminations of the *Histoire d'Adam* in Arsenal 3516 is provided in the hope that their close visual similarities may stimulate further investigation by specialists in French texts:

- fol. 4r (fig. 136): Temptation and Fall. Adam and Eve, standing, flanking the tree of knowledge, Eve plucking the apple, and both covering themselves with fig leaves. Cf. the north rose panel K-3 (fig. 118, middle panel). Only the lower half of this panel, which resembles the miniature, survived to the nineteenth century. The upper half, which was

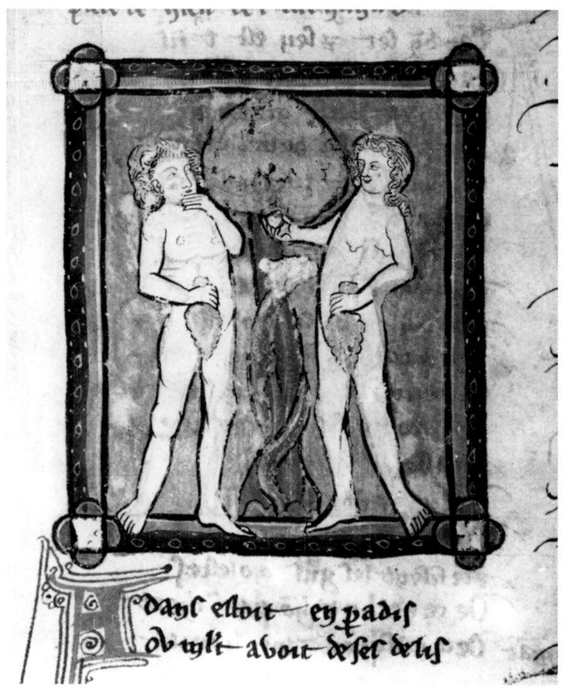

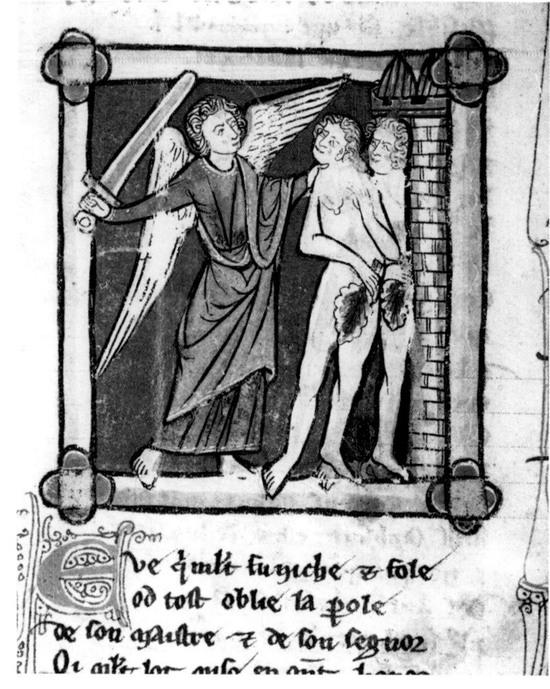

FIG. 136 Temptation and Fall. "L'estoire d'Adan" (Paris, Arsenal 3516), fol. 4r.

FIG. 137 Expulsion from Paradise. "L'estoire d'Adan" (Paris, Arsenal 3516), fol. 4v.

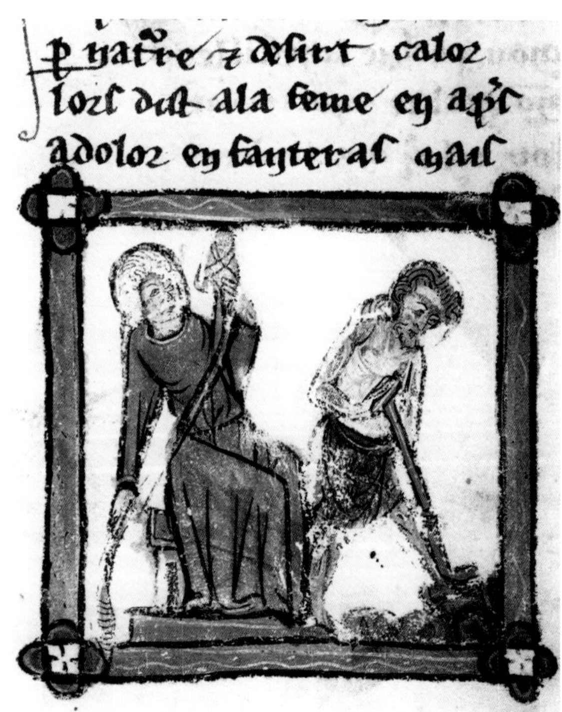

FIG. 138 Adam digging and Eve spinning. "L'estoire d'Adan" (Paris, Arsenal 3516), fol. 5r.

by that era filled with a stopgap, was replaced by Oudinot in 1872.

- fol. 4v (fig. 137): Expulsion from Paradise. An angel raises a sword (left); Eve and Adam move to the right. Cf. the rose panel I-3, originally in C-3 (fig. 115, bottom, tracing made after the 1872 restoration). The arrangement of figures is very close. As the heads and much of the upper bodies of Adam and Eve were restored in 1872, it is impossible to know whether Eve was originally next to the angel, as in the miniature.
- fol. 5r (fig. 138): Adam digging (right) and Eve spinning (left). Cf. the rose panel E-3, originally in I-3, which shows Adam digging (fig. 122). He wears more clothes but otherwise is very close to the figure in the miniature. The image of Eve spinning is the only one of the miniature scenes that has been significantly expanded in the rose, where the quatrefoil at D-3 shows her spinning but with the addition of a very large toddler, Cain, in her lap (fig. 125). This addition no doubt results from the emphasis on Cain and sin in the rose program.
- fol. 5r (fig. 139, top): Eve's maternity. Eve is in

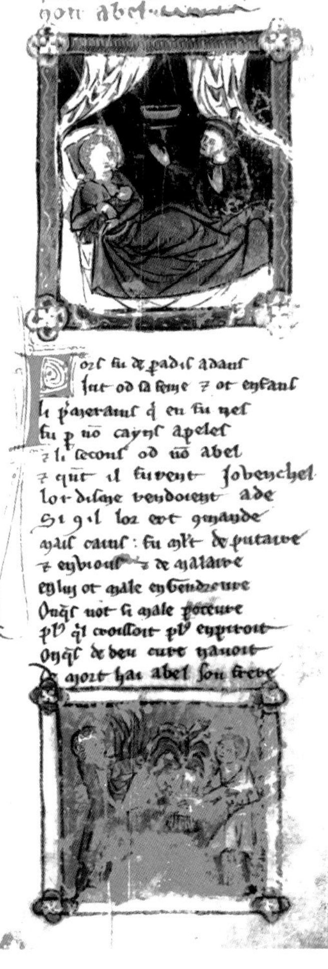

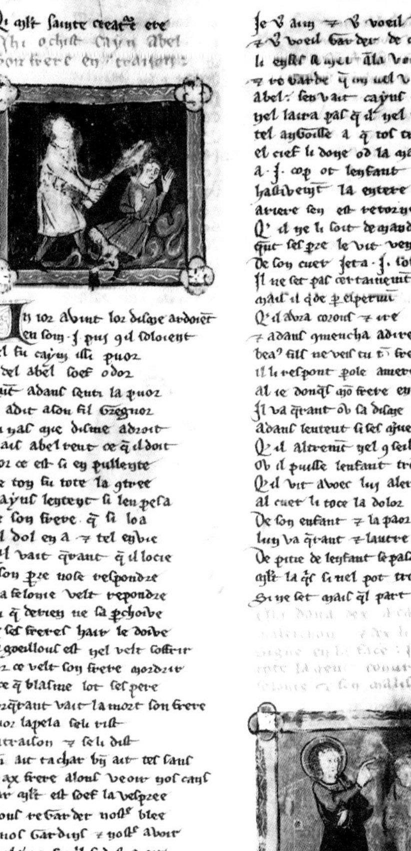

FIG. 139 Eve's maternity; Sacrifice of Cain and Abel. "L'estoire d'Adan" (Paris, Arsenal 3516), fol. 5r

FIG. 140 Cain murdering Abel; God cursing Cain. "L'estoire d'Adan" (Paris, Arsenal 3516), fol. 5v.

childbed, nursing a babe, while Adam sits to the right. Both Cain and Abel are mentioned in the text. Cf. the rose's image that I have identified as Eve nursing Abel (M-9, originally E-3), notably the profile head of the nursing babe-in-arms (fig. 126).

- fol. 5r (fig. 139, bottom): Sacrifices of Cain (right) and Abel (left). Each holds up his offering. The rose's panel of Abel's sacrifice is very similar (fig. 123, H-3).
- fol. 5v (fig. 140, top left): Cain (left) murders Abel, who is crumpling to the right. The rose's panel G-3 is very similar (fig. 119).
- fol. 5v (fig. 140, bottom right): God (left) curses Cain (right), who gestures to the right. The rose's panel F-3 is very similar (fig. 124).

Considering the long tradition and the variety and popularity of these scenes in medieval art, the similarities in the choice of scenes as well as in their visual arrangement in Arsenal 3516 and the Reims rose cannot, I believe, be fortuitous. The Arsenal volume is well over a generation later than the original lost bestiary manuscript made by Pierre de Beauvais for Philippe de Dreux and, in its present mutilated form, a less luxurious work than one would suppose such a volume to have been. But its evidence suggests that Philippe's book or a copy made for his family, probably lavishly illuminated and presumably bound with the *Histoire d'Adam,* inspired the north rose.

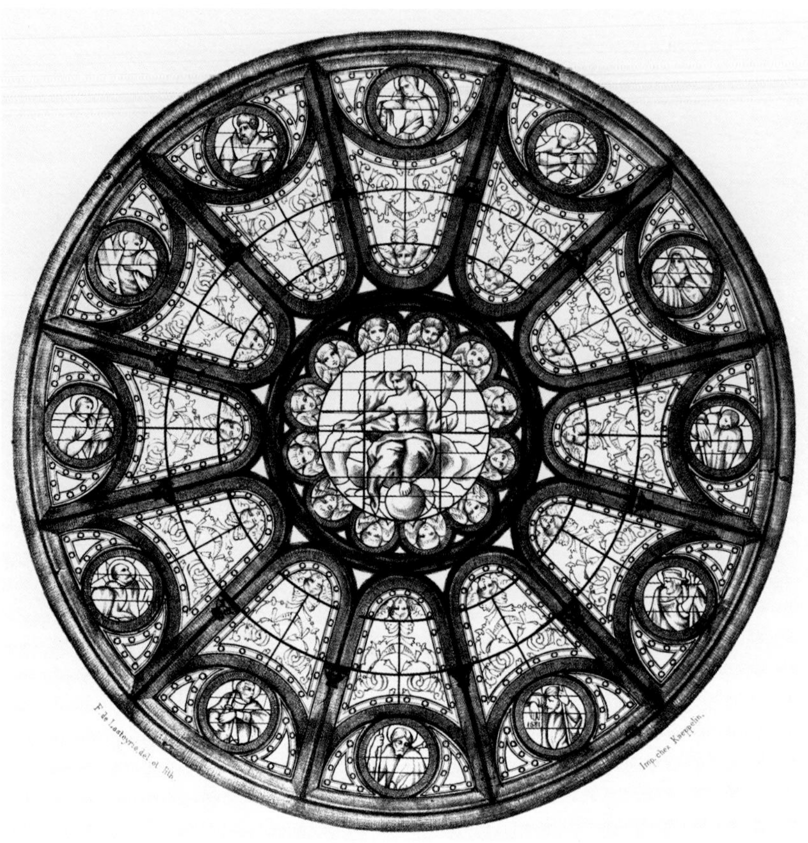

FIG. 141 South rose (lost). Glazing of 1581 by Nicolas Dérodé; drawing by Ferdinand de Lasteyrie, ca. 1850 (after Lasteyrie, *Histoire de la peinture sur verre*).

The Lost South Rose

The south rose of Reims was blown out in a storm in 1580[98] and received new glass by Nicolas Dérodé the following year (fig. 141). Dérodé's rose was destroyed in World War I, and new glazing was made by Jacques Simon in 1936. Ravaux points out, on the basis of the accounts of early writers, that the original stone tracery was also lost and replaced in 1581.[99] This was apparently well known in the nineteenth century but had been ignored in more recent scholarship. In my study of centripetal rose windows I proposed that the lost tracery of the south rose developed the form introduced by the Reims north rose, and influenced the designs of several later roses, notably the north rose of Châlons-en-Champagne, the transept rose of Burgos, and the tympanum rose of the Reims west facade.[100] Like these three surviving rose traceries, the original masonry of the Reims south rose was undoubtedly more elaborate than its sixteenth-century replacement and provided smaller areas for more numerous glass medallions than at present. Dérodé's rose that was destroyed in World War I is known from a drawing published in 1853 by Ferdinand de Lasteyrie (fig. 141). It depicted Christ enthroned in the center, surrounded by cherubim, the "petals" of the rose filled with a circle of heads and with large areas of foliate ornament, and finally a circumferential ring of the apostles. These themes probably reflect but also simplify the original rose program.

There are two additional clues to that program. The first lies in the sculpture surrounding the exterior of the south rose, in the same location as on the north. Just as the north rose's archivolt sculpture has a Genesis theme (fig. 117), maintained some years later in the glass (though with a different emphasis), it is likely that the sculpture surrounding the south rose also related to the glass of that rose (fig. 142). Two large standing figures, one to each side of the rose, depict Ecclesia and Synagoga (cf. Adam and Eve on the north). Above them in the archivolt framing the rose are eleven apostles and a number of Old Testament worthies including Moses, Job, and Jonah.[101]

The north rose of the cathedral of Châlons (figs. 143, 144), which copies and elaborates the tracery of the south rose of Reims, also probably reflects its original iconographic program.[102] Many of its subjects also appear in the sculpture of the Reims south rose as well as in Dérodé's later glass. Large stained-glass figures of Ecclesia and Synagoga fill the pierced spandrels below the Châlons rose, translating those motifs of the Reims south rose from the medium of sculpture into glass. Apostles fill the triforium lancets below the Châlons rose, like those in the archivolts of the Reims south rose and again in Dérodé's glazing. Prophets appear in the lights between the triforium and the rose at Châlons, recalling the Old Testament figures in the Reims archivolt. The center of the Châlons rose contains Christ in Majesty, large areas in the "petals" are filled with foliage, and a circle of heads frames the circumference, all found as well in the Dérodé glazing at Reims.

FIG. 142 Exterior of south rose: Ecclesia (left), Synagoga (right), eleven apostles, and Old Testament figures (archivolt above). The tracery was remade after the 1580 storm.

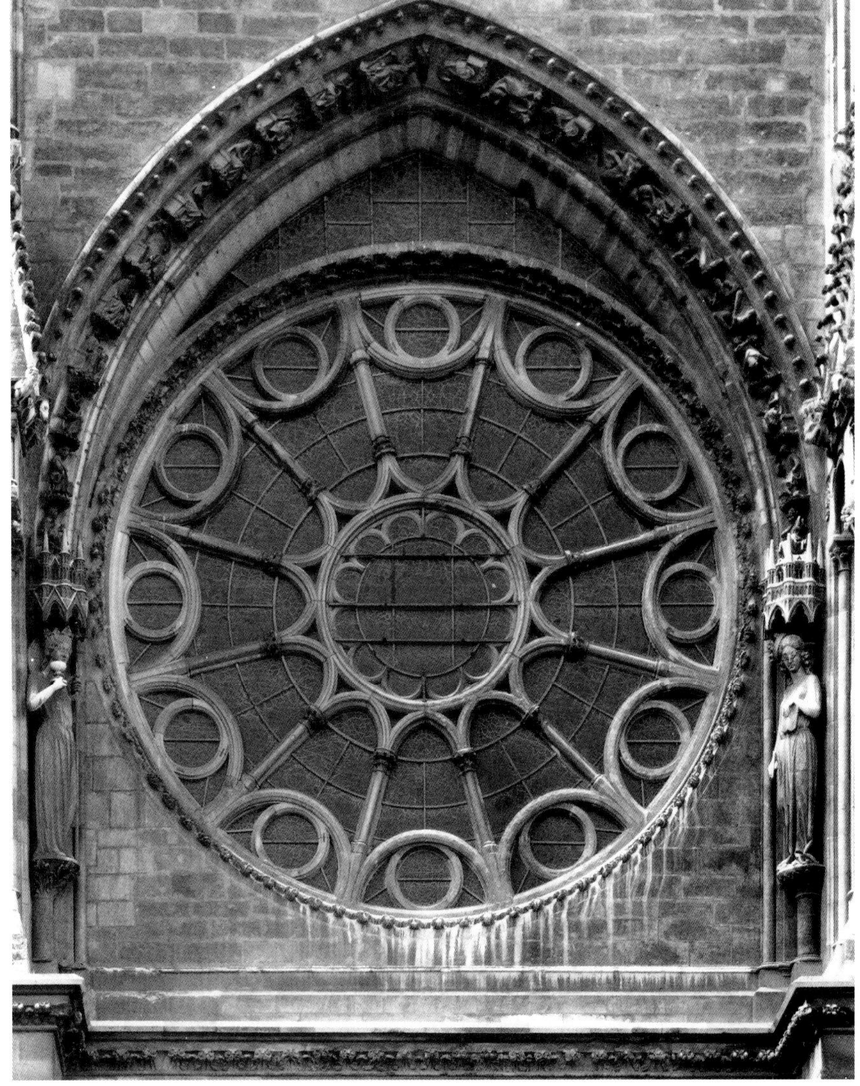

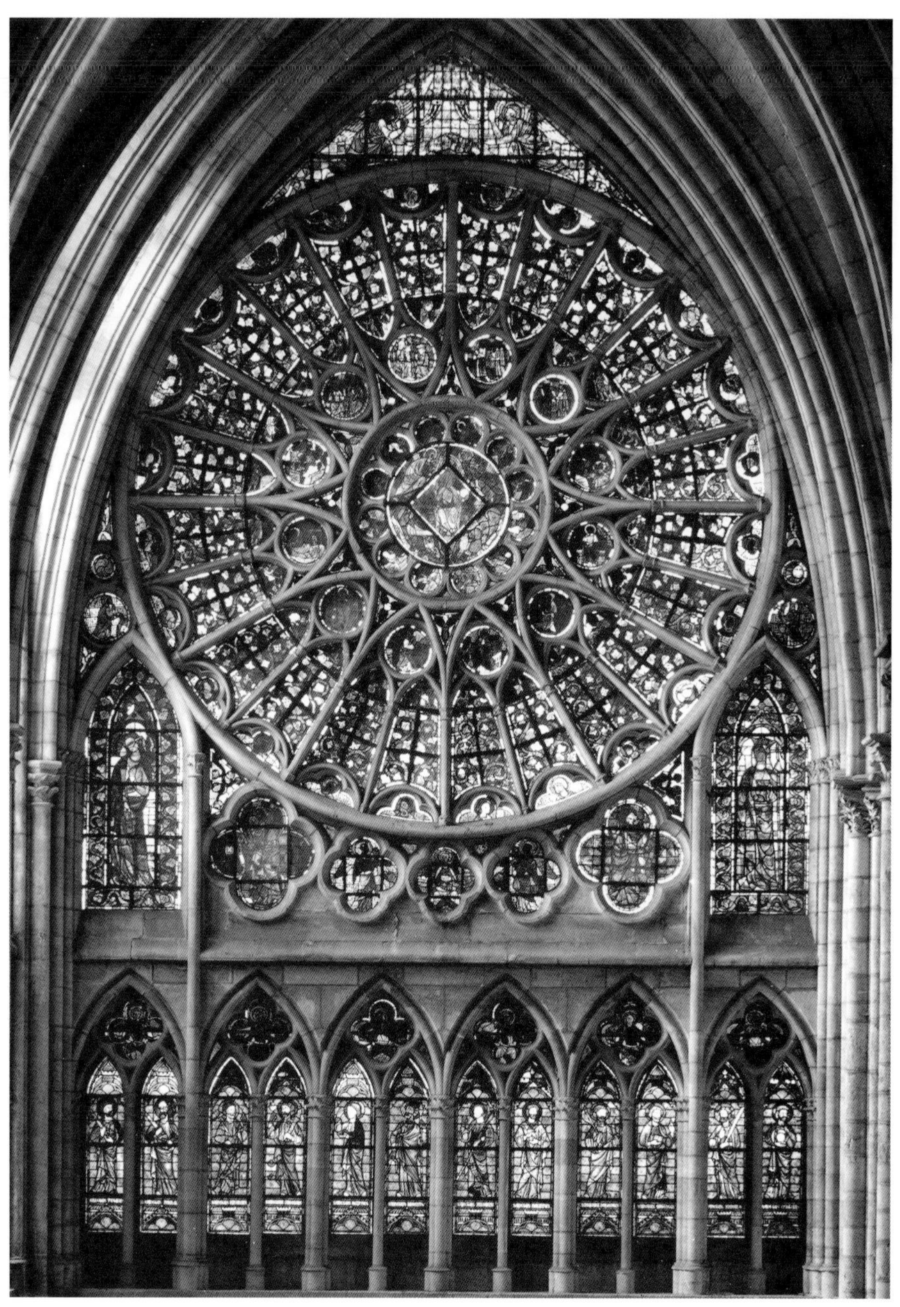

FIG. 143 Châlons-en-Champagne, cathedral, north rose, ca. 1255–60.

Added to those themes at Châlons is a ring of medallions of the Infancy of Christ and a Last Judgment sequence (angels blowing oliphants and dead rising from their tombs). I have interpreted the Châlons program as the Heavenly Jerusalem (i.e., Ecclesia) as it exists both in present time, as a result of the Incarnation, and in the future, at the Second Coming. Yves Christe's studies of the Apocalypse in medieval art have stressed this temporal duality of the theme.[103]

At Reims the north rose depicts Genesis, the beginning of Creation—created time. The south rose facing it almost certainly touched in some way on the end of created time, that is, the Last Judgment

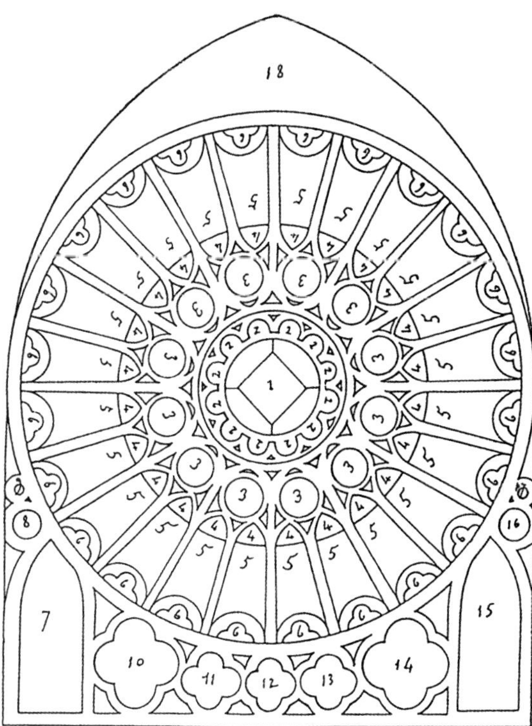

FIG. 144 Châlons cathedral, north rose, chart of subjects: (1) Majestas Domini with Evangelist symbols; (2) six angels with oliphants, six dead rising from tombs; (3, 4) Infancy of Christ; (5) foliage of ivy and vine; (6) heads of the blessed; (7) Synagoga; (8, 10, 14, 16) prophets; (9) sun; (11, 13) angels with censers; (12) angel with crowns; (15) Ecclesia; (17) moon; (18) modern (after Paul Lucot, *Les verrières de la cathédrale de Châlons, église Saint-Étienne*, 1907).

and/or the Apocalypse. An important aspect of that theme was the eventual and inevitable triumph of Ecclesia at the end of time.[104] Such a program would be entirely appropriate as a statement for the chapter of Reims to make following the penitential ceremonies imposed on the civic insurgents, the final such event occurring in August of 1240. The Reims transept roses fit together in an even subtler theological interpretation, however. Among other Church Fathers, the Venerable Bede equated the days of Creation with the various epochs of history.[105] The north rose presents chiefly the fifth and sixth days of Creation: birds, fish, animals, mankind. The creation of Eve at the apex of the Creation scenes (A-3, fig. 115) symbolized God pulling Ecclesia from the side of Christ.[106] The Church on earth, that is, between Christ's Incarnation and his Second Coming, occupied the sixth day, while God's repose on the seventh day signified that return, the Last Judgment. The latter concept was extended—for example, in the glosses of the Moralized Bibles—to encompass the Coronation of the Virgin (Ecclesia) by Christ in heaven.[107] The Reims north-rose program concluded with the commencement of the sixth day, and the south rose continued the theme to the end of time on the seventh. Further evidence for this interpretation is provided by the sculpted gables atop the two transepts, above the roses. Surmounting the north transept is the Annunciation to the Virgin, culmination of the north-rose program and beginning of the sixth day.[108] The gable of the south-transept facade bears a sculpture of the Assumption of the Virgin, her bodily translation to heaven—where, as the climax of the seventh day, she will be crowned in triumph.[109]

The Châlons north rose, which I believe takes its cue from the lost south rose of Reims, is a unique creation in its cathedral, of a theological complexity as well as iconographic and stylistic range far beyond the other Gothic arts remaining there.[110] How much of its richness reflects the lost glazing of the south rose of Reims can only be guessed. The same fertile and imaginative programming, however, is tangible in the Reims north rose, as I hope to have demonstrated earlier in this chapter—suggesting that the loss of the south rose is a very great loss indeed.

Even without a stylistic analysis of the lost rose, the tightness of the iconographic program in the transept suggests that the roses were planned together and probably glazed in sequence. The initial choice of an Old Testament theme for glass on the north (hence dark) side of a church and those of the New Testament on the south was fairly traditional, and the Genesis story of the creation of mankind, as it appears in the sculpture around the north rose's outer circumference, takes the rising form of a sacred genealogical tree such as the Tree of Jesse.[111] The recasting of the program in the stained glass of that rose reflects the trauma of the years of civic rebellion in Reims. Its program delivers a more pointed indictment, the narrative taking a downward direction emphasizing the punishment of the rebellion of Eve, and the first murder, by Cain. The creatures of God's creation were selected as a rich commentary underlining the moral themes of this narrative. The use of the bestiary in this way is unique, and I have suggested that such a manuscript owned by the archbishop may have passed into the canons' hands at his death, at a moment when the program of the transept roses was on the agenda. Although grisaille, introduced (as I believe) after his death in order to hasten the building's closure, was extended throughout the transept clerestories, the roses are the chief ornament of that space.

The roses speak with the chapter's voice. As the canons entered their exquisite new cathedral, the south rose, with its promise of Ecclesia Triumphant, hovered before them; as they left their stalls to exit into the often hostile world outside, the north rose declared their own song of triumph, after the trauma of insurrection, exile, and finally what amounted to civil war. Was the message received and understood by those who had been in rebellion, or aimed as a warning to the town's citizenry in general? In my view the application of "reception theory" too precisely to creations of the Gothic centuries is misguided.[112] The complexity and sophistication of the transept rose programs, no less than the exquisite beauty of the rose that remains to us, cannot be reduced to propaganda. While it is too much to say that it did not matter if the message was "received," for churchmen of the Middle Ages—indeed, for medieval secular lords in power as well—the statement was the reality, the main thing.[113] It was a reaffirmation of what was, for them, God's inarguable truth.

The Addendum: *Belles Verrières* in the South Transept

Inserted at an unrecorded date into one of the clerestory grisailles of the south transept (fig. 145, Bay 118) were four recycled images for which I have adopted the medieval term *belles verrières:* an enthroned Virgin and Child, an enthroned archbishop-saint, a smaller standing figure of John the Baptist, and a most unusual image depicting a Gothic church facade (figs. 146–48). This facade image is identified by inscription as "ECCLESIA RENENSIS [*sic*] METROPOLIS," that is, the cathedral of Reims (fig. 148). The stained-glass facade image in Bay 118, with its portals, gables, rose window, crenellations, flying buttresses, and charming gargoyles, is shown flattened frontally, like the thirteenth-century architectural drawings on parchment in the Strasbourg Musée de l'Oeuvre Notre-Dame as well as on the so-called Reims palimpsest.[114] In the medium of stained glass the only other examples of such frontal facade images are to be found in Reims itself—the famous series in the choir clerestories presenting "facades" of the suffragan cathedrals forming the archdiocese of Reims (e.g., figs. 71, 81).[115]

As discussed in chapter 3, scholars have long assumed that these south-transept images (or at least all but the smaller Baptist figure) are remains of a hypothesized original glazing of the cathedral's axial bay (Bay 100).[116] According to this universally accepted theory—which I am attempting to dislodge—the present Bay 118 spolia would have first glazed Bay 100 and would have been replaced by the archbishop Henri de Braine between 1235 and his death, in 1240. The present axial bay (fig. 69, Bay 100) depicts his named image in archiepiscopal regalia, paired with another facade image of the cathedral of Reims (labeled "ECCLESIA REMENSIS"),[117] beneath the Virgin and Child and the Crucifixion. Thus three of the four elements of Bay 100 (Virgin and Child, enthroned archbishop of Reims, "facade" of Reims) replicate those now inserted into Bay 118, which Reinhardt includes in his "first choir program." My doubts about his proposed program have been investigated in chapter 3.[118] As for the Bay 118 *belles verrières,* I believe that they never were part of that (or any) choir program.

The Four Reused Images: Date and Original Location

Scholars have unanimously agreed with Reinhardt's judgment that the four images inserted into Bay 118 are in the earliest style in the cathedral.[119] The faces are oval, the necks thick and columnar, the eyes greatly enlarged, and the vigorous color harmony is based on red, blue, and green (see

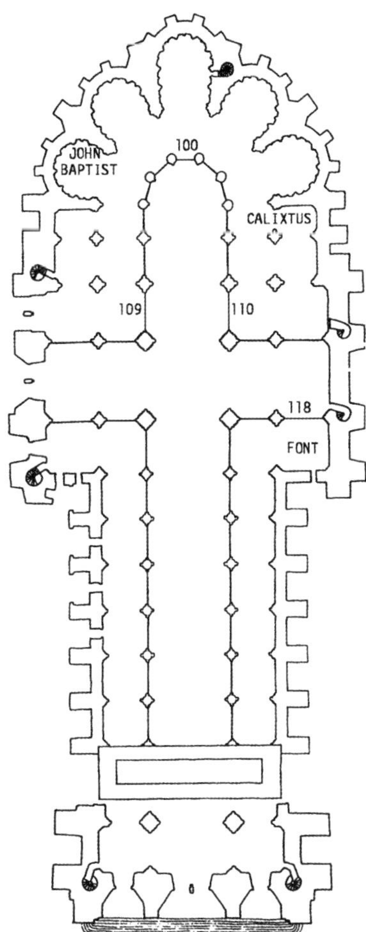

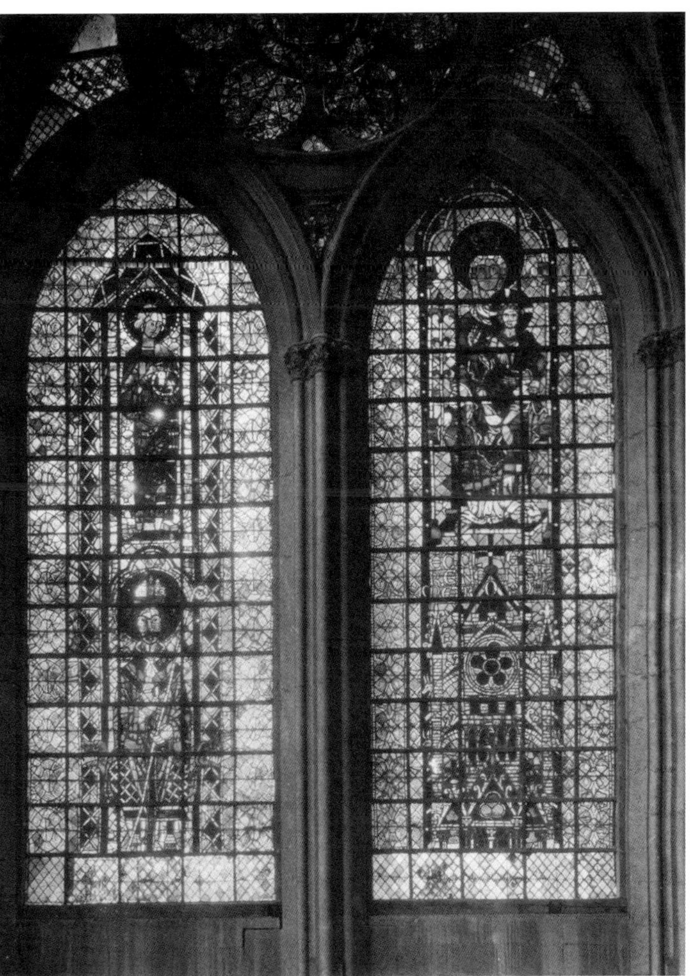

FIG. 145 Reims cathedral, plan with reconstruction of the original project conserving Archbishop Samson's twelfth-century facade. Bay numbers and locations indicated are those mentioned in this discussion (after Kurmann, *La façade de la cathédrale de Reims*).

FIG. 146 Bay 118 (1915).

particularly the pre-restoration photos, figs. 149, 150). The Virgin and the archbishop-saint, both enthroned frontally, impose a hieratic, sober mood. Draperies are of the soft, wrinkled type associated with the classicizing style in vogue in the early thirteenth century (*Muldenfaltenstil*). A date often proposed for them is about 1220–25, that is, preceding the reign of Archbishop Henri de Braine, which commenced in 1227. As early as 1911 Paul Simon, of the famous family of restorers in charge of the cathedral's glass for generations, commented on the thickness of the glass and even considered that the spolia might have come from the cathedral that burned around 1210.[120]

I suggest that it is more likely that these four images were made about 1220, perhaps as part of a refurbishment of the cathedral (a construction site since 1211, if not before) in anticipation of the coronation of Louis VIII, which took place on August 6, 1223. In 1220 King Philippe Auguste was fifty-five, in the fortieth year of his reign. His father, Louis VII, had reigned for forty-three years, Louis VI for thirty-nine, and Philippe I for forty-eight. Philippe Auguste's son Louis VIII had been married for twenty years and was a vigorous man of thirty-three who had fathered eight children, four of whom were still alive—and male. Contemplating Louis's eventual coronation would

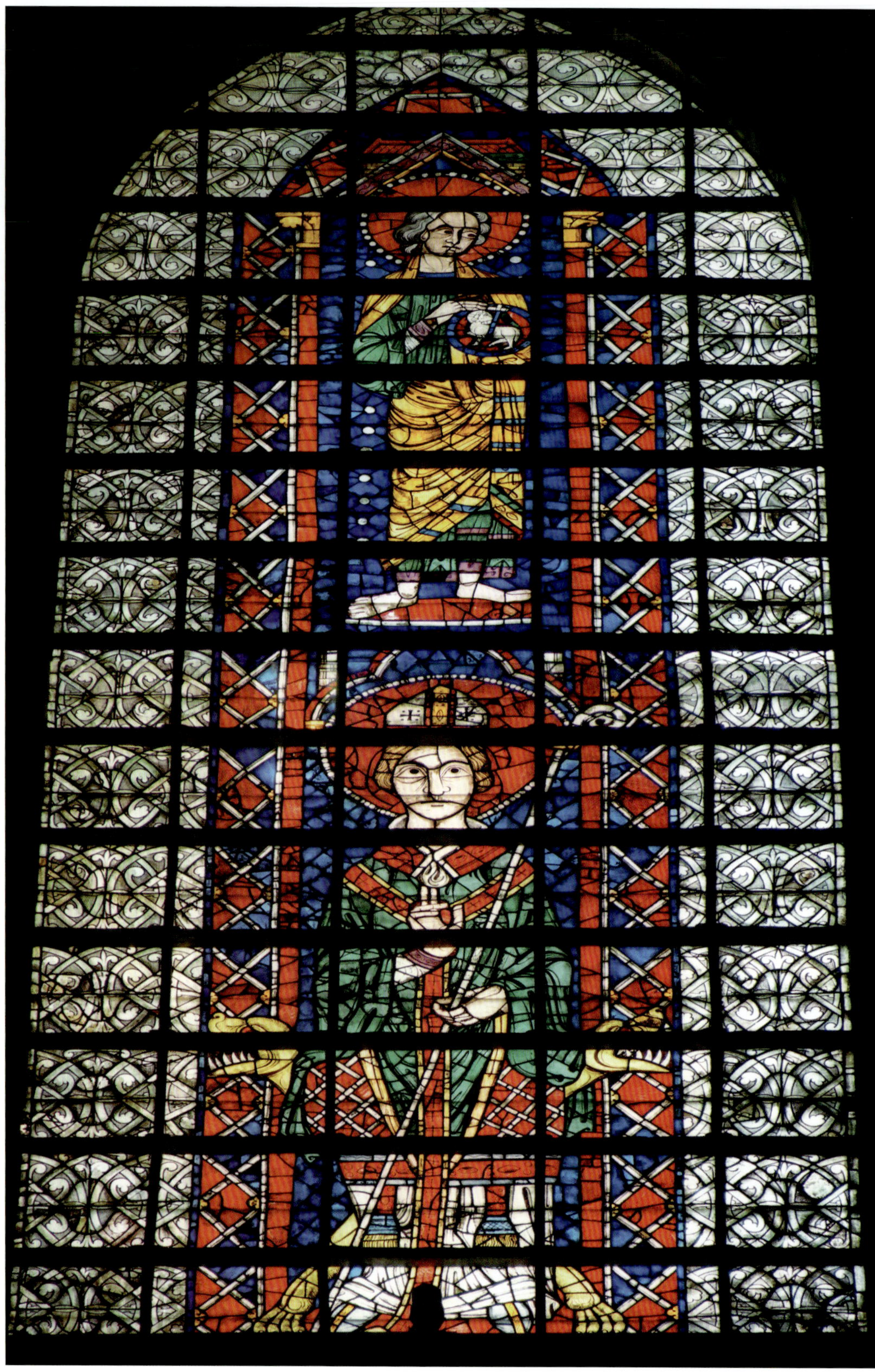

FIG. 147 Bay 118, left lancet: John the Baptist (above); an archbishop-saint here identified as St. Remi (below).

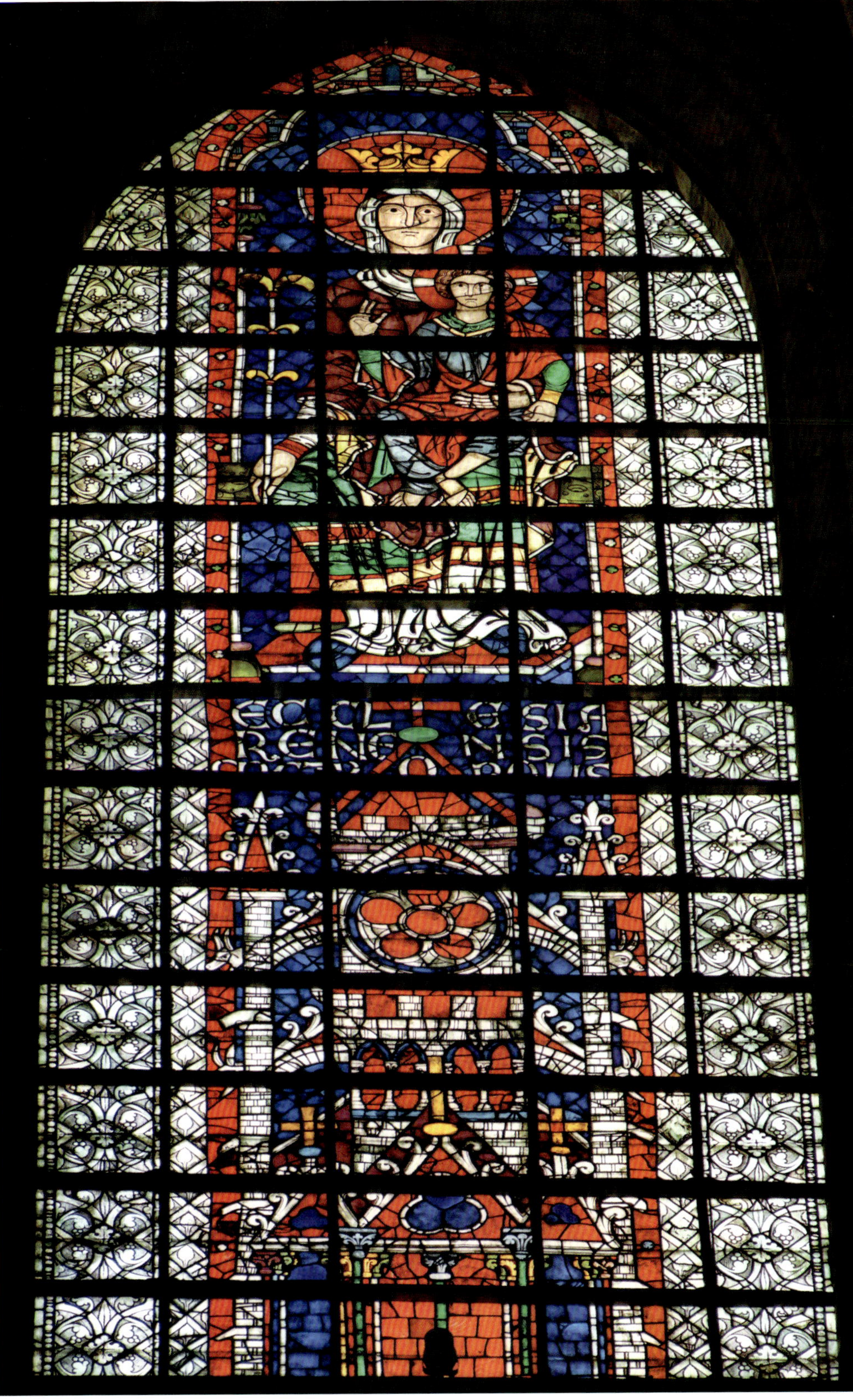

FIG. 148 Bay 118, right lancet: Virgin and Child; "facade" of Reims cathedral.

FIG. 149 St. Remi, Bay 118, left lancet, lower row. Autochrome by Henri Deneux, 1915.

FIG. 150 "Facade" of Reims cathedral, Bay 118, right lancet, lower row. Autochrome by Henri Deneux, 1915.

FIG. 151 John the Baptist, Bay 118, left lancet, top row, detail.

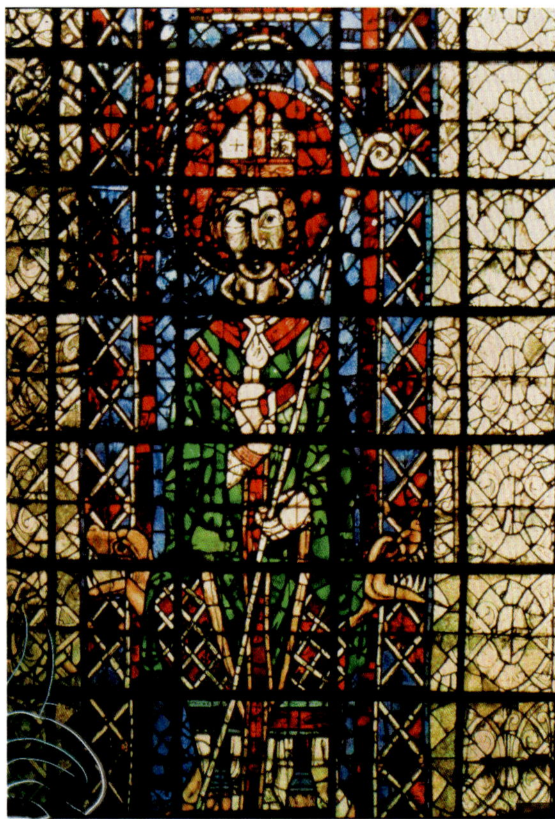

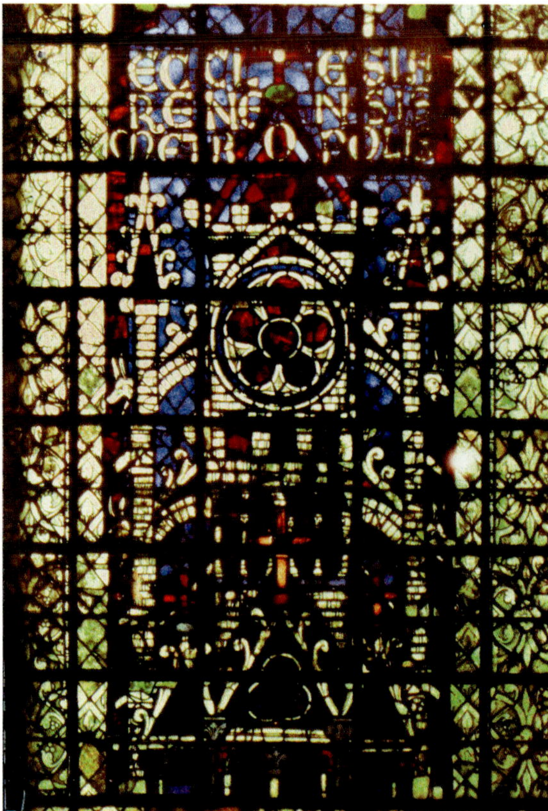

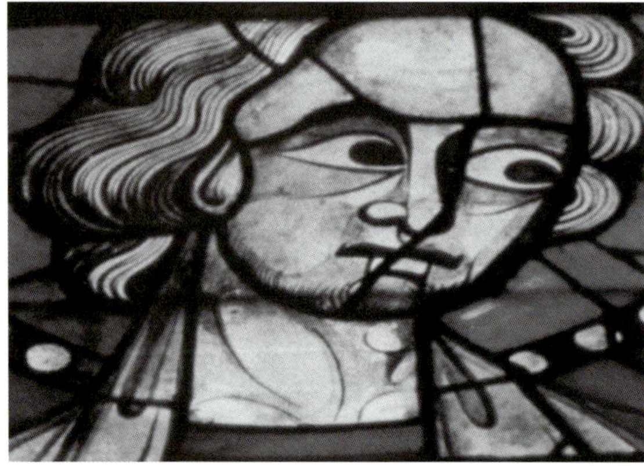

have been expected at Reims about 1220, and documents suggest new expenditures and a need for funds beginning in that year.[121] Moreover, Reims had not yet established itself definitively as the coronation site[122] (as will be discussed below). Although the Capetians had generally favored Reims, Louis VI had been crowned by the archbishop of Sens at Orléans in 1108, when the *rémois* archdiocese was *sede vacante* (that is, during an interregnum of the archbishopric). Since the time of Suger, the abbey of Saint-Denis had been actively promoting its claim to coronations based on the alleged feudal relationship of French kings to its patron, St. Denis. Though Philippe Auguste had been crowned at Reims in 1179, during his father's lifetime, after the latter's death the young king had insisted on being crowned again on the occasion of his marriage (and his queen's coronation) by the archbishop of Sens at the abbey of Saint-Denis. And in 1219 Reims was once again *sede vacante,* the cathedral was an active building site, and it had an older nave in need of sprucing up.

But where were the four spolia located in such a refurbishment? Reinhardt, who measured them, pointed out that the colored elements of Bay 118 would fit perfectly into the axial bay, 100, although it puzzled him that there would be no room at all for any kind of border.[123] Stained glass of the

Gothic era without borders is more than an anomaly—it is unthinkable. The four *belles verrières* have clearly been truncated not only in width but also in height, in order to compose a double row in Bay 118 (figs. 147–48), matching all other figural clerestories of the cathedral. As Balcon has pointed out, the Virgin's framing canopy has lost its crowning architectural motifs, found in all other cathedral glass.[124] This is true of the archbishop-saint's canopy as well, and the gabled frame over the Baptist is particularly awkward and misaligned. Evident, too, are the patching and rearrangement of the grisaille. There is now no grisaille border, an element found in all other transept clerestories, and the narrow grisaille strips flanking the Virgin (and the "facade" below her), a lozenge design similar to that in the borders of the transept's Bays 112 and 113, may be the remains of the original grisaille border of Bay 118. A rough comparison of the Virgin and Child in Bay 118, the largest design of the four images, with the same subject in Bay 100 reveals that the former is seven panels in height, the latter only six.

There can be no doubt that the spolia of about 1220 were patched into Bay 118 sometime after the transept clerestories were glazed in the years around 1241, and that, in their new double-row format, they were too tall to fit without some truncation. They cannot have originated in Bay 100, which is the same height as Bay 118 (10.5 m). It might be asked why they were stripped of their original borders. Clearly they were remade to conform to the new format employed in Bays 109 and 110 (figs. 99–100), grisaille flanking a vertical column of figures, though the colored spolia are much wider than the choir figures. Conformity to a new format was similarly imposed on the famous twelfth-century *Belle verrière* of Chartres, for example, when it was reused in the High Gothic chevet.[125]

I believe that the *belles verrières* were made for the other end of the cathedral of Reims as it stood about 1220—that is, for the facade windows of the twelfth-century cathedral of Archbishop Samson, the western nave of which was still in use at the time of Louis VIII's coronation.

Samson's Facade

Archbishop Samson (r. 1140–60) had added a new chevet and a new western block to the Carolingian cathedral about 1152, probably in imitation of Suger's additions to Saint-Denis, where he had attended the consecration of the choir in 1144. Like Suger's chevet, Samson's had a double ambulatory with seven radiating chapels, and, like Suger's facade, Samson's had two towers. It is a reasonable assumption that Samson was motivated to emulate Saint-Denis by that abbey's public-relations campaign, referred to above, to become the coronation site of the French kings.[126] Little is known about the appearance of Samson's facade block, which was situated beyond the Carolingian nave, approximately in the second and third bays of the present Gothic nave (fig. 145). The abbey of Saint-Remi in Reims also added a new chevet and facade onto an older nave structure, about 1165–70, and its facade (fig. 152) may provide a reflection of Samson's lost cathedral design of about 1152. Only the two lower levels at Saint-Remi are useful for comparison, since the slender towers were retained from a previous structure and the rose level above has been drastically restored and altered.[127]

Peter Kurmann has proposed that when the Gothic chevet was begun, around 1210, the original plan was to retain Samson's twelfth-century facade and join it to a new nave (fig. 145). He has further hypothesized that about 1215–20 it was embellished by large new statues—the six prophets now reused as jamb figures in the south portal of the Gothic facade begun about 1255.[128] I would like to adopt his scenario of the embellishment of Samson's facade at that time and suggest the addition of five stained-glass windows, the remains of which were moved to Bay 118 when the twelfth-century facade was replaced by the present Gothic one.

The six prophet statues discussed by Kurmann are all almost three meters tall, including their socles, much larger than the jamb statues of the north-transept portals. Kurmann suggests that Samson's facade had five windows, like the facade of Saint-Remi, and that the six statues were located between those bays, similar in placement to the two statues of about 1170–80 on the abbey's west front. The six cathedral figures, representing Old Testament worthies, are not of equal height. In their current arrangement as jamb statues on the right portal, those to the far right and left of the group, the tallest, are Simeon and Aaron, and each turns in; next in size are the Baptist and Abraham, adjoining them; and the shortest, the two in the middle, are Isaiah and Moses. Their location on the facade would probably have been similar, with the largest at the far sides and the shortest flanking the central bay. The directions in which their heads turn strongly support this arrangement. They form a Marian group, appropriate for a cathedral dedicated to the Virgin, and have long been compared with the Chartres north-transept jambs. In Kurmann's reconstruction, the three on the left (Simeon, the Baptist, and Isaiah) announce the Messiah, while the group on the right (Moses with the brazen serpent, Abraham sacrificing Isaac, and Aaron immolating the Pascal lamb, the *Mactatio Agni*) prefigures the Passion.[129]

Kurmann further suggests that the original iconographic program of Samson's facade, with its very shallow portal embrasure, would have been carried by mid-twelfth-century glazing. His comparison—and comparisons are not numerous—is to the Chartres facade (Tree of Jesse, Infancy, Passion windows). If so, I believe that any original glass of Samson's facade (possibly damaged in the ca. 1210 fire?) was replaced by new windows about 1220. The prophet statues imply a program honoring the Virgin Mary, to whom the cathedral is dedicated. The spoliate glass images, as we shall see, celebrate the Ecclesia of Reims, site of St. Remi's baptism of the Frankish king Clovis—whose name, we sometimes forget, is Louis.

To return to the four images inserted into Bay 118, I propose the following reconstruction of the (re)glazing of Samson's facade ca. 1220 (fig. 153). The five windows in the Saint-Remi facade (fig. 152) are of graduated height, and only the central three can be seen when viewing the facade from the interior of the main nave. The two outer

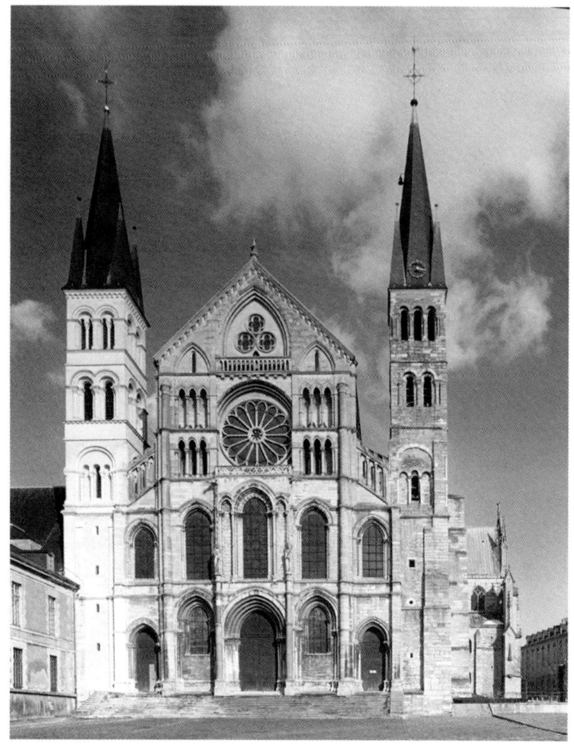

FIG. 152 Reims, abbey church of Saint-Remi, facade.

windows are above the left and right portals, on the axes of the side aisles; they are thus somewhat separate from the main trio. Two more windows flank the main door below. If Samson's facade was similar, the largest, central bay would be the obvious location for the patroness of the cathedral, the enthroned Virgin and Child now in Bay 118. This figure is the tallest and probably was the widest of the four *belles verrières,* since the flanking columns of the Virgin's canopy are now nearly sliced off, the cushion of her throne is awkwardly truncated at the ends, and she has no border of any kind. Flanking her were probably the two images of equal size: the archbishop-saint and the stained-glass "facade" of Reims.[130]

In the position of honor at the Virgin's right hand (thus on the left, or south) was probably the stained-glass "facade," identified by inscription as the cathedral of Reims: "Ecclesia Remensis Metropolis." The reference is at one level to the cathedral itself, of course, but more basic is the reference to the concept of Maria-Ecclesia. As in

A.

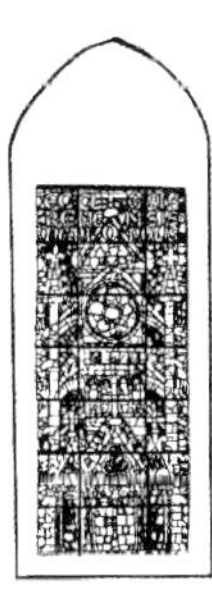

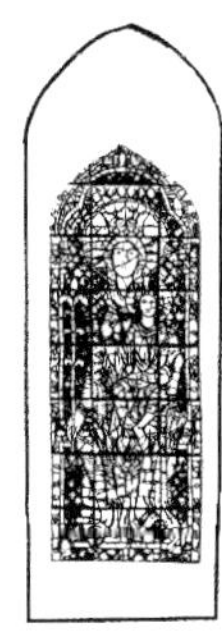

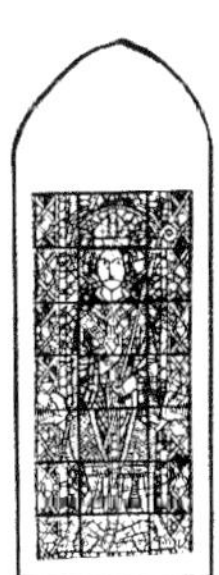

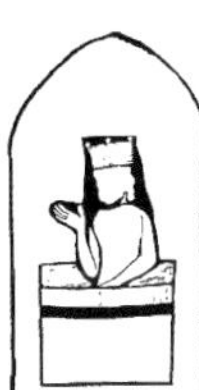

B.

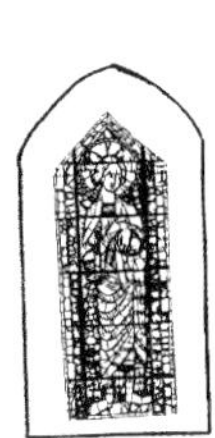

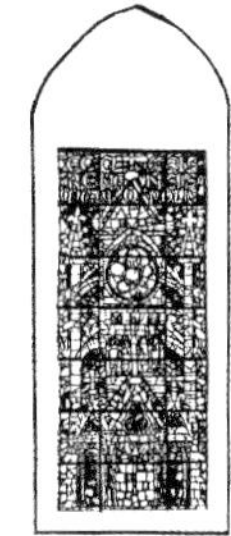

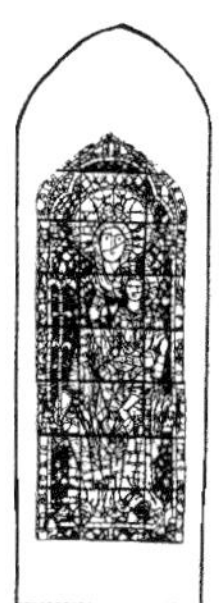

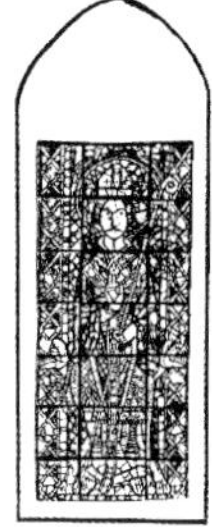

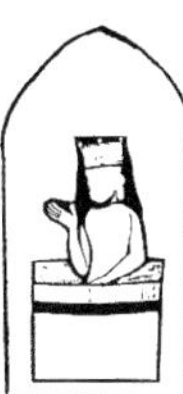

FIG. 153 Two possible reconstructions of the glazing of Archbishop Samson's facade, Reims cathedral, ca. 1220.

the elaborate iconography of the north-transept portals of Chartres, contemporary with this program, the Virgin is celebrated both as human mother and as the Church.[131]

To the Virgin's left (north) on Samson's facade was most likely the equally frontal and enthroned archbishop-saint. Who is he? If he ever had an inscription below him, it has been lost. A photograph of 1915 (fig. 146) shows the bay with the lower row of glass panels replaced by clear glass in a plain lozenge pattern. Such a substitution undoubtedly occurred well before the French Revolution, when, for the coronations of Louis XIV and Louis XV—and no doubt earlier—the lower panels of all clerestories were removed. Numerous engravings commemorating those events—for example, figures 5 and 6—show people watching through the openings thus created.[132] Victor Tourneur quotes a ceremonial of the cathedral of 1637, in a chapter entitled "Comment on se doibt gouverner en l'Eglise de Reims arrivant ung sacre pour empêcher le désordre": "Fault ouvrir aux vitres hautes deux panneaux de vitres de haulteur et les porter dans la plomerie haulte."[133] (To impede disorder, the advice was to remove the two lower panels from the clerestories.) Writing in the 1850s, Tourneur mentions that more lower panels of many windows were then broken, damaged, or misplaced than the ones above (see, e.g., figs. 7, 146). Modern restorations have eliminated this evidence.

Recent literature has often referred to this enthroned archbishop (fig. 147) as Henri de Braine, but this cannot be so, since the figure is nimbed—as was noted by several nineteenth-century observers.[134] He is, I believe, one of the sainted bishops of Reims, most probably St. Remi, who baptized Clovis in 496. He wears an archbishop's pallium, as he does on the 1219 seal of the abbey (fig. 154), although before Tilpin in 779 the prelates of Reims were bishops, not archbishops. Some images of the High Gothic era distinguish between the two offices by what prelates hold, treating the objects as what art historians call attributes; a bishop (or an abbot) has a crozier, whereas an archbishop can hold a cross-staff, although in "real life" his staff was born by an attendant (see fig. 18). The saint in Bay 118 holds a crozier. It might be pointed out that the named image of Archbishop Henri de Braine in Bay 100 also has a crozier, but his cross-staff is held by the angel atop the facade of his cathedral in the paired lancet (fig. 69). A contemporary image that I have identified as Archbishop Henri de Braine—with both cross-staff and crozier!—survives in Châlons cathedral.[135] The distinction between bishops with croziers and archbishops with cross-staffs does seem to have been honored in the series of prelates in the nave windows of Reims, where Tourneur saw (before World War I) figures in four or five bays on both sides holding cross-staffs, whereas all the rest held croziers.[136] The identification of the saint of Bay 118 as St. Remi will be pursued below.

The fourth of the *belles verrières,* the smaller standing figure of John the Baptist holding the disk of the Agnus Dei (fig. 147), turns to the right. He was probably located on Samson's facade in a bay to the south, either adjoining the Ecclesia facade image or in a bay flanking the portal, as can be seen on the facade of Saint-Remi (fig. 153). At one level of meaning he may stand in for the crowd of Old Testament worthies commonly associated with the Virgin (as in the group of six statues at Reims mentioned above, as well as on portals of the Coronation of the Virgin at Chartres and elsewhere). But I believe his chief significance here is to underline the idea of baptism, specifically baptism at Reims. Unlike most medieval images of the Baptist, this one does not have a long shaggy beard but only a youthful beard indicated by a fringe of hairs that follows the jawline (fig. 151)—resembling the youthful enthroned archbishop-saint whom I identify as St. Remi (fig. 147).[137] The similarity emphasizes the latter's pivotal role in a miraculous baptism (see below). Moreover, it is generally recognized that events in the Life of St. Remi parallel those of the Baptist.[138]

Thus it is probable that the missing fifth stained-glass figure decorating Samson's facade, located at the opposite (north) side, before or possibly adjoining St. Remi (fig. 153), was Clovis. The lost stained-glass figure of Clovis at Saint-Remi, seen in a facade window there in the early nineteenth century, comes to mind.[139] The baptism of Clovis, king of the Franks, with his two sisters and his three thousand soldiers, by St. Remi, bishop of Reims, is recounted by Gregory of Tours.[140] The legend of the Holy Ampulla, which was attached to this event only later, was given its most persuasive form by Archbishop Hincmar of Reims in the Carolingian era. It recounts how, when crowds prevented the delivery of the necessary chrism to St. Remi at the altar, a dove descended over the font carrying in its beak an ampulla of miraculous chrism. Richard Jackson comments that "the story was more or less forgotten outside of Reims, and not until the reign of Saint Louis did it resurface to make its impact upon the coronation ceremony."[141] In effect, it first appears in the Ordo of Reims, which Jackson dates between 1226 and 1250, preferring ca. 1230; it has been dated as early as 1215.[142] If, as I believe, Samson's facade was embellished with stained glass about 1220 in anticipation of the coronation of Louis VIII, its emphasis on the baptism of Clovis predates the Ordo of Reims perhaps only slightly and thus forms part of the Reims propaganda campaign to ensure its right to the coronation of the kings of France.[143]

To return to the arrangement of stained-glass images in my reconstruction of Samson's facade (fig. 153). John the Baptist at the left would represent, on one level of meaning, that baptism is a sacrament of the Church; the window above (or next to) him is Ecclesia Remensis (fig. 148). The pairing of St. Remi and Clovis that I propose for the right side of Samson's facade will be explored below. One can point out here that these images together emphasize the history of the sacrament of baptism locally, but more specifically the actual spot where the baptism of Clovis took place in St. Remi's cathedral. For, as we will see, the baptismal font at Reims had always been located, up to that time, at the west end of the nave.

The Baptistery

Excavations at Reims since 1991 have extended and modified the information obtained from those of Henri Deneux, begun in 1919, and interpreted by Reinhardt.[144] Built over Roman baths, the paleochristian baptistery of the late fourth–early fifth century was located on axis with the present cathedral, beneath the fifth bay of the present nave. It was approximately nine meters square in plan, with an immersion tank roughly three meters square in the center. Reached by four access stairways, it was decorated with mosaics. Whether it was freestanding or annexed on its east side to the basilica is uncertain. When, about 750, the cathedral was enlarged, the baptistery area was enclosed within the nave. In the early ninth century Archbishop Ebbo constructed the enlarged Carolingian cathedral, the nave of which was extended with a *Westwerk* at the facade end, a massive block of two stories and five vaulted chambers. The baptismal font was moved to this *Westwerk*. This structure was consecrated under Archbishop Hincmar in the presence of the emperor Charles the Bald. Ebbo's *Westwerk* was reworked, or possibly even replaced, by Adalberon about 976 with a central tower-porch. This structure enclosed three altars, the central one dedicated to St. Calixtus and those on the sides to St. Maurilius and to John the Baptist.[145] Next, Archbishop Samson, about 1152, reconstructed the west end of the nave again, replacing the single-tower structure with a twin-towered facade. Presumably the Baptist's altar and font were retained within Samson's facade block as well.

As discussed above, Kurmann has presented a strong argument that, when the present cathedral was undertaken, the original plan was to retain Samson's facade and to annex it to a new Gothic nave and that it was redecorated with the earliest Reims statuary of large scale (and/or, as I believe, with the stained-glass images now in Bay 118). By 1230, however, a decision had been reached to remove Samson's facade—eventually—and to extend the Gothic nave beyond it (see fig. 145). Work did not begin on that area, however, until midcentury.[146] The liturgical functions that had taken place in Samson's facade block would have had to be moved. Documentation of new chaplaincies, as well as the chapel names indicated on the cathedral plan by Jacques Cellier of 1583–87, suggests that the altars of St. Calixtus and the Baptist were probably moved into the chapels of the new Gothic choir at a fairly early date (fig. 199).[147] But a baptismal font needs to be located in an accessible and fairly public area of the church. According to Cellier's plan, the font was moved to the western aisle of the south transept.[148] I suggest that it was left functioning in Samson's facade block until the last possible moment and that the move of the font took place ca. 1250. The stained glass of Samson's facade was probably moved with it, to Bay 118, at the same time, since Bay 118 is the clerestory directly above the font in the completed Gothic cathedral (fig. 145).

Thus would be solved the mystery of why the four images were inserted into such an obscure location in the west wall of the south transept, hardly a major focal point in the building's interior.[149] The aisle bay where the font was located is a fairly accessible space directly down the nave's south aisle, large enough (with the south transept area adjoining it) to accommodate even a large group of people assembled for an important baptism, yet sufficiently out of the way to afford some privacy for such a ceremony. Another mystery would be solved as well. Bay 118 is one of the widest bays in the building.[150] One might wonder why the *belles verrières* were inserted into such a wide bay when width was not required, since the extra space had to be patched with grisailles, and since narrower transept bays were equally available. I submit that the precise location above the newly moved baptismal font in the Gothic transept was the deciding factor in the choice to place the spoliate windows in Bay 118, when Samson's facade was dismantled in the 1250s.

Several observations follow this line of reasoning. First, as noted earlier, the arrangement of the reused images in Bay 118 in two vertical columns, set within a grisaille field (figs. 147–48), copies the composition of windows already in place in choir Bays 109 and 110 since 1241 (figs. 99–100, 102). Second, Henri de Braine's axial bay (Bay 100, fig. 69) of ca. 1227–30[151] replicated—intentionally—designs of glass that had, by then, decorated Samson's facade at the other end of the building for up to a decade. Henri had himself depicted as the "successor of St. Remi." The reason is not hard to imagine. Each new archbishop of Reims spent the eve of his solemn entry into the city at the abbey of Saint-Remi and on the following day was escorted to his cathedral, where the abbot presented him to the chapter with the words "Ecce pastor vester, successor Beati Remigii."[152]

The Foldstool of St. Remi

A key to the missing fifth figure, of Clovis,[153] may be provided, I propose, by the beast-headed foldstool in the spoliate window of the archbishop-saint Remi (fig. 147). This detail is unique in the cathedral. Neither the image of Henri de Braine in Bay 100 nor that of any of his suffragans in the surrounding choir copied this detail, and none of the surviving prelates in the nave did either (though a few of the kings there sit on foldstools).[154] The beast-headed foldstool long carried royal connotations, of course, from the bronze throne of Dagobert to the seals of many Capetians, including Philippe Auguste, Louis VIII, and Louis IX. The *sella curulis,* or lion-headed folding chair, had since ancient times symbolized secular power and by the thirteenth century had become an emblem of the pastoral authority of the pope, used, for example, by Innocent III.[155]

Madeline Caviness has studied the foldstool in the context of the choir glazing of the abbey of Saint-Remi, planned about 1175, where some of the archbishops of Reims sit on foldstools and others on cushioned thrones. She indicates that on seals, bishops normally stand. In the archiepiscopal seals of Reims, only Archbishop Henri de France (d. 1175), who was of royal blood, appears enthroned on a foldstool; archbishops before and after him, throughout the entire thirteenth century, are depicted standing.[156] Likewise, on the seals of the abbey of Saint-Remi, those of Abbots Pierre de Celle (1170) and Simon (1182–98) have foldstools, while later seals, of Abbot Milon (1206) and Abbot Pierre (1239), show them standing.[157] More significant for the argument here is the seal of the abbey itself, in use until at least 1265 (fig. 154). It shows what Caviness suggests to be a consciously archaic image: the patron saint Remi enthroned on a foldstool. It was the abbey's second seal, and the date this seal was put into use can be established by documentation of the destruction of the damaged matrix, in bone or ivory, of the abbey's first seal. That date is 1219.[158]

Moreover, the abbey's new seal of 1219 is unusual in that it includes, in addition to St. Remi enthroned on a foldstool, an image to the left under his blessing hand: Clovis immersed in his baptismal font. In the iconography of the baptism of Clovis, he is depicted in his font several times in sculpture at Reims cathedral and often in other media, but in all cases the baptism is in progress and the baptizing saint stands next to the font, either blessing or receiving the Holy Ampulla.[159] This is true in the cathedral's north-transept tympanum and even in the static, iconic figural group of the gallery of kings added to the top of the Reims facade in the fourteenth century. Only on the new seal of the abbey of Saint-Remi is Clovis, immersed in his font, placed under the blessing hand of an enthroned St. Remi seated on a fold-stool. I propose that the abbey's new seal, introduced in 1219, was the model from which the images on Samson's facade were drawn.

More Seals

Just as the abbey's 1219 seal underlies the images of St. Remi and Clovis from Samson's facade, so too do other contemporary ecclesiastical seals associated with Reims help to explain the remaining *belles verrières.* The image of the Virgin and Child (fig. 148) replicates the seal of the chapter of the cathedral. Both the chapter's first seal, a rigid Romanesque image of about 1155–60 (fig. 155), and the second seal, introduced about 1200 (fig. 156), depict the frontal enthroned Virgin and blessing Child. On the earlier seal the Virgin holds a long-stemmed flowering scepter, while on the seal in use about 1220 she is crowned—as in the Bay 118 spolium.[160]

As for the figure of the Baptist, an Agnus Dei disk served as the seal for the officiality, or office, of grand archdeacon (*archidiaconus remensis*) when that post was held by Hugues de Bourgogne (from April 1218 until his resignation in 1225) (fig. 157). The grand archdeacon of Reims was the chief prelate under the archbishop and assumed the latter's duties in his absence. Hugues, a canon from 1206 until his death in 1231, was also a master of arts. Though not unique to the seal of his tenure as grand archdeacon, the Agnus Dei was not used on the only earlier archdeacon's seal to survive, and it was uncommon thereafter.[161]

The most striking of the stained-glass images in Bay 118, the "facade" of Reims cathedral, is related to a most unusual seal of the cathedral's chapter (fig. 158). This seal was used only *sede vacante,* that is, for periods of interregnum of the archbishopric.[162] Ecclesiastical seals depicting buildings are a somewhat unusual type, called monumental or *topographique,* and principally used for officialities, chapters, and some abbeys.[163] The inscription on this seal, "SIGILL' REM ECCLE METROPOLIS" (fig. 158), furnished the inscription on the glass, "ECCLESIA REMENSIS METROPOLIS" (fig. 148). The seal's image, however, is of the pre-Gothic cathedral, as will be discussed below. The facade image in Bay 118 brings the architecture up to date, since by about 1220 the great new cathedral had been in construction for at least a decade. The glass "facade" shows the new cathedral's double flying buttresses embellished with crockets, as well as the pierced spandrel in the ogives above the transept rose windows.[164]

This unique seal (fig. 158) was in use in 1242 and 1244, during the long interregnum following the death in 1240 of Henri de Braine. It shows the cathedral facade with two slender towers, as on the spolium "facade." Because the seal image is considered to represent the pre-Gothic cathedral, Pierre Desportes and Pierre Bony assume that it was created during the two-year interregnum following the death of Archbishop Guillaume de Champagne in 1202. If the *sede vacante* seal was created in 1202 and again used in the 1240s, I suggest that it is also likely that it was used by the chapter following the death, in Pavia, of Archbishop Aubry de Humbert at the end of 1218.[165] Appointed by the pope, as was the archbishop before him, Aubry was infrequently at Reims, often away on the king's or pope's business; he was on crusade from the spring of 1217 until he died while returning through Italy at the end of 1218. Following his death the cathedral was *sede vacante* until June 1219, when his successor Guillaume de Joinville took power, under a cloud of difficulties continuing until he too died on crusade in 1226 (see below). It is likely that when the news of the death of Archbishop Aubry reached Reims from Italy, the chapter envisioned yet another disputed election and extended interregnum. Although no dispute is recorded over the election of Archbishop Guillaume de Joinville in 1219, during his inauguration ceremony he refused to take the oath to maintain the chapter's rights and privileges, and the complaint against him was only settled, finally, in 1224.[166] The relevance of this situation to the present argument is clear. If Reims were *sede vacante* when Louis VIII was to be

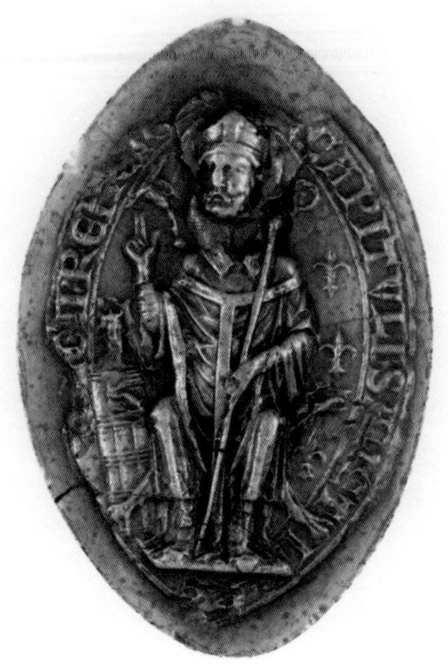

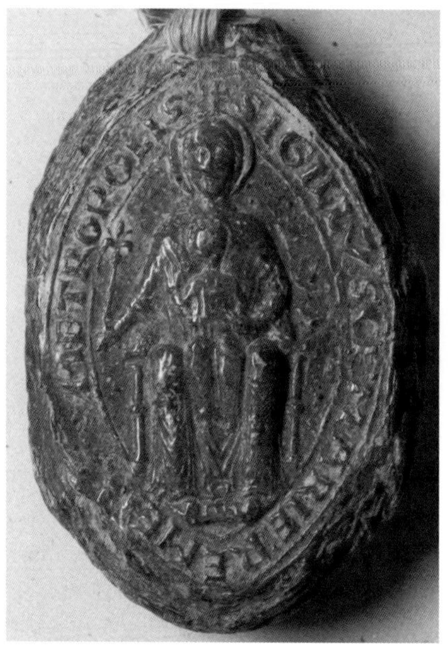

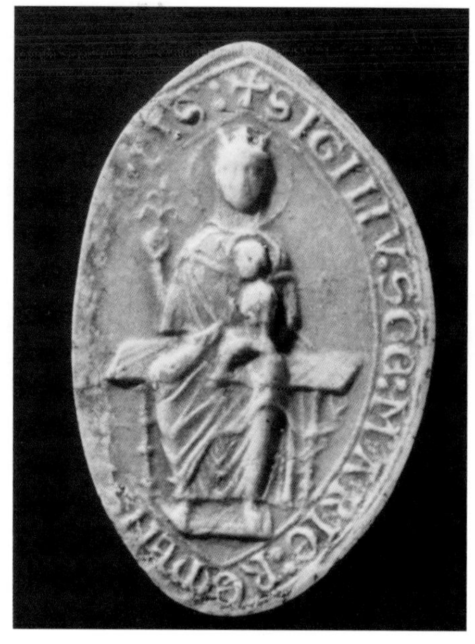

FIG. 154 Second seal of the abbey of Saint-Remi, Reims, put into use in 1219. Document of Archives nationales, Paris: Douët-d'Arcq, Supplément no. 2153.

FIG. 155 First seal of the Reims cathedral chapter, in use ca. 1155–60. Archives dépt. de la Marne, annexe Reims, 2 g 422 (pièce 7), 1192.

FIG. 156 Second seal of the Reims cathedral chapter, in use ca. 1200. Document of Archives nationales, Paris: Douët-d'Arcq no. 7289, ca. 1220.

crowned, another bishop—and another site—would probably be selected for the coronation.

The seals that furnished models for the stained glass of Samson's facade were all in use about 1219 and represent the authority of the cathedral: the chapter, the grand archdeacon, and the office—if not the person—of the archbishop. It is not as surprising as it might seem that the seal of the abbey of Saint-Remi (fig. 154) played such a major role in the cathedral's glazing program. It, like the seals of the chapter *sede vacante* (fig. 158) and the archdeacon (fig. 157), could, in a manner of speaking, stand in for the archbishop. Historical and symbolic associations between the archbishop and the abbey were strong. The abbey had been founded by Archbishop Tilpin (748–94), and until 945 the archbishop and the abbot were the same person. At his consecration each archbishop was heralded as the "successor to St. Remi," and he was enthroned in his cathedral on the so-named throne of Saint Remi.[167] There were contemporary associations as well. Through the twelfth century, the archbishop maintained power over the abbey, a relationship that only gradually weakened about 1260. In the years around 1219, the archbishop's *garde particulière* over the abbey was still in full force.[168]

Conclusion: The Power of the Seal

If, as I believe, Samson's facade received its decoration about 1220 in anticipation of the eventual coronation of Louis VIII, it seems obvious that the glazing was intended to confront the new-made king with a statement of Reims's power: its historic power to anoint, founded on the baptism of Clovis, and its contemporary power, invested in those ecclesiastical institutions and officers imbued with sacral authority. The judicial power of the seal to validate, to guarantee authenticity, was invoked and publicly displayed.

The king, freshly crowned and enthroned on high for all to see,[169] for the public acclamation at the conclusion of the ceremony, could enjoy a perfect view of this display. On the Gothic facade that later replaced Samson's facade, the concept of a sermon to greet the eyes of the king was retained in the unique sculptural display on the facade's verso, while all the themes of the stained glass of about 1220 were translated into sculpture inside and outside. The Virgin and Child maintained a central position as trumeau of the facade's main portal. The Baptist's life unfolded inside, along the inner lintel and wall to the right of that door,[170] and

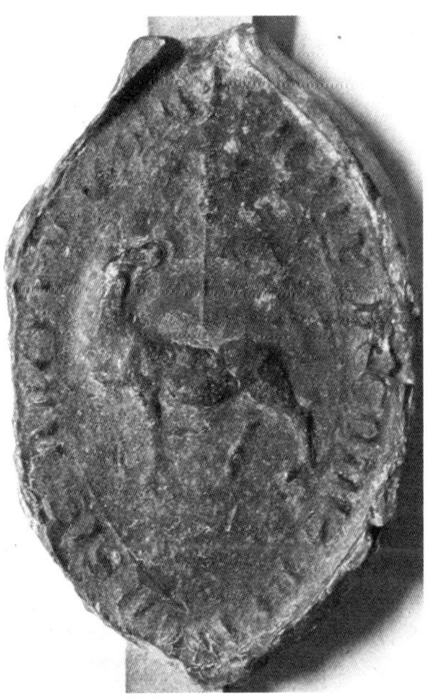

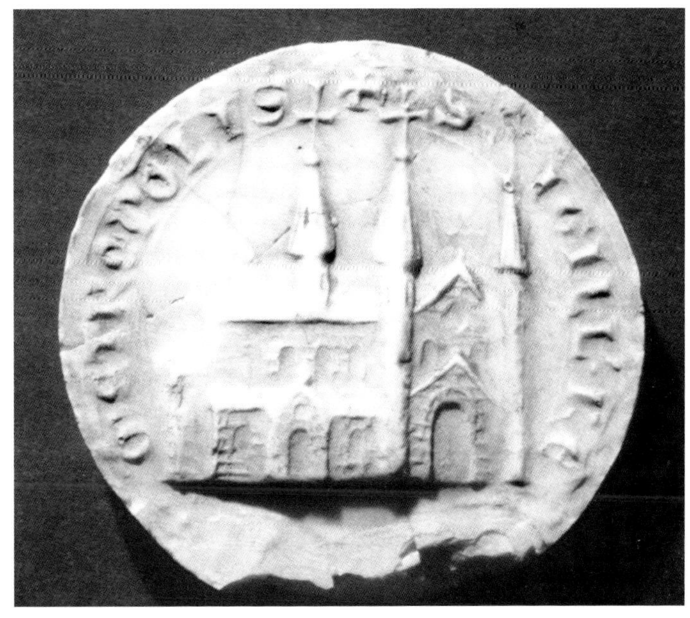

FIG. 157 Seal of officiality of Hugues de Bourgogne, grand archdeacon of Reims cathedral, 1218–25. Archives dépt. de la Marne, annexe Reims, 56 H 175 (pièce 1), 1221.

FIG. 158 Seal of the Reims cathedral chapter, *sede vacante,* probably in use in 1202. Document of Archives nationales, Paris: Douët-d'Arcq no. 7012, 1244.

his figure was among the prophets reused as jambs of the south portal. St. Remi, surely one of the bishops among the Gothic jamb statues, reappeared with Clovis in his font as the central group of the gallery of kings above, added in the fourteenth century. And the concept of Maria-Ecclesia (implicit in the unique stained-glass "facade" inscribed "ECCLESIA REMENSIS METROPOLIS") was underlined by a paired Ecclesia and Synagoga and was reassociated with the liturgical theme of the Triumph of the Virgin across the portal gables of the Gothic facade.[171]

Around 1227–30 in the chevet, Archbishop Henri de Braine copied the motif of the facade image for his axial choir window (Bay 100, fig. 71) and shortly thereafter for the synod of suffragan dioceses surrounding him in the chevet clerestory (e.g., figs. 73, 79, 81). Those stained-glass "facades" also function as seals, identifying, validating, and authenticating the prelates owing allegiance to the cathedral of Reims.

Medieval seals, which proliferated during the twelfth and thirteenth centuries, have long been recognized as mechanisms to validate and authenticate.[172] This concept resonated strongly in the twelfth century, when theologians like Hugh of Saint-Victor and Bernard of Clairvaux applied metaphors of the seal to the soul in the image of God.[173] While the pervasiveness of this sign system in art has not been fully explored by art historians, whose work has concentrated on discussions of such concepts as portraiture and realism, in Gothic stained glass it seems undeniable that real seals were actually employed as models for heraldic coats of arms in windows as well as occasionally for donor images such as kings in majesty and equestrian knights.[174] The *belles verrières* at Reims were based on seals proclaiming not individuals but offices, social structures of power. Thus they parallel precisely the rise in the adoption of seals by "la plupart des institutions et juridictions . . . ecclésiastiques," such seals of "juridiction" functioning as marks and icons of public power.[175] On the facade of the coronation cathedral as it stood in the year 1220, these icons of power proclaimed the authority and privilege of Ecclesia Remensis—whether or not there was an archbishop occupying the throne.

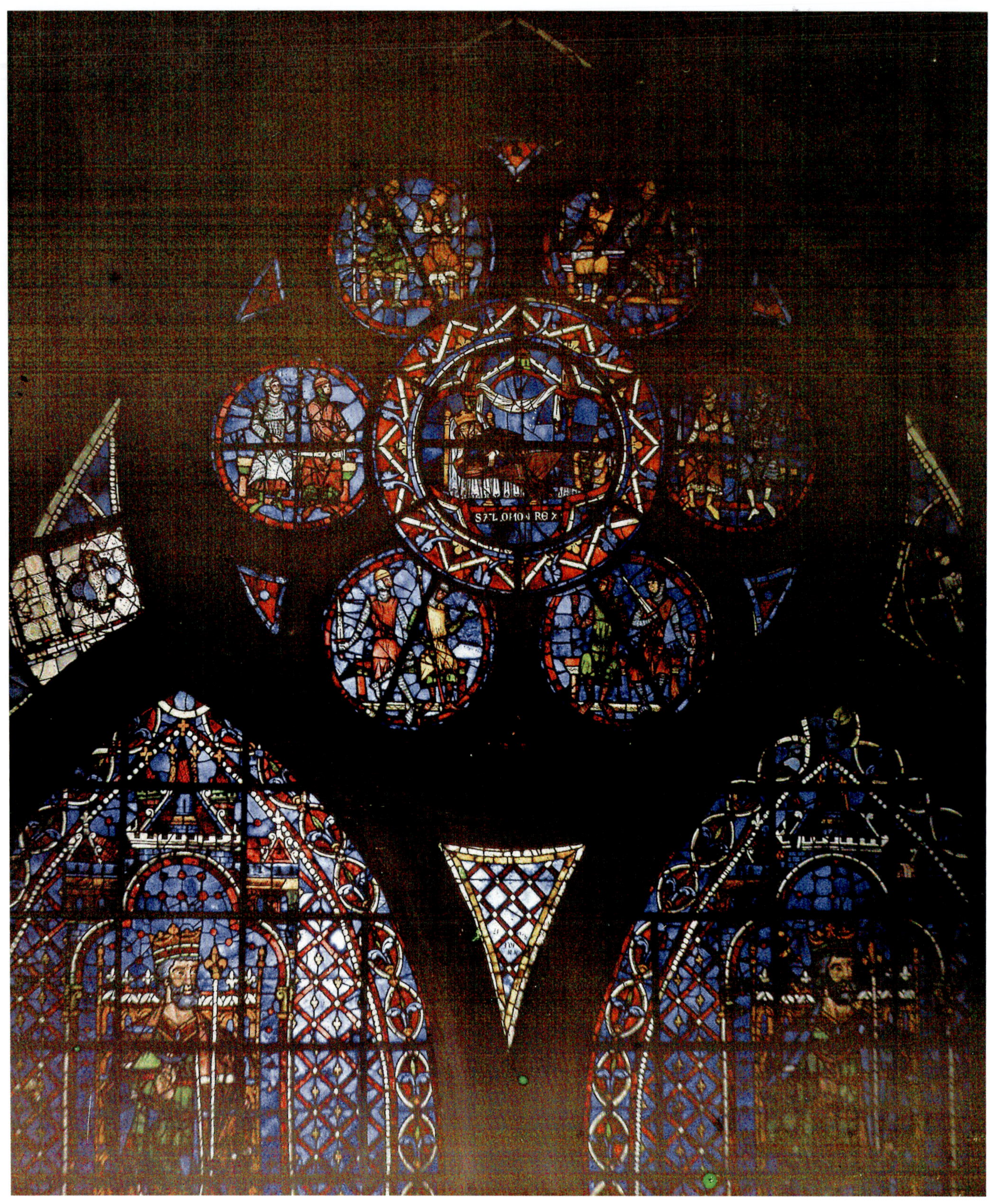

FIG. 159 Bay 121, rosace, King Solomon in Bed. Autochrome by Henri Deneux, 1915.

CHAPTER 5

THE ROSACES OF THE NAVE

Just as the rosaces of the chevet present and expand on the themes of the eastern bays—that is, apostolic succession and Ecclesia's power to combat the sins of disbelief and disobedience—the nave rosaces, beginning with Bay 121 (fig. 159), perform the same function for the ensemble west of the crossing. The power underlined here is the distinctive prerogative of Ecclesia Remensis to anoint and crown the kings of France. It will be argued in this chapter that the themes of the nave ensemble derive from two distinct, though certainly related, sources. These twin sources are the coronation liturgy as it was developed by 1250, when the glazing was planned, and the numerous writings—some of them obscure—of the Carolingian archbishop Hincmar (r. 845–82). Hincmar, as is well known and as clearly was recognized by the canons of the Gothic cathedral, profoundly shaped the Capetian coronation ceremony as developed and recast by the mid-thirteenth century. And Hincmar was an untiring defender of the historic centrality of Reims as "kingmaker."

The sophistication of the program of the nave rosaces outdoes even the "messages" embedded in the rosaces of the chevet, although no specific moment, action, or object of the coronation ceremony as such is depicted. Rather, those cathedral spaces in which the ceremony took place received themes reflecting the two main parts of the long ritual: first, the liturgy before the king-to-be was anointed, crowned, and enthroned; and second, when he had been empowered and was truly king. Thus are grouped the themes of the first three eastern bays of the nave—above the site of the liturgy, in the canons' choir (see fig. 160, Bays 121 through 126)—and then those of the remainder of the western nave, where the new-made king first received acclamation.

Outlined below are the events that constituted the ritual in the Ordo of 1250. The long day began with "the acts of waking the king, helping him out of bed, and leaving the [archbishop's] palace."[1] Within the church, the ceremony had eight phases:

1. Entry—procession to the altar and seating of participants.
2. Holy Ampulla—processional delivery by the abbot and monks of Saint-Remi.
3. Contracts—formulaic oaths by the king (peace, justice, and mercy) and his acceptance by "the people."
4. Knighting—the king, having disrobed, receives from various peers the sandals, spurs, and sword.
5. Unction—the archbishop anoints the king with oil from the Holy Ampulla, on the head, chest, between and on the shoulders, on the elbows, and hands.
6. Conferring the insignia—the king receives the tunic, surcoat, ring, scepter, "hand of justice," and

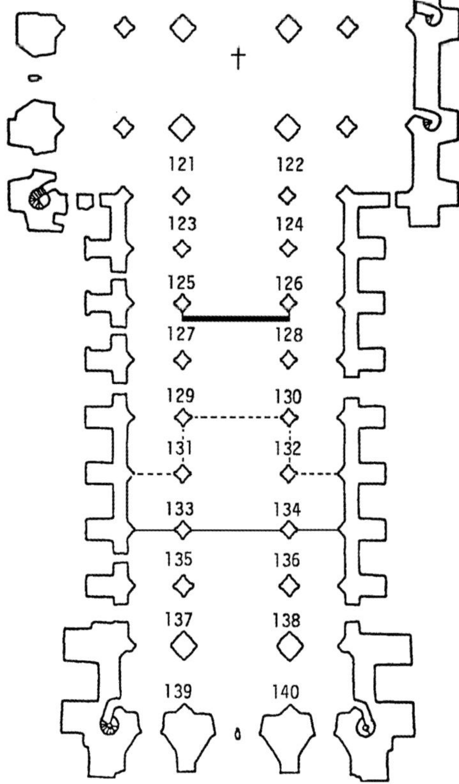

FIG. 160 Reims cathedral, plan of the nave. The heavy line indicates the choir screen (later, *jubé*). The dotted line denotes the *coupure Tourneur*, the division between the original nave construction and the extension to the new facade; it is indicated here at clerestory level. The thin straight line marks the location of the Romanesque facade (adapted after Kurmann, *La façade de la cathédrale de Reims*).

crown, and is seated upon the throne. He receives the kiss of peace and fealty; bells are rung and the Te Deum sung in celebration.

[end of the first part]

7. Mass—High Mass, in which the king receives Communion in both species like a priest.
8. Final rites—the king exchanges the heavy ceremonial crown for a lighter one and processes to the palace, preceded by the chamberlain, holding the unsheathed sword.

The shift in power occurred between phases 6 and 7. From the throne, located on a platform at the west end of the canons' choir (Bays 125 and 126), the new-crowned monarch could be seen and acclaimed by those occupying the remainder of the nave. That is the juncture of the two segments of the iconographic program of the nave rosaces (see fig. 161): episcopal authority shepherding wise rulership in the east, and beyond the *jubé* the king's power under Christ's ultimate authority.

Study of the nave glass is complicated by its extensive damage and uneven survival. Only the four easternmost bays of the nave, adjacent to the transept (121 through 128), were restored following the First World War. Nineteenth-century descriptions and drawings and Deneux's 1915 autochrome photos are thus of utmost importance for the study of the nave glazing. The arrangement of immense enthroned figures of kings (above) and bishops (below), now surviving in fragmentary form, originally filled the nave lancets. As scholars have recognized, the higher placement of the kings reflects the *laudes* of the coronation liturgy.[2] The arrangement also reflects the writings of Archbishop Hincmar, who—at the Synod of Sainte-Macre de Fismes in 881—specifically detailed the distinction between king and priest as well as the duties imposed on each:

> As we read in Holy Scriptures, two authorities rule the world, the holy priesthood and the royal power. Indeed, only Christ could truly be king and priest. Thus, after his *Incarnation* and *Resurrection* and *Ascension* into heaven, neither might a king assume priestly dignity nor a priest exercise kingly power. The offices are distinct, Christian kings needing priests for eternal life, and priests using kingly authority in temporal affairs. . . . The priesthood has greater dignity because it anoints kings, . . . while the burden of caring for the honor and defense and peace of the church through law and by arms has been imposed on the royal power by the King of Kings.[3]

Hincmar and other ninth-century theorists ultimately tipped this careful balance in favor of the power of the king.[4] I have provided his words here and have added the emphasis to three of them because they constitute one of the chief foundation blocks of the rosace program.

The Program of the Nave Rosaces

With perhaps only one exception, the subjects of these tracery rosaces—as they can be reconstructed

NORTH	SOUTH
121 King Solomon in Bed (fig. 159) 12 armed guards	122 nimbed bishop enthroned 6 bishops enthroned (fig. 162)
123 nimbed bishop enthroned (fig. 163) 6 angels with censers	124 Judgment of Solomon (fig. 164): King enthroned with scepter 4 seated counselors (upper lobes); executioners with baby (middle); 2 women, officers (lower)
125 bishop enthroned (fig. 165) 6 angels with censers, candles	126 Last Judgment (fig. 166): Christ with showing wounds; 6 angels with oliphants, passion symbols
----------------------- Jubé	-----------------------
127 Christ vested & enthroned, pointing up & down (fig. 167); Peter with keys & cross; angels	128 Virgin & Child (fig. 168) 6 angels with censers, candles
129 Virgin & Child 4 angels censing; 2 men praying	130 Resurrection: Christ stands, shroud 2 holy women w. vases (middle); 4 evangelists with symbols
....	....
131 ? Virgin & Child (fig. 211) 6 angels censing	132 Christ seated, holding orb 6 angels censing
133 ? Christ standing, in white apostles with scrolls	134 Transfiguration: Christ, Elias, Moses 4 sleeping apostles; 2 censing angels
135 ? Christ enthroned apostles with scrolls	136 Last Judgment: Christ showing wounds angels with oliphant, censer, passion symbols; 2 dead rising
137 Ascension: Christ's feet in cloud 12 apostles & Virgin watching	138 Last Judgment (center lost by 19th c.) angels with 2 oliphants, 2 crowns; dead rising
139 grisaille	140 grisaille

FIG. 161 Chart of the rosaces, nave clerestory, subjects reconstructed from the evidence of nineteenth-century observers and photos of World War I damage. The bracketed bays (Bays 121–28) survive or have been remade. The dashed line indicates the location of the *jubé*. The dotted line indicates the so-called *coupure Tourneur,* the last clerestory built before the decision to extend the nave and replace the old facade of ca. 1150. The Romanesque facade was located at Bays 133–34.

- Bay 122: All nineteenth-century observers saw a bishop in the center. The Christ of the Last Judgment now there was probably a replacement before 1914.
- Bay 127: Erroneously called a Resurrection in Recensement IV. The subject more probably is Christ, as lord of heaven, establishing the Church on earth; two angels are vested as deacons. Charles Cerf states that the lobes contained Peter (surviving), three figures with crosses, and two angels with crowns. The lobe of an angel with the crown of thorns is a replacement, not mentioned by nineteenth-century witnesses.
- Bay 128: Recensement IV erroneously states that this Virgin and Child was formerly in Bay 129. François de Guilhermy and Victor Tourneur noted a Virgin and Child in each bay, and this one (Bay 128) appears in a war-damage photo.
- Bay 137: Not to be confused with the Ascension panel installed in Bay 39, north nave aisle. Guilhermy noted both Ascension panels.

from nineteenth-century evidence—appear at first glance to be totally without order or sequence, a heterogeneous and even routine assemblage of enthroned bishops or kings, angels, the Virgin and Child, the Last Judgment, and isolated Christological scenes (Transfiguration, Resurrection, Ascension)[5] (see fig. 161). While the message of the great lancets below is easy to grasp—kings over bishops—the program of the rosaces is so subtle and complex as to be almost obscure. Although it is certainly possible and even likely that various panels already had been moved around before the nineteenth century, when they first were recorded, one can still essay some general observations. The following discussion of the nave rosaces is based on the descriptions of nineteenth-century witnesses.

A number of nineteenth-century observers noted a distinction in color or design between the easternmost "four or five bays" and the remainder of the nave.[6] A difference in campaigns between the glazing of the east nave bays and that of the west would be solidly supported by architectural evidence of the direction and pace of construction. There is strong evidence that the initial plan (discussed further in chapter 6) was to build the new nave to join with the surviving facade of the previous cathedral (see figs. 3, 160); the old facade was torn down and the Gothic nave extended no earlier than the midcentury. The subjects of the rosaces (fig. 161), however, divide most logically into those eastern bays that were over the area of the church where the coronation ceremony actually took place—that is, above the canons' stalls—and the western, public area of the nave. Although the permanent *jubé,* in place until 1744, was not constructed until 1416, Willibald Sauerländer and Jacques Le Goff stress that the medieval ceremony included a temporary structure for the enthronement at precisely the same location, that is, at the screen at the western end of the canons' choir occupying Bays 121 to 126.[7] Within this eastern nave area the rosaces—discussed below—depict, in addition to two scenes devoted to King Solomon (figs. 159, 164), numerous bishops and angels. However, beyond the *jubé* (and the new king's throne, upon it), all the rosaces were solely devoted to emblems of Christ's power and glory in one form or another.

This development from east to west parallels the Capetian coronation office in which, as noted by Richard Jackson, Christ is hardly mentioned until the actual anointing has occurred and thereafter is heavily emphasized.[8] Quite clearly the Christological scenes of the rosaces west of the *jubé* were not narrative in intent. Rather, they presented the themes of Christ's kingship, in presiding over the Last Judgment (Bays 126, 136, and 138; see figs. 161, 166); Christ's priesthood, in establishing the Church (Bays 127, 133, and 135; see fig. 167); and, specifically, Christ's Incarnation (the Transfiguration[9] in Bay 134 as well as the Virgin and Child in Bays 128, 129, and 131; see figs. 168, 211), Resurrection (Bay 130), and Ascension (Bay 137).[10] It cannot be fortuitous that these themes are precisely the ones voiced in Hincmar's statement of 881, quoted above: "Only Christ could truly be *king* and *priest.* Thus after his *Incarnation* and *Resurrection* and *Ascension* into heaven, . . . [t]he offices are distinct" (emphasis added). Symbolically no less than physically, the rosaces west of the *jubé* surmounted, most appropriately, the great lancets of kings and bishops beneath them. That is, the western rosaces established Christ's basis for the kingship and priesthood displayed in the lancets of the nave, as Hincmar had laid it out.

East of the *jubé,* within the area of the canons' choir at the eastern part of the nave (fig. 160), the rosaces relate to the pre-anointing part of the coronation rite. Three of these (Bays 122, 123, and 125) present enthroned bishops (figs. 162, 163, 165). In Bay 122 the central bishop (lost since the nineteenth century) was nimbed and surrounded by six more bishops seated in the encircling lobes (fig. 162). This image, too, reflected both of the sources for which I am arguing: Hincmar and the Gothic coronation liturgy. The Ordo of Charles the Bald, written (and performed) by Hincmar for that monarch's coronation as king of Lorraine at Metz in 869, included seven concelebrating bishops: "The liturgy is peculiar in that some of the

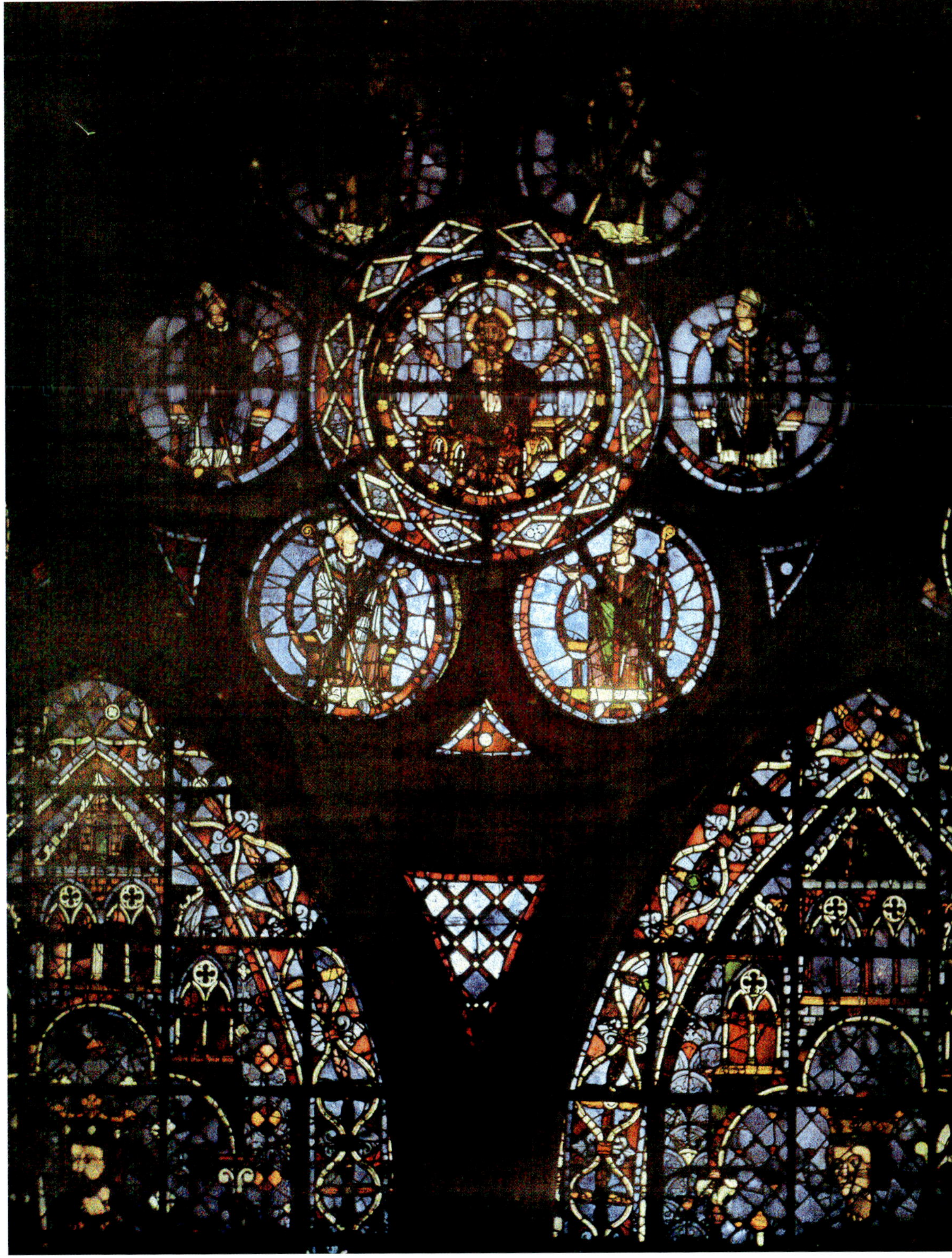

FIG. 162 Bay 122, rosace. The central medallion (Christ of the Last Judgment) is a stopgap replacement; all nineteenth-century observers saw there a bishop, nimbed and enthroned (St. Remi?). Lobes: six enthroned bishops. Autochrome by Henri Deneux, 1915.

FIG. 163 Bay 123, rosace: nimbed, enthroned bishop; censing angels.

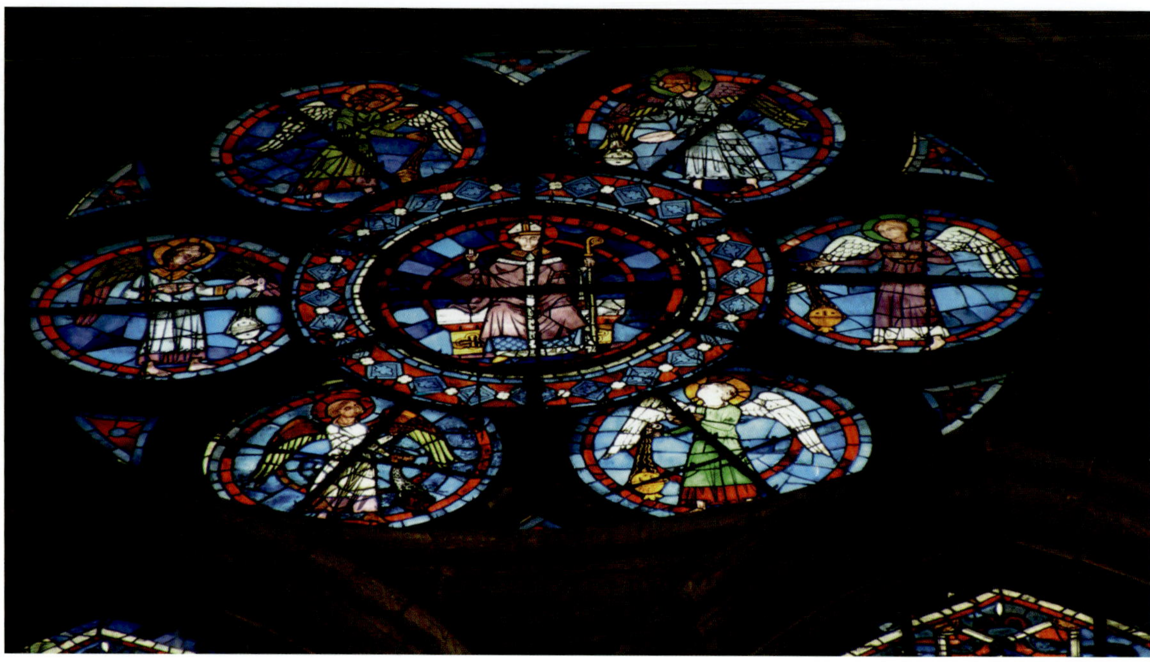

formulas are spoken by six assisting bishops, a practice specifically mentioned in no other ordo."[11] The six bishops in the lobes of the Bay 122 rosace, however, equally reflect the *pairs de France*. They were introduced into the Capetian coronation ceremony with the Ordo of Reims, dated by Jackson ca. 1230, and they are depicted participating in the ceremony in the Ordo of 1250 (fig. 169). The peers were a Gothic invention, and their number fluctuated until reaching an ideal of twelve (six ecclesiastical and six lay peers). After about 1225 the ecclesiastical peers consisted of the archbishop of Reims and the bishops of Langres, Beauvais, Châlons, Noyon, and Laon.[12] In this rosace (Bay 122) the lost nimbed bishop of the central medallion was surely St. Remi, whose baptism of Clovis with the Holy Ampulla in 496 had become fundamentally integrated into the French kings' coronation by the thirteenth century and—like the peers of France—first appears in the Ordo of Reims.[13]

Enthroned bishops, one nimbed and one not, appear in two more rosaces, those of Bays 123 and 125. This emphasis on bishops reflects the constant stress by Hincmar, who served as counselor to several monarchs, on the importance to kings of the counsel of bishops. See again his 881 oration at the Synod at Fismes: "And we read in the sacred histories [Deut. 17] that because priests anoint kings to rule, crown them, and give them the law, that they may know how to govern their subjects, kings should honor the priests of God."[14] The bishops in Bays 123 and 125 are encircled by angels with candles and censers (figs. 163, 165). Reims has often been called the cathedral of the angels, who figure prominently in its many decorative ensembles. Art historians have proposed chiefly Apocalyptic references for many of them.[15] Here again, the rosaces of the nave can be related more logically to Hincmar and to the Gothic coronation rite. Jackson notes the profusion of angels in both the cathedral and the coronation liturgy.[16] One of Hincmar's prayers, found in his ordines for Charles the Bald (869) and Louis the Stammerer (877) and reused in coronation rites for many centuries thereafter, requested God to "place his good angels for the protection of [the king], to precede, accompany, and follow [him] everywhere always, and by their power deliver [him] from the sword and from the risk of all perils."[17]

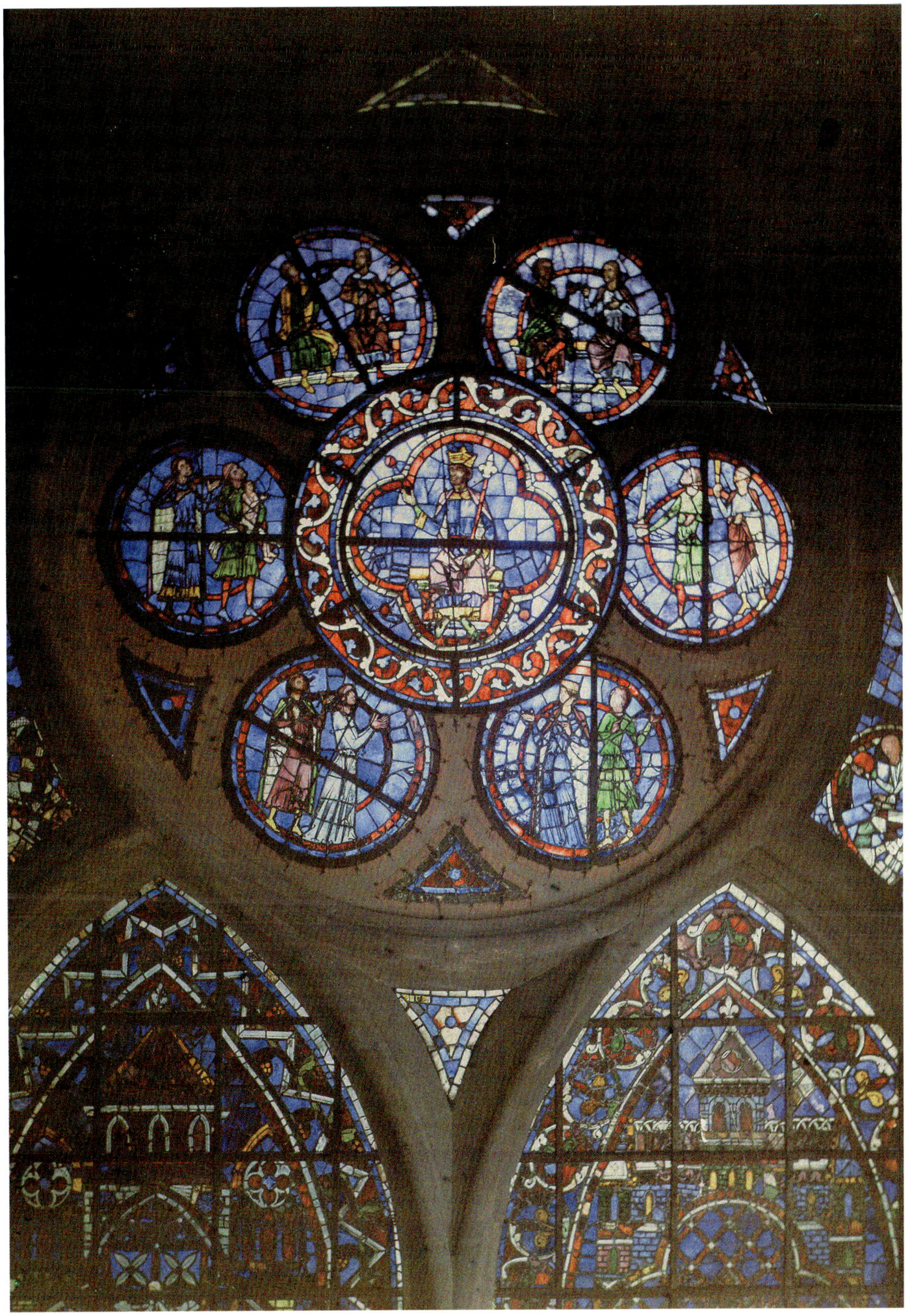

FIG. 164 Bay 124, rosace: the Judgment of Solomon. Autochrome by Henri Deneux, 1915.

FIG. 165 Bay 125, rosace: enthroned bishop; four angels with candles and two with censers.

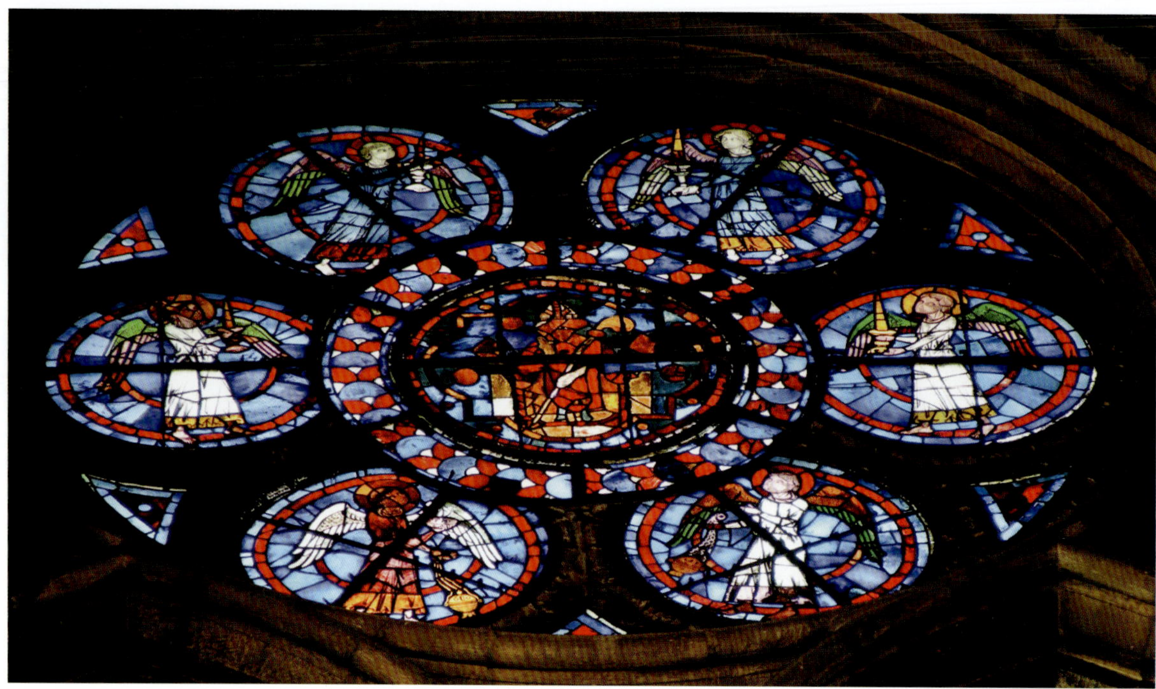

Solomon, Wise and Peaceful

Two rosaces of the nave clerestory present King Solomon. In Bay 121 (fig. 159) is the image of Solomon in Bed, so strange a theme that the programmer has provided the label "SALOMON REX," the only inscription in any of the nave rosaces.[18] In Bay 124 (fig. 164) is the much more familiar theme of the Judgment of Solomon (3 Kings 3:16–28). The identification of Bay 124 as the judgment, suggested by Hans Reinhardt, is undoubtedly correct.[19] It is accompanied in Bay 126 by the Last Judgment (fig. 166), of which it is the standard prototype. All the personae of the Judgment of Solomon appear in the Reims window:[20] the enthroned king (center); four king's counselors, seated and disputing (upper lobes); two pleading women, richly dressed as courtesans (lower lobes); and two types of royal agents. Three figures in vair-lined cloaks, clearly of some authority and status, as well as three policing figures of lower rank, bareheaded and wearing short green tunics, also appear. One of the latter brandishes a sword (center right lobe), and another (center left) presents the baby in a white cloth.

While the allegorical significance of the Judgment of Solomon normally involves Christ's choice of Ecclesia over Synagoga,[21] nothing in the nave glazing program would support an interpretation of the two Solomon scenes as typology in that mode, and both present the scenes in modern dress. No other Old Testament figures appear in the Reims stained-glass program (except Adam and his family in the north-rose Genesis), though many Old Testament worthies feature prominently in the sculpture of the cathedral's facade inside and out as well as around the transept roses. Even the Judgment of Solomon appears in the sculpted archivolts around the great west rose—as part of a series of images, now badly damaged, of the lives of David and Solomon.[22] Numerous authors have invoked the coronation in discussions of the Reims facade program, and indeed Christian monarchs were almost routinely compared to David, Solomon, and other Old Testament heroes. What is unusual about the two rosaces of Bays 121 and 124 is the exclusion of those others—the unique focus on Solomon. I will return to this point.

In the Judgment of Solomon, in Bay 124, the enthroned king holds a scepter very prominently

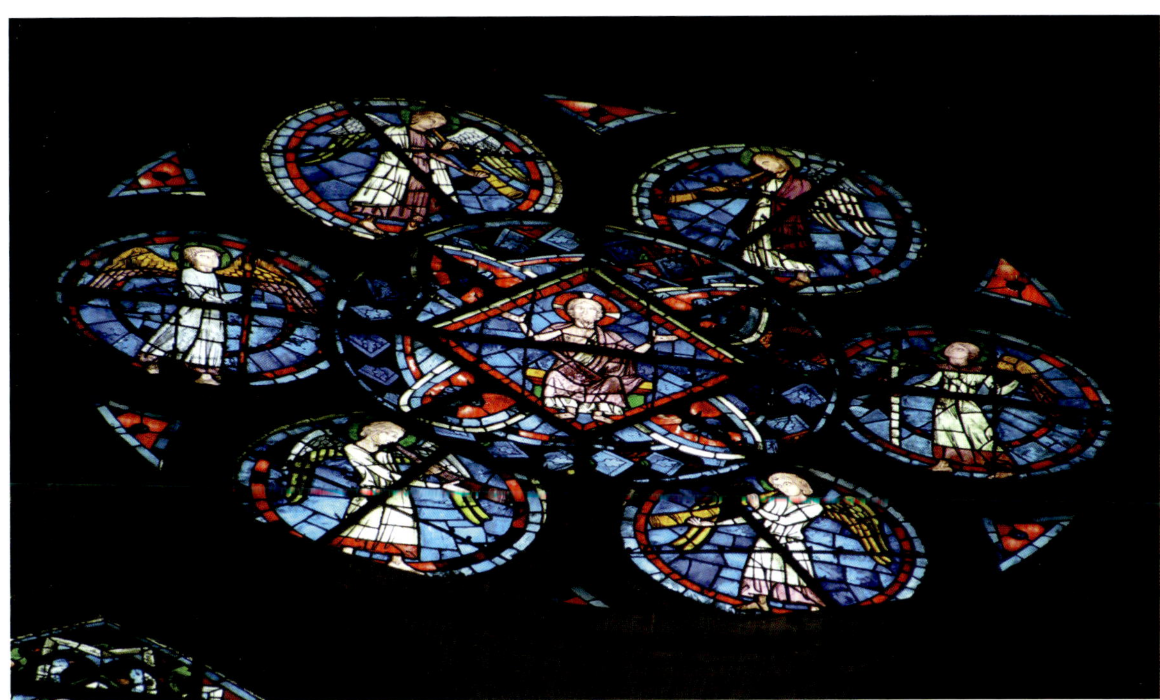

FIG. 166 Bay 126, rosace: the Last Judgment, Christ showing his wounds, four angels with oliphants, two with symbols of the Passion.

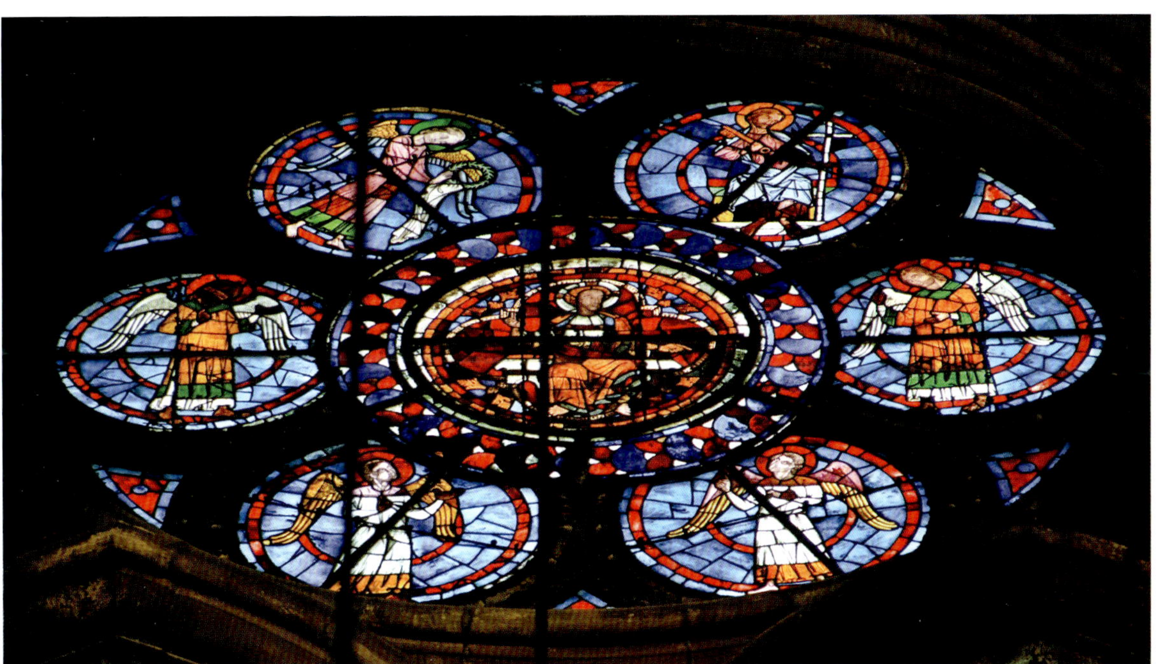

FIG. 167 Bay 127, rosace: Christ vested, enthroned, pointing up and down (that is, establishing the Church); Peter with keys and cross-staff (top right); angels, two of them vested as deacons. The angel with the crown of thorns (top left) is a stopgap replacement.

FIG. 168 Bay 128, rosace: Virgin and Child, four angels with censers, two with candles.

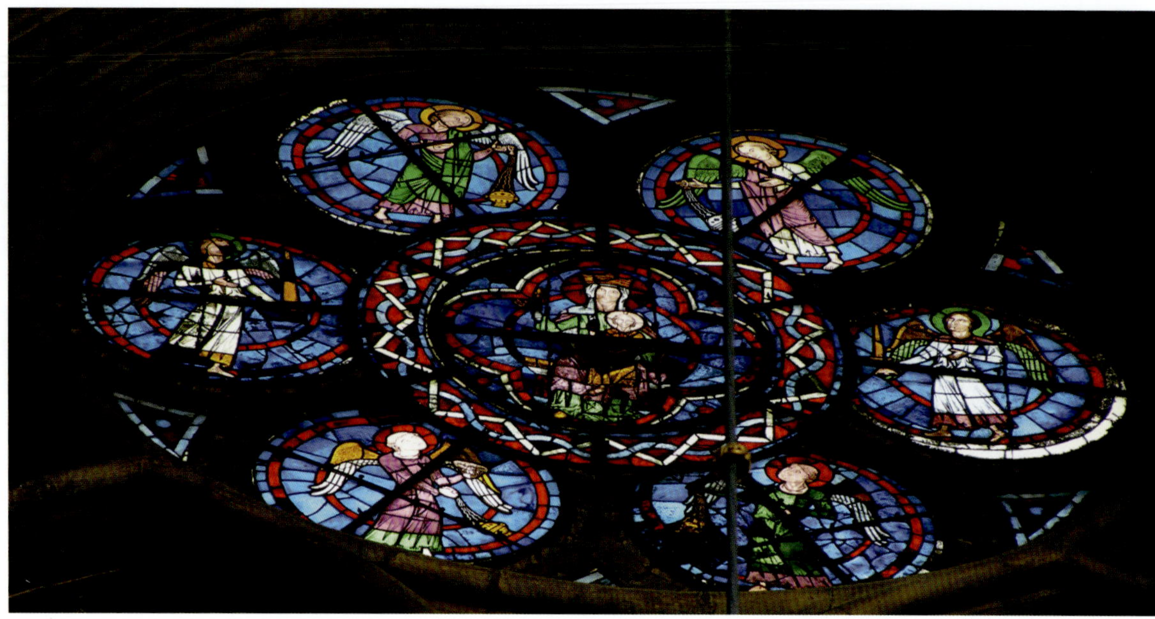

(fig. 164), suggesting another specific reference to Hincmar. In his ordo for the coronation of Louis the Stammerer in 877, Hincmar introduced a "liturgical novelty" for the investiture of the scepter, calling it "the sign of kingly power . . . by which the monarch should . . . defend the people from the wicked, punish evildoers, and lead the upright."[23] Another new formula in the 877 ordo, adopted universally thereafter, was Hincmar's consecration prayer. After mentioning Abraham, Moses, Joshua, and David, this new liturgical formula culminates in a plea to God—"You who have enriched Solomon with the ineffable gifts of wisdom and peace"[24]—to bless the king. Wisdom and peace are, in fact, the themes of this eastern group of rosaces. Wisdom is certainly the theme of the Judgment of Solomon (underlined by the accompanying Last Judgment, for which it is the prototype; figs. 164, 166). But the emphasis on peace is noteworthy. Peace—peace in strength—is encapsulated in the image in Bay 121 of the heavily guarded king reclining in bed (fig. 159).

The sharp focus on Solomon, omitting David and all other patriarchs, suggests a contemporary reference to the "New Solomon," St. Louis, king of France when the nave of Reims was glazed. Daniel Weiss has stated, "Renowned for the wisdom and justice of his leadership, Louis IX . . . earned the title *Ludovicus Justus* in his own lifetime, and he quite naturally came to be associated with Solomon, a typological fit indeed so appropriate that it was widely and enthusiastically endorsed."[25] Among numerous contemporary references to Louis IX's wisdom and justice, the testimony of Gautier Cornut upon witnessing the king wearing the crown of thorns is especially pertinent. Calling Louis IX "the True Solomon, the peacemaker," Cornut exclaimed, "And so with our hearts unable to believe the vision of our eyes, we could picture to ourselves the son of God crowned with thorns for our salvation! This is what the Holy Spirit invites us to do when, in the Song of Songs he addresses the faithful souls thus: 'Come out, daughters of Sion, and behold King Solomon wearing the diadem with which his mother crowned him.'"[26] This is verse 11 of Song of Songs 3 (see below). Verses 7 and 8 present Solomon in Bed—subject of the rosace of Bay 121—while verses 9–10 describe King Solomon's litter (the bed?).

King Solomon in Bed: The Theme in Art

An assessment of the Bay 121 rosace begins most usefully with the text of Song of Songs 3:7–11:

7 Behold threescore valiant ones of the most valiant of Israel surrounded the bed [*lectulus*] of Solomon!
8 All holding swords, and most expert in war: every man's sword upon his thigh, because of fears in the night.
9 King Solomon hath made him a litter [*ferculum*] of the wood of Libanus.
10 The pillars thereof he made of silver, the seat [*reclinatorium*] of gold, the going up [*ascensum*] of purple; the midst [*media*] he covered with charity for the daughters of Jerusalem.
11 Go forth, ye daughters of Sion, and see king Solomon in the diadem wherewith his mother crowned him.

This is the Douay-Rheims translation of the Bible, made from the Vulgate, and I have provided Latin terms as required for the discussion to follow (see also appendix 7). First, however, it will be useful to set the theme in context.

The passage describing King Solomon's repose, primarily verses 7 and 8, was not illustrated in the art of either Byzantium or western Christendom until the twelfth and thirteenth centuries, and it fell into an equal obscurity thereafter (see appendix 6). As Todor Petev has noted, "Here in fact we witness an interesting paradox; though the *Song of Songs* is one of the most widely commented upon texts in the high Middle Ages, it very rarely became a subject of visual representation."[27] Rare examples in Byzantine art (e.g., fig. 256) as well as what seems to be the first appearance in the West, in the *Hortus Deliciarum* of Herrad of Landsberg (fig. 255), associate the scene of the well-guarded bed of Solomon with the Virgin as part of the developing Marian iconography of the twelfth century.[28] In two unique cases in thirteenth-century Gothic art that have been mentioned in scholarly literature, other meanings are implied. It is hardly surprising that the first comprises the extravagantly illustrated Moralized Bibles associated with Louis IX; there the scene's commentary relates the sixty guardians to preachers who bring peace to the Church by combating enemies visible and invisible (fig. 257). The second case is quite different, though also understandable, as it was the personal selection of a king: Henry III's choice of the guardians (sans Solomon) for paintings near his own beds in both Winchester Castle and the Painted Chamber of the Palace of Westminster (fig. 258).

The extraordinary appearance of this theme in the coronation cathedral involves totally different meanings. Although Reims dates roughly from the same era as the Moralized Bibles and Henry III's bedroom decorations, and all are associated with monarchs, the significance of the theme of Solomon in Bed and the circumstances of its selection for Reims are considerably more complex. Reims does not reflect a personal preference, even of such a special person as a monarch. It is now generally accepted that the French kings, who did not contribute to the vast resources needed to build and ornament the Gothic cathedral, were the intended audience of some of its iconographic messages. While the same might be said of the Moralized Bibles, commissioned by monarchs and intended for their use, the Bibles present a predictable and solidly conservative message emphasizing the supremacy of theology and the dangers of heresy. At Reims, in a fundamental sense, the monarchy of France was a basic theme of the cathedral's program of imagery, indeed, one of its main subjects.

Another contemporaneous monument where monarchy forms a basic theme is, of course, the Sainte-Chapelle of Louis IX, and the contrast with Reims could hardly be greater.[29] The scene of Solomon in Bed (from the Song of Songs) does not occur, since the few appearances of Solomon are drawn from the book of Kings. Solomon appears only briefly in the king's chapel and in a distinctly negative light, as a worshipper of idols, incurring God's displeasure and bringing on the subsequent breakup of his kingdom.[30] The windows of the Sainte-Chapelle offer narratives—

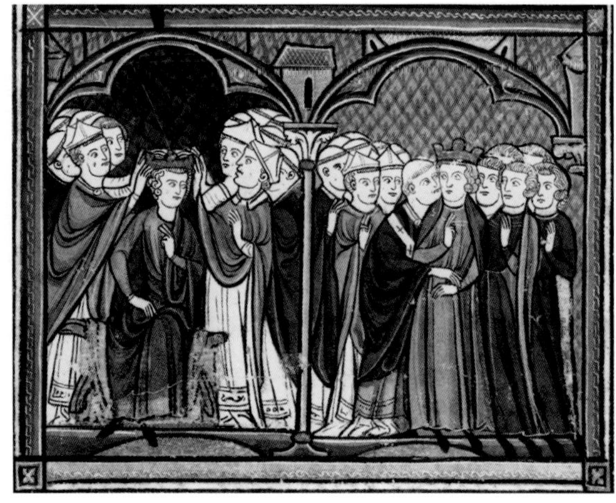

FIG. 169 The Ordo of 1250 (Paris, BnF, lat. 1246), fol. 26r, detail. The peers of France hold the crown over the king's head; the king, surrounded by the peers, receives the kiss of the bareheaded archbishop.

expanded, contracted—while the Reims nave glass presents themes, motifs, concepts. What then were the sources of these themes?

Solomon's Bed and Hincmar's *Carmen Figuratum*

Verse 3:7 of the Song of Songs (see above) describes "the most valiant of Israel [who] surrounded the *lectulus* of Solomon." Verses 9–10 describe his *ferculum* made "of the wood of Libanus." Whether or not the author intended the *lectulus* (small bed, couch) and the *ferculum* (litter, bed, or couch with shafts for transporting passengers) as the same piece of state furniture is not really at issue here. They occur in sequential verses, and both are places of repose for the monarch. As discussed in appendix 7, the Hebrew word for *ferculum* is a hapax legomenon; in the long history of commentary on the Song of Songs, it sometimes has been taken as the *lectulus* of verse 7, while at other times it has been given a totally different interpretation. In early Western Christian commentary, St. Ambrose conflated the two, and his text was readily available to iconographers in Gothic Reims.

Around 854–55 Hincmar, at an early point in his long career as archbishop, penned an exegetical work on verses 9–10 that is among the earliest Latin poems to be based on the Song of Songs, entitled *In ferculum Salomonis.* He dedicated the effort to Charles the Bald, who was often associated with Solomon in Carolingian texts.[31] Once labeled by scholars "a strange work," "bizarre," *"lourd exercise scolaire,"* Hincmar's poem has now been recognized as a *carmen figuratum.* That is, its 446 verses were apparently arranged on the page in visualization of the *ferculum*—with an accompanying prose *Explanatio* as a guide to the "word picture." While the *Explanatio* is known (*Patrologia Latina* 125, cols. 817–34), the poem it was meant to clarify has survived only in fragments discovered in recent times by Bernhard Bischoff,[32] allowing scholars to begin to grasp its form and to attempt a reconstruction.

The iconographer(s) in thirteenth-century Reims would have found in the text of Hincmar's tedious, banal, and convoluted poem of the ninth century a simple statement of Church dogma. It was a highly traditional exegesis of Solomon (as a type of Christ), of the Song of Songs (as Christ's love for the Church), and of verses 9–10 (as a description of the splendor of the Church). The poem is heavily larded with typically Carolingian number symbolism. Because Hincmar considered the *ferculum* a metaphor for the Church,[33] his difficult text was laid out on the page in a visual metaphor of the litter, with columns, *reclinatorium,* pillow, and so on. It must be acknowledged, however, that attempted reconstructions of Hincmar's image hardly strike the modern observer as depictions of a bed (see fig. 170). Ulrich Ernst has further suggested, from the *ferculum*'s central *media* (whatever it was), that the image was conceived as an *etimasia,* the throne (cf. Ps. 9:8 and Apoc. 22:1) used since the fifth century to indicate Christ's sovereignty over the world.[34]

The Gothic iconographer(s) of thirteenth-century Reims faced quite a challenge in drawing a stained-glass image from this cryptic and obscure poem. For identification they inserted an inscription in the glass, "SALOMON REX," the only inscription in any of the nave rosaces (fig. 159). And they clearly returned to the biblical text for assistance, finding in

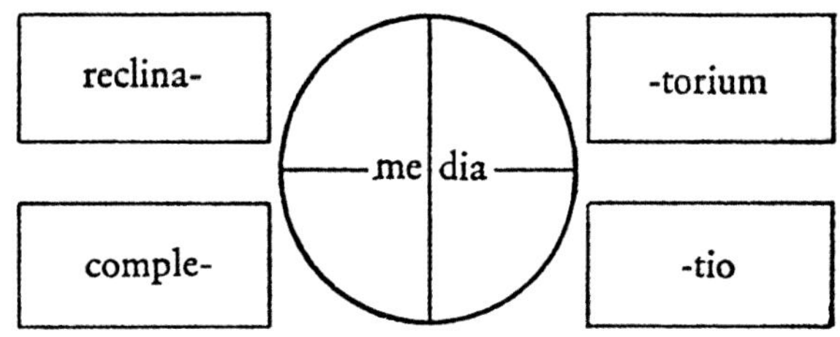

FIG. 170 Reconstruction of Solomon's bed from Hincmar's poem *In ferculum Salomonis* (after Burkhard Taeger, *Zahlensymbolik bei Hraban, bei Hincmar—und im "Heliand"? Studien zur Zahlensymbolik im Frühmittelalter*).

verse 7 the image for Bay 121—the scene of Solomon at peace, crowned, resting in his glorious bed,[35] and surrounded by guards.

The Sleeping King and His Guards

Like the biblical texts, the Gothic coronation liturgy provided the iconographers with useful detail. Of the Bible's sixty armed valiants, the rosace depicts only twelve (a pair in each of the six lobes, fig. 159), and only one of each pair holds a sword. They most probably are an additional reflection of the twelve peers of France (six lords and six bishops), who, as mentioned above, were introduced into the coronation liturgy ca. 1230 in the Ordo of Reims and who appear in the illustrations of the Ordo of 1250 (fig. 169). The motif of the peers dated only from the late twelfth century, and their number had not been set at twelve until around 1225. As Jackson has pointed out, "The college of the twelve peers had always been more ideal than real. . . . In 1202, Normandy reverted to the crown. Thus by the time the number of peers was set at twelve there were no longer twelve peers."[36] It has been argued that the idea was based on the twelve paladins of Charlemagne featured in *chansons de geste,* but the obvious parallel (of both) is to Christ and his apostles. Le Goff notes, "The peers, who help support the crown after the coronation and who accompany the crowned king to his throne, express . . . the participation of the feudal lords and their submission to the royal power."[37] They symbolize the vassals of the king, his loyal and trustworthy supporters, and they surround the new monarch in the Ordo of 1250 (fig. 169) like the valiants guarding Solomon.

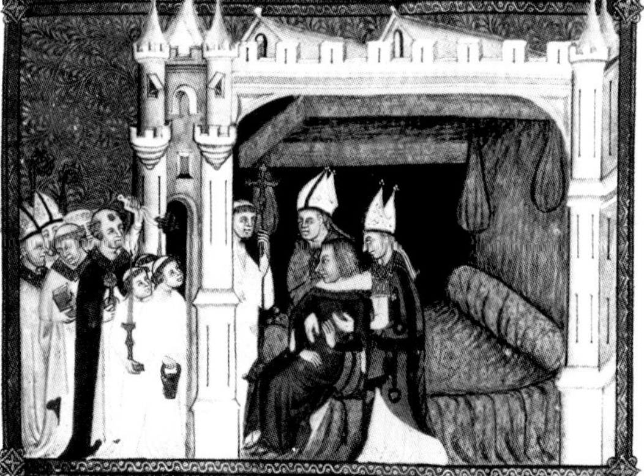

FIG. 171 Coronation Book of Charles V, 1365 (London, Brit. Lib., Cotton Tiberius B.VIII), fol. 44v, detail. King Charles in the archbishop's palace, roused by the bishops of Laon and Beauvais.

Yet another reference to the coronation liturgy is to be found, I believe, in the image of the sleeping Solomon himself. The very first event of the coronation day was a procession led by the first two of the episcopal peers, the bishops of Laon and Beauvais, to the archbishop's palace adjoining the cathedral for the ritual of rousing the sleeping king. An illumination depicting this ceremony in the Coronation Book of Charles V (fig. 171) accompanies the textual description:

> And the canons of the church of Reims . . . shall go to the archiepiscopal palace. And the Bishops of Laon and Beauvais . . . shall be in the said procession. And in the great chamber they shall seek the prince who is to be consecrated king sitting and half-lying on a bed [*sedentem et quasi jacentem supra thalamum*] properly appointed. When they arrive in the presence of the prince, the Bishop of Laon shall say this prayer: *Omnipotens sempiterne Deus [qui famulum tuum]*. . . .
>
> When this prayer is finished, the two bishops shall immediately and honorably support him on the left and the right and shall lead him reverently to the church.[38]

Jackson has traced the remote origins of the ritual of rousing the sleeping king to the early medieval German ordo of Mainz, ca. 961, in which first appear the prayer "Omnipotens sempiterne Deus, qui famulum tuum" and the two bishops leading the king to the church. The ceremony appears, among other places, in the Ratold Ordo of ca. 980 and from there was copied into the compilation known as the Ordo of 1250 (Paris, BnF, lat. 1246).[39] Although Jackson has noted that the king is not actually "asleep" until the coronation of Charles IX in 1561, Le Goff argues, concerning the Ordo of 1250, "At the beginning of the ceremonies, he is in his bed: *exeunte autem rege de thalamo*. . . . True, the ordo of 1250 says nothing of the king sleeping or being seized by two bishops, but it does say that when the king quits his bed, one of the bishops (not "a bishop," but "one of the bishops") is to say a prayer. . . . It seems reasonable to advance the hypothesis that the system of the two bishops—if not as rousers, at least as witnesses to the rising—was already in place."[40] The rosace of King Solomon in Bed provides further evidence that the ritual of the sleeping king formed part of the Ordo of 1250. This panel inaugurates the series of rosaces up to the *jubé,* with their liturgical references; it is located at the beginning of the series, that is, at the crossing and on the honorable dexter location on the north (at the right hand of the axial *Crucifixus*).[41] In the glazing, the coronation ceremony begins here.

The Ordo of 1250

The so-called Ordo of 1250, which exists in the single exemplar noted above, is only approximately dated. Originally called by Percy Schramm the "Compilation of about 1300," it received its present name from Jackson as a generic correction based on the appearance of the script and Robert Branner's dating of the numerous miniatures to ca. 1230–50.[42] Labeled by Jackson "the least harmonious, the worst conceived *ordo* in the whole history of the French rite,"[43] the Ordo of 1250 was not intended as a working liturgy and indeed could not be used as such. It is a compilation from at least four sources, with no attempt to mesh them into a serviceable whole. Jackson has outlined the many repetitions and misplacements of text that would make the manuscript unusable for any actual coronation ceremony; even some of the miniatures are repeated and out of order. The scene of the exchange of crowns (fol. 37v, preceding the Communion of the king and queen) reappears in a second, larger image on folio 42r, before the final procession to the palace.[44] Since the manuscript would be useless for a coronation, the question arises of why on earth it was composed. Jean-Claude Bonne reports that François Avril's preferred dating is now in the 1240s:

> The date neatly tallies . . . with the period between 1243 and 1248 when St. Louis decided to take the Cross and make meticulous arrangement for the governance of the realm during his absence. Given the precarious conditions of his own coronation and his desire to sacralize the image of the king of France, the achievement of an ordo focusing on these concerns fits neatly into the context of Louis's ordering of royal affairs to avoid crises that might be occasioned by his departure, including his death as a martyr of the Crusade.[45]

In any case the Ordo of 1250 seems to reflect an inquiry—or a series of inquiries—into the practices of coronation, their history, their meaning, their participants, and so on.

It is, I believe, unlikely that BnF, lat. 1246 was a royal commission. Perhaps it was a gift to the king? The illuminations, which seem to constitute a major element in the project, contain no gold, no fleurs-de-lis or castles of Castille, no *main de justice* or *grand sceptre,* and only generic types of crown and royal mantle, which do not particularly resemble the specific Capetian forms.[46] Although the text refers to the king of France, nothing in the illuminations makes this clear. The manuscript itself is a "fine copy" painted by a large atelier in Paris, one that, according to Branner, was popular with the clergy; the musical notation (on four or five lines) was standard in Paris but not used in Reims until much later.[47] However, it is generally accepted that its compilation of texts from four or more sources had been accomplished in Reims, possibly from manuscripts in the famous library of Saint-Remi (which burned in 1774). The illuminations highlight the central role of the archbishop of Reims in the ceremony, and they feature the Holy Ampulla; indeed, an entire large scene (fol. 4r) is devoted to the procession of the abbot and monks of Saint-Remi, in state, bringing the Holy Ampulla to the altar.[48]

Another strong regional connection is the litany, which contains all the important saints of Châlons-en-Champagne, though only Remi and Nicaise from Reims itself.[49] Châlons was a suffragan of Reims, and the bishop of Châlons was one of the six ecclesiastical peers who participated in the coronation ritual. If anything can be inferred from the manuscript's "Châlons connection," it is that the compilation of texts is more likely to have been made earlier than later. Connections between Châlons and Reims were particularly congenial throughout the 1230s, but not thereafter. Henri de Braine (r. 1227–40) had been elected bishop of Châlons in 1226 but, upon learning of the death of the archbishop, delayed his consecration and—after the first *élu* declined to serve—finally achieved the higher office he desired. He donated a stained-glass window to Châlons around 1236–37.[50] During the civic insurrections in Reims in 1233–36, Châlons had provided him with solid cooperation, which he did not receive from some of his other suffragans or from Louis IX. The archdeacon, dean, and succentor of Châlons, during this difficult time, acted as papal commissaries on Henri's behalf. The archdeacon in question was Jean Barat, who had been elected bishop of Châlons in two disputed elections (1201 and 1237) but never consecrated.[51] Henri de Braine died in mid-1240, Jean Barat about a year later, and thereafter the evidence indicates no special warmth between Châlons and Reims.

As for connections between Reims and the crown, Archbishop Henri de Braine's vainglory as direct descendant of King Louis VI poisoned his relations with Louis IX. Following Henri's death in 1240, the vacancy dragged on until 1245, when the pope appointed an outsider from western France, Juhel de Mathefelon. Archbishop Juhel took the cross with Louis IX about the same time but seems to have been too aged to leave with the king in 1248 and died in 1250. As a working hypothesis, a Châlons litany would be more likely if the compilation of texts was done in the late 1230s, whereas somewhat later, after 1245, Archbishop Juhel may have been instrumental in arranging for the production of BnF, lat. 1246 for his crusading monarch. While this hypothetical distinction is not necessarily pertinent to a precise dating for the manuscript, it is useful for the conception of the Reims stained-glass program.

The Program of the Reims Nave

Even the most casual perusal of the program of nave rosaces compiled in figure 161 establishes that the themes were not—at least not in the nineteenth century—presented in a nice, neat, orderly, or logical sequence. Even allowing for probable displacements over the centuries, one can discern no clear organizational arrangement that the various themes might originally have followed. The rosaces present concepts and seem to reflect a search for meaning (in biblical terms), for usage (in various liturgies from the Carolingian era onward), and for past authority, particularly in Hincmar's writings (even such a bizarre work as his *carmen figuratum*). The uncertain dating of the nave ensemble, or for that matter of the nave structure itself, offers little guidance. The traditional dating of the glass to ca. 1245–55, as provided in Recensement IV, places the nave windows directly after the final bays of the choir, there dated ca. 1235–45, and in any case applies only to the surviving and largely remade windows (Bays 121 to 128). A number of reliable nineteenth-century witnesses note a distinct difference between the appearance of the glass in the easternmost bays and that in the rest of the nave—that is, the windows totally lost in World War I. As the program is reconstructed, however, only the general reservation of Christological scenes for the area of the

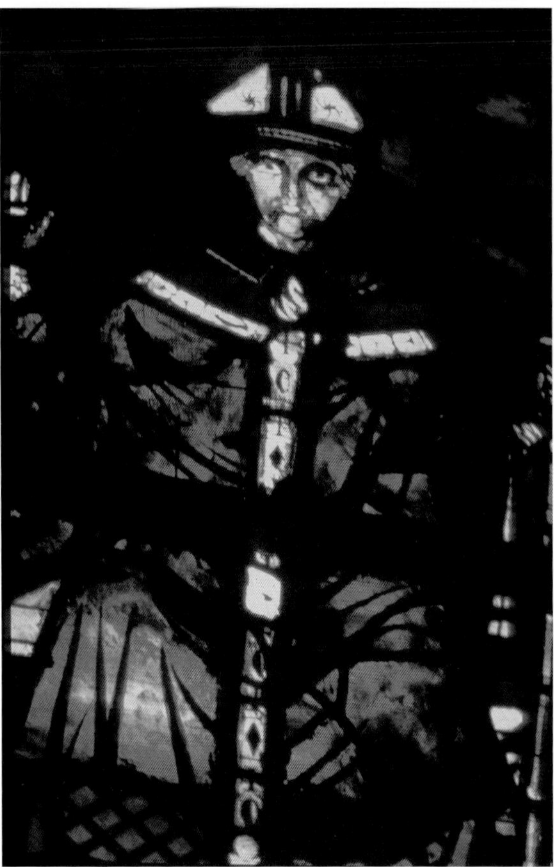

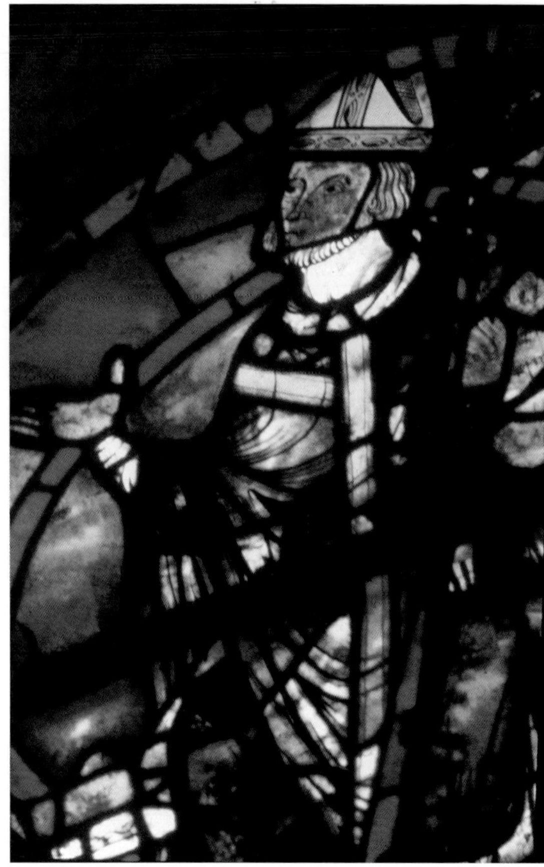

FIG. 172 Nimbed, enthroned bishop, Bay 123, rosace, central roundel, detail.

FIG. 173 Enthroned bishop, Bay 122, rosace, mid right lobe, detail.

nave west of the *jubé* seems to reveal any organizational principle.

Is it possible to clarify this puzzlement in any way? First, an observation on style.[52] A careful stylistic analysis of the nave windows—indeed of all Reims glass—undoubtedly will never be possible given the massive losses and equally massive interventions of the twentieth century (see figs. 177, 189).[53] With that caveat, it is obvious that the bishops in the rosaces of Bay 122 (fig. 173) and Bay 123 (fig. 172) represent distinctly different modes of glass painting. The heavy facial washes of the bishop in figure 172 are typical of many of the choir rosaces,[54] while the clean economical line employed for the bishop in figure 173 and his greater realism and immediacy are in a different style. It seems clear, at the least, that these two bishops were not products of the same glazing studio, a conclusion that suggests the execution of the nave program occupied some years. Another contrast can be noted between the rigid, axial figures of, say, Bays 122 and 126 (figs. 162, 166, 174) and the enthroned Christ of Bay 127 (fig. 175)—differences in palette, figure scale, and immediacy. Comparisons to the rosaces of the chevet are not that close either—for example, in the decorative vocabulary. The red circles in the grounds of lobes of Bays 102 and 108, as well as the north rose, reappear in nearly all the extant nave rosaces (Bays 122 through 128) (see figs. 34, 62, 162–68); however, the leading of a smaller lozenge-shaped center, introduced in the late choir rosaces (105, 107, 108, figs. 57, 64, 62), occurs only once in the nave (Bay 126, fig. 166).

The most obvious difference is the addition of framing devices around the central figures of the nave rosaces: quatrefoil frames in 121 and 124 (figs. 159, 164), and the later so-called *carré quadrilobé* form—a quatrefoil overlaid with a square or lozenge—in 122, 125, and 127 (figs. 162, 165, 167).[55] As for border designs, only the roundels of Bays 121 and 124 (the two Solomon rosaces) have borders of acanthus related generally to the chevet. Two new border types are introduced. The first is a chain of painted blue lozenges, variants of which appear in Bays 122, 123, and 126; the second is a simplified and unpainted fish-scale pattern of red and blue half- and quarter-circles, in Bays 125 and 127. Generally speaking, one can conclude that the nave rosaces are later by some years than those of the chevet, and generally simpler in design. Only the two Solomon rosaces (121 and 124) rise above this assessment. It is a good bet that they originally faced each other at the east end of the nave, inaugurating the program.

An anomaly in the subject program should be highlighted at this point. The Last Judgment in Bay 126 (fig. 166) is Christological in theme, and it is located east, not west, of the *jubé*. Its placement next to the Judgment of Solomon (Bay 124) is logical—but is it original? With Bay 122, at the crossing, these bays on the south are the only nave clerestories in which the large bishops in the lancets are named by inscription (as discussed in chapter 6). It is my belief that these bays were heavily damaged in the same 1580 storm that blew out the glass, and even the stone tracery, of the nearby south rose window and that the names of the large bishops were insertions during the succeeding restoration.[56] It is thus gratifying to learn that the restoration done on Bay 122 in 2000 by the atelier Simon-Marq discovered that, except for the ground, the glass in the figure of Viventius is a sixteenth-century restoration. Thus the present locations of the rosaces in Bays 122, 124, and 126 are possibly—indeed probably—not original. That solves the problem of the misplaced Last Judgment of Bay 126 at the least.

A further avenue of investigation, in establishing some coherence in the original program of the rosaces, is that of the dating and construction of the various sections of the nave. While there is almost no scholarly consensus about the chronol-

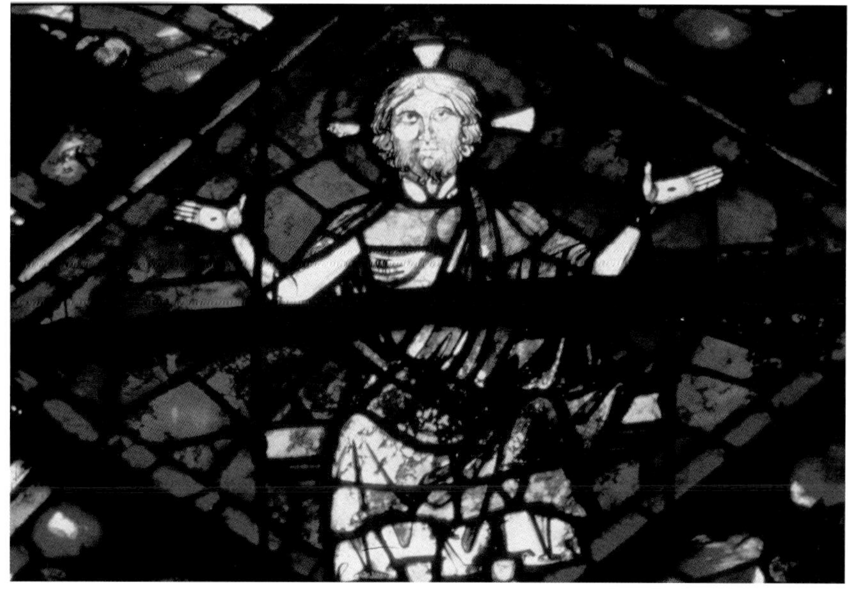

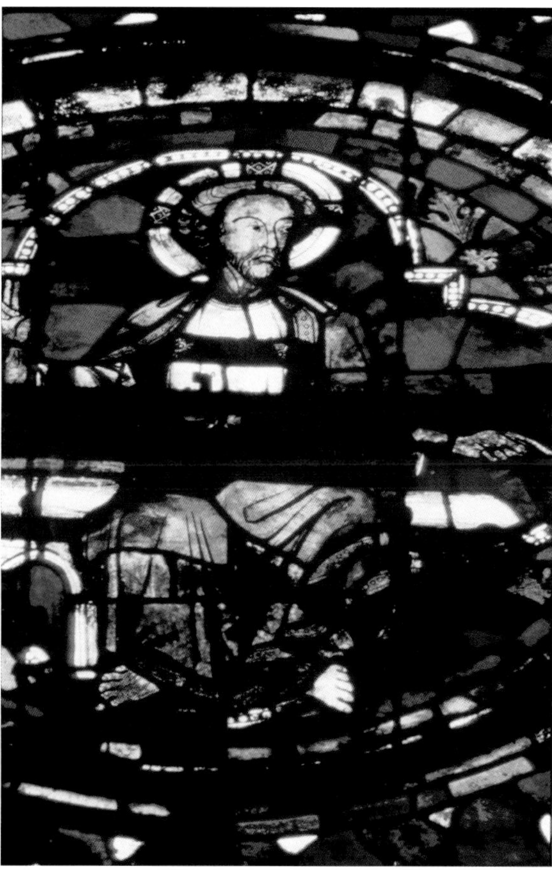

FIG. 174 Christ showing his wounds, Bay 126, rosace, central roundel, detail.

FIG. 175 Christ establishing the Church, Bay 127, rosace, central roundel, detail.

ogy of construction at Reims, it has been proposed that the "new choir" that the canons took possession of in 1241 was (or included) the three eastern bays of the nave.[57] My own view, as expressed in chapters 2–4, is that a temporary "canons' choir" was probably established for the opening of the new construction in 1241, perhaps occupying the chevet and transept. But that arrangement would have been pro tem. The location of the canons' choir in the new Gothic nave was, I would hasten to agree, always intended. Peter Kurmann assumes that the nave unit at issue here extended to the *coupure Tourneur* (see figs. 3, 160) and thus amounted at clerestory level to the five eastern bays. At least one more bay can be added to this group, preceding the Romanesque facade located at Bays 135 to 136.[58] Regardless of the actual moment(s) of construction of these bays, their conception as a unit seems likely, and thus the glass program for these nave bays also must have been conceived, at least, as a unit.

Then, in the 1250s, when the old facade was removed and the nave extended, that original glass program would have needed extending as well. Thus may be explained the puzzling repetitions in figure 161: three Virgin and Child images, three Last Judgments, two or three scenes of Christ enthroned, and so forth. So, if the program of the easternmost bays was a unit, and some allowance is made for misplacements over the centuries, what could the original nave program have been?

The group east of the *jubé* undoubtedly contained nearly all its present subjects, though possibly not in their present locations. The two Solomon scenes (Bays 121 and 124) certainly form a pair, as do the various nimbed and unnimbed bishops. Only missing is a sixth subject, probably destroyed in 1580 and replaced by the present Last Judgment in Bay 126.[59]

West of the *jubé* would have been six rosaces in the original program, those in Bays 127 to 132. They most probably presented those scenes that have been highlighted as most closely connected with Hincmar: the Virgin and Child (just one), the Transfiguration, the Resurrection, the Ascension, Christ vested and establishing his Church, and the Last Judgment. How these were arranged can be suggested. The first four would occupy two bays and thus is explained why—of Hincmar's trio of Incarnation, Resurrection, and Ascension[60]—the Incarnation was expanded to two images (Virgin and Child, and Transfiguration). Christ establishing his Church and then Christ judging it at the end of time form a fitting and final (as then planned) western pair of themes. The program of the nave rosaces of Reims was, at least in its conception, not as casual or incidental as has been thought.

Although the new facade and towers were not finished until much later, Kurmann dates to ca. 1275–99 the completion and vaulting of the bays of the nave extension.[61] Those were glazed with the mindless repetitions of the Virgin and Child, the Last Judgment, and the enthroned Christ (all lost in World War I). It is nonetheless likely that Kurmann's date applies to them as well. Beginning around 1280, an advanced and improved technology developed in the production of glass; larger pieces of stronger, thinner, and therefore clearer glass became standard.[62] Victor Tourneur in 1857 described exactly this difference in his discussion of the nave of Reims:

> All this stained glass is not of the same epoch. The first four or five bays on each side [the eastern nave] are of a darker, more harmonious color; the design, although poor, is more carefully done. They are of the first half of the thirteenth century. The remaining bays [the western nave] are very badly done. They are dominated by light tones, pale yellow, brilliant green, of a type . . . associated with a more advanced epoch. Their style is very different from that of the first bays; the forms are more broadly rendered, the pieces of glass larger. Besides, these windows fill the bays that are incontestably added to the original plan of the building. All this indicates that they certainly belong to the end of the thirteenth century.[63]

It is possible to delimit even further the date of the glass in the nave extension. The bays immediately inside the facade (Bays 139 and 140, fig. 238) were glazed in grisaille, since lighting there was obstructed by the towers.[64] Although those bays were in very bad condition by the nineteenth century, they still contained remnants of medieval grisaille, as well as borders of fleurs-de-lis and castles of Castille.[65] It is possible to date such borders, which reflect the political goals of Louis IX but definitely not those of Philippe le Bel, who came to power in 1285. Such borders last on in glazing practice only to about 1290 at the very latest.[66] Kurmann's dates for the completion of the nave extension can thus be considered "glass-included."

In sum: the glazing of the Reims nave was accomplished in two campaigns, the original one carefully planned and the later extension rather hasty and pro forma. The original program, established for the nave bays up to the old facade, was conceived in the 1240s (though perhaps completed slowly). It was a program heavily researched from Hincmar's writings and the Ordo of 1250. When the nave was extended to a new facade, glass was made for the new bays in the 1280s—when at least the memory of the original program was still retained—simply by repeating themes already present. The dense scholarship on the Gothic sculpture of Reims has established the French monarchy as one of its fundamental themes and the Gothic coronation liturgy as a basic source. It is hardly surprising that the same can be said of the stained-glass program in the nave of the cathedral, where the ceremony took place. The fascination is in the detail, invention, and complexity of the nave program, which is far more than the simple conjunction of images (kings, bishops, and standard religious images of angels, Virgin and Child, Last Judgment) that it has appeared to be.

Crucial to the program are the tracery rosaces. Their placement within the nave reflected the coronation ceremony as it unfolded in that space, before and after the king was anointed and took power. The importance of the coronation liturgies composed by Hincmar for various Carolingian events has long been recognized, but it seems undeniable that much of his other writing was consulted very carefully to establish the unique glass program. The rosaces, in fact, present Hincmar's message delivered at the synod in 881, where he declared that Christ was both king and priest but that, following his Incarnation, Transfiguration, and Ascension, those offices were distinct and in delicate balance. Kingship was to be supported by, and protective of, the priesthood.

The focus on Solomon to the exclusion of all other Old Testament worthies is a probable reference to the reigning monarch, Louis IX. The two Solomon scenes selected are less predictable: the popular Judgment of Solomon and the extremely rare scene of Solomon in Bed surrounded by guards, from Song of Songs 3:7–8. These two reverberate with references to both the coronation rite and to Hincmar and focus the message of the glazing program of the nave of Reims cathedral: wisdom and peace. The rare scene of King Solomon in Bed makes this message absolutely clear—peace in strength.

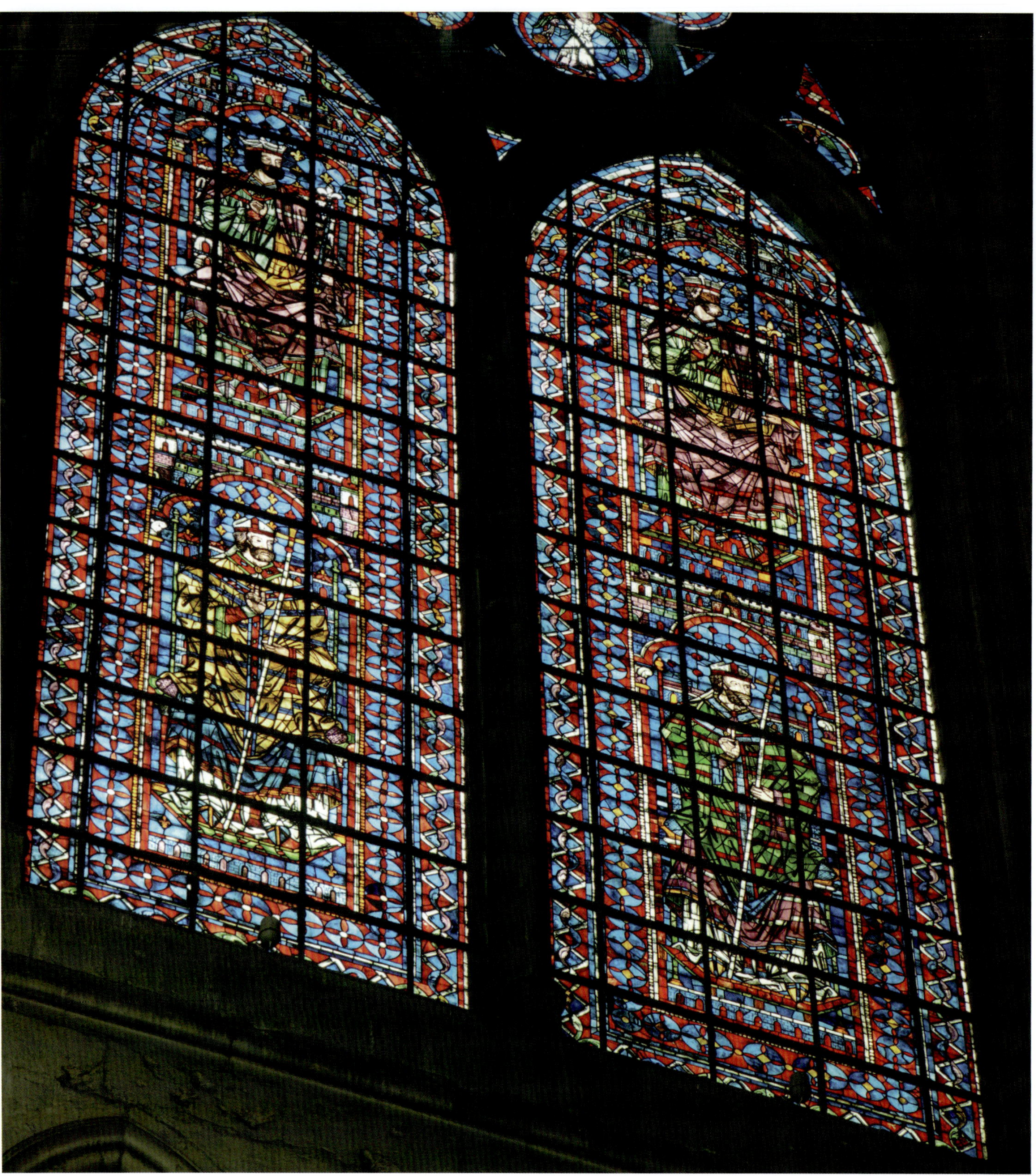

FIG. 176 Bay 125.

CHAPTER 6

THE LANCETS OF THE NAVE

The rosaces of the nave, like those of the chevet, provide rich matter for the comprehension of the clerestory ensemble of which they form a part, as well as insight into its program, sources, and goals—the larger picture, one might say. As shown in the previous chapter, the nave rosaces underline the Gothic coronation liturgy as origin and subject and also make clear the approach, which is in no way literal or representational but, rather, thematic and symbolic. That is, images are not provided of actions, events, or objects of the ceremony. The figures are not individuals but symbols. The images visualize concepts about kingship as imbedded in the thirteenth-century ordines and as found in the oeuvre of the Carolingian archbishop Hincmar. The study of the nave rosaces also makes clear the division between clerical and public space, behind and beyond the *jubé*. Another demarcation is indicated between those bays planned to connect to the Romanesque facade block and those added in the later extension of the Gothic nave to a new facade, the *coupure Tourneur* marking the division. And finally, a grouping is established between those bays that survive—if only in careful modern copies—and those knowable only from variable pre-1914 witness, if indeed at all.

Following the tragic damage to the nave windows in World War I and then the postwar restoration, stained glass now fills only the four easternmost bays of the nave, those adjacent to the transept. Predestruction descriptions, drawings, and photographs provide evidence that the program had consisted then, as it does now in fragmentary form, of immense enthroned figures of kings (above) and archbishops (below)[1] (see fig. 176). It is often noted that inscriptions name only one king, Karolvs, and six archbishops. One of the goals of this chapter is to eliminate these figures from the original program, thereby erasing the question of why the vast sequence of figures is unnamed. They are anonymous because they are signs, embodiments of power, not precise individuals. No action takes place. Their great size, their incessant repetition, and their repeated design (sometimes on the same cartoon) compose a great choral alleluia on the concept itself of French coronation, its *sine qua non* being a king to be crowned and an archbishop of Reims to crown him. The subject of the nave thus could be encapsulated as "coronation," specifically the *sacre* of the kings of France. The theme is no less site-specific to this particular church than are the chevet's images of its archbishop with his suffragan bishops and their cathedrals.

Thus the program of the immense clerestory lancets of the nave is seemingly very simple. But at Reims—unlike the similar glass arrangement at

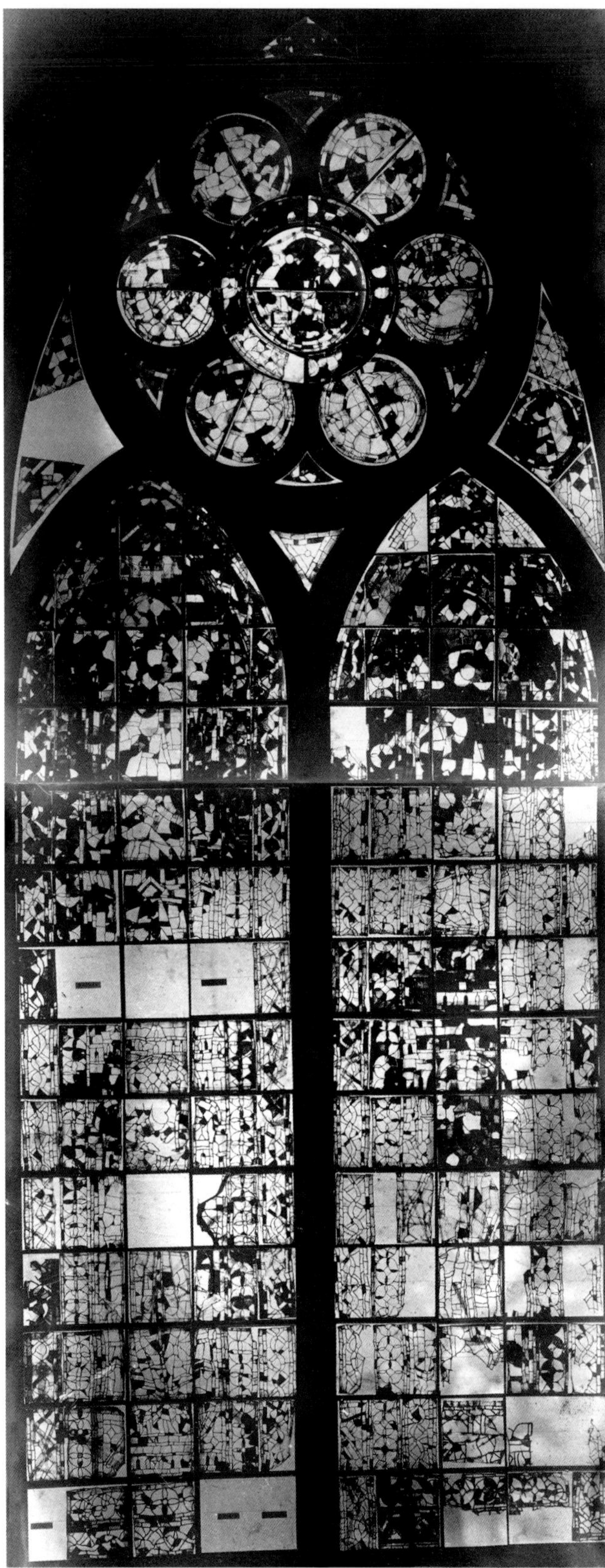

Saint-Remi, often assumed to be its model[2]—kings appear above archbishops. This arrangement reflects the thirteenth-century coronation liturgy. At its beginning the royal acclamations (*laudes regiae*) invoke kings before bishops, whereas at the finale, when the king ascends the throne, "the archbishop doffs his miter before the crowned king and respectfully kisses him."[3] The first mention of the *laudes* is the assertion by Flodoard (d. 966) that it was sung at the coronation of Louis the Pious in 816.[4] Anne Robertson, who has published the *laudes* from a Reims manuscript of ca. 1230 (Assisi, Biblioteca del Sacro Convento 695, fols. 41–43), analyzes its sections and affirms that, in addition to coronations, it was performed regularly on at least seven of the most important feasts during the year.[5] It was thus quite familiar to the ecclesiastical community of Reims. Moreover, the fact that the archbishops appear in the lower row of the lancets might well have appealed to the canons, who were in more or less continuous conflict with their prelates. Hincmar, in his writings for the Synod of Sainte-Macre de Fismes in 881,[6] attempts to separate and balance king and priest, but his elaborate ruminations on the balance of powers and those of other Carolingian theorists, based ultimately on the fourth-century Ambrosiaster, embroidered on a statement already succinctly put to the young Charlemagne in 775 in a letter from Cathwulf: "Thou art the viceregent of God, and the bishop is in the second place only, the viceregent of Christ."[7] There is, however, more to the lancet program than that.

Trustworthy Evidence?

It must be acknowledged at the outset that the study of the nave clerestories is fraught with problems. The nave originally contained thirty-six kings above thirty-six archbishops. Following the severe destruction of World War I only eight double-lancet clerestories were remade in the nave—that is, less than half of them. "Remade" is the most accurate word. Wartime photographs of damage (e.g., figs. 177, 189) make it clear that a number of presently extant figures had been demolished and are now wholly refabricated based on the tracings made in situ by the Simons during the nineteenth century.[8] Other nineteenth-century witnesses have been tapped in the discussions of the chevet and transept, chiefly the verbal accounts of Baron de Guilhermy and the clerics Tourneur and Cerf. Added to their descriptions are a number of drawings by cathedral visitors and the 1995 deposit to the Bibliothèque municipale of Reims of a precious group of pioneer color photographs made near the start of the war by Henri Deneux. These imperfect data do establish, as noted in the previous chapter, that the style and color of the easternmost nave bays (121 to 130) were more rich and somber than those clerestories added when the nave was later extended (from Bay 131 westward). Nonetheless, these nineteenth-century accounts, of course, record the glass with all the restorations and alterations of many previous centuries. The preliminary task of this chapter, then, is to root out and scrutinize such suspected changes to the original glazing program.

Six Named Archbishops

The glazing program of Reims has been among the group traditionally considered to reflect the great series of archbishops in the chevet of Saint-Remi, dated ca. 1175–80. There the prelates are all named.[9] In the cathedral nave only six have inscriptions, and nineteenth-century observers confirm that the number was not then higher.[10] The six are clustered in Bays 122, 124, and 126 in the south nave at the crossing. To compound the puzzle, it can be noted that these six named archbishops are quite insignificant prelates in the cathedral's past. The question is thus posed: just why should these six have been singled out for naming, and in this particular location?

Paul Simon, who was in charge of the upkeep of the cathedral windows for many decades, observed in 1911 that the glass on the south was in far worse condition than the rest.[11] This clue propels my investigation of the six named figures,[12] their design, vestments, gestures, thrones, and whatever history can tell us about their cults and importance. I argue that these names and figures are postmedieval in origin.

The numbering of archbishops comes from Flodoard (d. 966), *Historia Remensis ecclesiae,* whose catalogue, Duchesne has established, had already become traditional by the time of Archbishop Hincmar (d. 882) and was recited in the Mass at Reims.[13] Comparisons below are made to other cathedral arts as well as to glass surviving or known from Deneux's photographs, as well as from the nineteenth-century accounts.

• Bay 122, left lancet: St. Donatianus, seventh archbishop (late fourth century) (figs. 178–79).[14] Although Donatianus was the seventh archbishop chronologically speaking, here he commences the series in the nave. His body and cult, however, had been transferred to Bruges in the ninth century, hundreds of years before this window was made. The figure in the bay, haloed and beardless, sits on a high-backed throne and holds a crozier. Several details of this image are peculiar. His pose is rigidly frontal, unlike that of any other prelate in the entire nave, but similar to some bishops in the earlier chevet series. His blessing hand differs from those of all other bishops of the cathedral glass, including those of the chevet and south transept. It is placed far to the side, against the ground, while all other blessing hands are contained within the body silhouette. Like a few other archbishops in the nave—those of Bays 127 and 129, now lost—he wears the breastplate called a rational.[15] However, it is not rectangular but almost square, and peculiarly decorated in a lozenge pattern colored alternately like a checkerboard.

The rational in use at Reims in the Middle Ages was an uncommon type, "a rectangular pectoral studded with twelve jewels that continued in use until late in the fifteenth century, as indicated in the 1470 inventory of the cathedral."[16] The archbishop wore it only on solemn feast days. Sculpted examples appear on the north transept, where jamb statues of the archbishop-saints Remi and Nicaise wear rationals on the Calixtus portal,

FIG. 177 Bay 125, montage of war damage, after 1918.

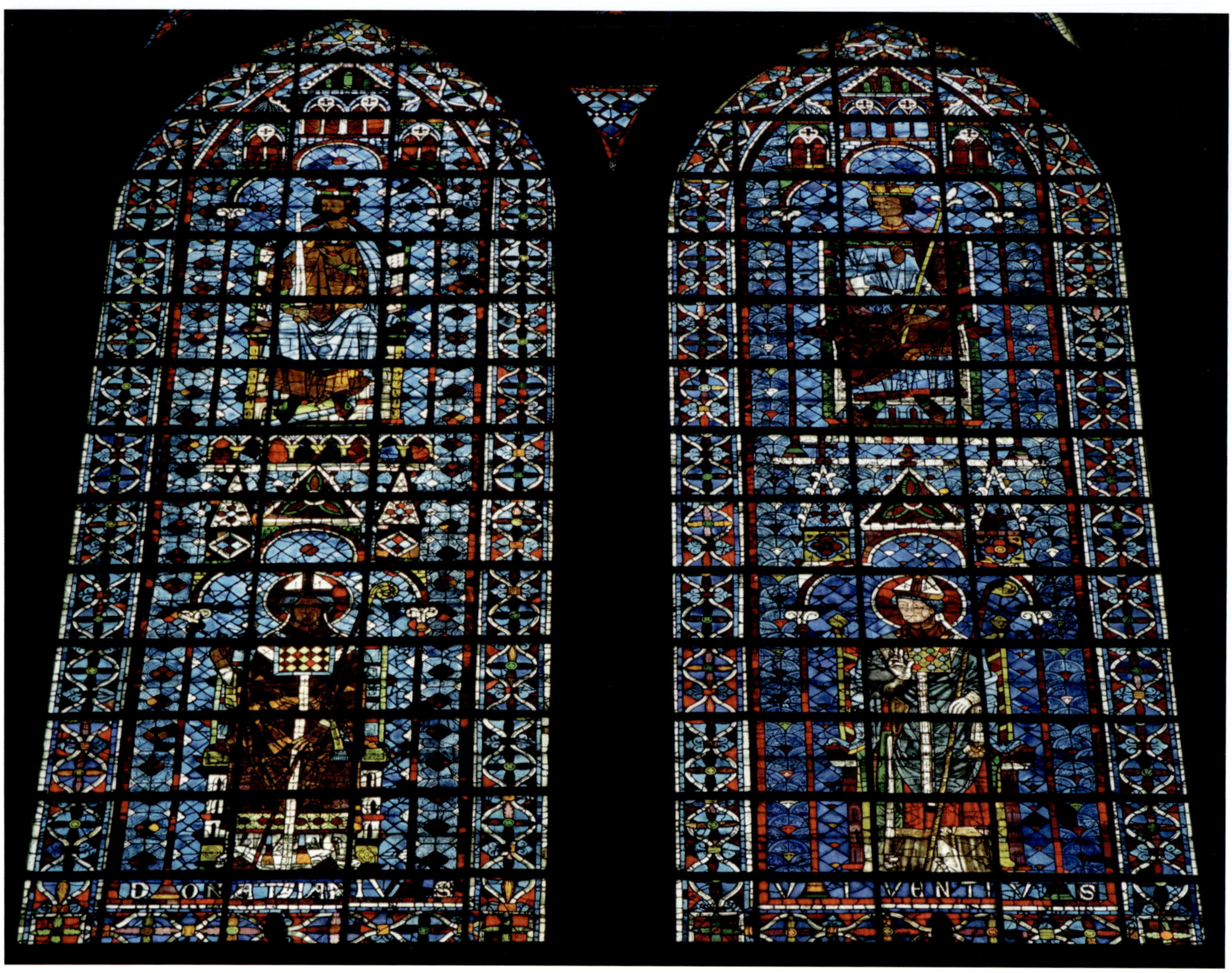

FIG. 178 Bay 122: the archbishop-saints Donatianus and Viventius.

as does the pope St. Calixtus there on the trumeau and later on the west facade. In stained glass, besides the now lost archbishops of Bays 127 and 129,[17] the rational appears on the highly visible image of Archbishop Henri de Braine (d. 1240) in the cathedral's axial bay. At Saint-Remi the rationals worn by several archbishops are somewhat smaller than the typical cathedral type, but they always have twelve jewels clearly indicated.[18] The rational worn by Donatianus in Bay 122 resembles none of these.

• Bay 122, right lancet: St. Viventius, eighth archbishop (late fourth century) (fig. 180).[19] According to Flodoard, Viventius's body was transferred in the ninth century to Braux (Ardennes), where his posthumous miracles included restoration of sight to the blind and the ability to walk to drunkards. Viventius is slightly bearded, and like Donatianus in the left lancet, he is haloed, sits on a high-backed throne, blesses, holds a crozier, and wears a rational. He turns toward the altar, as do the prelates in Bays 121, 123,

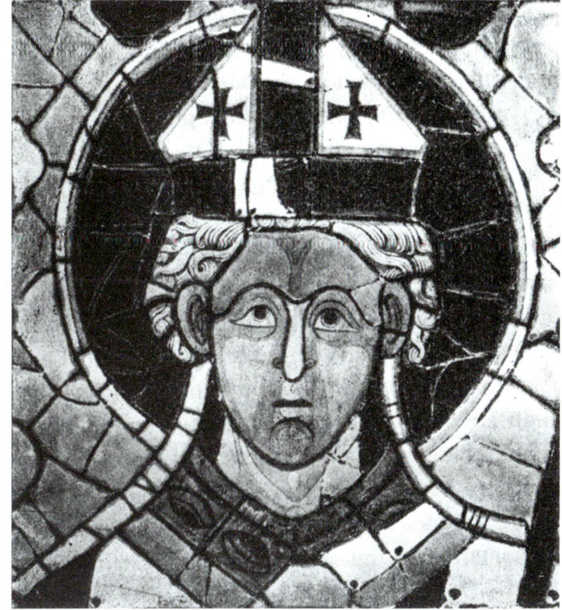

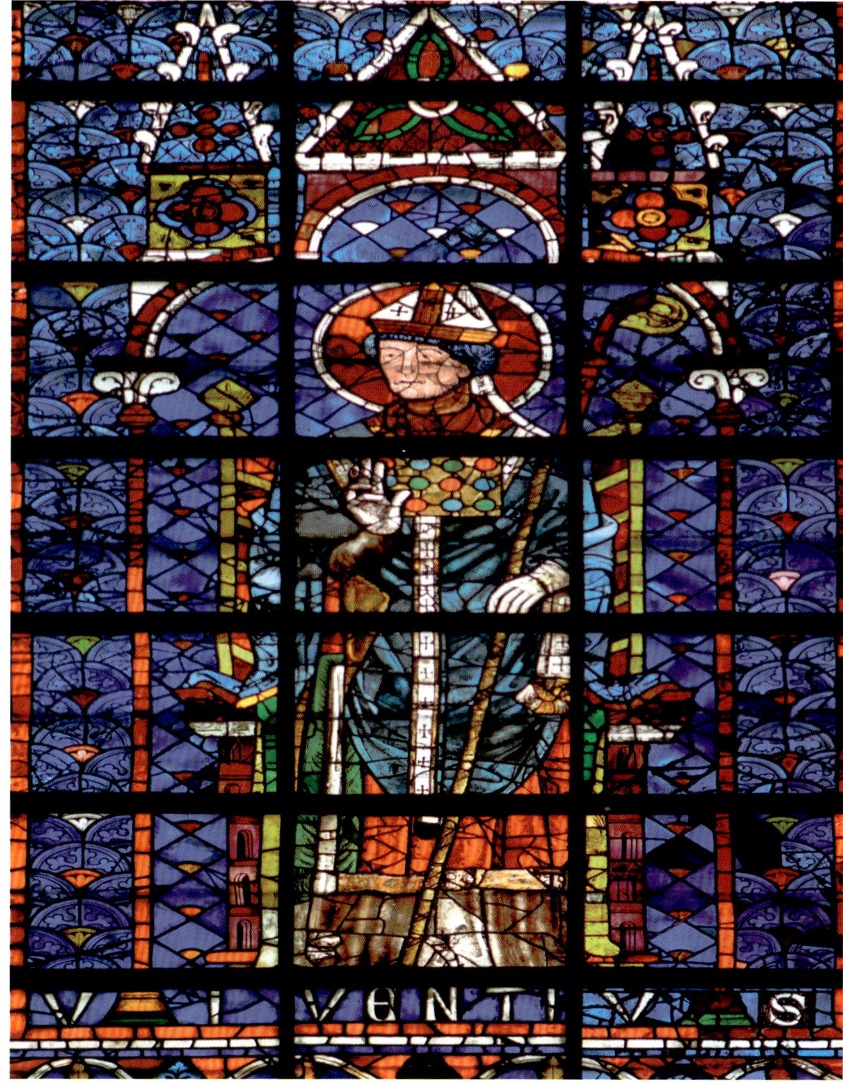

and 125 on the opposite, north side of the nave. His rational is the standard type with twelve jewels. This figure was restored in the studio of Benoît Marq in 2000, when it was discovered that, except for the ground, it is the work of a sixteenth-century restoration.[20]

The archbishops following Viventius—Severus (ninth) and the important *rémois* saint Nicaise (tenth)—are skipped over in the group of named prelates under discussion. This is particularly surprising since the thirteenth century "witnessed the heyday of the cult of St. Nicaise," especially from midcentury onward—that is, precisely when the stained glass of the nave was produced.[21] The chapels of Saints Nicaise and Remi flanked the axial chapel on the north and south; Nicaise was featured opposite St. Remi on the wings of Hincmar's golden jeweled retable on the cathedral's high altar; and their stories appear similarly balanced on the lintel of the Calixtus portal on the north transept. The nave, moreover, was the real site of Nicaise's cult in the cathedral, as William Hinkle has established. The so-called *rouelle,* a round marble stone set into the pavement marking the spot of his martyrdom, was situated in the middle of Bay 129–30, just west of the *jubé.*[22] A wrought-iron grill surrounded it, and a chandelier directly above it was lit on all feast days when processions moving from the high altar, passing through the *jubé,* paused for a station at the *rouelle.* If the group of named archbishops in the southeastern nave windows was indeed of medieval origin, St. Nicaise—and St. Remi, who would immediately follow the last named prelate in Bay 126—are inexplicable omissions. But succeeding Donatianus and Viventius in Bay 122, Bay 124 presents two archbishops named Baruc (or Barucius), about whose reigns nothing whatsoever is known.

FIG. 179 Archbishop Donatianus. Bay 122, left lancet, lower row. Tracing by Paul Simon from the exterior, here reversed as it appears from the interior (after Simon, "Notes sur les vitraux").

FIG. 180 Archbishop Viventius. Bay 122, right lancet, lower row.

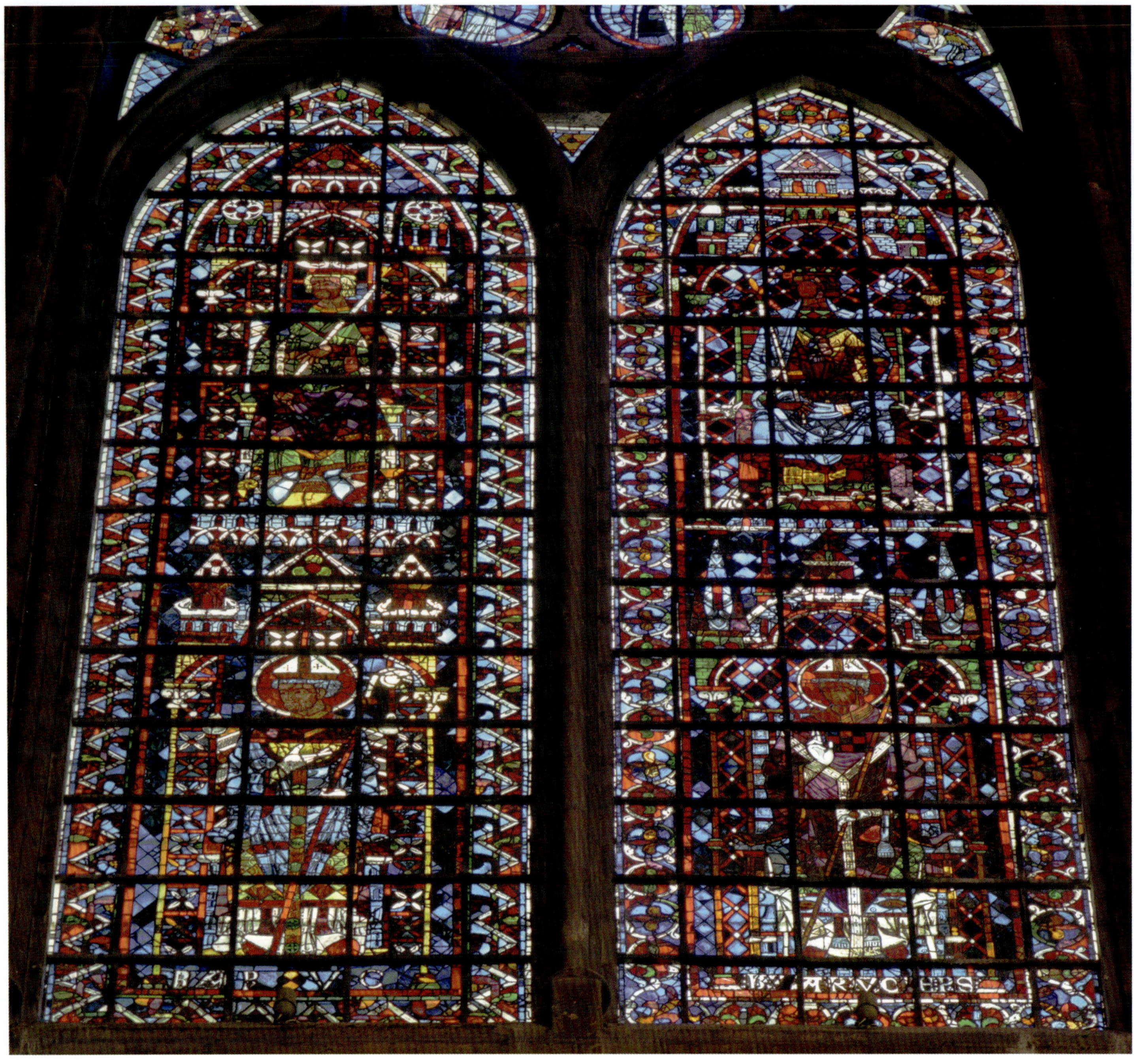

FIG. 181 Bay 124: Archbishops Baruc and Barucius.

• Bay 124, left lancet: Baruc, eleventh archbishop (ca. 408–20) (figs. 181, 182). Flodoard lists Baruc and Barucius as separate prelates, though modern scholars believe that the two names refer to the same individual.[23] The figure of Baruc, like the others listed above, is haloed, though in his case he was not a saint. He has a short beard and sits on a high-backed throne, holding a crozier in his left hand. His right hand, palm up, holds an object that has hitherto elicited no scholarly attention. Only Guilhermy remarks on the hand, with a long finger extended, saying that it points to the bishop in the paired lancet. But there is clearly an object in the hand. It is yellow and was more clearly distinguishable from the vestment behind it in the Deneux autochrome made in 1915 (fig. 182) than it is at present. It resembles a small balloon or bladder, and I suggest that it was intended to represent the *Sainte Ampoule,* which held the miraculous chrism used at coronations of the French kings. There is no reason why this obscure, early-fifth-century archbishop holds this object, and indeed historically he could not have done so, since the Holy Ampulla first appeared in history at the baptism of Clovis by St. Remi on Christmas day of the year 496.

The yellow object held by Archbishop Baruc in Bay 124 can be compared with several depictions of the *Sainte Ampoule* in the so-called Ordo of 1250, the coronation order probably compiled at Reims in the late 1230s (Paris, BnF, lat. 1246).[24] On folio 4r, in the miniature depicting monks of Saint-Remi bringing the *Ampoule* to the cathedral, the abbot carrying the golden Ampulla holds it in his palm, extending his fingers forward as in the window. On folio 17r, the archbishop anoints the king, holding the Ampulla in an upturned palm. This resemblance, however, need not establish the medieval authenticity of the design of Bay 124. No other prelates in the nave carry any kind of object specifically associated with the coronation ritual. Indeed, specificity seems to have been consciously avoided in the great parade of thirty-six kings and thirty-six bishops originally gracing the nave.

Richard Jackson has established that the earliest appearance of the Holy Ampulla in the coronation rite occurs in the Ordo of Reims, which he dates ca. 1230.[25] As Jackson has noted: "Until the Revolution, the legend of Remigius and the Holy Ampulla continued to be embedded at the heart of the coronation liturgy, where it had been placed in the late Middle Ages after completing its rise from the centuries-long obscurity in which it had lain before the early thirteenth century had brought it back to light."[26] The *Sainte Ampoule* was one of a number of specific additions to the coronation liturgy in the thirteenth century, such as the participation of the peers of France, that made the rite specifically French for the first time. The *Ampoule* grew in centrality during succeeding centuries. For Charles VIII's 1484 coronation, two new additions to the liturgy specified it: one a processional hymn as the Ampulla was borne from the cathedral door to the altar, and the second a text for the moment when it was placed upon the altar.[27] Also in 1484 a *tableau vivant* depicting the original miraculous transmission of the Holy Ampulla to earth was staged during the king's precoronation entry into the city. At the entry of Louis XIII for his coronation in 1610, one of the city gates received a painting showing the dove bringing the *Ampoule* to the altar.[28] Thus it is possible, even likely, that the depiction of the Ampulla in Reims Bay 124 is postmedieval. Of course, it goes without saying, and is irrelevant to

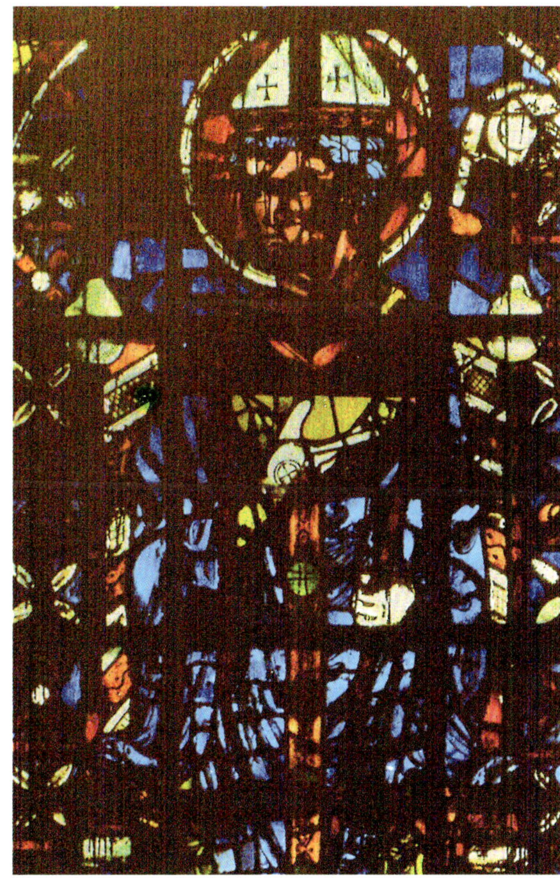

FIG. 182 Archbishop Baruc. Bay 124, left lancet, lower row. Autochrome by Henri Deneux, 1915.

FIG. 183 Archbishop Barucius. Bay 124, right lancet, lower row.

Opposite
FIG. 184 Bay 126: Archbishops Barnabas and Bennadius.

Below
FIG. 185 Archbishop Barnabas. Bay 126, left lancet, lower row.

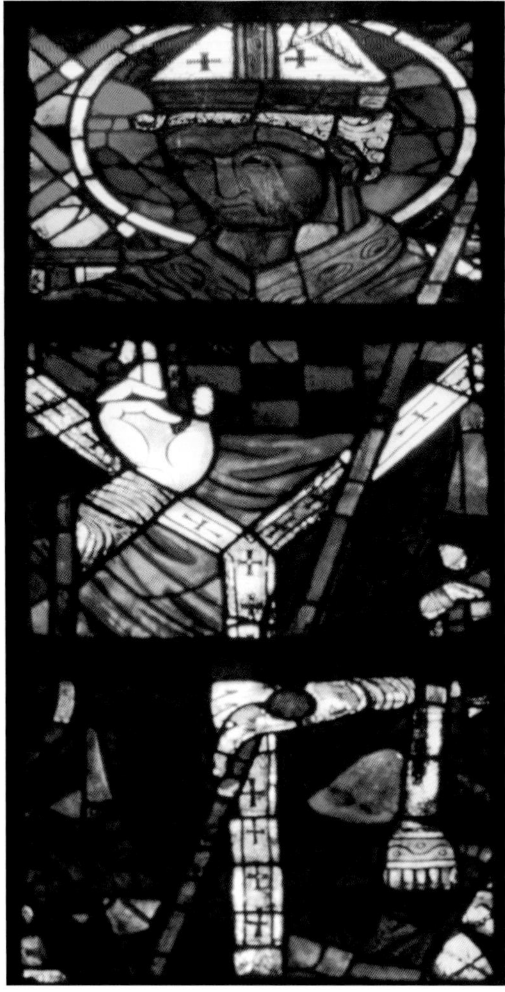

the argument, that neither of the Barucs ever used it in a coronation.

• Bay 124, right lancet: Barucius, twelfth archbishop (ca. 408–20) (figs. 181, 183).[29] Like Baruc I, he is haloed though not a saint. The figure, slightly bearded, sits on a high-backed throne, holds a crozier, and blesses. Like St. Donatianus in Bay 122, he wears a very strange rational, small and square rather than rectangular, with a "tic-tac-toe" pattern that is colored like a nine-square checkerboard. No thirteenth-century depiction of the rational in the cathedral looks like this. One might add that Barucius's maniple has a distinctly postmedieval, sixteenth-century shape; compare it, for example, to the maniples in figures 70, 73, 97, 100, 192.[30]

• Bay 126, left lancet: Barnabas, thirteenth archbishop (ca. 421–30) (figs. 184, 185).[31] Nothing is known about his reign except that he left a silver vase to his successor, Bennadius, whose own testament refers to Barnabas *sanctae recordationis.* The figure, like those of Bay 124, is haloed, though he was not a saint; he is beardless, sits on a high-backed throne, holds a crozier, and blesses. He wears another of the very peculiar "rationals" found in these bays with named prelates. In this case it is small, square, and formed of decorated lozenges.[32]

• Bay 126, right lancet: Bennadius, fourteenth archbishop (ca. 430–59) (fig. 184).[33] Flodoard states that his testament, in his own hand, gives his name as Bennagius. Like Barnabas, he is haloed although not a saint; he is bearded, sits on a low throne, holds a crozier, and blesses. Nothing is known about him except his testament, leaving money to repair the cathedral as well as sums to its many officers. He was buried in the cathedral. He was the immediate predecessor of the cathedral's most famous saint, Remi, who, like Nicaise—as noted above—is not among the six prelates identified by inscription in an ensemble that, until 1914, contained thirty-six archbishops in all.

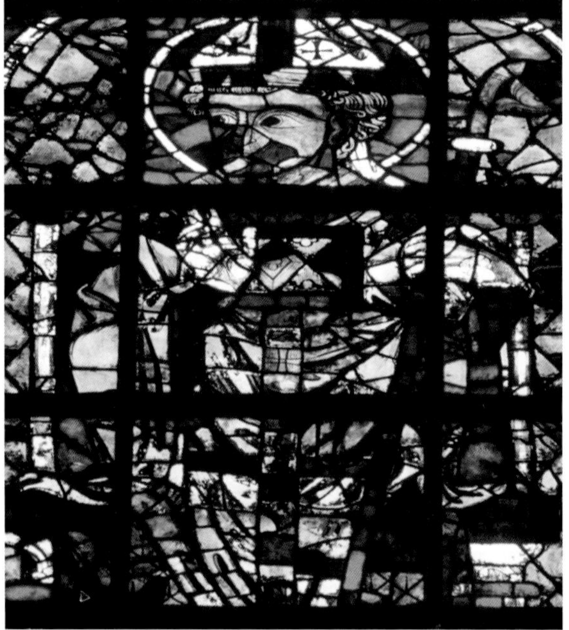

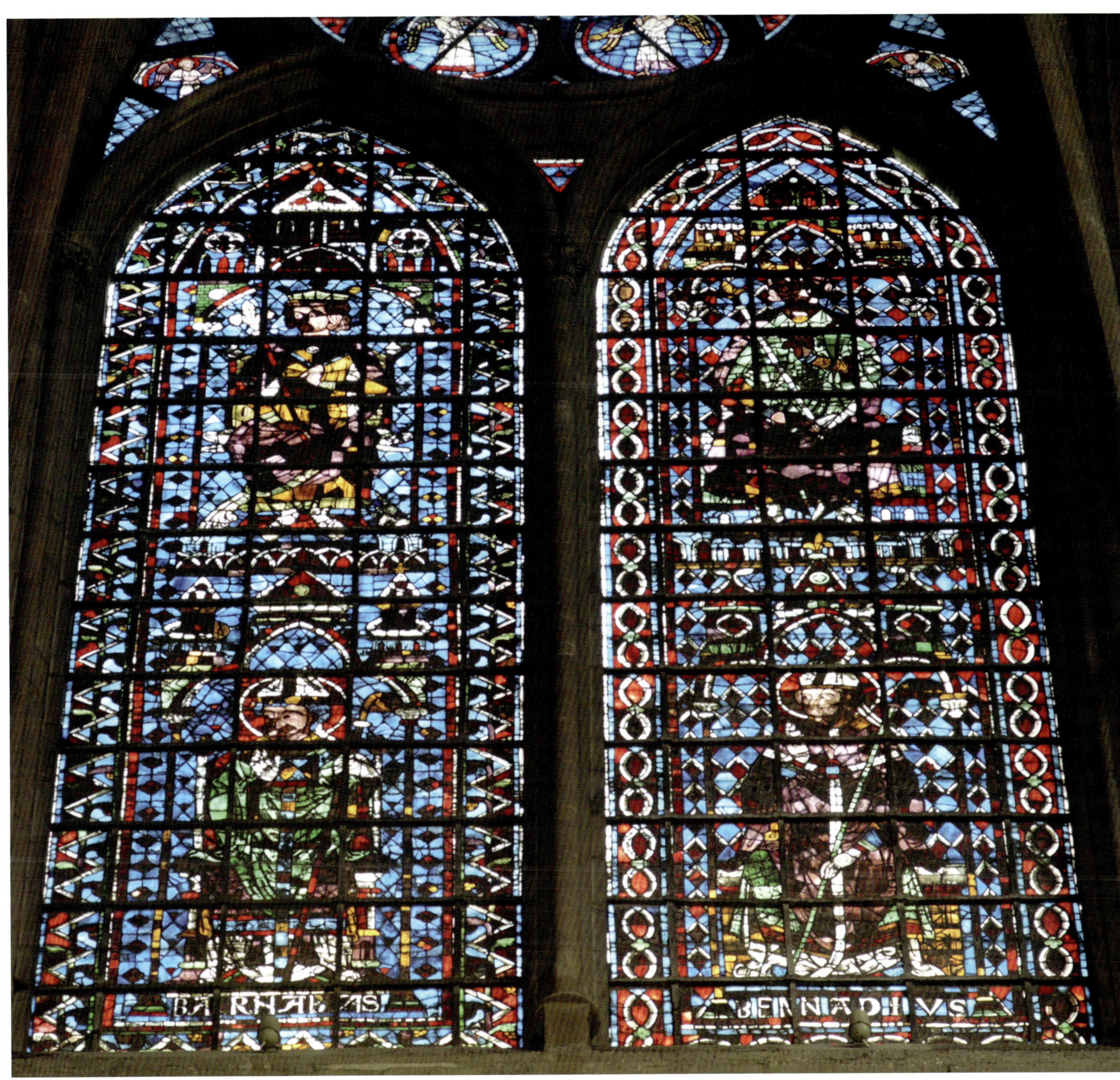

FIG. 186 King with bare sword. Bay 122, left lancet, top row.

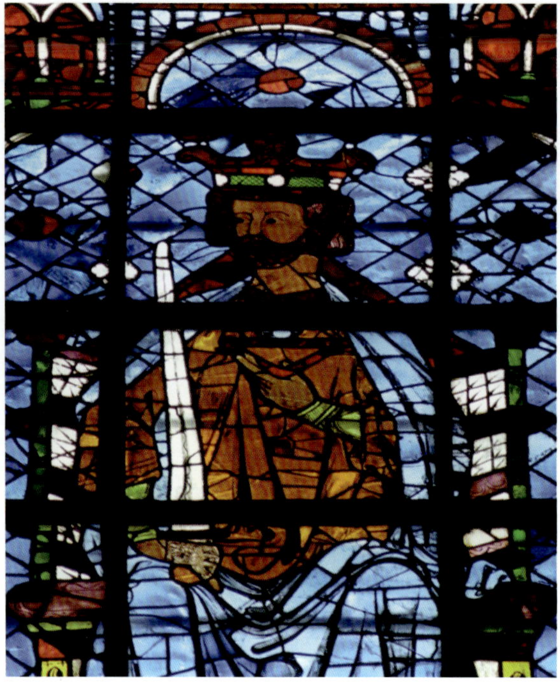

Funny Foldstools

One purpose of indicating the anomalies in the images of the six named archbishops is to establish that any postmedieval restoration did not simply reproduce original medieval designs. A word might be added here about similar peculiarities in the images of the six unnamed kings enthroned above them. The bare sword held point up by the left king in Bay 122 (figs. 178, 186) could be, like Baruc's *Sainte Ampoule,* a reference to the coronation.[34] However, only one other king, Karolvs, in Bay 128, holds such a sword (fig. 190); all other kings in the nave hold scepters. Bay 128, immediately adjoining the three south bays discussed above, is an obvious patchwork of disparate figures salvaged from elsewhere, and Karolvs is the oddest of the four, not just the only named king in the cathedral but rigidly frontal and smaller in scale. A hypothesis can be entertained that he was not originally in the Gothic nave but was moved there.[35] The left king of Bay 122 may copy him.

The most striking oddity is the type of throne provided for three of the kings in these southeastern nave bays, notably the left monarch in Bay 126 and the kings in the right lancets of Bays 122 and 124.[36] The left king in Bay 126 (fig. 184) sits on an animal-headed foldstool, but one provided with a high back. The monarchs in the right lancets of Bays 122 and 124 (figs. 178, 187) have straight-sided thrones with high backs, from the sides of which animal heads jut out incongruously. The combination of foldstool and high back does not seem to have existed in the Middle Ages.[37] Dagobert's throne from Saint-Denis, a foldstool that later was provided with low sides and a back, cannot even be considered an exception to this rule, since the reduced sides and the back gable in no way form a "high-backed throne."[38] Thus the odd thrones of these three kings in the southeastern nave bays, like the peculiar rationals in the same windows, can only be a postmedieval version of a medieval object that was no longer in current use. According to Ole Wanscher, "the ceremonial and symbolic importance of the genuine folding stool as the royal seat was waning during the later parts of the Middle Ages."[39] He describes a transitional, hybrid form of royal throne introduced in the fifteenth century: a large chair with nonfoldable crossed legs but retaining the foldstool's knobs or balls on the arms and also on its back supports. This description fits the Reims examples quite well.

Madeline Caviness's investigation of the history and use of the foldstool notes that it was traditionally associated both with rulers and with sacred imagery, including Sts. Jerome, Augustine, the Evangelist John, and the Virgin Mary.[40] Several bishops in the Saint-Remi windows are enthroned on foldstools. In the cathedral, the early archbishop-saint relocated to Bay 118 in the south transept sits on a particularly dramatic one (fig. 147). The association of rulers with foldstools is found on the seals of numerous Capetian kings, including Philippe Auguste and Louis IX.[41] Only two kings in the cathedral's nave windows, however, had foldstools, and they were also the only kings with haloes. These two were the monarchs in now lost Bay 129,[42] the most elaborate and impressive of the nave clerestories, occupying a pivotal location before the *jubé*. Its pre-1914 appearance is recorded in a Rothier photograph, and the king that survived World War I has now been relocated to the lower left lancet of Bay 127 (figs. 200, 202). Kings on high-backed thrones were much more common in the nave, most obviously all those monarchs in Bays 121, 123, and 125, on the north, facing the three bays under discussion here. The anomalous combination of foldstool with high-backed throne in these three southern bays thus conflates two medieval types that existed independently in cathedral images and carried somewhat different meanings.

Sixteenth-Century Repairs?

If the three nave bays containing named archbishops do include, as here suggested, extensive sixteenth-century repairs, these designs clearly were intended to blend with the medieval ensemble and have done so with great success. The search for evidence of the postmedieval artist's "handwriting" is complicated by the windows' long obscured condition and tortured history. Their designs were recorded by Paul Simon from 1875 to 1886 in colored tracings made in situ, and Westlake published the border of the right lancet of Bay 124 in 1881; in 1911 Simon warned that they were obscured by dirt and held precariously by weak eighteenth-century leading.[43] Deneux's post-1918 documentation of war damage indicates only minor loss to Bay 124 and somewhat more in Bay 126. Jacques Simon remade the bays from 1922 to 1926 using his father's tracings. Taken down in 1939, they were restored and reinstalled in 1946–47. Deneux's autochrome photos, made in 1915, indicate differences in minor detail, such as the glance of the eyes. Since both Paul and Jacques Simon commanded an archaizing style that has been taken for medieval work,[44] an accurate assessment must await the eventual publication by the French Corpus Vitrearum of restoration charts.

In 2000, Bay 122 was restored by the Simon-Marq atelier, and the recently cleaned figure of Viventius provides the clearest evidence of a postmedieval hand (fig. 180). The face and hands are modeled softly, the arms and fingers stubby and ill formed, and most noticeable is the shaded modulation of folds in the lower garments. Other draperies are indicated by crude, thick, black stripes or smears accompanied by thinner mat streaks, apparently imitating the shaded spoonfolds of thirteenth-century costuming. In general the ornament is based on medieval designs but applied with a heavier hand and postmedieval taste, as revealed, for example, in the three-dimensional crockets and the illogical alternation of left/right perspective in jewels, niches, and such decorative motifs.

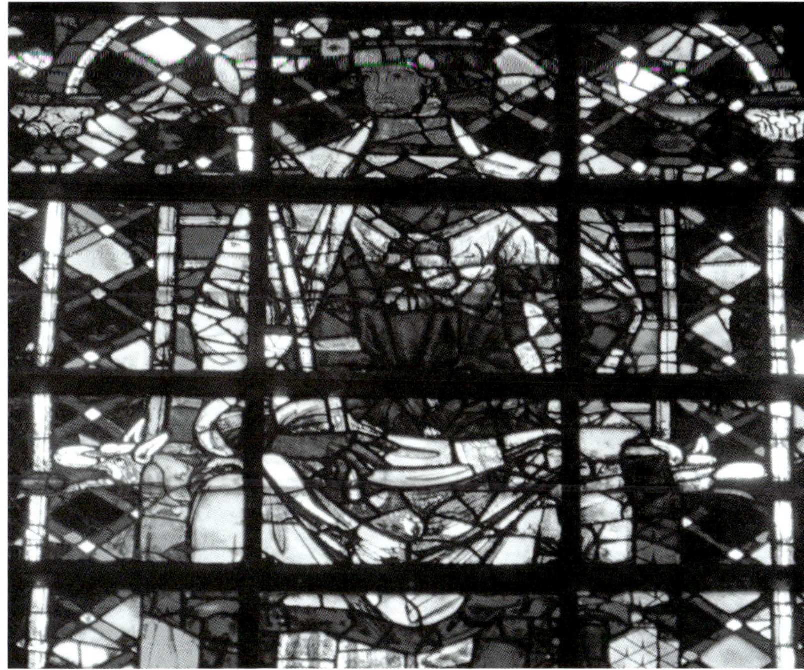

FIG. 187 King on high-backed throne with animal heads at the sides. Bay 124, right lancet, top row.

The need for such repairs over the years can be posited. One catastrophic event in the sixteenth century received mention in the otherwise laconic chronicles of the cathedral's past and also left an indelible mark on the building's fabric. This event was a violent windstorm, which caused the destruction of the south-transept rose window, both tracery and glass, as described in the seventeenth-century manuscript of Pierre Cocquault: "On Easter Day [1580] a great and very injurious windstorm caused a number of great ruins in several regions, and great buildings were brought down. In the church of Reims, the rose or O window on the side of the palace [the south] was violently blown in. The gable of the palace chamber with the large window was cast down. The pinnacles of the gables of the Augustinian and Carmelite churches were destroyed as well."[45] It is certainly arguable that such a powerful wind would have damaged nearby windows facing south, and Bays 122, 124, and 126 are directly west of the destroyed rose and at the same elevation. The more intense disorder of the southern clerestories of the Saint-Remi chevet, noted by Tourneur, might also receive the same explanation.[46]

The cathedral's south rose was remade the following year and the new glass, lost in World War I, bore the date 1581 and the name Nicolas Dérodé. His rose was in the Renaissance style, as attested by nineteenth-century observers and affirmed by the drawing published by Ferdinand de Lasteyrie (fig. 141); Guilhermy judged that "this window doesn't lack elegance."[47] Did Dérodé also repair the three south clerestories but in a very different, and successful, quasi-medieval style? If so, he presumably did so in order to maintain the integrity of the nave glazing.[48] Tourneur comments that Dérodé had been ignored by local biographers but that, besides his rose window, a self-portrait in oils owned by his descendants provided evidence of his talent. Cerf notes that Dérodé executed "peinture au portail" at the west facade in 1612, that is, thirty-one years after the rose glazing of 1581.[49] Certainly such a long career in art would have allowed him to develop a "medieval" style, though this hypothesis must remain pure conjecture.

Why These Archbishops?

The question remains: why begin the nave sequence with the cathedral's seventh archbishop (Donatianus) and continue with the obscure prelates succeeding him? Dom Guillaume Marlot, the "genial antiquarian"[50] who was a seventeenth-century prior of the abbey of Saint-Nicaise in Reims, offers a clue. Contrasting with Marlot's expansive description of the cathedral's sculpture, furnishings, relics, and so forth, his mention of the stained glass is brevity itself. He states that there are windows at two levels and that their glass, "pour estre espais et peints de diverses couleurs, causent quelque obscurité dans l'église."[51] As for the subjects, he devotes only the following paragraph, as remarkable for what it does not say as for what it does:

> In the windows are represented a whole series of ancient archbishops pontifically vested with their pallium, crozier, and miter, images that attract, by the light that shines through them, the eyes and spirit of those who come to pray, when considering them carefully, they recall the great virtues that they practiced well during their lives, God having established by his holy grace that the first bishops of each town were very eminent in holiness and like mirrors of perfection, so that posterity, coming to contemplate them, would be induced by affection to imitate them; which is why one has depicted them thus in the highest reaches of our churches, in imitation of those heroes that the ancients placed in the most eminent place in their chambers and that St. Charles [Borromeo] has revived at the Council of Milan, charging his suffragans to put portraits of their predecessors at the entry to the episcopal palace, removing all other representations made rather for the pleasure of the eye than for edification.[52]

In sum, at a moment when Reims cathedral still retained nearly its entire Gothic glazing program, Marlot gives not a nod to the glass of the aisles and chapels, the north and west rose windows, the thirty-six kings in the nave, or the unique series of suffragan cathedral facades in the clerestories of the chevet. For him the windows present the cathedral's "anciens archevesques," as per the widely disseminated teachings of St. Charles Borromeo.

Borromeo (d. 1585, canonized 1610) is recognized as one of the great leaders of the Counter-Reformation. Bishop of Milan from 1563, he held provincial councils there noteworthy for promoting religious renewal conforming to the decrees of the Council of Trent, which had concluded in 1563; "the amazing results [of his councils] are described in the *Acta ecclesiae Mediolanensis,* whose many editions published since 1582 have become the patrimony of the whole Church."[53] Reims, moreover, was involved with the reform from its beginning. The archbishop Charles de Guise, cardinal of Lorraine, had attended the Council of Trent and in 1564 held his own provincial council at Reims cathedral to promulgate its decrees. In 1583—that is, three years after the windstorm of 1580 mentioned above—his nephew Archbishop Louis de Guise convened yet another provincial council toward the same end.[54]

Looking at the windows of Reims through the eyes of the Counter-Reformation, Dom Marlot sees a procession of the cathedral's archbishops. Indeed, if one begins counting in the chevet following the axial bay, 100 (with its clearly labeled image of Archbishop Henri de Braine), the southern choir presents images of six prelates: one each in Bays 102, 104, 106, and 108, and two in Bay 110. Bay 110 is the last clerestory in the chevet, and over the crossing in the first clerestory of the nave (Bay 122), Marlot would have seen Donatianus, the seventh. The idea can be entertained that the repairs required by the storm of 1580 were made following the instruction of the great contemporary reformer-saint and cardinal-bishop Charles Borromeo.

In Marlot's defense one must allow that the inscriptions of the choir clerestories, identifying their prelates as bishops of Laon, Soissons, Beauvais, Noyon, and so forth, were possibly in a state of disarray. Each of these inscriptions usually occupies the bottom of a window, and from 1637, if not earlier, it was the custom to remove the lowest two panels of the clerestories to provide increased viewing of the coronation ceremony. Tourneur notes that these panels were "beaucoup plus brisés, endommagés et raccommodés que les autres."[55] Engravings of the coronations of Louis XIV (1654, fig. 5) and Louis XV (1722, fig. 6) illustrate this practice; Le Pautre's engraving made in 1654, during Marlot's lifetime, of the *sacre* of Louis XIV shows numerous witnesses hanging out of the clerestories of both choir and nave (fig. 5).[56]

To return briefly *da capo,* to the oft-found hypothesis that the Reims clerestories reflect those of Saint-Remi: the opposite is more likely to be the case. None of the six named archbishops of the cathedral appears in Caviness's appendix establishing the inscriptions at the abbey before extensive late-nineteenth-century restoration.[57] Following that work, which altered and added names and reordered the prelates, three of the six archbishops appear: Donatianus (Saint-Remi bay N.IIb), Viventius (S.IIb), and Bennadius (N.IVc).[58] Flodoard is certainly the ultimate source, but as Caviness points out, "a selection of archbishops had to be made, since the thirteenth-century list . . . includes forty-eight primates down to William of Champagne, whereas there was room for only thirty-three in the retrochoir."[59] The almost unknown Barnabas and the two Barucs, listed in Flodoard, were rejected in favor of the two saints Donatianus and Viventius and of Bennadius, who was buried in the cathedral. It is arguable that the restorer's selection of names for Saint-Remi was influenced by the named archbishops among the otherwise anonymous procession of thirty-six then visible in the nave of the cathedral. In the cases of both abbey and cathedral, the Gothic visitor would have seen something else.

+ KAROLVS

In several discussions in this book I have suggested that it is not unreasonable to assume that the glazing of Saint-Remi—and for that matter that of the Gothic cathedral—reflects in various ways the program of Archbishop Samson's Romanesque church. The enthroned king identified as Karolvs in the right lancet of Bay 128 (fig. 188), in the window immediately adjoining the three bays of named archbishops discussed above, is possibly the only remnant from that twelfth-century glazing. This section investigates clues supportive of this hypothesis.

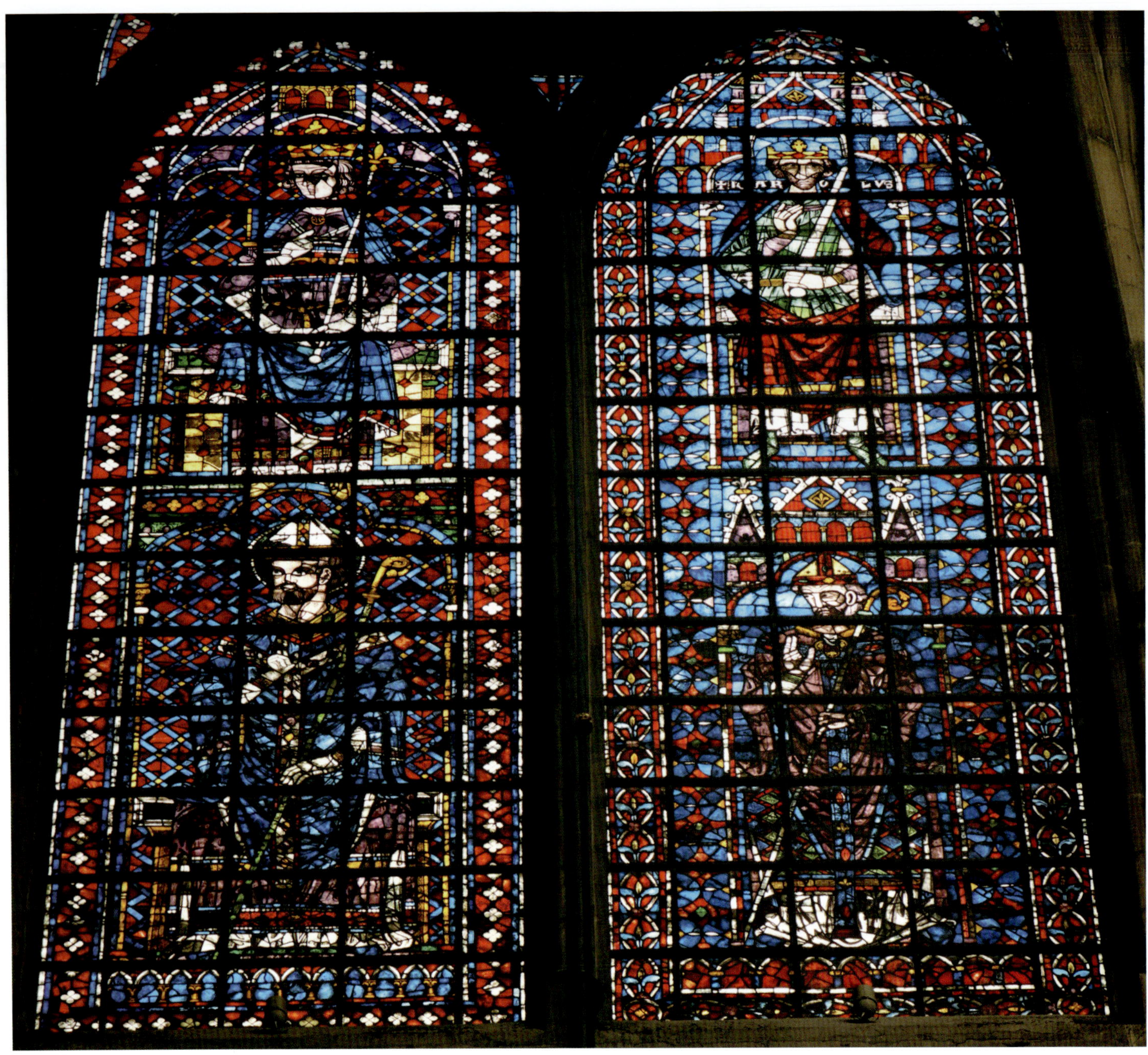

FIG. 188 Bay 128: Karolvs, right lancet, top row.

FIG. 189 Bay 128, montage of war damage, after 1918.

Karolvs is not only the single named king but the only rigidly frontal one in the cathedral, the only monarch not to turn at least his head. He is slender and slope-shouldered, the form based on a succession of triangles on a strong central axis.[60] He makes a particularly incongruous companion to the other figures in Bay 128. Those in the left lancet are notably larger in scale, while the archbishop below him has a much more massive physique. The color is also clearer and more lucid, particularly Karolvs's tunic, in a medium green not found elsewhere.

The present figure is modern. Deneux's photomontage of war damage indicates empty leads surviving in only a few of Karolvs's panels (fig. 189). The Deneux autochrome made before the destruction (fig. 190) confirms the color but also shows that the eyes of the king were staring forward hypnotically rather than in the shifty, Machiavellian, slightly apprehensive gaze the restorer has given the modern figure.[61] It is perhaps this modern, evasive look that has impeded recognition that this figure resembles mid-twelfth-century glazing much more closely than that of a century later in the Reims nave. Kings in twelfth-century glazing include the series in the nave of Saint-Remi and the so-called Charlemagne from Strasbourg cathedral, as well as the several frontal monarchs in the north nave aisle there, recycled from the previous nave glazing.[62] The closest stylistic parallel to Karolvs, however, is the "petit St. Remi" now in the tribune of Saint-Remi (bay Nt.11b, fig. 191). While he is much smaller, the saint has the same extremely pointed triangular face, rigid frontal pose, long straight nose, down-turned mouth, eyes with irises indicated, and narrow forehead beneath flattened headgear. Caviness has dated the figure to the mid–twelfth century, suggesting an origin in the apse of the previous abbey church, of Abbot Odo (d. 1151).[63] Karolvs's flattened crown can be compared to one in the Bible from Saint-Thierry, Reims, of the second half of the twelfth century (Reims, Bibl. mun., MS 23, fol. 69v). The inscription behind his head appears in numerous examples at Saint-Remi and other twelfth-century sites.[64]

If it can be allowed that Karolvs probably originated in the Romanesque cathedral of Archbishop Samson, where might he have come from, and when might he have been "translated"? Samson (r. 1140–61) had participated in Abbot Suger's consecration of the new Gothic chevet of Saint-Denis on June 11, 1144.[65] In 1152 he began constructions, like Suger's, at the west and east ends of his own Carolingian church. Onto the nave he added a connecting bay with a two-towered facade, while he replaced the apse with an enlarged chevet with ambulatory and five radiating chapels.[66] Shortly thereafter Abbot Pierre de Celle

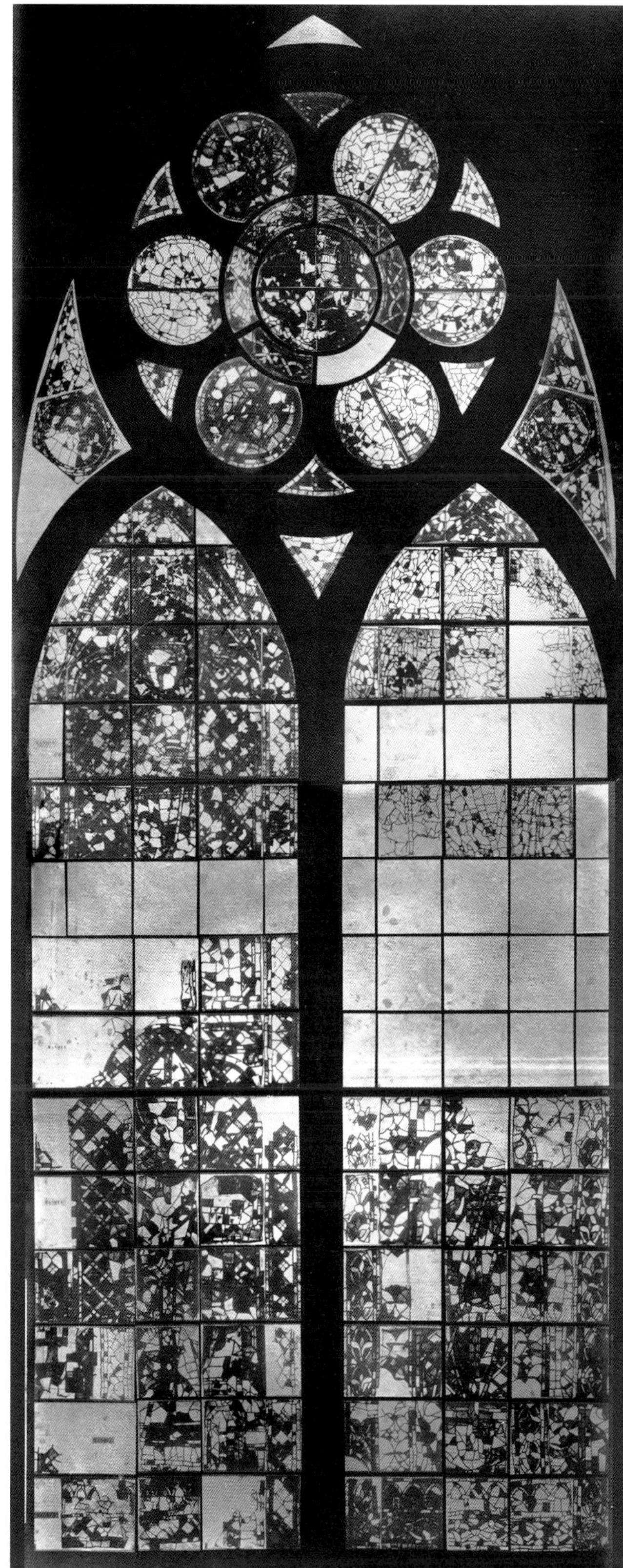

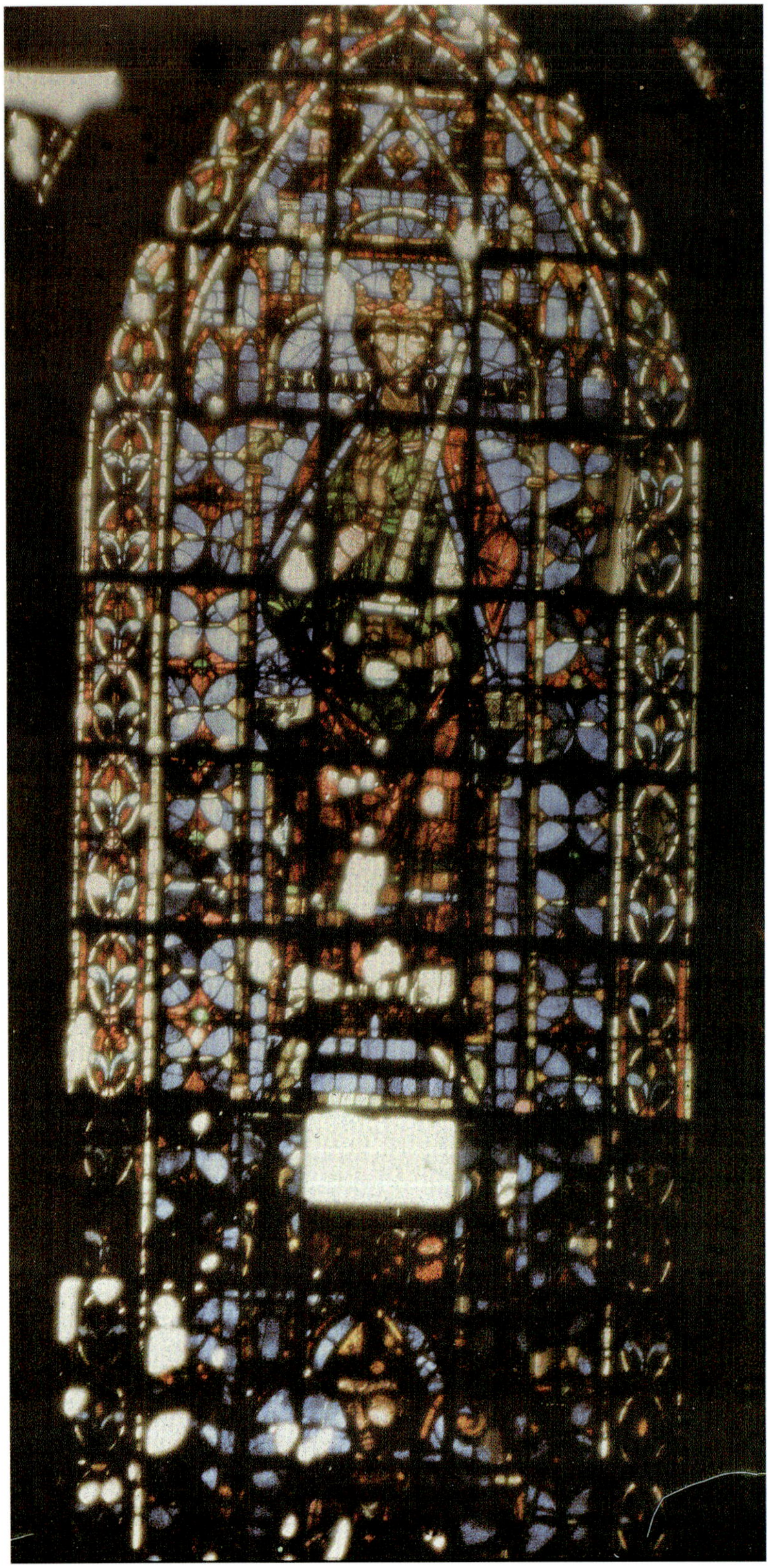

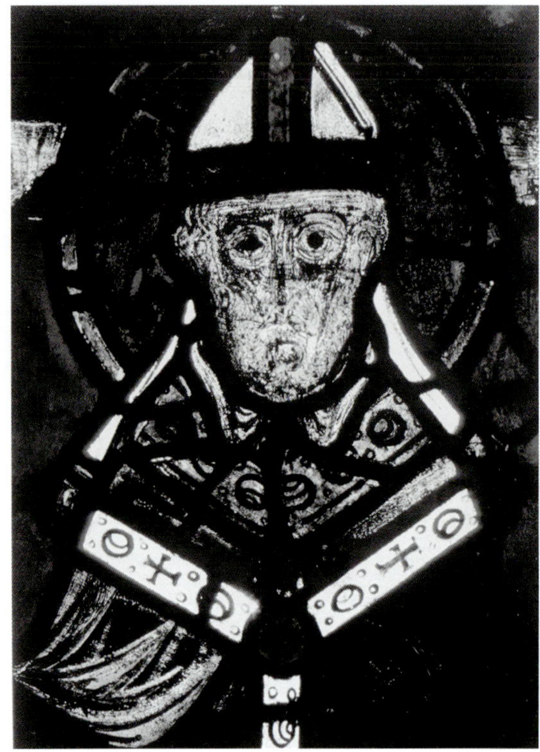

(1152–81) instigated rebuilding at the two ends of Saint-Remi. The sculptural detailing of Samson's construction was of admirable quality,[67] and it is hard to imagine that Samson's imitation of Suger would not have extended to a program of stained glass, though documentation and evidence are lacking. Since the western area of Samson's building became the locus of church services for several decades following the cathedral's fire ca. 1210, the damage to that area must have been less severe. On the basis of the twelfth-century programs of monarchs in the pre-Romanesque naves of Saint-Remi and Strasbourg, one can suggest an original location for Karolvs somewhere in the nave of Samson's cathedral.

The question of when Karolvs was moved—assuming he was moved just once[68]—would thus depend on the sequence of destruction and replacement of the old nave, a matter of intense disagreement among scholars. The glass of Bays 127 and 128 (which face one another), even omitting Karolvs from the equation, is (and was) not uniform in style.[69] The figures in the eastern lancets of those bays are larger in scale than those in the adjoining lancets. Perhaps a temporary wall interfered at this juncture? A final insoluble problem is exactly who Karolvs is. Only one thing seems certain: surely he is not the only monarch named Charles who was crowned in Reims before the Gothic era, Charles III the Simple in 893. Thus, if Karolvs was part of a series of windows, it did not simply honor *rémois* coronations. Charlemagne and Charles the Bald, neither of them crowned at Reims, are the only possibilities, and there are arguments supporting both candidacies. The evidence tilts in favor of Charles the Bald but is far from conclusive.

Although Charlemagne was not added to the cathedral's feasts until the mid–fourteenth century,[70] the great emperor was of course a legendary figure. At least two dozen *chansons de geste* identify Reims as his capital.[71] As for Charles the Bald, his significance to Reims was through Archbishop Hincmar, his constant advisor. Flodoard reports that he attended Hincmar's dedication of the refurbished cathedral in 862.[72] In 869 Hincmar crowned him king of Lorraine, at Metz, and inserted into the ordo that he wrote for the occasion a mention of the anointing of Clovis and the *Sainte Ampoule.*[73] I have suggested that a number of Hincmar's writings, some dedicated to Charles the Bald or even written at his request, were later to be tapped for the Gothic glazing programs of the cathedral.[74]

However, the main reason to highlight either monarch in Samson's Romanesque cathedral would no doubt have been that he was at the time in high profile at the abbey of Saint-Denis. Hinkle has summarized the attempts by the abbey during the twelfth century to become the locus of coronations.[75] An investigation of the importance of Charlemagne and/or Charles the Bald at Saint-Denis during the years of Samson's reign at Reims (1140–61) is thus the next task. The treasury of Saint-Denis once contained Charlemagne's crown, sword, scepter, cross, *"escrain,"* and chess pieces as well as, associated with him, the horn of Roland. Modern scholarship has established that none of these objects could have been a gift of the emperor. Several of them are Carolingian in date but were donations from Charles the Bald; only from the fifteenth century on did the *souvenir* of Charlemagne at the abbey begin to supplant that of the other monarch.[76] For example, the "splendidly useless piece of decoration, known as the 'Escrin de Charlemagne,' . . . was probably a gift of Charles the Bald," and Suger, who writes about it in *De administratione,* does not attribute it to either of them.[77]

Around 1140 the so-called Chronicle of Pseudo-Turpin (*Historia Karoli Magni et Rotholandi*) was composed, a "merry and gripping tale of strange times of yore" in which Charlemagne bestows many privileges on the abbey, including one specifying that no king was to be crowned in France without the abbot's counsel.[78] Often associated with it by scholars is the famous—or infamous—forged charter of Charlemagne, which conferred a long list of favors on Saint-Denis including its establishment as the required locus for coronations. Elizabeth A. R. Brown has argued that the Pseudo-Turpin chronicle was an extravagant romance largely ignored by the monks of the abbey until the period when it began to be taken seriously elsewhere, that is, in the thirteenth century. As for the forgery, she states that its text was first published by Doublet in 1625; Belleforest, a major critic of the Pseudo-Turpin, did, however, mention in 1579 having seen the charter at the abbey. Brown suggests that Doublet may have invented it, or perhaps it was created for Belleforest's abbey visit, or,

> if the forger worked in the twelfth or thirteenth century, he had a keen sense of humor and took pleasure in poking fun at the pretensions of the house and its abbots, going so far as to assert that no kings should be crowned save at the abbey. The flagrant ostentatiousness of the claims it contained would explain why it was not directly invoked and extensively quoted in Dyonisian compilations and histories. On the other hand, a forger who

FIG. 190 Karolvs. Bay 128, right lancet, top row. Autochrome by Henri Deneux, 1915.

FIG. 191 St. Remi, detail, mid–twelfth century. Reims, Saint-Remi, bay NtIIb.

produced the masterpiece for Belleforest's visit would have been trying to impress that author; if afterwards, to validate claims made on that occasion that Belleforest had subsequently published. Any of these hypotheses is arguable.[79]

Brown's revisionist stance, however, has been rejected by Lindy Grant, who dates the forgery to the late 1120s under Suger's abbacy.[80] Finally, there is the Charlemagne window added to the new Saint-Denis chevet, but when? Grant prefers 1147, in conjunction with the ceremony in which Louis VII received the *Vexillum* of Saint-Denis, marking the start of the crusade. Brown and Cothren prefer a date in the late 1150s.[81] In this case, however, either date would be within Archbishop Samson's tenure in office at Reims.

To turn to Charles the Bald and his importance at Suger's Saint-Denis: Charles was buried in the middle of the monks' choir near the matutinal altar. Among his numerous gifts to the abbey was the golden frontal of the main altar, which Suger embellished with sides and back of the same precious material. Around 1140 the abbot reestablished in the monastery monthly celebrations of Charles's anniversary, including a fine meal for his monks. In short, during Suger's tenure in office Charles the Bald was featured as the abbey's greatest benefactor.[82] Within the matutinal altar were his gifts of armbones of Sts. James, Stephen, and Vincent, and on October 9 of 1140 or 1141 Suger hosted a grand ceremonial spectacle to dismantle the altar and have goldsmiths open the reliquaries in the presence of "archbishops and bishops from diverse Provinces . . . , a conflux of abbots and monks or clerics as well as of noblemen; but also an innumerable crowd of people of both sexes."[83] Among those at the party was Archbishop Samson of Reims.

Thus various circumstantial evidence weights toward the identification of Karolvs with Charles the Bald, the monarch most likely to have been commemorated in the windows of the mid-twelfth-century cathedral of Reims. But there we must leave it.

The Original Gothic Glazing Program: Evidence and Assumptions

In sum: of the seventy-two figures originally filling the nave lancets of the Gothic cathedral, thirty-two remain at least in some reconstructed form at present, and perhaps nearly half that number, primarily those on the south, cannot be trusted to provide evidence of the Gothic glazing program. Therefore the discussion that follows concentrates on the extant northern bays, with recourse, wherever possible, to nineteenth-century observations and drawings and to a number of the pioneer autochrome photographs taken by Henri Deneux around 1915. A chronological assessment of the nave glazing will be assayed at the chapter's conclusion.

Originally the Gothic nave was planned to be joined to the twelfth-century facade block, and only several decades later was it decided to remove the Romanesque facade and extend the nave beyond it, to the present west facade.[84] The masonry line between the original work and the extension is called the *coupure Tourneur,* after the man who first identified it (figs. 3, 160). In figure 160 the dotted line shows the *coupure Tourneur* at clerestory level. Nineteenth-century observers were unanimous in noting a difference in glazing style at that point; in other words, the original program occupied clerestories from Bays 121 and 122 (at the crossing) through Bays 129 and 130. The three easternmost nave vaults rise above the canons' stalls; the fourth is a transitional space occupied in part by the closure to that area (and ultimately the late Gothic *jubé* and associated altars); and the fifth, Bays 129 and 130, is the first full compartment of the nave of the laity. Bays 129 and 130 were the location of the *rouelle* of St. Nicaise, a processional station, as well as of the Porte du Cerf, in the south aisle, an entry to the nave from a public court of the archbishop's palace ground. This fifth space was the prime focus of the "public nave" and was glazed accordingly.

The original program was extended westward starting with Bays 131 and 132, but not a great deal of time can have elapsed. Patrick Demouy has proposed that the nave was enclosed about 1285, when boy choristers were installed for the chanting of offices.[85] He is certainly correct about the date, since the westernmost bays, 139 and 140, within the facade towers, were glazed with grisailles bordered in the arms of Castille (gold castles on red). That border design became politically meaningless with the death of Philippe le Hardi in that year, 1285. The castles linger on in stained glass for no more than a few years, but by 1290, if they appear at all, they appear as mere decorative motifs using nonheraldic colors. The point of this observation is that the original nave program would certainly have been available during the entire glazing, which is datable roughly from around 1250 to 1285—that is, within one generation.

General observations include the following. All the kings and bishops are enthroned. Kings hold a scepter with one hand and tug at the strap of their mantle with the other, in the so-called "royal gesture."[86] Bishops usually bless with their right hand and hold a crozier with their left, but there are numerous variations on these formulae—and it is the details that are meaningful. If we can accept the argument of the beginning of this chapter, that the original figures did not represent historical personages, it follows that they embody concepts of power and its nuanced visualization.

Above the Canons' Stalls: The Evidence of Bays 121, 123, and 125

The study of the nave rosaces in chapter 5 makes clear the division between clerical and public space. The coronation ceremony took place in an enclosed area of the eastern nave extending from the altar (in the transept crossing) to the *jubé* (partway into the area at Bays 127 and 128), with canons' stalls running along the sides. From 1416 to 1764 the *jubé* was permanent; previously, the steps and platform were erected for each coronation.[87] Beyond doubt some sort of low closure existed at this point, between the canons' stalls on either side, previous to the construction of the *jubé*. The ritual enacted within this contained area was a semiprivate affair. Only at the climax of the ceremony did the newly crowned king climb the stairs to sit enthroned in majesty on top of the *jubé*, in full regalia, for all to see. From there he participated in the coronation Mass that followed, after which he moved in procession through the nave, receiving the acclamation of all. The site of the *jubé* marks the division between restricted and public space, and the stained-glass rosaces reflect this division. What then are the distinctive features of the kings and archbishops of these eastern nave bays? Because of the repairs from the 1580 windstorm in the southern lancets, discussed above, the observations to follow are based primarily on evidence from the clerestories on the north (121, 123, 125; figs. 176, 192–96).

In these eastern nave bays, all figures turn to the east, in the direction of the altar and site of the actual coronation. All sit on high-backed thrones (see fig. 208). All are bearded and none are haloed. All kings hold scepters and finger the straps of their mantles. All prelates bless and originally held cross-staffs,[88] mark of their archiepiscopal status, emphasizing the signal importance of the archbishop of Reims to the ceremony: he is the one who actually anoints and crowns the monarch. The cross-staff is the emblem of an archbishop, but in real life he never ever carried it himself; it was not a substitute for, but an addition to, the crozier, which he did carry. The cross-staff was carried before him in solemn procession and declared the office and authority of the archbishop. Cartoons are repeated within each bay. As Michael Cothren has noted:

> The first three windows west of the crossing in the north nave clerestory at the Cathedral of Reims (windows 121, 123, and 125 . . .) offer . . . [an] instance of two groups of clerestory figures that are fundamentally related stylistically but also separated by differences in conception. Here the delineation of faces and hair follows the same convention, and color harmonies are constant. In one window [125, figs. 176, 196] the voluminous

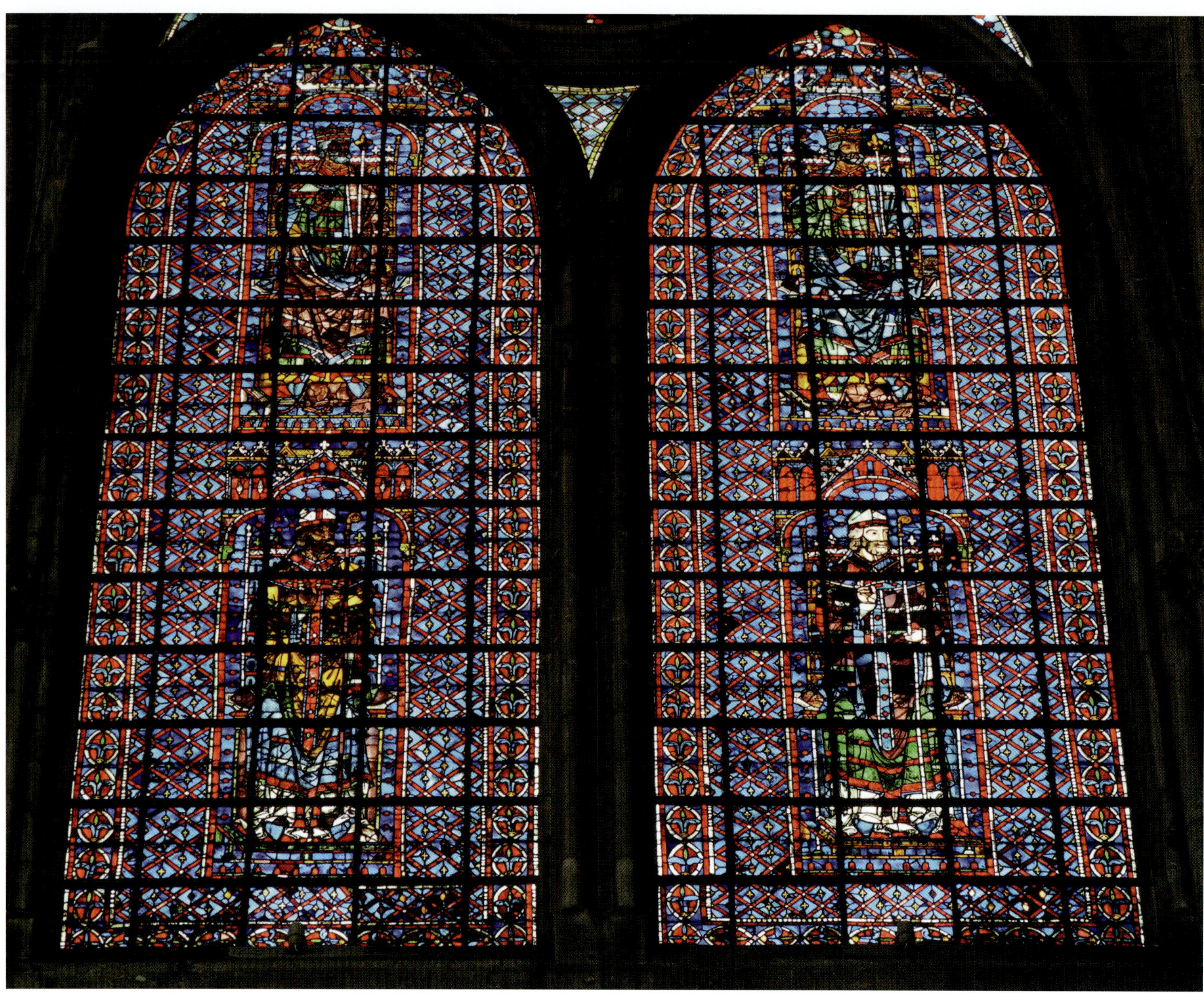

FIG. 192 Bay 121.

figures with small heads express clear silhouettes with spacious environments; there is an emphasis on decorative pattern through ornamental drapery bands and elaborate canopies. But the other two windows [figs. 159, 192–95] contain expressive and monumental figures with large heads. Canopies are smaller, borders are wider, and there are fewer decorative stripes on the clothing. This could indicate production within a single shop by artists of varying temperament.[89]

The glazier responsible for Bays 121 and 123 can be connected with the choir by a design convention: persons or creatures placed as socles beneath the figures' feet. The kings in Bay 121 rest their feet on lions (fig. 197), while the prelates in the next bay step on crouching figures (fig. 198), another emphasis on the great power of the archbishop of Reims. Such socles, similar to those in Bays 101, 102, 105, and 106 of the choir,[90] do not appear elsewhere in the nave.

Above the *Rouelle*: Bays 127 Through 130

Bays 127/128 and 129/130 were the last areas vaulted and glazed according to the original plan to join the Gothic nave to Samson's Romanesque facade block. The nave at Bays 127/128, just beyond the canons' choir, was partially occupied with some kind of "rood screen" or closure to that area, at the spot where the scaffolding was erected for coronations until the permanent *jubé* was constructed in 1418. On either side of the closure's central entrance was an altar, one dedicated to St. Paul and

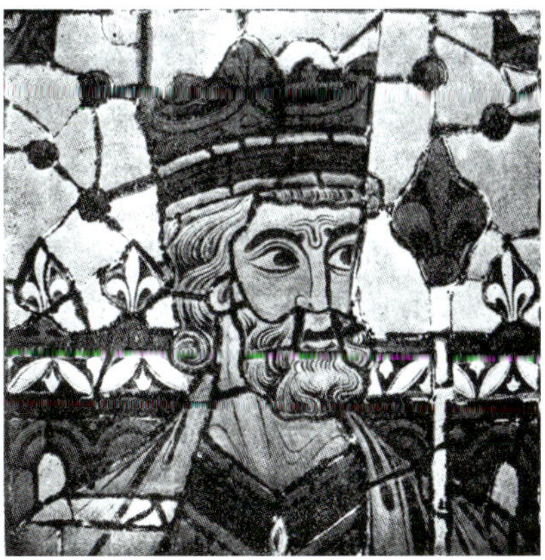

FIG. 193 King. Bay 121, left lancet, top row. Tracing by Paul Simon from the exterior, here reversed as it appears from the interior (after Simon, "Notes sur les vitraux").

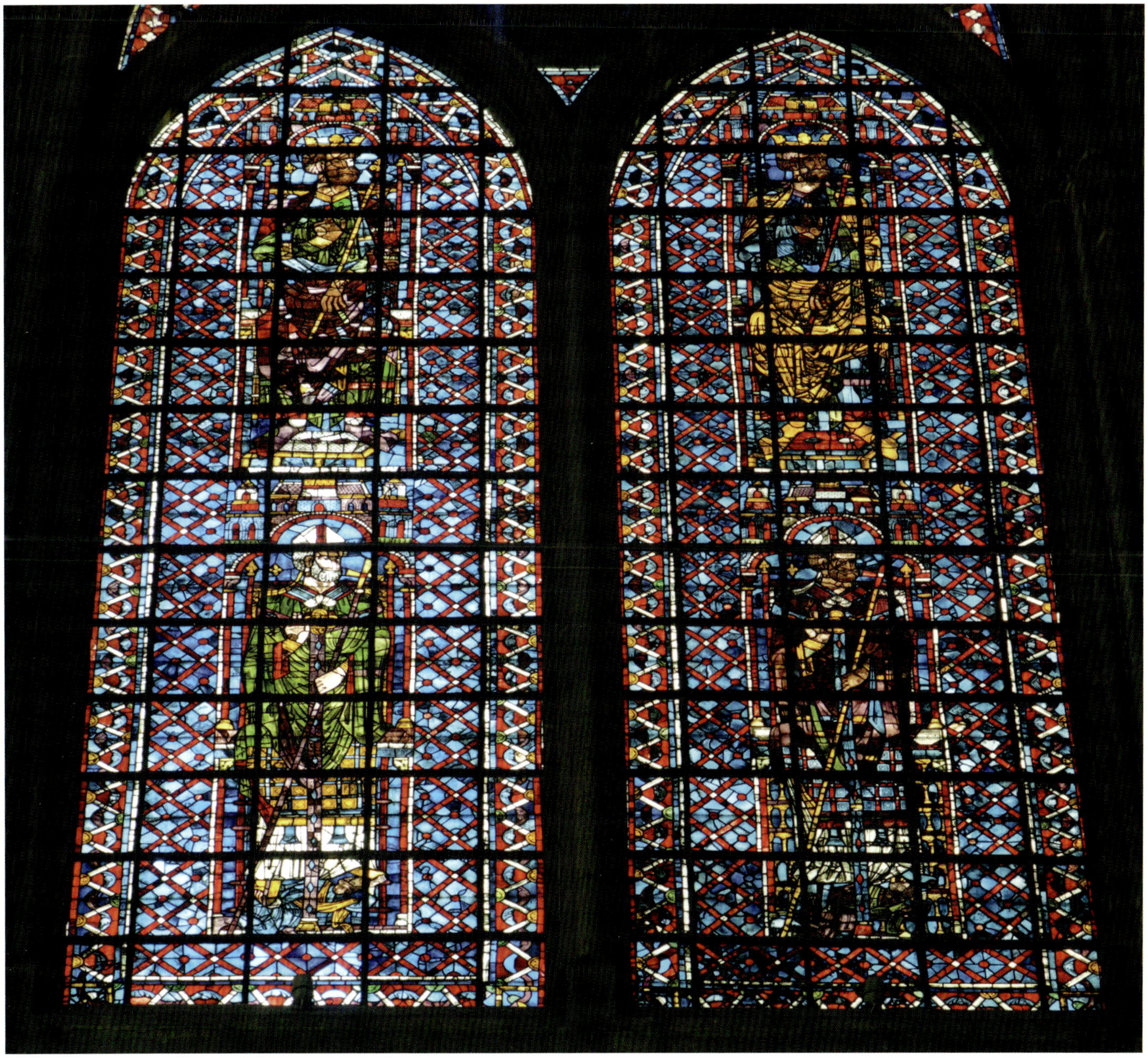

FIG. 194 Bay 123.

FIG. 195 Archbishop. Bay 123, lower row (1881) (after Westlake, *A History of Design in Painted Glass*).

FIG. 196 King. Bay 125, right lancet, top row. Autochrome by Henri Deneux, 1915.

FIG. 197 Lion(?), socle beneath the feet of a king. Bay 121, right lancet, top row.

FIG. 198 Man, socle beneath the feet of an archbishop. Bay 123, right lancet, lower row.

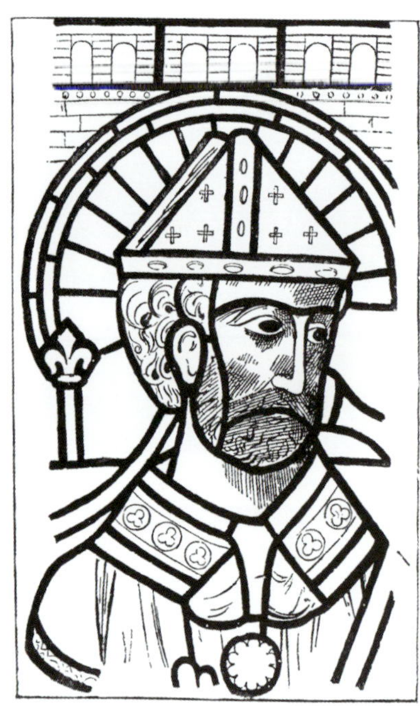

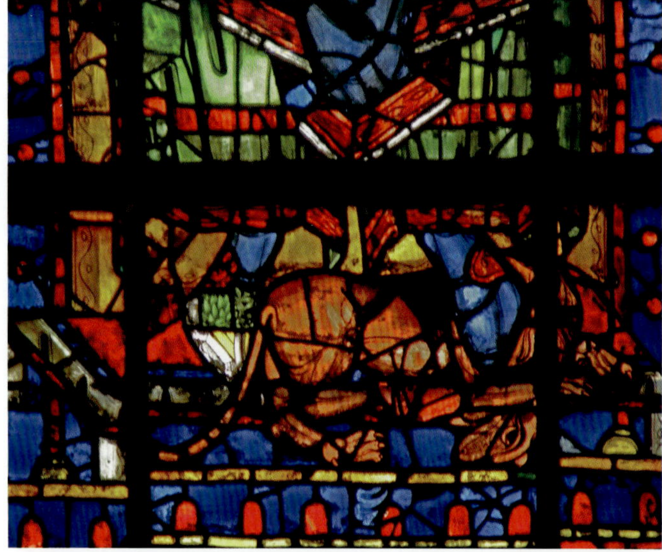

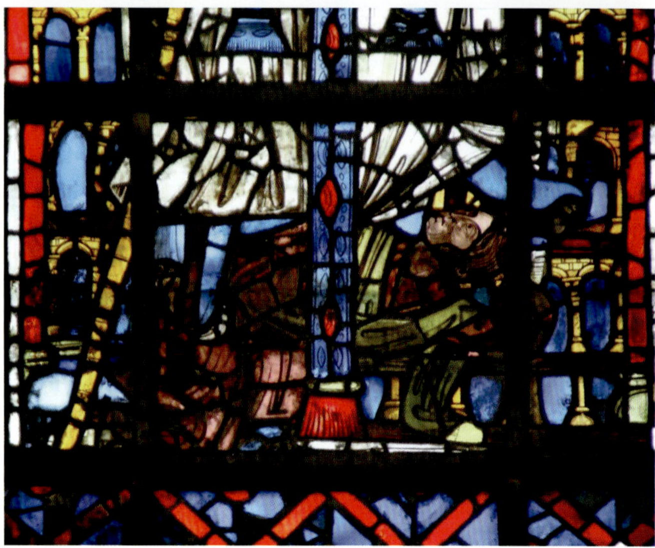

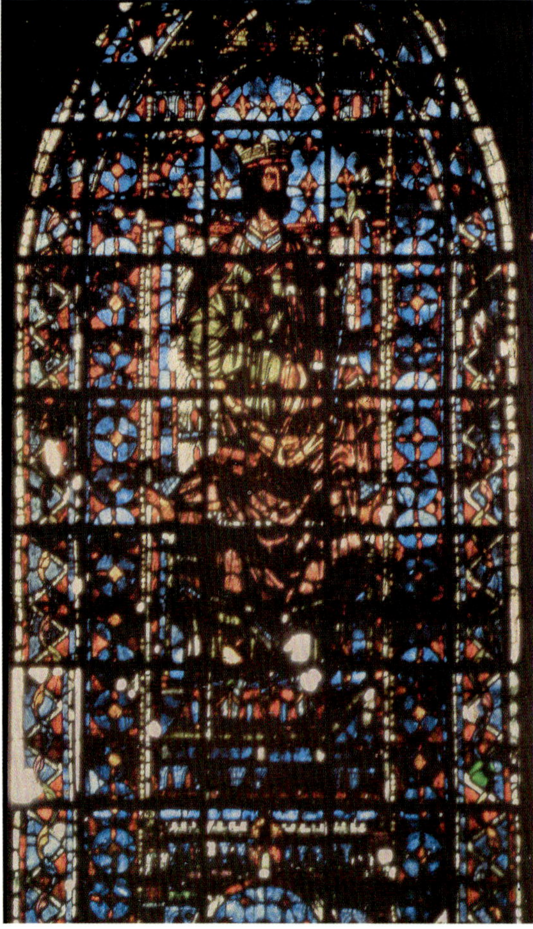

the other to the Holy Spirit (also called the altar of the *rouelle*).[91] Bays 129 and 130 thus lighted the first complete bay in the public area of the nave, beyond the canons' choir. It was the focal point of the public nave, site of the *rouelle* of St. Nicaise as well as the entrance in the south aisle known as the Porte du Cerf. Both appear on the earliest plan of the cathedral, by Jacques Cellier (1583–87, fig. 199), but both were much more ancient.

The *rouelle* was a round marble slab set into the pavement, marking the spot where St. Nicaise was martyred.[92] It was surrounded by a wrought-iron grill and was lit by a chandelier hanging directly over it. All major processions leaving the canons' enclosure stopped here to sing a first station, and this would no doubt have been true of the triumphal procession of the freshly crowned king following the coronation Mass. St. Nicaise was second only to St. Remi in importance to the Gothic cathedral. His cult was expanding rapidly at exactly the years when the nave was being glazed. In the cathedral's ambulatory, chapels of Saint Nicaise and Saint Remi flanked the axial one to the north and south. Both saints appeared on Hincmar's golden altarpiece. In 1213 the cranium of St. Nicaise received a new silver-gilt reliquary. In 1231 Archbishop Henri de Braine laid the foundation stone for the new cathedral-scale church of the abbey of Saint-Nicaise in Reims, a construction project not finished until ca. 1294 and one that attracted even royal contributions.[93] When the nave of the cathedral was extended and the new facade built, the inner side of the trumeau of its central portal received a statue of St. Nicaise facing the *rouelle*.

A door in the nave's south aisle opened to the area of the *rouelle* from the outer court of the bishop's palace. It was called the Porte du Cerf because that public court contained a large bronze sculpture of a stag.[94] The bronze stag had been installed by Archbishop Gervais (1055–67), the prelate who anointed and crowned Philippe I in Reims cathedral in the year 1059. The bronze bore an inscription with the name of the artist Osmundus and another quatrain glorifying Gervais. The archbishop's prisons were located across the court on the south, and thus the stag became the symbol of the ecclesiastical court of justice and the archbishop's secular power. At least by the late Middle Ages, the bronze stag during coronation festivities emitted free wine to the milling crowds.

The area of the *rouelle* was thus the focus of the nave of the laity. The clerestories lighting this area, Bays 127 to 130, were part of the original nave plan. War damage here was heavy, and Bays 127 and 128 were the last to be remade following 1918 (figs. 188–89, 200–201). The two lower figures now in Bay 127 were salvaged from the otherwise lost Bays 129 and 130, and discussion of the latter's glazing is

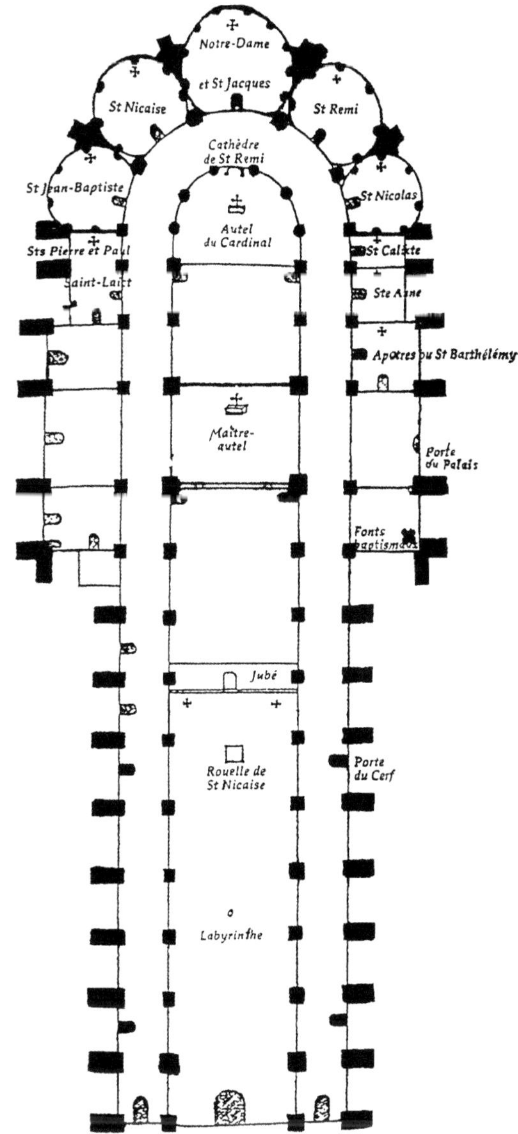

FIG. 199 Reims cathedral, plan, after Jacques Cellier, 1583–87.

possible on the basis of these two surviving figures, several prewar photographs (see fig. 202), and the verbal witness of Guilhermy and Cerf. Judging from the extant evidence, Bays 127/128 and 129/130 were completely different—from each other and from everything else in the nave. The first pair seems to have been a hodgepodge of disparate elements, while the second (129/130) included a masterpiece, the most handsome glass in the nave, the visual focus of the laity's church. Figures in the eastern lancets of 127 and of 128, that is, those in the half of each window closest to the canons' choir, were notably larger in

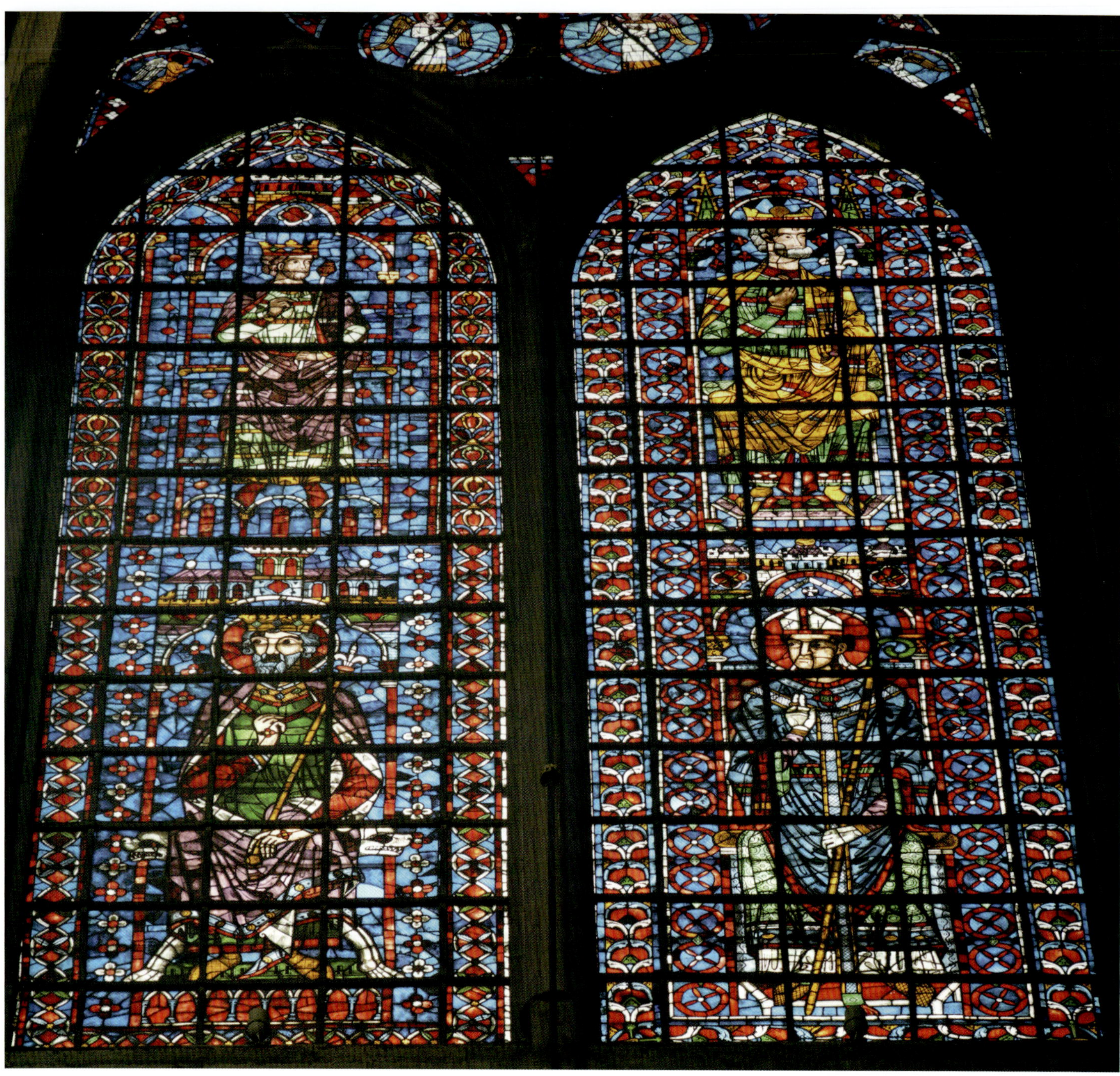

FIG. 200 Bay 127. The two lower figures salvaged from Bays 129 and 130 (otherwise lost).

scale than those in their paired lights, and the ornament, color, and design were simpler and bolder. The difference is enough to suggest some hiatus in glazing between the eastern and western lancets. Could this indicate a temporary wall of some kind, during construction, just beyond the canons' choir?

Stylistically these unmatched lancets do not compare closely with either the windows east of them (discussed above) or the extraordinary Bays 129 and 130 (see below). Moreover, complicating the issue, Bay 128 is the clerestory containing Karolvs, which I have suggested is an older, reused image.

127		128	
LEFT (WEST)	RIGHT (EAST)	LEFT (EAST)	RIGHT (WEST)
KING: smaller	KING: larger	KING: larger beardless very tall crown	KING (Karolvs): smaller frontal
ARCHBISHOP (lost): smaller no halo crozier rational (Cerf)	ARCHBISHOP (lost): larger red halo cross-staff (Guilhermy) rational (Cerf)	ARCHBISHOP: larger green halo crozier	ARCHBISHOP: smaller no halo crozier

Prewar figures of Bays 127 and 128

Like the figures to the east (Bays 121, 123, and 125; see above), those in 127 and 128 (all but Karolvs) looked eastward, all kings held scepters and fingered their mantle straps, and all bishops blessed (figs. 206, 207). Like most figures to the west (at least those for which we have data), those of Bays 127 and 128 sat on low thrones (fig. 208). And like the western figures, too, three of the four bishops carried croziers, not cross-staffs, as to the east (fig. 209). To sum up the varied types of evidence, noteworthy details recorded about the prewar figures of Bays 127—now restored with two figures salvaged from lost nave bays—and 128 can be charted as above.

The introduction of haloes and rationals connected Bays 127 and 128 with the pivotal Bays 129 and 130 to be discussed below (figs. 209, 210). To sum up: there were distinct differences in detail between the glazing above and that beyond the canons' choir enclosure; there were innovations of detail in the bays at the *rouelle;* and the transitional bays (127–28) were incoherent in conception, perhaps indicative of a hiatus in production and possibly some kind of temporary physical barrier just beyond the enclosure of the canons' stalls.

Striking are the polish and focal intensity of the designs that filled Bays 129 and 130, directly above the *rouelle,* insofar as they can be recovered. A lost Rothier photograph of Bay 129 was published twice around World War I, in London and in Paris (fig. 202).[95] Since no other photos of the cathedral's lancets by the famous Reims photographer are known, the choice of this bay to record and by others for publication would seem to indicate that those responsible, both French and English, considered this nave bay to be the most remarkable. This precious photo supplements verbal testimony of Guilhermy and Cerf from the mid–

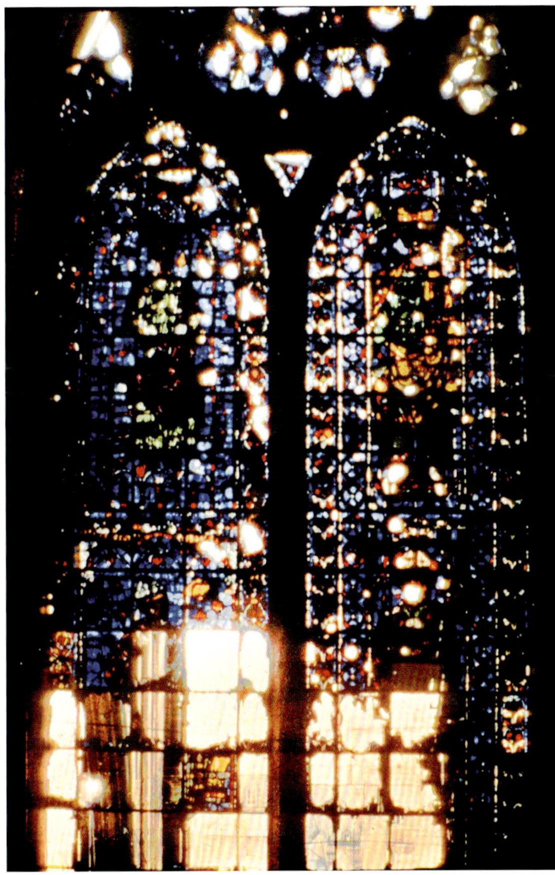

FIG. 201 Bay 127 (1915). Autochrome by Henri Deneux (?), obtained from Lucien Mary.

FIG. 202 Bay 129 (before 1914), now lost. Photo by François Rothier (after Arthur J. de Havilland Bushnell, *Storied Windows*).

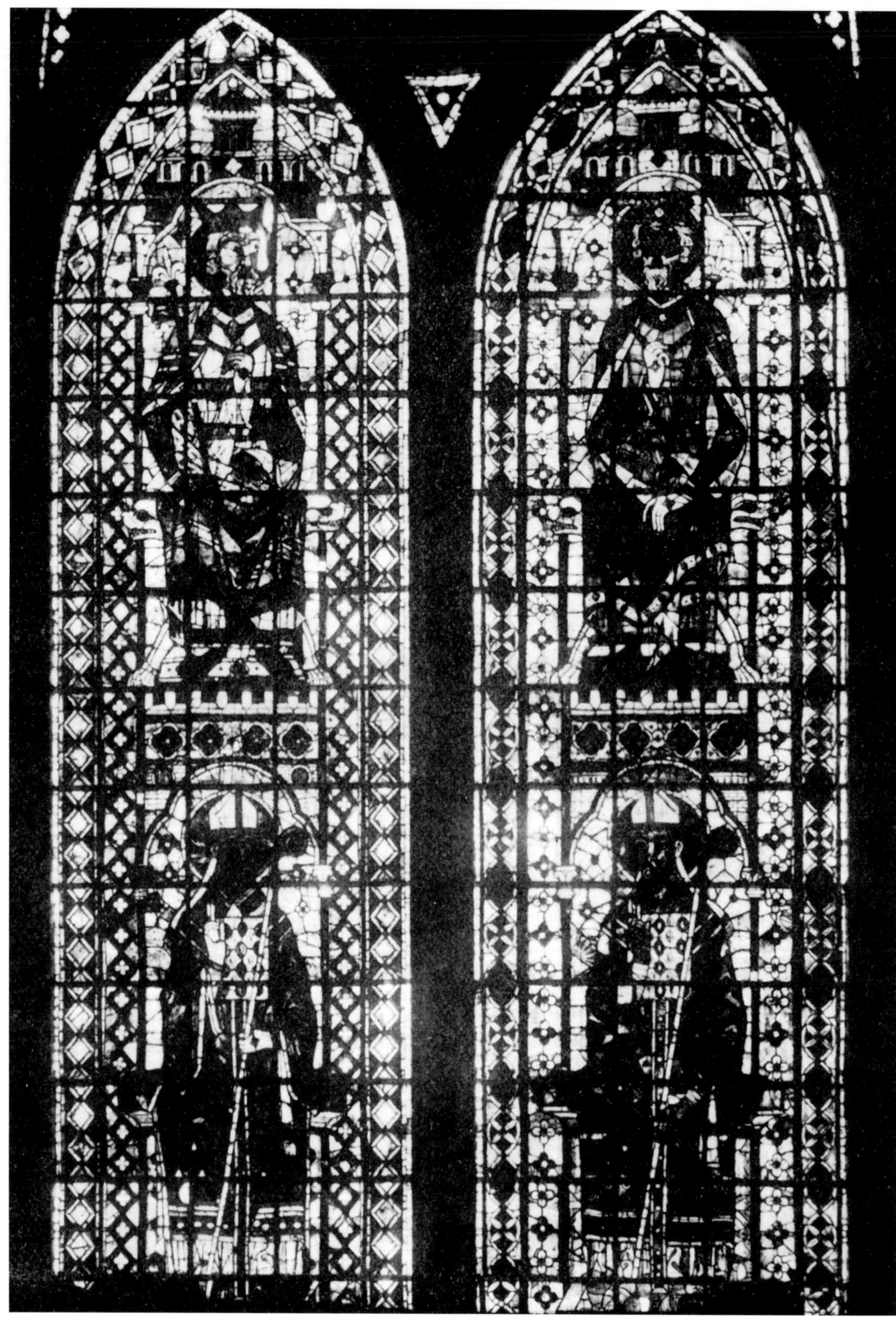

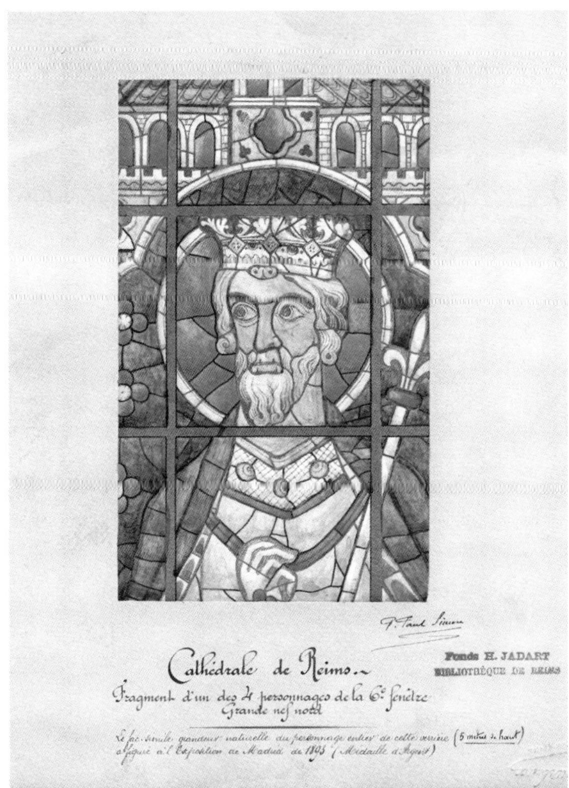

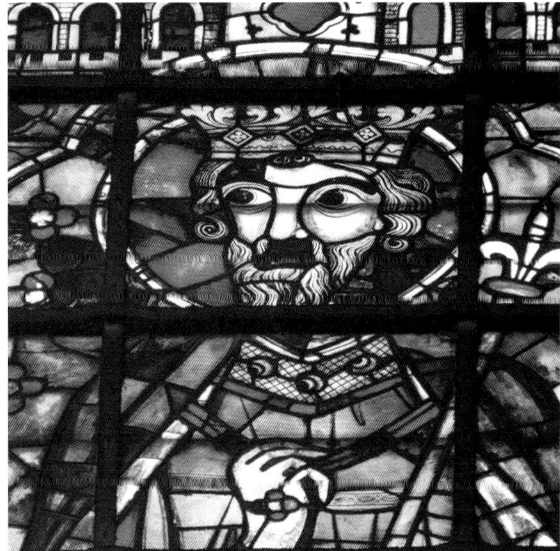

FIG. 203 King. Originally in Bay 129, right lancet, top row, replaced in Bay 127, left lancet, lower row. Watercolor by Paul Simon, before 1893, 15.7 × 9.6 cm, *Fragment d'un des quatre personnages de la sixième fenêtre, grande nef nord,* Reims, Bibl. mun., XV II a 27-BMR 14-036.

FIG. 204 King. Originally in Bay 129 and now in Bay 127, left lancet, lower row.

FIG. 205 Archbishop. Originally in Bay 130 and now in Bay 127, right lancet, lower row.

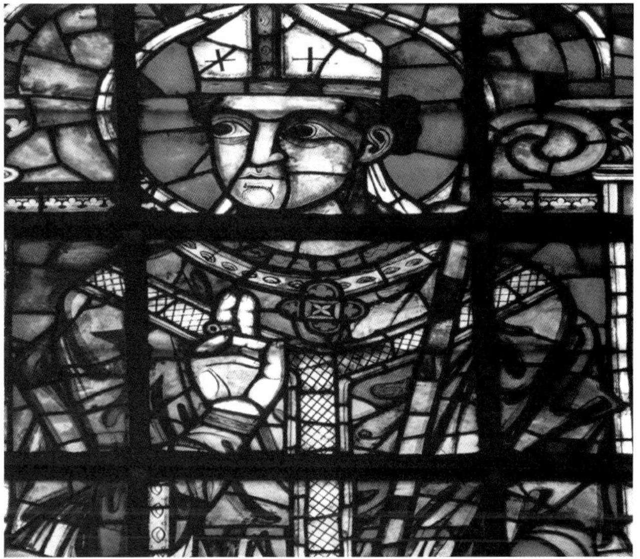

nineteenth century and allows the identification of the king originally in the right lancet. Before the war, this figure was photographed by Deneux, and Simon's tracing of him (fig. 203) was published.[96] The postwar restoration salvaged him and placed him in the lower left lancet of Bay 127 (frontispiece, fig. 204). Installed next to him in the right lancet is an archbishop (fig. 205) comparable in scale, color, and boldness of drawing, as well as in the power and dynamism of the characterization. Prewar photos indicate that this prelate was not originally in Bay 127 or 129, and Guilhermy's observations allow a firm identification of his original location in Bay 130.[97] The largely lost Bays 129 and 130 can therefore be considered together.

The Rothier photo establishes that all the figures in Bay 129 turned to honor each other rather than toward the altar, as do nearly all other figures in the nave (fig. 206). All four had haloes. These two kings were the only nimbed monarchs in the nave,[98] while the haloed archbishops were clustered in this bay and the next (fig. 210). Each Bay 129 archbishop also wore a rational (fig. 209), the spectacular gem-studded breastplate assumed by the prelate only for the most solemn festivals.[99] And finally, these two kings were the only ones in the nave enthroned on foldstools (fig. 208).[100] Bay 129 was arguably the first clerestory really visible to the newly crowned monarch when he was enthroned on the platform or *jubé.* He sat there on a foldstool. The foldstool appears in the glass of Saint-Remi, and Caviness has indicated that it was associated not only with rulers—for example, on

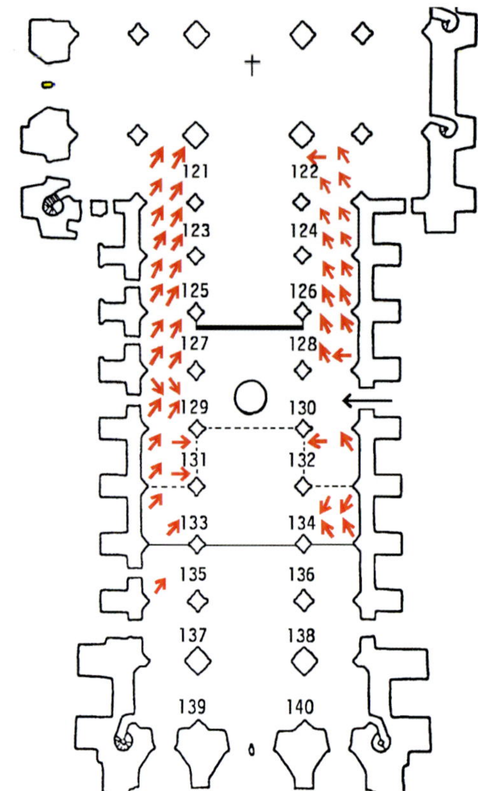

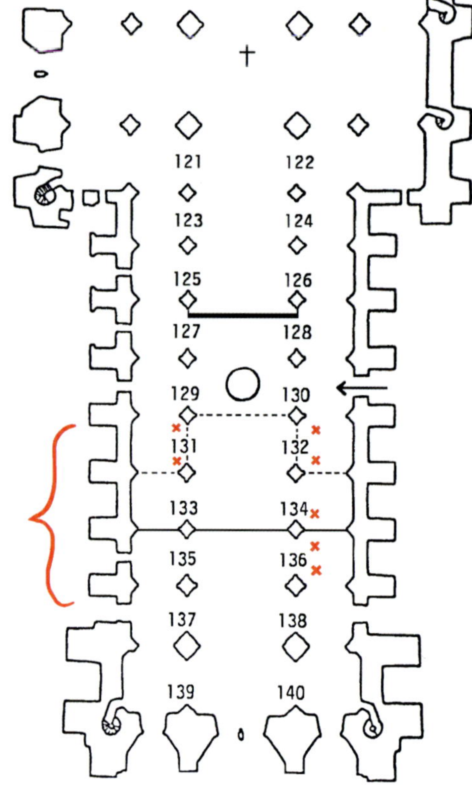

FIG. 206 Chart of the directions in which the nave figures face (those omitted cannot be established). The arrow through the right, south flank of the nave indicates the Porte du Cerf; the dotted line locates the *coupure Tourneur*.

FIG. 207 Chart of archbishops who do not bless (all others do, as far as can be established).

Opposite
FIG. 208 Chart of thrones: H = high-backed; L = low; F = foldstool.

FIG. 209 Chart of archbishops wearing rationals and of archbishops holding cross-staffs (all others have croziers, as far as can be established).

FIG. 210 Chart of figures with haloes and of figures waving.

the seals of many Capetian kings—but also traditionally with saints, including John the Evangelist and the Virgin Mary. St. Remi sat on a foldstool, I have argued, in Samson's Romanesque facade (fig. 147).[101]

The two survivors from Bays 129 and 130—the king (129) and the archbishop (130) now installed as the lower row of Bay 127—are so close in style and so different from the remainder of the nave glazing that there can be little doubt that the two facing bays at the *rouelle* received their glass at the same time. Thus it is unexpected that, from our limited information about the appearance of Bay 130, it was not as "fancy" as Bay 129. Why not? The surviving archbishop (fig. 205) wears a pallium but, unlike those that were in Bay 129 (fig. 202), no rational. Guilhermy lists the kings of Bay 130 without comment and notes only that the bishops have croziers and haloes. Cerf reports, concerning Bay 130, "rien qui puisse fixer l'attention."[102]

Bay 129, then, was unquestionably special: filled with saints both royal and episcopal, acknowledging each other and vested and enthroned in their most ceremonial splendor. It was a fitting ornament to greet the first appearance of a newly anointed monarch as he emerged in triumphant procession from behind the *jubé* at the close of the long coronation ceremony. It would have been the first clerestory facing anyone coming into the church from the Porte du Cerf in the south nave aisle, and a constant reminder of the unique and hallowed space he or she was entering. Its uniqueness suggests a particular moment and a special purpose behind its creation, which are pursued below.

Coronation and Chronology

Bays 121, 123, and 125 of the nave have been dated ca. 1245–55,[103] a judgment indicated by numerous

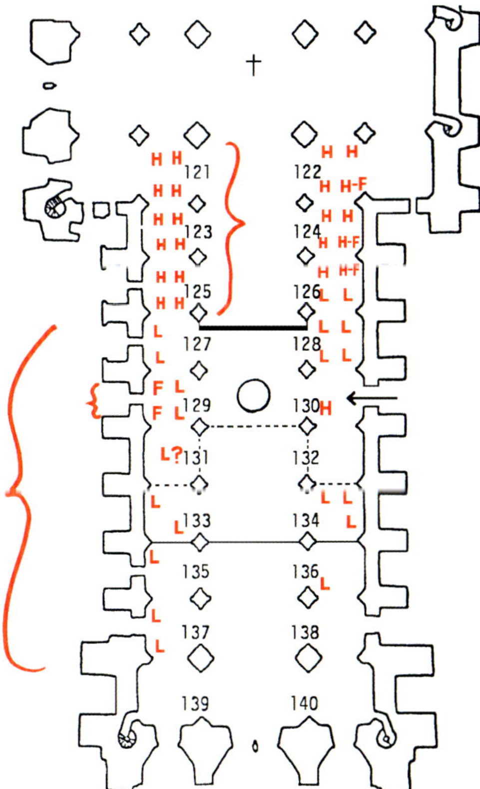

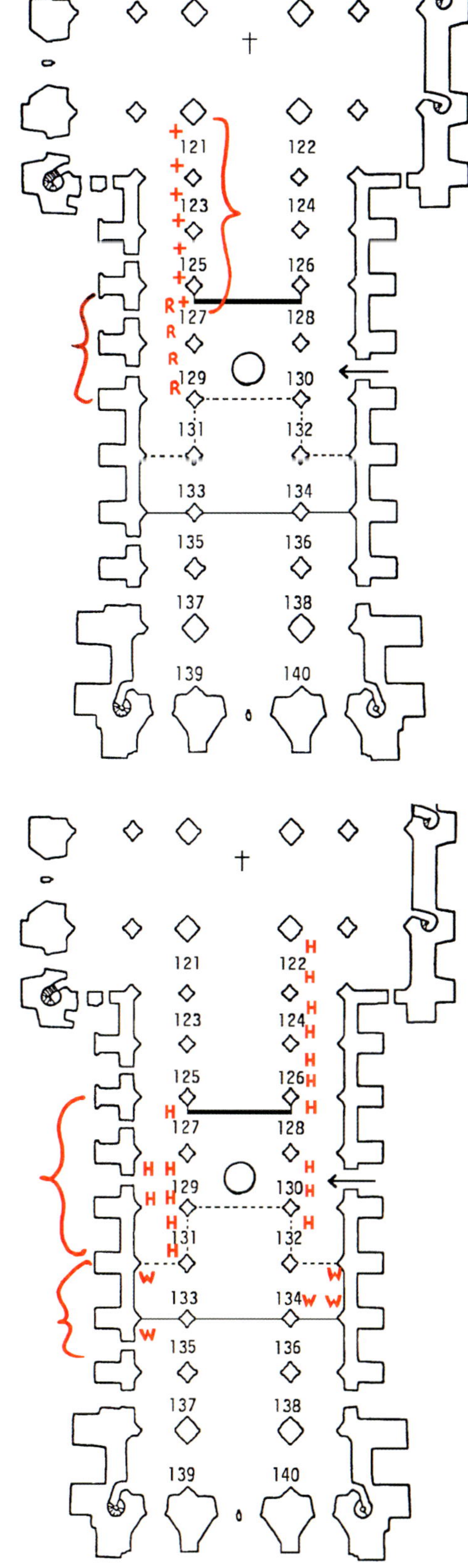

details of style. Certainly no great length of time separated them from Bays 105 through 108 in the chevet, which I argued in chapter 3 were made sporadically during the several years preceding the death of Henri de Braine, in 1240. Grodecki believed that the same artists were responsible.[104] A number of the border and ground patterns of the eastern nave bays repeat types found in the chevet,[105] and Bays 121 and 123 include creatures as socles for several figures, as found in Bays 101, 102, 105, and 106 of the chevet.

General comparisons to other monuments support this chronology. The rich, deep tonality of blue and red in Bays 121, 123, and 125—as well as the many fleurs-de-lis incorporated into their ornament—suggests a date following the Sainte-Chapelle. The socle creatures beneath the figures' feet appear in such an otherwise unrelated monument as Le Mans in the early 1250s.[106] None of the figures' canopies in the eastern bays of the nave has crockets,

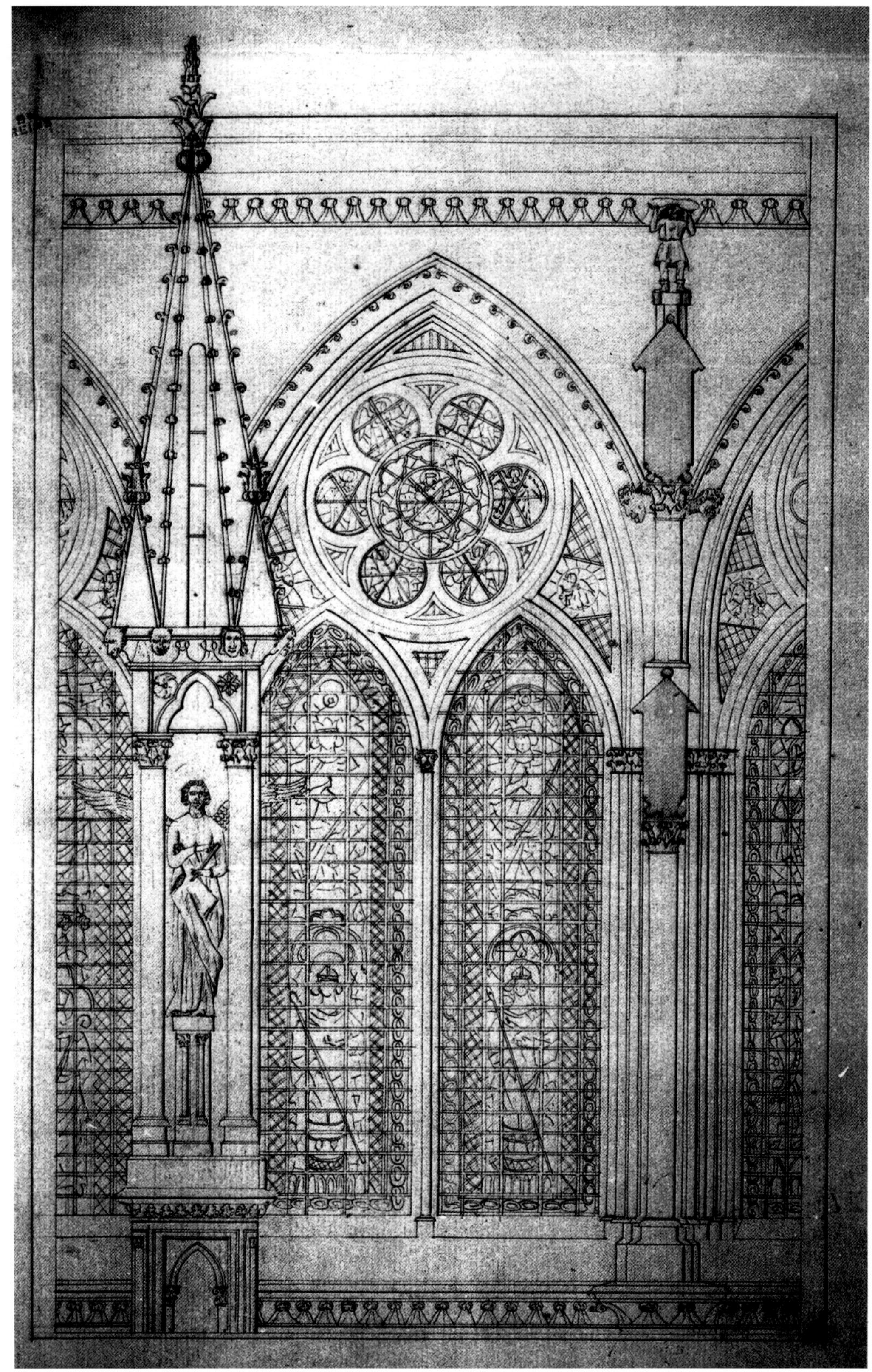

FIG. 211 Bay 131 (lost). Rosace has Virgin and Child; six censing angels. In the lancets, kings finger their mantle straps; nimbed archbishops hold closed books. Drawing by Leblan, before 1858.

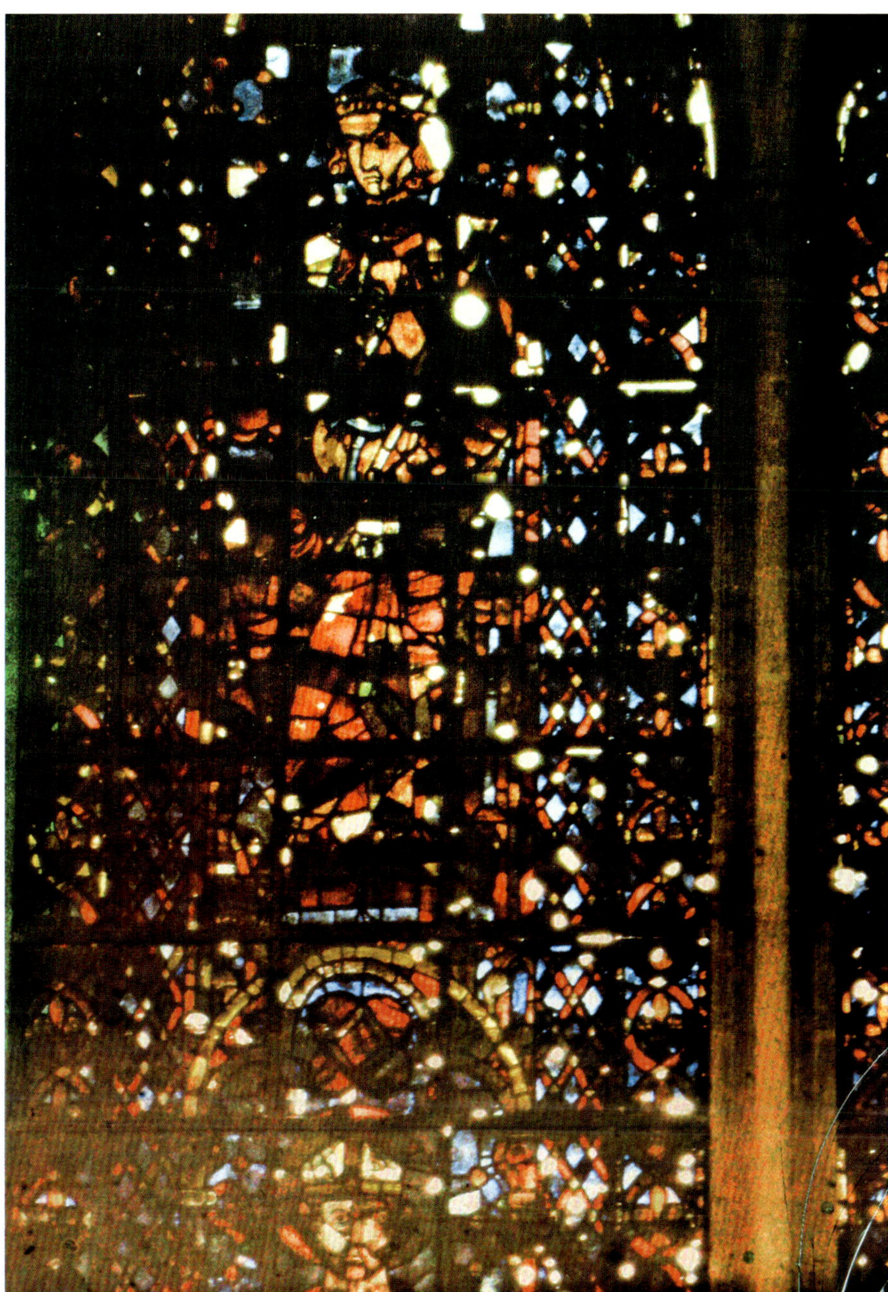

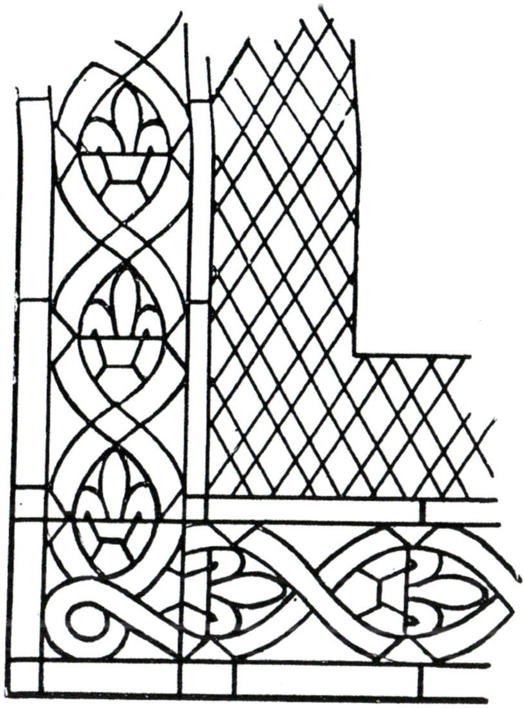

FIG. 212 King, waving; archbishop, frontal, nimbed in red. Bay 132 (lost), left lancet, top row. Autochrome by Henri Deneux, 1915.

FIG. 213 Border of fleurs-de-lis, Bay 132 (after Louis Ottin, *Le vitrail: Son histoire, ses manifestations a travers les âges et les peuples*, 1896).

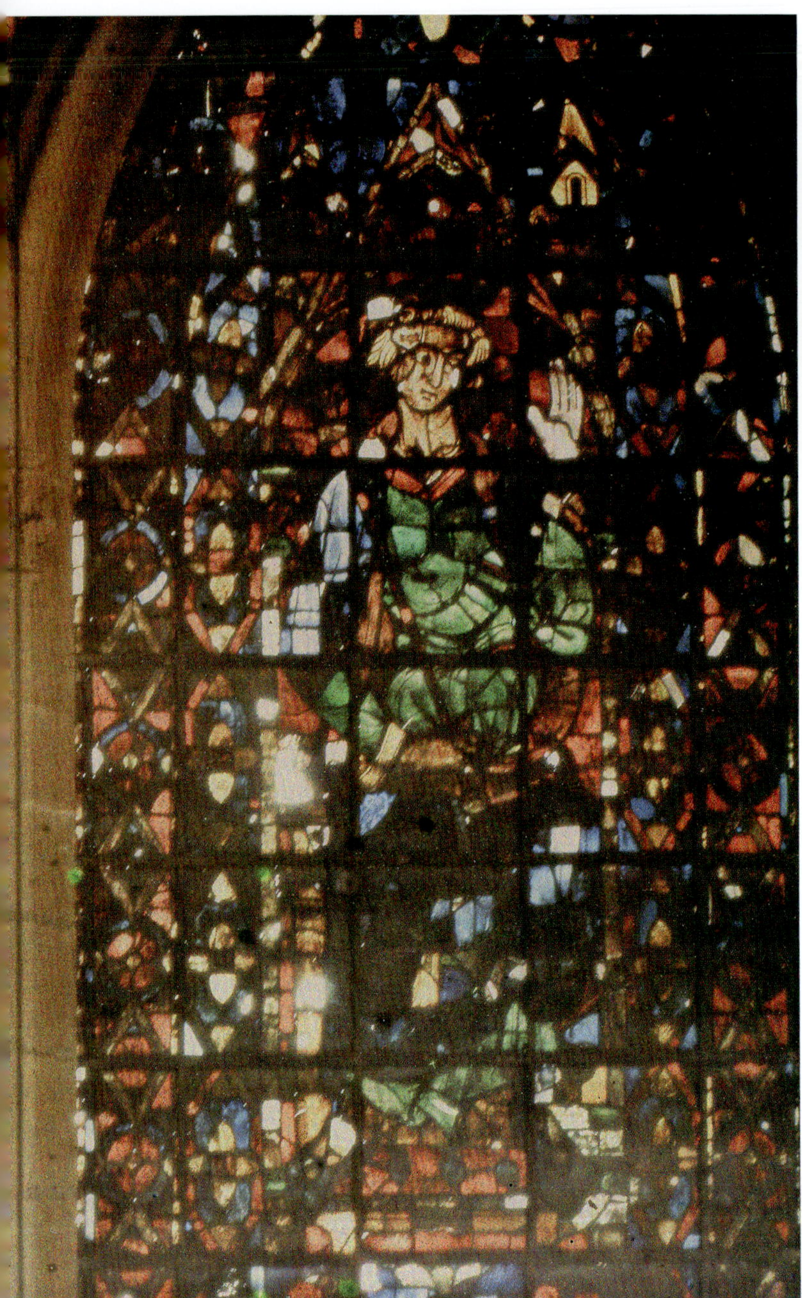

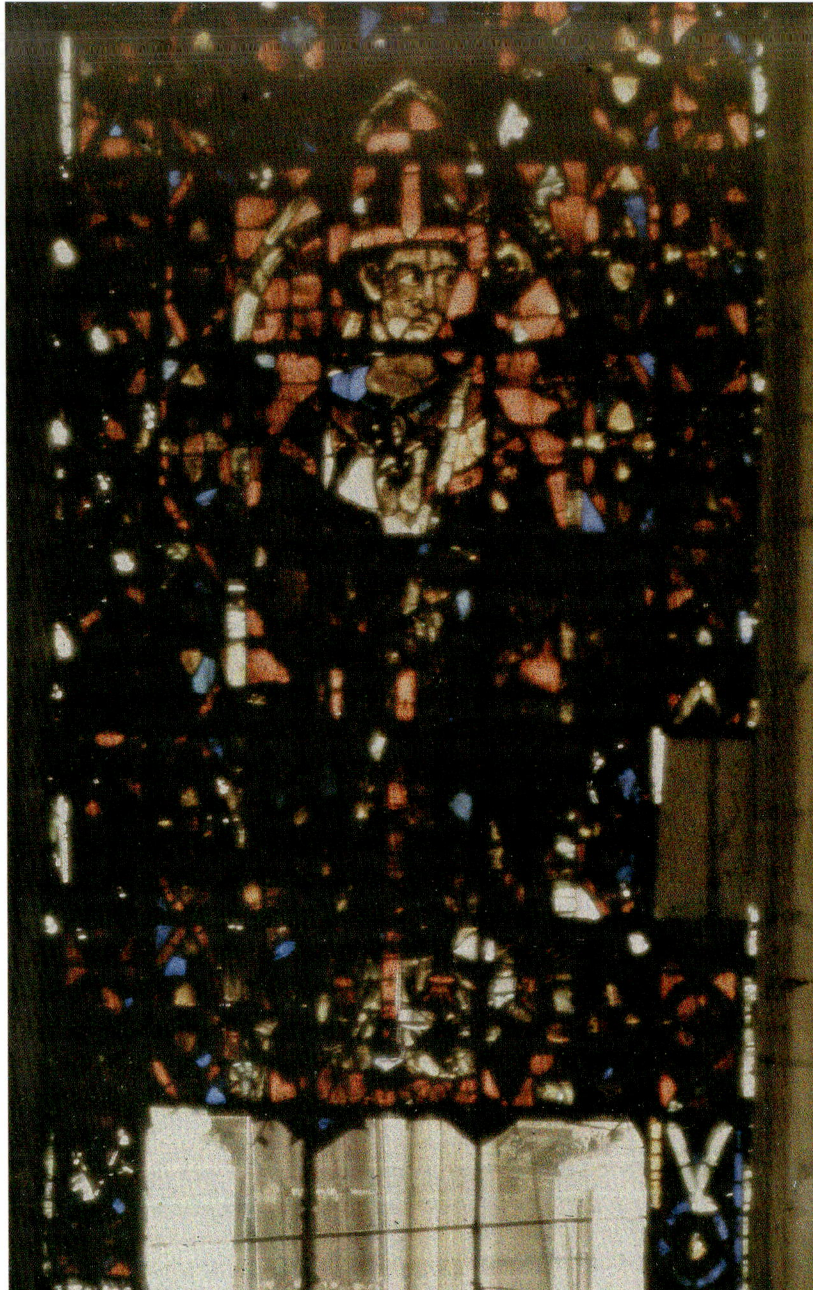

FIG. 214 King, waving. Bay 133 (lost), right lancet, top row. Autochrome by Henri Deneux, 1915.

FIG. 215 Archbishop, blessing. Bay 133 (lost), left lancet, lower row. Autochrome by Henri Deneux, 1915.

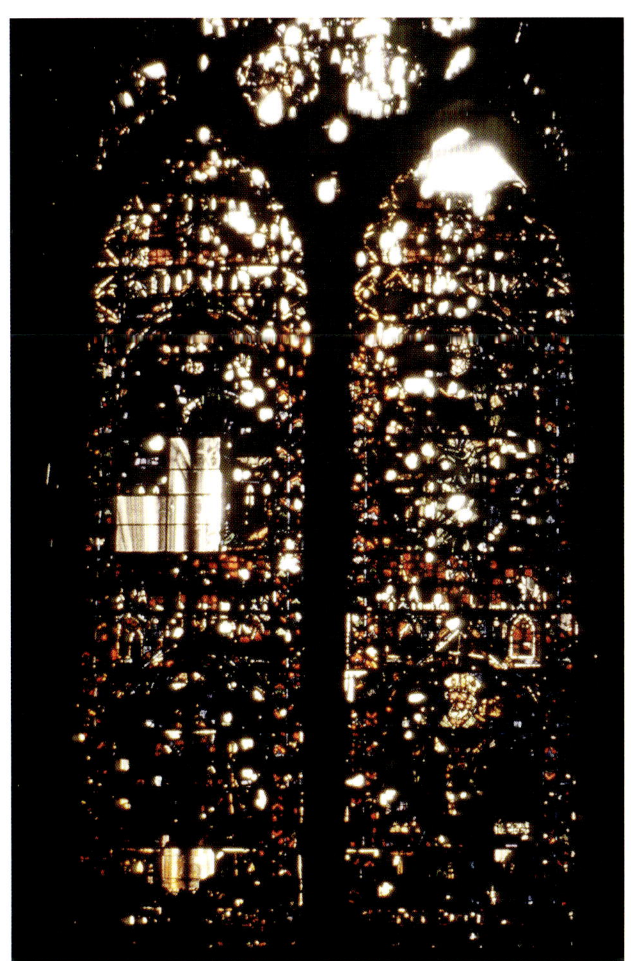

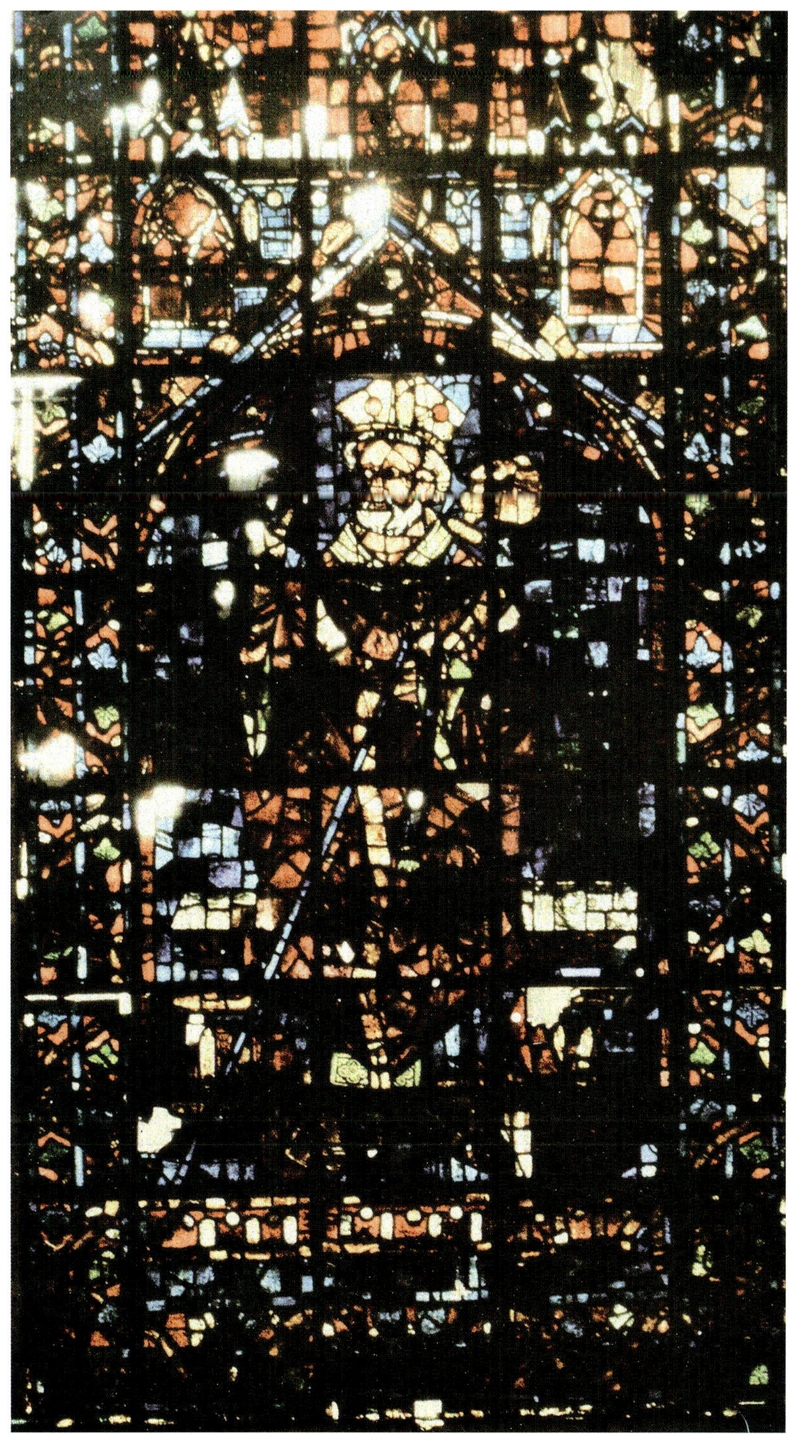

FIG. 216 Bay 134 (lost), 1915.

FIG. 217 Archbishop, waving. Bay 134 (lost), right lancet, lower row. Autochrome by Henri Deneux, 1915.

with the exception of that over the right bishop of Bay 121, and there the crockets are tightly curled palmettes, tilted backward, for which a general date at the midcentury would be expected.[107]

The nave, commenced ca. 1245, was completed at the new facade around 1285.[108] The arguments of this chapter have divided the nave glazing east of the *coupure Tourneur* into a coherent group of rich, somber windows above the canons' stalls (surviving chiefly on the north) and the problematic bays beyond that enclosure (127 through 130). Bays 127 and 128 (see chart above) were an incoherent jumble of mismatched styles, while Bays 129 and 130 were of high artistic merit, though 129 was rather fancier than 130. The glass beyond the *coupure Tourneur,* now lost, will be discussed below and can be dated roughly ca. 1275–85 on the basis of evidence about its canopies, lighter color, and other stylistic criteria.

What major event falling between the 1250s and 1285 could account for the observations above? Only the *sacre* of Philippe III le Hardi, in 1271. Unlike other coronations in the thirteenth century, it could have been anticipated, at least from the moment when Louis IX took the cross in 1267—an extremely unpopular move made by a monarch who had by then reigned forty-one years and clearly was not in the best of health.[109] It seems likely that, in the late 1260s, the canons of Reims assessed the situation in the building site that was, still, their cathedral. There may have been a temporary wall at the west end of their choir enclosure to shelter it from the ongoing building activity further west. Several of the bays of the new nave extension may have been vaulted but not glazed, and there was no usable western portal. Thus would be justified the clearing and improving of an area just west of the canons' stalls to provide not only passage through the Porte du Cerf from the archbishop's court but also a sacred area at the *rouelle* suitable for procession. Such a hypothesis even explains why the handsome Bays 129 and 130 resembled each other but why 129—directly opposite the Porte du Cerf—offered the more dazzling display.

Above the Extension to the Nave: Bays 131 Through 140

Bays 129 and 130 were the last of the original group of glazed clerestories in the nave, before the *coupure Tourneur.* The final western bays, 139 and 140, were glazed with grisaille since their lighting was hampered by the facade towers. Their original Castille borders would indicate a date not much later than 1285 for their completion.[110] The eight colored bays in between, Bays 131 through 138, were often described before World War I as of a different, later style: less rich and *soigné* in design, the figures larger, composed of bigger pieces of glass, in a color palette marked by light yellow and brilliant green.[111] About these sixteen lost kings and sixteen lost prelates information is sparse but not totally nonexistent (see below). Five figures were photographed by Deneux; another was published in a tracing by Simon; several other images exist; and we have brief descriptions made chiefly by Guilhermy (fols. 398r–v). Taken together, this information, in which images confirm the verbal evidence of prewar observers, produces the following list:[112]

131—(fig. 211): KINGS, beardless, finger their mantle straps
BISHOPS, nimbed in red, hold books
BORDER of fleurs-de-lis (Guilhermy)
132—KING (left lancet) waves (fig. 212)
BISHOP (left lancet) nimbed in red, faces forward
BISHOPS hold something (?) in the right hand (Guilhermy)
BORDERS of fleurs-de-lis (fig. 213)
133—KINGS beardless; KING (left lancet) waves (fig. 214)
BISHOP (left lancet) blesses (fig. 215)
BORDER of lozenges
134—(fig. 216): KINGS, bearded, wave and seem to speak (Guilhermy)
BISHOP (right lancet) waves (fig. 217)
BISHOP (left lancet) blesses
BORDER "à rinceau courant," of quasi-naturalistic leaves and berries (fig. 218)

Bay 134 differs notably in style from Bay 133 opposite as well as the others in the western nave.

The figures are smaller, the canopies more elaborate (fig. 216). The figures face each other rather than all to the east. It was probably an early restoration. The shape of the right bishop's miter, with diagonal sides but still wider than it is tall, suggests a date in the early fourteenth century.[113] Compare it to the miter in figure 220 among many others in the cathedral glazing.

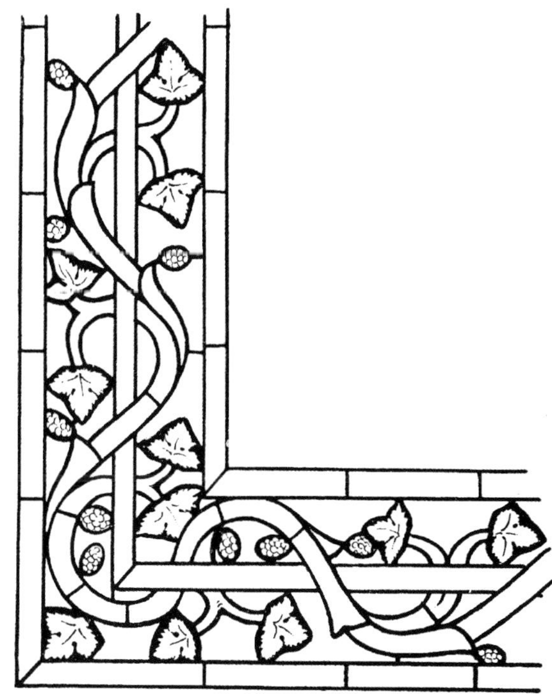

FIG. 218 Border of quasi-naturalistic leaves and berries, Bay 134 (after Louis Ottin, *Le vitrail: Son histoire, ses manifestations à travers les âges et les peuples*).

135—KINGS bearded; KING (right lancet) waves (fig. 219)
BISHOP blesses, holds crozier (fig. 220)
BORDER of fleurs-de-lis
136—KINGS bearded
BISHOPS hold their croziers with both hands
BORDER of quatrefoils
(Guilhermy)
137—KINGS beardless, on low thrones
BISHOPS under trilobed arches
(Guilhermy)
138—KINGS beardless
BISHOPS with croziers
BORDER of lozenges (fig. 221)
(Guilhermy)
139—Grisaille, with later coats of arms inserted, and oil-painted with circles and stars for the 1825 coronation (Cerf, *Histoire,* 2:287; fig. 238)
140—Like Bay 139 opposite (Guilhermy)

All the images but those of Bay 134 show figures each with a long neck, rounded head, and strong, well-defined features, including a long straight nose, small down-turned mouth, and the glance of the eyes sharply focused on something. Deneux's autochromes of Bays 132 and 133 establish that they were closely related in style; the emphatic facial painting is markedly similar. Unfortunately no image of the Bay 131 figures is adequate for comparison (see fig. 211). However, Tourneur states that some cartoons were repeated, and two images bear out his observation: the autochrome photo of a bishop in Bay 133 and the tracing of a bishop in Bay 135 (figs. 215, 220).

Some of the images show the canopies over these figures (fig. 220). These canopies are several obvious steps further in development from those few in the eastern nave windows. A gable embellished with spiky, upright crockets surmounts a pointed trefoil arch. The development of crockets from 1250 to 1300 in France proceeds from none at all to palmette crockets curled back, to more natural leaf forms such as ivy or maple in frontal silhouette and at a more spiky, stiffened angle, to the final type, which lasts well into the fourteenth century, the "frayed cabbage" leaves of fleshy or wilted appearance and curling not back but forward toward the *épi* at the peak of the gable.[114] At Reims the crockets are not yet naturalistic, but they stand crisply upward with only the slightest tilt backward; a general date for them would be ca. 1275–85. This dating fits nicely with the evidence of the final grisaille bays of the nave, 139 and 140, datable by their Castille borders to no later than about 1285.

Certainly the kings and archbishops in the nave extension were more casual and relaxed. Guilhermy comments that many of the prelates no longer blessed but held books (Bay 131) or other

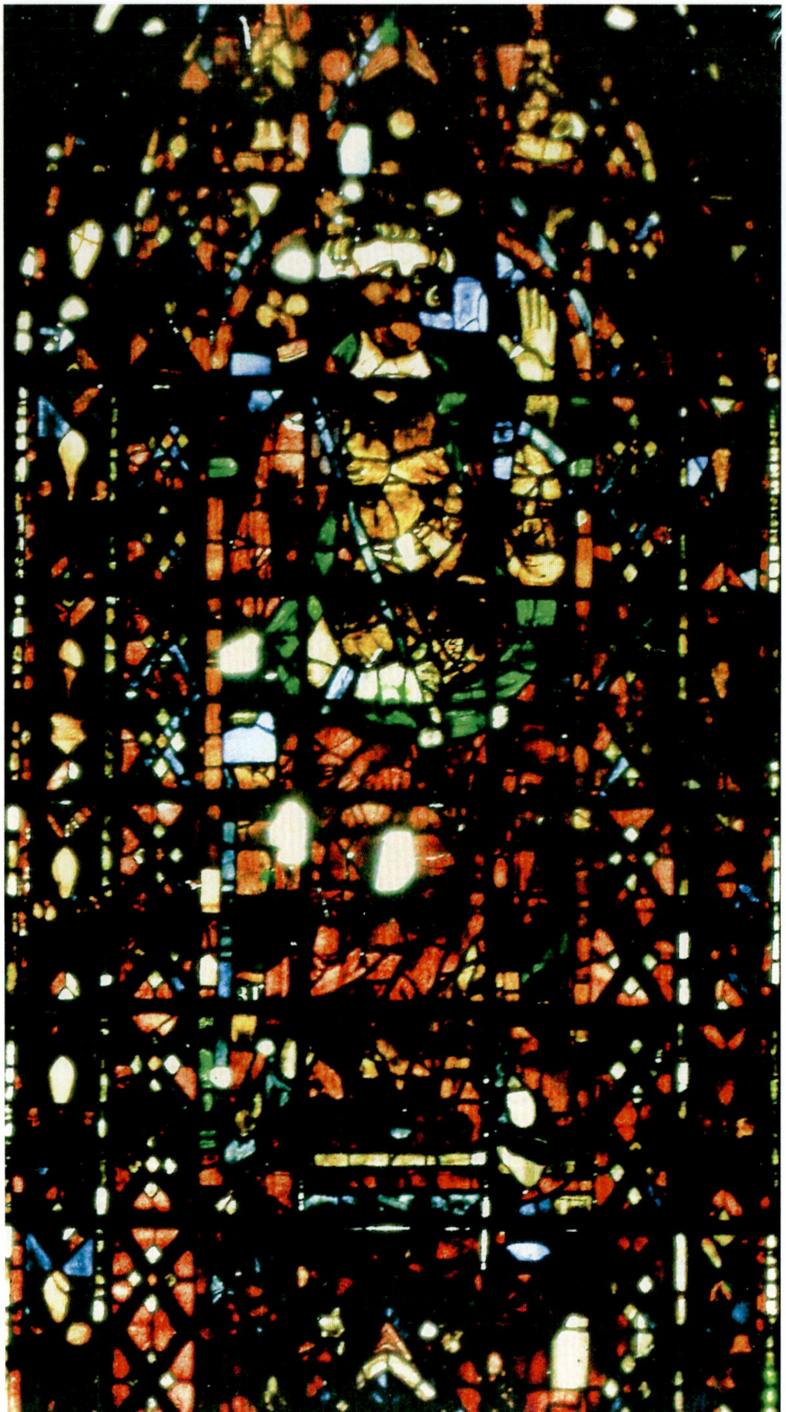

FIG. 219 King, waving. Bay 135 (lost), left lancet, top row. Autochrome by Henri Deneux, 1915.

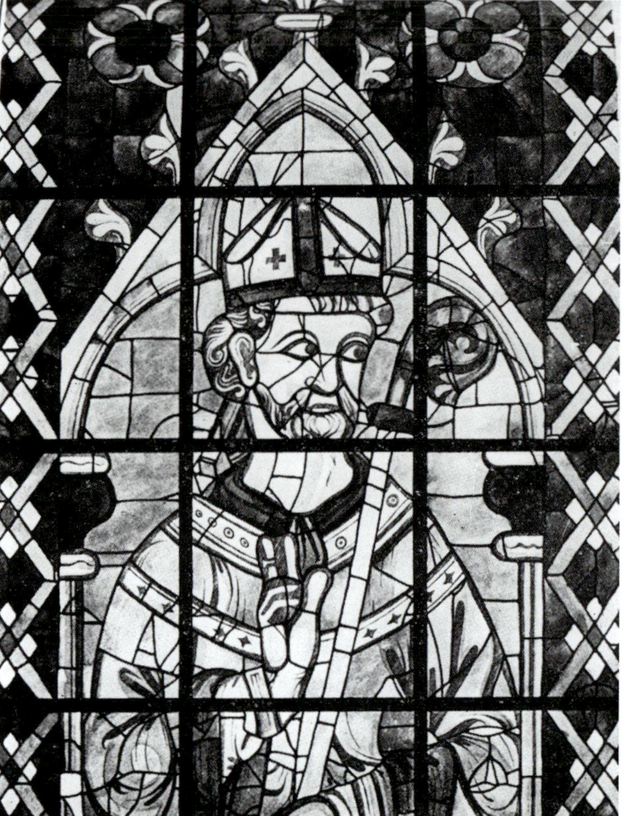

FIG. 220 Archbishop, blessing. Bay 135 (lost). Tracing by Paul Simon, before 1911 (after Simon, "Notes sur les vitraux").

objects, and in two cases (Bay 136) they grabbed their croziers with both hands. The long ceremony was over. They were seated on low benches rather than the elaborate high-backed furniture of the eastern bays. They turned toward the east and the *jubé*—where the new-made king would appear. At least half of them are recorded as making a hand gesture of affirmation that could almost be described as a wave (figs. 212, 214, 217, 219).[115] The music in the air may well have been the Gothic equivalent of the United States Marine Band playing "Hail to the Chief"!

The references to the coronation liturgy in the nave clerestories are subtle and universal rather than specific. The windows present themes of the ceremony rather than detailed objects or actions. The original stained-glass lancets dwelled on the *sine qua non* of a French coronation: a king to be anointed and crowned and an archbishop of Reims to anoint and crown him. As Richard Jackson, Jacques Le Goff, and others have stressed, the power and authority of the king and of the archbishop were maintained in a delicate balance during the long ritual. Only at the finale was that balance tipped in favor of the secular power—when the archbishop removed his miter to kiss the king and the new-made king appeared out beyond the *jubé* to receive the acclamation of his subjects, with the bare sword held high before him. The clerestories of the nave provided a great choral descant to the earthly proceedings beneath them—a vast cloud of celestial witnesses, participating in, and sealing with divinely sanctioned authority, the solemn actions of the mere mortals below.

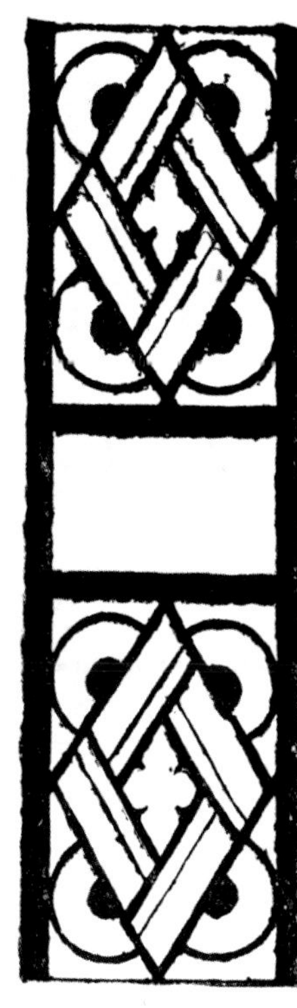

FIG. 221 Border of lozenges, Bay 137 or 138? (before 1881) (after Westlake, *A History of Design in Painted Glass*).

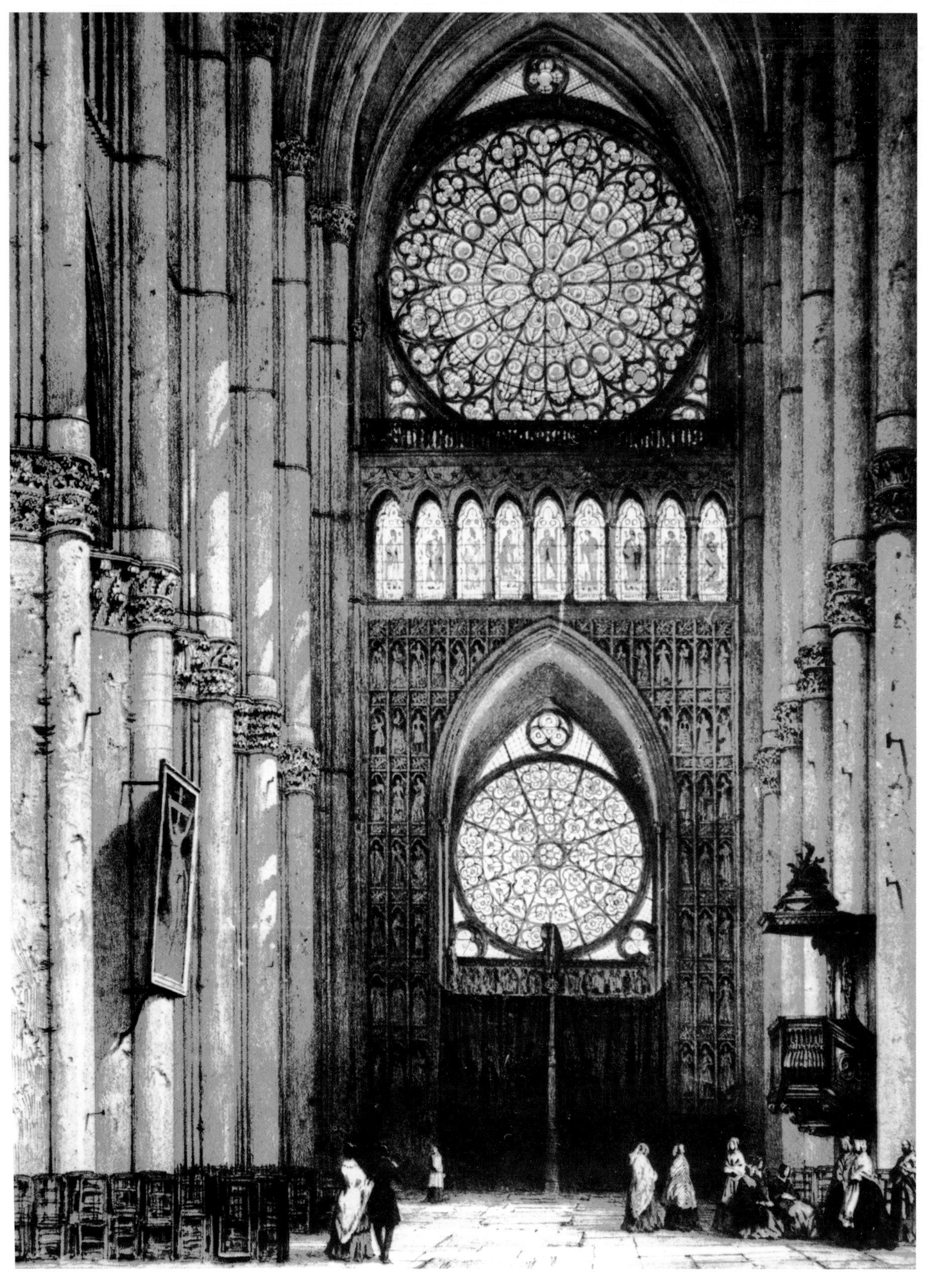

FIG. 222 Reims cathedral, interior of the west facade, 1845. The glazing in the small rose was installed in 1784–87. The far left and far right lancets of the gallery appear as they did before being half-blinded in the late nineteenth century, for stability (after Charles Nodier and Isidore Taylor, *Voyages pittoresques et romantiques dans l'ancienne France, Champagne*).

CHAPTER 7

THE GLAZING OF THE WEST FACADE

The creative unicum that is the inner facade of Reims Cathedral (fig. 222) can only be described in Mozartian terms: a masterpiece of clarity and lucidity, harmonic variety, rhythmic pulse, thematic reflection and inversion, balance, economy, surprise. Nothing in Gothic architectural design approaches its rich disciplined complexity, the consummate micro/macrocosm of colored light in the two roses sustained by the insistent *basso continuo* of the row upon row of niche statuary. The tranquil perfection of the verso composition actually contravenes its component parts; the regular grid of sculpture is actually in shallower relief as it rises, while the elements of the small centripetal rose converge to a focal centerpoint in contrast to the great rose's centrifugal explosion.[1] The glazing—the activating component of this master design—is the subject of this chapter. The discussion must commence with the unavoidable prologue, a recitation of its history of calamities.

The Lost Glazed Tympana

Concerning the lowest level of glazing on the facade, the tympana of the three western portals, we are seeking after *neiges d'antan.* In the nineteenth century the flanking tympana over the portals, at the west end of the nave aisles, contained fragmentary debris composed largely of sixteenth-century scenes on white glass, "cameaux blancs."[2] In the north tympanum was the Presentation of the Christ-child in the Temple, above the Assumption of the Virgin amid an angelic choir, while the south one included the Last Supper over the Crucifixion, between Mary and John. The origin of this debris cannot be guessed, and since the subjects do not conform to the themes of the sculpted gables of those portals—Crucifixion on the north, Last Judgment on the south—the installation of debris was probably haphazard. World War I destroyed it all.

The original glass of these tympana was probably removed during the eighteenth century when the cathedral lost all its aisle glass, sporadically, between 1730 and 1768.[3] The ironwork was retained. Seventeenth-century images of the facade (figs. 223, 224) show the same ironwork in the flanking tympana, a trefoil over a quatrefoil. The glazing indicated in this ironwork appears to have been ornament, perhaps grisaille like that in the westernmost clerestories of the nave (Bays 139 and 140) and some of the lower windows.[4]

The small rose forming the central portal's tympanum also lost its glass during the eighteenth century. The result, however, must have been disruptive even to the taste of that age, since around 1784–87 it was reglazed, even though the art of stained glass was then at its nadir.[5] The design (fig. 222), which survived until the First

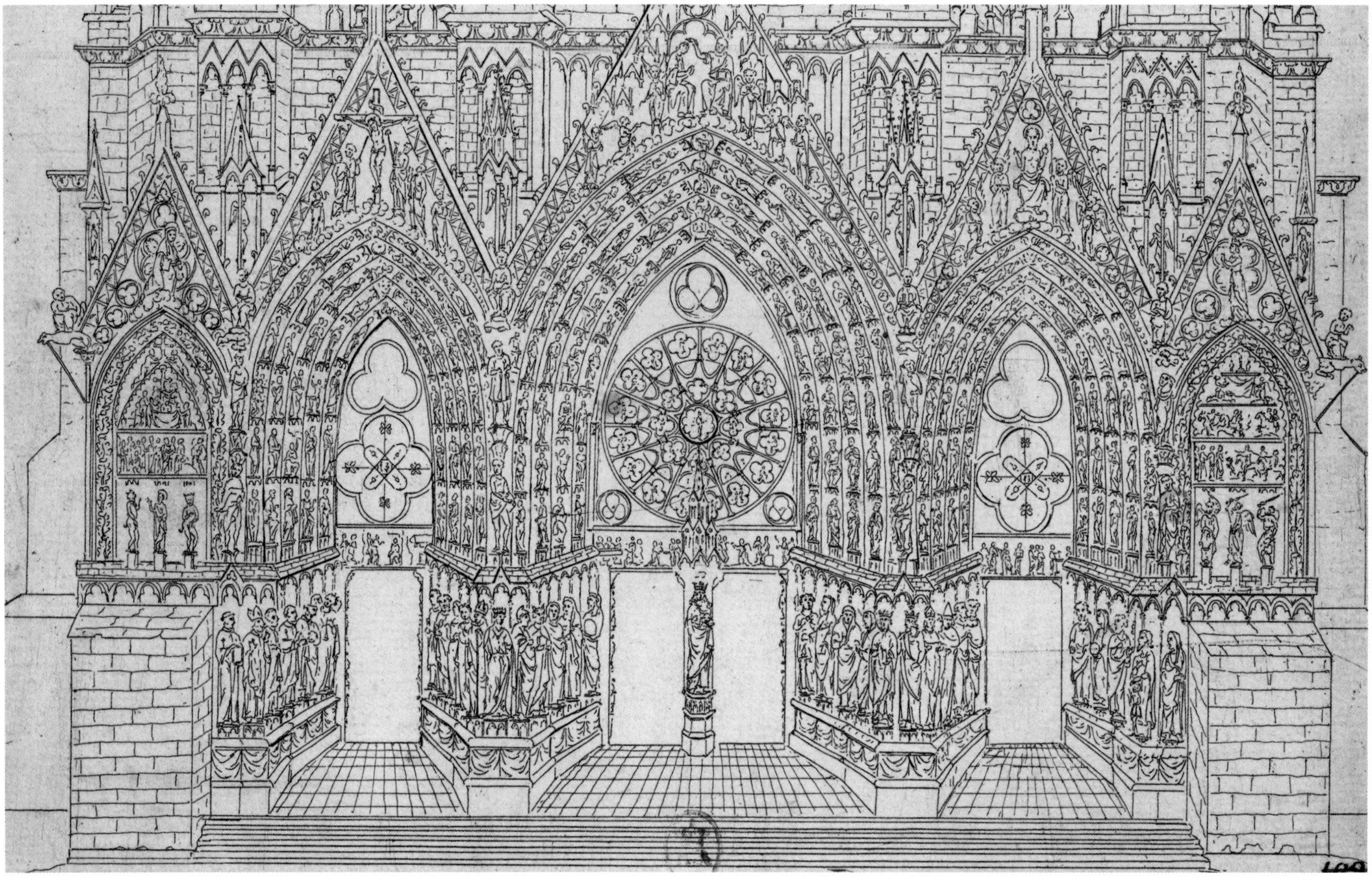

FIG. 223 West facade, portals, 1654, engraving by Androuet du Cerceau, detail, Paris, BnF, Est., VA 51 (15) 1 fol-H134406.

FIG. 224 West facade, tympanum of the north portal, 1625: *Le somptueux frontispice de l'église Notre Dame de Reims, ville du Sacre,* engraving by Nicolas de Son, detail, Reims, Bibl. mun., X II a 15-BMR 9-323.

World War, was limited to circles, rosettes, stars, and sunbursts created in pale tones of blue, green, yellow, and rust brown, painted without firing.[6] Already by the late 1840s a project had been planned for Henri Gérente to replace it with a Tree of Jesse, though nothing came of it following his death, in 1849. Sixteenth- and seventeenth-century images of the facade indicate some sort of medallions originally filling the small rose (figs. 223, 225). The central light probably contained the Virgin and Child. Since the tracery divides the rose into eight sections, the inner circle may have shown the Liberal Arts and Philosophy, as in the north rose of Laon, or perhaps the Virtues and Vices. Both subjects appear in the eight-lobed rosaces of Auxerre (bays 101, 102).[7] Another comparison would be to the west rose of Notre-

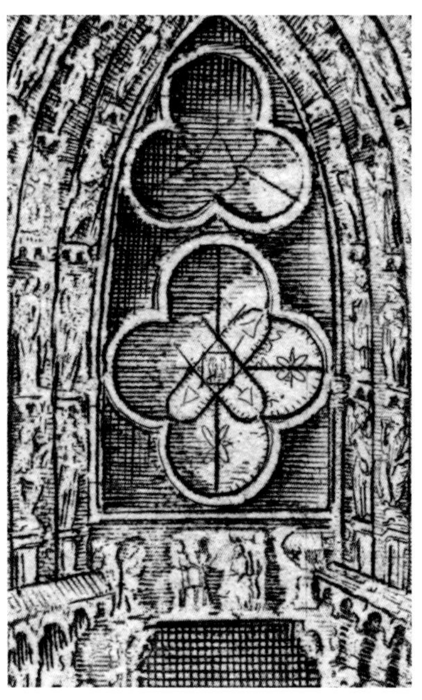

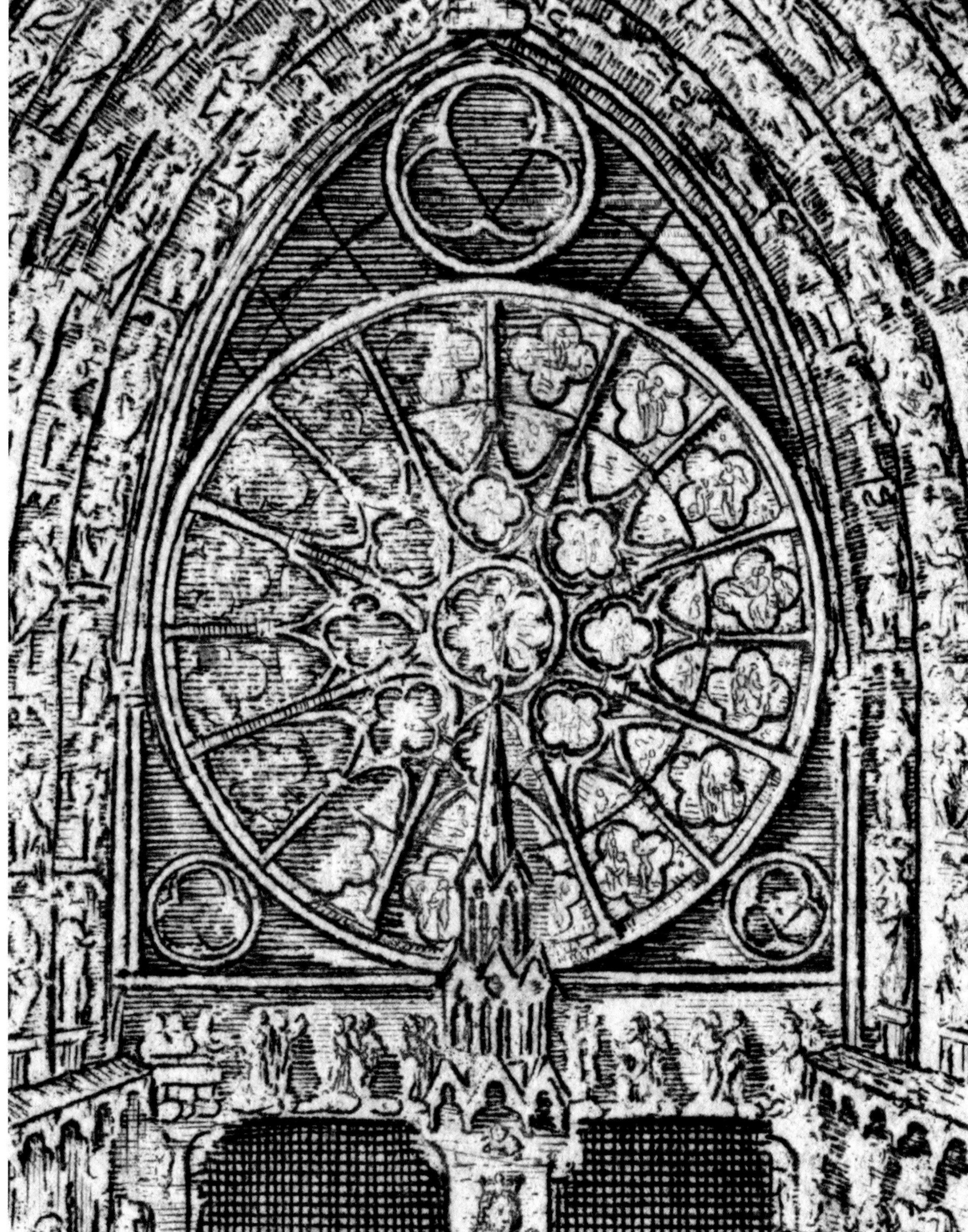

FIG. 225 West facade, tympanum of the central portal, 1625, showing the original glazing of the small rose: *Le somptueux frontispice de l'église Notre Dame de Reims, ville du Sacre,* engraving by Nicolas de Son, detail, Reims, Bibl. mun., XII a 15 BMR 9-323.

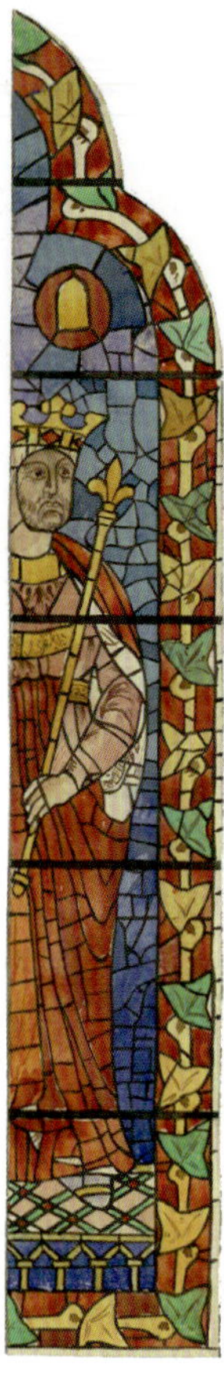
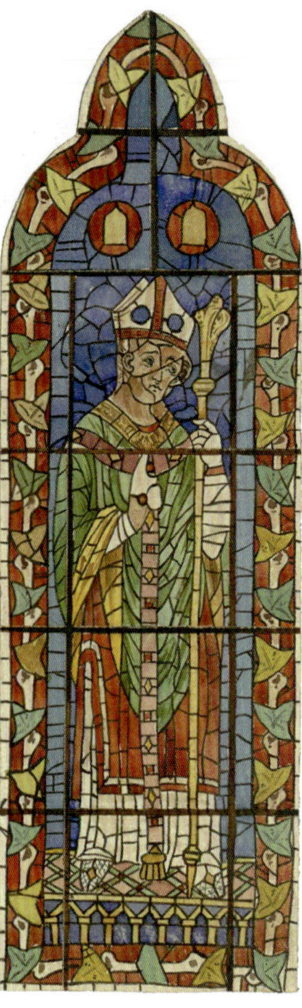
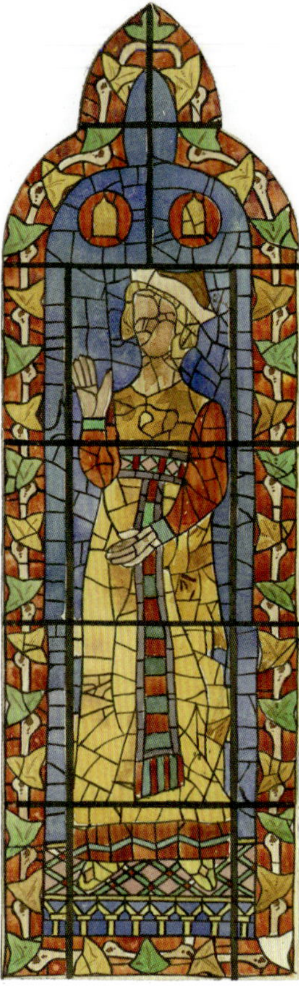
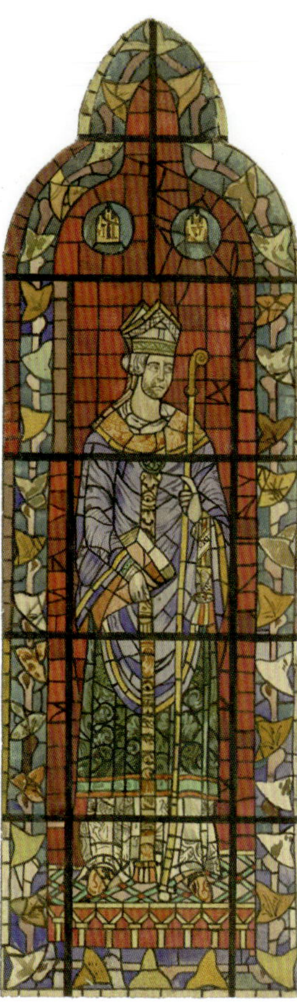

FIG. 226 West facade gallery, watercolors by Henri Deneux, 1914: (left to right) (A) king and archbishop; (B) aristocratic youth and archbishop; (C) king and archbishop; (D) aristocratic youth and archbishop; (E) king. The far left and right lancets were partially blinded in the late nineteenth century. *Les vitraux de la cathédrale Notre Dame de Reims: Galerie du revers de la façade occidentale*, Reims, Bibl. mun., Fonds Deneux, L066–L070.

Dame, Paris (ca. 1220), where the central Virgin and Child are surrounded by apostles (who appear at Reims in the great rose), Virtues and Vices, and the zodiac and labors of the months.[8] Of course a cycle of Infancy scenes would be another Marian possibility, the overarching theme of the Reims facade—capped by the sculpted gable of the central portal—being the Triumph and Coronation of Mary/Ecclesia.[9]

The West Gallery: Dating by the Castles of Castille

Triumph and coronation, here referencing the *sacre* of the French kings, declares itself in the glazing of the west gallery located between the two Marian roses of the facade. Nine larger-than-life figures occupy the arched lancets forming this gallery (figs. 222, 226). Heavy restoration is evident. The date 1550 appears on the sleeve of the far left figure, and sixteenth-century fragments appear in the draperies, while a more thorough restoration in 1834 is indicated by an inscription on one of the gallery's two central columns naming the workman as Oudet.[10] The clear orange and pink glasses doubtless date from that time.

The nine lancets present ecclesiastical and lay figures surrounding the central image of a king. Bareheaded and garbed in a blue sleeveless surcoat covered with large gold fleurs-de-lis, he holds a bare sword point upward (fig. 226C, 227). In the nineteenth century, popular tradition held the subject of the gallery to be Jeanne d'Arc at the *sacre* of the dauphin Charles VII, in 1429. Tourneur maintained that it was the baptism of Clovis by St. Remi, while Cerf refined this call and relabeled it the coronation of Clovis accompanied by his wife, St. Clotilde, and one of his sisters as well as

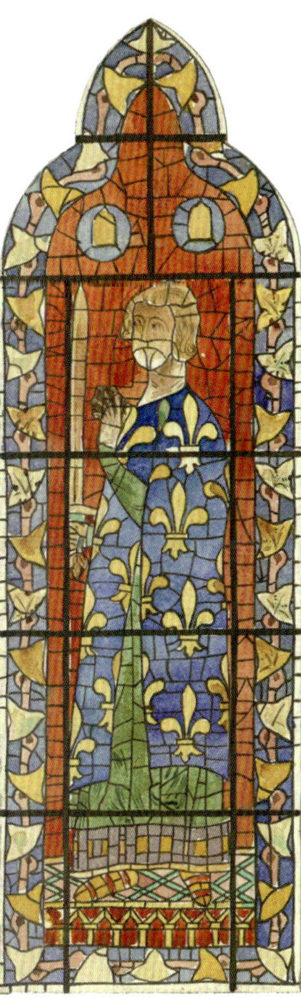
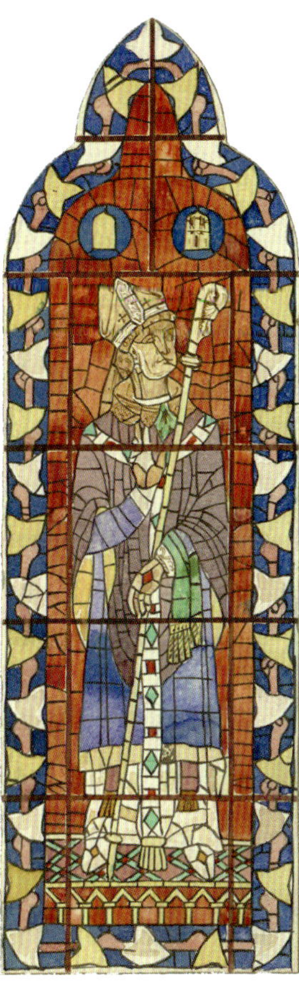
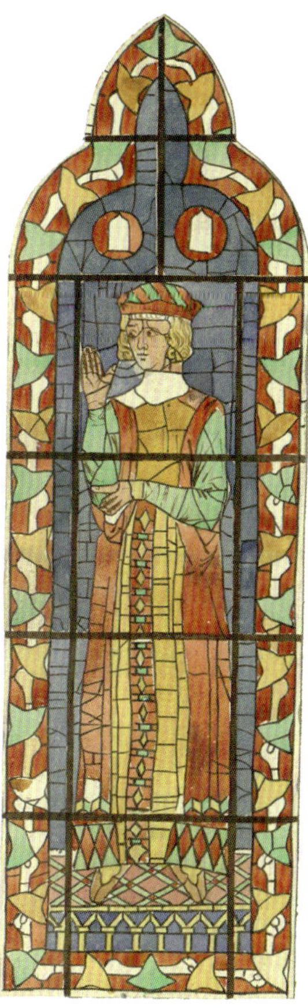
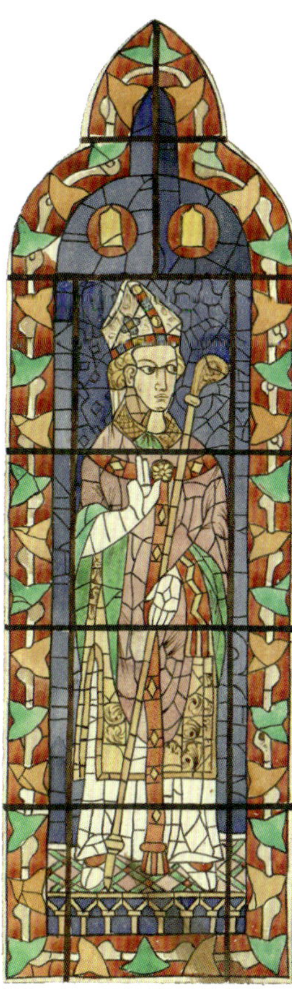
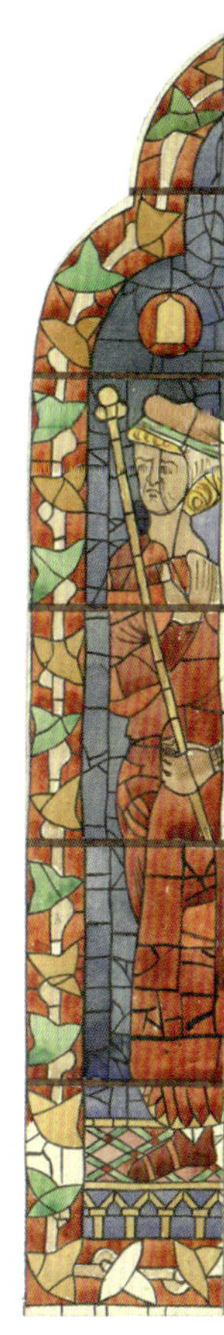

ecclesiastical and lay peers of the realm.[11] But Clovis's baptism, of which several depictions survive at Reims, always shows him at least partially nude, while the rare scene of Clovis enthroned, found in the St. Remi window at Chartres (bay 12), depicts him seated on a high-backed throne and crowned.[12] The central figure in the west gallery, however, stands bareheaded. Prosper Tarbé believed that the gallery presented the coronation of Louis IX in 1226, an opinion based on the inclusion of roundels over the figures' heads containing gold castles of Castille. Tarbé's identification at least had the merit of proffering some explanation for the figure at the far left, a crowned king holding a scepter (fig. 226A). In Tarbé's scenario he would be Jean de Brienne, king of Jerusalem, who attended St. Louis's coronation.[13] However, there is yet another sceptered king (badly damaged) in the gallery, balancing this figure at the far right (fig. 226E). So what is really going on in the west gallery lights? My hypothesis, elaborated below with arguments based on several details, is that the west gallery glazing was a gift of King Philippe IV le Bel at a date around 1290.

Tarbé's explanation, however—though no doubt inaccurate—does pinpoint a clue to a more precise dating of the west-facade glazing: the gold castles located above the figures' heads. The dating of the Reims facade by architectural historians remains fluid. To cite just two opinions: Ravaux's campaign for completion of the cathedral dates ca. 1266–ca. 1275, although he notes that Bernard de Soissons, the architect who is shown in the labyrinth designing the rose window, is cited in *rémois* documents of 1282 and 1287. Kurmann dates the final construction from ca. 1275 to slightly before 1299.[14] Approaching the question from a different perspective, Patrick Demouy has shown that in

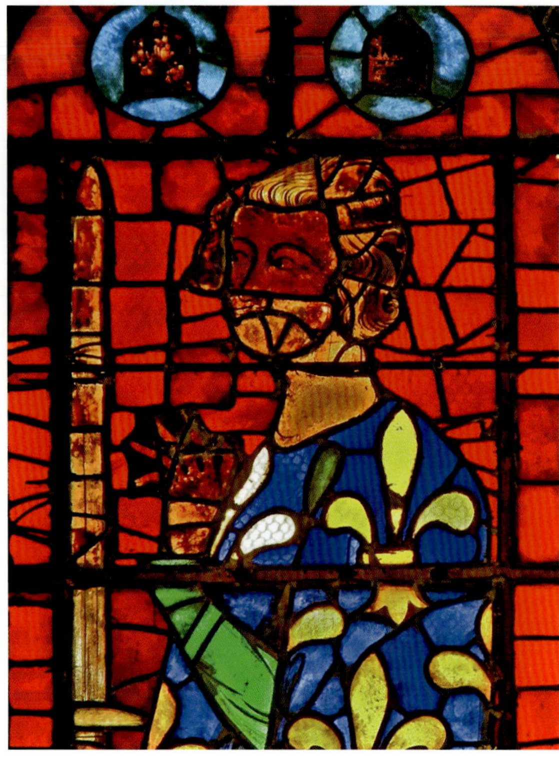

FIG. 227 King, west facade gallery, central lancet, detail.

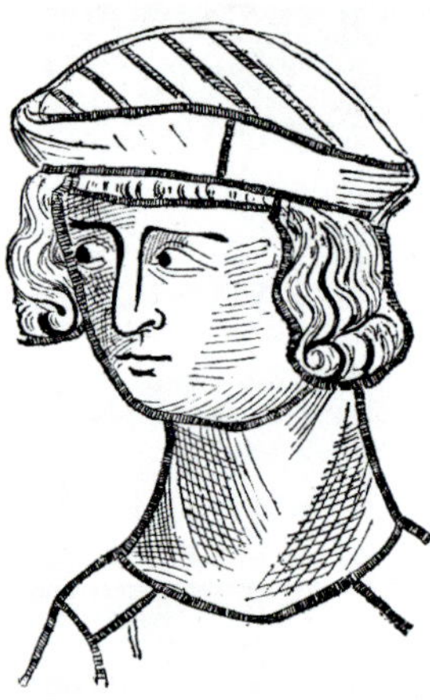

FIG. 228 Aristocratic youth, west facade gallery, right side, detail (1881) (after Westlake, *A History of Design in Painted Glass*).

August 1285 the performance of the liturgy was overhauled by the establishment of remuneration for a dozen clerics trained in singing and probably of a *maîtrise* (training program) for four resident choirboys, to assure the level of performance of the daily offices. He interprets this action to indicate the completion of the Gothic cathedral, not merely to address the constant problem of canons' absenteeism.[15] Can the glazing contribute to this dating discussion? To return to the gold castles in the west gallery, note that some are placed on blue grounds (fig. 227) and thus have no heraldic reference. A brief survey of such armorial emblems in glass will help to set the stage here.

Gold castles (on red), with the gold fleurs-de-lis of France (on blue), are well-known heraldic motifs found abundantly in Louis IX's Sainte-Chapelle in the 1240s as well as earlier in the north rose window of Chartres. Pinoteau has established that the emblems of Castille do not indicate direct involvement by Louis's mother, Blanche de Castille. Rather, they display the political pretensions of St. Louis, his father (Louis VIII), and his children to the throne of Castille.[16] Nine Castillian nobles had written Louis VIII that Blanche's father, Alfonso VIII, on his deathbed in 1214, had declared that if his son Henri died without issue (which happened in 1217), the crown should pass to the son of Blanche. Louis IX preferred to avoid war—against other Christians—and married several of his children into the Castillian house in a policy intended eventually to join the two crowns. In 1255 he affianced his eldest son, Louis (d. 1260), to the Castillian *infanta,* and in 1269 he married his daughter Blanche to the Castillian prince Ferdinand de la Cerda. As Pinoteau concludes, "All this to attempt to explain the presence of the castles [of Castille] in places where they have, one might say, no business: stained glass, seals (for the cadets) and enamels proclaim that St. Louis and his family are of Castillian blood."[17]

In 1276 the sons of the 1269 marriage were abruptly and illegally disinherited. Their uncle and St. Louis's heir, Philippe III, threatened war but was unable to move his army across the Pyrenees.[18] As late as 1284, the year before Philippe died, the claim of the eldest of the sons—Alfonso de la Cerda—was recognized but proved to be unenforceable without the military muscle of the next French king, Philippe IV, which he would be totally disinterested in providing. In effect the policy of Louis IX and Philippe III was directed toward Spain, while that of the latter's son Philippe IV, who came to power unexpectedly in his teens in

1285, upon his father's premature death, was definitely not. Thus "heraldic" castles in French windows were beginning to reflect a dead letter in the late 1280s.[19]

To sum up the accounts concerning the question of castles and fleurs-de-lis in French stained glass: the expansion of French influence under St. Louis, not to mention his national and international prestige, contributed fundamentally to the popularity of the motifs, which lessened hardly at all under his son Philippe le Hardi. Beginning in 1286 with that king's successor, however, the castles no longer carried any political significance, as Philippe IV le Bel was quick to reverse the tilt toward Spain that had marked the foreign-policy aspirations of his grandfather and father.[20] It has been my observation that fleurs-de-lis and castles last on in glazing after 1285 for perhaps five years, but that in the 1290s they are increasingly rare and usually changed in color, thus transmuted into simple nonheraldic ornament.[21]

The sequence outlined above applies quite well to Reims. Closest to the Sainte-Chapelle (1240s) are the heraldic ground patterns found in the surviving nave bays 121 and 125 (figs. 192, 176). Bay 121 has a lozenge grid enclosing fleurs-de-lis comparable to the ground in Sainte-Chapelle bay D; in Bay 125 the fleurs-de-lis that are set into the ground above the figures' heads resemble the ground pattern in Sainte-Chapelle bay M.[22] Next at Reims would be a lost grisaille datable ca. 1260–70 (fig. 229), the narrower fleur-de-lis border and naturalistic foliage indicating a location most probably in the nave aisles west of the *coupure Tourneur.*[23] In the lost Bays 131, 132, and 135—all of them west of the *coupure Tourneur*—Guilhermy reported fleurs-de-lis.[24] The precious Deneux autochrome photos include sections of Bays 132 and 135 (figs. 212, 219), allowing us to see that the fleurs-de-lis that Guilhermy saw were not simply repeated in lean border designs (as in the Sainte-Chapelle). Rather, they were incorporated into the wide borders maintained in the Reims clerestory, along with the broad lancets of the doublet-and-rose design, throughout the cathedral's entire construction. A drawing of the Bay 132 border was published

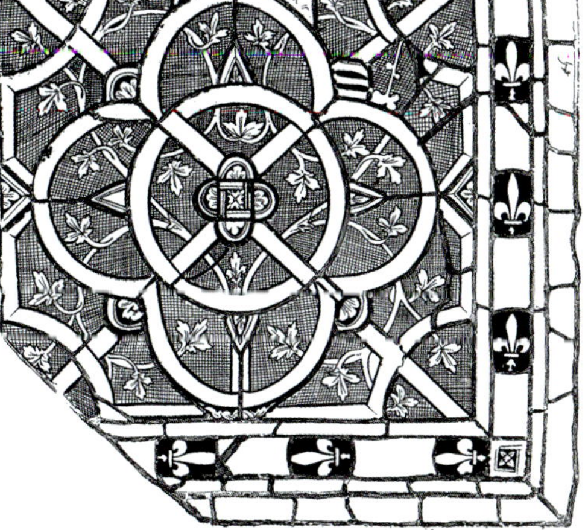

FIG. 229 Grisaille (lost) of naturalistic foliage within fleurs-de-lis borders, probably from the western nave aisles, 1895 (after Olivier Merson, *Les vitraux*).

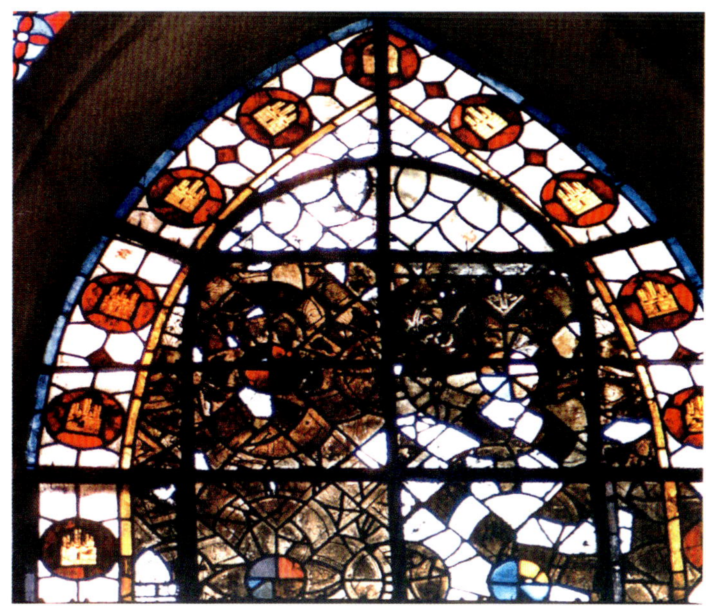

FIG. 230 Bay 39, debris of grisaille and Castille borders, probably from Bays 139–40.

in 1896 (fig. 213).[25] The final clerestories, 139 and 140, at the west end of the nave, contained grisailles within borders of castles of Castille.[26] Fragments of this glazing can now be identified in the lancets of Bay 39 directly below (fig. 230); the borders are fifteen centimeters wide.[27] The gold castles are set in red circles, recalling Sainte-Chapelle bay M and also found there in bays C, H, and O.[28]

These exact same circles enclosing castles reappear in the west gallery of the Reims facade, above the heads of the figures. But there they are worn with a difference. While the six flanking lights (three left and three right), which have blue grounds, display gold castles in red circles like those of the border fragments under discussion (now preserved in Bay 39), the three central lights of the west gallery, which have red grounds, display gold castles set in blue circles (figs. 226B–C). Heraldically speaking, they are meaningless. Such ornament would only have been possible after 1285, when Philippe IV came to power and the trained singers were established to perform the new cathedral's liturgy.

The West Gallery: Dating of the Fashion in Heraldic Display

Other details of the west-gallery glazing deserve attention in regard to dating. The central figure—unquestionably a French king—wears a deep blue robe covered with huge gold fleurs-de-lis (figs. 226C, left, and 227). The royal ceremonial regalia mentioned in thirteenth-century ordines are fleurs-de-lis-covered stockings or small boots, tunic, and surcoat or mantle. Their color is hyacinth—violet in the early French translation of the Ordo of Reims. The reference is to the hyacinth robes of the high priest Aaron in Exodus 28:31: "Facies et tunicam superumeralis totam hyacinthinam."[29]

The coronation ceremony is illustrated in some detail in the so-called Ordo of 1250 (Paris, BnF, lat. 1246), a manuscript most probably compiled before Louis IX left for crusade in the late 1240s.[30] While the text, as mentioned above, describes the king's garments as hyacinth decorated with gold fleurs-de-lis, the numerous illustrations in the manuscript (e.g., fig. 169) nowhere depict the monarch thus attired. He wears plain robes, sometimes red, sometimes blue. This may not be an artist's lapse but rather a reflection of the tastes of Louis IX, a notably simple dresser among kings. Even on occasions when he did dress up—for example, at the knighting of his brother Alphonse in 1241[31]—he did not wear garments with heraldic ornament. In the midst of the abundant heraldic emblems lavished on the Sainte-Chapelle, the glazing of bay A depicts figures of Louis IX and his family wearing plain, undecorated clothing.[32] Upon his return from crusade until his death in 1270, his dress was even more austere. It seems probable that Louis IX regarded the fleurs-de-lis-covered garments worn at the coronation to be sacramental vestments and thus not dress appropriate for other occasions. In 1261, at any rate, he regularized the custom of returning the regalia of the *sacre* to Saint-Denis "between coronations."[33]

Philippe III was crowned in 1271. He surely wore fleurs-de-lis-covered robes, as did all monarchs thereafter, and his regalia were undoubtedly hyacinth in color as prescribed by the ordines composed during his father's reign. However, the next ordo manuscript to contain illuminations, the Coronation Book of Jeanne d'Evreux, of 1326, depicts the king in fleurs-de-lis on dark blue throughout, as does the heavily illustrated Coronation Book of Charles V, of 1365 (where others are similarly garbed, including the archbishop of Reims).[34]

A change in "fashion" occurred somewhere between Philippe III's *sacre* (1271) and the fourteenth century. When and how this happened is difficult to pinpoint. Nevertheless, the coronation of Philippe III almost certainly reflected the preferences of his father, Louis IX. As Fawtier put it, "Philip III was a man of small intelligence who struggled along faithfully in St. Louis' footsteps."[35] The Last Capetian Ordo of ca. 1250–70, used for Philippe III's coronation, had certainly been overseen by Louis IX. And Philippe's coronation would have been anticipated for some time. When Louis IX took the cross in 1267, he was weak and ill.[36] And when he left in 1270 for his ill-fated second crusade he was fifty-six years old and forty-four years had passed since his own *sacre,* hastily organized and ill attended in the construction site that had been Reims cathedral in the mid-1220s.[37] Jean de Joinville's testimony, datable before 1309, indicates the shift:

> He [Louis IX] often said that people ought to clothe and arm themselves in such a way that men of riper age would never say they had spent too much on dress, or young men say they had spent

> too little. I repeated this remark to our present king [Philippe IV le Bel] when speaking of the elaborately embroidered tabards that are in vogue today. I told him that, during the whole of our voyage oversea, I had never seen such embroidered tabards, either on the king or on any one else. He said to me that he had several such garments, with his own arms embroidered on them, and they had cost him eight hundred *livres parisis.* I told him that he would have put his money to better use if he had given it to God, and had his clothes made of good plain taffeta bearing his arms, as his father [Philippe III] had done.[38]

Another witness brings the date of the shift in fashion even closer: the extended and increasingly hysterical deathbed confession in 1292 of the princess Jeanne de Châtillon. St. Louis had affianced his son Pierre d'Alençon to her in 1263; she was thus a younger sister-in-law of Philippe III. A good Christian woman, she died while still young, having spent her enormous fortune during eight years of widowhood on charitable works. Nonetheless her conscience tortured her: minstrels, music and dancing, wines, meats, and bonbons, the company of great lords and ladies, fine curtained beds, jewels, elegant palace rooms, and, not least, the memory that "j'ai voulu tout mon lignaige surmonter, & . . . les fleurs de lys de France en mes parements peindre & démonstrer."[39]

Elsewhere I have introduced the argument that ostentatious heraldic trappings entered the Capetian court in 1274 with Philippe III's second wife, that Jacqueline Kennedy of Gothic France: Marie de Brabant. Novels and at least one play, in verse in five acts, have been written about that gay intriguer (the phrase is Frederick Powicke's), young, beautiful, witty, and intelligent, who created around her a brilliant court supporting literati and Sorbonne astronomers alike.[40] She brought with her the strong heraldic and genealogical tastes of the Brabantine court of her father, Duke Henri III, and then her brother Duke Jean I. The frontispiece of the poem *Cléomadès,* by Adenès li rois (Paris, Arsenal, MS 3142, fol. 1, datable after 1285 and before 1290), shows the famous *trouvère* performing with his rebec for Queen Marie. She is reclining, accompanied by her nephew and the Capetian princess Blanche de France, all of them resplendently garbed in full heraldic display.[41] Although Philippe IV le Bel detested his stepmother Marie de Brabant, he could not resist the change in fashion, as Jean de Joinville's conversation with him, quoted above, makes clear. Evidence of it once lay in the city of Reims itself, where in the lost church of Saint-Nicaise, next to the chapel containing Queen Marie's window of ca. 1284–85, glass depicted Philippe IV and his queen and their seven children all wearing heraldic finery.[42]

A date no earlier than the late 1280s is also reasonable for the west-gallery glazing of Reims cathedral, where the figure of the king (figs. 226C, left, and 227) wears a long sleeveless surcoat of rich deep blue covered with huge golden lilies. The west gallery does not depict a coronation ceremony. The king's tunic is emerald green. He is bareheaded—no crown in sight—and with his right hand holds an unsheathed sword, point upward. The king only touches the sword for two brief moments during the coronation ceremony. The ritual of the sword begins as the archbishop girds the king with the sheathed sword, then removes the bare sword and hands it to the king, who places it on the altar; the archbishop then returns it to the king, who passes it to the *grand sénéchal,* who carries it point upward before the king for the remainder of the ceremony and then for the return to the bishop's palace. Nothing of the sort is happening in the west gallery,[43] where the central king himself holds the sword and the archbishop facing him holds a crozier and book. Food for thought: in the cathedral ca. 1290, only Karolvs (Bay 128) held up such a sword.[44]

Although the ritual of the sword, just described, was a well-established element of the coronation liturgy, Philippe III was the first king to use Charlemagne's sword, Joyeuse, part of the Saint-Denis treasury, as reported by Guillaume de Nangis.[45] Robert II d'Artois, the new king's cousin, carried Joyeuse before him during the last section of the ceremony. Philippe III's coronation, in August 1271, perhaps needed some pomp. He was a widower, Isabelle d'Aragon having died in January, and as Reims was *sede vacante,* he was crowned by the bishop of Soissons. The coronation of his son Philippe IV le Bel—somewhat like that of Louis IX—followed the unexpected early death of his father and was certainly carried out as traditionally and orthodoxly as possible.

The west gallery, then, does not depict an actual coronation, either real and historical or idealized and timeless. So who are the other eight figures around the king and what then is the subject, or theme?[46] The four figures to the king's right (to the south, our left), whom he is facing, all turn toward him. First is the archbishop mentioned above, holding a crozier and book (fig. 226B, right). Behind him is a badly damaged figure, flipped in Deneux's watercolor (fig. 226B) but facing right, as at present, in pre-1914 photographs. This figure is often identified as a "princess" or possibly a cleric. He is neither—not in clerical vestments and not female, since the robe reveals too much of the feet and the fragmented head reveals a noble adolescent male's short haircut under a soft-brimmed hat. This lay figure raises his hand in acclamation in the same manner as do a number of kings and bishops in the lost western nave bays, now known from Deneux autochromes (figs. 201, 212, 214, 217, 219). Next comes another archbishop. And the final figure at the far left is a crowned king, dressed in red, holding a scepter (fig. 226A, left).[47] The four figures behind the central king (to our right, on the north) mirror the types opposite them. Behind the central king is another archbishop in pallium with crozier (fig. 226C, right). Then comes another "nonprincess," a figure surviving in good enough condition for us to appreciate his fancy striped hat and pageboy haircut (figs. 226D, left, and 228). Like the lay youth on the south, he raises a hand in acclamation. Then follows yet another archbishop, blessing, and finally, at the far right, another king holding a scepter (fig. 226E). This quartet of figures on the north, behind the central king, forms two pairs. Each archbishop seems to accompany and bless the figure next to him. What a strange congregation we have here! Each of the four archbishops wears the pallium identifying that office. The two lay figures are richly dressed and youthful. Both sceptered kings, forming the parentheses of the lineup, wear red.

This is not a coronation ceremony and equally not a symbolic statement relating to such an event: too many archbishops, for one thing. The oddity of the program cannot be stressed too much. Here we find no saints, angels, or prophets, but rather three kings, four archbishops, and two fancy young men. Indeed the lineup is—I submit—too idiosyncratic to be the creation of an educated churchman. The central figure of the king brandishing the bare sword seems enough evidence to support that supposition. Is the west-gallery glazing, then, a lay donation? There is no record of any others in the cathedral. Given the total void in documentation, it would be audacious to make a guess, but if one ventured to do so, the best guess would be King Philippe IV le Bel, the only contemporary "interested party" with the necessary arrogance and determination. His own hasty and unexpected coronation in 1286, at the age of seventeen, was probably held in the cathedral building very close to completion. New singers had just been engaged to assure daily services of some quality, and the architecture of the facade may have been nearly complete. The facade glazing was not all in place for his coronation, however, judging from the appearance in the west gallery of the nonheraldic "castle" ornaments, a development that followed the demise of Philippe III and of his (and St. Louis's) Spanish involvement and the subsequent shift in policy of his son's reign.

If indeed Philippe le Bel donated the glass of the west gallery, who or what did he intend all these bizarre figures to represent, and when did he make his gift? The central king, bareheaded—in "humility"?—but wearing unmistakable heraldic identification, wields the symbol of his secular power. Joseph Strayer's assessment of the king's character may be useful in comprehending the meaning of this audacious image:

> Philip the Fair was brought up in . . . a strongly religious tradition, and [he] was a pious Christian, as far as he understood piety. . . . But Philip's piety was conventional and limited; it is doubtful that he ever went beyond formal observances to true religious experience.
>
> Philip the Fair also learned another religion at his father's court—the religion of monarchy. This religion made a deeper impression on him than Christianity; or, to put it in his terms, Christianity obviously supported the religion of monarchy. The king of France was the Vicar of God, the chief supporter of the Church. He was anointed with oil that had been sent down from Heaven; he could cure the sick; he had inherited the insignia and the holy mission of Charlemagne. He was the greatest king in Christendom, subject to no temporal authority. To oppose such a king was not only evil, it was sacrilegious. . . . Philip understood and practiced this religion rather better than he did Christianity.[48]

Thus the two sceptered kings of the west gallery (figs. 226A, left, and E)—lurking on the periphery like ghosts of Christmas Past—are possibly his father and grandfather, though any precise identification is not really necessary. They are kings of France, and each has his archbishop, as do all the kings in the clerestory bays of the long cathedral nave. The two aristocratic youths in the west gallery (figs. 226B, left, and D, left) are much more puzzling, since they seem far too frivolous to be peers of France at a *sacre.* If Philippe IV had anyone specifically in mind, perhaps the noble youth behind his back might be his elder brother, Louis (d. 1276), original heir to the throne. The young man facing him might be Philippe IV's own son Louis Hutin, born 1289. French kingship—past, present, and future—would then form the theme.

Philippe IV had been married, in 1284, to Jeanne de Navarre, heiress to the county of Champagne in which Reims is located. Between 1289 and 1293, when she bore them a second son, Jeanne gave a window to the abbey church of Saint-Nicaise in Reims. It depicted her presenting her bay to St. Nicaise, accompanied by her son Louis Hutin (no more than age three) wearing a hyacinth robe with fleurs-de-lis.[49] If there ever was a moment when her husband—"Vicar of God, the high priest of the religion of monarchy"—would have donated glass to Reims cathedral, 1290, upon the birth of his royal heir, may have been it. Moreover, from 1288 to 1290 he was at odds with the Church, pope, and several French bishops; the compromise reached in 1290 was largely in his favor. From 1290 until 1296 things were calm, but about 1296–97 the king's relationship with the northern archbishoprics, including Reims, deteriorated.[50] Many things point to 1290 as the moment when the west gallery received its strange glazing and to Philippe le Bel as its donor.

The Great Rose: Prologue

The west gallery and the great rose above it (fig. 231) have each suffered so much damage and remaking, and are ensembles of such different types and scales, that stylistic analysis can now provide few conclusions. It can be stated, however, that ornament connects the final nave glazing with that of the facade. As noted above, the castles set in circles that formed borders in Bays 139 and 140 reappear in the west gallery (figs. 230 and 226A, D). And the robust quasi-naturalistic ivy borders of the nine gallery lights, in vivid gold and green, are akin to several foliage patterns in the great rose (figs. 226, 249). Not a great deal of time can have elapsed between these projects.

Nineteenth-century witnesses noted the magnificent color and dominant red of the rose while deploring—even before the 1886 hailstorm, and well before the First World War—the state of degradation, illegibility, and ruin. Lucien Magne summed it up with "la rose occidentale n'est plus formée que de débris," and Paul Simon pronounced midcentury illustrations of the rose "fantaisiste quant aux médaillons et à la disposition des fonds mosaïques" (see figs. 233–35).[51] While little of its original glass survives at present,[52] the great rose benefited from an exhaustive study and reconstruction in 1909 by Paul Simon, before the incendiary bombs arrived in 1914, and a second

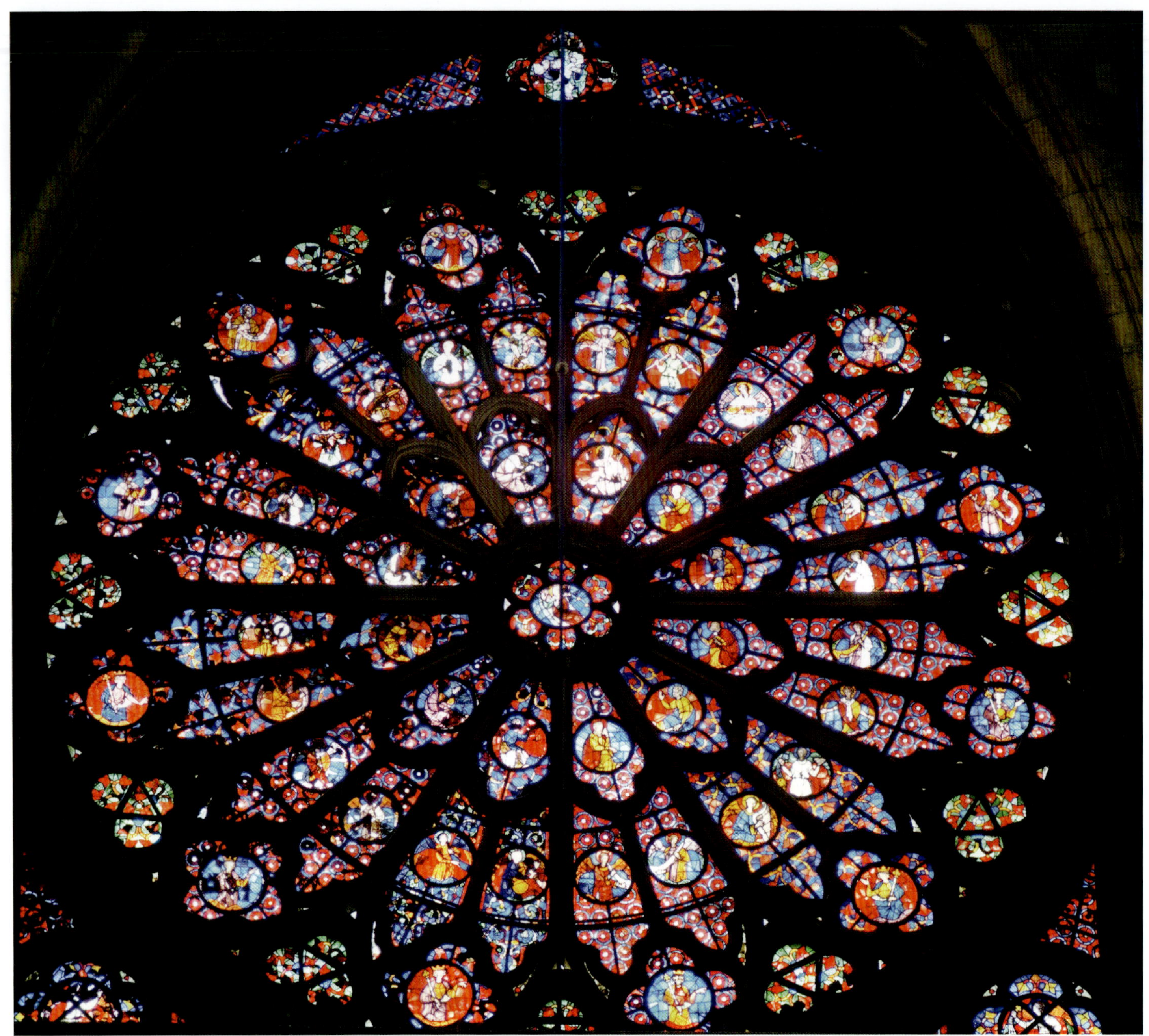

FIG. 231 West rose.

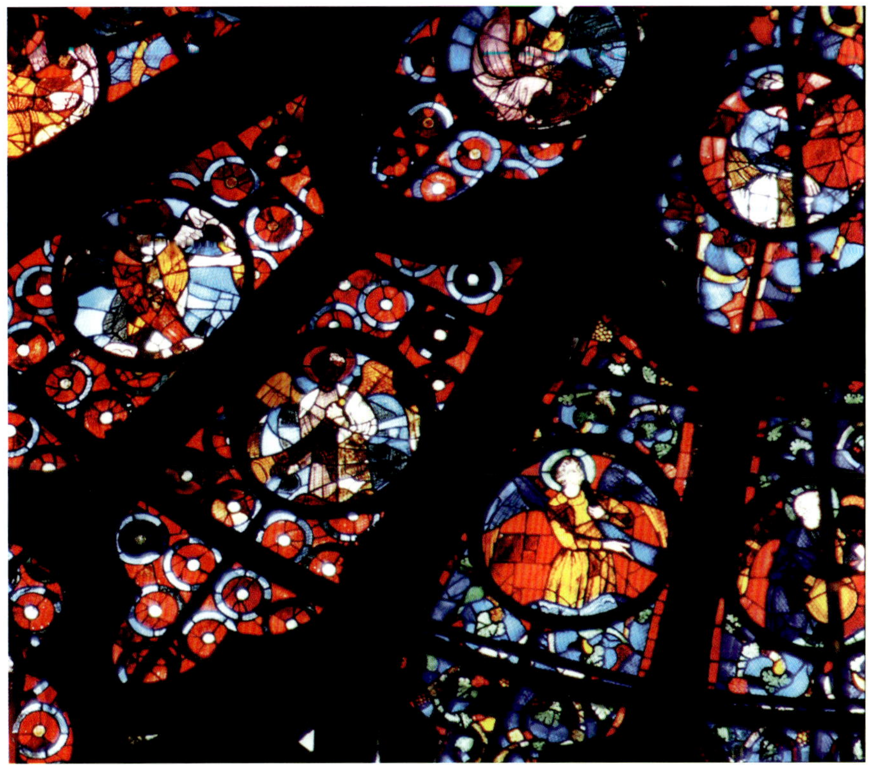

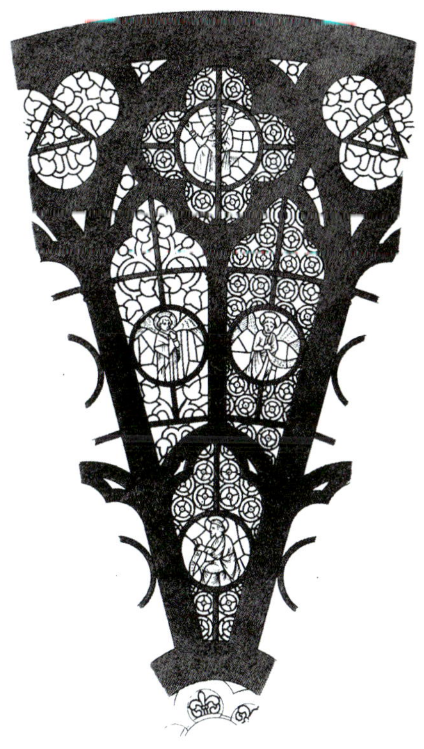

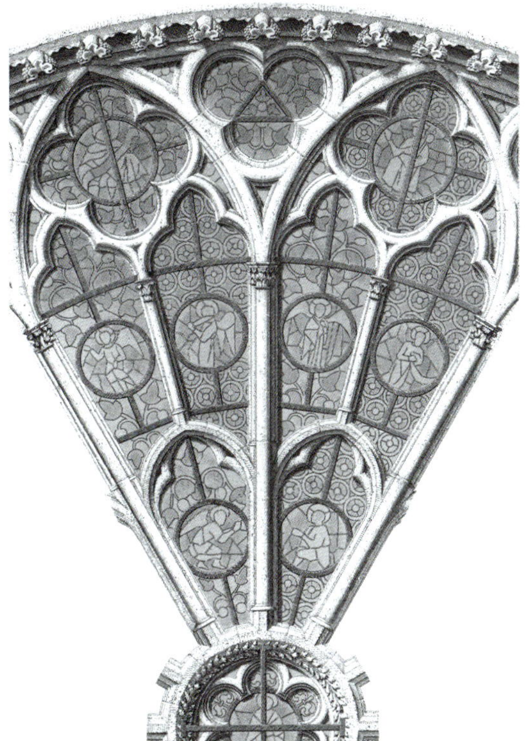

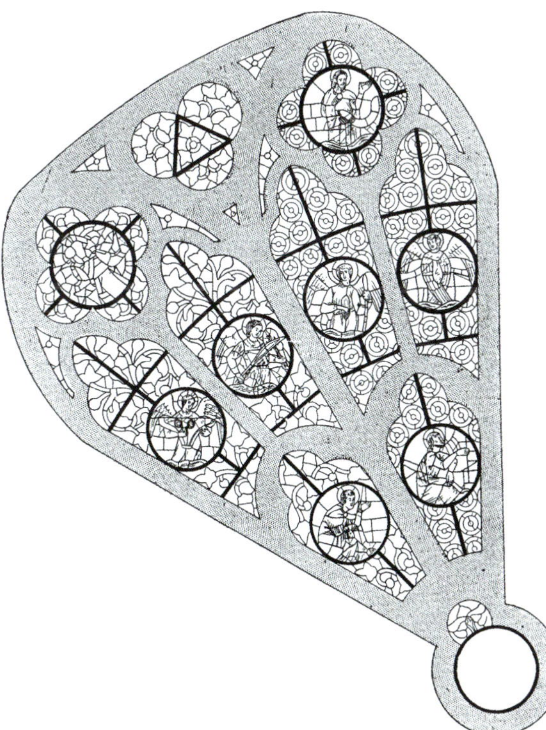

FIG. 232 West rose, lower left quadrant: lancet 12, trial design.

FIG. 233 West rose, detail, 1857 (after Victor Tourneur, *Histoire et description des vitraux*).

FIG. 234 West rose, detail, 1858 (after Jules Gailhabaud, *L'architecture du Ve au XVIIe siècle*).

FIG. 235 West rose, detail, 1895 (after Olivier Merson, *Les vitraux*).

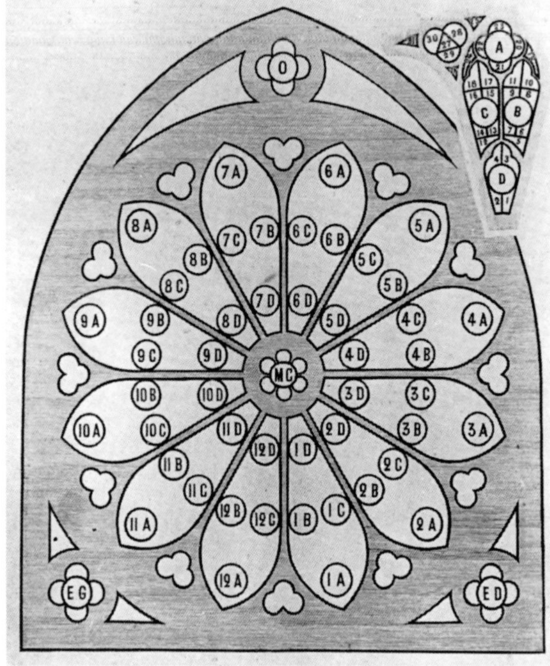

FIG. 236 Chart of the west rose, by Paul Simon (after Simon, *La grande rose*).

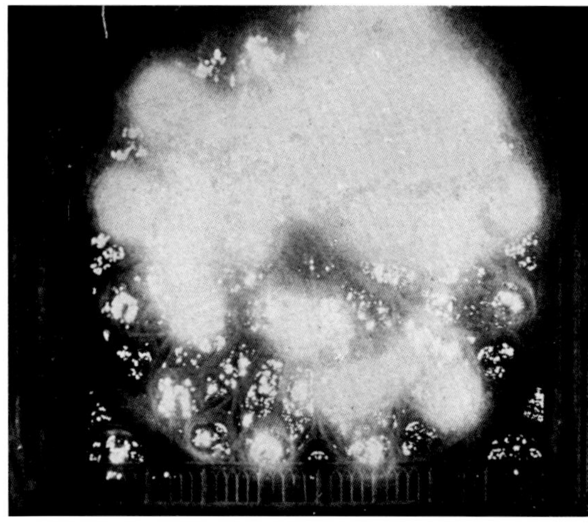

FIG. 237 West rose. Amateur photo taken several hours after the 1886 hailstorm (after Paul Simon, *La grande rose*).

complete restoration, employing the same cartoons, by his son Jacques Simon after 1925. These two twentieth-century restorations were based on the remarkable set of tracings of the glass commenced by Pierre Simon, Paul's father, in 1848 and continued by Paul from 1875 to 1886 (figs. 241–45). The book published in 1911 by Paul Simon describes in exquisite detail his study of the glass and the reconstruction of the original iconographic arrangement, the methods, materials, and results of this labor, documenting the procedures completely and illustrating the various states of completion with tracings or scale drawings made in the studio. His numbering system (fig. 236) has been adopted here to facilitate reference to these illustrations in the present discussion.[53]

Simon's second chapter sketches the history of damage and repair, beginning with some kind of consolidation with ironwork in 1611. A storm in 1768 required the dismounting and releading of the rose by his ancestor François Simon. Repairs were made in situ from ladders from 1853 to 1854 by Pierre Simon. The ogive light, then at risk of falling, was the only one dismounted to the studio, where a tracing of it was made (fig. 241)—the first of the valuable series to come. Damage from a severe hailstorm in 1886 (fig. 237) was repaired by Paul Simon, again in situ, by gluing large pieces of thick painted glass over the damaged areas, "travail . . . très peu couteaux, et fort solide néanmoins, puisqu'il permit d'attendre 22 ans."[54] Then in 1908–9 he undertook the project, clearly a labor of love, of complete restitution that is documented in his book (fig. 238). His work was largely destroyed by 1918 (fig. 239). His son Jacques repeated the task after 1925, and the glass was dismounted for safety during the summer of 1939.

The rose is devoted to the Assumption of the Virgin. It forms the logical complement to her Coronation in the central gable outside and is clearly—unlike the west gallery but like the entire cathedral glazing, as far as we know, otherwise—the undertaking of the ecclesiastical community. Just as no document records Philippe IV's involvement, which I have hypothesized, in the west-gallery glazing, no archival evidence identifies the interest of a specific churchman in the great rose. It is worth noting, nonetheless, that the 1285 seal of Archbishop Pierre Barbet (r. 1273–98) shows him standing on a pedestal decorated with a small rose, beneath a Gothic canopy with a larger rose. The counterseal shows the Coronation of the Virgin by Christ.[55] The confluence of a small rose below a large rose, on the front of the seal, with the

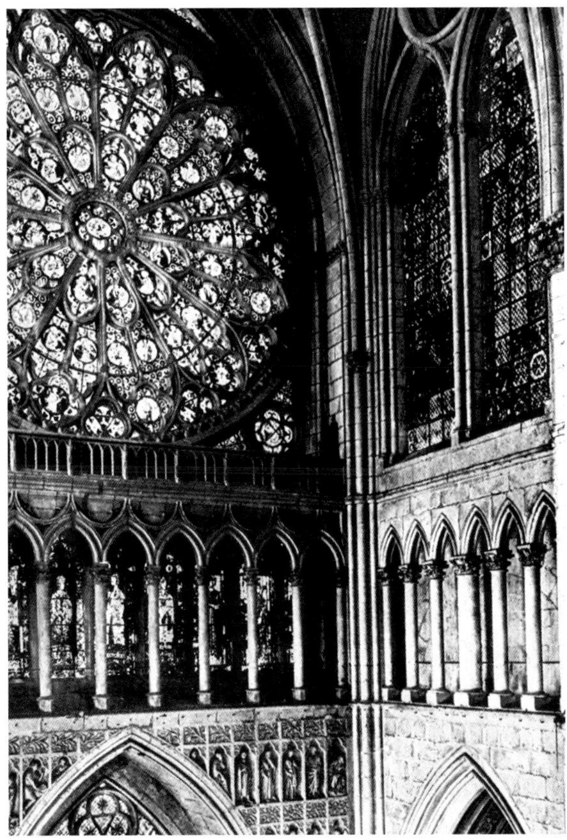

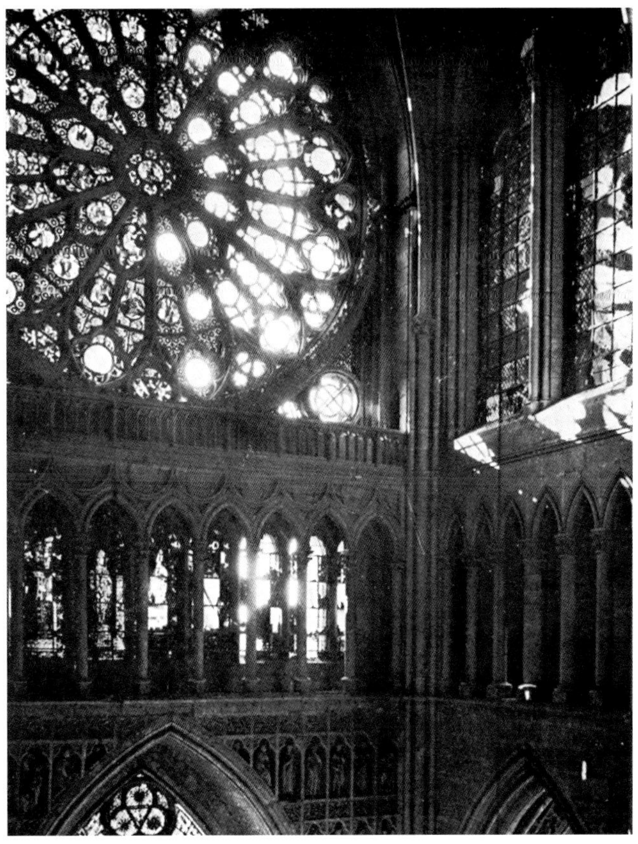

FIG. 238 West rose and gallery, and Bay 139. The grisaille of Bay 139 retains the cold painting applied for the 1825 coronation. Photo by Jacques Doucet, before 1914 (after Étienne Moreau-Nélaton, *La cathédrale de Reims*).

FIG. 239 West rose and gallery, and Bay 139. Photo by Abbé Remy Thinot, before February 1915 (after Maurice Landrieux, *The Cathedral of Reims: The Story of a German Crime*).

Coronation of the Virgin, on the verso, at the date of 1285—the year when Philippe IV became king—is suggestive. Pierre Barbet was a Parisian bourgeois, favored by Philippe III and then involved in "diverses missions diplomatiques pour le compte de Philippe le Bel."[56] It would not be surprising if Archbishop Pierre Barbet had taken a particular interest in the glazing of the west facade, but there we must leave it.

The Great Rose: Design and Ornament

The rose comprises twelve centrifugally radiating petals, or lancets, glazed with alternating ground patterns of ornamented circles and ivylike foliage (fig. 249). Both circles and foliage carry underlying religious import, which by the late thirteenth century had largely become a matter of traditional usage. Circle patterns had long represented the unity of the Godhead, while foliage in Christian art gave form to the divine gift of eternal life.[57] Tracery in each of the twelve petals divides it into a "doublet-and-rose" pattern matching the form of all bays of the cathedral, above and below. Thus are provided, in the rose, three concentric rings of circular medallions framing the central light of the Virgin (fig. 236). While the program does have anomalies, in general terms the inner ring (D on the chart) presents the twelve apostles (e.g., figs. 242 [2D, 12D], 249 [10D]); the middle ring (B–C) depicts musical angels (figs. 243, 244) and seraphim (figs. 245, 246); and the outer ring (A) includes kings in the lower half of the rose and prophets above, thus forming a reference to the Jesse Tree (figs. 242 [3A, 9A], 248 [12A]).[58]

As Simon reports, one of the twelve petals (no. 12 in his chart, see figs. 232, lower right, and 248, top center) has a different foliate ground pattern—composed of smaller, fussier leafage—which is also found in its adjacent outer trefoil as well as in the

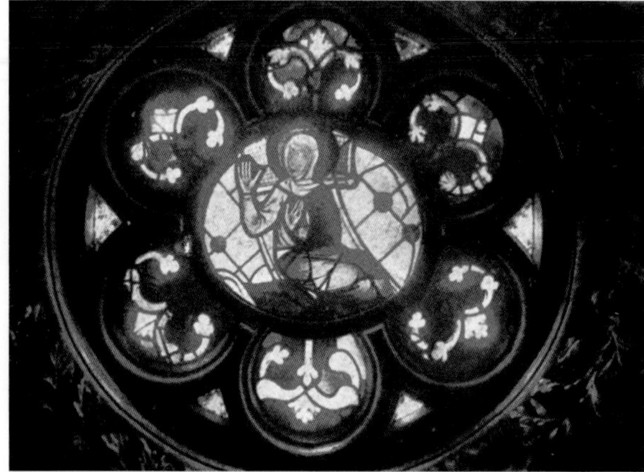

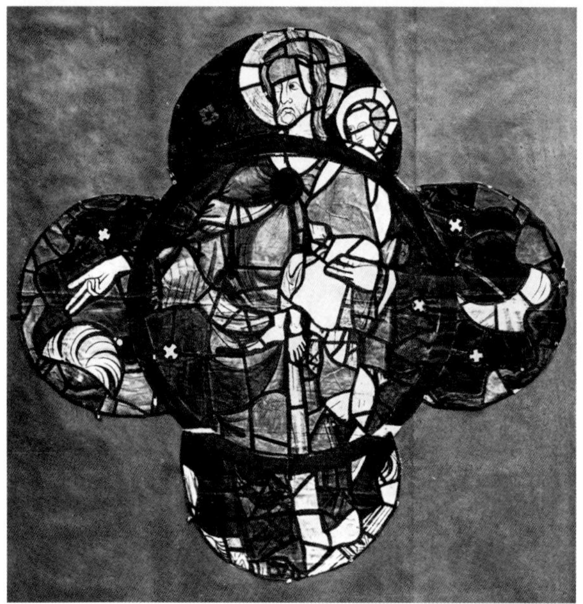

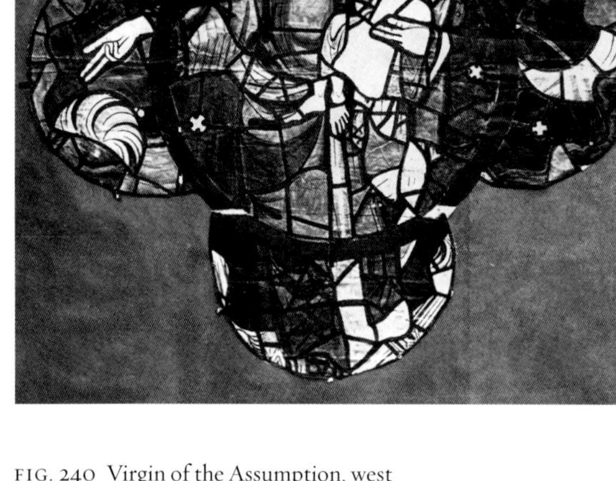

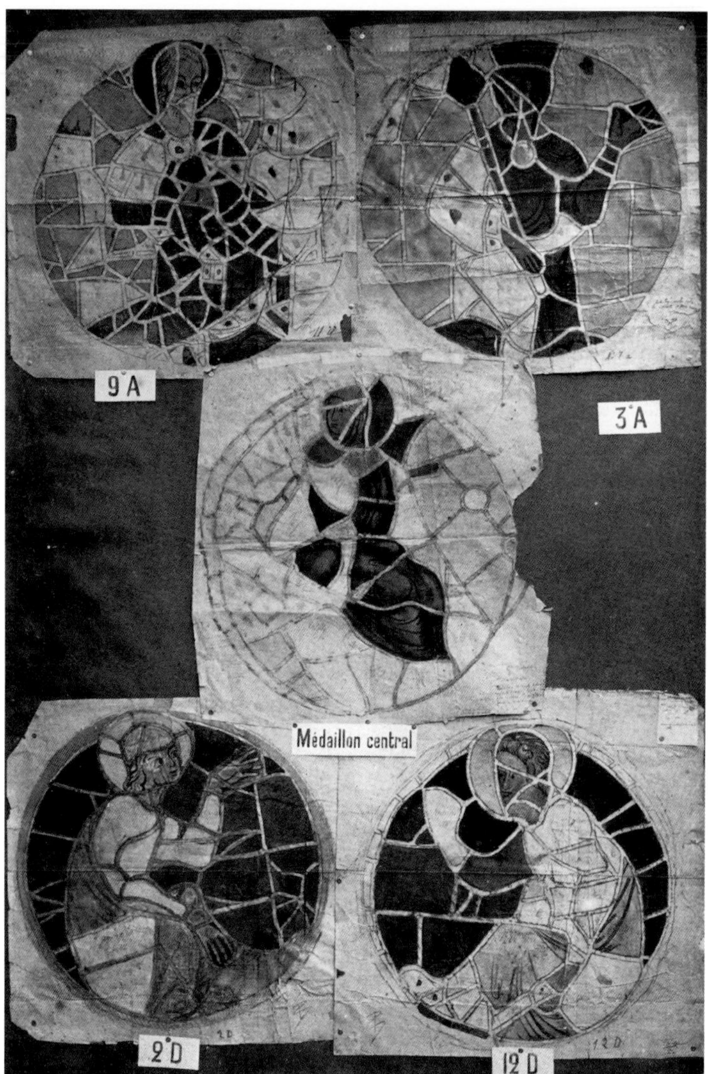

FIG. 240 Virgin of the Assumption, west rose, central medallion. Photo by François Rothier, before 1914 (after Louis Bréhier, *La cathédrale de Reims: Une oeuvre française*).

FIG. 241 Christ in heaven holding the Virgin's soul, ogive over the west rose. Tracing made by Pierre Simon in 1853 (after Paul Simon, *La grande rose*).

FIG. 242 West rose, tracings made in situ between 1875 and 1886: central medallion, 3A, 9A, 2D, 12D (after Paul Simon, *La grande rose*).

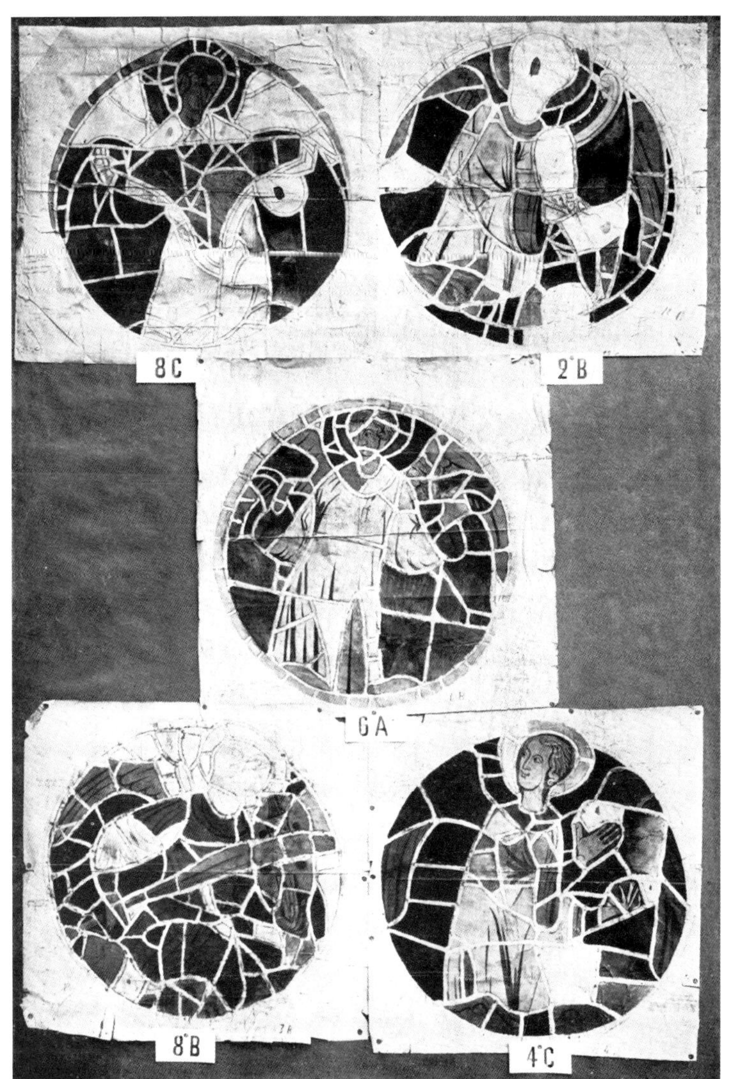

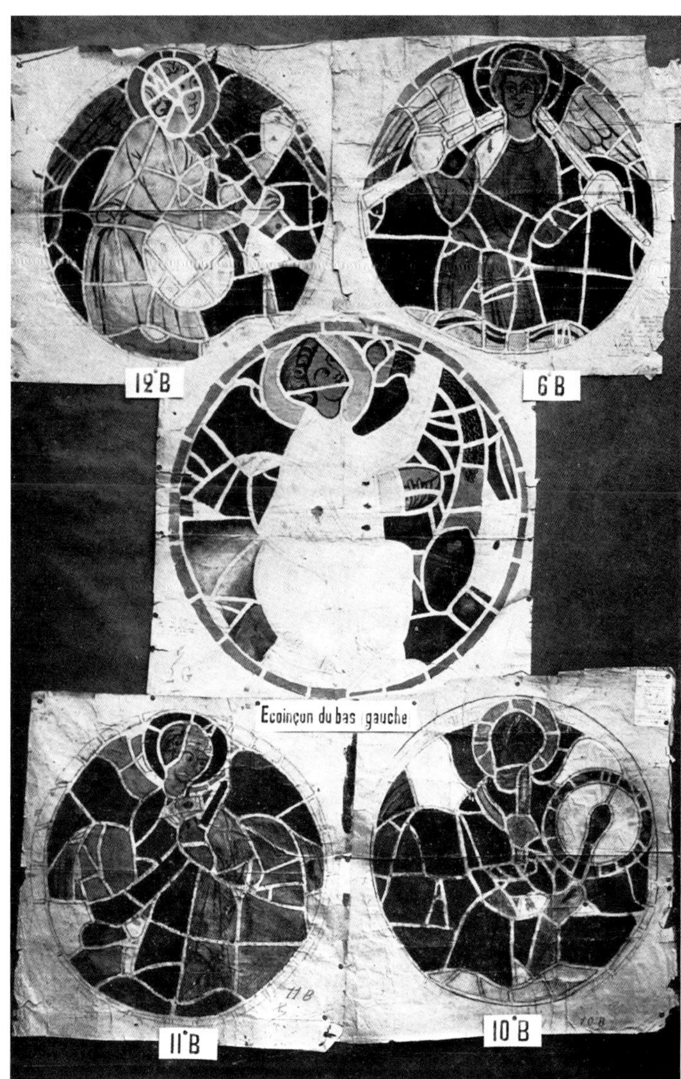

FIG. 243 West rose, tracings made in situ between 1875 and 1886: 6A, 2B, 8B, 4C, 8C (after Paul Simon, *La grande rose*).

FIG. 244 West rose, tracings made in situ between 1875 and 1886: left corner medallion, 6B, 10B, 11B, 12B (after Paul Simon, *La grande rose*).

FIG. 245 Seraph (11C), west rose, tracing made in situ between 1875 and 1886 (after Paul Simon, *La grande rose*).

FIG. 246 Seraph (7B), largely an early restoration, west rose, tracing made after the 1886 hailstorm (after Simon, *La grande rose*).

FIG. 247 West rose, tracings made after the 1886 hailstorm: 1A, 1B, 2C, 2D, 3C, 3D, 4B, 4D, 6C (after Simon, *La grande rose*).

Opposite
FIG. 248 West rose, watercolors by Henri Deneux showing medallions 1A and 12A, 1914. *Les vitraux de la cathédrale Notre Dame de Reims,* Reims, Bibl. mun., Fonds Deneux, L072–L073.

FIG. 249 West rose, watercolors by Paul Simon of restored panels ca. 1910: 8B, 8C, 10D, and examples of both lancet grounds (after Simon, *La grande rose*).

FIG. 250 West rose, watercolors by Paul Simon of restored panels ca. 1910: 2B, 4C, 5C, 10B, left corner medallion (after Simon, *La grande rose*).

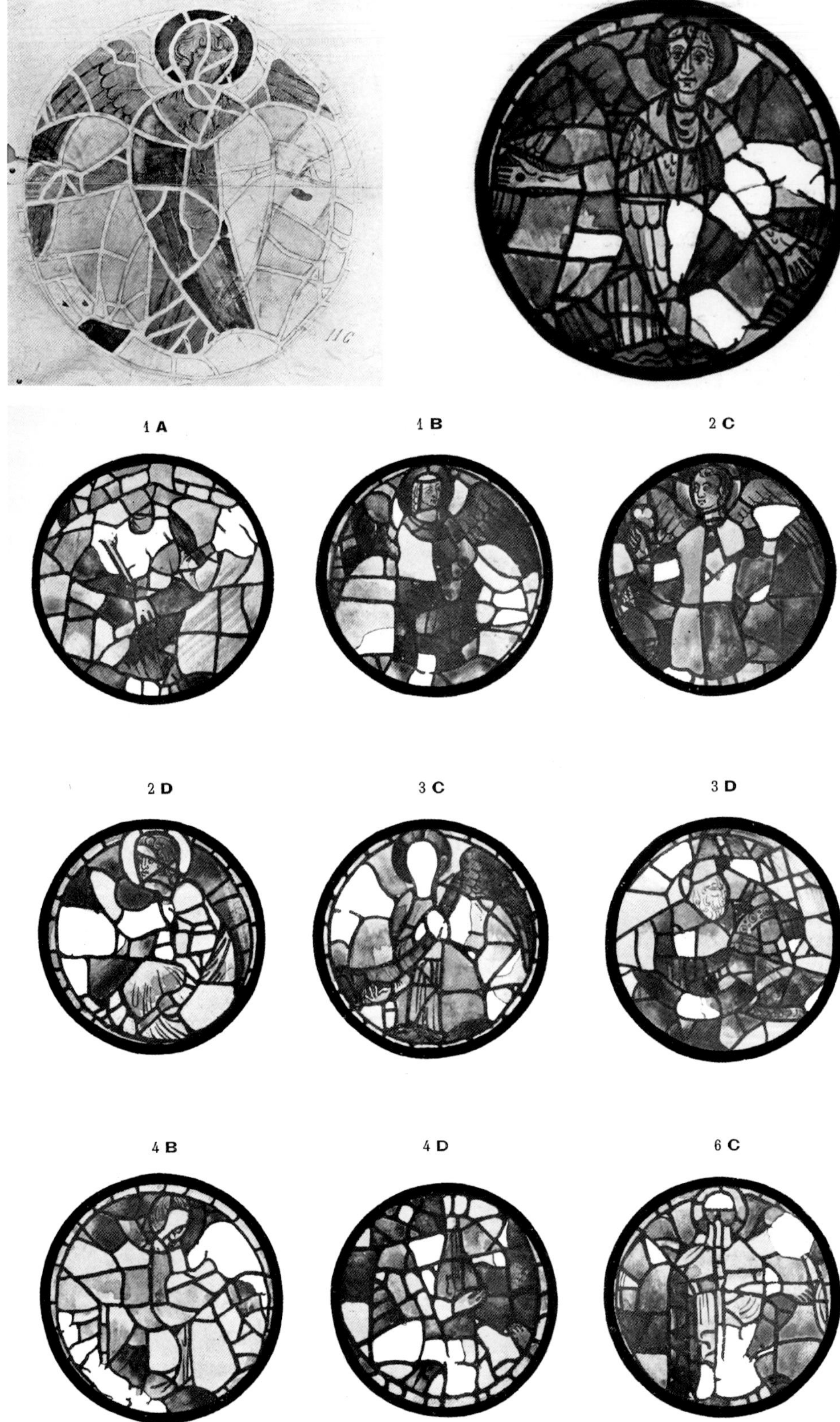

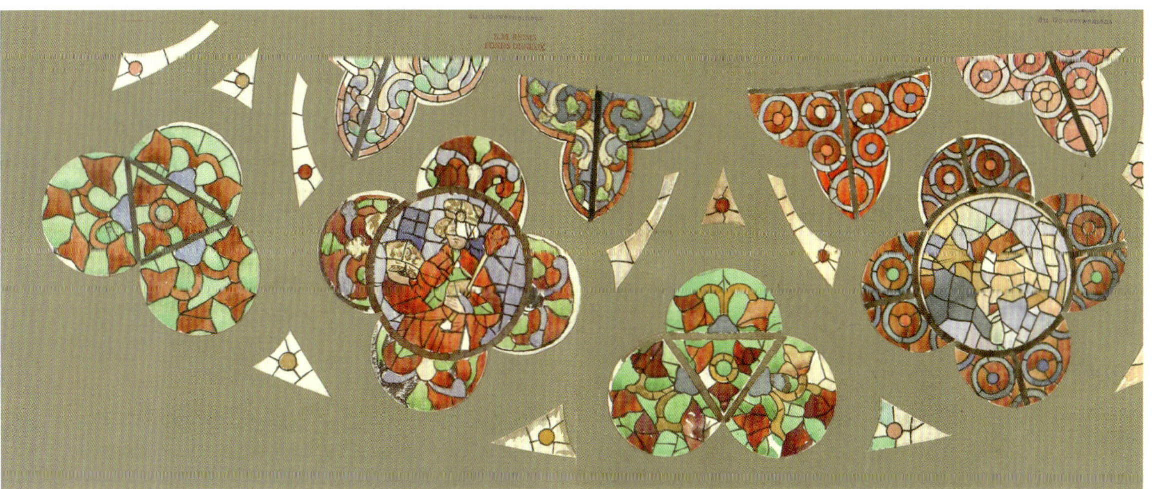

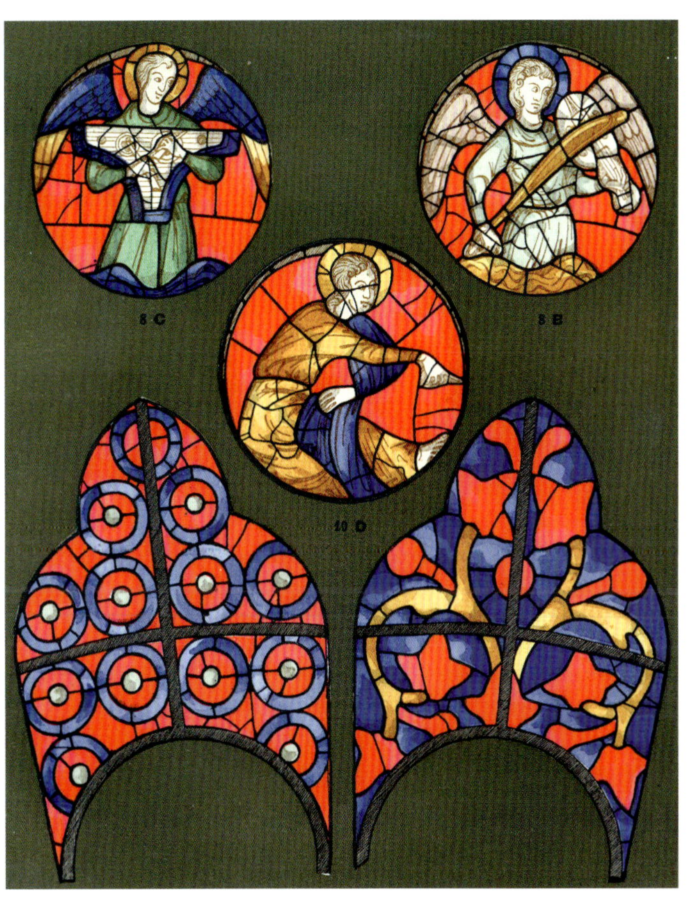

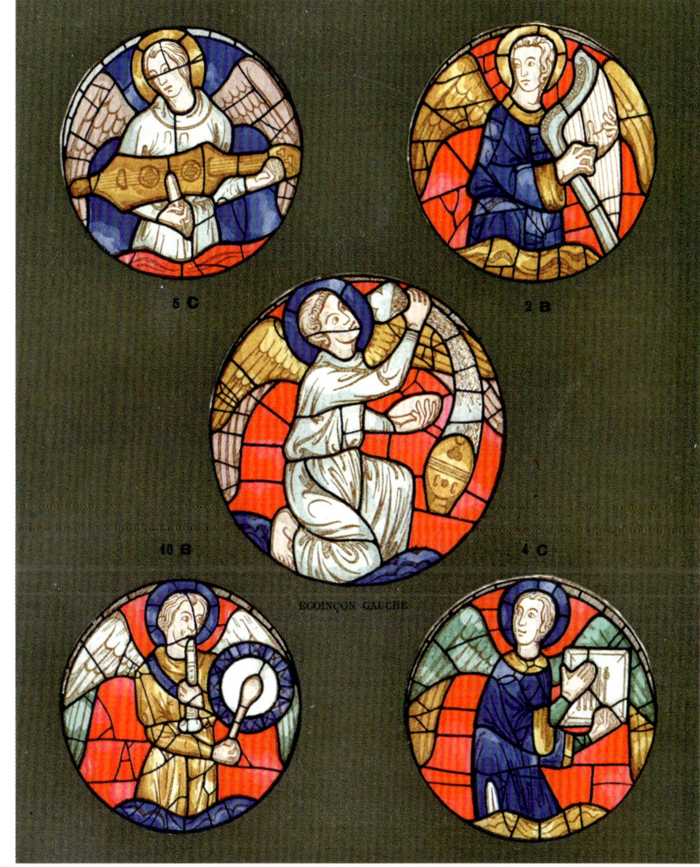

six small lobes surrounding the central light. Following Givelet, he interpreted this as a trial design. He notes that it does not make as striking an effect as the ground designs adopted thereafter and also that its fabrication would have entailed greater time and expense. Simon kept it in his 1909 restoration, "malgré son peu d'importance, en raison de son authenticité."[59] Their theory of trial work is undoubtedly correct. I have posited a similar trial situation for Bay 101 in the chevet, as has Caviness for the northwest clerestory of the Saint-Remi chevet.[60] It is possible, though certainly not provable, that a lapse of time is indicated since the foliage of the trial work—a generic, desiccated, and knobby medieval "acanthus"—looks to the past while the type adopted is a vigorous quasi-naturalistic ivy heralding the future of Gothic ornament.[61]

The Great Rose: Iconographic Surprises

A number of unexpected details indicate that the subject of the Assumption of the Virgin here is unconventional. In essence the rose strays far from the typical French Gothic formula for the Triumph of the Virgin sequence, though its climax in the Coronation of the Virgin sculpture in the exterior gable is orthodox enough. I argue that Hincmar again provides the source. But first, to detail the rose's iconographic peculiarities: a Virgin in bed at the point of death (center), surrounded by twelve apostles (inner ring, D) and Christ holding her soul (ogive above), presents all the elements of a Dormition (Koimesis). However, under closer examination, the Virgin in the central light sits back on a pillowed bed and looks above her, raising both hands upward (fig. 240).[62] In the ogive light directly over the rose and above this central Virgin, Christ, standing and holding her soul, his right hand lowered in blessing, is flanked by the sun and moon (fig. 241).[63] He is thus not at her deathbed on earth but in heaven. Surrounding the rose's central light, the apostles are often in wildly agitated poses, gesturing and staring upward.[64] They are clearly not so much comforting the Virgin, whom they surround, as reacting to the appearance of Christ with her soul above them.

Thus, while the Dormition—that is, the Koimesis scene as introduced to the West through Byzantine ivories in the tenth century—is referenced, it is not actually depicted here. In the Dormition the Virgin lies prone in bed, "asleep," surrounded by the apostles, who had miraculously flown in to comfort her in her last moments, while Christ stands behind her bed holding her soul.[65] The scene appears from the late twelfth century in French art. Examples in glass include bay 123 of Angers Cathedral (ca. 1180) and Chartres bay 42 (ca. 1205–15), and in sculpture the Chartres north-transept tympanum (ca. 1205–10) and the Strasbourg south-transept tympanum (ca. 1230). The scene remains in both France and Germany in fourteenth-century art but ultimately is reduced to the figure of Christ carrying his mother's soul.[66] In contrast to the Dormition, then, the ogive light at Reims specifically depicts Christ's reception of the Virgin's soul in heaven.

So what does the rose itself depict? The seated Virgin in the central light, eyes open and hands in a quasi-orante position, seems to refer to her bodily Assumption, but again, the image does not "follow the rules" of typical Gothic iconography. Mary's bodily Assumption appeared in the Latin West in the fifth century in the widely diffused apocryphal text by Pseudo-Melito, *Transitus Mariae*.[67] However, the Pseudo-Melito includes, after the Dormition at the Virgin's deathbed, an extended narrative about her funeral procession and tomb, whence occurs her bodily Assumption—a dubious theological matter. The Virgin in the Reims west rose is not in or on a tomb, and thus her bodily resurrection as found in Pseudo-Melito is not the subject here.

A hint to explain the Virgin's strange image may be found in the cloud of rejoicing angels in the rose as well as the Tree of Jesse (kings and prophets) surrounding the Virgin. These suggest another source, one connected with the Carolingian archbishop of Reims, Hincmar. The reliance on Hincmar would be supported by the evidence that has been presented of the serious study and use of

Hincmar's varied and extensive oeuvre as bases of the sophisticated programs of both the choir and nave glazing earlier at Reims.[68] Between his election in 845 and 849, Hincmar had his craftsmen copy and luxuriously bind, in wood covers faced with gold and ivory plaques, a manuscript devoted to the Virgin Mary.[69] He presented this luxury codex, now lost, to the treasury of his cathedral. In addition to an apocryphal text on the Virgin's nativity, this precious manuscript contained Pseudo-Jerome's letter IX to Paula and Eustochium, which is a long and impassioned sermon for the feast of the Assumption of the Virgin.[70] The Pseudo-Jerome epistle enjoyed enormous prestige in Carolingian France, forming the liturgy—even replacing the Gospel—for Assumption day in such important monasteries as Cluny, Corbie, and Saint-Bénigne de Dijon. Phrases from it survived in that office as well as that of the Immaculate Conception into the twentieth century. Hincmar, consumed in the early years by devotion to the Virgin, contributed to his gift a hundred-line dogmatic poem of his own to Mary.[71] It is not unlikely that Hincmar's luxurious manuscript survived in the cathedral's treasury or library in the late thirteenth century, when the program of the west rose was undertaken.

Thus Philippe Verdier, noting that Hincmar's luxury manuscript had an ivory cover, wonders if that cover could have represented the Assumption of the Virgin. He points out that the earliest form of that subject was the *Virgo orans* and cites the ivory carved by the monk Tuotilo ca. 900 that serves as the lower cover of Saint-Gall codex 53.[72] It seems possible that the Virgin in the Reims rose may be a Gothic "interpretation" of the unfamiliar *orans* posture found on Hincmar's Carolingian ivory.

The text of the Pseudo-Jerome letter, though ducking a direct statement on Mary's bodily Assumption, diffused "une imagerie si obsédante qu'elle réduisait à un débat purement spéculatif le problème de l'assomption intégrale, en corps et en âme de la Vierge. . . . [L'épître] entre dans un paroxysme verbal quand il évoque l'entrée glorieuse au ciel de la Vierge et son accession au trône du Christ."[73] Its growing crescendo of lyric metaphors for the joy expressed in heaven and the multitudes of lauding angels finds visual form in the Reims rose's middle ring of twenty-four angels and seraphim. The Pseudo-Jerome text also contains a reference that would justify the kings and prophets forming the outer ring of medallions: "Ascendebat autem Dei genitrix de deserto praesentis saeculi virga de radica Jesse olim exorta."[74]

The Great Rose: Gothic Innovation

Thus far the Reims west rose can be compared in general terms with, for example, the Chartres north rose, where encircling the enthroned Virgin and Child is first a ring of angels and seraphim, while in the lights beyond appear kings of Judah and prophets.[75] But as with the Hincmariana that formed the basis of the sophisticated nave program, the witness of the famous Carolingian archbishop becomes the foundation for unexpected iconographic innovation. The two clearly unusual features of the west-rose ensemble are the central Virgin's alert but semi-reclining posture in bed and the orchestra of instrument-playing angels surrounding her. As discussed above, the central Virgin (fig. 240) is neither dead nor asleep, nor is she being bodily elevated from her tomb (or indeed from anywhere else). Her unusual posture in bed is not found in Carolingian ivories of the *Virgo orans.* I would like to offer the hypothesis that the Virgin, in her Gothic form at the center of the rose, is depicted at the commencement of her "ritual" of coronation—which culminates in her crowning and enthronement on the exterior gable—and that her posture was understood as a reference to that introductory moment in the coronation ordo of the French *sacre.* That is, her semi-reclining posture in bed refers to the commencement of the French king's long coronation day (see fig. 171), when the bishops process to the archbishop's palace to find him in bed, "sedentem et quasi jacentem supra thalamum."[76] The phrase describes her posture precisely.

Such an image would be meaningful only to a small, elite group in Reims. The angel philharmonic, on the other hand, participates in a much broader iconographic development in art—and at the very beginning of that development. While choirs of singing angels have been sighted regularly in religious literature from the Bible onward, ensembles of angel instrumentalists appeared only in the latter thirteenth century, and in scenes associated with the Triumph of the Virgin. In the Golden Legend, dated ca. 1260–67, Voragine quotes a homily describing the Virgin's welcome to heaven by the nine choirs of angels: Thrones, Dominations, Principalities, Cherubim, and so on. Among them, the Powers are playing upon the lyre (*potestates citharisando*).[77] And a long German poem by Brother Philipp from the Carthusian monastery of Seitz in southeastern Austria, dated to the beginning of the fourteenth century, describes the same scene with singing and dancing, including the Seraphim "mit gîgen [*Geigen* = fiddles] und mit harpfen klange" (line 9807), all conducted by the archangels Michael and Gabriel.[78] Note that these instruments are all *bas* (soft), as opposed to *haut* (loud), a medieval distinction.

Ensembles of angel-musicians appear at around the same time in art, the earliest French example usually identified as the apse fresco of Vernais (Cher) dated ca. 1285–90—that is, exactly contemporary with the Reims facade glazing under discussion. In the fresco a sextet of angels accompanies the Coronation of the Virgin, the first on the left plucking a cittern (citole), then angels bowing a rebec and playing cymbals, and on the right a shawm and probably another fiddle (the last figure now illegible).[79] Thus this small angelic combo includes both *haut* and *bas* instruments: plucked and bowed strings, percussion, and a loud piercing wind instrument. Monumental examples are not numerous until well into the fourteenth century, when in glass one could cite a rosace of the Coronation of the Virgin in Beauvais (ca. 1340s) and the *occhio* of the same subject at Santa Maria Novella in Florence, by Andrea di Buonaiuto (ca. 1365).[80] Both of these angelic ensembles are also fairly limited in personnel.

Thus it is surprising that the full symphony orchestra in the Reims west rose has not drawn attention in the scholarly literature. Before taking a closer look and listen, one might mention two unusual musician groups in Reims in sculptural ensembles that were roughly contemporary with the rose. The first comprises the sculptures on the famous House of the Musicians, a bourgeois shop/residence that stood in the rue de Tambour until World War I. It has been dated only very approximately, to around 1260.[81] Five life-size seated statues (fig. 251) adorned the upper facade, four of them now in the Musée de Saint-Remi. Flanking the central figure of a youthful falconer were, on the left, a musician playing a reed pipe and tabor (small drum) and another with a bagpipe, while to the right were figures with a harp and a vielle (medieval fiddle) with bow.[82]

The statues of the House of the Musicians are all secular figures, while those in the second *rémois* sculptural group, on the central portal of the cathedral (fig. 252), can be assumed to have religious significance, and they must predate the glazing above them, though perhaps not by too long. Archivolts include kings playing a double-reed pipe, cymbals, and a variety of stringed instruments, including dulcimers played on the lap with hammers, bowed rebecs, and plucked gitterns. Kurmann poses the question why most of the ancestors of Christ are represented with musical instruments. He suggests a possible "contamination" from the iconography of the Elders of the Apocalypse (who wear crowns), concluding, "C'est une question qui n'a pas encore été étudiée."[83] None of these musical archivolt figures are angels. The same portal, however, does offer one angelic example: a console beneath the jamb statue of the Virgin of the Annunciation portrays an angel plucking a psaltery hugged to his chest. For this isolated angel-musician a symbolic meaning is probable, the psaltery having been a reference to Christ's Incarnation for the Church Fathers, repeated as late as Honorius of Autun (fl. 1106–35).[84]

The instruments played by the consort in the west rose are much more varied and numerous—and they are played not by laymen, Elders, or kings of Judah, but exclusively by angels. Simon's 1909 reconstruction of the rose contained eighteen

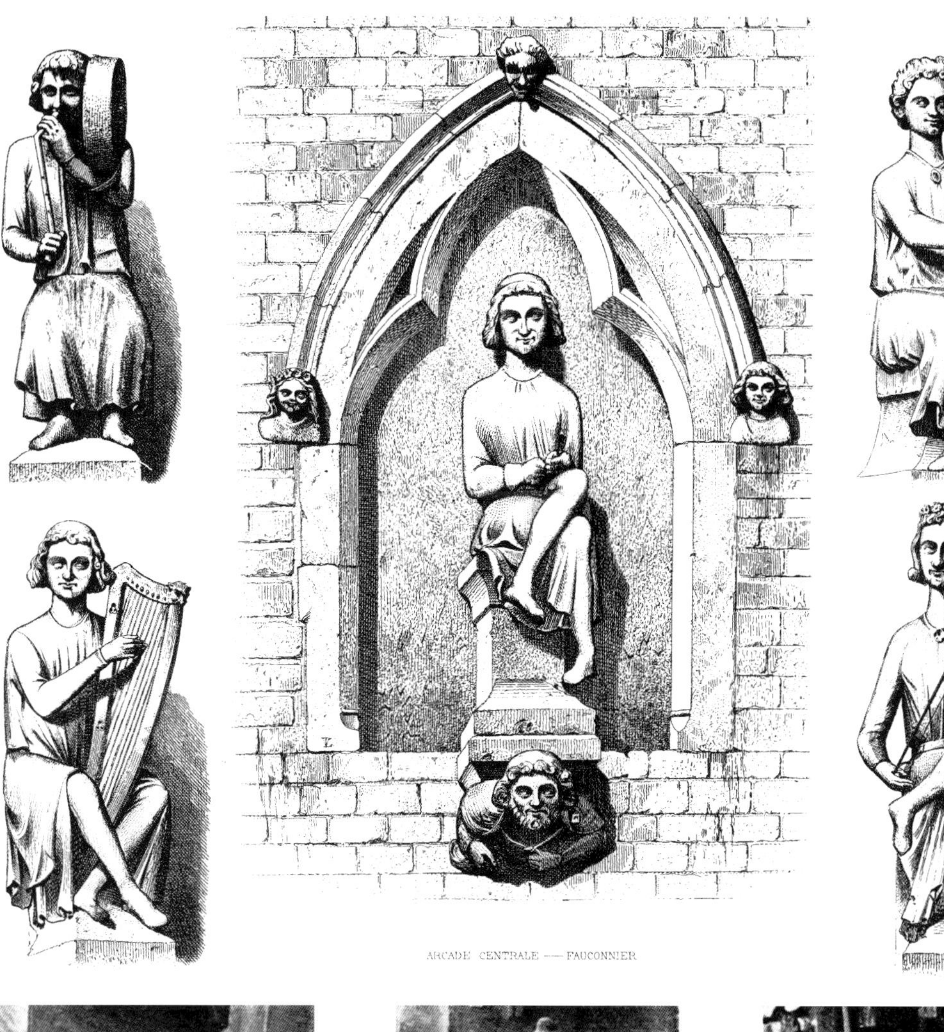

FIG. 251 Sculptures from the facade of the House of the Musicians, rue de Tambour, Reims, now in the Musée de Saint-Remi (after Aymar Verdier and François Cattois, *Architecture civile et domestique*).

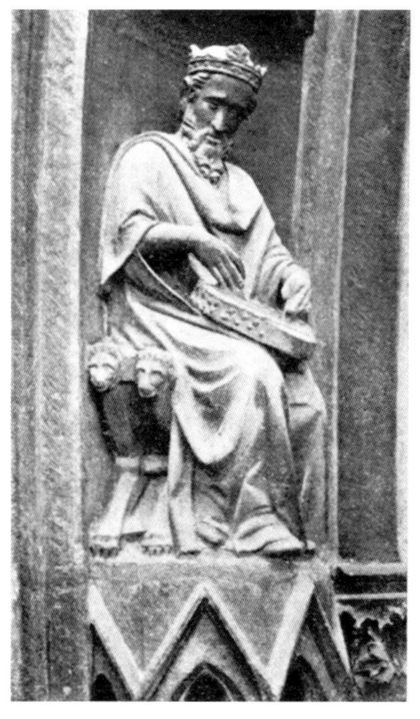

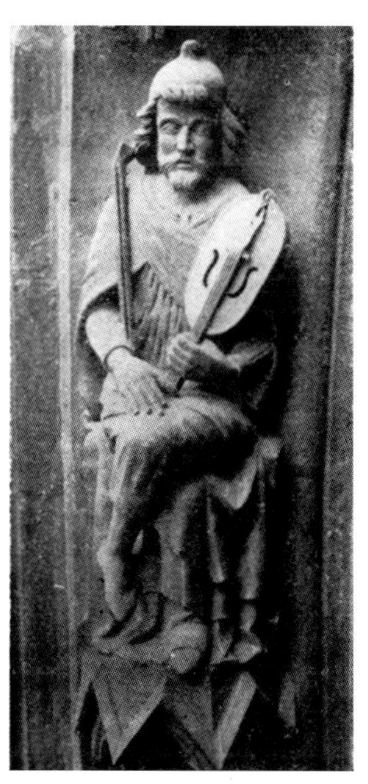

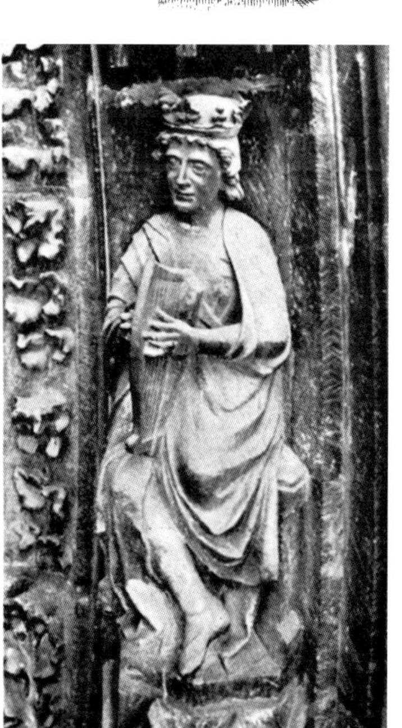

FIG. 252 Royal musicians, Reims cathedral, west facade, central portal (after Louis Bréhier, *La cathédrale de Reims: Une oeuvre française*).

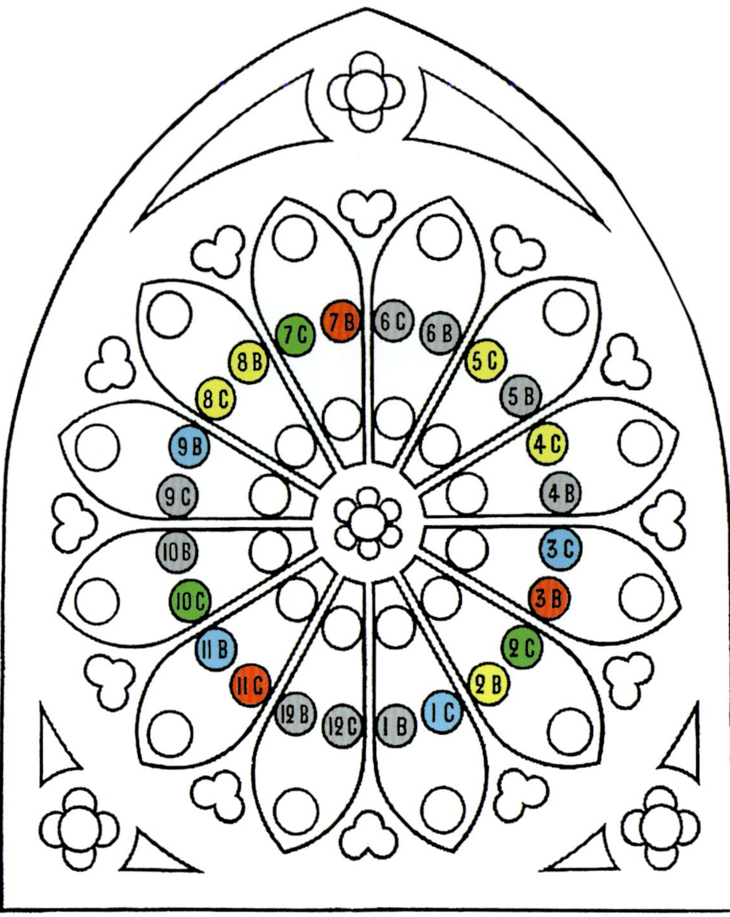

FIG. 253 Chart of the angels in the west rose, in Simon's reconstruction, 1909: (yellow) stringed instruments; (gray) wind instruments; (blue) oliphants, held but not played; (green) censers [2C, 10C], instruments of the Passion [7C]; (red) seraphim. Only the three seraphim reveal a pattern, dividing the twelve petals evenly. The postwar restoration strengthened this pattern by switching 11C with 11B.

musical angels in the ring of twenty-four. Their arrangement reveals no obvious pattern (fig. 253). Four of them, 1C, 3C, 9B, and 11B, held—but did not play—massive oliphants (figs. 247 [3C], 244 [11B]), undoubtedly a temporal reference to the Last Judgment and appropriate to a western rose.[85] Five angels blew other types of wind instruments: 1B and 5B, curved gemshorns; 12C, a longer curved horn; 4B, a small shawm with finger holes; and 6C, a very long shawm (fig. 247 [1B, 4B, 6C]). Other wind instruments were played by 6B, double pipes; 12B, bagpipes; 10B, reed pipe and tabor (fig. 244 [6B, 10B, 12B]); and 9C, shawm and three bells.[86] Stringed instruments were just as varied. Angel 2B played a harp; 4C plucked a square psaltery (fig. 243 [2B, 4C]); 5C played a waisted gittern with plectrum (fig. 250); 8C had a large snout-shaped psaltery and two plectra; and 8B bowed a medieval vielle or fiddle (figs. 243, 249 [8B, 8C]).[87]

The size of the rose's angelic orchestra is exceptional for its time, and in French art for a very long time to come. Not until the late fifteenth and sixteenth centuries are such groups found in rose windows.[88] Just as exceptional for its early date is the mix, cheek by jowl as it were, of the soft (*bas*), mostly stringed, instruments with such a large group of *haut* instruments. Music historians are unanimous in stating—and indeed common sense asserts—that these instruments would never have been played together. Emanuel Winternitz advises that "angel orchestras depicted in *trecento* and *quattrocento* art . . . for instance . . . four trumpets pitted against a few soft string instruments should be taken *cum grano salis*."[89] David Monrow concurs, remarking about "the dazzling variety of musical instruments shown in the hands of angels by religious painters of the fourteenth and fifteenth centuries [that] such angel concerts belong not to this world but to paradise and they bear little relation to contemporary church music practice."[90]

Edmund Bowles's study of medieval textual references to *haut* and *bas* instruments affirms that, under some circumstances, both groups would be present but that they would play at different moments.[91] His numerous texts suggest these scenarios. Drums and horns would be played outdoors, while shawms and the pipe and tabor were used at banquets where even trumpets, after the fanfares at entries, occasionally provided dinner music. Harp and lute were aristocratic instruments to accompany song at such festivities; the vielle was a widespread supplement to or substitute for the voice. A twelfth-century poem describes the psaltery and monochord played at the coronation banquet of King Arthur, and at the Feast of Westminster in 1306, in honor of the future Edward II, the seventy-five minstrels entertained on the psaltery, bowed rebec and fiddle, bells, as well as the small organ suitable for dancers and mummers.[92] One might add to his references a particularly pertinent literary example, the instruments described on the day of wedding and coronation in *Cléomadés,* written by Adenès li rois between 1275 and 1280 and presented to Marie de Brabant, queen of France: "Vièles et sauterions, / Harpes, gigues, et canons, / Leüs, rubebes et kitaires. / Et ot en pluseurs lieus nacaires / Qui moult très grant noise faisoient; / Mais fors des routes mis estoient. / Cymbales, rotes, timpanons, / Et mandoires, et micanons / I ot, et cornes et douçaines, / Et trompes et grosses araines. / Cors sarrazinois et tabours."[93]

Certainly the instruments of the Reims great rose would never have actually joined forces in any single piece of music, either processional out of doors or accompanying a song inside. The cacophony of such an angelic ensemble one shudders to imagine; heavenly exultation is clearly in the eye, not the ear, of the beholder. The precocious size and variety of the angel orchestra of Reims at such an early date for such a theme do—I propose—hint at some special impetus at work. Just as I have suggested that the Virgin in the central light, "sitting and half reclining" on her Dormition bed, may reflect the commencement of the French king's coronation day, I wonder if the piercing sounds of the shawms and the clamor of cymbals, nakers, and bagpipes, as well as the light beat of the pipe and tabor-drum, soft-toned dulcimers and rebecs and vielles, may not reflect the variety of celebrations—both public and private—that regularly climaxed the end of that long day's ceremonial.

As a fitting epilogue I should mention a noteworthy appreciation of this most extraordinary rose window by the famous poet and composer Guillaume de Machaut (ca. 1300–1377), who for forty years was a canon of Reims cathedral, in the generation succeeding the completion of the cathedral. His early poem *Remede de fortune* was, it is believed, written for and about Bonne de Luxembourg, daughter of a king and married in 1332 to the heir to the French throne, Jean le Bon.[94] The setting is named Hesdin, the pleasure castle of the Artois branch of the French monarchy, a place frequently visited by royalty. The final section of the poem begins with a Mass in "a very beautiful chapel, painted . . . with the finest colors I'd ever seen." A feast followed, with musical entertainment thereafter, the performers arranged "all in a circle" and playing thirty-two different types of instruments. The poet continues: "And it certainly seemed to me that such a melodious sound had never been perceived or heard; because I heard and perceived each one of them, according to the pitch of his instrument—vielle, guitar, cittern, harp, trumpet, horn, flute, pipe, bladder pipe, bagpipe, naker, tabor, and whatever could be played with finger, pick, or bow—performing in perfect harmony there in the little park."[95] Not only does the music follow Mass in a beautifully colored church, but the musicians are in a circle, playing *bas* and *haut* instruments, and, as Bowles comments, "through the author [Machaut]'s fancy they are all heard being performed together."[96] Guillaume de Machaut, an expert musician and an informed churchman as well as a sensitive poet, must have observed the great innovative rose crowning the facade of his cathedral often—and very carefully.

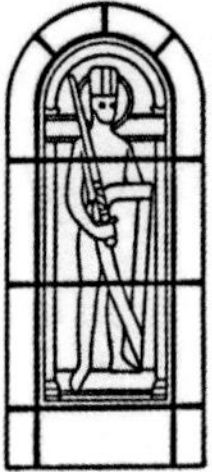
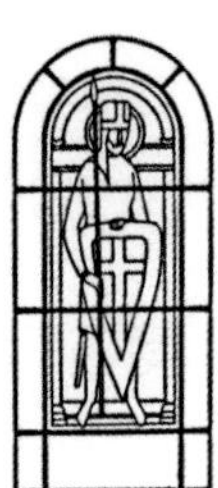
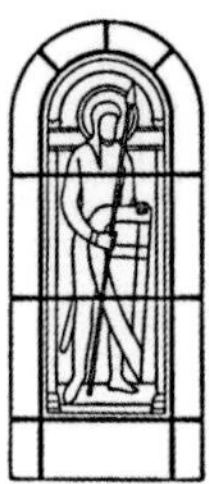
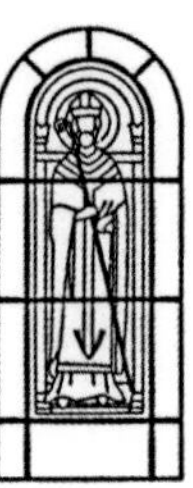
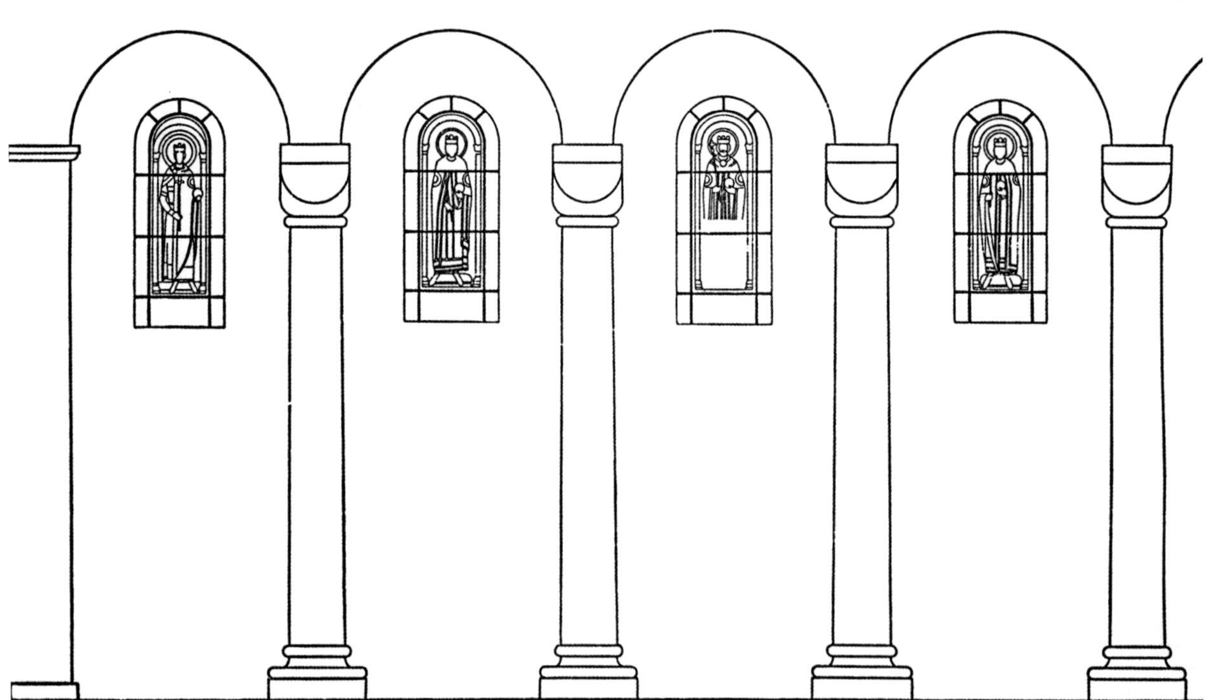

FIG. 254 Strasbourg cathedral, reconstruction of glazing in the Romanesque nave, detail (after Fridtjof Zschokke, *Die romanischen Glasgemälde des Strassburger Münsters*).

CODA

Comparanda

Indeed there are no *comparanda*. Reims is unique, not only in the grand clerestory and rose programs but in innumerable minutiae and nuances of meaning. The singularity of its glazed sequences of suffragan bishops and their cathedral "facades" has long been recognized; the first full set of apostles' lives (chapter 2), the first angel-musicians (chapter 7), and the first and only image of King Solomon in Bed (chapter 5) are no less noteworthy. The loss of the lower windows, of course, complicates comparisons. To consider, then, the upper glazing ensembles of High Gothic cathedrals preceding and coeval with Reims—Chartres, Bourges, Auxerre, Troyes: major saints and prophets, local prelates and venerations, Marian, Christological, and biblical themes, and donors form the standard and fairly predictable fare. An attempt has been made to link a few of the Chartres clerestory figures with relics and the locations of altars.[1] The majestic processions of apostles, prophets, and local saints at Bourges are tidier and more straightforward.[2] Auxerre's smaller clerestory program draws on the same themes. Troyes, while unusual in employing large medallion frames and narrative, presents an ad hoc mix of core Christological subjects and local venerations.[3] And except for Chartres, this Gothic figural glazing is limited to the chevets. While suffragan cathedrals of Reims such as Laon, Soissons, Châlons, and Amiens have suffered enormous losses, their surviving windows draw from the same ecclesiastical vocabulary. Reims, even missing its lower windows, commands attention.

Like the High Gothic cathedrals noted above, Reims depicts apostles and central Marian and Christological themes. Also found are local prelates, though, unlike those elsewhere, they are, in all but isolated cases, unnamed and unnimbed.[4] The windows of Reims include no prophets and indeed no Old Testament personae, except for Adam's immediate family in the north rose (e.g., fig. 118) and Solomon in the rosaces of Bays 121 and 124 (figs. 159, 164).[5] What Reims does have are kings, and like the prelates they are nameless.[6] The lack of specificity implies universality, timeless continuity, a more abstract level of significance.

Reims is notable for its lack of donor images, excepting only Archbishop Henri de Braine in the axial bay (fig. 70) and the royal gift I have proposed in the facade gallery (fig. 227). Also strange is the near total absence of Old Testament figures and of local saints either named or provided with identifying attributes. Would the lost aisle glazing alter this assessment if we still had it? The only certain subjects were the Tree of Jesse, a stopgap removed from the north rose in the 1870s and preserved only in a tracing, and the Ascension still found in Bay 39 (fig. 20).[7] Dom Guillaume Marlot, writing in the 1660s, states only that the lower windows of the cathedral, like the upper ones, were glazed with thick, dark glass, obscuring vision.[8] His total disregard for the aisle windows seems surprising in view of his detailed observations of donors and some of the unusual narratives in the glazing of the abbey church of Saint-Nicaise.[9] Of course, he was *grand prieur* of Saint-Nicaise. It does suggest, however, that the cathedral's aisle windows included no donors or, at the least, no heraldry or noteworthy inscriptions.

The Gothic cathedral of Reims was never challenged as the site of coronation of the French monarchy. Of the earlier, would-be kingmakers of the twelfth century—Sens cathedral and Saint-Denis—the original glazing ensembles cannot be recovered. The abbey of Suger (d. 1151) may possibly have had windows of kings, since the *rayonnant* upper structure that was later replaced over his ambulatory is reported to have had in the choir's glazed triforium a figure of Pepin le Bref.[10] At any rate, Archbishop Samson's mid-twelfth-century building at Reims arguably copied Suger's architectural projects at Saint-Denis, adding a choir with ambulatory and radiating chapels to one end of the Carolingian nave and a western towered block to the other.[11] The cathedral of Samson (r. 1140–60) just as probably inspired, in its turn, the later-twelfth-century rebuilding at both ends of the Carolingian nave of the *rémois* abbey of Saint-Remi. Art historians have agreed in affirming Saint-Remi's glazing as the main source for that of the High Gothic cathedral. Caviness's study of the abbey's windows has put our understanding of that unusual program on firm footing.[12] The abbey had a series of probably named kings, now fragmentary, below Old Testament figures, and in the spectacular new chevet a row of prophets (in the straight bays) and apostles (hemicycle) above a row of archbishops of Reims, all identified by inscription. Although there are significant variants in the High Gothic cathedral glass, its similarity to Saint-Remi seems undeniable, not only in subjects but more basically in the double-row format.

In this book I have proposed that one might look further: that the inspiration for the unique glazing of Saint-Remi, like the very idea of its additions to the east and west ends of an ancient nave, was Archbishop Samson's cathedral nearby. Its twelfth-century chevet was destroyed in the fire ca. 1210 or pulled down immediately thereafter, while the Carolingian nave stood and did service for several decades during the High Gothic construction. I have suggested in chapter 6 that the figure of Karolvs now in Bay 128 (a modern copy; see figs. 188–90), smaller than the surrounding monarchs and the only one named, came from Samson's building. In sum, the glazing of Samson's building would have been the most likely source for the unusual program at Saint-Remi as well as for themes and variations in the thirteenth-century cathedral that succeeded it.

Before I leave these musings, I want to invoke Fridtjof Zschokke's oft-repeated proposal that Saint-Remi was the source for the cycle of kings originally in the eleventh-century nave of Strasbourg cathedral.[13] Zschokke's reconstruction of those figures (fig. 254) may provide the best general indication available of the appearance of the glazing of the nave of Archbishop Samson's cathedral of Reims, an image of which is preserved on the chapter's seal of ca. 1202 (fig. 158). The small, undivided clerestory openings in those naves, like those in Jean Bony's reconstructions of Saint-Denis and Sens, would have accommodated only single figures.[14] To put it another way: the chief debt of the High Gothic cathedral of Reims to the glazing of Saint-Remi was most reasonably the insistent format of two rows of figures that dominates the monument and unifies its messages and its dramatic effects. The triple rows of Troyes and Châlons might be considered a development, but the midcentury introduction of grisaille and the band window disrupted further diffusion.[15]

It is generally agreed that the architecture and sculpture of Reims influenced Gothic arts in undeniable and fundamental ways. The traceable influence of the glass, on the other hand, seems minimal. Innovations like the representation of an archdiocese's power by references to its suffragans produced no copies, nor did the visualizations of those cathedrals in the series of "facades." It is worth pondering why the "facades," which we find so charming, did not. The answer must lie in the representation itself, so closely allied to the newly developing facade drawings of specialized, professional, Gothic architects. Most cathedral viewers simply did not think of cathedrals that way; the doll-size churches often presented by Gothic donors are visualizations in a proto-perspective, as is, for example, the image of Reims itself on the seal of ca. 1202 (fig. 158).

Implied is a higher degree of intellectualization, that is, of specialized research and scholarly investigation, than we usually expect in cathedral programs. The study of the lives of the apostles in the Pseudo-Abdias (proposed in chapter 2), the bestiary lessons in the north rose (chapter 4), and the close study of Hincmar's wide array of writings evidenced throughout the church (chapters 2, 5, 6, 7) buttress this argument. Little was left to chance in the visual message of the cathedral's glazing. A message for whom? The glazing does not target the ordinary churchgoer, or even monarchs upon the rare events of their coronations (as does the facade's sculpted verso). The stained glass of Reims is an authoritative and ceremonial affirmation, a medieval summation—before God and man—of the essence, privilege, and unique calling of this place.[16] This great chorale of power and continuity would successfully resound until the social and industrial revolutions of modern France.

APPENDIX I

Heresy in Champagne

Because heresy in the Middle Ages is so strongly associated with southern France and Lombardy, this appendix collects evidence for the accusation in Champagne as well as occasions in which the archbishops of Reims took part. It also presents evidence from those events for the connection of heresy with usury, at least in the minds of the accusers; usury was the initial complaint against the rich merchants of Reims during the 1230s, when the cathedral's chevet windows were glazed. Heresy first appears in documents in this region in the mid-eleventh century and by 1245 has virtually disappeared. Between 1043 and 1048 Roger II, bishop of Châlons-sur-Marne, a suffragan of Reims, wrote to the bishop of Liège for advice on how to deal with "Manichaeans" (the dualist heresy combatted by Augustine). Tolerance was advised.[1] In 1049 a provincial council called by the archbishop at Reims excommunicated heretics there. A century later—March 1145—dualist heretics were reported to have come to Liège from Mont-Aimé, some forty-five kilometers south of Reims.[2] And for the following century every archbishop of Reims was obliged to confront the problem.

In 1148 Archbishop Samson (r. 1140–60) held a council in Reims that tried and burned Manichaeans said to have come from Brittany; he called another such council in Reims in October 1157.[3] Samson, however, forbade trial by fire in his diocese and preferred imprisonment to death or mutilation. The cases up to this point seem to have involved rustics, itinerant weavers,[4] or even madmen. However, in 1162 Archbishop Henri de France (1162–75) reported to his brother King Louis VII that while he was traveling in Flanders a group of accused heretics had offered him a bribe of 600 silver marks. In 1172 he participated in a trial in Arras, one of his suffragan dioceses, which burned a heretical cleric. Sometime before 1180 Archbishop Guillaume aux Blanches-Mains (1176–1202) held a trial of two women, dualist heretics. One was a young girl who had rejected the advances of the lascivious young cleric Gervais de Tilbury and had been denounced by him, while the other was her older mentor, who debated her accusers vigorously and knowledgeably. Both were condemned, though the *magistra* was reported to have escaped by magic (accomplices?).[5] In 1182–83, Guillaume presided over a trial in Arras of Manichaeans: "nobles et non-nobles, clercs, chevaliers, ruraux, vierges, veuves et femmes mariées."[6] In 1205 Archbishop Gui Paré (1204–6) held a trial in Braine, less than forty kilometers northeast of Reims, attended by Count Robert II de Dreux and his countess, Yolande de Coucy. A number of heretics were burned, including Nicolas, "the most famous painter in France." This event is all the more significant because the future archbishop Henri de Braine (1227–40), who figures so prominently in the Reims chevet glazing, was the son of Robert and Yolande. He was born at Braine around 1196 and probably spent his childhood there. In 1205 he would have been about nine years old. Whether he attended the heretics' execution with his father and mother is unrecorded.[7]

Innocent III called the Albigensian crusade in March 1208. It was heavily recruited in Champagne, and recruitment had to be renewed annually. Among those who left to fight with Simon de Montfort in the south were Archbishop Aubry de Humbert

(1207–18) in 1209—and in 1210 Count Robert II de Dreux and his brother Philippe de Dreux, bishop of Beauvais, the father and uncle of Archbishop Henri de Braine.[8] In 1215 Uncle Philippe—an infamous warrior—joined the future Louis VIII on his first campaign against the southern Cathars.[9] Philippe de Dreux was his nephew's mentor, and it is likely that Henri de Braine, then aged nearly twenty, was already placed among his uncle's canons at Beauvais, since in the following year (1216) he was awarded his first ecclesiastical post, as treasurer.[10] In 1223 the last archbishop of Reims to precede Henri de Braine, Guillaume de Joinville (1219–26), met with a large group of prelates in Paris to plan the southern crusade. In 1226 he left with Louis VIII for Avignon, participated in the siege there, and died two days before the king did. The peace treaty was signed in April 1229.[11]

Malcolm Barber has noted that during the twenty years of southern crusading the Cathars in northern France "chose to maintain a low profile," with only one trial recorded (Cambrai, a suffragan diocese of Reims, in 1217).[12] In the following decade, the 1230s—that is, for most of the reign of Henri de Braine at Reims—the pursuit of heresy intensified and broadened in scope. The archbishop's council held in Reims, probably in 1230, condemned and burned Echard the baker and forbade the circulation of vernacular translations of the Bible. Echard was not a Manichaean dualist but a poor preacher of the Waldensian sect (the Poor Men of Lyon).[13] It has been argued that many of those condemned in the early years were not Cathars or even heretics but "anticlerics" objecting to abuses of the clergy highlighted by the Gregorian reforms. And certainly the violent anticlericism of the *rémois* bourgeois in the thirteenth century is made vivid by the *Ménestrel de Reims*.[14] A clear list of dualist Cathar beliefs, however, is attributed to heretics probably in La Charité-sur-Loire in Burgundy around 1200, as well as in the description of the Reims council of ca. 1176–80.[15] Barber concludes: "There is no doubt that the orthodox believed that they were battling with adherents of some kind of dualist belief. . . . In the sources these people are variously called Manichaeans, Publicans, Patarines, Piphiles, Textores, Bulgars, and, from the 1160s, Cathars. It seems safe to assume that writers using any of these terms meant some form of dualistic belief."[16]

Whether or not the merchants of Reims were unbelievers or just hostile to perceived abuses by the Church's ministers, two developments had given them real cause for fear by 1230. One was the long association of heresy with weavers. Bernard de Clairvaux (d. 1152) had sermonized against *textores,* and Archbishop Samson's council in Reims in 1157 condemned *abjectissimos textores* explicitly. *Textor* had become a synonym in Champagne for heretic, and the wealth of the merchants of Reims was derived from textiles, chiefly fine linens and serge traded internationally.[17] The second development was the increasing connection between heresy and usury (avarice) by Church and Crown. Preachers—including Philippe, chancellor of the University of Paris, and Jacques de Vitry, papal legate—connected the two in their sermons.[18] Letters of Innocent III in 1199 and 1208 joined the two accusations in specific cases.[19] In the royal accounts of Louis IX, "it is often difficult to determine in a given case whether the word [*Bulgari, bougri, bogrii*] refers to heresy, usury, or unnatural vice; one of these crimes was frequently supposed to involve the others."[20]

Pierre Desportes indicates 1230 as the year when both pope and king turned the spotlight on usury. For Reims the moment was Henri de Braine's provincial council of August 1231. This council ruled that accused usurers would be treated in the same manner as heretics, that is, investigated on rumor, without knowing their accusers and without legal counsel, unless the lawyer would swear—on pain of being barred from the courts—that he believed the one he defended was innocent.[21] In 1231–32 Gregory IX began using Dominicans as inquisitors, and in April of 1233 he commissioned Robert le Petit—the infamous Dominican and converted heretic known as Robert le Bougre—to try heretics in the north, at La Charité-sur-Loire. Labeled "un maniaque homicide" by modern historians, Robert, according to Matthew Paris, tended to confound heretics and usurers and to punish the simple and innocent along with the wicked.[22] Because of complains by bishops, the pope called him off for eighteen months (February 1234 to August 1235) but then reinstated him with broader powers in the provinces of Reims and Sens. Early in 1234 Archbishop Henri de Braine had annulled a lucrative loan made by the city's rich merchants, and had moved his law courts—where heresy trials were held—to the fortified Porte de Mars (fig. 17). Chronicles record that the bourgeois involved began to fear accusation as usurers, and they apparently expected the cathedral chapter to support them. When no support materialized, they turned in frustration on the canons as traitors, and their physical attacks had by November sent the latter into a twenty-six month exile.

Before pursuing here the further trajectory of the inquisitor Robert le Bougre, some discussion is needed about why the canons, who were by and large highly educated and sophisticated men from wealthy families, would have followed "church policy" so submissively. The connection of usury (= avarice) with heresy (= disbelief, idolatry) had a long history in the Church, based on St. Paul's enigmatic assertion that "greed is idolatry" (Eph. 5:5 and Col. 3:5). This argument was maintained in the early Church, also by Bede (ca. 672–735), and even Peter Damian (1007–72).[23] However, of particular importance for the chapter of Reims would have been one of the most popular writings of Archbishop Hincmar (845–82), *De cavendis vitiis et virtutibus exercendis,* written around 860 at the request of Charles the Bald.[24] Hincmar's treatise denounces avarice as the root of all evil, condemns heresy, and recommends penitence and the Eucharist as the surest ways to avoid the consequences of vice. *De cavendis,* which survives in numerous manuscripts from the ninth through the sixteenth centuries, was Hincmar's most frequently copied work and would unquestionably have been known to the canons of Reims. The evidence of the canons' research into various other, much more obscure works of Hincmar for the glazing programs of the nave and the facade suggests that *De cavendis* served them as a foundation for the chevet program of the 1230s. Chief among its main themes are disbelief (heresy), avarice (usury), and punishment for the physical abuse of men of the Church.

To return to the immediate threat to the bourgeois of Reims posed by Robert le Bougre: he began a second campaign in 1235 in Châlons-sur-Marne, located forty kilometers to the southeast, where he burned the first group, more than sixty. One accused at Châlons, Jean Chevalier, who managed to establish his orthodoxy, was condemned to elaborate public penance anyway and further warned by the Dominican "that if he ever took usury or visited Lombardy he would be considered as a heretic and treated accordingly."[25] In some ten weeks' time the inquisitor had persecuted his way as far as Cambrai, another suffragan diocese of Reims, where the trial was attended by Archbishop Henri de Braine and his bishops of Cambrai, Tournai, Arras, and Noyon; all but Noyon were also present at the next trial, in Douai. Robert le Bougre then seems to have marched through Flanders, but the climax of his career of terror was a weeklong *auto da fé* in May of 1239 back in Champagne at the fortress of Mont-Aimé, just south of Reims. The castle there, reconstructed in 1210, had no doubt been chosen not only for its history as a center of heresy[26] but for its facilities to accommodate in style a great many dignitaries as well as for its prisons to confine the accused brought from their territories for trial.[27] Present were the archbishop and ten of his eleven suffragans as well as many other prelates, the count of Champagne, and important barons. Between 180 and 187 persons were burned.

Robert le Bougre's career came to an ignominious end, but evidence of exactly when varies from 1239 to 1244–45 or even later.[28] Thereafter the issue of heresy was over in the north, generally speaking. Certainly in Reims—once Archbishop Henri de Braine had died in exile, in July 1240—the canons and the bourgeois hastened to settle differences, lift the excommunication, and establish peace.

APPENDIX 2

Genealogy of Archbishop Henri de Braine

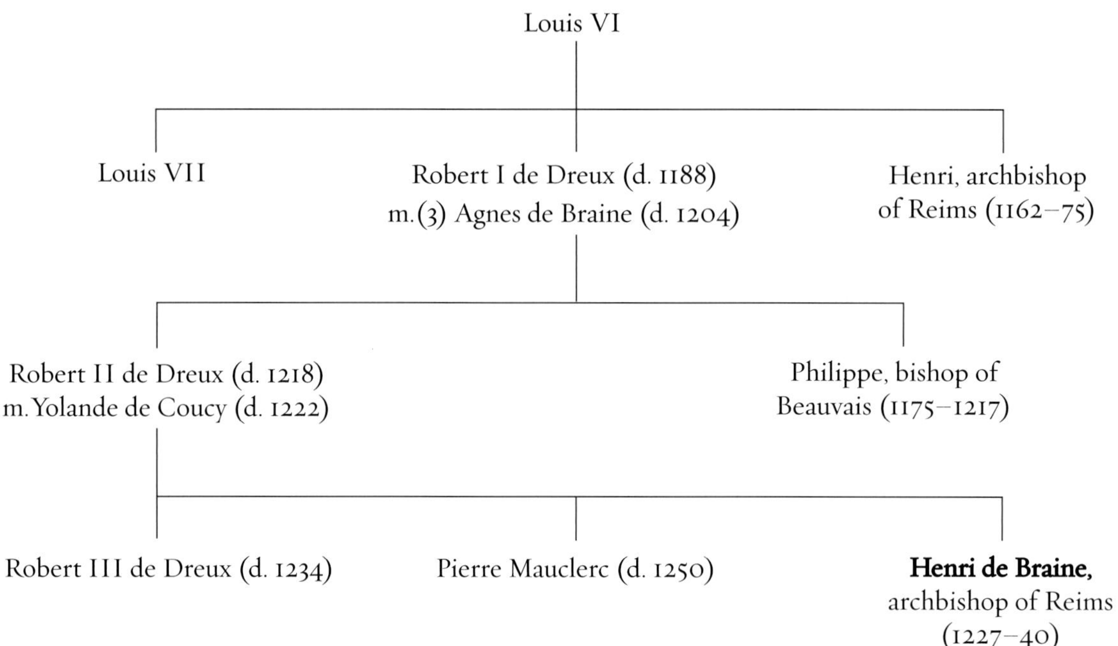

Chart adapted from Painter, *Scourge of the Clergy*. A number of children have been omitted.

APPENDIX 3

Ogive Glass of Bays 100 Through 104

The ogive lights above the narrow hemicycle bays (100 through 104) are large enough to be glazed with subjects, and the high visibility and focal importance of these clerestories suggest that the images would have been selected with care. The original program was probably a Trinity flanked by angels. All but one of these five elements still exist, though not all now in logical locations. The axial bay (100) has, in the upper ogive light, a bust of the Godhead (with cruciferous halo) blessing and holding an orb (see figs. 13, 24). In the place of honor, to dexter, Bay 101, is a bust of Christ blessing, a figure with much less beard than that in Bay 100, in order to distinguish the Son (fig. 28). The dove of the Holy Ghost, which one would expect in the next most honorable position—the ogive of Bay 102—is now in Bay 104, while the ogive light of Bay 102 contains an angel holding a crown, looking in the direction of the axial bay. These two lights seem to have been interchanged at some unrecorded time in the past, previous to the 1840s, when all the ogive lights were recorded as at present (see fig. 8).

The fifth ogive, that of Bay 103, presumably might have had another angel but in fact contains a smaller medallion of the beheading of a kneeling saint by an executioner with sword who grabs him by the hair (see figs. 49, top, and 51). Since the rosace below it is devoted to Thomas (the three lobes to the right and originally the central roundel)[1] and Philip (left lobes), the beheading usually has been identified as the martyrdom of Thomas. Neither Thomas nor Philip, however, was beheaded by a single executioner. Thomas was martyred, but either by a high priest or by a group of soldiers. In Bourges bay 16 (ca. 1210–15), a pagan priest strikes a kneeling Thomas in the midback with a lance.[2] Chartres bay 23 (ca. 1220–30) shows the apostle standing and the priest of the sun striking him in the neck with a sword, as later recounted in the Golden Legend.[3] The Pseudo-Abdias, which I believe to have been the source for the Reims series of rosaces, has Thomas pierced by four soldiers with lances (bk. 9).[4] In short, it is likely that this medallion of a beheading, smaller in scale than the lobes of the rosace below,[5] is a stopgap from the bays of the aisle windows, which are narrower than the clerestories. The glass of the ground floor was removed in the early eighteenth century, but some of it was saved to make repairs in the remaining windows.[6]

The ogive images in most cases can be connected stylistically to the lancets of the hemicycle beneath them. The Godhead in Bay 100 (figs. 13, 24) closely matches the lancets below in the red/blue palette. Its blue ground leaded in a latticework also appears below, as does the facial painting: eyes with both the pupils and irises indicated (cf. the archbishop in Bay 100), long straight nose, covered ears. The halo in the ogive, however, contains jewels, and the long drooping mouth is leaded into the beard area. These details do not appear in Bay 100 but are found in 101, which was in my opinion the next bay to be made. This suggests that the glazier of Bay 101 produced at least part of the bust in the ogive of Bay 100, perhaps on the cartoon of the glazier of the Bay 100 lancets.

The ogive light of Bay 101 contains a bust of the blessing Christ, second person of the Trinity (fig. 28). The artist and design differ from those of both Bay 100 and the lancets of Bay 101. The ground here is adorned with curving foliage like the borders below, but the shape of the face, the enlarged eyes, and the leading across the eyebrows all resemble these same features in the lancets of Bays 103 and 104.

The dove of the Holy Ghost (now in Bay 104 but presumably intended for Bay 102; barely visible in fig. 39) contains a simple network ground of white against red. This type of latticework ground appears in the left lancet of Bay 101, in red against blue. The red ground behind the dove and the red ground of the latticework are unusual at Reims, appearing otherwise only in a small area of Bay 101 (behind the bishop's head), as well as in the unique rosace of 107 and one of the apostles of Bay 110 (right lancet).

The angel in Bay 102 (fig. 34, top) is framed in a lozenge flanked by a slightly more elaborate latticework ground, and the same ground appears in the ogive of Bay 103 (the smaller medallion of the beheading). This kind of latticework is found only in Bay 108, a network of red against blue, with white scintillants in the corners.

As stated above, these ogive images all appear in the Cahier and Martin engraving published in the 1840s (fig. 8). Until the glass is deposed for examination, it is impossible to guess whether the several anomalies result from restoration over the centuries or might reflect part of the breakdown of the chevet program that one observes beginning with Bay 105.[7] In any case, I do not believe that the smaller medallion of the beheading was intended for Bay 103, or indeed for any location in the clerestories. An original program featuring the Trinity over the hemicycle bays is most probable.

APPENDIX 4

The "Spanish Connection": Legends of the Apostle James, Translations by Pierre de Beauvais, and the Family of Archbishop Henri de Braine

Because St. James receives such unexpected and unusual iconographic treatment in Bay 101 of the Reims chevet, immediately adjoining the axial bay containing the likeness of Archbishop Henri de Braine, this appendix investigates the possible interests of the prelate's family in Compostela and the Jacobus legend and cult. The archbishop's uncle and mentor, Philippe de Dreux, bishop of Beauvais, made the pilgrimage to Compostela in 1182, at the beginning of his episcopate.[1] This famously bellicose cleric also participated vigorously in several crusades to the Holy Land as well as two against the Albigensian heretics, was captured and imprisoned by the English, and fought in the Battle of Bouvines. Somehow he also found time to amass an impressive personal library, which at his death in 1217 he willed to his nephew Henri, who was then in his first ecclesiastical post, as treasurer at Beauvais cathedral.[2]

Bishop Philippe's pilgrimage may have provided an occasion to make some additions to his library, as Max Berkey suggests.[3] One may have been the *Historia Compostellana,* a work begun ca. 1111–13 and continued by several writers. The final author was Girardus (d. ca. 1140), a canon and teacher of Santiago who had originated in Beauvais.[4] Girardus extensively reorganized the previous matter in addition to incorporating new material, including a "slightly reworked *Translatio Beati Jacobi,*" the popular account—in the form of a letter attributed to Pope Leo—of the translation of the apostle's remains from Jerusalem to Compostela.[5] Girardus identifies himself in book II, chapters 6, 8, 10, and 19, and his French name supports the supposition that he is the speaker in book I, chapter 109, "who wishes during the communal revolution of 1117 he were back in Beauvais."[6] Bishop Philippe, newly consecrated, may have been drawn to this *gesta* as the product of a priest from his diocese of Beauvais.

Another work that may have come to Bishop Philippe's attention in Santiago is the *Codex Calixtinus,* a five-volume composite dated from around 1137 to before 1173.[7] The earliest exemplar is a luxurious illuminated manuscript of that date (or those dates) in the cathedral archives of Santiago de Compostela. Book I presents the liturgy for feasts of St. James, including the sermon *Veneranda Dies* (see below). Book II presents twenty-two miracles of the apostle from 1080 to 1135. Book III provides several versions of the *translatio* of the apostle's relics from Jerusalem to Spain. Book IV is the famous and popular Pseudo-Turpin, "a magical chronicle of Charlemagne's fabulous campaigns in Spain."[8] And book V is the well-known Pilgrim's Guide.

We are on firmer ground concerning the bishop's library in discussing the translations made for him and his family over some years by Pierre de Beauvais. While Pierre's precise identity is unknown, his name is attached to some dozen works, including a bestiary composed for Bishop Philippe (d. 1217) and a *Mappemonde* for his elder brother Count Robert II de Dreux (d. 1218).[9] Three works associated with Pierre's name present material about St. James and Charlemagne and matter found in *Codex Calixtinus,* books II–IV. Pierre did not work from the Latin texts as found in the *Codex Calixtinus,* however, which suggests that while Bishop Philippe may have learned of the *Codex Calixtinus* in 1182, he did not bring home a copy of that work from his pilgrimage.[10]

In 1212 at Beauvais, in the time of Bishop Philippe, Pierre specifies that he was commissioned by the countess Yolande to produce a French version of the *Translation and Miracles of Saint Jacques,* the matter of books II–III of the *Codex Calixtinus.*[11] The patron is now usually identified as Yolande de Coucy, sister-in-law of Bishop Philippe—that is, wife of Count Robert II and mother of Henri de Braine.[12] Another work by Pierre is the *Voyage de Charlemagne à Constantinople,* his translation of the Latin text known as the *Descriptio.*[13] The purpose of the Latin *Descriptio* was "to authenticate and to make famous above all rivals" the nail and crown of thorns of Charlemagne given to Saint-Denis, and Pierre states at the beginning of his translation that he found his source at Saint-Denis.[14]

Also at the beginning of Pierre's *Voyage,* St. James is inserted as agent. The *Voyage* (recounting Charlemagne's exploits to the east) is paired in the manuscript tradition with Pierre's adaptation of the Pseudo-Turpin (recounting Charlemagne's exploits to the west, in Spain) in the French translation made by one Johannes, which Pierre also reports to have found at Saint-Denis.[15] Of the eight French translations made of the rousing Turpin saga in the thirteenth century, the Johannes version (as made popular by Pierre de Beauvais) is the second, dated no later than 1205.[16] The Turpin name, familiar from the *Chanson de Roland,* was identified with the historical figure (Tilpinus, Tulpinus) who had been a monk and officer at Saint-Denis before his election ca. 751 as archbishop of Reims.[17]

The bellicose reputation of Bishop Philippe de Dreux of Beauvais strongly suggests that he would have felt real kinship with the warrior-prelate who was Pseudo-Turpin. In 1202–4 he was one of the candidates—and the one backed by King Philippe Auguste—contending to fill the vacancy of the archbishopric of Reims; the post had been held previously by their uncle, the prince Henri de France (d. 1175). Indeed he was elected archbishop, but his election was ultimately disputed on the basis of his warlike repute.[18] It is hard to imagine a more logical moment for him to acquire a French translation of the Pseudo-Turpin from his customary author Pierre de Beauvais.

Finally, the "Spanish connection" of the family of Archbishop Henri de Braine may explain a rare detail in the rosace devoted to James (Bay 101, central roundel, fig. 30). The saint and Christ sit side by side, each grasping one end of the same bicolored staff or pole. As discussed in chapter 2, the scene has frequently been misidentified. It visualizes a local folk belief circulated among Santiago pilgrims that Christ gave James a branch half stripped of bark, saying that those who came to his sanctuary in the spirit of prayer would be cleansed of sin as the branch had been cleaned. The "fabula" is among those castigated in the sermon *Veneranda Dies,* found in book I, chapter xvii, of the *Codex Calixtinus.*[19] Reims is one of the earliest examples of this rare scene.[20] The theme does not appear in texts, and it seems to have quickly merged with the introduction of James's pilgrim staff in the later thirteenth century. It does appear to have gained currency in Reims, however, on the evidence of the *Ménestrel de Reims* (fl. before 1260). One of the most popular oaths of his many chivalric characters is "Par la lance saint Jaque!"[21]

APPENDIX 5

Pierre de Beauvais and the Bestiary

Pierre de Beauvais, who was introduced in appendix 4, composed a French version of the Latin bestiary known as the *Physiologus* for his patron Philippe de Dreux, bishop of Beauvais.[1] Bishop Philippe, elected in 1175 and consecrated in 1180, died in 1217. Pierre's *Bestiaire* exists in two forms, a "short version" found in four manuscripts, and a "long version" known in five plus two leaves from a sixth. The "short version" manuscripts are as follows:[2]

Paris, BnF, nouv. acq. fr. 13521, fols. 22r–31r (late thirteenth century)
Paris, BnF, fr. 834, fols. 39r–48v (beginning of the fourteenth century)
Paris, BnF, fr. 944, fols. 14r–34v (beginning of the fifteenth century)
Louvain, Bibl. der Godgeleerdheid, Fonds Groot-seminarie Mechelen 32, fols. 1r–23r (fifteenth century)

The "long version" exemplars:[3]

Paris, Arsenal 3516, fols. 198v–212v (ca. 1267?) (figs. 128, 135)
Ex-Phillipps 6739, 51 fols. (late thirteenth century) (present location unknown)[4]
Montpellier, Bibl interuniv., Section médicine, H 437, fols. 195r–250r (1340–41)
Vatican, Biblioteca apostolica vaticana, Regina lat. 1323, fols. 2r–36r (1475)
Brussels, Bibliothèque royale, II 6978, fols. 22r–62v (1482)

Bishop Philippe is named as the patron in one of the "short version" manuscripts (Paris, BnF, fr. 944).[5] This dedication is repeated in all five of the "long versions."[6] Another "short version" manuscript (Louvain, BG, Mechelen 32) names the patron as "Conte Robert," most probably Philippe's elder brother and devoted companion in arms, Robert II de Dreux (d. 1218).[7] Count Robert was the father, and Bishop Philippe the uncle and mentor, of Henri de Braine, archbishop of Reims from 1227 to 1240, and the bishop willed his extensive library to his nephew.[8] For these reasons I suggest in chapter 4 that Henri de Braine owned a copy of Pierre de Beauvais's *Bestiaire,* either his uncle's manuscript willed to him in 1217 or one made for other members of the family, perhaps as gifts. Some of the archbishop's manuscripts may have come to the cathedral upon his unexpected death in exile, in July 1240.

The relationship of Pierre de Beauvais's "short version" *Bestiaire* to the "long version" has puzzled scholars for over a century, even the basic question of which came first. The "short version" is now believed to have been the original, and must date before the death of its patron, Bishop Philippe, in 1217. The same dedication as well as the thirty-eight chapters of the "short version" appear in the "long version," expanded to a total of seventy-two—that is, nearly doubled in the number of creatures. Based on study of the added material, Craig Baker has now dated the "long version" between 1246 and 1268 and attributed it, in spite of its text naming the author as Pierre de Beauvais, to an anonymous writer.[9] Thus Archbishop Henri de Braine's hypothetical manuscript would have been a "short version" *Bestiaire.*

The earliest of the four exemplars of the "short version" (Paris, BnF, nouv. acq. fr. 13521) is dated to the late thirteenth century.[10] It is also the only one of the four to be illuminated, although French-language bestiaries normally were.[11] On the other hand, of the six "long version" manuscripts existing in whole or in part, only the two fifteenth-century exemplars are unillustrated. The earliest is Paris, Arsenal 3516, a through-composed volume, the script and miniatures (those not cut out) consistent throughout, dated 1267 or possibly earlier.[12] It seems fairly certain that the archbishop's hypothetical manuscript would have been illuminated.

Among the texts other than the bestiary that are included in Arsenal 3516 is "L'estoire d'Adan" (fols. 4r–6v), which is a part of the *Bible anonyme,* a twelfth-century work by an anonymous monk of Saint-Denis.[13] Illustrating this section of Arsenal 3516 are the Genesis scenes described in chapter 4 (figs. 136–40), which are so close to their counterparts in the Reims north rose. The same text of the *Histoire d'Adam* with the same scenes illustrated also appears in another "long version" manuscript: Montpellier, H437 (dated 1340–41).[14] The connection of this Genesis text with Saint-Denis is significant because, as Paul Meyer has noted, Pierre de Beauvais states in several works that he did research at Saint-Denis.[15] In other words, it is not unlikely that Pierre's original *bestiaire* (e.g., in the archbishop's hypothetical manuscript) was conjoined to the *Histoire d'Adam* from the beginning. This connection would be in line with Ron Baxter's observations on the development of the bestiary from the *Physiologus,* in the arrangement of chapters "in increasingly legible orders to users familiar with the Genesis myth."[16]

Worth mentioning is one visual oddity that may connect Arsenal 3516 and Montpellier H437 with the Reims north rose, a detail of the image of the caladrius. Folio 199v of Arsenal 3516 has a strange textual addition that Cahier reports as probably an interpolation, since it is written above the line. The caladrius is described as having two straight horns like a goat's. The image in the accompanying miniature had two long horns added later to the bird's head (fig. 128).[17] Similarly, a small horned caladrius illustrates the Montpellier manuscript.[18] The caladrius in the Reims north rose (originally J-9, now K-9, fig. 130) has two small bumps on its head; however, these might simply be areas of missing grisaille paint; certainty would require an examination of the panel dismounted and on a light table.

I have constructed this elaborate hypothesis to explain (a) the unusual and unexpected use of bestiary material in a cathedral rose and (b) the visual similarity between the Genesis scenes of that rose and those in a manuscript containing the *bestiaire* attributed to Pierre de Beauvais, a work associated with the family of Archbishop Henri de Braine. However, Baker's recent assessments of the "long version" of that work demonstrate that a major link is missing—one associating that later version with Pierre's original composition of before 1217. I hope that my observations about the Reims north rose may be of help to textual scholars in investigating that relationship.

APPENDIX 6

King Solomon in Bed (Song of Songs 3:7–8)

The rosace of Bay 121 of the nave depicts the extremely rare scene of King Solomon in Bed (Song of Songs 3:7–8):

7 Behold threescore valiant ones of the most valiant of Israel surrounded the bed of Solomon!
8 All holding swords, and most expert in war: every man's sword upon his thigh, because of fears in the night.

In both Byzantine and Western art this strange scene finds perhaps a half dozen examples in all.[1] It did not occur in art before the twelfth century, and after the mid–fifteenth century it all but disappeared. Moreover, the Reims rosace resembles none of these idiosyncratic artworks in its interpretation or, of course, its style. This appendix surveys the visual examples of this obscure theme with an exploration of their meanings, which can vary considerably from case to case.[2]

The *Hortus Deliciarum* and Byzantine Images

The earliest image in Western art appears to have been in the *Hortus Deliciarum.* This manuscript, destroyed with the municipal library of Strasbourg in 1870, was composed by Herrad of Landsberg, abbess of the Augustinian nunnery of Hohenbourg, Mont-Sainte-Odile, in Alsace, largely between 1175 and 1185.[3] The authoritative pair of volumes edited by Rosalie Green reconstructs and makes available all of this manuscript's images surviving in copies as well as the recorded text inscriptions. A highly eccentric work, the *Hortus Deliciarum* is described by Green as "a great triptych whose centre is a narrative life of Christ," framed by allegorical material. Commencing with Genesis, the first section drew largely on the Old Testament, while the third section concluded with the Last Judgment. Following the central life of Christ, this last portion began with an elaborate Psychomachia, succeeded by a series of rare scenes of King Solomon, including, on folio 204v, the one here under discussion.

Solomon, crowned and asleep, lies on a richly appointed bed behind which stands a horde of warriors in medieval helmets and chain mail (fig. 255). An inscription states that "Rex salomon requiescit in lectulo, id est ecclesia" (King Solomon rests in bed, which is the Church). On the following page (fol. 205r) an explanatory text further elaborated the interpretation. Although the source of the passage was not given, scholars have identified it from book 3 of Rupert of Deutz's *Commentaria in Canticum canticorum* (written 1117–26): "Now what is the bed of the true and truly peaceful King Solomon, who re-established peace between us and the Lord, if it is not that of Him in whom the divine nature was joined with human nature? What is this bed, if it is not Mary's virginal womb for it was there that the Divinity, the Word of God, the Lord, was enclosed and was inseparably united in his unique Person, to the human formed from the flesh of the Virgin?"[4] In the *Hortus Deliciarum* the Solomon scenes following the Psychomachia represent, in general, the peace following the war against vice, and more specifically the union of Christ (antitype Solomon) with his Church, Ecclesia. The two texts noted above, the first relating the bed to the Church and the second relating it to the Virgin, reflect the interpretations of the Song of Songs that were standard up to Herrad's time. The reading of the biblical book as an expression of the love of Christ and the Church (or Christ and the individual soul) was established from the earliest Christian commentary, that of Origen, in the third century. The Marian interpretation, while vastly extended in Rupert of Deutz's treatise, had been introduced in the liturgy of the Virgin's feasts quite early and can be traced as far back as St. Ambrose. In textual exegesis "there is no 'non-allegorical' Latin tradition of Song of Songs commentary."[5] This is true in the Byzantine church as well. The literal interpretations of the late fourth century, by Theodore, bishop of Mopsuestia, and by the Roman Jovinian, were both condemned as heretical. A literal interpretation does not recur until the advent of Protestantism and appears in a Catholic treatise only with Bossuet in the 1690s.[6] It should be emphasized, however, that—unlike the two inscriptions—the image in the *Hortus Deliciarum* (fig. 255) depicts a literal version of the biblical text. The scene is played in modern dress, with twelfth-century armor, but it is played straight.

This is not true of the rare Byzantine images of Solomon's bed, the earliest of which predate Herrad's manuscript by perhaps a generation or more. These are in two manuscripts each containing the same set of six homilies on the Virgin, written by the monk Jacobus of the monastery of Kokkinobaphos (near Bursa, modern Turkey) and probably illustrated in Constantinople. Jeffrey Anderson ascribes their illustration to one artist, whom he dubs the Kokkinobaphos Master; he dates one manuscript (Paris, BnF, gr. 1208) to the artist's early career in the 1120s–1130s, and the other (Vatican, Biblioteca apostolica vaticana, gr. 1162) to his mature years around the 1140s–early 1150s.[7] In these manuscripts the image of the bed of Solomon (fig. 256) is one of a series of Marian typologies or prefigurations forming introductory frontispieces for each of the homilies; the others are Jacob's ladder, Moses and the burning bush, Gideon's fleece, and Aaron's flowering rod. These pictures do not illustrate and are only loosely connected to the text. It is organized to present events of the Virgin's life, many of them apocryphal, and uses (without attribution) passages, chiefly from St. Gregory of Nyssa, that are not at all Marian in interpretation.[8] The commentary of St. Gregory (late fourth century) on the Song of Songs interprets the Sponsa as the soul of man; no Byzantine commentary interpreted the Virgin as the Sponsa until the fifteenth century.[9] However, the Bed of Solomon, as an epithet applied to the Virgin in Byzantine hymns, can be traced as far back as Marian homilies of the early eighth century by St. John of Damascus and others. The two Kokkinobaphos images under discussion are visual metaphors and do not illustrate literally the biblical text of Song of Songs 3:7–8 (see fig. 256). Christ (not his antitype Solomon) lies in the bed, and the sixty armed men are a celestial guard, their long hair bound by the white ribbons appropriate to Byzantine angels.

Is the *Hortus Deliciarum* dependent on such a Byzantine source? Green strongly asserts this position. She notes, besides a general similarity of format, specifically the ornamentation of the bed cover (cf. figs. 255 and 256), which is different from and more elaborate than other beds depicted in Herrad's manuscript.[10] But she does not pursue the logistics. It is almost certain that neither of the two extant manuscripts by the Kokkinobaphos Master served as the model: BnF gr. 1208 was obtained for that collection from the Seraglio Library in Constantinople in the late 1660s, while Vat. gr. 1162 arrived in Rome from the Near East to first appear in that library's catalogue of 1475.[11] Gérard Cames struggled mightily with obscure genealogical and historical data to spin numerous hypotheses of possible contact by Herrad with imagined Byzantine manuscripts, based on the presence—in exile or as Hohenstaufen brides—of various Sicilian and Byzantine princesses in Alsace or southern Germany. Unfortunately, any such proposed connections fell before Herrad's abbacy or in its final year and thereafter, causing him to date the *Hortus Deliciarum* as late as 1205.[12] That view has found little support. Whether the beds in figs. 255 and 256 are similar enough to warrant such nebulous speculation will be left to the judgment of the reader.

Only one other, quite idiosyncratic depiction of Solomon's bed occurs in Byzantine art: a fresco of 1295 in St. Clement, Ohrid (now Macedonia), part of an extended cycle of Marian typologies in the narthex.[13] Placed in a bed under a transparent bedcover, and guarded by a mass of armed soldiers, appears not Solomon or even Christ but a small, square, painted icon depicting the Virgin and Child. Such a peculiar image had no future. The Marian allegory of the Bed of Solomon lived on in Byzantine art in another guise. As late as the eighteenth century a painting manual instructs that the figure of King Solomon must be represented holding in one hand a scroll with Marian inscription and in the other—as a sort of attribute?—a small bed.[14]

The King as Audience: The Capetian Moralized Bible

In contrast to the Marian typologies of Byzantium, the *Hortus Deliciarum* image of Solomon in Bed forms part of a narrative sequence devoted to King Solomon's life. The *Hortus* depiction (unlike its textual commentaries) is literal and "historical," albeit in modern dress. Solomon, antitype of Christ, was also the obvious "historical" prototype of the wise king and in Gothic art is always related to contemporary, earthly royalty. Anointed king with "a horn of oil out of the tabernacle" (3 Kings 1:34, 39, 45), Solomon made a fitting model. Both the French and English kings were anointed in a consecration ceremony as part of their coronation.[15] Like the familiar themes of the Judgment of Solomon[16] and the Throne of Solomon,[17] the rare scene of Solomon in Bed serves, in Gothic art, as a kind of Mirror of Princes.

The luxury volumes known as *Bibles moralisées,* four of which were produced in France in the first half of the thirteenth century, have always been associated with princes. Their very cost would suggest as much. Suzanne Lewis believes that they were most probably produced at the abbey of Saint-Victor in Paris, while John Lowden "demolishes any notion that the texts that accompany the images were fashioned by learned masters of the University of Paris, or indeed by anyone of much learning at all."[18] The third and fourth Moralized Bibles are of importance to this study. They contain the scene of Solomon in Bed, and both may have been commissioned by Queen Blanche de Castille (d. 1252).[19] The third Bible, a lavish three-volume work in Toledo (Tesoro del Cabildo de la catedral, MSS 1–3), was most probably made for her son Louis IX during his minority under her regency between 1226 and 1234.[20] Solomon in Bed appears on folio 77 of volume 2. The fourth Moralized Bible, begun later but finished in conjunction with the third, is dated around 1235. Lowden believes that it was made for Louis IX's wife, Marguerite de Provence, while Daniel Weiss has argued that it was taken on Louis's Crusade in 1248.[21] This Bible is now divided between Oxford (Bodleian, MS 270b), Paris (BnF, lat. 11560), and London (Brit. Lib., Harleian 1526 and 1527), and the scene of Solomon in Bed—a close copy of Toledo's—appears within the Song of Songs in the Paris manuscript, folio 77v (fig. 257). Nine armed guards surround the sleeping king.

In the Moralized Bibles, each biblical scene is paired with an image and text giving the meaning. The solidly conservative message consistently emphasizes the supremacy of theology over all other knowledge and stresses the dangers of heresy.[22] In the Toledo and Paris manuscripts (fig. 257) the moralizing scene paired with King Solomon in Bed depicts a bishop-saint, enthroned with a book on his knees, flanked by a Dominican and a Franciscan both holding books and preaching.[23] The barefoot figure leaning on the bishop's breast is Christ, since the text states that Solomon's bed signifies eternal beatitude and also the good company of the saints, in which Christ reposes. The text then compares the armed warriors to preachers who bring peace to the

Church, combating enemies visible and invisible—that is, heretics and unbelievers.

The Moralized Bible image, made for regal readers, lived on to the fifteenth century in several versions made for highborn patrons. The Oxford/Paris/London Bible was copied in a manuscript of ca. 1277–94 (London, Brit. Lib., Add. 18719), which was copied with an added French text in a manuscript of 1349–52 (Paris, BnF, fr. 167), which was in turn then copied in the incomplete Paris, BnF, fr. 166, begun in 1402 and still being worked on in 1492. These manuscripts follow their models almost page by page, and Solomon in Bed appears on folio 151v in Add. 18719, BnF fr. 167, and BnF fr. 166.[24]

The figure of Solomon in Bed is a type of Christ in the Moralized Bibles, as in earlier examples, but there is no Marian allusion here. The emphasis has now shifted to the armed warriors and the protection they provide. An example in which the warriors are even more central appears in Gothic England.

The King as Patron: Henry III's Bedchambers

Henry III (1216–72) has been called "one of the most art-loving monarchs that have ever reigned over England," and "that great champion of Gothic art in England."[25] Though survivals of his art commissions are scarce, a considerable number can be discussed on the basis of documents of his reign in the Public Record Office, excavations, eyewitness accounts of occasional visitors, and most notably antiquarian drawings and notes. The scenes depicted in wall painting, stained glass, tiles, and other art forms that he ordered for his castles span a broad range of religious and secular subjects. Among them are Old and New Testament stories, parables, allegories, saints, and history—classical, mythological, and nearly contemporary (i.e., the Third Crusade). His personal preferences have been noted and include Dives and Lazarus, the Old Testament story of Joseph, the Wheel of Fortune and Tree of Jesse, and Edward the Confessor.

Among these repeated subjects in art commissioned by Henry III is that of the militant guardians of King Solomon's bed, which he ordered for two of his bedchambers. The first was for Winchester Castle, where he had grown up, and where on December 29, 1250, a painting of these guards was commanded for the "table of the King's bed."[26] At the time of the commission the King's Hall at Winchester already contained images of a Wheel of Fortune, *mappa mundi,* a series of painted heads, and unspecified Bible stories, while later additions included the saints George and Edward, a good deal of royal heraldry, and possibly a stained-glass panel of the "Nativity of the Blessed Mary." The casual, heterogeneous, and unorganized character of these various decorations is an indication that these were subjects the king liked to look at and probably that the chamber functioned more as private than as public space.

For Henry III's second painting of the guardians of Solomon's bed, Paul Binski's in-depth monograph on the Painted Chamber at Westminster—where the images were located—provides a thorough investigation of the room's structure, layout, and probable function, the arrangement and chronology of its painted decor, and a clearer idea of the reasons for the selection and placement of subjects. Note that King Solomon himself does not appear at either Winchester or Westminster.

Westminster's Painted Chamber,[27] which burned down in 1834, was the upper floor of a rectangular hall of twelfth-century date, oriented east–west. After Henry III had rearranged its apertures, it had windows on three sides, including two new handsome bays on the east wall overlooking the Thames. The main public entrance was at the other end, at the west corner of the south wall, while doors at the eastern end opened onto a chapel and the queen's chamber. The main focus of the room was the bed, "a piece of state furniture" situated between a fireplace and the chapel door at the east end of the north wall, thus diagonally opposite the main entrance. It was a posted, canopy bed, elaborately ornamented, its columns painted green with gilt stars, with matching green bed linens. Green was Henry III's favorite color, and while Binski suggests that the green color might allude to Song of Songs 1:15 (*lectulus noster floridus*), this is not certain.[28] Although the King James Bible (where it is verse 16) has "our bed is green," the Douay-Rheims Bible translates the Vulgate as "our bed is flourishing," and it is often referred to as the flowery bed.

In Henry III's time the room was decorated as follows. On the wall at the head of the bed was an *al secco* wall painting depicting, almost life-size, the Coronation of St. Edward the Confessor, the scene incorporating in its wall area a quatrefoil window opening into the adjacent chapel directly from the bed. Binski's reconstruction of the bed area (fig. 258) shows the mural of St. Edward's Coronation visible to someone in bed when the bed curtains were closed, as well as to viewers in the room when the curtains were pulled open. Flanking the Coronation were two guardians of Solomon's bed. In 1819 the one that then survived (on the left, near the fireplace) was copied by Edward Crocker in watercolors now housed in the Ashmolean Museum, Oxford, and the Department of Prints and Drawings of the Victoria and Albert Museum. The two guardians were the same scale as the Coronation scene and were placed under the same painted arcading. Unlike Edward's Coronation, however, the guardians could not have been seen by someone lying in the curtained bed but appropriately would have remained visible then to any viewers in the room.

In the splays of the window opposite the bed were figures of the same size representing St. Edward holding out a ring as alms to St. John the Evangelist disguised as a pilgrim/beggar. The story was the most popular of Edward's legend,[29] and it certainly related to the scene of his Coronation located over the bed. The remaining window splays depicted large standing figures of Virtues, shown as female figures in crowns and chain mail crushing Vices beneath their feet (that is, the Psychomachia). Binski is surely correct in assuming that the St. Edward scenes, the two guardians, and the victorious Virtues formed an iconographic program reflecting Henry III's concept of his monarchy. In addition to Binski's persuasive arguments, one might note that the ensemble is visually coordinated even in detail,[30] since the Virtues and the guardians have chain mail and shields, and the Virtues and St. Edward wear crowns. The preferred date for this program of images is the last decade of the king's life, from the 1263 fire (that necessitated a new campaign of wall painting) until Henry's death in 1272.[31]

Previously, the *Hortus Deliciarum* had conjoined the Psychomachia (Virtues/Vices) with the scene of the guardians of Solomon's bed. The new factor in the equation is thus St. Edward, and St. Edward was probably Henry III's favorite subject. In addition to a string of his documented commissions at many castles,[32] he named his eldest son after him. Edward the Confessor, to Henry III, was the model of the virtuous and wise king, an English Solomon. The comparison appears in the beautiful manuscript of the saint's life probably made for Henry's queen ca. 1255–60, *La Estoire de Seint Aedward le Rei* (Cambridge, Univ. Libr., MS Ee.3.59), vv. 890–91: "Much he resembles King Solomon of great fame, of great renown."[33]

The cult of St. Edward the Confessor was developed at Westminster in the twelfth century, and all of the Anglo-Norman vitae rely on the only Latin life of wide circulation, written by the Cistercian abbot Ailred of Rievaulx for the translation of the saint in 1163.[34] The comparison of St. Edward to King Solomon, however, is older. It appears in the very first life, composed in 1065–67, just after the saint's death, a work otherwise presenting a view of his reign totally different from Ailred's Anglo-Norman perspective:[35]

You shall be first to sing King Edward's song.
Describe him thus, this English king, so fair
In form, so nobly fine in limb and mind;
How at his coming, with all grief repressed,
A golden age shone for his English race,
As after David's wars came Solomon and peace.

In the Painted Chamber the large scene over the bed depicted St. Edward's Coronation. It is unfortunate that, by the time the early-nine-

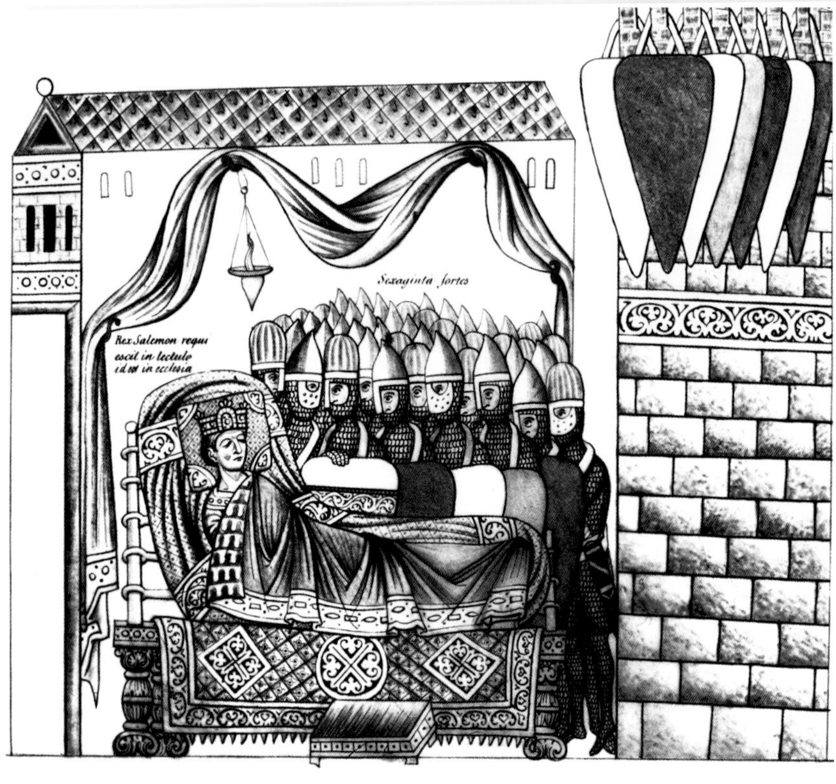

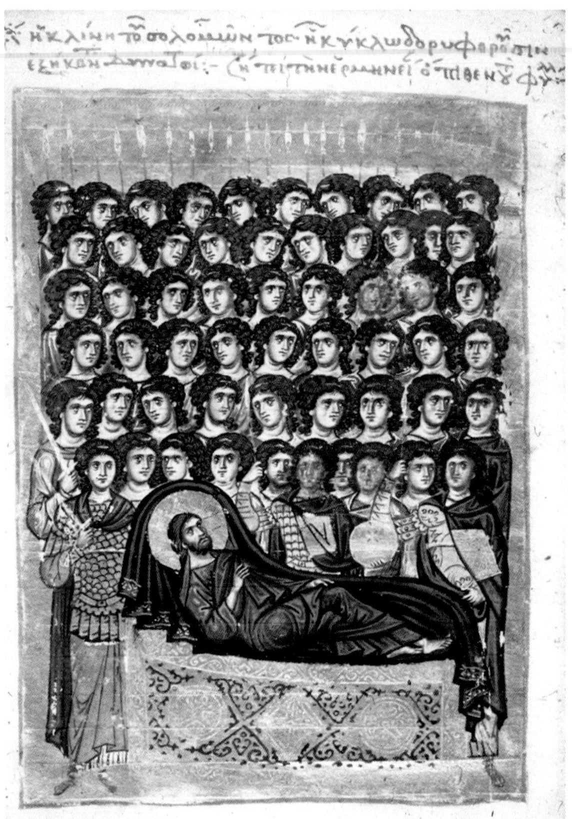

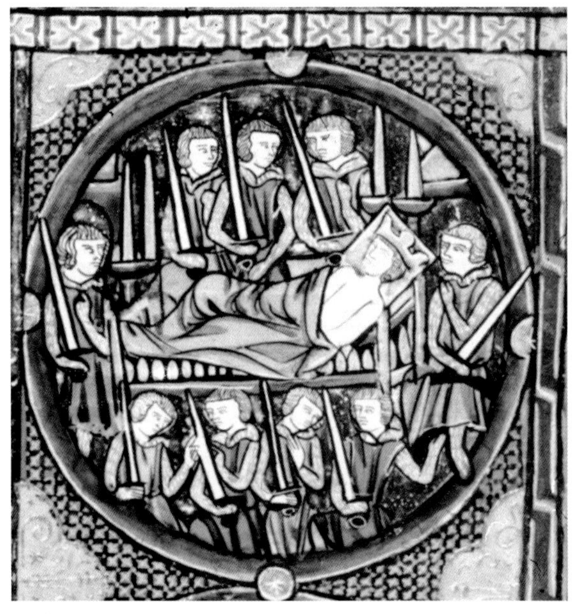

FIG. 255 King Solomon in Bed. Herrad of Landsberg, *Hortus Deliciarum,* fol. 204v, ca. 1175–85 (destroyed). Tracing copy made by Auguste de Bastard d'Estaing ca. 1840 (Paris, BnF, Est. Ad 144a Fol, pl. 85a, 1 [detail]) (after Sirarpie Der Nersessian, "Le lit de Salomon").

FIG. 256 King Solomon in Bed. Homilies on the Virgin, by the monk Jacobus of Kokkinobaphos, Constantinople, ca. 1130 (Paris, BnF, gr. 1208), fol. 109v (after Sirarpie Der Nersessian, "Le lit de Salomon").

FIG. 257 King Solomon in Bed. Moralized Bible, ca. 1235–45 (Paris, BnF, lat. 11560), fol. 77v, detail (after Alexandre de Laborde, *La Bible moralisée conservée à Oxford, Paris et Londres*).

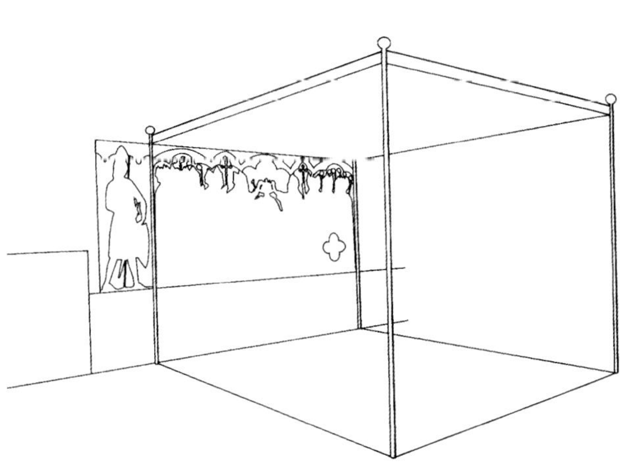

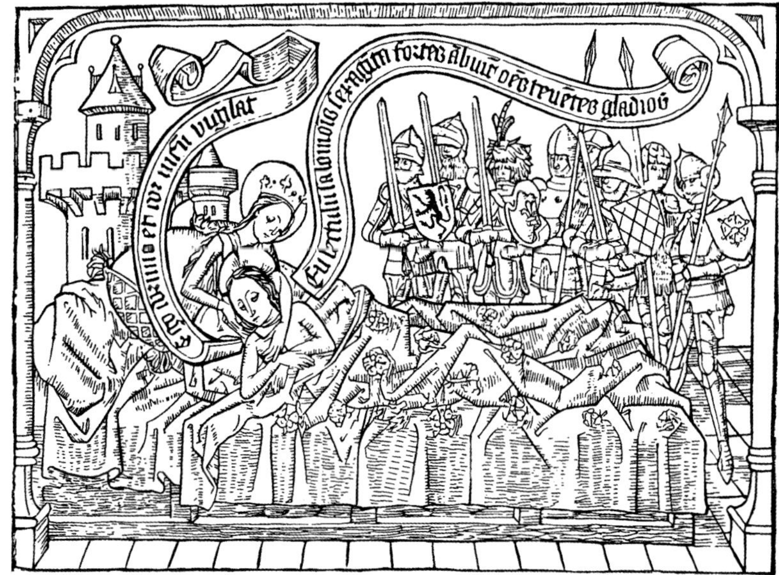

FIG. 258 Westminster, Painted Chamber. Conjectural view of the bed enclosure of the king's chamber, showing murals of the Coronation of St. Edward and (to the left) one of the Guardians of Solomon's bed, ca. 1263–72 (after Paul Binski, *The Painted Chamber at Westminster*).

FIG. 259 King Solomon in Bed. *Canticum canticorum* block-book, ca. 1465 (Munich, Bayerische Staatsbibliothek, Xylograph 32), fol. 15v (after Adrien Jean Joseph Delen and M. Meertens, eds., *Canticum canticorum*).

teenth-century copies were made, the painting had deteriorated to illegibility in the area of the throne. Francis Wormald, in marshaling evidence from several of Henry III's commissions (a new throne, a royal chair for Windsor, the Great Seal) has concluded that the design for the English throne reflected the iconography of the Throne of Solomon as described in 3 Kings 10:18–20 and 2 Chronicles 9:17–19.[36] This connection is built into the coronation ceremony, in the antiphon *Unxerunt Salomonem,* sung during the anointing of the new king, on the text "Zadok the priest and Nathan the prophet anointed Solomon king" (3 Kings 1:38–39, 45).[37] Wormald continues: "Henri III was much interested in defining his position as king, particularly in relation to the anointing, as we know from a letter addressed to him by Robert Grosseteste, Bishop of Lincoln. The king had consulted the bishop about the effect of the anointing and had asked whether it made him like a priest. The bishop replied in the negative."[38] Henry III's disappointment is not recorded.

The King as Subject: Reims, Bay 121 of the Nave

Coeval with the Moralized Bibles and with Henry III's bedroom decorations is the Reims rosace of Bay 121 (fig. 159). In chapter 5, I argue for the greater complexity of sources and meanings for the subject at Reims.[39] The highlighting of King Solomon refers without much doubt to the reigning monarch, Louis IX, often identified by contemporaries with Solomon. The rosace stands adjacent to the transept, thus forming the beginning of the nave series, and appropriately references the initial event of the coronation day, when the king was roused from his bedchamber. The number and depiction of guardians derive from the peers of France (six bishops and six secular lords), newly introduced into the coronation liturgy around 1230. Among the references in the cathedral to the oeuvre of that Carolingian kingmaker Archbishop Hincmar, this scene derives from one of his most eccentric and obscure compositions, a *carmen figuratum* written for Charles the Bald and entitled *In ferculum Salomonis.* The identification of the bed (*lectulus,* vs. 7) with the litter (*ferculum,* vs. 9 and Hincmar's poem) would have been buttressed by Hincmar's own copy of Bede's commentary on the Song of Songs (now Reims, Bibl. mun. 434) as well as by the commentaries of St. Ambrose available in a famous compilation by the abbot Guillaume de Saint-Thierry and kept at his abbey of Saint-Thierry in Reims (now Reims, Bibl. mun. 142, fols. 1–60).[40] In other words, the theme was uniquely tailored to the program of a coronation cathedral, and careful research contributed to its realization.

Coda: The Blockbook *Canticum Canticorum*

The waning Middle Ages saw a return to Marian interpretation of the scene of King Solomon in Bed in the unique blockbook *Canticum canticorum* of ca. 1465. It survives in twenty-nine copies, of two editions, with watermarks of Basel, Metz, and Épinal. At the beginning of the second edition is an inscription in Dutch: "This is the omen of Mary, the Mother of God, which is called in Latin the *Canticum.*"[41] All of its thirty-two images were copied by the Regensburg illuminator Berthold Furtmeyr to illustrate the Song of Songs in his Old Testament manuscript of 1468–72 (Augsburg University, Cod. I.3.2°IV, fols. 76r–83r).[42] Such full illustration of the biblical book is extremely rare, and the blockbook also differs from other devotional blockbooks in that no commentary is provided. The only texts are abbreviated biblical quotations from the Vulgate, included in scrolls within the scenes. These images are arranged as sets of four on each pair of facing pages and are not in strict biblical sequence. While the blockbook form itself can be related to the devotional tradition of the *Biblia pauperum* and *Speculum humanae salvationis,* the *Canticum canticorum* blockbook "does not seem to have had a direct pictorial precedent," and the lack of textual commentary may indicate that its usage was chiefly monastic.[43] Todor Petev's comparison to the Moralized Bibles, however, is unfounded—at least for the image and iconography of the scene of King Solomon in Bed.

Beds are mentioned in three places in the Song of Songs: 1:16, 3:1, and the passage of 3:7 that has occupied this study. Many beds, sixteen in fact, appear in the blockbook, accompanied by a wide variety of texts. In other words, the artist was not producing illustrations of the Song per se but concocting visual images for meditation, clearly for readers who knew the text well. The image of Solomon in Bed appears in the blockbook on the bottom of folio 15v (fig. 259). A crowned and haloed female figure sits in the bed and embraces a recumbent haloed sleeper, guarded by eight knights in full plate armor and weaponry. The two inscriptions make clear that the image is composite. While above the warriors and bed is a scroll with the text "En lectulum salomonis sexaginta fortes ambuint tenentes gladios" (abbreviated from Song of Songs 3:7), the text framing the crowned woman, "Ego dormio et cor meum vigilat" (Douay-Rheims: I sleep and my heart watcheth), is from Song of Songs 5:2. And the bedcover, which is decorated with roses, is a blatant visual reference to the flowery bed, the *lectulus noster floridus,* of Song of Songs 1:16. Petev has pointed out that the image of the couple "would have resonated in mood and iconography with contemporaneous *Andachtsbilder,* like the Pietà."[44] The resemblance to the Virgin embracing the dead Christ was reinforced in the Munich copy of the blockbook (Bayerische Staatsbibliothek, Xylograph 32, fol. 15v), where an artist who provided hand coloring on the images added stigmata to the hands of the sleeping Sponsus.

Da Capo

The survey of images of King Solomon in Bed underlines what has been observed about the Song of Songs: that there never was a tradition in the visual arts for this most commented-upon book of the Bible. Illustration was almost always limited to an illuminated initial at the beginning of the Song of Songs. According to Judith Wechsler, these initials typically showed the Sponsus and Sponsa (Christ and Ecclesia), until the rise of the Virgin's cult in the twelfth and thirteenth centuries substituted an image of the Virgin and Child—and this in spite of the fact that maternity receives no mention at all in the Song's text.[45] The scene of King Solomon in Bed is thus a rare exception, a scene from the Song that was chosen for illustration from time to time, under vastly different circumstances. And excluding oddities in Byzantium, the Western Christian images of King Solomon in Bed do not reflect the Marian change that Wechsler noted, until the blatant Mariology of the unique mid-fifteenth-century blockbook. On the contrary. While the text of the twelfth-century *Hortus Deliciarum* is drawn from the early Mariological writing of Rupert of Deutz, the accompanying image is literal—and in modern dress. There is no Marian element in the Moralized Bible image, the wall paintings of Henry III, or the stained glass of the Reims rosace.

In Christian textual commentary the Song of Songs was always an allegory. The poetry of the Song, however interpreted, has provided a constant stimulus to widely divergent interpretations. Medieval exegesis considered the bed as the Church, the human soul, the eternal repose of heaven, the womb of the Virgin, and so forth, but in art it remains a piece of royal furniture. While interpretations of the warriors ranged from angels to friars preaching against heresy, to the bedtime fairies of King Henry III of England, to the *pairs de France,* they are recognizable as protectors by the chain mail and plate armor of their times. Arguably the most multivalent, original, and profound of these rare and unique images is the rosace of Reims, where the primary message—peace in strength—is one for all time.

APPENDIX 7

Lectulus and *Ferculum* (Song of Songs 3:7, 9)

As discussed in appendix 6, Bay 121 presents King Solomon in Bed (Song of Songs 3:7–8), one of the sources for which, I have argued, was Archbishop Hincmar's *carmen figuratum* entitled *In ferculum Salomonis* (based on Song of Songs 3:9–10):[1]

7 Behold threescore valiant ones of the most valiant of Israel surrounded the bed [*lectulus*] of Solomon!
8 All holding swords, and most expert in war: every man's sword upon his thigh, because of fears in the night.
9 King Solomon hath made him a litter [*ferculum*] of the wood of Libanus.
10 The pillars thereof he made of silver, the seat [*reclinatorium*] of gold, the going up [*ascensum*] of purple; the midst [*media*] he covered with charity for the daughters of Jerusalem.

The question whether Solomon's bed (Vulgate: *lectulus,* Song of Songs 3:7) and his litter (*ferculum,* 3:9) were the same thing or different objects thus deserves investigation. The translations and commentaries on the Song of Songs are voluminous and never ending. The intention of its author must be sought in the original Hebrew, whereas medieval interpretations could draw on a rich accumulation of sources. This appendix indicates briefly the range of interpretative positions in Hebrew commentary and then provides a few examples of Latin exegesis pertinent to the Carolingian and the Gothic eras important to this study. Although the common view by the thirteenth century was that the *lectulus* and *ferculum* were separate entities, in libraries in Reims commentaries of the Fathers as well as contemporary theologians were available to support the view that they were the same thing.

In Hebrew commentary, interpretation seems to hinge on whether verse 6, immediately preceding the text under consideration in this study (Song of Songs 3:7–10), is included in the poetic unit under consideration. Verse 6 is a question: "Who is she [what is this] that goeth up by the desert, as a pillar of smoke of aromatical spices, of myrrh and frankincense, and of all the powders of the perfumer?" If verse 7, concerning Solomon's bed, is taken as the answer to this question—that is, if "who is she" can be translated "what is this"—then the bed of verse 7 is portable or ambulatory and equated with the litter of verse 9.[2] The Hebrew term in verse 7 is *miṭṭāh,* which is used in the Old Testament for both stationary beds or couches and portable litters or biers.[3] Whether it is the same thing as the object in verse 9 is a judgment call, since the Hebrew word for litter in verse 9, *'appiryon,* is a hapax legomenon, and the description of it in verse 10 (mentioning pillars and seat) includes another hapax (Vulgate: *reclinatorium*). The latter has been rendered as "bed," "dais," "roof," "support," and probably a good many other terms. In other words, what Solomon's *ferculum* of verses 9–10 actually was is debatable in Hebrew, and one interpretation is that it was ambulatory and identical with the *lectulus* of verse 7.

The opposite position also has had its advocates. This camp insists that 3:7 is not an answer to the question in 3:6, "but the beginning of a new, thematically self-contained unit," and that the bed and litter are different objects.[4] These scholars translate the litter of verse 9 as a (nonambulatory) "pavilion," possibly even a building or palace, since it has "pillars of Solomon," traditionally assumed to be massive. The elusive hapax that describes it in verse 10 (Hebrew *repidato,* translated as *reclinatorium* in the Vulgate), is taken for upholstery or couch coverings. The interpretation of Solomon's litter as a royal pavilion or throne, and nonambulatory, is heightened by the last phrase of verse 10, which speaks of its paving (the literal translation of the Hebrew is "its interior paved with love from, or by, the daughters of Jerusalem"). A luxury mosaic stone pavement seems indicated, and the obscure term "love" has been considered a distortion from "stone," "ebony," or even "leather."

In the Middle Ages the idea that the "litter" of verses 9–10 was stationary (a bridal canopy or room) is found in Gersonides (d. 1344) and Abraham ben Isaac Halevi (Gerona, d. 1393).[5] Indeed in rabbinical commentaries both the "bed" and "litter" could be portable or stationary. Jerome's choice of the terms *lectulus* and *ferculum* for his translation of the Bible seems to have come about by his use of different sources.[6] His explanation appears in his *Commentarii in Isaiam Prophetam* 3.7: "The Hebrews used words from nearly all the languages: it is like that in the Cantica Canticorum, from the Greek *phoreion,* that is the *ferculum* that Solomon made for himself, and we read it in the Hebrew thus."[7] Jerome translated the Old Testament from the Hebrew (thus, *mittāh* "bed" became *lectulus*), but when faced with the hapax of verse 9, he turned to the Greek Septuagint, where the word is *phoreion* "litter, sedan chair," thus Latin *ferculum.* Christian exegesis has had to contend with the consequences ever since.

Bede, the most important source used by Hincmar in the *carmen figuratum* discussed in chapter 5, groups the *lectulus* and *ferculum* together in his *In Cantica canticorum* 2.3.7: "Therefore he climbed up onto the *lectulus,* the *ferculum,* of Solomon, that is, of the peaceful king, namely, of our Lord and Savior, that is to say the *lectulus* on which [we hope] he may rest forever in peace, truly the *ferculum* from which life is restored by feasts without end."[8] The codex containing Bede's commentary that scholars believe was the one used by Hincmar, with "the regular Hincmar bookmark" on numerous folios, survives and is now Reims, Bibl. mun., MS 434.[9]

A contemporary of Hincmar, Haimo of Auxerre, continues in similar fashion in his *Commentarium in Cantica canticorum:* "As above, concerning Solomon's *lectus,* here now called a *ferculum,* that is to say the holy Church, in which, as it were, the saints of God rest, and, as it were, recline on a *lectus* at the banquet of eternal satiety."[10] By the Gothic era, the standard interpretation of Song of Songs 3:6–11 was that the bride is being transported to the *lectulus* in the *ferculum,* the latter understood by "the majority of interpreters . . . as designating some sort of litter or portable throne."[11] Other meanings included a fixed structure (palace, building of some sort), Solomon's throne (1 Kings 7:7), or even—based on classical Latin usage—a table, dinner tray, or dish.[12] A few commentaries, however, continued to meld the two, for example, Honorius Augustodunensis, *Sigillum Beatae Mariae ubi exponuntur Cantica canticorum:* "Solomon, Christ, the true peaceful king, made for himself a *ferculum,* that is, a *lectus* for a banquet, from the wood of Lebanon."[13] In his *Expositio in Cantica canticorum,* Honorius elaborates thus: "It was fitting for King Solomon [to have] a *ferculum* of the wood of Lebanon, that is, a *lectus* of cedar. The columns of this *lectus* he made of silver; the headrest he made of gold; the ascensum, that is to say the footstool [for climbing onto it], he made of purple."[14]

A slightly later author, Alain de Lille (who died at Cîteaux in 1202), wrote in the same vein: "*Ferculum* in the strict sense. It could be called a tribunal [raised platform] that is carried from place to place or a *lectus,* according to which signification it is explained literally as can be found in Cant."[15]

In the city of Reims in the thirteenth century, however, one probable and authoritative source for the Gothic iconographers to have used would have been the Church Father Ambrose. While Ambrose never wrote a commentary on the Song of Songs as such, he covered almost all of it in one or another of his writings, and his comments were collected in a well-known compilation that was, moreover, easily available in Reims. It has been argued that Ambrose (d. 397) may have used a pre-Vulgate biblical text; Jerome, who began revision of the Gospels and Psalms in 383, left Rome in 385 and translated the rest of the Old Testament ca. 391–406. At any rate, Ambrose discusses the *ferculum* of verse 9 as a bed (*De virginibus* 3.5): "For Solomon made himself a *lectus* from the wood of Lebanon. Its columns were of silver; its armrests [?] were of gold; and its back was a layer of gems. What is this *lectus,* if it is not a type of our body?"[16]

Guillaume de Saint-Thierry (ca. 1085–1148), probably during his abbacy, 1119–35, of the monastery of that name at Reims, compiled Ambrose's references into a lengthy and popular collection entitled *Commentarius in Cantica canticorum e scriptis S. Ambrosii.*[17] Guillaume's compilation was easy to use, since it deals with the text of the Song in biblical sequence, and it was famous—he himself referred to it as "opus grande et inclytum."[18] The original manuscript of his compilation was kept at the abbey of Saint-Thierry in Reims, and it survives in that city to this day: now Reims, Bibl. mun., MS 142, fols. 1v–60v.[19]

Thus it is not an unreasonable hypothesis that the Gothic iconographers of the stained-glass program of the Reims nave would have consulted Hincmar's copy of Bede or the famous collection of the commentaries of Ambrose kept at Saint-Thierry. Both of them were, then as now, in the city of Reims.

APPENDIX 8

Two Seraphim Attributed to Reims in U.S. Collections

Two half-circular panels now in American museums, each depicting the half figure of a seraph, have been published recently with restoration charts and the attribution to the west rose window of Reims cathedral. The first is in the museum of the University of Michigan, Ann Arbor, published in the American volume of the Corpus Vitrearum including that museum.[1] It was purchased for the museum in 1979 from the Paris dealer Brimo de Laroussilhe. The second panel was purchased by the J. Paul Getty Museum, Los Angeles, from the London dealer Sam Fogg and published in his catalogue of 2002.[2] Their measurements are almost identical, around 35–36 cm high and 66–69 cm wide.[3] The knotted neck scarf of the Getty seraph, which is so close to that of the Michigan panel, is modern, suggesting that repairs were made copying one from the other. This supposition gains support from information in the files of the Ann Arbor museum indicating that their seraph was one of a pair at the time of sale. The attribution of the Michigan panel to the facade rose window of Reims originates, apparently, with the late Jane Hayward. The Getty panel follows this presumed provenance based on the close resemblance of the two panels. However, there are several reasons why these two seraphim are unlikely to have come from the Reims west rose.

The rose now has three seraphim in its circle of twenty-four angels, all listed and discussed in the book written by the restorer Paul Simon about his work on the rose from 1906 to 1909.[4] They were the only seraphim in the rose in the nineteenth century, and he accounts for all of the remaining twenty-four angel medallions. He illustrates two of the three seraphim in tracings made to scale from the panels, one before and the other just after the 1886 hailstorm (figs. 245, 246).[5] His restoration was the first, except for makeshift measures, following that damage; the rose was again remade by his son Jacques Simon following the massive destruction of World War I. Paul Simon found the seraphim in locations 3B, 7B, and 11C (see fig. 253). His son Jacques moved the seraph at 11C to 11B so that the three would divide the ring of angels equally into three groups of seven each, and his correction seems justified by the medieval significance of the numbers three and seven.

The seraphim in the Reims rose are not as close to the museum panels as has been suggested. Although exact dimensions are unavailable, they are probably somewhat larger, and they are full circles, not divided by irons into an upper and lower lunette. They do not have acanthus fronds flanking their heads, although this detail is associated with seraphim—for example, in the north rose of Chartres.[6] The Reims seraphim have longer, more widespread upper wings, and their neck scarves fall well below the midpoint of their panels. The middle wings covering the torso do not bulge into a heart shape as those on the museum panels do (and also at Chartres), but conform more to the body, in a shield shape. Finally, since Paul Simon's restoration of the Reims rose was his lifetime achievement and a labor of love, it is difficult to imagine that two panels in as fine condition as the museum seraphim would not have been carefully reinstated in the rose if they had indeed come from there.

Furthermore, there is the question of date. The Michigan panel has been dated ca. 1280–early

1300s, based largely on the presumed architectural chronology of the Reims rose. On the other hand, Michael Michael, discussing the Getty panel, observes: "But the distinctive large eyes and wide faces, combined with the troughed folds of the drapery, suggest an earlier date, and more work on the chronology of the Reims West Rose may be required."[7] He suggests ca. 1275–99. My study of the west-facade glazing in chapter 7 dates the gallery below the rose to ca. 1290–92 and the rose itself no earlier. Physical evidence from the Michigan panel would corroborate Michael's judgment that the museum panels predate 1280. The Michigan glass is described by Virginia Raguin and Helen Zakin as "of a thick hand-blown variety characteristic of the thirteenth century."[8] It measures approximately 0.9 cm in thickness, according to the museum. Fragments that fell from the west rose in the 1886 hailstorm were only from 0.3 cm to 0.5 cm thick.[9] Now, an improvement and refinement in glass production and quality began to appear around 1280, which changed the nature of the craft. Glass after that time was thinner and came in larger pieces, and perhaps not just anyone had the skill to produce it. This change would account for the new specialization in practice; craftsmen now making windows purchased glass from different craftsmen who made and sold the glass from fixed workplaces.[10]

In short, the seraphim in the University of Michigan and Getty Museums are handsome survivors, almost certainly from France and probably datable in the third quarter of the thirteenth century. But they do not come from the Reims west facade.

Notes

Prolegomena

1. Whitney W. Stoddard, *Monastery and Cathedral in France* (Middletown, Conn., 1966), 199; his book was written as an introductory textbook for his students at Williams College and reprinted numerous times. The following appreciation is drawn from his remarks on pages 197–209. The dimensions he gives for Reims are 123 ft. (37.5 m) to the vault, 44½ ft. (13.5 m) wide; for Chartres, 7 ft. (2 m) less in height, 53½ ft. (16.3 m) wide.

2. Paul Simon, "Notes sur les vitraux de la cathédrale de Reims," *Congrès archéologique* 78, pt. 2 (1911): 294 n. 1. Recensement IV, 386–90, gives 10.50 m for the height of the chevet and transept clerestories, 11 m for those of the nave. If these height measurements do not include the rosaces, the discrepancy disappears. The Recensement width measurements vary only slightly from Simon's.

3. On the fragments, recently discovered, most of them heads from the lower windows, see chapter 1, at note 45. They have been published by Balcon-Berry (Balcon).

4. See my selected bibliography. Reims cathedral is covered in Recensement IV, 383–91.

5. See my selected bibliography, publications under Balcon and Balcon-Berry.

6. On the tracings, see the remarks from the Académie de Reims reprinted in Paul Simon, *La grande rose de la cathédrale de Reims* (Reims, 1911), 84–85. For Simon tracings and drawings reproduced in this book, including those made from panels after restoration, see figs. 13–16, 22, 65, 77–78, 82–83, 115, 127, 179, 193, 203, 220, 241–47, 249, 250.

7. "AVISTA at Kalamazoo 2010: Sylvie Balcon-Berry, Stained Glass and the Chronology of Reims Cathedral," *AVISTA Forum Journal* 20, no. 1/2 (Fall 2010): 66; eadem, "Les vitraux du Moyen Âge," in *La grâce d'une cathédrale: Reims*, ed. Thierry Jordan et al. (Strasbourg, 2010), 236, 536 n. 327, 537 n. 343. The preservation and study of these drawings have long been advocated: Peter Kurmann, "En guise de conclusion: Du 'rémecentrisme' à l'approche pluridisciplinaire," 194, in *Nouveaux regards sur la cathédrale de Reims* ed. Bruno Decrock and Patrick Demouy (Langres, 2008); Anne Prache in *Congrès archéologique* 185 (1977): 44. I proposed this project to the DRAC-Champagne/Ardenne in 1990.

8. Kurmann, "En guise de conclusion," 203 and n. 30.

Chapter 1

1. The sources are cited most completely in Jean-Pierre Ravaux, "Les campagnes de construction de la cathédrale de Reims au XIIIe siècle," *Bulletin monumental* 137 (1979): 7–66. On recent reinterpretations of the documents, see William W. Clark, *Medieval Cathedrals* (Westport, Conn., 2006), 88–92; Jean-Pierre Ravaux, "Le texte de 1241 et son importance dans la chronologie de la cathédrale de Reims," in *Nouveaux regards sur la cathédrale de Reims*, ed. Bruno Decrock and Patrick Demouy (Langres, 2008), 63–66; Jean Wirth, *La datation de la sculpture médiévale* (Geneva, 2004) (see his chaps. 3 and 5 on the document of 1252).

2. Anne Prache, "Le début de la construction de la cathédrale de Reims au XIIIe siècle: L'apport de l'archéologie et de la dendrochronologie," in *Nouveaux regards*, 41–52; Willy Tegel and Olivier Brun, "Premiers résultats des analyses dendrochronologiques relatives aux boulins de construction," in ibid., 29–40. On the vagaries of medieval dating, see Robert Bartlett, *The Hanged Man: A Story of Miracle, Memory, and Colonialism in the Middle Ages* (Princeton, 2004), 55–58.

3. Dom Guillaume Marlot, *Histoire de la ville, cité et université de Reims*, vol. 3 (Reims, 1846), 524. He wrote in French but only published a shortened Latin version (1666–71). The longer original French text first appeared in print in the 1840s. For a survey of the glass and its history, see now Recensement IV, 384–86, more or less accurate.

4. See chapter 4, at notes 132–33.

5. Orin E. Skinner, "Restoring the Stained Glass Treasures of Rheims Cathedral," *American Architect* 131, no. 2520 (May 5, 1927): 559–63, reprinted in *Stained Glass, Bulletin of the Stained Glass Association of America* 22, no. 7 (August 1927): 6–9. See Prolegomena at notes 6–7.

6. The architect Henri Deneux (1874–1969) was in

charge of Reims cathedral from 1915 until his retirement in 1938 and oversaw the postwar excavations and reconstruction. See Delphine Quéreux-Sbaï, "Henri Deneux, restaurateur et photographe de la cathédrale," in *Mythes et réalités de la cathédrale de Reims de 1825 à 1975* (Paris, 2001), 114–23; *Rebâtir Reims: La collection photographique Henri Deneux 1870/1938* (Châlons-sur-Marne, 1988).

7. See, e.g., Louis Grodecki and Catherine Brisac, *Gothic Stained Glass, 1200–1300* (Ithaca, 1984), 117–18, 256.

8. Hans Reinhardt, *La cathédrale de Reims: Son histoire, son architecture, sa sculpture, ses vitraux* (Paris, 1963), 183–92.

9. Kurt Weitzmann, *Illustrations in Roll and Codex: A Study of the Origin and Method of Text Illustration* (Princeton, 1947), 205.

10. John Gage, *Color and Meaning: Art, Science, and Symbolism* (Berkeley and Los Angeles, 1999), 9.

11. See Robert Neuss and Walter Berry, "La cathédrale de Reims: Archéologie du site," in *Reims: La cathédrale,* ed. Patrick Demouy (La Pierre-qui-vire, 2001), esp. 41, 52–59.

12. Anne Prache, *Saint-Remi de Reims: L'oeuvre de Pierre de Celle et sa place dans l'architecture gothique* (Geneva, 1973); Madeline H. Caviness, *Sumptuous Arts at the Royal Abbeys in Reims and Braine: Ornatus elegantiae, varietate stupendes* (Princeton, 1990); Patrick Demouy, "L'image des archevêques dans l'abbatiale Saint-Remi de Reims du XIIe siècle," in *Architektur und Monumentalskulptur des 12.–14. Jahrhunderts, Produktion und Rezeption: Festschrift für Peter Kurmann zum 65. Geburtstag,* ed. Stephan Gasser, Christian Freigang, and Bruno Boerner (Bern, 2006), 627–39.

13. William M. Hinkle, *The Portal of the Saints of Reims Cathedral: A Study in Mediaeval Iconography* (New York, 1965), 28–30, 36–37; Demouy, "L'images" 631–32.

14. The most famous example is *Notre-Dame de la Belle Verrière* at Chartres, the twelfth-century image saved from the fire of 1194 and located at the top of the left lancet of bay 30, in the south chevet. See Chantal Bouchon, Catherine Brisac, Claudine Lautier, and Yolanta Zaluska, "La 'Belle-verrière' de Chartres," *Revue de l'art* 46 (1979): 16–24. Another example comprises fragmentary scenes reset in the north nave of Rouen: Michael Cothren, "The Seven Sleepers and the Seven Kneelers: Prolegomena to a Study of the 'Belles Verrières' of the Cathedral of Rouen," *Gesta* 25 (1986): 203–26. In regard to sculpture, Dale Kinney limits the term "spolia" to works taken from an alien context and employed in a new way: see Dale Kinney, "The Concept of Spolia," in Conrad Rudolph, ed., *A Companion to Medieval Art* (Oxford, 2006), 233–52, with bibliography.

15. Simon, "Notes sur les vitraux," 301–2.

16. See chapter 4, at notes 164–6. On Aubry de Humbert (r. 1207–18), see Pierre Desportes et al., *Fasti ecclesiae Gallicanae: Répertoire prosopographique des évêques, dignitaires et chanoines de France de 1200 à 1500,* vol. 3, *Diocèse de Reims* (Turnhout, 1998), 156–58.

17. Peter Kurmann, *La façade de la cathédrale de Reims: Architecture et sculpture des portails, étude archéologique et stylistique* (Lausanne, 1987), 1:48–59. He dates the six prophets to ca. 1210–15.

18. Pierre Desportes, *Reims et les rémois aux XIIIe et XIVe siècles* (Paris, 1979), 78–82 (Samson), 82–85 (Henri de France and the 1166–67 insurrection), 85–88 (Guillaume de Champagne and the *Willelmine*). For the latter, see also Desportes et al., *Fasti,* 151–53.

19. On these archbishops, see Desportes et al., *Fasti,* 154–61; Desportes, *Reims et les rémois,* 155–56. On Guy Paré at Braine: Caviness, *Sumptuous Arts,* 69–70. On Philippe de Dreux, bishop of Beauvais: Hercule Géraud, "Le comte-évêque," *Bibliothèque de l'École des chartes* 5 (1843–44): 8–36 passim; William Mendel Newman, *Les seigneurs de Nesle en Picardie (XIIe–XIIIe siècle): Leurs chartes et leur histoire,* vol. 1 (Paris, 1971), 227.

20. E.g., Robert Branner, "Historical Aspects of the Reconstruction of Reims Cathedral, 1210–1241," *Speculum* 36 (1961): 23–37; Barbara Abou-El-Haj, "The Urban Setting for Late Medieval Church Building: Reims and Its Cathedral Between 1210 and 1240," *Art History* 11 (1988): 17–41; eadem, "Program and Power in the Glass of Reims," in *Radical Art History, Internationale Anthologie, Subject: O. K. Werckmeister,* ed. Wolfgang Kersten (Zurich, 1997), 23–33, 226–33 (illus.). The basic account is by the historian Desportes, *Reims et les rémois,* 155–67.

21. Pertinent entries in the *Annales de Saint-Nicaise* are translated in Clark, *Medieval Cathedrals,* 236–37.

22. Emile Chénon, "L'hérésie à La Charité-sur-Loire et les débuts de l'inquisition monastique dans la France du nord au XIIIe siècle," *Nouvelle revue historique de droit français et étranger,* 3rd ser., 40 (1917): 304, 321.

23. Because persecution of heresy is not generally associated with the North of France, I have assembled information pertaining to Champagne in appendix 1.

24. Mary C. Mansfield, *The Humiliation of Sinners: Public Penance in Thirteenth-Century France* (Ithaca, 1995), 253, 269–77.

25. Anne Walters Robertson, *Guillaume de Machaut and Reims: Context and Meaning in His Musical Works* (Cambridge, 2002), 34.

26. Patrick Demouy, "Vie d'une cathédrale," in *Reims: La cathédrale,* 68. For the location of the cloister chapel of Saint-Michel, see Desportes et al., *Fasti,* 56, fig. 2.

27. Desportes, *Reims et les rémois,* 167.

28. Caviness, *Sumptuous Arts,* 133–35. For the Chartres south rose, see Recensement II:40. For Henri de Braine's

windows in Saint-Nicaise and Châlons cathedral: Meredith Parsons Lillich, "Heraldry and Patronage in the Lost Windows of Saint-Nicaise de Reims," in *L'art et les révolutions: XXVIIe Congrès international d'histoire de l'art,* vol. 8 (Strasbourg, 1992), 76 and n. 17, reprinted in *Studies in Medieval Stained Glass and Monasticism* (London, 2001), 441–42; eadem, "Remembrance of Things Past: Stained Glass Spolia at Châlons Cathedral," *Zeitschrift für Kunstgeschichte* 59 (1996): 488–93 and figs. 20–21, reprinted in ibid., 231–32, 249–54.

29. Branner, "Historical Aspects," 33.

30. On Juhel de Mathefelon, see Desportes et al., *Fasti,* 162–63; Desportes, *Reims et les rémois,* 167–68. According to Branner, "Historical Aspects," 36, he was "one of the poorest administrators in the history of the see."

31. Desportes, *Reims et les rémois,* 175; Branner, "Historical Aspects," 36.

32. Despite recent and intensive study of BnF, lat. 1246, no consensus has been reached on such important questions as when, where, why, by whom, for whom, and for what reason it was made. I am offering my own judgment on these matters here and in chapter 5.

33. On these archbishops, see Desportes et al., *Fasti,* 163–66.

34. The *vidimus* was discovered by Jean-Pierre Ravaux, who documents the find in "Les campagnes," 11–12 and n. 49. Wirth, *La datation,* 47–49, 289, interprets it as a document required for litigation following the houses' destruction.

35. The glazing craft was changing around 1280, and the quality of glass seems to indicate improvements in the process of glassmaking as well, subjects that have only begun to be investigated. See Meredith Parsons Lillich, "Gothic Glaziers: Monks, Jews, Taxpayers, Bretons, Women," *Journal of Glass Studies* 27 (1985): 87–89, reprinted in *Studies,* 16, 29–31.

36. Patrick Demouy, "Les *pueri chori* de Notre-Dame de Reims: Contribution à l'histoire des clergeons au Moyen Âge," in *Le clerc séculier au Moyen Âge: XXIIe Congrès des médiévistes de l'enseignement supérieur, Amiens, 1991* (Paris, 1993), 139, 141, 143. For Philippe IV's lack of interest in Spain and the resultant disappearance of castles of Castille from glazing, see chapter 7.

37. On Queen Jeanne de Navarre's window at Saint-Nicaise, see Lillich, "Heraldry and Patronage," 75, 85, reprinted in *Studies,* 441, 449–50.

38. Victor Tourneur, *Histoire et description des vitraux et des statues de l'intérieur de la cathédrale de Reims* (Reims, 1857), 59–62; Charles Cerf, *Histoire et description de Notre-Dame de Reims* (Reims, 1861), 2:315–17. The removal of the lower windows may have begun before 1730 and was completed perhaps in 1768.

39. Numerous corroded grisaille fragments have been excavated along the cathedral's north flank, where they were used for fill: Sylvie Balcon-Berry, "Les vitraux de la cathédrale de Reims à la lumière de recherches récentes," in *Nouveaux regards,* 156.

40. Demouy, "Vie d'une cathédrale," in *Reims: La cathédrale,* 92.

41. François de Guilhermy, "Notes sur diverses localités de la France," Paris, BnF, nouv. acq. fr. 6106, fols. 399v–400r. He reports (fol. 398r) another example of the Ascension, showing only Christ's feet, in the rosace of Bay 137, now lost. See fig. 161. That glass dated later, ca. 1280.

42. Balcon-Berry, "Les vitraux," 152; Sylvie Balcon, "Les vitraux," in *Reims: La cathédrale,* 335–42.

43. Robert Deshman, "Another Look at the Disappearing Christ: Corporeal and Spiritual Vision in Early Medieval Images," *Art Bulletin* 79 (1997): 518.

44. Illustrations: Émile Van Moé and Jean Lafond, "Le psautier Leber 6 de la Bibliothèque de Rouen," in *Les trésors des bibliothèques de France,* vol. 1 (Paris, 1926–27), 88–97, fol. 218v (unnumbered plate); Henry Martin, *Les joyaux de l'Arsenal,* vol. 1, *Psautier de saint Louis et de Blanche de Castille* (Paris, 1909), pl. XXXIII; Victor Leroquais, *Le psautier de Jully: 1re moitié du XIIIe siècle* (Lyon, 1923), pl. XI. The Jully Psalter includes St. Francis, canonized in 1228; for the other dates, see Robert Branner, *Manuscript Painting in Paris During the Reign of Saint Louis* (Berkeley and Los Angeles, 1977), 204, 208.

45. Balcon-Berry, "Les vitraux," 170–71, 211; eadem, "Moyen Âge," 232, 234–5; Balcon, "Les vitraux," 339, pls. 133–35; eadem, "Marne: Cathédrale de Reims, découverte de vitraux du début du XIIIe siècle," *Bulletin monumental* 156 (1998): 179–81. See also *Mythes et réalités de la cathédrale de Reims de 1825 à 1975* (Paris, 2001), 127, fig. 4.

46. Accession C8e1. See Elizabeth Emery, "The Martyred Cathedral: American Attitudes Toward Notre-Dame de Reims During the First World War," in *Medieval Art and Architecture After the Middle Ages,* ed. Janet T. Marquardt and Alyce A. Jordan (Newcastle upon Tyne, 2009), 331; Madeline H. Caviness, "Boston: Isabella Stewart Gardner Museum," in *Stained Glass Before 1700 in American Collections,* vol. 1, *New England and New York (Corpus Vitrearum Checklist 1),* Studies in the History of Art, vol. 15, Monograph Series 1 (Washington, D.C., 1985), 44. The entry, unillustrated, states in error that the panel contains three heads.

47. See, e.g., Peter Kurmann, "Un colosse aux pieds d'argile: La chronologie de la sculpture française du XIIIe siècle repose-t-elle sur des dates assurées?" in *Épigraphie et iconographie: Actes du colloque tenu à Poitiers les 5–8 octobre 1995,* ed.

Robert Favreau (Poitiers, 1996), 143–51; Wirth, *La datation,* 103–23 and 285–93 passim; Fabienne Joubert, "Proprement gothique?" in *Architektur und Monumentalskulptur,* 723–39; Paul Williamson, *Gothic Sculpture, 1140–1300* (New Haven, 1995), 51–52.

Chapter 2

1. In 1995 a partial view of the Bay 101 rosace appeared in Humbert Jacomet, "L'énigmatique odyssée de saint Jacques," *Archeologia* 318 (1995): 62; and the following year I published two details (of the rosaces of Bays 103 and 104) in "Remembrance of Things Past: Stained Glass Spolia at Châlons Cathedral," *Zeitschrift für Kunstgeschichte* 59 (1996): 491, 493, figs. 23–24, reprinted in *Studies in Medieval Stained Glass and Monasticism* (London, 2001), 234. The rosaces were not included in the scale montages of photographs made in the Archives photographiques in Paris after World War II.

2. Victor Tourneur, *Histoire et description des vitraux et des statues de l'intérieur de la cathédrale de Reims* (Reims, 1857), 50–53; Charles Cerf, *Histoire et description de Notre-Dame de Reims* (Reims, 1861), 2:270–81; Hans Reinhardt, *La cathédrale de Reims: Son histoire, son architecture, sa sculpture, ses vitraux* (Paris, 1963), 183–84. Recent sources repeating these mistakes include Recensement IV:383–89 passim and the oft-reproduced chart found, for example, in Pierre Desportes et al., *Fasti ecclesiae Gallicanae: Répertoire prosopographique des évêques, dignitaires et chanoines de France de 1200 à 1500,* vol. 3, *Diocèse de Reims* (Turnhout, 1998), 49.

3. Émile Mâle, *Les saints compagnons du Christ* (Paris, 1954), 211, refers to "the rosace of Simon and Jude"; however, the rosaces of Simon (Bay 106) and Jude (Bay 105, in which Simon appears twice) face each other across the chevet. Similarly, Louis Réau cites the Reims rosace of Judas Thaddeus; however, Jude shares the rosace of Bay 105 with Matthew: Réau, *Iconographie de l'art chrétien,* vol. 3, pt. 2 (Paris, 1958), 765.

4. Walter Horn and Ernest Born, *The Plan of St. Gall* (Berkeley and Los Angeles, 1979), 1:131, figs. 89 (Merovingian), 90 (eighth century), 91 (thirteenth-century monastic barn), and 92 (Pennsylvania Dutch barn). The authority on European examples is Patrik Reuterswärd; on the six-petaled compass rosette, see his "Forgotten Symbols of God (II)," *Konsthistorisk Tidskrift* (1985): 17–63—reprinted (as essay no. 3, paginated separately) in *The Forgotten Symbols of God,* Stockholm Studies in History of Art, 35 (Uppsala, 1986)—esp. 48–50. Historians of Byzantine art have worked more extensively on such symbols. According to Carl Sheppard, these "motifs up to at least the seventh century possessed meaning. Afterward they retained the ability to evoke qualities of meaning without being specific": Sheppard, "Byzantine Carved Marble Slabs," *Art Bulletin* 51 (1969): 66 n. 10. See also Henry Maguire, "Magic and Geometry in Early Christian Floor Mosaics and Textiles," *Jahrbuch der österreichischen Byzantinistik* 44 (1994): 265–74 passim, on the eight-part rosette (which he calls an eight-rayed ring sign) and six-part rosette (a star made of a circle with a dot in the middle and triangular projections around the circumference). His fig. 2 includes both types.

5. Adolf Katzenellenbogen, "Tympanum and Archivolts on the Portal of St. Honoré at Amiens," in *De Artibus Opuscula XL: Essays in Honor of Erwin Panofsky,* ed. Millard Meiss (New York, 1961), 1:281. On routine episcopal duties that fall under these three categories, see Michael W. Cothren, *Picturing the Celestial City: The Medieval Stained Glass of Beauvais Cathedral* (Princeton, 2006), 52–54.

6. Katzenellenbogen, "Tympanum," 287–88, 290, citing Sts. Ambrose and Augustine and, closer in time, Peter Lombard.

7. In both cases the Flagellation is on the left, whereas at Reims it is on the right. At Chartres (bay 37, ca. 1205–15), where the Flagellation is also on the right, the Crowning with Thorns appears to the left: Colette Manhès-Deremble, *Les vitraux narratifs de la cathédrale de Chartres: Étude iconographique,* Corpus Vitrearum, France, Études, II (Paris, 1993), 352–53, medallions 9 and 10. For Troyes, see Elizabeth C. Pastan and Sylvie Balcon, *Les vitraux de choeur de la cathédrale de Troyes (XIIIe siècle),* Corpus Vitrearum, France, II (Paris, 2006), 253, fig. 355. For Sens, see ibid., 292, fig. 253, where the Crowning with Thorns is in the row below.

8. For ninth-century examples, see Gertrud Schiller, *Iconography of Christian Art,* vol. 2 (Greenwich, Conn., 1972), 66: Utrecht Psalter (Utrecht, Universiteits-bibliotheek MS 32), fol. 85v, ca. 830 (Schiller, fig. 359); Stuttgart Psalter (from Saint-Germain-des-prés) (Stuttgart, Landesbibliothek, Cod. Bibl. 2°23), fol. 43v, ca. 820–30 (Schiller, fig. 225).

9. For Saint-Julien-du-Sault, see Pastan and Balcon, *Troyes,* 254, fig. 215; for Sens, ibid., 254, fig. 214.

10. For Chartres, see Manhès-Deremble, *Les vitraux narratifs,* 41, fig. 13 (medallion 12). For the Sainte-Chapelle: Louis Grodecki in Marcel Aubert et al., *Les vitraux de Notre-Dame et de la Sainte-Chapelle de Paris,* Corpus Vitrearum Medii Aevi, France, I (Paris, 1959), pl. 49 (H31 and H32).

11. Émile Mâle, *Religious Art in France: The Thirteenth Century,* 458 n. 52. For Bourges, see Recensement II:170; Hervé Benoît, *Les grands vitraux du déambulatoire de Bourges* (Paris, 1995), pls. K and P (after p. 28).

12. For Saint-Julien-du-Sault and the Lyon south rose, see Recensement III:168 and 299 (bay 116); for Lyon, see also Painton Cowen, *The Rose Window: Splendour and Symbol*

(London, 2005), 36 (ill. cut off at bottom of the page). For Troyes and Sens: Pastan and Balcon, *Troyes,* 253, fig. 355; 292, fig. 253. For the Sainte-Chapelle: Aubert et al., *Les vitraux de Notre-Dame,* 203–4 (H38, H45, H46). For the Tours windows: Recensement II:123, 126; Henri Boissonnot, *Les verrières de la cathédrale de Tours* (Paris, 1932), pls. XVIII and VIII (drawings). For the Lorraine examples: Meredith Parsons Lillich, *Rainbow Like an Emerald: Stained Glass in Lorraine in the Thirteenth and Early Fourteenth Centuries* (University Park, 1991), 24, 31; pls. II 6a, II 6c. An extremely late example is at Saint-Père de Chartres (bay 217, ca. 1305–15): eadem, *The Stained Glass of Saint-Père de Chartres* (Middletown, 1978), pl. XII (opp. p. 192); Recensement II:52.

13. For Poitiers, see Louis Grodecki, *Le vitrail roman* (Fribourg, 1977), 71–74, 286.

14. William H. Forsyth, *The Entombment of Christ: French Sculpture of the Fifteenth and Sixteenth Centuries* (Cambridge, Mass., 1970), 9. The motif of the three holes became increasingly decorative as artists did not understand its *raison d'être:* see Lillich, *Saint-Père,* 152 and notes.

15. Anne Prache, "Le début de la construction de la cathédrale de Reims au XIIIe siècle: L'apport de l'archéologie et de la dendrochronologie," in *Nouveaux regards sur la cathédrale de Reims,* ed. Bruno Decrock and Patrick Demouy (Langres, 2008), 42, 46–47.

16. Louis Grodecki, "A Stained Glass *Atelier* of the Thirteenth Century," *Journal of the Warburg and Courtauld Institutes* 11 (1948): 108 n. 4; Meredith Parsons Lillich, *The Armor of Light: Stained Glass in Western France, 1250–1325* (Berkeley and Los Angeles, 1994), 227–28, fig. VII.5.

17. Jacobus de Voragine, *The Golden Legend: Readings on the Saints,* trans. William Granger Ryan, 2 vols. (Princeton, 1993). See also Sherry L. Reames, *The "Legenda aurea": A Reexamination of Its Paradoxical History* (Madison, 1985).

18. It has been suggested that earlier sets survive only in part, for example, the four Nazareth capitals depicting scenes of Peter, Thomas, James Major, and Matthew. However, a full set in the Church of the Annunciation could not accommodate more than another four apostles. See Jaroslav Folda, *The Art of the Crusaders in the Holy Land, 1098–1187* (Cambridge, 1995), 434 and pl. 10.5.

19. Otto Demus, *The Mosaics of San Marco in Venice,* vol. 1, *The Eleventh and Twelfth Centuries,* text vol. (Chicago, 1984), chap. 17, esp. 220 and n. 11. Six of the twelve, those on the north, are now seventeenth-century replacements; the original mosaics, on the south, depict James the Less, Philip, Bartholomew, Matthew, Simon, and Jude.

20. For the Stuttgart (or Zweifalten) Passional (Stuttgart, Württembergische Landesbibliothek, Cod. Bibl. 2° 56–58, 3 vols., ca. 1120–35), see Sigrid von Borries-Schulten, *Die romanischen Handschriften der Württembergischen Landesbibliothek Stuttgart, 2.1: Provenienz Zweifalten* (Stuttgart, 1987), nos. 34–36; Albert Boeckler, *Das Stuttgarter Passionale* (Augsburg, 1923). For the Regensburg Martyrology (Munich, Clm 13074, ca. 1175): Elisabeth Klemm, *Die romanischen Handschriften der Bayerischen Staatsbibliothek,* vol. 1, *Die Bistümer Regensburg, Passau und Salzburg,* text vol. (Wiesbaden, 1980), 68–71; Albert Boeckler, *Die Regensburg-Prüfeninger Buchmalerei des XII. und XIII. Jahrhunderts* (Munich, 1924), 49–53; it includes the saints Christopher, Mark, and Luke and omits apostles John and Philip, since neither died in martyrdom (the latter according to Western legend only).

21. See the discussion at notes 120–23 below. I propose in this chapter that the rich library of Saint-Thierry, near Reims, was the locus for the research on the program for the rosaces. The patron of Saint-Thierry was St. Bartholomew, and three of his vitae were in their library.

22. Justification for this chronology is presented in this chapter below and in chapter 3. In Bay 104 James the Less appears, very much alive, under attack by a fuller with his club (fig. 47). The ogive light over Bay 103 contains a beheading, which I believe is a stopgap from the lower windows (see appendix 3).

23. Manhès-Deremble, *Les vitraux narratifs,* 58–60, suggests that windows devoted to Peter and to Philip may have been lost, but even if so, only nine apostles would be included. While she admits that, as Yves Delaporte believed, the cathedral's liturgical texts provided some source material, she emphasizes the use of various forms of apocryphal legends; however, the only apostle window she studies in detail is the bay of John the Evangelist (bay 48). See her pp. 76–77, 115–17, 136, 182–90, 205–7. Bourges has narrative windows for Peter and Paul together, James Major, John, and Thomas, which also include apocryphal material.

24. The thirteenth-century liturgical books of the cathedral accord Peter, Paul, Andrew, James Major, and John simplex feasts of nine lessons with nine candles; the remainder had simplex feasts of nine lessons with seven candles. See Anne Walters Robertson, *Guillaume de Machaut and Reims: Context and Meaning in His Musical Works* (Cambridge, 2002), 39–42 (table 1-1) and 354 n. 50. Reims possessed relics of Peter, Paul, John, and Bartholomew, displayed with those of other saints in a "vénérable bric-à-brac" to the left of the altar: Patrick Demouy, "Vocables, reliques et processions. Sources d'une étude iconographique de la cathédrale de Reims au XIIIe siècle," in *Nouveaux regards,* 114.

25. Demus, *The Mosaics,* 1:219–20. The location at San Marco is appropriate, since the apostles' evangelizing followed Pentecost.

26. Ibid., 225.

27. On Paris, BnF, lat. 5563, see *Catalogus codicum hagiographicorum latinorum antiquiorum saeculo XVI qui asservantur in Bibliotheca nationale Parisiensi,* ed. Albertus Poncelet, vol. 2 (Brussels, 1890), 468–69 (as eleventh-century); François Dolbeau, "Typologie et formation des collections hagiographiques d'après les recueils de l'abbaye de Saint-Thierry," in *Saint-Thierry: Une abbaye du VIe au XXe siècle; Actes du colloque international d'histoire monastique, 1976,* ed. Michel Bur (Saint-Thierry, 1979), 161–62, 164, 177 (as eleventh-century); Eric Junod and Jean-Daniel Kaestli, *Acta Iohannis,* Corpus Christianorum, Series Apocryphorum, 2 (Turnhout, 1983), 2:756 (as tenth-century).

28. See note 21 above. On the Saint-Thierry manuscript (now Reims, Bibl. mun., MS 142) that was probably consulted for the complex nave program, see appendix 7. On the Saint-Thierry library: Jean Leclercq, "Livres et lecteurs à Saint-Thierry au XIIe siècle," in *Saint-Thierry,* 103, 110–11.

29. A succinct statement about the five Early Christian acts is found in James Keith Elliott, *The Apocryphal New Testament* (Oxford, 1993), 229–30. Some of the differences between the five early Acts are discussed by Christine M. Thomas, *The Acts of Peter, Gospel Literature, and the Ancient Novel: Rewriting the Past* (Oxford, 2003), 11–12, 81.

30. Neither has a modern edition. The Pseudo-Abdias is described briefly in Montague Rhodes James, *The Apocryphal New Testament* (Oxford, 1966), 438. The assessment of the Pseudo-Melito and Pseudo-Abdias that follows here draws heavily from Eric Junod and Jean-Daniel Kaestli's intensive study of the *Acts of John:* Junod and Kaestli, *L'histoire des actes apocryphes des apôtres du IIIe au IXe siècle: Le cas des actes de Jean,* Cahiers de la Revue de théologie et de philosophie, 7 (Geneva, 1982), 4, 102–7; eidem, *Acta Iohannis,* 2:750–58, 764–72, 793–95. Note that Junod and Kaestli refer to the Pseudo-Abdias as the *Virtutes apostolorum* and the Pseudo-Melito as the *Passiones apostolorum.*

31. Junod and Kaestli, *L'histoire,* 105.

32. Although the boiling-oil episode was known to Tertullian, Jerome, and Bede, it was not localized in Rome until very close to the time of the Pseudo-Melito itself: Junod and Kaestli, *Acta Iohannis,* 2:772–81.

33. Mâle, *Thirteenth Century,* 293–94. On the Golden Legend, see Junod and Kaestli, *L'histoire,* 107.

34. See note 30 above. Early editions of the Pseudo-Abdias vary the number of books as well as the order of the apostles, which in the Saint-Thierry manuscript (as well as many others) is Peter, Paul, James the Less, Philip, Andrew, James Major, John, Thomas, Bartholomew, Matthew, Simon and Jude. Two of the ten manuscripts catalogued in Junod and Kaestli, *Acta Iohannis,* 2:755–57, dating from the ninth to thirteenth centuries, have a slightly different order; the editors could not account for the rationale behind any of the orders. Friedrich Nausea's edition (Cologne, 1531) combines Peter and Paul as well as Simon and Jude and adds Barnabas from a different source, in the following order: Peter and Paul, Andrew, James Major, John, Thomas, Bartholomew, James the Less, Philip, Matthew, Simon and Jude, Barnabas. The much better known edition by Wolfgang Lazius (Basle, 1552), reprinted often in the sixteenth century and later by Fabricius (Hamburg, 1703), initiated the sobriquet "Pseudo-Abdias" and ordered the apostles as Peter, Paul, Andrew, James Major, John, James the Less plus Simon and Jude, Matthew, Bartholomew, Thomas, Philip. Elliott, *Apocryphal,* 525–26, lists this edition's contents as well as the meager modern translations available. The oft-cited study of these apocryphal texts by Richard Adalbert Lipsius (1883–90; reprinted Amsterdam, 1976) is heavily criticized by Junod and Kaestli in *Acta Iohannis,* 2:750–57. For purposes of simple convenience I have cited below the French translation by Jacques Paul Migne, *Dictionnaire des apocryphes,* vol. 2 (1856; reprinted Turnhout, 1989), which is somewhat more accessible and provides the apostles' lives in alphabetical order.

35. See the discussion above, at notes 21–22.

36. On the apostolic succession, see above, at note 5. On the civic strife in Reims during the 1230s, see chapter 1.

37. See also the evidence in the lancets below the rosace, chapter 3.

38. János Bollók, "The Description of Paul in the Acta Pauli," in *The Apocryphal Acts of Paul and Thecla,* ed. Jan N. Bremmer (Kampen, 1996), 1–15. On *The Acts of Paul and Thecla,* see Elliott, *Apocryphal,* 353, 364 (3); Wilhelm Schneemelcher, ed., *New Testament Apocrypha,* trans. and ed. Robert McLachlan Wilson, vol. 2 (Louisville, Ky., 2003), 239 (3).

39. See Luba Eleen, *The Illustration of the Pauline Epistles in French and English Bibles of the Twelfth and Thirteenth Centuries* (Oxford, 1982), 3.

40. On Paul as preacher, see ibid., 66–69. On the Reims facade sculpture: Peter Kurmann, *La façade de la cathédrale de Reims: Architecture et sculpture des portails, étude archéologique et stylistique* (Lausanne, 1987), 1:194–96; vol. 2, pls. 369–70. On the Rouen window: Recensement VI:343; illustrated in Georges Ritter, *Les vitraux de la cathédrale de Rouen* (Cognac, 1926), pls. XXIV–XXVI.

41. Migne, *Dictionnaire,* col. 661 n. 614.

42. On Pseudo-Linus, see Eleen, *Pauline Epistles,* 19, 101–2; Elliott, *Apocryphal,* 388; Schneemelcher, *New*

Testament, 439. For Poitiers, see note 13 above; for Chartres, Manhès-Deremble, *Les vitraux narratifs,* 304–5; for Rouen, Ritter, *Rouen,* pl. XXVI. In bay 204 at Troyes (ca. 1235–40), Paul is not blindfolded but clutches Plautilla's bloody kerchief (though he has not yet bled): Pastan and Balcon, *Troyes,* 422, fig. 365.

43. Eleen, *Pauline Epistles,* 103–4. One type does not seem to supersede the other. The "restrained form" also appears in glass at Bourges (bay 9, ca. 1210–15; Recensement II:172), at Saint-Julien-du-Sault (bay 1, ca. 1235–40; Recensement III:168), and twice at Saint-Père de Chartres (bay 221, ca. 1280, and bay 201, ca. 1295–1300; Recensement II:50, 54; Lillich, *The Armor,* 315, fig. IX.9A).

44. *Butler's Lives of the Saints,* ed. Herbert Thurston and Donald Attwater (New York, 1963), 3:183.

45. On the Pseudo-Abdias text, see Migne, *Dictionnaire,* esp. cols. 265, 272–74; Elliott, *Apocryphal,* 527–28 (English summary by M. R. James); Schneemelcher, *New Testament,* 477.

46. E.g., Bourges bay 18, ca. 1210–15 (preaching, beheading; Recensement II:173); Chartres bay 5, ca. 1210–25 (all three scenes; Manhès-Deremble, *Les vitraux narratifs,* 306–7); Auxerre bay 16, ca. 1235–45 (confrontation with Herod, beheading; Virginia Chieffo Raguin, *Stained Glass in Thirteenth-Century Burgundy* [Princeton, 1982], 144–45); Tours bay 5, from Saint-Martin de Tours, ca. 1250 (confrontation, beheading), and Tours bay 210, ca. 1260–70 (all three scenes; Recensement II:123 and 129).

47. Cerf, *Histoire,* 2:276; Reinhardt, *La cathédrale,* 184; Recensement IV:387.

48. On Chartres bay 5 and bay 111 (which was lost in 1773), see Yves Delaporte and Étienne Houvet, *Les vitraux de la cathédrale de Chartres,* text vol. (Chartres, 1926), 308–9, 481–82, and, following him, Mâle, *Les saints compagnons,* 167, and Manhès-Deremble, *Les vitraux narratifs,* 77, 306–7. On Tours and Le Mans: Linda Papanicolaou, "Stained Glass Windows of the Choir of the Cathedral of Tours" (Ph.D. diss., New York University, Institute of Fine Arts, 1979), 107–8; her identifications, however, were not adopted in Recensement II:129–252. The Troyes-cathedral example was not identified correctly in Recensement IV:229 or Pastan and Balcon, *Troyes,* 472.

49. Humbert Jacomet, "L'énigmatique odyssée de saint Jacques," *Archeologia* 318 (1995): 58–67; see also Alison Stones, *Le livre d'images de Madame Marie* (Paris, 1997), 74 n. 3. See appendix 4.

50. Émile Mâle, *Religious Art in France: The Twelfth Century,* trans. Marthiel Mathews from the rev. ed. of 1953 (Princeton, 1978), 296–98. The Santiago statues are illustrated in Vera Hell and Hellmut Hell, *The Great Pilgrimage of the Middle Ages: The Road to St. James of Compostela* (New York, 1964), pls. 155, 160; Brian Tate and Marcus Tate, *The Pilgrim Route to Santiago* (Oxford, 1987), 147, 151.

51. The modern head in the bottom lobe (James preaching) was copied from the balding St. Paul.

52. For Amiens, see Kurmann, *La façade,* vol. 2, pl. 967. For the Château de Rouen panel, see Sophie Lagabrielle, *Vitraux: Musée nationale du Moyen Âge, Thermes et Hôtel de Cluny* (Paris, 2006), 55 (ill.). Lagabrielle, based on manuscript comparisons (52–53), dates the James panel too late; for a stylistic analysis with comparable stained glass, see Lillich, *The Armor,* 65–66, 344 n. 76.

53. The translation appears in William Melczer, *The Pilgrim's Guide to Santiago de Compostela* (New York, 1993), 10. For the Latin entry, see Baudoin de Gaiffier, "Le Breviarium Apostolorum (BHL 652): Tradition manuscrite et oeuvres apparentées," *Analecta bollandiana* 81 (1963): 108–9. The mid-eighth-century Parisian manuscript (Paris, BnF, lat. 7193) was discovered by E. A. Lowe, who documents the find in "The Vatican MS of the Gelasian Sacramentary and Its Supplement at Paris," *Journal of Theological Studies* 27 (1925–26): 357–73; the *Breviarium Apostolorum* section on James Major is on 369 (fols. 55r–v).

54. The recent literature on the Santiago pilgrimage and the manuscripts involved in promoting it is dauntingly vast. For the development of the cult, see Robert Plötz, "Peregrinatio ad Limina Sancti Jacobi," in *The "Codex Calixtinus" and the Shrine of St. James,* ed. John Williams and Alison Stones, Jakobus-Studien, 3 (Tübingen, 1992), 37–49; Jan van Herwaarden, "Saint James in Spain up to the 12th Century," in *Wallfahrt kennt keine Grenzen,* ed. Lenz Kriss-Rettenbeck and Gerda Möhler (Munich, 1984), esp. 238–41.

55. Louis Duchesne, "Saint Jacques en Galice," *Annales du Midi* 12 (1900): 179.

56. See note 24 above. It should be noted that the axial chapel, open in 1221, was dedicated to James as well as the Virgin; a chaplaincy for James in the Romanesque cathedral dated to 1190. See Jean-Pierre Ravaux, "Les campagnes de construction de la cathédrale de Reims au XIIIe siècle," *Bulletin monumental* 137 (1979): 8–9; the 1221 document is printed in full in his n. 16.

57. See appendix 4.

58. The Reims north rose may also be based on a manuscript written by Pierre de Beauvais for the archbishop's family, a bestiary. See appendix 2 and chapter 4.

59. For illustrations of the Laon north rose (ca. 1190–1200) and east rose (ca. 1200), see Cowen, *The Rose Window,* 70, 72, 227. For restoration charts of these roses: Françoise Perrot, "Les vitraux médiévaux de la cathédrale: État d'une recherche," in *Laon: Une acropole à la française,*

Cahiers du patrimoine, 40, vol. 1 (Amiens, 1995), 338 (fig. 379), 342 (fig. 383). The earlier dating given here has been proposed in Claudine Lautier, "Les vitraux du chevet de la cathédrale de Laon: Première approche," *Österreichische Zeitschrift für Kunst und Denkmalpflege* 54, 3/4 (2000): 257–64.

60. In the mid-nineteenth-century engraving in Charles Cahier and Arthur Marie Martin, *Monographie de la cathédrale de Bourges* (see my fig. 8), the left lobes at the bottom and middle are interchanged. This could be either a mistake in the drawing or an earlier error in installation. The present arrangement, with the enthroned Nero in the middle lobe observing Peter's crucifixion, seems clearly to have been the original arrangement.

61. *Butler's Lives of the Saints,* 2:666–67.

62. Carolyn Kinder Carr, "Aspects of the Iconography of Saint Peter in Medieval Art of Western Europe to the Early Thirteenth Century" (Ph.D. diss., Case Western Reserve University, 1978), 138–39; Cyrille Vogel and Reinhard Elze, *Le pontifical romano-germanique du dixième siècle,* vol. 2 (Vatican, 1963), 137, 277. For the Pseudo-Abdias, see Migne, *Dictionnaire,* col. 700. The feast of Peter in Chains at Reims in the thirteenth century was only simplex with nine lessons and seven candles: Robertson, *Guillaume de Machaut,* 40.

63. Carr, "Aspects," 139–43, citing Cluniac examples in Meyer Schapiro, *The Parma Ildefonsus: A Romanesque Illuminated Manuscript from Cluny and Related Works* (New York, 1954), 44 n. 177.

64. Nero's name is inscribed on a Moissac capital (east gallery, no. 20): Meyer Schapiro, *Romanesque Art* (New York, 1977), fig. 45, opp. p. 167. In early texts Agrippa orders Peter's crucifixion; on the textual shift from Agrippa to Nero, see Thomas, *The Acts of Peter* (as in note 29 above), 51–54. Nero is the tyrant in only two early texts, the Pseudo-Hegesippus (a Latin translation of Josephus's "Jewish Wars," ca. 370 C.E.) and the Marcellus text (fifth–sixth centuries); on these texts, see Thomas, *The Acts of Peter,* 10, 106–7. The section in the Pseudo-Abdias from chapter 16 to the end copies the Pseudo-Hegesippos almost word for word: Elliott, *Apocryphal,* 429; Migne, *Dictionnaire,* col. 709 n. 695. The Pseudo-Marcellus can be discounted as a source for Reims because it states that Peter was nailed to the cross (see note 65 below).

65. For Tertullian, see *Scorpiace* 15.3, translated in Geoffrey D. Dunn, *Tertullian,* The Early Church Fathers (London, 2004), 114. For the Pseudo-Marcellus: Carr, "Aspects," 162 (note that she refers to this text as the *Passio Sanctorum Apostolorum Petri et Pauli*); Elliott, *Apocryphal,* 428; Schneemelcher, *New Testament,* 440–41. The earliest known image of Peter's crucifixion shows him seminude and nailed: mosaic of ca. 705 in the Oratorio of John VII, Old Saint Peter's, known by a sixteenth-century Grimaldi drawing illustrated in Josef Wilpert, *Die römischen Mosaiken und Malereien der kirchlichen Bauten vom* IV. *bis* XIII. *Jahrhundert* (Freiburg im Breisgau, 1917), text vol., 399, fig. 136.

66. See my discussion of the nailed formats, in Lillich, *Saint-Père,* 105–7, 166–67; eadem, *The Armor,* 43–44. The article by Tony Sauvel, "Le crucifiement de saint Pierre," *Bulletin monumental* 97 (1938): 337–52, should be used with great caution.

67. For the Lyon bay 7 rosace, see Recensement III:298, fig. 263; Catherine Brisac, "La peinture sur verre à Lyon au XIIe siècle et au début du XIIIe siècle," *Dossiers de l'archéologie,* no. 26 (January–February 1978): 41–42, 48, ill. p. 39. Note that the crucifixion of Peter in the lancet of Lyon bay 7 is modern. For Clermont-Ferrand (bay 12, b6 in Saint Anne chapel, southwest radiating chapel): Catherine Brisac, "The Romanesque Panels in the Cathedral of Clermont-Ferrand," in *Studies on Medieval Stained Glass,* ed. Madeline Caviness and Timothy Husband, Corpus Vitrearum, USA, Occasional Papers 1 (New York, 1985), 15 and 17–23 passim; Henri du Ranquet, *Les vitraux de la cathédrale de Clermont-Ferrand* (Clermont-Ferrand, 1932), 203, colored drawing opp. p. 196. For Troyes (bay 14, ambulatory): Pastan and Balcon, *Troyes,* 151, fig. 111. On Troyes bay 204, however, see note 68 below. For Bourges (bay 9): Recensement II:172; Cahier and Martin, *Bourges,* vol. 2, pl. XIII.

68. For Troyes bay 204, see Pastan and Balcon, *Troyes,* 239 (fig. 200), 421–23. For Auxerre bay 7: Recensement III:114; Raguin, *Burgundy,* 161–62.

69. The Simon Magus story does not appear in Bay 102, contrary to assertions found in Recensement IV:387; Mâle, *Les saints compagnons,* 105; and Louis Bréhier, *La cathédrale de Reims* (Paris, 1916), 250. Here is a list of some of the numerous examples of the Simon Magus legend in French glass before and after Reims:

- Poitiers bay 2 (ca. 1160–80): Louis Grodecki, "Les vitraux de la cathédrale de Poitiers," *Congrès archéologique* 109 (1951): 147
- Troyes bays 10 and 14 (ca. 1200): Pastan and Balcon, *Troyes,* 96–98, 151, 345–47
- Chartres bay 4 (ca. 1210–15): Manhès-Deremble, *Les vitraux narratifs,* 304–5
- Bourges bay 9 (ca. 1210–15): Recensement II:172
- Rouen bay 14 (ca. 1220–30): Recensement VI:343
- Angers bay 107 (ca. 1225–35): Recensement II:290
- Saint-Julien-du-Sault bay 1 (ca. 1240–45): Recensement III:168
- Auxerre bay 7 (ca. 1250): Recensement III:114
- Le Mans bays 101 and 108 (ca. 1255–65): Recensement II:249, 251
- Tours bay 203 (ca. 1260–75): Recensement II:126
- Saint-Père, Chartres, bay 221 (ca. 1280 and after 1305): Recensement II:54; Lillich, *Saint-Père,* pl. VI, opp. p. 64

70. For Chartres bay 2 (medallions 27 and 31), see Manhès-Deremble, *Les vitraux narratifs,* 302–3. For Auxerre bay 13 (medallion 16): Recensement III:117; Raguin, *Burgundy,* 131–32.

71. Schneemelcher, *New Testament,* 109. On its fame and popularity in the Middle Ages, see Charlotte Denoël, *Saint André: Culte et iconographie en France (ve–xve siècles)* (Paris, 2004), 165–66.

72. Elliott, *Apocryphal,* 262; cf. Dennis Ronald MacDonald, *The Acts of Andrew and the Acts of Andrew and Matthias in the City of the Cannibals* (Atlanta, Ga., 1990), 405, 409–15; Schneemelcher, *New Testament,* 148. The version of Andrew's prayer in the Pseudo-Abdias (bk. 3, chap. 40) is much longer: Migne, *Dictionnaire,* col. 91. The Pseudo-Abdias follows Gregory of Tours, whose version stops at the martyrdom, and for that material uses another source, the identification of which is disputed: Elliott, *Apocryphal,* 235, 525; Denoël, *Saint André,* 30–33, 165 (where the Pseudo-Abdias is called *Virtutes Apostolorum*).

73. Denoël, *Saint André,* 114, 155, 166, lists only one twelfth-century example, a metalwork triptych of Saint Andrew (ca. 1150) in the Trier cathedral treasury. For the lost panel of Angers, see the illustration in Louis de Farcy, *Monographie de la cathédrale d'Angers,* vol. 1 (Angers, 1910), 152 (pl.); Recensement II:292. For Notre-Dame, Dijon: Recensement III:36. For Troyes bay 11: Pastan and Balcon, *Troyes,* 349–51, fig. 305.

74. I have found only one example of such a reduced format, in the Pamplona Bible (Amiens, Bibl. mun., lat. 108, ca. 1200), fol. 208r, a work that seems to be a unicum: François Bucher, *The Pamplona Bibles: A Facsimile Compiled from Two Picture Bibles with Martyrologies Commissioned by King Sancho el Fuerte of Navarre (1194–1234)* (New Haven, 1970), vol. 2, pl. 465.

75. Denoël, *Saint André,* 166, provides only two isolated examples of phylacteries: in the twelfth-century Trier triptych (see note 73 above) and the Gradual of Gisela von Kerssenbrock, a manuscript of ca. 1300 (Osnabrück, Diözesanarchiv, Inv. no. Ma 101; see Denoël, *Saint André,* fig. 38).

76. Herbert Norris, *Church Vestments: Their Origin and Development* (New York, 1950; reprint, Mineola, N.Y., 2002), 70; stoles were worn by deacons, priests, and all higher clergy (8); priests were allowed to wear their stoles at all times and were obliged to when celebrating Mass (89–91).

77. Denoël, *Saint André,* 196. For general comments on the various forms of Andrew's cross, see also Lillich, *Saint-Père,* 108–9, 114–15 nn. 36–44; Cothren, *Picturing the Celestial City,* 239 n. 44.

78. Denoël, *Saint André,* fig. 27; *Les plus beaux manuscrits de la Bibliothèque municipale de Reims,* exh. cat. (Paris, 1967), 18, no. 10; Charles Samaran and Robert Marichal, *Catalogue des manuscrits en écriture latine portant des indications de date, de lieu ou de copiste,* vol. 5, *Est de la France,* text vol. (Paris, 1965), 245. The earliest example of Andrew's upright cross given by Denoël, *Saint André* (fig. 37), is the ninth-century Drogo Sacramentary (Paris, BnF, lat. 9428), fol. 98v; the upright cross remains the longest in Italian art. A textual hypothesis may support its antiquity and southern orientation. The late-second-century Greek *Acts of Andrew,* source of the Latin recensions, is theorized to have drawn heavily from Homer's *Odyssey;* the upright cross would relate to Odysseus lashed to the mast of his ship. Almost none of the Homeric references were transmitted to the Latin recensions: Dennis Ronald MacDonald, *Christianizing Homer: The Odyssey, Plato, and the Acts of Andrew* (Oxford, 1994), 281–82. And Thomas, *The Acts of Peter* (as in note 29 above), 12, maintains that no Early Christian Greek-speaking readers ever understood these Homeric allusions!

79. Denoël, *Saint André,* 231–32; Bucher, *Pamplona,* vol. 2, pl. 460, color pl. 10.

80. For Lyon, see Recensement III:298, fig. 263, where the fragment is identified as "mise en croix de saint Pierre, fin du XIIe s." For a list of thirteenth-century windows of Andrew's horizontal crucifixion, see Cothren, *Picturing the Celestial City,* 239 n. 44; to his list can be added Notre-Dame de Dijon bay 15, ca. 1230–35 (Raguin, *Burgundy,* fig. 160). There are two examples at Le Mans, ca. 1255, which (like that at Lyon) have been identified as Peter's crucifixion: Lillich, *The Armor,* 336 n. 144. A more challenging puzzle is Tours cathedral bay 7, the panels of which were removed from the church of Saint-Martin, Tours, in the Revolution. Recensement II:123–24 identifies the bay's subject as the lives of Peter and Paul; Louis Grodecki, in Marcel Aubert et al., *Le vitrail français* (Paris, 1958), pl. 120, identifies part of the bay as the life of Andrew. Actually, included in these Saint-Martin spolia are four crucifixions, all tied, three of them horizontal and one diagonal (one with a clothed saint, three with seminude saints). Repetitions also occur of ruler-saint confrontations and of executioners brandishing weapons over saints. This glass would repay close study. Originally the series may have represented martyrdoms of the apostles at an interesting iconographic moment just previous to the composition of the Golden Legend.

81. The head of James the Less in the bottom lobe of Bay 104 is an innocuous modern restoration.

82. A modern edition of the Pseudo-Abdias, book 5 (John), has been published by Junod and Kaestli, *Acta Iohannis.* One of the group of manuscripts on which Junod

and Kaestli based their edition (see ibid., 2:756) was the manuscript from Saint-Thierry near Reims (now Paris, BnF, lat 5563), which I propose as the main source used by the Reims programmer. A résumé of the stories in book 5 of the Pseudo-Abdias, chapter by chapter, appears on 2:760–61; the Latin text of the three scenes at Reims is on 2:799, 823–32. Note that Junod and Kaestli refer to book 5 as the *Virtutes Iohannis* and to the entire Pseudo-Abdias as the *Virtutes apostolorum* (2:750). The Pseudo-Melito (which they call *Passio Iohannis*), written independently, slightly earlier than the Pseudo-Abdias, and probably in Rome, omits both the boiling oil and the "installation de Jean dans la fosse et sa mort" (2:764 n. 3).

83. On the tonsuring of the Reims canons, see Robertson, *Guillaume de Machaut,* 345 n. 105. What is unusual in the rosace of Bay 104 is that John is always tonsured. In medieval art he is sometimes tonsured, sometimes not, and in series of apostles rarely. See Suzanne Lewis, *Reading Images: Narrative Discourse and Reception in the Thirteenth-Century Illuminated Apocalypse* (Cambridge, 1995), 36; for an example of the tonsure in glass, see bays 3 and 212 at Tours: Papanicolaou, "Stained Glass Windows of the Choir of the Cathedral of Tours" (as in note 48 above), 117. The poor condition of the later facade sculpture at Reims makes it difficult to tell if John is always tonsured there: Kurmann, *La façade,* vol. 2, pls. 381, 383, 384.

84. To limit the vast field to stained glass, lists of Gothic windows devoted to John are in Raguin, *Burgundy,* 134, and Manhès-Deremble, *Les vitraux narratifs,* 183. Note that, of the examples in these lists, Lyon is modern and many others are incomplete or fragmentary. The cycle of John in the nave of San Francesco in Assisi (ca. 1275) is consistently different in detail from the French examples: Giuseppe Marchini, *Le vetrate dell'Umbria,* Corpus Vitrearum Medii Aevi, Italia, I (Rome, 1973), 46–47, pl. XLII.

85. Lewis, *Reading Images,* 26–28; the Bible is Bodleian MS Auct. D.4.8. On the life of John in English Apocalypse manuscripts, see Lewis's chap. 1, esp. 19, 25, 28, 31. For Troyes bay 202, see Pastan and Balcon, *Troyes,* 240–44, 413–16; Recensement IV, color pl. XII (opp. p. 221).

86. The rosace scene is not specified in the literature, except erroneously (as John on Patmos) by Barbara Abou-El-Haj, "Program and Power in the Glass of Reims," in *Radical Art History, Internationale Anthologie, Subject: O. K. Werckmeister,* ed. Wolfgang Kersten (Zurich, 1997), 29 n. 48. Only Bourges bay 22 includes John's author portrait with eagle rather than John on Patmos, also regularly misidentified: Recensement II:174. The Pseudo-Abdias only refers in passing to John's authorship of the Fourth Gospel, in John's final prayer before he climbs into his tomb: "and I wrote the works that I've seen with my eyes and the words that my ears have heard from your mouth": Migne, *Dictionnaire,* col. 355 (bk. 5, chap. 23).

87. Cothren, *Picturing the Celestial City,* 248 n. 125. For illustrations of Gospel portraits in early Reims manuscripts, see *Trésors de la Bibliothèque municipale de Reims,* exh. cat. (Reims, 1978), no. 9, color pl. II (Matthew in Reims MS 7, fol. 21r, late ninth century, from Saint-Thierry); no. 16, pl. V (Luke in Reims MS 9, mid–eleventh century, from Saint-Remi); no. 17 (Mark in Reims MS 13, late eleventh century, from the cathedral chapter). Also *Les plus beaux manuscrits* (as in note 78 above), pl. I (Matthew in Reims MS 7); pl. III (John in Reims MS 9).

88. Migne, *Dictionnaire,* col. 329 (bk. 5, chap. 2). Tertullian, *De praescriptione haereticorum,* chap. 36, trans. Peter Holmes in *The Ante-Nicene Fathers,* ed. Alexander Roberts and James Donaldson (1867–72; reprint, Grand Rapids, Mich., 1993), 3:260. My paragraph is based on Junod and Kaestli, *Acta Iohannis,* 2:775–81 passim. Note that the mosaics of the portico of the Lateran, sometimes stated to be seventh-century (and thus the earliest cycle with this scene in art), are correctly dated 1159–81 C.E.: Wilpert, *Die römischen Mosaiken,* text vol., 211–12.

89. Sens, e.g., is crowded with figures: Recensement III:176, fig. 153. The only manuscript closely related to the scene depicted at Reims is the Pamplona Bible (ca. 1200): Bucher, *Pamplona,* vol. 2, pl. 454.

90. Large bowls appear in the windows of Auxerre bay 12, ca. 1235–40 (Pastan and Balcon, *Troyes,* 242, fig. 204); and later at Saint-Julien-du-Sault, bay 3, ca. 1240–50 (Raguin, *Burgundy,* fig. 93) and Tours, bay 3, ca. 1250, and bay 212, 1264–67 (Recensement II:123, 129). Earlier examples at Chartres, bay 48, ca. 1205–15 (Manhès-Deremble, *Les vitraux narratifs,* 188, fig. 83) and Bourges, bay 22, ca. 1210–15 (Recensement II:174) have large bowls with at least a short stem or foot. Closest to the chalice at Reims is Troyes bay 202, ca. 1235–40 (Pastan and Balcon, *Troyes,* 241, fig. 203).

91. On the variants, see Manhès-Deremble, *Les vitraux narratifs,* 189 n. 653.

92. On Chartres MS 500, see Yves Delaporte, *Les manuscrits enluminés de la Bibliothèque de Chartres* (Chartres, 1929), 35–37. The scene was on folio 18v. Delaporte notes the mediocre execution of rather ill-proportioned figures and identifies the scene as John "descending into his tomb." The Bibliothèque de Chartres informs me that it has no reproduction of this folio, and it is unclear how Manhès-Deremble (see note 91 above) knows about it. She compares it to Saint-Julien-du-Sault but does not mention Reims.

93. Demus, *The Mosaics,* vol. 1, pl. 8; he lists the other examples on 223 and 362 n. 39.

94. Migne, *Dictionnaire,* cols. 275–82. Eusebius copied the late-second-century account of Hegesippus: Schneemelcher, *New Testament,* 478; Elliott, *Apocryphal,* 528.

95. Demus, *The Mosaics,* 1:222–23; Boeckler, *Regensburg* (as in note 20 above), Abb. 56–57.

96. Demus, *The Mosaics,* 1:220, 222–23, pl. 357. Demus (362 nn. 38–39) also lists the Stavelot Altar and six manuscripts, among them the Regensburg Martyrology (Boeckler, *Regensburg,* Abb. 57), the Stuttgart Passional (Boeckler, *Stuttgarter,* fig. 30), the Pamplona Bible (Bucher, *Pamplona,* fig. 467a), and the Zweifalten Martyrology (ca. 1161). For the Zweifalten Martyrology (Stuttgart, Landesbibliothek, Cod. Hist. 2° 415), fol. 39r, see von Borries-Schulten, *Die romanischen* (as in note 20 above), 97, illustrated in Wolfgang Kemp, *The Narratives of Gothic Stained Glass* (Cambridge, 1997), 55, fig. 26.

97. See note 103 and the text at notes 106–7 below. An older repair, in my opinion a spolium, is the medallion, in the ogive light above the rosace, depicting an executioner grabbing a kneeling saint by the hair and wielding a sword to behead him, similar to the executions of Paul and James in lobes of Bay 101. See appendix 3.

98. Schneemelcher, *New Testament,* 323–24, 453–55; Elliott, *Apocryphal,* 439–46.

99. For Bourges, see Benoît, *Bourges* (as in note 11 above), 36–38, color pl. U. For Chartres: Manhès-Deremble, *Les vitraux narratifs,* 334–35. For Tours: Recensement II:129–30. The cycle in the nave of Assisi is later and quite different in detail: Marchini, *Vetrate dell'Umbria,* 46–49.

100. The Golden Legend states that as a Jew Thomas did not eat or drink at the banquet: Jacobus de Voragine, *The Golden Legend,* 2:30. In the Pseudo-Abdias version Thomas, noticed as a Jew by a Jewish girl entertainer at the feast, stares at her and is slapped for that: Migne, *Dictionnaire,* cols. 990–91.

101. The Sens panel is an isolated fragment: Recensement III:176. For the Porte des Bleds tympanum at Semur-en-Auxois, see Willibald Sauerländer, *Gothic Sculpture in France, 1140–1270,* trans. Janet Sondheimer (New York, 1972), pl. 291b.

102. Augustine's three mentions appear in *Contra Adimantum* 17.2.5 ("Answer to Adimantus, a Disciple of Mani," in *The Works of Augustine: A Translation for the 21st Century,* pt. 1, vol. 19, *The Manichean Debate,* ed. and trans. Roland Teske [Hyde Park, N.Y., 2006], 207); in *De sermone Domini in monte* 1.19.65 (*Commentary on the Lord's Sermon on the Mount,* trans. Denis J. Kavanagh, The Fathers of the Church, vol. 11 [New York, 1951], 92); and in *Contra Faustum* 22.79 ("Reply to Faustus the Manichaean [Contra Faustum Manichaeum] A.D. 400," trans. Richard Stothert, in *A Select Library of the Nicene and Post-Nicene Fathers of the Christian Church,* vol. 4, ed. Philip Schaff [1886; reprint, Grand Rapids, Mich., 1989], 304), the fullest account.

103. Cahier and Martin, *Bourges* (see my fig. 8); also Bréhier, *La cathédrale* (as in note 69 above), 251. A photo by the architect Deneux dated October 2, 1914, taken from the exterior, shows this roundel still in place: Paris, Arch. phot., Deneux cl.00519.

104. Migne, *Dictionnaire,* cols. 993–95. There actually was a king by the name of Gundaphorus around 46 C.E.: Elliott, *Apocryphal,* 440.

105. For Chartres, see Manhès-Deremble, *Les vitraux narratifs,* 334–35; for Semur, Sauerländer, *Gothic Sculpture,* pl. 291b. The heavenly palace is not included in the medallion window at Bourges (Benoît, *Bourges,* 36–38, color pl. U), which is surprising since the glass was given by the masons. For the right portal of the facade at Poitiers, see Sauerländer, *Gothic Sculpture,* pl. 299 (where the portal is dated ca. 1250–55). This part of the facade is dated later, to the "7e campagne," by Yves Blomme, "La construction de la cathédrale Saint-Pierre de Poitiers," *Bulletin monumental* 152 (1994): 57, fig. 45G.

106. Cerf, *Histoire,* 2:277.

107. Perhaps in the present Simon-Marq studio in Reims? If, on the other hand, the panel was destroyed in the war, it does not necessarily follow that the surrounding lobes, made with earlier and thicker glass, would also have been damaged. A similar trauma occurred at Evron (Mayenne) when in 1974 the vaults fell, destroying Renaissance repairs but not the original parts of the figures; see the illustration in Lillich, *The Armor,* 283, fig. VIII.12. At La Trinité, Vendôme, an explosion in the 1870 Franco-Prussian War destroyed all but one of the Renaissance windows in the choir but did not severely damage the Gothic glass filling the space immediately beneath them: see the illustration in ibid., 223, fig. VII.2.A.

108. Robertson, *Guillaume de Machaut,* 40. On their feast day, see de Gaiffier, "Breviarium" (as in note 53 above), 102 n. 4.

109. On the Pseudo-Abdias, see Schneemelcher, *New Testament,* 473; Migne, *Dictionnaire,* cols. 687–90. On the Regensburg Martyrology: Boeckler, *Regensburg,* 49–52. John is omitted for the same reason.

110. Jacobus de Voragine, *The Golden Legend,* 1:267. Isidore of Seville, *Liber de ortu et obitu patriarchaeum,* ed. J. Carracedo Fraga, Corpus Christianorum, Series Latina 108E (Turnhout, 1996), 69 (chap. 50.2). For the *Breviarium Apostolorum* (fols. 55v–56r), see de Gaiffier, "Breviarium," 92, and Lowe,

"Vatican," 369–70 (both as in note 53); also Schneemelcher, *New Testament*, 472–73. On the Greek upside-down crucifixion: Elliott, *Apocryphal*, 517; Schneemelcher, *New Testament*, 468–73; *Actes de l'apôtre Philippe*, ed. and trans. Frederic Amsler, François Bovon, and Bertrand Bouvier (Turnhout, 1996), 91–221. For the Stavelot Altar: Hanns Swarzenski, *Monuments of Romanesque Art* (Chicago, 1967), fig. 374.

111. Demus, *The Mosaics*, 1:223 and color pl. 8.

112. *Trésors de la Bibliothèque*, no. 20, second illustration.

113. Boeckler, *Stuttgarter* (as in note 20 above), 20, Abb. 51 (Cod. Bibl. 2° 57, fol. 49v).

114. Michael Camille, *The Gothic Idol: Ideology and Image-Making in Medieval Art* (Cambridge, 1989), 67, 97–98, fig. 198r.

115. On the Cathars, see Malcolm Barber, *The Cathars: Dualist Heretics in Languedoc in the High Middle Ages* (New York, 2000), and Malcolm D. Lambert, *The Cathars* (Oxford, 1998).

116. The proconsul Tyrannographos (or Tyrannognophos) was married to Nicanora, one of Philip's converts. The Greek text is translated in *Actes de l'apôtre Philippe*, 215 (Act 15:1).

117. Migne, *Dictionnaire*, cols. 149–60.

118. Victor Beyer, *Les vitraux de l'ancienne église des Dominicains de Strasbourg*, Corpus Vitrearum, France, IX 2 (Strasbourg, 2007), 66–77, esp. 72.

119. Marchini, *Vetrate dell'Umbria*, 63–65, pls. LII (a4–5, a8), LIII, LIV.

120. Jacobus de Voragine, *The Golden Legend*, 2:112. The Greek texts are listed in Max Bonnet, "La passion de S. Barthélemy: En quelle langue a-t-elle été écrite?" *Analecta bollandiana* 14 (1895): 354. The brief entries devoted to Bartholomew in the *Breviarium Apostolorum* and Isidore of Seville's *De ortu et obitu patrum* are printed side by side in de Gaiffier, "Breviarium" (as in note 53 above), 107.

121. On Anastasius, see *New Catholic Encyclopedia*, 2nd ed. (Washington, D.C., 2003), 1:389–90. On Theodore the Studite: Alice Gardner, *Theodore of Studium: His Life and Times* (London, 1905); R. J. Schork, "Theodore the Studite, St.," in *New Catholic Encyclopedia*, 13:877–78; Daniele Stiernon, "Teodore Studita, confessore, santo," in *Bibliotheca sanctorum*, vol. 12 (Vatican, 1969), cols. 265–70.

122. A third copy, now Reims MS 299, has been dated to the second half of the thirteenth century and thus is probably too late to have served as a source for the Reims rosace. See Ulla Westerbergh, *Anastarius Bibliothecarius Sermo Theodori Studitae de Sancto Bartholomeo Apostolo: A Study* (Stockholm, 1963), 21–22, 59–60, 68–69, 75–76, 119–20; also Marie-Pierre Laffitte, "Esquisse d'une bibliothèque médiévale: Le fonds de manuscrits de l'abbaye de Saint-Thierry," in *Saint-Thierry*, 97–100, also 163–64, 177. On Reims MS 1407, see Samaran and Marichal, *Catalogue* (as in note 78 above), text vol. 5, 309.

123. Dolbeau, "Typologie" (as in note 27 above), 164.

124. Demus, *The Mosaics*, 1:223–24.

125. For the knife attribute, see Mâle, *Thirteenth Century*, 305, 308–9. For the Chartres jamb statue: Sauerländer, *Gothic Sculpture*, pl. 111. For the Reims jamb statue: Kurmann, *La façade*, vol. 2, pl. 212.

126. The manuscripts are the Pamplona Bible (Bucher, *Pamplona*, vol. 2, pl. 469) and the Saint Elisabeth Psalter (Cividale, Museo archeologico nazionale, Codici sacri 7, fol. 5r: *Mostra storica nazionale della miniatura*, ed. Giovanni Muzzioli, exh. cat., 2nd ed. [Florence, 1954], 109–10, no. 152, ca. 1200–1217). The Psalter was probably made in the monastery of Reinharsbrun, Mainz. Examples later than Reims include the glass of the Strasbourg Dominican church (see note 118 above) and Saint-Père de Chartres (ca. 1295–1300). On the latter, see Lillich, *Saint-Père*, 110.

127. Migne, *Dictionnaire*, cols. 939–52.

128. Demus, *The Mosaics*, 1:220, 225, pls. 361, 373. Manhès-Deremble, *Les vitraux narratifs*, 300–301. Simon and Jude together receive four scenes in the Regensburg Martyrology: Boeckler, *Regensburg* (as in note 20 above), 52, Abb. 64–65 (fols. 120r–v).

129. See note 87 above; also Amedée Boinet, *La miniature carolingienne, ses origines, son développement* (Paris, 1913), pls. LXXV–LXXVII.

130. A more likely source in Hincmariana for the chevet program is suggested in the text below, at note 163. In chapters 5 and 7, I have proposed the influence of Hincmar's poetic compositions, and his large contributions to the coronation liturgy form the basis for the nave glazing.

131. Branner, *Manuscript Painting*, 89–90, 199 n. 10, fig. 255. Another near-contemporary example showing Matthew writing his Gospel is the sculpture from the Chartres *jubé* now in the Louvre (ca. 1240), which does include the angel: Sauerländer, *Gothic Sculpture*, 438–40, ill. 61.

132. Pseudo-Abdias, bk. 7, chaps. 1–13: Migne, *Dictionnaire*, cols. 549–62. The Golden Legend's entry for Matthew is largely an abridgment of the Pseudo-Abdias.

133. References for these cycles are in the succeeding notes.

134. See Jaraslav Folda, *The Nazareth Capitals and the Crusader Shrine of the Annunciation* (University Park, 1986), 79 n. 74. On the popularity of Matthew's martyrdom, see Demus, *The Mosaics*, 1:220, 224.

135. For the Regensburg Martyrology, see Boeckler,

Regensburg, 52, Abb. 60 (fol. 90r). For the spolium in the south rose, Notre-Dame, Paris: Recensement 1:17, pl. 1a; Jean Lafond in Aubert et al., *Les vitraux de Notre-Dame,* 64 (F-17). For Assisi: Marchini, *Vetrate dell'Umbria,* 65, color pl. LII (b7). For Saint-Ouen bay 27: Jean Lafond, *Les vitraux de l'église Saint-Ouen de Rouen,* Corpus Vitrearum Medii Aevi, France, IV-2, 1 (Paris, 1970), 118, pl. 26.

136. See F. A. Sullivan, "Apostolic Succession," in *New Catholic Encyclopedia,* 1:589–92, esp. 591.

137. Grodecki, *Le vitrail roman,* 114, 116 (fig. 95), 286; Lafond in Aubert et al., *Les vitraux de Notre-Dame,* 65 (I-17).

138. See above, at note 127. Schneemelcher, *New Testament,* 482, suggests that Simon's prominence may reflect the origin of the legend in the ancient *Acts of Peter,* through an accidental or deliberate confusion of Simon Peter with Simon the Canaanite.

139. V. L. Kennedy, *The Saints of the Canon of the Mass* (Rome, 1938), 148–49.

140. Lowe, "Vatican" (as in note 53 above), 358, 360, 368–70.

141. Ibid., 373 n. 3; *Trésors de la Bibliothèque,* cat. no. 3 with bibliography.

142. Robertson, *Guillaume de Machaut,* 39–42.

143. Schneemelcher, *New Testament,* 443–47; on the few Latin versions, 446.

144. Jacobus de Voragine, *The Golden Legend,* 1:166–71.

145. The online Index of Christian Art lists three twelfth-century Eastern manuscripts plus the famous Rabbula Gospels, now of disputed date and composition. See Massimo Bernabò, ed., *Il Tetravangelo di Rabbula: Firenze, Biblioteca Medicea Laurenziana, plut. 1.56; L'illustrazione del Nuovo Testamento nella Siria del VI secolo* (Rome, 2008).

146. Jacobus de Voragine, *The Golden Legend,* 1:169–70.

147. For the *Hortus Deliciarum,* see Herrad of Hohenbourg, *Hortus Deliciarum,* ed. Rosalie Green et al. (London, 1979), 1:184; vol. 2, pl. 104 (no. 239). For the Zweifalten Martyrology, see note 96 above; illustrated in Karl Löffler, *Schwäbische Buchmalerei in romanischer Zeit* (Augsburg, 1928), 49, pl. 24.

148. One example at Châlons is in the north-rose gallery (ca. 1255–60): Meredith Parsons Lillich, "La 'rose verte' de la cathédrale de Châlons," *Cahiers archéologiques* 49 (2001): 125, fig. 15. The second, probably originally from the south-transept clerestory (ca. 1263–70), is now in nave bay 24: eadem, "More Stained Glass Spolia at Châlons Cathedral," *Cahiers archéologiques* 45 (1997): 127, figs. 10, 12C, reprinted in *Studies,* 274, 289, figs. 10, 12C.

149. For a summary of the Parisian controversy over Pseudo-Dionysius resulting in the condemnations of the 1240s, see Meredith Parsons Lillich, "Monastic Stained Glass: Patronage and Style," in *Monasticism and the Arts,* ed. Timothy Verdon (Syracuse, 1984), 224–25 and notes, reprinted in *Studies,* 322, 337–38.

150. On the masons who built a Reims-type rose window at Cluny, see Willibald Sauerländer, "Über einen Reimser Bildhauer in Cluny," in *Gedenkschrift Ernst Gall,* ed. Margarete Kühn and Louis Grodecki (Munich, 1965), 257, 260, fig. 160. On the influence of Reims sculptors: idem, "Reims und Bamberg: Zu Art und Umfang der Übernahmen," *Zeitschrift für Kunstgeschichte* 39, 2/3 (1976): 167–92, reprinted in *Cathedrals and Sculpture,* vol. 2 (London, 2000); Dieter Kimpel and Robert Suckale, *L'architecture gothique en France 1130–1270* (Paris, 1990), 289 and 494 n. 45; Wirth, *La datation,* 70–71, 87. Reims sculptors have been suggested even earlier, in Hungary at Pannonhalma, consecrated 1224: Imre Takács, "Die Erneuerung der Abteikirche von Pannonhalma im 13. Jahrhundert," *Acta Historiae Artium* 38 (1996): esp. 52–65.

151. Kennedy, *Saints of the Canon,* 148–49; Henri Quentin, *Les martyrologes historiques du Moyen Âge* (Paris, 1908; reprint, Aalen, 1969), 51, 586.

152. For the Pseudo-Marcus, see Schneemelcher, *New Testament,* 465–66; Elliott, *Apocryphal,* 524. An English translation is in *The Ante-Nicene Fathers,* vol. VIII, ed. Alexander Roberts and James Donaldson (New York, 1903), 493–96. The version in the Golden Legend is considerably briefer: Jacobus de Voragine, *The Golden Legend,* 1:321. Voragine (319) reports a tradition according to which the Latin translator was Bede, although no such work survives.

153. For the Stuttgart Passional, see Boeckler, *Stuttgarter,* Abb. 50 (Cod. Bibl. 2° 57, fol. 90r). For the Regensburg Martyrology: Boeckler, *Regensburg,* Abb. 67 (fol. 140r). For the Psalter/Hhours (New York, Pierpont Morgan M 92, fol. 110r): Branner, *Manuscript Painting,* 58, 207 (on dating, 65).

154. Schneemelcher, *New Testament,* 466.

155. The hands appear this way in the tracing of this lobe published before World War I by Simon, "Notes sur les vitraux," opp. p. 300. Although the gestures resemble medieval number reckoning (right hand = 9,000, left hand = 8), nothing in the legend relates to this: Elisabeth Alfoeldi-Rosenbaum, "The Finger Calculus in Antiquity and in the Middle Ages: Studies on Roman Game Counters, I," *Frühmittelalterliche Studien* 5 (1971): esp. Taf. IV, VII; J. Hilton Turner, "Roman Elementary Mathematics: The Operations," *Classical Journal* 47, no. 2 (November 1951): 67–68.

156. For Barnabas's Christian hosts, see *Ante-Nicene Fathers,* VIII: 494–95; Migne, *Dictionnaire,* cols. 145–47.

157. For the cap with barbette, see Herbert Norris,

Medieval Costume and Fashion (London, 1927; reprint, Mineola, N.Y., 1999), 119. For the widow: *Ante-Nicene Fathers,* VIII:495. In Migne, *Dictionnaire,* col. 146, the old widow is poor.

158. *Ante-Nicene Fathers,* VIII:495 n. 7. Voragine calls him "Eusebius, a prominent and powerful man who was related to Nero": Jacobus de Voragine, *The Golden Legend,* 1:321. In Migne, *Dictionnaire,* cols. 147–48, he is "Jébussaeus, parent de l'empereur Néron."

159. *Ante-Nicene Fathers,* VIII:495; Migne, *Dictionnaire,* col. 145; Jacobus de Voragine, *The Golden Legend,* 1:321. Because Barnabas's legend differs, notably at the end, from the rosace, I investigated the legend of the Evangelist Mark, who was also dragged by a rope around his neck (the large figure in the lancets below the rosace is occasionally identified as Mark, though I believe erroneously; see chapter 3). Nothing in Mark's legend can account for the scenes in the Bay 107 rosace, nor for that matter can the legend of Luke.

160. For another example of the "sweetening" of a religious story, see Anne Rudloff Stanton, "Queen Mary and Her Psalter: A Gothic Manuscript in Tudor England," in *Medieval Art and Architecture After the Middle Ages,* ed. Janet T. Marquardt and Alyce A. Jordan (Newcastle upon Tyne, 2009), 23, fig. 2. Rachel survives Benjamin's birth and lives to visit Joseph in Egypt.

161. See chapter 1, which (like this paragraph) is based on Desportes, *Reims et les rémois,* 157, 162–67; a succinct summary of the years 1234–40 is on 169.

162. Robertson, *Guillaume de Machaut,* 29; for the location of the chapel of Saint-Michel, see 33 (plan).

163. Here Hincmar is borrowing from, and improving upon, St. Paul (Col. 3:5), who says "simulacrorum servitus." See Hincmar, of Reims, *De cavendis vitiis et virtutibus exercendis,* Monumenta Germaniae Historica, Quellen zur Geistesgeschichte des Mittelalters, 16 (Munich, 1998) 132.

Chapter 3

1. Henri Deneux, "Des modifications apportées à la cathédrale de Reims, au cours de sa construction, du XIIIe au XIVe siècle," *Bulletin monumental* 106 (1948): 126–28, fig. 6.

2. Jean Bony, *French Gothic Architecture of the Twelfth and Thirteenth Centuries* (Berkeley and Los Angeles, 1983), 270–71, 504 n. 19. For a discussion of Villard's drawing (Paris, BnF, fr. 19093, fol. 31v), see William W. Clark, "Reims Cathedral in the Portfolio of Villard de Honnecourt," in *Villard's Legacy: Studies in Medieval Technology, Science, and Art in Memory of Jean Gimpel,* ed. Marie-Thérèse Zenner (Aldershot, Hampshire, 2004), 48–49; Carl F. Barnes, Jr., *The Portfolio of Villard de Honnecourt (Paris, Bibliothèque nationale de France,* MS *Fr 19093): A New Critical Edition and Color Facsimile* (Burlington, Vt., 2009), 198–200, color pl. 65.

3. Jean-Pierre Ravaux, "Les campagnes de construction de la cathédrale de Reims au XIIIe siècle," *Bulletin monumental* 137 (1979): 8–9 and 59 n. 16 (1221 document and publication of its text), 37 (dating of choir clerestory and vaults); Dieter Kimpel and Robert Suckale, *L'architecture gothique en France 1130–1270* (Paris, 1990), 288–90; Peter Kurmann, *La façade de la cathédrale de Reims: Architecture et sculpture des portails, étude archéologique et stylistique* (Lausanne, 1987), 1:65–68.

4. For an example where the clerestory windows do include an added strip to heighten them, see Meredith Parsons Lillich, *The Stained Glass of Saint-Père de Chartres* (Middletown, 1978), 39.

5. The suggestion that the choir glass may have been installed once the roof was in place, before the high vaults were constructed, is not in my opinion likely. See Peter Kurmann, "L'archevêque Henri de Braine: Son rôle à la cathédrale de Reims," in *Mémoire de Champagne,* vol. 1, *Actes du 2e Mois médiéval* (Langres, 2000), 133; Brigitte Kurmann-Schwarz and Patrick Demouy, "Les vitraux du chevet de la cathédrale de Reims: Une donation de l'archevêque Henri de Braine," in Pierre Desportes et al., *Fasti ecclesiae Gallicanae: Répertoire prosopographique des évêques, dignitaires et chanoines de France de 1200 à 1500,* vol. 3, *Diocèse de Reims* (Turnhout, 1998), 47. Michael W. Cothren has considered the question at Beauvais and seems less convinced than I am that this procedure would not have occurred in the thirteenth century: Cothren, *Picturing the Celestial City: The Medieval Stained Glass of Beauvais Cathedral* (Princeton, 2006), 102 and n. 2. Considering Jean Bony's observation (quoted above, at note 2) that the Reims choir clerestories were "built from the start" to the greater height, the issue cannot be tied to the question of when the decision was made to raise the vaults. Jean Lafond once commented that clerestory glass sometimes predates aisle or chapel glass, since its installation would have been more economical when the scaffolding for the high vaults was still in place. But to endanger glass of this richness and expense while the masons had not yet completed work on the vaulting is, I believe, not a reasonable scenario. The case of Amiens, where the axial window bears the date 1269 but recent dendrochronological evidence dates the choir roof to 1284–85, is not in my opinion conclusive. Stained-glass windows can be designed once the templates for their bays exist (and financing is assured?), which may have happened in 1269. If the construction sequence of the monument was not ready for the glass when the latter was completed, it would be stored for safekeeping until such time.

6. Sylvie Balcon-Berry, "Les vitraux de la cathédrale de Reims à la lumière de recherches récentes," in *Nouveaux regards sur la cathédrale de Reims*, ed. Bruno Decrock and Patrick Demouy (Langres, 2008), 161; Sylvie Balcon, "Les vitraux," in *Reims: La cathédrale*, ed. Patrick Demouy (La Pierre-qui-vire, 2001), 345; eadem, "Les vitraux de la cathédrale d'après les documents du fonds Deneux conservés à la Bibliothèque municipale de Reims," in *Mythes et réalités de la cathédrale de Reims de 1825 à 1975* (Paris, 2001), 48–49.

7. The thirteen images are details of Bays 100 (two), 101 (one), 102 (three), 104 (one), 108 (two), and 110 (four). Balcon also lists Bay 109, but unfortunately neither of the two lost bays (105, 109) is among the Deneux autochrome photographs given to the Reims *bibliothèque*.

8. Hans Reinhardt, *La cathédrale de Reims: Son histoire, son architecture, sa sculpture, ses vitraux* (Paris, 1963), 185–86. For my study of the Bay 118 images, see chapter 4.

9. Peter Kurmann and Brigitte Kurmann-Schwarz, "Französische Bischöfe als Auftraggeber und Stifter von Glasmalereien: Das Kunstwerk als Geschichtsquelle," *Zeitschrift für Kunstgeschichte* 60 (1997): 438; Kurmann-Schwarz and Demouy, "Les vitraux du chevet," 48; Kurmann, "L'archevêque Henri de Braine," 127, 130.

10. Peter's crucifixion finds a small place at the bottom of the axial bay of the cathedral of Saint-Pierre, Poitiers, where the major areas of the design are devoted to Christ, as expected: Louis Grodecki, *Le vitrail roman* (Fribourg, 1977), 71–74, 286; see my fig. 26. Cathedrals dedicated to St. Stephen, such as Bourges and Châlons-en-Champagne, include the saint in the axial bay along with Christ and the Virgin; the sense is clear at Bourges, where Stephen carries a model of the cathedral bearing his name. For Bourges, see Recensement II:178 (baie 200); for Châlons, see Meredith Parsons Lillich, "St. Memmie, Apostle of Châlons, and Other Bishop Saints in the Gothic Windows of Châlons Cathedral," *Studies in Iconography* 19 (1998): 78, reprinted in *Studies in Medieval Stained Glass and Monasticism* (London, 2001), 175.

11. Peter has "eyeglasses" leading around his eyes, and a beautiful Deneux autochrome photo clearly shows the unique shaded drapery painting that is found only in Bay 102 (even in the rosace there). See the discussion below.

12. Balcon-Berry, "Les vitraux," 158; eadem, "Les vitraux du MoyenÂge," in *La grâce d'une cathédrale: Reims*, ed. Thierry Jordan et al. (Strasbourg, 2010), 241, 244; Balcon, "Les vitraux," in *Reims: La cathédrale*, 357, 359–60, 366.

13. François de Guilhermy, "Notes sur diverses localités de la France," Paris, BnF, nouv. acq. fr. 6106, fol. 400v, noted that James Major stands, and 1844 image (see my fig. 8) clearly shows it. John the Evangelist and James Major were brothers (Matt. 4:21). James's priestly vestments have been noted by Cerf, who, however, gives a mistaken explanation; see note 109 below.

14. He omitted the Baptist, for whom he could assign no original position: Reinhardt, *La cathédrale*, 186.

15. Madeline H. Caviness, "Modular Assemblages: Reconstructing the Choir Clerestory Glazing of Soissons Cathedral," *Journal of the Walters Art Gallery* 48 (1990): 57–68. On Saint-Remi, see eadem, *Sumptuous Arts at the Royal Abbeys in Reims and Braine: Ornatus elegantiae, varietate stupendes* (Princeton, 1990), and Anne Prache, *Saint-Remi de Reims: L'oeuvre de Pierre de Celle et sa place dans l'architecture gothique* (Geneva, 1973).

16. On Châlons, see Lillich, "St. Memmie," reprinted in *Studies*, 168–201.

17. On Henri de Braine, see Desportes et al., *Fasti*, 102, 161, 320; William Mendel Newman, *Les seigneurs de Nesle en Picardie (XIIe–XIIIe siècle): Leurs chartes et leur histoire* (Paris, 1971), 1:227, 242; Père Anselme, *Histoire généalogique et chronologique de la maison royale de France*, 3rd ed., vol. 2 (Paris, 1726; reprint, New York, 1967), 5; Jean-Pierre Ravaux, "Les évêques de Châlons-sur-Marne des origines à 1789," *Mémoires de la Société d'agriculture, commerce, sciences et arts du département de la Marne* 98 (1983): 94; Sidney Painter, *Scourge of the Clergy: Peter of Dreux, Duke of Brittany* (Baltimore, 1937), genealogical chart after p. 155, also 3–4, 45–47, 74–75, 79. On Henri de Braine's family, see also appendixes 2 and 4 in this volume.

18. This theory has been posited by Kurmann-Schwarz and Demouy, "Les vitraux du chevet," 47; Kurmann, "L'archevêque Henri de Braine," 132. I am now of their opinion; in former publications I occasionally provided a general date in the early 1230s for Bay 100 with the chevet program.

19. Meredith Parsons Lillich, "Early Heraldry: How to Crack the Code," *Gesta* 30 (1991): 44, reprinted in *Studies*, 423 (see also 438 n. 4). The Chartres north rose, on the other hand, given by Louis IX (and not by Blanche de Castille!) and iced with the king's heraldry (associated later with the Sainte-Chapelle), is dated ca. 1240 by Hervé Pinoteau, "Autour de la bulle 'Dei filius,'" in *Vingt-cinq ans d'études dynastiques* (Paris, 1982), 295–313. In 1227 Louis IX was thirteen years old, and Queen Blanche never used the heraldry found in the rose and the Sainte-Chapelle.

20. Meredith Parsons Lillich, "Heraldry and Patronage in the Lost Windows of Saint-Nicaise de Reims," in *L'art et les révolutions: XXVIIe Congrès international d'histoire de l'art* (Strasbourg, 1992), 8:76 and n. 17, reprinted in *Studies*, 441–42.

21. Meredith Parsons Lillich, "Remembrance of Things

Past: Stained Glass Spolia at Châlons Cathedral," *Zeitschrift für Kunstgeschichte* 59 (1996): 488–93 and figs. 20–21, reprinted in *Studies,* 231–32, 249–54.

22. For information about the Dreux family and their lavish arts, see Caviness, *Sumptuous Arts,* esp. 73–74, 88, 133–35, 150–51.

23. Reinhardt, *La cathédrale,* 187, grouped Bay 100 with Bay 105 to make up his third atelier, but they are not alike. Both have small heads and horizontal color bands in the drapery (the Virgin only in Bay 100), but the painting style is different. It should be noted that Balcon has established that Bay 105 is now largely a modern re-creation (see below, at note 145).

24. The spolium "facade" in Bay 118 (ca. 1219–20) has a rose resembling the Laon north rose, a circle of round medallions, while the Bay 100 "facade" has a centrifugal wheel. The tracery of the Reims transept roses had evidently not been designed by the late 1220s, when Bay 100 was probably made; the roses' tracery is strongly regional and centripetal: Meredith Parsons Lillich, "Observations on the Gothic Rose Window with Centripetal Tracery," in *Arte d'Occidente: Temi e metodi; Studi in onore di Angiola Maria Romanini,* ed. Antonio Cadei et al. (Rome, 1999), 1:198–99, fig. 2A, reprinted in *Studies,* 158–59. The tracery of the Reims south rose was blown out in a storm in 1580 and replaced in 1581 in a simplified form: Ravaux, "Les campagnes," 65 n. 114; Antoine Gilbert, *Description historique de l'église métropolitaine de Notre-Dame de Reims* (Reims, 1825), 22.

25. On the two Marian seals, see chapter 4, at note 160; also Desportes et al., *Fasti,* 20–21.

26. On *la chaire de saint Remy,* which was not a foldstool, see Dom Guillaume Marlot, *Histoire de la ville, cité et université de Reims,* vol. 1 (Reims, 1843), pièces justif., 711, and vol. 3 (1846), 524n; also Kurmann-Schwarz and Demouy, "Les vitraux du chevet," 50; Patrick Demouy, "Synodes diocésains et conciles provinciaux à Reims et en Belgique seconde aux XIe–XIIIe siècles," in *La Champagne et ses administrations à travers le temps: Actes du colloque d'histoire régionale Reims/Châlons-sur-Marne, 1987* (Paris, 1990), 105.

27. *Sceaux et usages de sceaux: Images de la Champagne médiévale,* ed. Jean-Luc Chassel (Paris, 2003), 68 and color ill. 61; see also the review of this catalogue by Arnaud Timbert in *Bulletin monumental* 163 (2003): 303–4. For the seal of Archbishop Henri de Braine, see Desportes et al., *Fasti,* 162; Patrick Demouy, "Les sceaux des archevêques de Reims des origines à la fin du XIIIe siècle," in *L'encadrement religieux des fidèles au Moyen-Âge et jusqu'au Concile de Trente,* Actes du 109e Congrès nationale des sociétés savantes: Section d'histoire médiévale et philologie, vol. 1 (Paris, 1985), no. 14.

28. A good detail photograph showing four of the five lancet borders is in Painton Cowen, *The Rose Window: Splendour and Symbol* (London, 2005), 245.

29. Kurmann-Schwarz and Demouy, "Les vitraux du chevet," 48; Caviness, *Sumptuous Arts,* 46, 118, 132, pl. 110.

30. Grodecki, *Le vitrail roman,* 72, 286, fig. 58.

31. Émile Mâle, *Religious Art in France: The Thirteenth Century,* trans. Marthiel Mathews from the 9th ed., 1958 (Princeton, 1984), 198, 458 n. 52. For Bourges, see Recensement 11:170; illustrated in Hervé Benoît, *Les grands vitraux du déambulatoire de Bourges* (Paris, 1995), pls. K and P (after p. 28).

32. On Troyes, see Elizabeth C. Pastan and Sylvie Balcon, *Les vitraux de choeur de la cathédrale de Troyes (XIIIe siècle),* Corpus Vitrearum, France, 11 (Paris, 2006), 253, fig. 355. On Saint-Gengoult, Toul (ca. 1255–61), and Ménillot in the Toul suburbs (after 1263): Meredith Parsons Lillich, *Rainbow Like an Emerald: Stained Glass in Lorraine in the Thirteenth and Early Fourteenth Centuries* (University Park, 1991), 24, 31, pls. 11 6a, 11 6c.

33. On the Châlons pre-1147 Crucifixion, see Grodecki, *Le vitrail roman,* 120–23, 278–79; Lillich, "Remembrance," 465, 468–70, 481–82, 496, reprinted in *Studies,* 206, 210–11, 242–43, 257. For the clerestory Crucifixion at Châlons: Louis Grodecki and Catherine Brisac, *Gothic Stained Glass, 1200–1300* (Ithaca, 1984), 119, fig. 105; Lillich, "St. Memmie," 77–79, reprinted in *Studies,* 171–72, fig. 4. Another suffragan cathedral, Laon, has an axial Passion window (Bay 0, ca. 1210–15), which includes the Crucifixion and the Marys at the Tomb: Recensement 1:162–63.

34. For Troyes, see Pastan and Balcon, *Troyes,* 406–9. For Auxerre: Virginia Chieffo Raguin, *Stained Glass in Thirteenth-Century Burgundy* (Princeton, 1982), 78. For Beauvais: Cothren, *Picturing the Celestial City,* 108–10, pl. 117.

35. Pierre Desportes, *Reims et les rémois aux XIIIe et XIVe siècles* (Paris, 1979), 156.

36. Two more of the five were their cousins, Enguerrand III de Coucy and Mathieu II de Montmorency; the fifth was Philippe Hurepel, half-brother of Louis VIII and the queen's brother-in-law. Yolande's father, Mauclerc, had promised her to King Henry III of England in late 1226. Either union would have required papal dispensation. In May 1227 the pope forbade the marriage of Yolande to Jean d'Anjou, but Queen Blanche insisted that she not be returned to her father until Jean did reach age fourteen. Jean died soon, probably in 1227. See Painter, *Scourge,* 41, 45–47, 59.

37. Desportes, *Reims et les rémois,* 157, 159 n. 26. Mauclerc had done homage to the English king again in 1229.

38. Painter, *Scourge,* 74–75, 78–79.

39. Although in principle annual events, provincial

councils were not infrequently skipped or were so pro forma as to have left no records. Henri's next council was probably in 1233. Demouy, "Synodes diocésains," 104, 109 n. 32; Kurmann-Schwarz and Demouy, "Les vitraux du chevet," 50–51.

40. Barbara Abou-El-Haj, "Program and Power in the Glass of Reims," in *Radical Art History, Internationale Anthologie, Subject: O. K. Werckmeister,* ed. Wolfgang Kersten (Zurich, 1997), 27, remarks that this "arrangement [of the apostolic succession] I think of as an administrative version of Pentecost or the Mission of the Apostles." The traditional part (apostles flanking the Virgin and Crucifixion) was copied at Beauvais, a *rémois* suffragan cathedral, in the more advanced band-window format: see Cothren, *Picturing the Celestial City,* 110–11.

41. Anne Walters Robertson, *Guillaume de Machaut and Reims: Context and Meaning in His Musical Works* (Cambridge, 2002), 354, based on Reims, Bibl. mun. 221, fol. 60r (twelfth century), and Troyes, Bibl. mun. 1951, fol. 60v (late twelfth century).

42. At present, Matthew and Jude (Bay 105) are interchanged and turn their backs on one another, which never happens in medieval art. Evidence from the nineteenth century indicates that this error was committed in the post–World War I restoration. They appear correctly in the engraving in Cahier and Martin, *Bourges,* vol. 2, Études XIX (my fig. 9), and Guilhermy, "Notes," fol. 400r, describes them in that order.

43. Demouy, "Synodes diocésains," 105, seems to suggest a glazier's error. Dany Sandron, "La cathédrale et l'architecte: À propos de la façade occidentale de Laon," in *Pierre, lumière, couleur: Études d'histoire de l'art du Moyen Âge en l'honneur d'Anne Prache,* ed. Fabienne Joubert and Dany Sandron (Paris, 1999), 143 n. 35, thinks it was probably not a glazier's error but admits "la raison de cette inversion complète nous échappe."

44. Lillich, "St. Memmie," 77 and n. 8, reprinted in *Studies,* 171. At Reims the entrance was on the south, but the throne was always situated on axis.

45. See, e.g., Recensement IV:388–89; Kurmann-Schwarz and Demouy, "Les vitraux du chevet," 51; Balcon, "Les vitraux," in *Reims: La cathédrale,* 364. Both Barnabas and Matthias appear at Bourges, but Barnabas eventually became more popular as attributes developed, probably because his attribute, a flame, is so distinctive. See Lillich, *Saint-Père,* 101 n. 23 (to the list can be added the Breviary of Philippe le Bel, Paris, BnF, lat. 1023, fol. 332v), also 102 n. 35, 118–19; eadem, *The Armor of Light: Stained Glass in Western France, 1250–1325* (Berkeley and Los Angeles, 1994), 236, 301, 303, fig. IX.2, color pls. 50A, 61.

46. Cothren, *Picturing the Celestial City,* 233 n. 56; Lillich, *Saint-Père,* 83–84, 96–98, 118–21. For example, the Saint-Père hemicycle (early fourteenth century; see ibid., 93) comprises sixteen apostles, including Paul and Barnabas, and there may have been more, since the four figures in the western bay on the south are now lost.

47. Mâle, *Thirteenth Century,* 309.

48. At the suffragan cathedral of Châlons, attributes are markedly more developed in the north-rose gallery (ca. 1255–60) and in the group of apostles from the south transept, now in bay 24 (ca. 1263–70): Meredith Parsons Lillich, "La 'rose verte' de la cathédrale de Châlons," *Cahiers archéologiques* 49 (2001): 125, fig. 15; eadem, "More Stained Glass Spolia at Châlons Cathedral," *Cahiers archéologiques* 45 (1997): 126–27, figs. 10, 12, reprinted in *Studies,* 273–74, 289. The suffragan cathedral of Beauvais, however, has a series of apostles with quite conventional attributes, datable ca. 1255–60 up to 1272: Cothren, *Picturing the Celestial City,* 102, 110–11. The lack of more advanced attributes seems to me to support his earlier dating.

49. Demouy, "Synodes diocésains," 104, suggests the least prestigious to be the most recently established and furthest geographically from Reims (Arras, 1093, and Tournai, 1146), or perhaps the tiny diocese of Senlis, or Cambrai, which was the only one not in France.

50. None of the lists coincide exactly, and they obviously include guesswork. For example, Ferdinand de Lasteyrie gives an inscription for the Beauvais "facade" (Bay 104), while François de Guilhermy states that it had "plus d'inscription," and none appears in the Cahier-Martin engraving: Lasteyrie, *Histoire de la peinture sur verre d'après ses monuments en France,* vol. 1 (Paris, 1857), 88; Guilhermy, "Notes," fol. 400v; Cahier and Martin, *Bourges,* vol. 2, Études XVIII (my fig. 8). Also consulted were Victor Tourneur, *Histoire et description des vitraux et des statues de l'intérieur de la cathédrale de Reims* (Reims, 1857); Charles Cerf, *Histoire et description de Notre-Dame de Reims,* 2 vols. (Reims, 1861); and Étienne Povillon-Piérard, *Description historique de l'église métropolitaine de Notre-Dame de Rheims* (Reims, 1823).

51. The reversal of Matthew and Jude in Bay 105 is, however, modern. See note 42 above.

52. The reversal of bishop and "facade" in Bay 106 is not a modern error; it appears in Cahier and Martin, *Bourges,* vol. 2, Études XIX (my fig. 9).

53. Guilhermy, "Notes," fol. 400r; Cerf, *Histoire,* 2:280; Tourneur, *Histoire,* 48; Cahier and Martin, *Bourges,* vol. 2, Études XIX (my fig. 9).

54. On illiterate glaziers, see Meredith Parsons Lillich, "Gothic Glaziers: Monks, Jews, Taxpayers, Bretons, Women," *Journal of Glass Studies* 27 (1985): 75 and n. 17,

reprinted in *Studies,* 5; eadem, *The Armor,* 52; eadem, "St. Memmie," 80, 85–86, reprinted in *Studies,* 173, 182.

55. Cerf, *Histoire,* 2:271–72. Eva Frodl-Kraft, "Zu den Kirchenschaubildern in den Hochchorfenstern von Reims: Abbildung und Abstraktion," *Wiener Jahrbuch für Kunstgeschichte* 25 (1972): 57–75 passim.

56. Stephen Murray, *Notre-Dame, Cathedral of Amiens: The Power of Change in Gothic* (Cambridge, 1996), 67.

57. For Laon, see William W. Clark and Richard King, *Laon Cathedral: Architecture,* vol. 1, Courtauld Companion Text, 1 (London, 1983), 47, 52, 54. For Soissons: Dany Sandron, *La cathédrale de Soissons, architecture du pouvoir* (Paris, 1998), 131, 139. For Amiens: Murray, *Amiens,* 95, 102. For Noyon: Charles Seymour Jr., *Notre-Dame of Noyon in the Twelfth Century: A Study in the Early Development of Gothic Architecture* (New Haven, 1939; reprint, New York, 1968), 66–67, 140, fig. 75.

58. For Beauvais, see Stephen Murray, *Beauvais Cathedral: Architecture of Transcendence* (Princeton, 1989), 10–12, where the author discusses the Basse-Oeuvre, which excavations have established had some sort of porch, or *Westwerk.* For Châlons, whose facade, dated by Ravaux either ca. 1150–60 or ca. 1186 and replaced only in 1628, had three portals and two unfinished towers, see Jean-Pierre Ravaux, "Les cathédrales de Châlons-sur-Marne avant 1230," *Mémoires de la Société d'agriculture, commerce, sciences et arts du département de la Marne* 89 (1974): 60–63. For Tournai, whose mid-twelfth-century nave facade now has a postmedieval porch and sculpture, a later wheel window, and no towers, see Xavier Barral I Alter, ed., *L'art du vitrail XIIe–XIIIe siècle* (Paris, 2004), 248 (ill.); for dating, see Bony, *French Gothic Architecture,* 487 n. 22.

59. Frodl-Kraft, "Kirchenschaubildern," 71–72; see now Sandron, "La cathédrale et l'architecte," 141–44.

60. Peter Kurmann, "Architecture, vitrail et orfèvrerie: À propos des premiers dessins d'édifices gothiques," in *Représentations architecturales dans les vitraux: Actes du XXIe colloque du Corpus Vitrearum,* Dossier de la Commission royal des monuments, sites et fouilles, 9 (Liege, 2002), esp. 35–36, 39–40.

61. Frodl-Kraft, "Kirchenschaubildern," 66–67; Sandron, "La cathédrale et l'architecte," 142 n. 32; Kurmann, "Architecture, vitrail," 36; Abou-El-Haj, "Program and Power," 29.

62. Frodl-Kraft, "Kirchenschaubildern," 70 n. 28, 73; Sandron, "La cathédrale et l'architecte," 142 n. 32; Kurmann, "Architecture, vitrail," 36. For a color plate of the Tournai "facade," see Martine Callias Bey, Véronique David, and Michel Hérold, *Vitrail: Peinture de lumière* (Lyon, 2006), 57.

63. Kurmann, "Architecture, vitrail," 35, 39, figs. 3–4; Abou-El-Haj, "Program and Power," 29; Sandron, "La cathédrale et l'architecte," 142 n. 32.

64. Kurmann, "Architecture, vitrail," 36 n. 28.

65. Alain Villes, *La cathédrale Saint-Étienne de Châlons-en-Champagne* (Langres, 2002), 219, figs. 16, 147; Kurmann, "Architecture, vitrail," 35. See the engraving showing the Châlons twelfth-century facade and two transept towers: Alain Villes, "La concurrence entre la cathédrale Saint-Étienne et la collégiale Notre-Dame-en-Vaux de Châlons-en-Champagne, son intérêt pour l'archéologie et l'histoire de l'art," in *Architektur und Monumentalskulptur des 12.–14. Jahrhunderts, Produktion und Rezeption: Festschrift für Peter Kurmann zum 65. Geburtstag,* ed. Stephan Gasser, Christian Freigang, and Bruno Boerner (Bern, 2006), 105–6, fig. 4. The eighty-meter wooden spire on the north tower, shown in the engraving, was constructed in 1520 and destroyed by lightning in 1668.

66. Kurmann, "Architecture, vitrail," 35–36, figs. 5–6. This part of Beauvais cathedral is discussed and dated in Murray, *Beauvais,* 66–67, 83.

67. Clark, "Reims Cathedral in the Portfolio"; see also Barnes, *The Portfolio,* 223–24.

68. James S. Ackerman, "Villard de Honnecourt's Drawings of Reims Cathedral: A Study in Architectural Representation," *Artibus et Historiae* 18, no. 35 (1997): 48.

69. Henri Deneux, "Signes lapidaires et épures du XIIIe siècle à la cathédrale de Reims," *Bulletin monumental* 84 (1925): 125, figs. 19–20; Robert Branner, "The North Transept and the First West Facades of Reims Cathedral," *Zeitschrift für Kunstgeschichte* 24 (1961): 231–33, fig. 11.

70. Kurmann, "Architecture, vitrail," 33–37. Alanus de Rosceio was a canon in 1192: Desportes et al., *Fasti,* 567, no. 1053.

71. Frodl-Kraft, "Kirchenschaubildern," 57, 67–71, figs. 5, 11. She also mentions the gargoyles and the buttresses with double flyers in the spolium "facade" (cf. her figs. 11 and 12), and that both Reims "facades" have crenellations on the roof.

72. Kurmann, "Architecture, vitrail," 35–36. For Villard's fol. 32v, see Barnes, *The Portfolio,* 209–10, color pl. 67; Clark, "Reims Cathedral in the Portfolio," 28, fig. 2.3(a).

73. Lillich, "Observations," reprinted in *Studies,* 155–67.

74. For the Beauvais "facade" (Bay 104), see Kurmann, "Architecture, vitrail," 40, fig. 6, which illustrates the Beauvais south transept, east aisle, where the rose has been rebuilt; for examples of simple centrifugal wheels in the same elevation see Murray, *Beauvais,* pls. 42 (north transept, east aisle) and 46 (south transept, east side of east aisle). None of the Beauvais wheels is on a major facade; they light

lower levels of the complex Beauvais elevation. For "Noyon" (Bay 106), see Abou-El-Haj, "Program and Power," 29, where the author has noted that the "Noyon" wheel window resembles the small rose on the cathedral treasury north of the chevet, dated ca. 1170–75, and is again not a major facade window. On the Noyon-treasury rose, see Lillich, "Observations," 198, reprinted in *Studies,* 156.

75. Branner, "The North Transept," 231–32, notes that the engraved scale drawings on the transept's triforium wall could not have been made from the completed triforium passage "unless he [the man who made them] were a giant or were standing on a platform in the passage. . . . This was probably before the triforium arcade had been put in place, for only at such a moment would the rear walls of the passage have presented extensive, accessible surfaces." A scaffold must have been present in the transept at the time.

76. Willibald Sauerländer, "Über einen Reimser Bildhauer in Cluny," in *Gedenkschrift Ernst Gall,* ed. Margarete Kühn and Louis Grodecki (Munich, 1965), 257 (fig. 160) and 260; Kimpel and Suckale, *L'architecture,* 514–15.

77. The north-rose glazing (chapter 4) dates to the 1240s, and the tracery and glass may have been installed from the same scaffolding. The south rose window was blown out in a storm in 1580 and rebuilt in simpler fashion: Lillich, "Observations," 201–2, reprinted in *Studies,* 162. See note 24 above and chapter 4.

78. Lillich, "Observations," 199, reprinted in *Studies,* 159.

79. See above, at notes 57 and 61.

80. Barnes, *The Portfolio,* 198–200; Clark, "Reims Cathedral in the Portfolio," 49, fig. 2.16 (left). The second text on fol. 31v: "On the caps of the piers there must be angels. In front of these there must be flying buttresses." This does not correspond exactly to their location as built.

81. Tourneur, *Histoire,* 47, first noted that the angel in Bay 100 holds the archbishop's cross-staff. On cross-staffs, see Norris, *Church Vestments,* 141, pls. III (opp. p. 15) and XVI (opp. p. 77), fig. 204 (p. 140). See also my fig. 18.

82. Reinhardt, *La cathédrale,* 186, first identified this theme.

83. Peter Kurmann, "Le portail apocalyptique de la cathédrale de Reims: À propos de son iconographie," in *L'Apocalypse de Jean: Traditions exégétiques et iconographiques, IIIe–XIIIe siècles,* ed. Yves Christe (Geneva, 1979), 254–55.

84. Yves Christe, "Cuncto tempore saeculi: Théophanies présentes et futures dan l'iconographie monumentale du haut Moyen Âge," in *Atti del XXIV Congresso internazionale di storia dell'arte,* vol. 1 (Bologna, 1979), 140; idem, *L'Apocalypse de Jean: Sens et développements de ses visions synthétiques* (Paris, 1996), 161.

85. A simpler explanation might be that, since "Amiens" shares Bay 105 with the bishop of Senlis, the absence of an angel on the roof could be another indication of the eventual breakdown in the achievement of the choir program, discussed below. I think the shadow of a sophisticated programmer is worth considering, since the rosace scenes are so unusual and carefully studied and chosen. To return to the puzzlement of scholars over Bay 105, Cerf, *Histoire,* 2:279, suggests that the telamon seated on a mound or cushion above "Amiens" is its angel, and Guilhermy, "Notes," fol. 400r, actually calls it a half-figure angel. But the creature has no wings, sits stoically supporting his apostle, and in no way resembles an angel. He is a "socle," like the one below the bishop in the same bay (a lioness?). More "socles" appear in Bays 101, 102, and 106 (the latter a pair of telamons). The apostles in the upper row of Bay 105, Matthew and Jude, are presently reversed but occupied their correct lancets in the nineteenth century (see note 42 above). The telamon could support either of them.

86. Reinhardt, *La cathédrale,* 186; Frodl-Kraft, "Kirchenschaubildern," 78, 82. Frodl-Kraft called the "facade" in Bay 107 "Morinie," since the bishop in that bay is so named in inscription. The "facade," however, is unidentified by inscription. See above, at note 53.

87. Christe (in "Cuncto," 139, and *L'Apocalypse de Jean,* 161) states that the "Soissons" angel makes a gesture of benediction, but this is clearly not the case: see the comment of Adolphe Napoleon Didron, *Christian Iconography: The History of Christian Art in the Middle Ages,* trans. E. J. Millington (London, 1851; reprint, New York, 1965), 1:407n. Cerf, *Histoire,* 2:271, states that the angel holds a book, but the Cahier-Martin engraving clearly shows a scroll: Cahier and Martin, *Bourges,* vol. 2, Études XVIII (my fig. 8). In the Apocalypse sculptures on the south portal of the main facade, several decades later, the angels of the seven churches hold open scrolls: Kurmann, "Le portail apocalyptique," 254, 292 (fig. 12). No angel in the entire text of the Apocalypse is described therein as holding a scroll. I believe the scroll identifies this angel as the seventh, making the prophecy of doomsday (see below).

88. Yves Christe, "The Apocalypse in the Monumental Art of the Eleventh Through Thirteenth Centuries," in *The Apocalypse in the Middle Ages,* ed. Richard Emmerson and Bernard McGinn (Ithaca, 1992), 235, 240; Robert E. Lerner, "The Medieval Return to the Thousand-Year Sabbath," in ibid., 55–56; E. Ann Matter, "The Apocalypse in Early Medieval Exegesis," in ibid., 50. Peter the Chanter (d. 1197) was originally from Reims: Beryl Smalley, *The Study of the Bible in the Middle Ages* (Oxford, 1952; reprint, Notre Dame, 1978), 257. On the Chanter, see Smalley's chap. V passim; on Richard of Saint-Victor (d. 1173), 106–11.

89. Christe, "The Apocalypse in the Monumental Art," 255; also Lerner, "The Medieval Return," 54–55.

90. On the six trumpeting angels in present (or past) time, see Christe, "The Apocalypse in the Monumental Art," 237–38, 240, 257; Lerner, "The Medieval Return," 54.

91. William W. Clark, "Reading Reims, I: The Sculptures on the Chapel Buttresses," *Gesta* 39 (2000): 140–41. This article contains fine illustrations of them all.

92. Raguin, *Burgundy,* 60–63; Recensement III:114, 121–23; Meredith Parsons Lillich, "The Band Window: A Theory of Origin and Development," *Gesta* 9, pt. 1 (1970): 28–29, reprinted in *Studies,* 70–72. In this work of *jeunesse* I followed Grodecki in including the Saint-Remi tribune windows (n. 17); Caviness has now established that the figures there were later insertions: Caviness, *Sumptuous Arts,* 49, pls. 92–93. In my opinion this type of grisaille/color combination began at Notre-Dame in Paris in the clerestories newly enlarged after ca. 1225, and the change was theologically driven: Lillich, *The Armor,* 6–8; Cothren, *Picturing the Celestial City,* 112–13.

93. See chapter 1. The archbishop was in a power struggle with Louis IX from 1233 to January 1236, and troubles with *rémois* bourgeois came to a boil in spring 1235, when they attacked the archbishop's law court, recently moved to the Porte de Mars, and killed his marshal.

94. Reinhardt, *La cathédrale,* 186. Even by his own criteria the other figures he includes in the "first atelier" (Bays 109 and 110 and the apostles in 108) do not form a coherent group; see the discussion below. Unfortunately, the adoption of his theory in Recensement IV:384 has given it new life. Among numerous errors of detail in the latter work, the bishops in Bay 109 are called archbishops (389). Neither one has a pallium, rationale, or cross-staff, the only items distinguishing an archbishop from a bishop.

95. Caviness, *Sumptuous Arts,* pls. 145–55, 157–60, color pls. 5–7.

96. Ibid., 104–5, pls. 81 and 86.

97. Kurmann, *La façade,* 1:66, and Kimpel and Suckale, *L'architecture,* 290, believe that the old nave was removed in the early or mid 1220s. Ravaux, "Les campagnes," 10–11, 39, prefers a date around 1241.

98. Victor Beyer, Christiane Wild-Block, and Fridtjof Zschokke, *Les vitraux de la cathédrale Notre-Dame de Strasbourg,* Corpus Vitrearum, France, IX-1 (Paris, 1986), 26, 28–29 (figs. 10–11), and 150–51; Caviness, *Sumptuous Arts,* pls. 9a–b.

99. On the other hand, I believe the famous Karolvs in Bay 128 was salvaged from Samson's cathedral, perhaps the nave. The figure is presently modern, having been destroyed in the First World War. The Deneux autochrome of 1915 shows the eyes more detached, less "shifty" and side-glancing. See chapter 6.

100. Cothren, *Picturing the Celestial City,* 96–99, 193–94. He dates them to the 1240s.

101. The archbishop's conflicts with his monarch, his canons, and his bourgeois only began to occupy him around 1233. See chapter 1.

102. Caviness has suggested the same thing at Saint-Remi, where bay N.VI differs from the other clerestories, employing working procedures that seem to have been judged unsatisfactory once the glass was installed: Caviness, *Sumptuous Arts,* 110–11. A similar suggestion can be made about the decoration in the rays of the Reims west rose; see chapter 7 at note 59.

103. The glazier copied this detail from the Reims "facade" of ca. 1219–20, where the gargoyle heads are much larger but no rainwater spews from them (see fig. 148). Installed in Samson's facade, the panel would not have been as far from the viewer as are the present chevet clerestories.

104. For Chartres, see Marcel Aubert et al., *Le vitrail français* (Paris, 1958), 135 (fig. 102). For Strasbourg: Beyer, Wild-Block, and Zschokke, *Strasbourg,* figs. 165, 526, pl. V. For Beauvais: Cothren, *Picturing the Celestial City,* 117–18, 185–86 (pls. 123–24, 202b, 203a).

105. Lewis Day, *Windows: A Book About Stained and Painted Glass,* 3rd ed. (London, 1909), 40. The mouths, severe straight lines, are also leaded in, as noted by Reinhardt, *La cathédrale,* 186. The other hemicycle bays do not adopt this method, but it does recur in Bay 106. See the discussion of Bay 106 below.

106. The glazier may be copying the arrangement of the Reims "facade" of ca. 1219–20, where the inscription is also placed above, although it is much more regular and legible. See figs. 73, 148.

107. The painting on Paul's yellow mantle, which appears more heavily laid on, is a modern restoration; cf. the Deneux autochrome of 1915 (fig. 74). This mantle, inexplicably, is said to be red by Cerf, *Histoire,* 2:276.

108. For illustrations of gargoyles on the cathedral, see Alain Erlande-Brandenburg, *La cathédrale de Reims: Chef-d'oeuvre du gothique* (Arles, 2007), 73; Kurmann, *La façade,* vol. 2, pls. 21, 115–16. Tourneur, *Histoire,* 45, reports that James's "socle" is a duck and that Cahier and Martin considered it "an emblem of St. James's peregrinations."

109. The only author to undertake an explanation is Cerf, *Histoire,* 2:276, who says that James wears priestly vestments because he was bishop of Jerusalem. This is a patent error, since it was James the Less, not James Major, who was bishop of Jerusalem and indeed is depicted that way in his rosace (Bay 104).

110. Ravaux, "Les campagnes," 9. A chaplaincy under James's patronage was established in 1190 in the previous cathedral.

111. For the rosace, see chapter 2.

112. See appendix 4.

113. In an unconvincing paragraph John Gage has asserted that in medieval art Peter was normally clothed in a blue tunic and yellow cloak or "related hues". Gage, *Color and Meaning: Art, Science, and Symbolism* (Berkeley and Los Angeles, 1999), 70–71. Among the related hues Gage mentions are green (tunic) and light pink (cloak), similar to those found in Bay 102. Peter wears these colors in the left lancet as well as in one of the lobes of the rosace, but so does the emperor Nero there. I prefer to see these as the colors the artist chose to unify his composition. Green plays a major role in the ornament of the rosace, which is unusual, and the large blocks of color in the lancets are all repeated in the rosace.

114. Note however that the chasuble of the bishop of Soissons is now largely remade. See the Deneux photo, reproduced in Balcon-Berry, "Moyen Âge" (as in note 12 above), 238, fig. 24.

115. Variants of both types of borders occur earlier in the Chartres clerestory, contemporary with Reims in the Troyes clerestory, and, in simplified forms, later at Beauvais.

116. Good details are found in Balcon-Berry, "Moyen Âge", 239, fig. 25 (Châlons bishop) and 241, fig. 27 (John); Aubert et al., *Le vitrail français,* 143, fig. 107, and Raguin, *Burgundy,* fig. 90 (Philip); Caviness, "Modular Assemblages," 61, fig. 9 (Thomas); and Lillich, "Remembrance," figs. 23–24, reprinted in *Studies,* 234 (rosaces).

117. No relationship between Modena and Reims is intended, just a recognition of two comparably powerful artists. For Wiligelmo's jamb figures, see Roberto Salvini, *Wiligelmo e le origini della scultura romanica* (Milan, 1956), figs. 17–22 (between pp. 16 and 17).

118. John is writing his Gospel. He is not on Patmos addressing the seven churches of Asia, as sometimes stated; see, e.g., Abou-El-Haj, "Program and Power," 29 n. 48.

119. Epernay, Bibl. mun., MS I. The Evangelist portraits are on fols. 18v, 60v, 90v, and 125v; the book's patron was Archbishop Ebbo, ca. 816–35. See Florentine Mütherich and Joachim Gaehde, *Carolingian Painting* (New York, 1976), 25, 59, pl. 15.

120. Didron, *Christian Iconography,* 2:395; see also 1:407–8, figs. 21, 24, 49, 52; on the "Guide to Painting," 2:189–91. On the Greek gesture of benediction, see also Norris, *Church Vestments,* 183–84.

121. The architects pictured in the lost Reims labyrinth have most often been identified, in order, as Jean d'Orbais, Jean le Loup, Gaucher de Reims, and Bernard de Soissons. See Ravaux, "Les campagnes," 57; Robert Branner, "The Labyrinth of Reims Cathedral," *Journal of the Society of Architectural Historians* 21, no. 1 (March 1962): 18–25. Erlande-Brandenburg, *La cathédrale,* 124–25, lists scholars who have studied this problem and their conclusions concerning the order of architects.

122. Recensement IV:386. For Paul Simon's tracing of the panel, see Louis Demaison, *La cathédrale de Reims* (Reims, 1913), 115.

123. Robert Branner, "Jean d'Orbais and the Cathedral of Reims," *Art Bulletin* 43 (1961): 131–33.

124. Chartres bay 16 (Sts. Margaret and Catherine, traditionally dated 1220–27) was given by several donors including Marguerite de Lèves: Colette Manhès-Deremble, *Les vitraux narratifs de la cathédrale de Chartres: Étude iconographique,* Corpus Vitrearum, France, Études, II (Paris, 1993), 15–17. The rosace of bay 116 (St. Denis giving the oriflamme to Jean Clément de Mez) shows John the Baptist and the arms of Clément: Recensement II:39. Another possible example would be the lost bay 111 (life of the Baptist), given by a queen of Castille, perhaps Jeanne de Dammartin: Mâle, *Thirteenth Century,* 321; Yves Delaporte and Étienne Houvet, *Les vitraux de la cathédrale de Chartres* (Chartres, 1926), text vol., 432–33.

125. Manhès-Deremble, *Les vitraux narratifs,* 28. She gives no source for this information.

126. François Garnier, *Le langage de l'image au Moyen Âge,* 2 vols. (Paris, 1982–89). On finger reckoning, see Elisabeth Alfoeldi-Rosenbaum, "The Finger Calculus in Antiquity and in the Middle Ages: Studies on Roman Game Counters, I," *Frühmittelalterliche Studien* 5 (1971): 4–9, Taf. I–VIII; J. Hilton Turner, "Roman Elementary Mathematics: The Operations," *Classical Journal* 47, no. 2 (November 1951): 66 (ill.).

127. Roland Bechmann, "The Saracen's Sepulcher: An Interpretation of Folio 6r in the Portfolio of Villard de Honnecourt," in *Villard's Legacy* (as in note 2 above), 121–34, esp. 130; Barnes, *The Portfolio,* 54. Note that Bechmann describes the master's gesture as made by the right hand, with index and little finger extended, thumb and two middle fingers folded. However, careful examination of folio 6r reveals that only the thumb and ring finger are bent in, as with the gesture made by St. John in Bay 104. Bechmann identifies his source as Renauld Beffeyte, who, however, in the same volume (pp. 97, 99) has made more fundamental errors, misinterpreting the Latin gesture of benediction made by Christ, bishops, and so forth, as the gesture for eight—which can only be made with the left hand (see the previous note). More standard theories

concerning the "Saracen's Tomb" are listed in Barnes, *The Portfolio*, 53–54.

128. On the reused images in Bay 118, see chapter 4; on the proposed "first atelier," see Reinhardt, *La cathédrale*, 186–87. He includes, besides Bays 103 and 104, the upper row of Bay 108 as well as Bays 109 and 110 (discussed below). These figures do not form a coherent stylistic group in any detail of his description of the atelier. The leading of faces, for example, is similar in Bays 108 through 110, but does not resemble that of Bays 103 and 104. Reinhardt states that the color of the "group" is *clair*, but some windows have a decidedly somber palette, e.g., Bay 103.

129. Kurmann, *La façade*, 1:167.

130. These characteristics are adopted from the initial paragraph of Robert Branner, *Manuscript Painting in Paris During the Reign of Saint Louis* (Berkeley and Los Angeles, 1977), chap. 2.

131. On this conflict, see Cothren, *Picturing the Celestial City*, 55 and notes; Desportes et al., *Fasti*, 161; Desportes, *Reims et les rémois*, 157.

132. Desportes et al., *Fasti*, 161, 320; Ravaux, "Les évêques de Châlons" (as in note 17 above), 94.

133. On the involvement of the officers of Châlons in diplomacy with the king in 1233–35, see Thomas Gousset, *Actes de la province ecclésiastique de Reims*, vol. 2 (Reims, 1843), 363–67 passim; Desportes, *Reims et les rémois*, 163. On Henri de Braine's window at Châlons: Lillich, "Remembrance," 488–93, reprinted in *Studies*, 232 (fig. 21), 249–54.

134. It is particularly evident in the drawing in Lasteyrie, *Histoire*, vol. 2, pl. XV (my fig. 85). The leading around the Beauvais bishop's head (Bay 104) is too irregular to allow the same conclusion. However, there is a peculiar mistake in his vestments. The red vertical orphrey down the front of his chasuble disappears (as it should) on the dalmatic below but seems to reappear on the white alb below that, where two ends of the stole should be. A stupid mistake, a poor restoration, or evidence of reworking to eliminate an archbishop's pallium? The postwar re-creation of these windows renders close examination of the glass inconclusive, but the pre-1914 Simon tracing might provide evidence when it becomes available.

135. On the close relations between the archbishop and Châlons at this time, see chapter 5.

136. Caviness, *Sumptuous Arts*, and eadem, "Modular Assemblages," passim.

137. See notes 157–58 below. The nave clerestory glazing developed along the same path as the straight chevet, but it could hardly predate Bays 105 through 110.

138. Ravaux, "Les campagnes," 37.

139. Desportes, *Reims et les rémois*, 167. The chapter only agreed to the archbishop's demand to cease church services altogether in mid-1240, a week before he died.

140. Ibid., 161–62.

141. Lillich, *The Armor*, 6–8; eadem, "Monastic Stained Glass," 225–33, reprinted in *Studies*, 338–45. White glass was not necessarily cheaper to produce: *Studies*, 313 n. 36, 395 n. 2.

142. Bartholomew's skinning (Bay 106) is of course the exception, but like Peter's upside-down crucifixion (Bay 102), it was among the very commonest and earliest images of martyrdom to develop in art: Mâle, *Thirteenth Century*, 305, 307. Besides, perhaps even the canons of Reims could not imagine that their fellow citizens would skin them!

143. Compare figs. 32 (105, Matthew) and 33 (106, Simon) in Balcon-Berry, "MoyenÂge," 245, with the caveat that 105 is modern (ibid., 239; note 145 below).

144. Cerf, *Histoire*, 2:274, 279, mentions, with some errors, all of the "socles" in Bays 105 and 106 except Simon's duck monster. It appears in the engraving in Cahier and Martin, *Bourges*, vol. 2, Études XIX (see my fig. 9).

145. Balcon-Berry, "Les vitraux," 161; Balcon, "Documents du fonds Deneux," 49; eadem, "Les vitraux," in *Reims: La cathédrale*, 346. Unfortunately, there are no Deneux autochrome photos of either Bay 105 or 106.

146. Desportes, *Reims et les rémois*, 166.

147. The apostle with palm (Bay 108) is identified as Mark by Frodl-Kraft, "Kirchenschaubildern," 83, pl. 44, and in Recensement IV:389. The same figure is called Luke by William M. Hinkle, *The Portal of the Saints of Reims Cathedral: A Study in Mediaeval Iconography* (New York, 1965), app. J, and by Balcon, "Les vitraux," in *Reims: La Cathédrale*, 363–64. And vice versa for the apostle with scroll (Bay 107).

148. Robertson, *Guillaume de Machaut*, 33.

149. Most of the haloes in the rosaces of Bays 105 and 106 have an almost invisible jeweled pattern, in no way similar to the emphatic pearling of the Bay 108 rosace (which is painted in stickwork on a variety of colored glasses). For Alsatian examples, see Recensement V:137, fig. 129 (Strasbourg, John the Baptist and John the Evangelist, late twelfth century); 139, fig. 130 (Wissembourg, late twelfth century); 175, fig. 155 (Niederhaslach, ca. 1275); for an example close in date to Reims, see Beyer, Wild-Block, and Zschokke, *Strasbourg*, 131, pl. IV (New Testament rose, south transept, ca. 1235). For the comparable red circles at Laon, see Cowen, *The Rose Window*, 72; Grodecki and Brisac, *Gothic Stained Glass*, 38, fig. 24; in Reims Bay 102, my fig. 34; in the Reims north rose, my figs. 122–23, 129–32, 134.

150. Professor Jürgen Michler kindly allowed me to use his measured drawings for figure 27. See Michler, "Fenster- und Masswerksysteme in der nordfranzösischen Gotik des 13. Jahrhunderts," *Wallraf-Richartz Jahrbuch* 62 (2001):

77–78, fig. 6. Recensement IV:386–89 gives the width of the hemicycle bays as 3.40 m, of Bays 105 and 106 as 4 m, of Bays 107 and 108 as 5.20 m, of Bays 109 and 110 as 6.40 m.

151. Reinhardt, *La cathédrale,* 186–87. Bays 103 and 104 have antiquizing "wet drapery," while the line is spare and softer in Bay 108. The Deneux autochrome of the apostle with palm (Bay 108) does not show the obsessive, heavy spoon-folds in his drapery, which are modern; and they do not appear in the other figures in the bay.

152. Reinhardt, *La cathédrale,* 187, grouped him in his final, fourth atelier, which he called "more evolved." See the color illustration in Balcon, "Les vitraux," in *Reims: La cathédrale,* pl. 128 (after p. 348).

153. Balcon reports that Bay 107 is largely original, having been down for restoration during World War I: Balcon-Berry, "Les vitraux," 161; Balcon, "Les vitraux," in *Reims: La cathédrale,* 345; eadem, "Documents du fonds Deneux," 48–49.

154. The pearled haloes are a traditional Romanesque type; see above, at note 149.

155. Frodl-Kraft, "Kirchenschaubildern," 82, Taf. 36.

156. Demouy, "Synodes diocésains," 104. On the bishop of Senlis, in Bay 105, see above, at notes 142–43. He is unlikely to be an insert there: his vestments have horizontal color bands like those of the apostles above him; like Matthew, he has a "socle" beneath his feet; and the ground pattern is so complex that inserting a figure into it would be time-consuming and difficult. His inscription, to either side and extending into the borders, could be an afterthought.

157. As reported by Ravaux, this phrase and date appear in the so-called Annals of Saint-Nicaise, Paris, BnF, lat. 9376: "1241, hoc anno in vigilia nativitatis beate Marie virginis, intravit capitulum Remense chorum suum novum." See Ravaux, "Les campagnes," 8, 58 n. 8, 61 n. 43.

158. The Annals (see the previous note) do not specify the location of "their choir" in the building. Kurmann, *La façade,* 1:64, and Kimpel and Suckale, *L'architecture,* 289, believe that "their choir" signifies its final location in the eastern bays of the nave. However, "their choir" could have occupied a temporary location during extended years of construction. For several possible locations of the canons' stalls, see Erlande-Brandenburg, *La cathédrale,* 42. I do not, however, subscribe to his view that the shift to a location in the eastern nave was made by Henri de Braine.

159. Recensement IV:389; Balcon, "Les vitraux," in *Reims: La cathédrale,* 359, 361–62.

160. For a discussion of the process of making a window from a full-scale cartoon drawn on a glazing table, see Sarah Brown and David O'Connor, *Medieval Craftsmen: Glass Painters* (Toronto, 1991), 52–54. A single medieval glazing table has survived, discovered by Vila-Grau and now in the Gerona Museu d'art: see Joan Vila-Grau, "La table de peintre-verrier de Gérone," *Revue de l'art,* no. 72 (1986): 32–34; Joan Ainaud I de Lasarte et al., *Els vitralls de la catedral de Girona,* Corpus Vitrearum, Espanya 7, Catalunya 2 (Barcelona, 1987), 78–82.

161. Balcon-Berry, "Les vitraux," 161–62; Balcon, "Documents du fonds Deneux," 49, 53; eadem, "Nouvelles appréciations sur les vitraux de la cathédrale de Reims comportant des représentations architecturales à partir de documents d'archives," in *Représentations architecturales dans les vitraux: Acts du* XXIe *colloque du Corpus Vitrearum,* Dossier de la Commission royale des monuments, sites et fouilles, 9 (Liege, 2002), 67–68, 70. Unfortunately none of the Deneux autochrome photographs of 1915 shows the lost Bay 109, while four of them show Bay 110.

162. Compare Recensement IV:388, fig. 372 (109, right lancet) with Balcon-Berry, "Moyen Âge," 244, fig. 31 (110, right bishop).

163. On the "first choir program," see Reinhardt, *La cathédrale,* 185–86. On Henri Deneux: Delphine Quéreux-Sbaï, "Henri Deneux, restaurateur et photographe de la cathédrale," in *Mythes et réalités de la cathédrale de Reims,* 115–23, esp. 115–17; Isabelle Pallot-Frossard, "Henri Deneux et la cathédrale de Reims: Un face à face de 23 ans," in *Rebâtir Reims: La collection photographique Henri Deneux 1870/1938* (Châlons-sur-Marne, 1988), 29–34. On the stained-glass restorations under Deneux's direction: Balcon, "Documents du fonds Deneux," 49.

164. Robert Branner, review of *La cathédrale de Reims,* by Hans Reinhardt, *Art Bulletin* 45 (1963): 375; see also Reinhardt, *La cathédrale,* 2, and his book dedication.

165. Reinhardt, *La cathédrale,* 186. His criteria are (1) round or triangular faces with long thick necks, (2) eyes painted on a single piece of glass (by which he means no "eyeglasses" leading), and (3) a palette of green, blue, and red. Bays 109 and 110 have no round faces; the palette has large areas of golden yellow and purple-brown, while green is not particularly stressed. The other bays in his group do not conform to these criteria well either; for example, the spolia in Bay 118 have oval faces (Virgin, saint-bishop) and a bright cheerful palette.

166. See the illustrations in Caviness, *Sumptuous Arts,* and eadem, "Modular Assemblages."

167. Auxerre: frontal St. Stephen in bay 6; frontal saint-bishop Amâtre (bay 102): Raguin, *Burgundy,* figs. 86, 97. Saint-Quentin: frontal saint (bay 201): Cothren, *Picturing the Celestial City,* 121, pl. 126c; for dating, 236 n. 121. Amiens: two frontal angels (bay 200): Nathalie Frachon-

Gielarek, *Amiens: Les verrières de la cathédrale,* Images du patrimoine, 214 (Amiens, 2003), 32–33.

168. This opinion is based upon the present study. It is a revision of my general remarks in previous publications, which were based on the scholarly consensus before I began the present examination. See, e.g., Meredith Parsons Lillich, "The Stained-Glass Spolia in the South Transept of Reims Cathedral and Rémois Ecclesiastical Seals," *Gesta* 46 (2007): 2, 3, 16 n. 18.

169. See above, at notes 92 and 141. Illustrations of Auxerre's examples: Recensement III:122 (Bay 104); Lillich, "The Band Window" (as in note 92 above), 27–30, figs. 2–7, reprinted in *Studies,* 64–65, 70–74.

170. It is, in fact, another mode of glazing. An important example is the glazing of Sées cathedral, where the repetition of cartoons was standard and produced a rhythmic, repeating ornamental display that is quite effective: Lillich, *The Armor,* 180, fig. VI.9; 213–17, color pls. 44–46. Cothren, *Picturing the Celestial City,* 236 n. 117, comments on the glazing of Amiens, where two designs produce four angels (Bay 200) and two cartoons serve for ten bishops (lower gallery of the south rose): "Rather than infusing these glazings with boring repetitiveness, the reuse of cartoons seems to lend a sense of rhythmic agitation."

171. On such shop models, see Robert W. Scheller, *Exemplum: Model-Book Drawings and the Practice of Artistic Transmission in the Middle Ages (ca. 900–ca. 1470),* trans. Michael Hoyle (Amsterdam, 1995), 48–53, cat. nos. 5 and 9 (for single-figure patterns).

172. Frodl-Kraft, "Kirchenschaubildern," Taf. 43–45, 39–41.

173. On Juhel de Mathefelon, see Desportes, *Reims et les rémois,* 167–68; Desportes et al., *Fasti,* 162–63.

Chapter 4

1. Meredith Parsons Lillich, "Monastic Stained Glass: Patronage and Style," in *Monasticism and the Arts,* ed. Timothy Verdon (Syracuse, 1984), 224–33, reprinted in *Studies in Medieval Stained Glass and Monasticism* (London, 2001), 322, 337–45, and notes. See also eadem, *The Armor of Light: Stained Glass in Western France, 1250–1325* (Berkeley and Los Angeles, 1994), 6–8.

2. On the "summer-and-winter" format, see Lillich, *The Armor,* 412 (entries in the general index under "grisaille and color combinations, Summer-and-winter format"). On Saint-Germain-des-Prés: Mary Shepard, "The St. Germain Windows from the Thirteenth-Century Lady Chapel at Saint-Germain-des-Prés," in *The Cloisters: Studies in Honor of the Fiftieth Anniversary,* ed. Elizabeth C. Parker (New York, 1992), 299 n. 3. For Sens, largely unpublished: Recensement III:181–82, which omits reference to the illustrations in Charles Cahier and Arthur Marie Martin, *Monographie de la cathédrale de Bourges* (Paris, 1844), vol. 2, Études XV–XVI (Sens bays 100–102, the colored apsidal windows) and Grisailles F (seven of the Sens grisaille patterns); the Cahier-Martin drawings of Sens bays 100–102 are reproduced in Elizabeth C. Pastan and Sylvie Balcon, *Les vitraux de choeur de la cathédrale de Troyes (XIIIe siècle),* Corpus Vitrearum, France, II (Paris, 2006), 292 fig. 253, but not the grisailles. For Châlons, see Meredith Parsons Lillich, "St. Memmie, Apostle of Châlons, and Other Bishop Saints in the Gothic Windows of Châlons Cathedral," *Studies in Iconography* 19 (1998).

3. See the interior views in Dieter Kimpel and Robert Suckale, *L'architecture gothique en France 1130–1270* (Paris, 1990), 281 fig. 286 and 284 fig. 289.

4. Bay 118 is the transept bay containing the four inserted *belles verrières,* discussed at the end of this chapter. The grisailles have been patched around the images, but it seems clear that they are remains of the original grisaille designs.

5. The transept bays at the crossing have a triforium arcade of four arches like Bays 107 and 108 in the chevet as well as the nave bays (up to Bays 139 and 140 at the facade). The transept bays flanking the roses have a triforium arcade of six arches. Measurements are not available; those provided in Recensement IV must be incorrect ("Bay 118, 5.8 m, and all other transept bays, 3 m").

6. A set of magnificent detail photos (e.g., my figs. 106–10) has allowed me to correct here a few observations in my description in Meredith Parsons Lillich, "The Stained-Glass Spolia in the South Transept of Reims Cathedral and Rémois Ecclesiastical Seals," *Gesta* 46 (2007): 2. Naomi Kline's early dating of the Reims grisaille can be discounted: Kline, "The Stained Glass of the Abbey Church at Orbais" (Ph.D. diss., Boston University, 1983), 192–93. Her judgment was probably based on the drawing attributed to Reims cathedral in Cahier and Martin, *Bourges,* vol. 2, Grisailles E, no. 7. This drawing is almost certainly mislabeled. It is an example of "ornamental colored glazing" similar to the design next to it (no. 6), from Saint-Remi, dated ca. 1170s–80s (cf. Madeline H. Caviness, *Sumptuous Arts at the Royal Abbeys in Reims and Braine: Ornatus elegantiae, varietate stupendes* [Princeton, 1990], 357–58, 363 [R.o.6]). Nothing remotely like it is known from the cathedral or is likely to have been there in the 1840s, when Cahier-Martin was published. Caviness (368) unearthed a mistake in labeling in R.b.7, and some similar confusion must be responsible for the misattribution of this drawing to Reims cathedral.

7. Eugène-Emmanuel Viollet-le-Duc, *Dictionnaire raisonné de l'architecture du XIe au XVIe siècle*, vol. 9 (Paris, 1858), 452. For the changes in grisaille design first introduced at midcentury, see Meredith Parsons Lillich, *The Stained Glass of Saint-Père de Chartres* (Middletown, 1978), 26–27. The Reims grisailles slightly predate the centripetal patterns found in the ca. 1240–45 campaign at Saint-Père as well as at Auxerre (see the illustrations in *Saint Père*, 28, 30). The Reims grisailles are later than Chartres bay 19 (Delaporte bay 44, ca. 1235–40) and definitely precede Chartres bay 25, right lancet (Delaporte bay 47, datable 1259): see Meredith Parsons Lillich, "A Redating of the Thirteenth-Century Grisaille Windows of Chartres Cathedral," *Gesta* 11/1 (1972): 11–14, 17, reprinted in *Studies*, 99–103, 106 (specifically on Reims, 100 and n. 13). This article uses Delaporte bay numbering; for Corpus Vitrearum numbering, see Recensement II:26.

8. His first act was to complain to the pope that the chapter had lifted the excommunication though the bourgeois still owed the archbishop (him now) the final installment of the royally arbitrated monetary penance for their previous insurgency, and the pope authorized him to revoke the absolution. The payment was made. Pierre Desportes, *Reims et les rémois aux XIIIe et XIVe siècles* (Paris, 1979), 167–68.

9. Pierre Desportes et al., *Fasti ecclesiae Gallicanae: Répertoire prosopographique des évêques, dignitaires et chanoines de France de 1200 à 1500*, vol. 3, *Diocèse de Reims* (Turnhout, 1998), 162–63.

10. Arthur J. de Havilland Bushnell, *Storied Windows* (Edinburgh, 1914), 295.

11. Colette Manhès and Jean-Paul Deremble, *Le vitrail du bon samaritain: Chartres, Sens, Bourges* (Paris, 1986). On Lyon, see Recensement III:299 (baie 116).

12. On the south rose, see below, at note 98.

13. Willibald Sauerländer, *Gothic Sculpture in France, 1140–1270*, trans. Janet Sondheimer (New York, 1972), 483.

14. On the 1980 restoration, see Benoît Marq, "Protection de vitraux du XIIe et du XIIIe siècle en Champagne-Ardenne et Picardie," *Vitrea* 7 (1991): 85–86. At that time the north rose was among the group given an external coating of the infamous Viacryl, a procedure that was abandoned thereafter: Isabelle Pallot-Frossard, "Petite histoire des verrières de protection ou comment un vitrail échappe à la clôture," *Dossier vitrail = Monumental: Revue scientifique et technique des monuments historiques*, semestriel 1 (2004): 93. The earliest discussion of restoration campaigns does not mention either 1600 or 1650: Victor Tourneur, *Histoire et description des vitraux et des statues de l'intérieur de la cathédrale de Reims* (Reims, 1857), 55–62. A proposed restoration of ca. 1600 is based on notes and rubbings the restorer Pierre Simon made in 1872, now in the possession of the atelier Simon-Marq in Reims. Simon's notes and rubbings were made available to Nathalie Frachon for her 1982 thesis, "La rose nord du transept de la cathédrale de Reims" (Mémoire de maîtrise, Université de Paris IV–Sorbonne); see 23–37. I am grateful to the late Catherine Brisac for access to this thesis. See now Recensement IV:384, 386.

15. "L'ensemble de cette composition appartient certainement au XIIIe siècle. On y retrouve le coloris de cette époque, la translucidité sans transparence, la naïveté du dessin, le caractère de son style et de sa disposition. Malheureusement, presque tous les sujets sont mutilés; c'est à peine si l'on en trouve deux ou trois dans leur entier. Les lacunes causées par la chute des vitraux du XIIIe siècle ont été comblées presque toutes par des fragments de bordures du XVIe, parfaitement reconnaissables à leur pâleur et à leur dessin." Tourneur, *Histoire*, 285, repeated by Charles Cerf, *Histoire et description de Notre-Dame de Reims* (Reims, 1861), 2:285. The rose is described as "beautiful and 13th c." in Étienne Povillon-Piérard, *Description historique de l'église métropolitaine de Notre-Dame de Rheims* (Reims, 1823), 140; see also Ferdinand de Lasteyrie, *Histoire de la peinture sur verre d'après ses monuments en France*, vol. 1 (Paris, 1857), 89–90, and François de Guilhermy, "Notes sur diverses localités de la France," Paris, BnF, nouv. acq. fr. 6106, fol. 402r. The report of Canon Thibaut in 1858, which states, "La rose nord est dans le plus mauvais état, elle menace ruine," is concerned with the stone tracery: "Rapport décrivant la cathédrale de Reims (edifice et mobilier) au ministère de l'Instruction publique et des cultes," Arch. dépt. Marne, annexe Reims, Fonds Thibaut 8J:44 (1858).

16. See Prolegomena at notes 6–7 and note 14 above.

17. See notes 14–15 above. Frachon, "La rose nord," 29, quotes 1872 correspondence of Pierre Simon concerning the rubbings: "Les estompages [rubbings] ont été fait par Sirop (ouvrier à la maison Simon), les empreintes à l'huile par Ch. DaVenne et les coloriages, retouches par moi, Paul et Marie [Simon]." A few Simon rubbings, and lithographs made from them, are accessible in the Bibliothèque municipale in Reims: *Catalogue iconographique: Dessins originaux, gravures, lithographies, photographies et autres documents concernant Reims des origines à 1930, conservés à la Bibliothèque* (Reims, 1982), 130: Section XV-11,a (Détail de l'intérieur, Vitraux). The rubbings were available to Oudinot, restorer of the figural medallions in 1872, but he did not make use of them. Cf. Recensement IV:384.

18. The angels flanking the central God might refer to the creation of light on the first day (Gen. 1:3–5): see Yves Christe, "L'Héxaméron dans les Bibles moralisées de la

première moitié du XIIIe siècle," *Cahiers archéologiques* 47 (1999): 179. The sun and moon were reversed before 1872, according to the Simon rubbing: Frachon, "La rose nord," pl. 12. Although the reversal of sun and moon in the north rose of the cathedral of Châlons-en-Champagne is a significant element of the iconographic program, the reversal at Reims was probably a simple error in installation. On Châlons, see Meredith Parsons Lillich, "La 'rose verte' de la cathédrale de Châlons," *Cahiers archéologiques* 49 (2001): 123.

19. Guilhermy, "Notes," fol. 402v, reports "a mutilated figure in a circle; it is God." For the nineteenth-century illustrations, see Tourneur, *Histoire,* lithograph by Boudié-Collin between pp. 42 and 43; Jules Gailhabaud, *L'architecture du ve au xviie siècle et les arts qui en dépendent,* vol. 1 (Paris, 1858), unnumbered pl. ("Transsept-Croisillon septentrional-Rose, etc."), dessin de E. Leblan, gravé par J. Sulpis; Nat Hubert John Westlake, *A History of Design in Painted Glass,* vol. 1 (London, 1881), 85, pl. XLVIIIa.

20. The selection of scenes of Adam, Eve, and their children, as well as their design, conforms to an astonishing degree with a French manuscript: Paris, Arsenal 3516. See below, at note 93.

21. The most complete list of archivolt subjects is provided by Victor Tourneur, *Description historique et archéologique de Notre-Dame de Reims* (Reims, 1880), 54. For the fullest illustration of them, see Paul Vitry, *La cathédrale de Reims,* vol. 2 (Paris, 1919), pl. LII (photos by Rothier). See my fig. 117.

22. Attempts to assign specific identities to the descendants have been inconclusive: Sauerländer, *Gothic Sculpture,* 483; Hans Reinhardt, *La cathédrale de Reims: Son histoire, son architecture, sa sculpture, ses vitraux* (Paris, 1963), 156; Charles Cerf, "La rose nord de la cathédrale de Reims," *Travaux de l'Académie nationale de Reims* 89 (1890): 276.

23. Marvin Trachtenberg, *The Campanile of Florence Cathedral: "Giotto's Tower"* (New York, 1971), esp. chap. IV.

24. Adam lies asleep to the right; God takes a rib from his side. See Simon"s tracing (from the exterior) in "AVISTA at Kalamazoo 2010: Sylvie Balcon-Berry, Stained Glass and the Chronology of Reims Cathedral," *AVISTA Forum Journal* 20, no. 1/2 (Fall 2010): 66, fig. 2. Nineteenth-century illustrations interpret the standing figure as God holding a small figure (see my fig. 116, bottom medallion). The panel was then nearly illegible, and Guilhermy, "Notes," fol. 402r, reports, "I think it is God creating man." The Creation of Eve was more common in art than that of Adam. The reason may be that, according to Augustine (*Enarratio in Psalmum XL,* in *Patrologia Latina* 36, col. 461), the creation of Eve prefigured the creation of the Church from the wound of Christ on the cross: see Adolf Katzenellenbogen, *The Sculptural Programs of Chartres Cathedral: Christ-Mary-Ecclesia* (Baltimore, 1959), 74. The iconographic type of God taking a rib from Adam's side is common in Carolingian art but rare by the Gothic period. See, e.g., the Grandval Bible (London, Brit. Lib. Add. MS 10546, Tours ca. 840), fol. 5v: Florentine Mütherich and Joachim Gaehde, *Carolingian Painting* (New York, 1976), pl. 20. The more common Gothic type, Eve rising from the side of Adam, appears in the exterior sculpture of the Reims rose (Sauerländer, *Gothic Sculpture,* 483). On the two types, see Jack M. Greenstein, "The Body of Eve in Andrea Pisano's *Creation* Relief," *Art Bulletin* 90 (2008): 577; Georges Sanoner, "La Bible racontée par les artistes du Moyen Âge, III: Création d'Eve," *Revue de l'art chrétien* 60 (1910): 241–46 passim.

25. Recensement IV:389 states in error that the panel showing Cain murdering Abel is modern, replacing a stopgap panel (the stoning of St. Stephen, fifteenth or sixteenth century). The stopgap was not in G-3 but in G-9 (of the outermost ring of medallions), and several nineteenth-century witnesses mention both it and Cain murdering Abel: e.g., Tourneur, *Histoire,* 43–44. Cain's head in F-3 (God cursing Cain) is beardless; see the excellent illustration in Recensement IV:389 fig. 373. (His head in G-3 is modern.) Although Ruth Mellinkoff has suggested that beardlessness was in rare examples "the mark of Cain," a beardless Cain is common in French Gothic art. See, e.g., the stained glass of Toul cathedral's bay 7 (late 1230s–1243) and the Psalter of Saint Louis, ca. 1258–70 (Paris, BnF, lat. 10525), fol. 2r, both illustrated in Meredith Parsons Lillich, *Rainbow Like an Emerald: Stained Glass in Lorraine in the Thirteenth and Early Fourteenth Centuries* (University Park, 1991), pl. 1.9. On Cain, see Ruth Mellinkoff, *The Mark of Cain* (Berkeley, 1981), 57–59.

26. The upper half of Adam and Eve seated in paradise (L-3) was lost by 1872 (Frachon, "La rose nord," 31, 44, 93). I suggest that the green "leaves" now near the figures' laps were provided by Oudinot when he fabricated the new upper half of the scene, since they are not mentioned by any witnesses before 1872. Frachon indicates that the bottom of the tree (center) and Eve's buttocks (on the right) are largely original. According to Tourneur, *Histoire,* 43, repeated by Cerf, *Histoire,* 2:286, "on ne voit plus que le tronc de l'arbre et les jambes des personnages." Both clerics would have had access to the upper passages of the cathedral. Observers from the cathedral floor were unclear about the identity of "Adam." Guilhermy, "Notes," fol. 402v, called the scene "God speaking to a nude figure," while Povillon-Piérard, *Description,* 141, thought it was the devil tempting Eve. Significantly, Cerf's article written following

the restoration ("La rose nord," 278, 280) states that Adam and Eve are "not nude" but "clothed." Green leaves in the figures' laps, if original, would identify the scene as Adam and Eve *after* the Fall. Since the Temptation-Fall (K-3), like L-3 under discussion here, survived to the nineteenth century with original glass only in the lower panel of the medallion, the two half-scenes could possibly have been interchanged in 1740, when debris was inserted above both to repair storm losses. However, I believe that L-3 depicted Adam and Eve in paradise *before* the Fall for two reasons: they appear the same way in the exterior sculpture; and the iconographic program as I have reconstructed it indicates that the Temptation-Fall (K-3) would have been inappropriate as one of the three uppermost scenes of the series. It is more likely that Oudinot in 1872 added green leaves when he designed new upper halves to complete these scenes.

27. In 1872, I-3 was interchanged with C-3, as part of Oudinot's new arrangement of the narrative. All nineteenth-century witnesses identify K-3, J-3, and I-3 as I have indicated.

28. See the previous note. All nineteenth-century witnesses place the Expulsion in C-3.

29. Povillon-Piérard, *Description,* 141; also Prosper Tarbé, *Notre-Dame de Reims,* 2nd ed. (Reims, 1852), 84; Tourneur, *Histoire,* 43; Cerf, *Histoire,* 2:286; Guilhermy, "Notes," fol. 402r, noted noncommittally "a figure" (D-3) and Eve seated, nursing a child (E-3). Among pre-restoration witnesses, E-3 is identified as the Virgin and Child by Jean-Baptiste-François Geruzez, *Description historique et statistique de la ville de Reims* (Reims, 1817), 2:711, and Antoine Gilbert, *Description historique de l'église métropolitaine de Notre-Dame de Reims* (Reims, 1825), 23. However, in his critique of the 1872 rearrangement, Cerf, "La rose nord," 278, seems to attribute the idea to Viollet-le-Duc (who presumably considered the medallion a stopgap from another window and moved it).

30. Virginia Chieffo Raguin, *Stained Glass in Thirteenth-Century Burgundy* (Princeton, 1982), 139.

31. Jewish legend attributed to Eve the weaving of bedcovers in paradise: Louis Ginzberg, *The Legends of the Jews,* vol. 1 (Philadelphia, 1942), 22. On Eve spinning in Christian art, see Hans Aurenhammer, *Lexikon der christlichen Ikonographie,* vol. 1, pt. 1 (Vienna, 1959), 49–50.

32. For San Zeno, see Christine Bornstein, *Portals and Politics in the Early Italian City-State: The Sculpture of Nicholaus in Context* (Parma, 1988), 151, fig. 217. For Ferrara: Lillich, *Rainbow,* 13 and pl. 1.8b. On Paris, BnF, lat. 8846 (late twelfth century): Nigel Morgan, *Early Gothic Manuscripts,* vol. 1, *1190–1250* (Oxford, 1982), 47, cat. 1.

33. For Vienna, ÖNB, MS 2554, see *Bible moralisée: Codex Vindobonensis 2554,* ed. and trans. Gerald B. Guest (London, 1995), 55 and fol. 2v of the facsimile. For Tours (ca. 1255–65): Linda Papanicolaou, "The Iconography of the Genesis Window of the Cathedral of Tours," *Gesta* 20, pt. 1 (1981): 179–80, 189 (Eve spinning = 3d, Birth scene = 4a). For Rouen (ca. 1280–1300): Louise Pillion, *Les portails latéraux de la cathédrale de Rouen* (Paris, 1907), 178, figs. 52, 59A. For Thann: Otto Schmitt, "Die Thanner Genesis und ihr Verhältnis zur gotischen Monumentalplastik Südwestdeutschlands," in *Festschrift für Hans Jantzen* (Berlin, 1951), 107, Abb. 19–20.

34. Papanicolaou, "The Iconography," 183–86 passim. The *Vita Adae et Evae* is mentioned on 179 and also by Schmitt, *Die Thanner Genesis,* 106–7; on this text, see Robert Henry Charles, *The Apocrypha and Pseudepigrapha of the Old Testament in English* (Oxford, 1973), 2:123–24.

35. Frachon, "La rose nord," 79, pl. 23 (rubbing, detail).

36. Sauerländer, *Gothic Sculpture,* pl. 259.

37. Frachon, "La rose nord," 61, 96–97, and restoration chart for M-9 (the cushion and upper "throne" are marked as replacements of 1600). This suggests that the "throne" may have been created in a postmedieval period when the figure was no longer understood to be Eve. The vegetal pattern to either side of the woman's legs is on original glass and is very clear in Simon's tracing of ca. 1875 (ibid., pl. 32).

38. Cf. Eve nursing Cain in Francis Joseph Tschan, *Saint Bernward of Hildesheim,* vol. 2 (Notre Dame, 1951), 194; vol. 3 (1952), pl. 121; and in the Grandval Bible (see note 24 above).

39. George Ferguson, *Signs and Symbols in Christian Art* (New York, 1966), 153.

40. Michel Pastoureau, *Couleurs, images, symboles: Études d'histoire et d'anthropologie* (Paris, 1989), 76–77; idem, *Figures et couleurs: Études sur la symbolique et la sensibilité médiévales* (Paris, 1986), 30, 34.

41. Ruth Mellinkoff, *Outcasts: Signs of Otherness in Northern European Art of the Late Middle Ages* (Berkeley and Los Angeles, 1993), 44; see 35–56 passim; for examples before and during the thirteenth century, 38, 44–46, 51, 252 n. 39.

42. On *Maria lactans,* see Gertrud Schiller, *Ikonographie der christlichen Kunst,* vol. 4, pt. 2 (Gütersloh, 1980), 20, 22, 180, 191–92 (the Liège relief is 186, Abb. 804). The early history of the motif is surveyed by Michael Mallory, "A Lost *Madonna del Latte* by Ambrogio Lorenzetti," *Art Bulletin* 51 (1969): 41 n. 1. Another unique early example of a nursing Child in Western art is in the Flight to Egypt, as it appears, for example, in a fresco of Petit-Quevilly, near Rouen (Winchester school, ca. 1160): Neil Stratford, "The Wall-Paintings of the Petit-Quevilly," in *Medieval Art,*

Architecture, and Archaeology at Rouen, ed. Jenny Stratford, British Archaeological Association Transactions, 12 (Leeds, 1993), 56; illustrated in Lillich, *Rainbow,* 98, pl. v.5b. Both Virgin and Child are nimbed.

43. On Chenu, see Françoise Perrot and Anne Granboulan, "The French 12th, 13th, and 16th Century Glass at Rivenhall, Essex," *Journal of Stained Glass* 18, no. 1 (1983–84): 1–14. On Chartres bay 138: Recensement II:42, fig. 28. On Chartres bay 30: Recensement II:32; Colette Manhès-Deremble, *Les vitraux narratifs de la cathédrale de Chartres: Étude iconographique,* Corpus Vitrearum, France, Études, II (Paris, 1993), 65, color ill. on the jacket. On Pontigné: Marie-Pasquine Subes, "Quelques parallèles entre deux arts monumentaux au XIIIe siècle: Peinture murale et vitrail," in *Pierre, lumière, couleur: Études d'histoire de l'art du Moyen Âge en l'honneur d'Anne Prache,* ed. Fabienne Joubert and Dany Sandron (Paris, 1999), 157, color ill. 9.

44. The ogive medallion (M) was filled with four fleurs-de-lis in a cross pattern within leads of ca. 1740 and was thus probably a creation of that restoration: Frachon, "La rose nord," 31. Among nineteenth-century witnesses only Guilhermy, "Notes," fol. 402v, records what he saw in the ogive: between adoring angels, in the center, a medallion *tout rouge.* He adds: "What is it?"

45. Guilhermy identified the damaged figure as God; see note 19 above.

46. Recensement IV:391. See chapter 7, at notes 62–66 and figs. 240, 241.

47. Recensement IV:386–87. See the drawing in Cahier and Martin, *Bourges,* vol. 2, Études XVIII (my fig. 8). Bay 102 has an angel with crown, and Bay 103 a saint's martyrdom (probably a stopgap). See appendix 3.

48. Adelheid Heimann, "Trinitas Creator Mundi," *Journal of the Warburg Institute* 2 (1938–39): 42, 45 n. 4, 47.

49. Émile Mâle, *Religious Art in France: The Thirteenth Century,* trans. Marthiel Mathews from the 9th ed., 1958 (Princeton, 1984), 159, 192–94.

50. Mellinkoff, *Outcasts,* 48, 133; Mâle, *Thirteenth Century,* 148, 159; Paul-Henri Michel, "L'iconographie de Caïn et Abel," *Cahiers de civilisation médiévale* 1 (1958): 195 (I could not verify his reference to the Gospel of Luke); Georges Sanoner, "Iconographie de la Bible d'après les artistes de l'antiquité et du Moyen Âge," *Bulletin monumental* 80 (1921): 211–13.

51. Ruth Mellinkoff, "Cain and the Jews," *Journal of Jewish Art* 6 (1979): 16–38; Pearl F. Braude, "'Cokkel in oure Clene Corn': Some Implications of Cain's Sacrifice," *Gesta* 7 (1968): 15–28. Eve is cast as an archtype of heretics in the so-called pastoral epistles (1 Timothy, 2 Timothy, Titus), but I have found no evidence that this idea survived in medieval texts: see Jouette Bassler, "Adam, Eve, and the Pastor: The Use of Genesis 2–3 in the Pastoral Epistles," in *Genesis 1–3 in the History of Exegesis: Intrigue in the Garden,* ed. Gregory Allen Robbins (Lewiston, N.Y., 1988), 43–65.

52. William Chester Jordan, *The French Monarchy and the Jews: From Philip Augustus to the Last Capetians* (Philadelphia, 1989); see the many references in the index under "Usury," "Heresy," and "heretics."

53. This scene will be revisited in the conclusion below.

54. See note 19 above, also the text at note 45. On L-9, see Frachon, "La rose nord," 111.

55. Willene Clark and Meradith McMunn, eds., *Beasts and Birds of the Middle Ages: The Bestiary and Its Legacy* (Philadelphia, 1989), 4. The introduction to this volume is particularly useful for the growing literature on bestiaries.

56. Florence McCulloch, *Mediaeval Latin and French Bestiaries* (Chapel Hill, 1960), 122–23. Typical illustrations: (a) Cambridge, Univ. Lib., MS II.4.26, ca. 1200 (griffin attacking a boar), for which, see Terence H. White, ed. and trans., *Bestiary: A Book of Beasts* (New York, 1960), 23; (b) Cambridge, Univ. Lib., MS KK.4.25, ca. 1220–40 (attacking a man), for which, see Ron Baxter, *Bestiaries and Their Users in the Middle Ages* (London, 1998), 138, pl. 38; (c) Oxford, Bodleian, MS Bodley 764, ca. 1240–50 (attacking a horse), for which, see *Bestiary: Being an English Version of the Bodleian Library, Oxford M.S. Bodley 764,* translated and introduced by Richard Barber (Woodbridge, Suffolk, 1992), 38.

57. The literature on Dante's griffin is extensive. See Piero Camporese, "Grifone," in *Enciclopedia Dantesca,* vol. 3 (Rome, 1971), 287. The revisionist interpretation offered by Peter Armour, *Dante's Griffin and the History of the World: A Study of the Earthly Paradise (Purgatorio, cantos xxix–xxxiii)* (Oxford, 1989), has not been well received; see the review by Peter S. Hawkins in *Speculum* 66 (1991): 840–41. On the Good Shepherd sarcophagus (Rome, Lateran Museums, second half of the fourth century), Christ (as the Good Shepherd) stands on a pedestal decorated with two griffins flanking a tripod (for the Trinity); see the illustration in Wolfgang F. Volbach, *Early Christian Art* (New York, 1961), pl. 6. Griffins abound in Romanesque sculpture: Victor Henry Debidour, *Le bestiaire sculptée du Moyen Âge en France* (Paris, 1961), 216–20, figs. 308–11. On the griffin's dual nature (in twelfth-century frescoes of San Pietro in Valle, Ferentillo), see Herbert Kessler, *Spiritual Seeing: Picturing God's Invisibility in Medieval Art* (Philadelphia, 2000), 26; for a contrary opinion, Mâle, *Thirteenth Century,* 52.

58. The two other birds now in the medallion were made by Oudinot in 1872: Frachon, "La rose nord," 110. The panel is discussed and illustrated in Marq, "Protection de vitraux" (as in note 14 above), 85–86.

59. Mâle, *Thirteenth Century,* 44–45, fig. 22. For Lyon, see Recensement III:296, baie 0; Baxter, *Bestiaries and Their Users,* 8–9, 13 (ill.). On the caladrius, see McCulloch, *Mediaeval Latin,* 99–101; Pamela Gravestock, "Did Imaginary Animals Exist?" in *The Mark of the Beast: The Medieval Bestiary in Art, Life, and Literature,* ed. Debra Hassig (New York, 1999), 129. Bestiaries usually depict the caladrius with a person in sickbed: see Baxter, *Bestiaries and Their Users,* 66–68 and pl. 13 (Brussels, Bibl. Roy., MS 10074, fol. 143r [*Physiologus,* eleventh century]), where the caladrius-sickbed is paired with the crucified Christ and Moses with the Brazen Serpent. A caladrius appears on his own, as at Reims, in the Aviary of Hugues de Fouilloy: Françoise Bibolet, "Portraits d'oiseaux illustrant le 'De avibus' d'Hugues de Fouilloy (manuscrit de Clairvaux, Troyes 177)," in *Mélanges à la mémoire du Père Anselme Dimier,* II, ed. Benoît Chauvin, vol. 4 (Arbois, 1984), 426–27, 443.

60. Brunsdon Yapp, *Birds in Medieval Manuscripts* (New York, 1982), 106–7, pl. 14; on the confused depiction of long-legged birds, 13–18, 42, 118–19. The texts could also be confused; see Guy R. Mermier, trans., *A Medieval Book of Beasts: Pierre de Beauvais' Bestiary* (Lewiston, N.Y., 1992), 81 (ibis-stork?) and 130 (heron-coot?).

61. Yapp, *Birds,* 15. Illustrations of bluish gray herons appear in Ann Payne, *Medieval Beasts* (New York, 1990), 68 (London, Brit. Lib., MS Harley 4751, fol. 41r, ca. 1230–40); *Bestiary: Being an English Version,* 132 (Oxford, Bodleian, MS Bodley 764, fol. 64v, ca. 1240–50); see also Bibolet, "Portraits d'oiseaux," 426 (no. 22).

62. The glass used in thirteenth-century France photographs as purple against a cloudy sky but brown against a blue sky and is often identified as purple-brown.

63. White, *Bestiary,* 125. In the twelfth-century Aviary of Hugues de Fouilloy and the Bestiary of Philippe de Thaon, the phoenix is described as purple: Willene Clark, *The Medieval Book of Birds: Hugh of Fouilloy's Aviarium* (Binghamton, N.Y., 1992), 231; Guy Mermier, "The Phoenix: Its Nature and Its Place in the Tradition of the Physiologus," in Clark and McMunn, *Beasts and Birds,* 76.

64. Bibolet, "Portraits d'oiseaux," 428 (no. 24); Clark, *The Medieval Book of Birds,* 39; see Payne, *Medieval Beasts,* 70.

65. Lactantius, *The Minor Works,* trans. Mary Francis McDonald, The Fathers of the Church, 54 (Washington, D.C., 1965), 218.

66. Brunetto Latini, *The Book of the Treasure (Li livres dou tresor),* trans. Paul Barrette and Spurgeon Baldwin (New York, 1993), 121–22.

67. Mermier, "The Phoenix: Its Nature," 73. On the text of the twelfth-century Vienna *Physiologus* (Vienna, ÖNB, lat. 1010), see McCulloch, *Mediaeval Latin,* 41–44.

68. Valerie Jones, "The Phoenix and the Resurrection," in *The Mark of the Beast,* ed. Hassig, 99–110.

69. For an excellent illustration of the Reims crane (labeled an "ibis"), see Recensement IV:389, fig. 374. Compare it, for example, to ibises and ostriches in many bestiaries: Bibolet, "Portraits d'oiseaux," 437, fig. 110 (ostrich); Yapp, *Birds,* 55 (ostrich); Payne, *Medieval Beasts,* 69 (ostrich); *Bestiary: Being an English Version,* 135 (ibis), 137 (ostrich); White, *Bestiary,* 119 (ibis), 121 (ostrich); Clark and McMunn, *Beasts and Birds,* 46 (ibis), 52 (ostrich).

70. Clark, *The Medieval Book of Birds,* 203–5; in a monastic context, the symbolism includes senior monks who protect and admonish their brethren.

71. Pierre Simon's diagram of the rose of 1872, before restoration, calls all three panels *poissons:* Frachon, "La rose nord," pl. 6. The eel is partly original glass, as are two of the three fish in the panel that was in D-9, but the third fish panel (now in F-9) is wholly from the 1872 restoration: ibid., 105–7. It is probably this new medallion that is represented in the rough sketch (reversed) published in Léon-Auguste Ottin, *L'art de faire un vitrail* (Paris, 1892), 65, fig. 53.

72. White, *Bestiary,* 206.

73. Ferguson, *Signs and Symbols,* 18. The fish symbol for Christ, the ichthys, a term derived acrostically from the Greek letters for Jesus Christ Son of God Savior, is an Early Christian theme and not mentioned in Gothic bestiaries.

74. Debra Hassig, "Sex in the Bestiaries," in *The Mark of the Beast,* ed. Hassig, 76–77. The Perfects of the Cathar heresy ate only fish for this reason, that is, because fish were "deemed to be free from the corruption that attached to mammalian intercourse": René Weis, *The Yellow Cross: The Story of the Last Cathars, 1290–1329* (New York, 2001), xxv.

75. White, *Bestiary,* 209.

76. Ibid., 206–7; Christe, "L'Hexaméron" (as in note 18 above), 178, 180, 189, 190. The large central fish was restored in 1930, according to Frachon, "La rose nord," 106.

77. The most reliable record is the glazier Pierre Simon's drawing before the 1872 restoration, which indicates a goat, dog, and "antelope"; the last two are now restored (Frachon, "La rose nord," 104, pl. 6). Early-nineteenth-century writers mention "a ram and other animals": Geruzez, *Description historique,* 2:711, and Gilbert, *Description historique,* 23. Tourneur, *Histoire,* 44, notes the goat (*chevreau*). Cerf's identification in 1890 (lion, *boeuf,* and stag) is hard to explain: Cerf, "La rose nord," 277.

78. McCulloch, *Mediaeval Latin,* 172–74; *Physiologus,* trans. Michael Curley (Austin, 1979), 58; Mermier, *A Medieval Book of Beasts,* 169–70.

79. *Theobaldi "Physiologus,"* ed. and trans. P. T. Eden

(Leiden, 1972), 49–51; White, *Bestiary,* 38–39; *Bestiary: Being an English Version,* 51–52; *The Medieval Bestiary,* trans. Thomas J. Elliott (Boston, 1970), unpaginated, "Cervus" (an Early Middle English text).

80. White, *Bestiary,* 66–67.

81. McCulloch, *Mediaeval Latin,* 120–22; Payne, *Medieval Beasts,* 41.

82. White, *Bestiary,* 40–43; see 74–75 for the he-goat, "a lascivious and butting animal who is always burning for coition."

83. *Bestiary: Being an English Version,* 90. On Oxford, Bodleian, MS Bodley 764, see Baxter, *Bestiaries and Their Users,* 160–61, 199–201. It is an extended Second-Family Latin bestiary and unusual in being of secular use, probably made for one of the Marcher lords rather than for a religious house.

84. *Bestiary: Being an English Version,* 97–98. Moreover, as with goats, bestiaries distinguish between the ass and the onager (wild ass). The onager "is the Devil": Guy R. Mermier, ed., *Le bestiaire de Pierre de Beauvais (version courte): Édition critique avec notes et glossaire* (Paris, 1977), 47; White, *Bestiary,* 83; Payne, *Medieval Beasts,* 56.

85. Kurmann, *La façade,* 1:27, 70; idem, "Mobilité des artistes ou mobilité des modèles? À propos de l'atelier des sculpteurs rémois au XIIIe siècle," *Revue de l'art* 120/2 (1998): 28. Kimpel and Suckale, *L'architecture,* 289–90. On the riots, see chapter 1; Desportes, *Reims et les rémois,* 157–67.

86. Bamberg and Mainz are also considered in Kimpel and Suckale, *L'architecture,* 494 n. 45. On Notre-Dame de Cluny, see Willibald Sauerländer, "Über einen Reimser Bildhauer in Cluny," in *Gedenkschrift Ernst Gall,* ed. Margarete Kühn and Louis Grodecki (Munich, 1965), 257, 260, fig. 160. An even earlier migration of Reims sculptors has been theorized by Imre Takács, "Die Erneuerung der Abteikirche von Pannonhalma im 13. Jahrhundert," *Acta Historiae Artium* 38 (1996): 52–65 passim (reviewed by Gergely László in *Bulletin monumental* 157 [1999]: 384). Sculpture at the Hungarian church, which was consecrated in 1224, is proposed as the work of sculptors who had worked on lower parts of the Reims north transept.

87. Meredith Parsons Lillich, "Observations on the Gothic Rose Window with Centripetal Tracery," in *Arte d'Occidente: Temi e metodi; Studi in onore di Angiola Maria Romanini,* ed. Antonio Cadei et al. (Rome, 1999), 1:197–204, reprinted in *Studies,* 155–67.

88. Sauerländer, *Gothic Sculpture,* 483, 486, pls. 258–59.

89. Braude, "Cokkel" (as in note 51 above), 19.

90. *Sancti Bernardi Opera,* vol. 2, *Sermones super Cantica Canticorum 36–86,* ed. Jean Leclercq, Charles H. Talbot, and Henri Rochais (Rome, 1958), 176, line 7. See Braude, "Cokkel," 28 n. 42.

91. See above, at note 8.

92. Baxter, *Bestiaries and Their Users,* 154. See appendix 5 for a summary account of Latin and French bestiaries as well as for information about the literary output of Pierre de Beauvais.

93. Patricia Stirnemann, "Where Can We Go from Here? The Study of French Twelfth-Century Manuscripts," in *Romanesque Art and Thought in the Twelfth Century: Essays in Honor of Walter Cahn,* ed. Colum Hourihane (University Park, 2008), 86–87.

94. Baxter, *Bestiaries and Their Users,* 209; see also 194. His comments are based chiefly on English monastic Latin bestiaries, particularly those of the First Family.

95. Ibid., 189–90.

96. See the useful lists in McCulloch, *Mediaeval Latin,* 63–65.

97. Willene B. Clark, "Twelfth- and Thirteenth-Century Latin Sermons and the Latin Bestiary," *Compar(a)ison: An International Journal of Comparative Literature* 1, *Bestiaires* (1996), ed. Christopher Lucken, 5–19, esp. 11–13, 17. I would like to thank Professor Clark for generous counsel on bestiaries.

98. See chapter 6, at note 45.

99. Ravaux, "Les campagnes," 65 n. 114. In addition to the early sources cited by Ravaux, see Gilbert, *Description historique,* 22. On the south rose, see Recensement IV:384–86; Balcon, "Les vitraux," in *Reims: La cathédrale,* 336, 379–80.

100. Lillich, "Observations," 200–202, reprinted in *Studies,* 161–67.

101. Sauerländer, *Gothic Sculpture,* 483.

102. On the north rose of Châlons, see Lillich, "La 'rose verte.'"

103. E.g., see Yves Christe, "The Apocalypse in the Monumental Art of the Eleventh Through Thirteenth Centuries," in *The Apocalypse in the Middle Ages,* ed. Richard Emmerson and Bernard McGinn (Ithaca, 1992), 235–40 passim.

104. See also Patrick Demouy, "La sculpture: Roses et pignons du transept," in *Reims: La cathédrale,* 225. Sculpted figures of the triumphant Ecclesia and defeated Synagoga amid apostles and patriarchs and intermeshed with Judgment themes also appear in the south transept of Strasbourg cathedral: the Angel Pier inside and the Judging Solomon originally between the twin portals of the facade.

105. *Hexaemeron;* see *Patrologia Latina* (online) 91, cols. 36–38, quoted in Katzenellenbogen, *The Sculptural Programs,* 134 n. 103. See also Christe, "L'Héxaméron" (as in note 18 above), 184, 198 n. 8.

106. See note 24 above.

107. Christe, "L'Héxaméron," 183, 193–94; also idem,

"Aux origines de l'Hexaéméron des Bibles moralisées: Le cycle de la création de la cathédrale de Laon," *Cahiers archéologiques* 40 (1992): 95–96.

108. Christe, "L'Héxaméron," 184. The Annunciation sculpture is a restoration made after the fire of 1481: Peter Kurmann and Alain Villes, *Reims: La cathédrale Notre-Dame* (Paris, 2001), 55.

109. Kurmann and Villes, *Reims: La cathédrale,* 56–57. This sculpture is a replacement, in Flamboyant Gothic style, made ca. 1502.

110. See Lillich, "La 'rose verte,'" 137, 142 n. 77.

111. Margot Fassler, "Mary's Nativity, Fulbert of Chartres, and the *Stirps Jesse:* Liturgical Innovation Circa 1000 and Its Afterlife," *Speculum* 75 (2000): 423.

112. Cf. Gerald B. Guest, "Structuring Old Testament History in the Psalter of Louis IX," in *Tributes to Lucy Freeman Sandler: Studies in Illuminated Manuscripts,* ed. Kathryn A. Smith and Carol H. Krinsky (London, 2007), 51–61, esp. the conclusion.

113. For example, Jacques Le Goff has remarked that the "people" were marginal and passive in the coronation ceremony: Le Goff, "A Coronation Program for the Age of Saint Louis: The Ordo of 1250," in *Coronations: Medieval and Early Modern Monarchic Ritual,* ed. Janos M. Bak (Berkeley and Los Angeles, 1990), 50.

114. On the Strasbourg parchments, see *Les bâtisseurs des cathédrales gothiques,* ed. Roland Recht (Strasbourg, 1989), 380–98. On the Reims palimpsest: ibid., 232–33; also Stephen Murray, "The Gothic Facade Drawings in the Reims Palimpsest," *Gesta* 17, pt. 2 (1978): 51–55. James S. Ackerman has argued that Villard de Honnecourt copied his Reims drawings from parchment sheets in the *chantier,* made by or for one of the cathedral's designers, and that "Reims was an incubator for the maturation of architectural drawing": Ackerman, "Villard de Honnecourt's Drawings of Reims Cathedral: A Study in Architectural Representation," *Artibus et Historiae* 18, no. 35 (1997): 41–49. On Villard's drawings, see now Clark, "Reims Cathedral in the Portfolio."

115. See chapter 3. Previous studies discussing the "facades" include Eva Frodl-Kraft, "Zu den Kirchenschaubildern in den Hochchorfenstern von Reims: Abbildung und Abstraktion," *Wiener Jahrbuch für Kunstgeschichte* 25 (1972); Sylvie Balcon, "Nouvelles appréciations sur les vitraux de la cathédrale de Reims comportant des représentations architecturales à partir de documents d'archives," in *Représentations architecturales dans les vitraux: Acts du XXIe colloque du Corpus Vitrearum,* Dossier de la Commission royale des monuments, sites et fouilles, 9 (Liege, 2002); Peter Kurmann, "Architecture, vitrail et orfevrerie: À propos des premiers dessins d'édifices gothiques," in ibid.

116. Based on Reinhardt, *La cathédrale,* 185–86. Previously Marcel Aubert, *Le vitrail en France* (Paris, 1946), 31, suggested that the "original glazing," which he dated ca. 1230, was replaced when the vaults of the choir were raised during construction (see note 124 below). In the nineteenth century it was believed that Bay 118 had served "d'essai et de modèle" for Bay 100, the axial bay: Victor Tourneur, "Notice sur les vitraux de la cathédrale de Reims," *Travaux de l'académie de Reims* 4 (1846): 231.

117. On Bay 100, see chapter 3. The inscription "ECCLESIA REMENSIS" is modern but probably reliable. Although no nineteenth-century source reports it, Guilhermy, "Notes," fol. 400v, notes the "confused letters" "RE ENS" below the feet of the archbishop (the inscription there now is also modern). The lowest panels of the lancets of Bay 100 had been interchanged, as reported by Tourneur, and this inscription almost certainly came from the adjoining lancet with the facade image: Tourneur, *Histoire,* 56–57.

118. On Reinhardt's proposed *premier atelier,* grouping the Bay 118 spolia with several apostles and bishops in the present choir ensemble, see Reinhardt, *La cathédrale,* 186, and my rebuttal in chapter 3. My view here is a revision of general remarks in earlier publications, before I had undertaken a close examination of the choir lancets; see, e.g., Lillich, "The Stained-Glass Spolia," 2, 3, 16 n. 18.

119. I would, with two provisos, concur with that part of his assessment. First, the Bay 118 images do not closely resemble the other figures he groups in his "first choir program" (see chapter 3), and second, I believe that the Karolvs in Bay 128 of the nave was a spolium from the twelfth-century church. "Was" is the operative verb here, since the present Karolvs was almost completely remade following World War I (see chapter 6).

120. Paul Simon, "Notes sur les vitraux de la cathédrale de Reims," *Congrès archéologique* 78, pt. 2 (1911): 301–2.

121. Robert Branner, "Historical Aspects of the Reconstruction of Reims Cathedral, 1210–1241," *Speculum* 36 (1961): 25, 30–31, 37.

122. For the threats to Reims as coronation site, see the discussion by William M. Hinkle, *The Portal of the Saints of Reims Cathedral: A Study in Mediaeval Iconography* (New York, 1965), 26–31, 36–37.

123. Reinhardt, *La cathédrale,* 185–86. Width measurements provided in Recensement IV:386–90 and given for doublet bays are 5.8 meters for Bay 118 and 3.4 meters for Bay 100. The transept's Bay 118 is narrower than the choir's Bays 109 and 110, at the crossing (6.5 m wide), where a similar format is employed (colored figures in a grisaille field), surrounded by a normal wide border, which is totally

lacking in Bay 118. Cf. figs. 100 and 146. On Bays 109 and 110, see chapter 3.

124. Balcon, "Les vitraux," in *Reims: La cathédrale,* 347. However, she misrepresents (347, 366) Deneux's evidence concerning the change in vaulting height in the choir and south transept. The vaults were raised (not lowered, as she states), and the clerestory windows of the choir were never taller than at present. See Henri Deneux, "Des modifications apportées à la cathédrale de Reims, au cours de sa construction, du XIIIe au XIVe siècle," *Bulletin monumental* 106 (1948): esp. 127, fig. 6. Jean Bony points out that the older vault design (1.7 m lower) would have provided a triforium and clerestory that together would have equaled the height of the main arcade, as in Villard de Honnecourt's drawing of Reims (Paris, BnF, fr. 19093, fol. 31v): Bony, *French Gothic Architecture of the Twelfth and Thirteenth Centuries* (Berkeley and Los Angeles, 1983), 270 and 504 n. 19. See also Kurmann, *La façade,* 1:65–66.

125. Chantal Bouchon, Catherine Brisac, Claudine Lautier, and Yolanta Zaluska, "La 'Belle-verrière' de Chartres," *Revue de l'art* 46 (1979): 16–24. It is Chartres bay 30 in the Corpus Vitrearum numbering (see Recensement II:32).

126. On Samson's facade, see Robert Neiss and Walter Berry, "La cathédrale du XIIe siècle," in *Reims: La cathédrale,* 41, 59; also Kurmann, *La façade,* 1:42, 47. Excavations have not established whether the two towers were flush with the facade or extended beyond it.

127. Kurmann, *La façade,* 1:49. The original rose of Saint-Remi was certainly smaller, and it may have been inserted only at the end of the twelfth century: Anne Prache, *Saint-Remi de Reims: L'oeuvre de Pierre de Celle et sa place dans l'architecture gothique* (Geneva, 1973), 52–55. The rose as focal element of facade design seems to have been introduced first in transept facades. The first example of a west-facade rose is that at Laon, ca. 1190–1205: Bony, *French Gothic Architecture,* 191, 494 n. 28; Kimpel and Suckale, *L'architecture,* 184, 486 n. 15.

128. Kurmann, *La façade,* 1:46–48, 58–59. Kurmann (48 n. 51) first suggested this in 1977. It was briefly proposed, independently, by Jan van der Meulen, "Sculpture and Its Architectural Context at Chartres Around 1200," in *The Year 1200: A Symposium* (New York, 1975), 513–14, and was reiterated without citation by Ravaux, "Les campagnes," 35.

129. Kurmann, *La façade,* 1:50–56 (on the directions of heads, see 51). The badly damaged statue at the far right, often called Samuel, was identified as Aaron by Léon Pressouyre, "La 'Mactatio Agni' au portail des cathédrales gothiques et l'exégèse contemporaine," *Bulletin monumental* 132 (1974): 62–63 and fig. 2.

130. The Saint-Remi facade is little help in regard to any cathedral glazing, its original glass having been lost. See Caviness, *Sumptuous Arts,* 25, 51–53, 55–56, 117, 139–40. It is tempting to believe that the lost stained-glass figures of Clovis and his queen, reported in the 1820s in the lower bays flanking the central portal, were then still in their original positions. The abbey's facade statue above the place where Clovis was located represents St. Remi, who baptized Clovis. My reconstruction of the cathedral program (see below, at notes 137–39) also includes St. Remi and Clovis. Caviness (298, fig. 201) has identified the lost Clovis of Saint-Remi with the drawing made by Viollet-le-Duc before 1868.

While measurements of Samson's facade can only be approximated, the three central windows—to be seen from the interior of the nave—would have occupied the space of the present west rose (12 m in diameter) and gallery beneath (14 m wide). See above, at note 123; according to Reinhardt, the spolium of the Virgin would exactly fit, as it is (that is, sliced and borderless), one of the lancets of Bay 100, approximately 1.5 meters wide (bay width 3.4 m, including the central stonework). The approximate surface width of the three spolia proposed for the nave would thus be, even with wide High Gothic borders added, perhaps about 6 meters.

131. The literature on the concept of Maria-Ecclesia, found in the liturgy, is vast. A good introduction to the subject is Katzenellenbogen, *The Sculptural Programs,* 59–60. See also Marie-Louise Thérel, *À l'origine du décor du portail occidental de Notre-Dame de Senlis: Le triomphe de la Vierge-Église; Sources historiques, littéraires et iconographiques* (Paris, 1984).

132. For Louis XIV, see also Willibald Sauerländer, "Observations sur la topographie et l'iconologie de la cathédrale du sacre," *Académie des inscriptions et belles-lettres, comptes-rendus des séances* (1992): 469 fig. 3. The practice is probably much earlier, since it was followed at Henri IV's coronation, in 1594 (uniquely held at Chartres): Brigitte Kurmann-Schwarz and Peter Kurmann, *Chartres: La cathédrale* (La Pierre-qui-vire, 2001), 133–34.

133. Tourneur, *Histoire,* 56–57.

134. The error apparently first appeared in Deneux, "Des modifications," 139. It was often repeated, for example, in Recensement IV, 390, and has now been corrected by Balcon, "Les vitraux," in *Reims: La cathédrale,* 346. The halo was noted in the nineteenth century by Guilhermy, "Notes," fol. 403; Tourneur, *Histoire,* 39; and Cerf, *Histoire,* 2:283.

135. Meredith Parsons Lillich, "Remembrance of Things Past: Stained Glass Spolia at Châlons Cathedral," *Zeitschrift für Kunstgeschichte* 59 (1996): 487, fig. 21, reprinted in *Studies,* 232,

249–53. A lost stained-glass image of Henri de Braine in Saint-Nicaise, Reims, was described ca. 1660 as "peint en habit d'archevêque": Dom Guillaume Marlot, *Histoire de la ville, cité et université de Reims,* vol. 3 (Reims, 1846), 331, also 573.

136. Tourneur, *Histoire,* 36. One of the surviving nave figures (an archbishop with cross-staff) is illustrated in Lucien Mary, *Rheims* (Colmar, 1984), 4. On the cross-staff of an archbishop, see Herbert Norris, *Church Vestments: Their Origin and Development* (New York, 1950; reprint, Mineola, N.Y., 2002), 138–40.

137. Both heads appear to be original and are close in style: Balcon, "Les vitraux," in *Reims: La cathédrale,* 347. The Baptist's fringe of facial hair is now invisible from the floor of the cathedral, which supports my hypothesis that the Baptist image was not originally intended for a clerestory. The youthful Baptist image here is totally unrelated to the apocryphal figure, which reached Italy from the Eastern Church during the second half of the thirteenth century: Marilyn A. Lavin, "Giovannino Battista: A Study in Renaissance Religious Symbolism," *Art Bulletin* 37 (1955): 85–101. St. Remi is often shown beardless, as here (Hinkle, *The Portal of the Saints,* figs. 35, 54–55, 65–66, 69–70, 77). He is bearded on the Calixtus Portal of the Reims north transept (ibid., figs. 42, 52, 63, 72); on the later dating of the Calixtus Portal, see note 143 below.

138. The descending dove in the Baptism of Clovis clearly relates to the baptism of Christ. Hinkle points out that Hincmar's Life of St. Remi connects the birth of Remi to those of Isaac and the Baptist, while Richier's Life of St. Remi (second half of the thirteenth century) compares the vision of the hermit before Remi's birth to the annunciations to Zacharias, Abraham, and the Virgin. Hinkle, *The Portal of the Saints,* 24, 45 n. 236.

139. See note 130 above.

140. *Historiae Francorum,* 2:31; *History of the Franks, by Gregory, Bishop of Tours,* trans. Ernest Brehaut (New York, 1969), 40–41.

141. Richard A. Jackson, *Vive le roi! A History of the French Coronation from Charles V to Charles X* (Chapel Hill, 1984), 26, 31–32.

142. Richard A. Jackson, "Manuscripts, Texts, and Enigmas of Medieval French Coronation Ordines," *Viator* 23 (1992): 54 and n. 81. On the Ordo of Reims, see Richard A. Jackson, ed., *Ordines coronationis Franciae: Texts and Ordines for the Coronation of Frankish and French Kings and Queens in the Middle Ages* (Philadelphia, 2000), 1:30 and 2:291–305.

143. On the rivalry between Reims and Saint-Denis, see above, at note 122. The scene of St. Remi baptizing Clovis appears on the Calixtus Portal, added to the center of the cathedral's north facade: Hinkle, *The Portal of the Saints,* fig. 52. The later dating of this portal, following the civic riots and canons' exile (November 1234 to January 1237), is convincing: Barbara Abou-El-Haj, "The Urban Setting for Late Medieval Church Building: Reims and Its Cathedral Between 1210 and 1240," *Art History* 11 (1988). Her note 6 provides citations for the earlier dating favored by previous scholars. I have argued in this chapter that the glass of the north rose window, directly above the Calixtus Portal, displays a similar post-riot iconography.

144. Walter Berry and Robert Neiss, "La découverte du baptistère paléochrétien de Reims," in *Clovis: Histoire et mémoire,* ed. Michel Rouche, vol. 2, *Le baptême de Clovis, son écho à travers l'histoire* (Paris, 1997), 869–88; Neiss and Berry, "La cathédrale de Reims: Archéologie du site," in *Reims: La cathédrale,* 40–44, 51, 53, 59. I would like to thank Walter Berry warmly for the detailed explanation of the baptistery excavations that he graciously provided me during a visit to the site. See previously Henri Deneux, *Dix ans de fouilles dans la cathédrale de Reims (1919–1930),* Conférence donnée à la Société des amis du vieux Reims, le 1er juin 1944 (Reims, n.d.); Reinhardt, *La cathédrale,* 15–22, 27–36, 55–60.

145. Reinhardt, *La cathédrale,* 26 n. 12, 41 n. 7, 43 n. 15.

146. See Jean Wirth, *La datation de la sculpture médiévale* (Geneva, 2004), 47–49, 286–93 passim, whose explanation of the need for a *vidimus* is sound; see previously Ravaux, "Les campagnes," 11–12; Kurmann, *La façade,* 1:22–24.

147. Both chapels are named in the choir on Cellier's plan, illustrated in *Reims: La cathédrale,* 79; see also 101 (the 1722 plan). The chapel adjoining that of Saint Calixtus, dedicated to Saint Anne, received chaplaincies between 1230 and 1239; chaplaincies for the Baptist's altar are dated ca. 1227 and 1238. See Ravaux, "Les campagnes," 9 and nn. 24–25.

148. It was still in the south transept in 1722 (see the previous note).

149. A previous attempt to explain the obscure location depends on the theory that Bay 118 was a rejected glazing of the axial bay, Bay 100, replaced by Henri de Braine in order to install his own named image there: Barbara Abou-El-Haj, "Program and Power in the Glass of Reims," in *Radical Art History, Internationale Anthologie, Subject: O. K. Werckmeister,* ed. Wolfgang Kersten (Zurich, 1997), 27. She suggested that the old and the new designs (Bays 118 and 100) would mark the archbishop's ceremonial route from his palace—or, more precisely, the door where he entered the cathedral—to his throne in the hemicycle. But Henri de Braine, who inserted his image into Bay 100, died in 1240. The present study proposes that the images inserted into Bay 118 were not moved there from Bay 100 but from Samson's

facade, which was not dismantled until the nave was extended in the 1250s. It could also be argued that the archbishop's entrance was not at Bay 118 but at the eastern end of the south transept: Robert Branner, "The North Transept and the First West Facades of Reims Cathedral," *Zeitschrift für Kunstgeschichte* 24 (1961): 221 (fig. 2), 225.

150. Bays 109 and 110, at the crossing, are wider. See notes 5 and 123 above.

151. See chapter 3, at note 18. This dating reflects my study of the chevet glazing and revises the dating given previously, on the basis of the scholarly literature, in Lillich, "The Stained-Glass Spolia," 11.

152. Patrick Demouy, "Le baptême de Clovis dans les monuments rémois (XIIIe–XVIe siècles)," in *Clovis: Histoire et mémoire,* 2:816, citing the *Ordo receptionum* from *Sacramentaire et martyrologe de l'abbaye de Saint-Remy: Martyrologe, calendrier, ordinaires et prosaires de la métropole de Reims (VIIIe–XIIIe siècle),* ed. Ulysse Chevalier (Paris, 1900), 226.

153. It is conjecture whether the figure of Clovis was turned (as shown in my fig. 153), like John the Baptist, or shown frontally, like the Virgin and the archbishop-saint.

154. Only the two kings in Bay 129, which was the focal point of the nave, had foldstools; see chapter 6, at notes 95–101. For foldstools, see chapter 6, at notes 40–41.

155. Seals of French kings are illustrated in Pierre Bony, *Un siècle de sceaux figurés (1135–1235)* (Paris, 2002), figs. 5 (Louis VI), 7 (Louis VII), 406 (Philippe Auguste), 409 (Louis VIII), 542 (Louis IX). He calls the foldstool "le trône capétien en X" (51–55 passim, 80). See also Brigitte Bedos-Rezak, "Suger and the Symbolism of Royal Power: The Seal of Louis VII," in *Abbot Suger and Saint-Denis: A Symposium,* ed. Paula Gerson (New York, 1986), 95–103. On the *sella curulis,* see Ole Wanscher, *Sella curulis: The Folding Stool, Ancient Symbol of Dignity* (Copenhagen, 1980); Thomas F. Mathews, *The Clash of Gods: A Reinterpretation of Early Christian Art* (Princeton, 1993), 104–8. Illustrations of the *sella curulis* of the papacy appear in Herbert Kessler and Johanna Zacharias, *Rome 1300: On the Path of the Pilgrim* (New Haven, 2000), 4 (fig. 1) and 129 (fig. 129).

156. Caviness, *Sumptuous Arts,* 59–60, pls. 116–18; Patrick Demouy, "Les sceaux des archevêques de Reims des origines à la fin du XIIIe siècle," in *L'encadrement religieux des fidèles au Moyen-Âge et jusqu'au Concile de Trente,* Actes du 109e Congrès nationale des sociétés savantes: Section d'histoire médiévale et philologie, vol. 1 (Paris, 1985), 689, 696–720; and *Sceaux et usages de sceaux: Images de la Champagne médiévale,* ed. Jean-Luc Chassel (Paris, 2003), 68, color figs. 60–61.

157. For Pierre de Celle, Simon, and Milon, see Caviness, *Sumptuous Arts,* 59–60, pl. 119. The seal of Abbot Pierre (1239) is no. 2152 of the typed supplement to the Douët-d'Arcq collection, Archives nationales, Paris (information graciously supplied by Pierre Bony).

158. P. Bony, *Un siècle de sceaux,* 12 n. 1, 40, 93, figs. 163 (first seal of Saint-Remi, the inscription of which was damaged ca. 1200), 493 (metal counterseal made for it at that time), 523 (second seal, metallic, which replaced the first seal, destroyed ca. 1219); and *Sceaux et usages,* ed. Chassel, 53, color fig. 44. The authenticity of the new seal being contested, the abbey issued a document attesting to the destruction of the first seal matrix by the dean of the cathedral chapter. The shape of the first seal and of the counterseal made for it ca. 1200 was described by Caviness, *Sumptuous Arts* (60 n. 205) as a "spinning top"; Pierre Bony (*Un siècle de sceaux,* 40) proposes that it was the shape of the Holy Ampulla kept at Saint-Remi and used to anoint kings in the coronation ceremony.

159. Hinkle, *The Portal of the Saints,* figs. 35, 52–56; Demouy, "Le baptême de Clovis," 807–15. This standard image of the baptism of Clovis is the one used on the counterseal of the abbey (see the previous note).

160. Desportes et al., *Fasti,* 20–21; *Sceaux et usages,* ed. Chassel, 75, color fig. 67 (first seal). The inscription on both seals is "SIGILLUM SCE MARIE REMENSIS METROPOLIS." The later stained-glass Virgin in the axial bay, Bay 100, Henri de Braine's window (my fig. 69), has a much shorter scepter and bends her arm at the elbow to hold it, as she does on the second seal. See chapter 3, at note 25. The chapter's first seal is Coulon inventory no. 1857 (see the following note).

161. On Hugues de Bourgogne, see Desportes et al., *Fasti,* 327, no. 1173. The seal of his officiality, used in 1221, is no. 1806 in Auguste Coulon, "Inventaire des sceaux de la Champagne" (typescript, Archives nationales, Paris). There is some confusion in Coulon's list, since he lumps all archdeacons together. Reims cathedral, however, had two archdeacons, the grand archdeacon (*archidiaconus remensis,* who was the principal auxiliary of the archbishop) and the petit archdeacon (archdeacon of Champagne, *archidiaconus ecclesie remensis*); see Desportes et al., *Fasti,* 15–16. For the list of holders of both offices, see ibid., 102–3. After Hugues de Bourgogne, the Agnus Dei was retained on seals during the brief tenure as grand archdeacon of Henri de Braine (December 1225 until his election as archbishop in February 1227) but not by the next officeholder, Hugues de Sarcus (ibid., 102, 335). The officiality seals used by Hugues de Sarcus (as archdeacon of Champagne, 1212–26, and archdeacon of Reims, 1227–44) all show an open tomb: Coulon, "Inventaire," nos. 1805 (misdated 1203), 1807 (1221), and 1810 (1235); *Sceaux et usages,* ed. Chassel, 80, fig. 75. I am most grateful to the late Pierre Bony for detailed information on these seals.

162. Desportes et al., *Fasti,* 21; P. Bony, *Un siècle de sceaux,* 76; Patrick Demouy, *Genèse d'une cathédrale: Les archevêques de Reims et leur église aux XIe et XIIe siècles* (Langres, 2005), 131–33. This seal was still in use in 1263.

163. Auguste Coulon, "Éléments de sigillographie ecclésiastique française: Type monumental," in Victor Carrière, *Introduction aux études d'histoire ecclésiastique locale,* vol. 2 (Paris, 1934), 162–65; Helen Rosenau, "Note on Some Qualities of Architectural Seals During the Middle Ages," *Gazette des beaux-arts* 90 (September 1977): 78–84. Ecclesiastical seals of this type are somewhat more common in England; see P. Bony, *Un siècle de sceaux,* figs. 95–99, 220, 386, 389–93, 540. For the officiality of Reims, see Brigitte Bedos-Rezak, "Les sceaux au temps de Philipppe Auguste," in *La France de Philippe Auguste: Le temps des mutations,* ed. Robert-Henri Bautier (Paris, 1982), 725, pl. 11/9 (dated 1224). Architecture is more frequently depicted on town seals, though not on the majority of them: Brigitte Bedos-Rezak, "Towns and Seals: Representation and Signification in Medieval France," *Bulletin of the John Rylands University Library of Manchester* 72/3 (1990): 44–46, figs. 6 (Cambrai, dated 1185), 12 (Bayonne, 1205), and many later examples.

164. Kurmann, "Architecture, vitrail," 36; Frodl-Kraft, "Kirchenschaubildern," 70 n. 17. The transept rose windows were probably only in the planning stages ca. 1220, since their distinctive centripetal tracery patterns do not appear in the Bay 118 facade image. On their tracery, see Lillich, "Observations," 198–99, fig. 2A, reprinted in *Studies,* 158–59, 164.

165. Archbishop Aubry de Humbert was the prelate who, in 1211, placed the first stone of the Gothic cathedral; on him, see Desportes et al, *Fasti,* 156–58. While he was on crusade his vicar was Milon de Nanteuil (ibid., 436, no. 1101). Highborn and ambitious, Milon had been passed over for archbishop in 1204 because of his youth, and in December 1217 he had been elected bishop of Beauvais, a suffragan diocese of Reims (he was consecrated only after November 1221). Surely he would have been interested in the archiepiscopal election. Similarly, Henri de Braine, elected bishop of Châlons in 1226, postponed his consecration when the archbishopric fell vacant (he was elected to the latter see in 1227).

166. Desportes et al., *Fasti,* 158–60.

167. On the so-called throne of Saint Remi, see ibid., 50. On the close relationship between the archbishops and the abbey, see Caviness, *Sumptuous Arts,* 58, and Prache, *Saint-Remi,* 4–5.

168. Desportes, *Reims et les rémois,* 169–72, esp. 170.

169. Until the *jubé* (destroyed in 1744) was constructed in 1416–17, a temporary platform was erected for each coronation where the screen separates the western part of the nave from the liturgical choir: see Richard A. Jackson, "Le pouvoir monarchique dans la cérémonie du sacre et couronnement des rois de France," in *Représentation, pouvoir et royauté à la fin du Moyen Âge,* ed. Joël Blanchard (Paris, 1995), 239. Such a platform is illustrated in the Coronation Book of Charles V (London, Brit. Lib., Cotton Tiberius B.VIII), fol. 64r: Carra Ferguson O'Meara, *Monarchy and Consent: The Coronation Book of Charles V of France* (London, 2001), pl. 26.

170. On the verso sculpture, see Donna Sadler, "Lessons Fit for a King: The Sculptural Program of the Verso of the West Facade of Reims Cathedral," *Arte medievale,* 2nd ser., 9, no. 1 (1995): 49–65. I submit that one reason for giving such unusual importance to John the Baptist on the verso (see Sadler's diagram, fig. 6) may have been to commemorate the traditional association of the baptismal font in Reims cathedral with that area of the western nave.

171. For the sculptural program of the Reims facade, see Sauerländer, *Gothic Sculpture,* 474–80, and Kurmann, *La façade.*

172. Michel Pastoureau, *Les sceaux,* Typologie des sources du Moyen Âge occidental, 36 (Turnhout, 1981), 22, 25.

173. On the seal metaphor, see Herbert Kessler, *Seeing Medieval Art* (Orchard Park, N.Y.), 2004, 179; Thomas E. A. Dale, "The Individual, the Resurrected Body, and Romanesque Portraiture: The Tomb of Rudolf von Schwaben in Merseburg," *Speculum* 77 (2002): 720–21, 743; idem, "Romanesque Sculpted Portraits: Convention, Vision, and Real Presence," *Gesta* 46 (2007): 112–13 and notes; and Brigitte Bedos-Rezak, "Medieval Identity: A Sign and a Concept," *American Historical Review* 105 (2000): 1504, 1522–30 passim.

174. Among numerous examples, see Lillich, *Studies,* 429, 449, 457–59 passim, 475, 502, 539–40, and eadem, *The Armor,* 97, 231. For other periods and media of medieval art, see Pastoureau, *Les sceaux,* 74–76; Dale, "The Individual," 721 n. 44; and François Eygun, *Sigillographie du Poitou jusqu'en 1515* (Poitiers, 1938), 98–100.

175. Pastoureau, *Les sceaux,* 27, 29–31.

CHAPTER 5

1. Jacques Le Goff, "A Coronation Program for the Age of Saint Louis: The Ordo of 1250," in *Coronations: Medieval and Early Modern Monarchic Ritual,* ed. Janos M. Bak (Berkeley and Los Angeles, 1990), 53; the list that follows is taken from 53–55. See also Jacques Le Goff, "La structure et la contenu idéologique de la cérémonie du sacre," in *Le sacre royal à l'époque de saint Louis d'après le manuscrit latin 1246 de la BNF,* ed. Le Goff et al. (Paris, 2001), 29–33.

2. See chapter 6, at notes 3–5.

3. Hincmar, "Acts of the Synod of Sainte-Macre de Fismes (881)," in *Patrologia Latina* (online) 125, col. 1071. See also note 14 below. I am grateful to Professor Mary Sommar for the skillful translation. See also Donna Sadler-Davis, "The Sculptural Program of the Verso of the West Facade of Reims Cathedral" (Ph.D. diss., Indiana University, 1984), 24. Having established the distinction between kings and bishops at the start, Hincmar attempts to keep them in balance, and excerpts from his oration have been isolated to support opposing positions; see, e.g., Janet L. Nelson, "National Synods, Kingships as Office, and Royal Anointing: An Early Medieval Syndrome," *Studies in Church History* 7 (1971): 55. Significant to my argument here is Jean Devisse's observation that Hincmar's views in this oration were particularly in tune with those in the circle of Louis IX: Devisse, *Hincmar, archevêque de Reims, 845–882,* vol. 2 (Geneva, 1975), 692, 722, 991–1004.

4. See chapter 6, at note 7.

5. I have established the chart in figure 161 on the basis of the complete lists of windows in François de Guilhermy, "Notes sur diverses localités de la France," Paris, BnF, nouv. acq. fr. 6106, fols. 398r–399v, and Charles Cerf, *Histoire et description de Notre-Dame de Reims* (Reims, 1861), 2:287–97, as well as the subjects highlighted by Victor Tourneur, *Histoire et description des vitraux et des statues de l'intérieur de la cathédrale de Reims* (Reims, 1857), 331–38. Guilhermy is the most reliable, though he undoubtedly was observing from the nave floor. Tourneur and Cerf were clerics and thus had the opportunity for sustained study, probably from the triforium. Tourneur gives an incomplete account with jumbled locations, corrected by Cerf, whose publication, though heavily reliant on Tourneur, is much more methodical and thorough. Where Guilhermy and Cerf agree, we are on solid ground. Unfortunately, they do not always agree.

For the four easternmost bays (comprising Bays 121 to 128) there is the additional evidence of photographs taken by Henri Deneux in 1915 (see note 53 below), as well as the glass presently restored in those bays and catalogued, not without errors, in Recensement IV:383–91. Among Deneux's photographs of war damage after 1918 are photomontages of some of the eastern bays, presumably made to aid in restoration: Paris, Archives photographiques, DNX 02891–02901. Bays 121 and 122 and the rosace of 124, presumably less damaged, are not included; the rosaces of Bays 123 and 125 (fig. 177) show more loss; the rosace of Bay 126 had completely lost its central panel and one lobe; the photomontages of Bays 127 and 128 (DNX 02899 and 02901) are switched (possibly through an error in labeling?), and damage was extreme, though the rosaces are recognizable. For Bay 128, see fig. 189.

6. Tourneur, *Histoire,* 3; Cerf, *Histoire,* 2:295–97; Lucien Magne, "Le vitrail," *Gazette des beaux-arts* 31 (1885): 159. N. H. J. Westlake and Paul Simon, both practicing glaziers, were far more appreciative of the nave ensemble as a whole, and they also distinguish between the four or five bays near the transept and the others: Westlake, *A History of Design in Painted Glass,* vol. 1 (London, 1881), 83–85; Simon, "Notes sur les vitraux de la cathédrale de Reims," *Congrès archéologique* 78, pt. 2 (1911): 295–300 passim. See also below, at note 63.

7. Willibald Sauerländer, "Observations sur la topographie et l'iconologie de la cathédrale du sacre," *Académie des inscriptions et belles-lettres, comptes-rendus des séances* (1992): 466–73 and fig. 1; Le Goff, "A Coronation Program," 50–51. See also chapter 4, note 169.

8. Richard A. Jackson, "Le pouvoir monarchique dans la cérémonie du sacre et couronnement des rois de France," in *Représentation, pouvoir et royauté à la fin du Moyen Âge,* ed. Joël Blanchard (Paris, 1995), 246.

9. At the Transfiguration the man Jesus was recognized as the incarnate Son of God (Luke 9:35). The image of the Virgin and Child is the standard medieval symbol of the Incarnation.

10. Of the bays listed in this sentence, 126, 127, and 128 survive in restored form.

11. Richard A. Jackson, "Manuscripts, Texts, and Enigmas of Medieval French Coronation Ordines," *Viator* 23 (1992): 39 (Ordo VII). See also idem, ed., *Ordines coronationis Franciae: Texts and Ordines for the Coronation of Frankish and French Kings and Queens in the Middle Ages* (Philadelphia, 2000), 1:87 and 106–7 (Ordo VII, nos. 18–24); and idem, "Who Wrote Hincmar's Ordines?" *Viator* 25 (1994): 40–46, 51. The seven concelebrating bishops are mentioned in William J. Diebold, "The Ruler Portrait of Charles the Bald in the S. Paolo Bible," *Art Bulletin* 76 (1994): 16 n. 60. By the coronation of Charles VIII, in 1484, at least ten concelebrants took part: Jackson, "Le pouvoir," 238.

12. On the Ordo of Reims, see Jackson, "Manuscripts, Texts, and Enigmas," 53–55 (Ordo XXA), and idem, *Ordines coronationis Franciae,* 2:291–92. On the ecclesiastical peers, see Le Goff, "A Coronation Program," 49–50, and Richard A. Jackson, *Vive le roi! A History of the French Coronation from Charles V to Charles X* (Chapel Hill, 1984), 158–59. Note that the number of participating peers varies in the illuminations of the Ordo of 1250 (Paris, BnF, lat. 1246); see my fig. 169 and the complete color illustrations in *Le sacre royal,* ed. Le Goff et al. On the Ordo of 1250, see Jackson, "Manuscripts, Texts, and Enigmas," 56–58 (Ordo XXI), and idem, *Ordines coronationis Franciae,* 2:341–43.

13. This legend is the topic of Hincmar's introductory discourse in the Ordo of Charles the Bald. See Jackson, "Manuscripts, Texts, and Enigmas," 39, 54; also his useful summary in *Vive le roi!* 31–32, and in "Who Wrote Hincmar's Ordines?" 33.

14. This is a later passage in the Hincmar oration cited at note 3 above. His writings abound in references to the importance of priestly (i.e., bishops') counsel. It is a major theme of the sculpted inner facade of Reims: see Donna Sadler, "Lessons Fit for a King: The Sculptural Program of the Verso of the West Facade of Reims Cathedral," *Arte medievale*, 2nd ser., 9, no. 1 (1995): esp. 64. On Hincmar's advice to Charles the Bald, see, e.g., John J. Contreni, "'Building Mansions in Heaven': The *Visio Baronti*, Archangel Raphael, and a Carolingian King," *Speculum* 78 (2003): 704 n. 116.

15. Yves Christe, *L'Apocalypse de Jean: Sens et développements de ses visions synthétiques* (Paris, 1996), 159–61 (read 1240 and 1250 for 1140 and 1150 passim); Sauerländer, "Observations" (as in note 7 above), esp. 473, 475; Peter Kurmann, "Le portail apocalyptique de la cathédrale de Reims: À propos de son iconographie," in *L'Apocalypse de Jean: Traditions exégétiques et iconographiques, IIIe–XIIIe siècles*, ed. Yves Christe (Geneva, 1979), 245–313.

16. Jackson, "Le pouvoir," 241.

17. "Angelos suos bonos semper et ubique, qui te praecedant, comitentur, et subsequantur, ad custodiam tui ponat, et a peccato seu gladio, et ab omnium periculorum discrimine, te sua potentia liberet": Jackson, *Ordines coronationis Franciae*, 1:107 (Ordo VII, no. 26). See also 1:122 (Ordo VIIIB, no. 25); Jackson, "Who Wrote Hincmar's Ordines?" 36, 40, 42, 52; and Diebold, "The Ruler Portrait" (as in note 11 above), 9–10, 16 n. 60.

18. This *rara avis* will be the subject of investigation below.

19. Hans Reinhardt, *La cathédrale de Reims: Son histoire, son architecture, sa sculpture, ses vitraux* (Paris, 1963), 190: "un roi entouré et de deux femmes semble figurer le Jugement de Salomon"; Sylvie Balcon, "Les vitraux de la cathédrale d'après les documents du fonds Deneux conservés à la Bibliothèque municipale de Reims," in *Mythes et réalités de la cathédrale de Reims de 1825 à 1975* (Paris, 2001), 53–54. The subject was not identified by nineteenth-century observers or in Recensement IV:390. Tourneur, *Histoire*, 36–37, grouped the rosace with several scenes "de jugement général." Cerf, *Histoire*, 2:294, noted six pairs of figures, "several" holding swords, and concluded, "On dirait plutôt les ducs qui accompagnent un roi." Guilhermy, "Notes," fol. 399v, mentioned a seated king and six groups of two figures but hazarded no guess regarding their identity.

20. Cf. Strasbourg stained glass and Chartres sculpture: Victor Beyer, Christiane Wild-Block, and Fridtjof Zschokke, *Les vitraux de la cathédrale Notre-Dame de Strasbourg*, Corpus Vitrearum, France, IX-1 (Paris, 1986), figs. 53–55, 345; Adolf Katzenellenbogen, *The Sculptural Programs of Chartres Cathedral: Christ, Mary, Ecclesia* (Baltimore, 1959), fig. 58. The scene is discussed in Claus Michael Kauffmann, "The Iconography of the Judgment of Solomon in the Middle Ages," in *Tributes to Jonathan J. G. Alexander: The Making and Meaning of Illuminated Medieval and Renaissance Manuscripts, Art, and Architecture*, ed. Susan L'Engle and Gerald B. Guest (Turnhout, 2006), 297–305.

21. Katzenellenbogen, *The Sculptural Programs*, 69–70. Reinhardt, *La cathédrale*, 191, offered just such a traditional allegorical interpretation of the rosace of Solomon in Bed according to the *Hortus Deliciarum*, with Solomon as a type of Christ.

22. The Judgment of Solomon occupies two voussoirs on the left frame of the great west rose. See Reinhardt, *La cathédrale*, 179, and Sauerländer, "Observations," 481; illustrated in Étienne Moreau-Nélaton, *La cathédrale de Reims* (Paris, 1915), pl. 65.

23. "sceptrum, regiae potestatis insigne, virgam scilicet rectam regni, virgam virtutis: qua . . . populum videlicet christianum tibi a Deo commissum, regia virtute ab improbis defendas, pravos corrigas, rectos . . . dirigas": Jackson, *Ordines coronationis Franciae*, 1:121–22 (Ordo VIIIB, no. 16). See also 1:112 and idem, "Manuscripts, Texts, and Enigmas," 40.

24. "Salomonem sapientiae pacisque ineffabili munere ditasti": Jackson, *Ordines coronationis Franciae*, 1:121 (Ordo VIIIB, no. 14). See also idem, "Manuscripts, Texts, and Enigmas," 40, and Sadler-Davis, "The Sculptural Program," 232.

25. Daniel H. Weiss, *Art and Crusade in the Age of Saint Louis* (Cambridge, 1998), 54–55. Weiss's assertion that Louis IX himself probably orchestrated his identification as "the New Solomon" has been criticized; see the review by Caroline Bruzelius in *Speculum* 76 (2001): 814. She suggests "the preachers and intellectuals of Paris," mentioning Bonaventure, the king's confessor Geoffroi de Beaulieu, and the Dominican Arnaud du Pré.

26. Translated in Weiss, *Art and Crusade*, 56, from Paul Riant, ed., *Exuviae sacrae Constantinopolitanae*, vol. 1 (Geneva, 1877), 47. Similarly, the sequence *Si vis vere gloriari*, created for the feast of the Crown of Thorns in 1239, includes the following: "The king [Louis IX] . . . revealed himself to us to be the true Solomon." See Meredith Cohen, "An Indulgence for the Visitor: The Public at the Sainte-Chapelle of Paris," *Speculum* 83 (2008): 880, citing Judith Blezzard, Stephan Ryle, and Jonathan Alexander, "New

Perspectives on the Feast of the Crown of Thorns," *Journal of the Plainsong and Mediaeval Music Society* 10 (1987): 40–41.

27. Todor Petev, "Typology and Format in the Netherlandish Blockbook *Canticum canticorum*, ca. 1465," *Visual Resources* 13 (1998): 348. My thanks to Marilyn Lavin for this reference.

28. See appendix 6 for literature on the artworks mentioned in this paragraph.

29. The programs of Reims and the Sainte-Chapelle are contrasted by Donna L. Sadler, "The King as Subject, the King as Author: Art and Politics of Louis IX," in *European Monarchy: Its Evolution and Practice from Roman Antiquity to Modern Times*, ed. Heinz Duchhardt et al. (Stuttgart, 1992), 53–67.

30. On the Sainte-Chapelle, see Alyce A. Jordan, *Visualizing Kingship in the Windows of the Sainte-Chapelle* (Turnhout, 2002), 18, 25–28, 40, 116–21. The strong emphasis on Solomon that Weiss believes was intended in the Sainte-Chapelle is totally absent from its architectural decoration (stained glass, sculpture, painted medallions): Daniel H. Weiss, "Architectural Symbolism and the Decoration of the Ste.-Chapelle," *Art Bulletin* 77 (1995): 308–20. See also note 25 above and Harvey Stahl, *Picturing Kingship: History and Painting in the Psalter of Saint Louis* (University Park, 2008), 298–99 n. 188.

31. Diebold, "The Ruler Portrait," (as in note 11 above), 12 n. 37. On Hincmar's poem, see, in addition to the references in the following note, Karin Lerchner, *Lectulus floridus: Zur Bedeutung des Bettes in Literatur und Handschriftenillustration des Mittelalters*, Pictura et Poesis, 6 (Cologne, 1993), 204–5, 212–13; E. Ann Matter, *The Voice of My Beloved: The Song of Songs in Western Medieval Christianity* (Philadelphia, 1990), 187; Maria Antonietta Barbàra, "Su alcune fonti dell'Explanatio in Ferculum Salomonis di Incmaro di Reims," *Itinerarium* 5 (1997): 21–27. Many thanks to Dr. Marilyn Lavin for the Lerchner reference and to Professor Matter for her kind assistance.

32. On the fragments discovered by Bischoff in Vercelli, MS CIX (written at Reims, mid–ninth century), see Burkhard Taeger, *Zahlensymbolik bei Hraban, bei Hincmar—und im "Heliand"? Studien zur Zahlensymbolik im Frühmittelalter* (Munich, 1970), esp. 141–47, and idem, "Zum 'Ferculum Salomonis' Hinkmars von Reims," *Deutsches Archiv für Erforschung des Mittelalters* 33 (1977): 154 n. 6.

33. The poem is a traditional exegesis of the litter as the Church, conceived as the sum total of its doctrines—including grace and predestination, the Trinity, the beatific vision, and so forth. The message to Charles the Bald would have been to find repose in the Church, like Solomon in his litter. Hincmar borrowed chiefly from Bede and Gregory the Great. Rabanus Maurus provided the initial idea, that the litter is a symbol of the movement of souls toward God, and thus of the Church, whose preaching facilitated that movement: Devisse, *Hincmar*, 1:56. On the poem's number symbolism, see Taeger, *Zahlensymbolik*, 89–192. Hincmar's poem is mentioned by Flodoard (d. 966) in *Historia Remensis ecclesiae*, bk. 3, chap. 15 (*Historia Remensis ecclesiae: Die Geschichte der Reimser Kirche*, ed. Martina Stratmann, Monumenta Germaniae Historica, Scriptores, 36 [Hanover, 1998], 241), as a treatise on the Eucharist: see André Wilmart, "Distiques d'Hincmar sur l'eucharistie? Un sermon oublié de S. Augustin sur le même sujet," *Revue bénédictine* 40 (1928): 87.

34. The *media* was composed of a cross and circle with the Lamb of God at the center. Ernst suggests the *etimasia*, listing several examples and illustrating one with flanking columns and a Chi-Rho Christogram on a fourth-century sarcophagus: Ulrich Ernst, *Carmen figuratum: Geschichte des Figurengedichts von den antiken Ursprüngen bis zum Ausgang des Mittelalters* (Cologne, 1991), 351–53, figs. 100, 102, also illustrated in Gertrud Schiller, *Ikonographie der christlichen Kunst*, vol. 3 (Gütersloh, 1986), fig. 556.

35. In the rosace, Solomon is swathed in purple, and the pillars of his bed are not silver (verse 10) but gold. Taeger, *Zahlensymbolik*, 143, notes that the Vercelli sheet also disregards the pillars' silver color.

36. Jackson, *Vive le roi!* 159; on the peers, see 157–60 and 217–18. The original twelve became "roles to be played" in the ceremony, represented by others.

37. Le Goff, "A Coronation Program," 49.

38. Jackson, *Vive le roi!* 133. See also idem, "The Sleeping King," *Bibliothèque d'humanisme et renaissance* 31 (1969): 528–32; Carra Ferguson O'Meara, *Monarchy and Consent: The Coronation Book of Charles V of France* (London, 2001), 79, 94, 140–43, 291–92, and pl. 3; and François Avril, *Manuscript Painting at the Court of France: The Fourteenth Century, 1310–1380* (New York, 1978), 92–93 (where the bishop of Laon is misidentified as the archbishop of Reims because of the presence of the cross-staff).

39. Jackson, *Vive le roi!* 133–34. The ceremony is also found in the coronation ordo of Roger II of Sicily, 1130, and it was part of the Polish coronation from the late thirteenth century. See Reinhard Elze, "The Ordo for the Coronation of King Roger II of Sicily: An Example of Dating from Internal Evidence," in *Coronations: Medieval and Early Modern Monarchic Ritual*, ed. Janos M. Bak (Berkeley and Los Angeles, 1990), 170, and, in the same volume, Aleksander Gieysztor, "Gesture in the Coronation Ceremonies of Medieval Poland," 157.

40. Le Goff, "A Coronation Program," 51.

41. The honorable location in the chevet is reversed

because the archbishop entered the cathedral from his palace to the south: see Meredith Parsons Lillich, "St. Memmie, Apostle of Châlons, and Other Bishop Saints in the Gothic Windows of Châlons Cathedral," *Studies in Iconography* 19 (1998): 77, 80, reprinted in *Studies in Medieval Stained Glass and Monasticism* (London, 2001), 171–72. Peter, leading off the apostles, appears on the south (Bay 102). (The subjects in the rosace of Bay 101 are misidentified in Recensement IV:387; Peter does not appear there.)

42. Robert Branner dated the atelier 1230–50 and suggested that the artist of the Ordo of 1250 also painted a Psalter datable between 1235 and 1253: Branner, *Manuscript Painting in Paris During the Reign of Saint Louis* (Berkeley and Los Angeles, 1977), 87–88, 91. My discussion of the Ordo of 1250 is based on Jackson, *Ordines coronationis Franciae,* 2:341–56, and idem, "Manuscripts, Texts, and Enigmas," 56–58. See also Le Goff, "A Coronation Program"; Jean-Claude Bonne, "The Manuscript of the Ordo of 1250 and Its Illuminations," in *Coronations: Medieval* (as in note 38 above), 63–67; *Le sacre royal,* ed. Le Goff et al.; and O'Meara, *Monarchy and Consent,* 90–99. Branner and O'Meara, following Victor Leroquais, refer to the manuscript as a pontifical, a view no longer supportable.

43. Jackson, "Manuscripts, Texts, and Enigmas," 56.

44. For color illustrations of fols. 37v and 42v, see *Le sacre royal,* ed. Le Goff et al., figs. XIV and XV; see also in the same volume Bonne's discussion, "Images du sacre," 183–86. On the misplacements in the text, see Jackson, *Ordines coronationis Franciae,* 2:341–42.

45. Bonne, "The Manuscript of the Ordo," 61. O'Meary, *Monarchy and Consent,* 98, suggests that the manuscript was compiled "with the intention of being used for a son of Louis, especially as it places such emphasis upon hereditary succession." Le Goff has recently taken this tack and revised his dating from the years of preparation for the crusade to the last years of Louis's reign, the project coinciding with the reorganization of royal tombs at Saint-Denis in 1263: *Le sacre royal,* ed. Le Goff et al., 16, 34; also Eric Palazzo, *L'évêque et son image: L'illustration du pontifical au Moyen Âge* (Turnhout, 1999), 301. The only art-historical support for such a late date for BnF lat. 1246 would be the *lettres filigranées* (pen-flourished initials), which according to Patricia Stirnemann could date "un peu plus tard que 1250" (as reported in *Le sacre royal,* 142 and n. 121). She has suggested that Louis IX could have ordered the manuscript as a gift for his son Philippe on the occasion of his marriage in 1262 at age seventeen (ibid., 203 and n. 189). But BnF lat. 1246 is hardly a royal marriage gift to an heir apparent. Small in format and without gold, it is painted in "un style assez moyen," "loin . . . de la très haute qualité esthétique" of the finest Paris production (ibid., 144). Readers can judge this for themselves by the color reproductions, to scale, of all the volume's pages containing miniatures (ibid., figs. I–XV). If the volume was intended for the hands of a prince, it is more likely that such a simple little picture book would have been made before Louis's departure on crusade in 1248, when his two sons were three and four years old.

46. These observations were made by Hervé Pinoteau in a letter to Richard Jackson of April 18, 1999. (My thanks to Professor Jackson and Baron Pinoteau for this, and previous, kindnesses.) In a recent review Anne Hedeman has suggested that BnF, lat. 1246 "may not come from a royal or perhaps even an episcopal milieu": *Speculum* 78 (2003): 1359.

47. Branner, *Manuscript Painting,* 87; Marie-Noël Colette, "Le chant dans l'ordo du sacre," in *Le sacre royal,* ed. Le Goff et al., 245–46.

48. Color illustration in *Le sacre royal,* ed. Le Goff et al., fig. II.

49. The Châlons saints are Memmius, Donatianus, Domitianus, Alpinus, Ludomirus, and Elaphius: Jackson, *Ordines coronationis Franciae,* 2:342–43. St. Donatianus, second bishop of Châlons (feast day August 7), is to be distinguished from St. Donatianus of Reims and Bruges (feast day October 14; see chapter 6, at note 14).

50. Meredith Parsons Lillich, "Remembrance of Things Past: Stained Glass Spolia at Châlons Cathedral," *Zeitschrift für Kunstgeschichte* 59 (1996): 488–93, reprinted in *Studies,* 249–53. Considering the solid support that Henri de Braine received from Châlons, one wonders if it is merely coincidence that the only suffragan bishop depicted with a sort of "halo" in the Reims choir windows (where Henri de Braine appears in the axial bay) is the bishop of Châlons. See figs. 84–85, but also fig. 73 (bishop of Laon).

51. The vacancy in Châlons beginning in 1237 ended in 1243/44 with the consecration of Bishop Geoffrey II de Grandpré (d. 1247), who previously had been a canon there; so also was his successor Pierre de Hans, not of noble birth, consecrated in 1248. On bishops of Châlons, see Jean-Pierre Ravaux, "Les évêques de Châlons-sur-Marne des origines à 1789," *Mémoires de la Société d'agriculture, commerce, sciences et arts du département de la Marne* 98 (1983): 91–92 and 94–97. On archbishops of Reims, see Pierre Desportes et al., *Fasti ecclesiae Gallicanae: Répertoire prosopographique des évêques, dignitaires et chanoines de France de 1200 à 1500,* vol. 3, *Diocèse de Reims* (Turnhout, 1998), 160–63.

52. Stylistic assessments of Reims by Louis Grodecki and Eva Frodl-Kraft are summarized in Recensement IV:384. Grodecki believed that the nave windows followed the choir directly and were by the same artists; Frodl-Kraft

identified two styles in the choir, an earlier one related to Chartres and Bourges, and a later one, close to Amiens and Paris. See the following note.

53. This chapter publishes all the nave rosaces that are included in the 1915 autochrome photographs by Henri Deneux, donated in 1995 to the Bibliothèque municipale in Reims. Unfortunately, none of the rosaces lost in World War I was among those photographs. The situation is somewhat better for the lancets below; a number of the lost kings and bishops (though by no means all) appear in the Deneux autochromes. On the autochromes, see Balcon, "Documents du fonds Deneux" (as in note 19 above). The eventual publication of the tracings and watercolors made by the Simons before World War I would contribute significantly to the study of this lost glazing. See my Prolegomena at notes 6–7.

54. Cf. the rosace of Bay 103 (fig. 50).

55. On the *carré quadrilobé* frame, see Meredith Parsons Lillich, *The Armor of Light: Stained Glass in Western France, 1250–1325* (Berkeley and Los Angeles, 1994), 55, 147, 342 n. 44.

56. For the discovery, during recent restoration, of the sixteenth-century glass, see Balcon, "Documents du fonds Deneux," 53. For the 1580 storm, see chapter 4 at note 98. On the inscriptions naming the bishops in Bays 122, 124, and 126, see chapter 6; Bay 128, which includes the enthroned Karolvs, may also reflect old restorations (see chapter 6 at notes 60–64).

57. Peter Kurmann, *La façade de la cathédrale de Reims: Architecture et sculpture des portails, étude archéologique et stylistique* (Lausanne, 1987), 1:64; Dieter Kimpel and Robert Suckale, *L'architecture gothique en France 1130–1270* (Paris, 1990), 289.

58. The *coupure Tourneur* (see figs. 3, 160) extends diagonally from the clerestory down through to the aisle of the next bay to the west. See Kurmann, *La façade,* 1:59–63. The last nave vault constructed was at Bays 129 to 130, before the decision to remove the Romanesque facade (located at Bays 135 to 136). Grisaille may have been planned for the clerestories abutting the Romanesque towers (it was used later for Bays 139 and 140, adjacent to the Gothic towers).

59. The central medallion of the rosace of Bay 126 (Christ enthroned, showing his wounds, figs. 166, 174) is now totally restored; the area is shown as completely destroyed in the Deneux photograph of war damage after 1918 (Arch. phot., DNX 02894; see note 5 above). All nineteenth-century witnesses report the same subject. It is possible that it had been moved from Bay 138 to Bay 126 in the late sixteenth century. The rosace in Bay 138, in the nineteenth century, was missing its center and one lobe, while in other lobes were a Last Judgment group of two angels with trumpets, two with crowns, and dead rising from their tombs: Cerf, *Histoire,* 2:296. Guilhermy, "Notes," fol. 398v, states that the lost central medallion of Bay 138 had been replaced by "un damier," a checkered pattern. That sort of filler, composed of salvaged colored glass, would have been a likely restoration following the 1580 storm.

The Christ of the Last Judgment presently in Bay 122 is a different story. The panel was there by 1914 (see fig. 162), but all nineteenth-century witnesses report an enthroned nimbed bishop. The replacement was possibly made ca. 1912. In 1911 Paul Simon, in charge of the cathedral's glass, stressed the precarious condition of the south nave glass and expressed the hope that restoration would continue year by year: Simon, "Notes sur les vitraux," 289, 294. That the present panel is a replacement seems clear, as it is too small for the ironwork and a wide red fillet with yellow rosettes was added to make it fit. Bay 122 (the bay adjoining the crossing) is wider than those of the rest of the nave. The only such panel (a Last Judgment) that is mentioned in nineteenth-century accounts was in the rosace of Bay 136 (destroyed in 1918). Perhaps the panel was salvaged from there?

60. On Hincmar's trio, see above, at notes 3, 9, and 10.

61. Kurmann, *La façade,* 1:129–30, 159.

62. Meredith Parsons Lillich, "Gothic Glaziers: Monks, Jews, Taxpayers, Bretons, Women," *Journal of Glass Studies* 27 (1985): 88, reprinted in *Studies,* 29–30. The refinement of glass material is noted by both art historians and archeologists and has just begun to be studied. See Recensement VI:21 n. 18.

63. Tourneur, *Histoire,* 38; see also above, at note 6. Cerf, *Histoire,* 2:293–97, puts Bays 121 to 130 in the early group and Bays 131 to 138 in the later one. The glazier in charge of the windows, Paul Simon, who made most of the tracings, found the western group simpler in ornament and painting, with most figures made from repeated cartoons: "Notes sur les vitraux," 298–300. However, cartoons are repeated with minor variations elsewhere in the cathedral. The difference in general effect between the eastern and western nave groups cannot have been obtrusive, since it is not even mentioned by Guilhermy, who knew the difference between thirteenth-century and fourteenth-century glazing.

64. Grisaille was inserted in the Chartres north transept, in a bay obscured by the tower (the clerestory flanking the north rose to the west), in the last quarter of the thirteenth century, with borders of the castles of Castille (like Reims Bays 139 and 140; see note 65 below):

Meredith Parsons Lillich, "A Redating of the Thirteenth-Century Grisaille Windows of Chartres Cathedral," *Gesta* 11/1 (1972): 11, 16, reprinted in *Studies,* 97–98, 105–6, 115 fig. 13. There I refer to the window by the Delaporte numbers (bays 146 to 148 for the doublet and rose); it is numbered bay 123 in Recensement II:40. Another example of grisaille is found in bay 137 in the north facade tower of Sens cathedral: Recensement III:186, and Françoise Gatouillat, "Vitreries de type cistercien dans l'Yonne," in *Archéologie, histoire et folklore du nord de l'Yonne,* Actes du 56e congrès de l'Association bourguignonne des sociétés savantes (Villeneuve-sur-Yonne, 1985), 63–64 and illustrations.

65. Tourneur, *Histoire,* 31–32, reports thirteenth-century grisaille, partly destroyed, with insertions including coats of arms of the fourteenth to sixteenth centuries, the whole covered in 1825 by oil painting of red, blue, and yellow circles and stars for the coronation of Charles X. The borders contained castles of Castille. Guilhermy, "Notes," fols. 398r–399r, reports that Bays 139 and 140 had castles and Bays 131, 132, and 135 had borders of fleurs-de-lis. Westlake, *A History of Design,* 83, also mentions such borders.

66. See chapter 7, at notes 16–19. I first started beating this drum in Meredith Parsons Lillich, *Rainbow Like an Emerald: Stained Glass in Lorraine in the Thirteenth and Early Fourteenth Centuries* (University Park, 1991), 88.

Chapter 6

1. Among nineteenth-century witnesses, see François de Guilhermy, "Notes sur diverses localités de la France," Paris, BnF, nouv. acq. fr. 6106, fols. 398r–399v; Charles Cerf, *Histoire et description de Notre-Dame de Reims* (Reims, 1861), 2:287–97; and Victor Tourneur, *Histoire et description des vitraux et des statues de l'intérieur de la cathédrale de Reims* (Reims, 1857), 331–38. In addition to these verbal accounts there are a few drawings, not always accurate, published by Nat Hubert John Westlake, in *A History of Design in Painted Glass,* vol. 1 (London, 1881); tracings and watercolors by Paul Simon; and the recently available autochrome photographs made by Henri Deneux before the severe war damage of 1917. These are cited below as appropriate.

2. See, e.g., Madeline H. Caviness, *Sumptuous Arts at the Royal Abbeys in Reims and Braine: Ornatus elegantiae, varietate stupendes* (Princeton, 1990), 57 and 133.

3. Jacques Le Goff, "A Coronation Program for the Age of Saint Louis: The Ordo of 1250," in *Coronations: Medieval and Early Modern Monarchic Ritual,* ed. Janos M. Bak (Berkeley and Los Angeles, 1990), 56.

4. Flodoard of Reims, *Historia Remensis ecclesiae,* bk. 2, chap. 19, ed. Martina Stratmann, Monumenta Germaniae Historica, Scriptores, 36 (Hanover, 1998), 178; Anne Walters Robertson, *Guillaume de Machaut and Reims: Context and Meaning in His Musical Works* (Cambridge, 2002), 64.

5. Robertson, *Guillaume de Machaut,* 64–67, 341–42 n. 38.

6. See chapter 5, at note 3.

7. Ernst H. Kantorowicz, *The King's Two Bodies: A Study in Mediaeval Political Theory* (Princeton, 1957), 77, 91 n. 12, 161; see also Joanna Story, "Cathwulf, Kingship, and the Royal Abbey of Saint-Denis," *Speculum* 74 (1999): 1–2.

8. The tracings of the north and west rose windows were complete, as were those recording the cathedral's colored borders. Paul Simon made watercolors of two nave rosaces (Bay 121, which survives, and Bay 133, now lost) as well as of "plusieurs personnages." See the review of the 1905 exhibition held by the Académie de Reims, reprinted in Paul Simon, *La grande rose de la cathédrale de Reims* (Reims, 1911), 84–85. I briefly saw the immense watercolors of the two roses in the basement of the Monuments historiques many decades ago, but not the others. Simon published a number of tracings, including one of a now lost figure from Bay 135: "Notes sur les vitraux," opp. p. 294, left image (my fig. 220). See my Prolegomena at notes 6–7.

9. Caviness, *Sumptuous Arts,* 17–18, 131–35 passim. Her appendix 3, 142–44, lists the name inscriptions recorded before and after the extensive late-nineteenth-century restorations, when names were renewed and added and figures moved in the apparent goal of imposing a stricter chronological order.

10. Guilhermy, "Notes," fols. 398r–399v; Tourneur, *Histoire,* 31–38; Cerf, *Histoire,* 2:287–98.

11. Simon, "Notes sur les vitraux," 294.

12. A seventh named bishop, Discolius, appears between Donatianus and Viventius in the list provided by Étienne Povillon-Piérard, *Description historique de l'église métropolitaine de Notre-Dame de Rheims* (Reims, 1823), 137, and, presumably following him, Prosper Tarbé, *Notre-Dame de Reims,* 2nd ed. (Reims, 1852), 82–83, and Ferdinand de Lasteyrie, *Histoire de la peinture sur verre d'après ses monuments en France,* vol. 1 (Paris, 1857), 88. De Lasteyrie erroneously cites Antoine Gilbert, *Description historique de l'église métropolitaine de Notre-Dame de Reims* (Reims, 1825), but gives the correct reference from Povillon-Piérard (a nonexistent page in Gilbert). According to Louis Duchesne, *Fastes épiscopaux de l'ancienne Gaule,* vol. 3 (Paris, 1915), 81 n. 2, a "Dyscolius" was among the signatories of a forged document of the false "council of Cologne." At any rate, "Discolius" was unknown in Reims in the Middle Ages.

13. Duchesne, *Fastes,* 76. On Flodoard, see *Dictionary of the Middle Ages,* ed. Joseph Strayer, vol. 5 (New York, 1985), 90–91. Authors in the nineteenth century numbered the

archbishops differently: Guilhermy, "Notes," fol. 399v; Tourneur, *Histoire*, 35; Cerf, *Histoire*, 2:292.

14. Flodoard, *Historia*, bk. 1, chap. 5, ed. Stratmann, 72; Alfred Baudrillat et al., eds., *Dictionnaire d'histoire et de géographie ecclésiastique*, vol. 14 (Paris, 1912), col. 654. Guilhermy, Tourneur, and Cerf number him eighth archbishop.

15. Cerf, *Histoire*, 2:293, states that the archbishops of Bays 127 and 129 wore rationals. For Bay 129, see below, at note 95, and my figure 202.

16. William M. Hinkle, *The Portal of the Saints of Reims Cathedral: A Study in Mediaeval Iconography* (New York, 1965), app. C, 70, figs. 5, 8, 9, and 42.

17. The lower row of Bay 127 is now filled with figures salvaged from other bays; see below, at notes 94–95.

18. Caviness, *Sumptuous Arts*, color pl. 6, pls. 147 and 158.

19. Flodoard, *Historia*, bk. 1, chap. 5, ed. Stratmann, 72; Henri Platelle, "Vivenzio," in *Bibliotheca sanctorum*, vol. 12 (Rome, 1969), col. 1318. Authors in the nineteenth century number him ninth.

20. Sylvie Balcon, "Les vitraux de la cathédrale d'après les documents du fonds Deneux conservés à la Bibliothèque municipale de Reims," in *Mythes et réalités de la cathédrale de Reims de 1825 à 1975* (Paris, 2001), 53; Sylvie Balcon-Berry, "Les vitraux du Moyen Âge," in *La grâce d'une cathédrale: Reims*, ed. Thierry Jordan et al. (Strasbourg, 2010), 237, fig. 21 (after the 2000 restoration). The question whether the sixteenth-century figure replicates a medieval original is considered below.

21. Hinkle, *The Portal of the Saints*, 21 and n. 98; also 11–12, 14–22, and 52. During these same years, the 1240s through the 1270s, the abbey church of Saint-Nicaise was being rebuilt at "cathedral scale," a project supported heavily by the bourgeoisie: Pierre Desportes, *Reims et les rémois aux XIIIe et XIVe siècles* (Paris, 1979), 176–77. As the cathedral nave construction was in direct rivalry with that project for contributions, it seems unlikely that Nicaise—source of numerous miracles at this time—would have been omitted from a thirteenth-century group of named archbishops in cathedral glazing.

22. Hinkle, *The Portal of the Saints*, 20–22. The *rouelle* appears on Jacques Cellier's cathedral plan of the 1580s (see my fig. 199). On the location of the *rouelle*, see also Louis Demaison, "Les cathédrales de Reims antérieures au XIIIe siècle," *Bulletin monumental* 85 (1926): 75–77.

23. Flodoard, *Historia*, bk. 1, chap. 9, ed. Stratmann, 79; Duchesne, *Fastes*, 81, follows Flodoard, adding a note that they might be identical. Baudrillat et al., *Dictionnaire*, vol. 6, col. 1055, considers them to be the same individual.

24. On this ordo, see Richard A. Jackson, ed., *Ordines coronationis Franciae: Texts and Ordines for the Coronation of Frankish and French Kings and Queens in the Middle Ages* (Philadelphia, 2000), 2:341–66. For color illustrations of the illuminations that include the *Sainte Ampoule*, see *Le sacre royal à l'époque de saint Louis d'après le manuscrit latin 1246 de la BNF*, ed. Jacques Le Goff et al. (Paris, 2001), pls. II and IV; in that volume, lat. 1246 is dated in the 1260s (pp. 16, 34). Le Goff's previous dating, in the 1240s, is preferable: see Le Goff, "A Coronation Program," 46–47, 61. See chapter 5, note 45. The earlier dating is also preferred by Cecilia Gaposchin in her review of *Le sacre royal*: *Speculum* 79 (2004): 514. Previous literature erroneously referred to lat. 1246 as the Châlons Pontifical, following Leroquais, a view no longer tenable.

25. Jackson, *Ordines coronationis Franciae*, 2:291–305.

26. Richard A. Jackson, *Vive le roi! A History of the French Coronation from Charles V to Charles X* (Chapel Hill, 1984), 43, also 31–32, 188–89, 195, and 204; Hinkle, *The Portal of the Saints*, 37–40.

27. Jackson, *Vive le roi!* 43.

28. Ibid., 176–77.

29. See note 23 above.

30. Cerf, *Histoire*, 2:293, states that on the south side only Donatianus and Viventius (Bay 122) wear rationals. Perhaps the "rationals" in Bays 124 and 126 are so odd that he did not recognize them as such. He does mention authentic rationals in Bays 127 and 129 (see my fig. 202), on the north. On the sixteenth-century maniple, no longer a long narrow band but broadened at each end into something like the form of a spade, see Joseph Braun, "Maniple," in *The Catholic Encyclopedia*, vol. 9 (New York, 1910), 601–2.

31. Flodoard, *Historia*, bk. 1, chap. 9, ed. Stratmann, 79; Duchesne, *Fastes*, 81; Baudrillat et al., *Dictionnaire*, vol. 6, col. 852. Tourneur, *Histoire*, 36, followed by Cerf, *Histoire*, 1:292–93, reports that the two bishops in Bay 126 were reversed, with Barnabas on the right, but this must be a mistake. Guilhermy, "Notes," fol. 399v, and the Deneux photomontage of war damage in 1918 (Arch. phot., Deneux 02892N) have Barnabas on the left.

32. See note 30 above.

33. Flodoard, *Historia*, bk. 1, chap. 9, ed. Stratmann, 79; Duchesne, *Fastes*, 81; Baudrillat et al., *Dictionnaire*, vol. 7, col. 1351.

34. On the sword and other regalia in the coronation liturgy, see Jackson, *Ordines coronationis Franciae*, 2:352–53. The bare sword appears several times in the Ordo of 1250 miniatures but never with the king holding it point up: *Le sacre royal*, ed. Le Goff et al., pls. VI, X, and XV. See chapter 7, at notes 42–43.

35. The identity and origin of Karolvs are discussed below. The figure, shown in a Deneux autochrome (my fig.

190), was destroyed in 1918 and remade thereafter (Recensement IV, fig. 369).

36. Cerf, *Histoire,* 2:291, states that all four kings of Bays 124 and 126 have foldstools, but these figures have survived with minimal damage and prove that Cerf was mistaken. Deneux autochrome photos of 1915 exist for Bays 122 (right king) and 126 (left king). See also Balcon, "Documents du fonds Deneux," 50 fig. 5 (Bay 122, right king).

37. Ole Wanscher, *Sella curulis: The Folding Stool, an Ancient Symbol of Dignity* (Copenhagen, 1980), 194, 200.

38. Ibid., 216, 220, 222, 329. The Dagobert throne is now dated to the late eighth century, with later additions possibly by Abbot Suger. See *Le trésor de Saint-Denis: Musée du Louvre, Paris, 12 mars–17 juin 1991,* exh. cat. (Paris, 1991), 63–68, no. 5.

39. Wanscher, *Sella curulis,* 210, 248, 262.

40. Caviness, *Sumptuous Arts,* 59–61; pls. 121, 124, and 125 (sacred figures on foldstools); pls. 114 and 158 (archbishops on foldstools).

41. Ibid., 58, pl. 115. For the seal of Philippe Auguste, see Wanscher, *Sella curulis,* 221A. For the seal of Louis IX, see *La France de saint Louis* (Paris, 1970), 17. See chapter 4, note 155.

42. See below, at notes 95–101.

43. Westlake, *A History of Design,* 86, pl. XLIXa; Simon, "Notes sur les vitraux," 294. Bays 122 and 124 have recently been cleaned.

44. Caviness, *Sumptuous Arts,* 34, 107–8 n. 60.

45. "Le jour de Pâques [1580] se fit un grand vent fort à oultrages qui causa plusieurs grandes ruines en plusieurs pays, et furent grands bâtiments mis par terre. En l'église de Reims, la rose ou l'O du côté du palais [the south] fut emporté par violence. Le pignon de la salle du Palais où est la grande vitre fut jeté en bas. Les sommets des pignons des églises des Augustins et des Carmes le furent également." Pierre Cocquault, "Histoire de l'église, ville et province de Reims," Reims, Bibl. mun., MS 1609, 4:453, as recorded by Tourneur, *Histoire,* 40.

46. Caviness, *Sumptuous Arts,* 144 note j, citing Victor Tourneur, "Mémoire," *Congrès archéologique* 28 (1861): 93–94.

47. Lasteyrie, *Histoire,* vol. 2, pl. XCII; Guilhermy, "Notes," fol. 403r; Tourneur, *Histoire,* 40–41, quoting Prosper Tarbé. See also chapter 4, at notes 98–100.

48. A similar type of postmedieval repair in "medieval" style has been hypothesized at Chartres by Roger J. Adams, "The Chartres Clerestory Apostle Windows: An Iconographic Aberration?" *Gesta* 26 (1987): 141–50.

49. Tourneur, *Histoire,* 54; Cerf, *Histoire,* 1:70 n. 1 and 2:284 n. 1.

50. The phrase is Hinkle's: *The Portal of the Saints,* 8.

51. Dom Guillaume Marlot, *Histoire de la ville, cité et université de Reims,* vol. 3 (Reims, 1846), 524.

52. "Dans les vitres sont représentés tout d'une suite les anciens archevesques revestus pontificalement avec leur pallium, croce et mitre, dont les portraits attirent, par la clarté qui brille à travers, les yeux et l'esprit de ceux qui viennent pour prier, lorsque les considérant avec attention, ils se souviennent des hautes vertus qu'ils ont heureusement pratiquées pendant leur vie, Dieu ayant fait par sa sainte grâce que les premiers évesques de chaque ville fussent très-éminents en sainteté et comme des miroirs de perfection, afin que la postérité venant à les contempler, fut portée d'affection à les imiter; d'où vient qu'on les a dépeints ainsi au plus haut de nos églises, à l'exemple de ces héros que les anciens plaçoient au lieu plus éminent de leurs cabinets, et que saint Charles [Borromeo] a renouvellés au concile de Milan, enjoignant à ses suffragants de mettre les portraits de leurs devanciers à l'entrée du palais épiscopal, en éloignant toutes autre figures faites plustost pour le contentement des yeux que pour l'édification." Marlot, *Histoire,* 3:524.

53. "Borromeo, Charles, St.," in *New Catholic Encyclopedia,* 2nd ed. (Washington, D.C., 2003), 2:540.

54. Cerf, *Histoire,* 1:306–12. See also Alain Erlande-Brandenburg, *La cathédrale de Reims: Chef-d'oeuvre du gothique* (Arles, 2007), 110.

55. Tourneur, *Histoire,* 56. He quotes from the cathedral's 1637 ceremonial and notes that the most glaring misplacements of panels had been corrected four or five years before his writing. Since lower panels were similarly removed for Henry IV's coronation at Chartres in 1594, it is likely that the practice was even older at Reims: Brigitte Kurmann-Schwarz and Peter Kurmann, *Chartres: La cathédrale* (La Pierre-qui-vire, 2001), 133–34.

56. A nineteenth-century lithograph shows people standing on the exterior clerestory ledge: Patrick Demouy, *Notre-Dame de Reims: Sanctuaire de la monarchie sacrée* (Paris, 1995), 28.

57. Caviness, *Sumptuous Arts,* 142–44.

58. Donatianus and Viventius have been lost since ca. 1895; see the foldout plan of Saint-Remi in Caviness, *Sumptuous Arts,* inside rear cover.

59. Ibid., 58.

60. The only rigidly frontal archbishop surviving in the nave is the left one in Bay 122, Donatianus, probably a postmedieval design. See above, at note 14.

61. Cf. also Simon's tracing (Balcon-Berry, "Moyen Âge," 247, fig. 35) to Hans Reinhardt, *La Cathédrale de Reims: Son histoire, son architecture, sa sculpture, ses vitraux* (Paris, 1963), pl. 45.

62. On the kings at Saint-Remi, see Caviness, *Sumptuous Arts,* 55–56. For Strasbourg: Victor Beyer, Christiane

Wild-Block, and Fridtjof Zschokke, *Les vitraux de la cathédrale Notre-Dame de Strasbourg,* Corpus Vitrearum, France, IX-1 (Paris, 1986), 548–50 ("Charlemagne"); 26–29, 142, 182–200 passim (kings from the Romanesque nave, dated last third of the twelfth century).

63. Caviness, *Sumptuous Arts,* 24–25, 58–59, 104–5, pls. 81, 86, 92.

64. For the Saint-Thierry Bible, see ibid., pl. 250. The significance of the + before the name is unclear. No inscription at Saint-Remi has such a cross except the modern one for "Noe" (ibid., 283, pl. 165). It does not indicate sanctity; there is one preceding the name of Pierre Mauclerc on his tomb (ibid., 229, pl. 63b).

65. *Abbot Suger on the Abbey Church of St.-Denis and Its Art Treasures,* ed. and trans. Erwin Panofsky, 2nd ed., ed. Gerda Panofsky-Soergel (Princeton, 1979), 112–13 (*De consecratione* VI), 197.

66. Robert Neiss and Walter Berry, "La cathédrale de Reims: Archéologie du site," in *Reims: La cathédrale,* ed. Patrick Demouy (La Pierre-qui-vire, 2001), 41, 57–59; Reinhardt, *La cathédrale,* 51–58 passim; Peter Kurmann, *La façade de la cathédrale de Reims: Architecture et sculpture des portails, étude archéologique et stylistique* (Lausanne, 1987), 1:42. Alain Villes has suggested that in elevation Samson's chevet resembled Sens rather than Saint-Denis: Villes, "La concurrence entre la cathédrale Saint-Étienne et la collégiale Notre-Dame-en-Vaux de Châlons-en-Champagne, son intérêt pour l'archéologie et l'histoire de l'art," in *Architektur und Monumentalskulptur des 12.–14. Jahrhunderts, Produktion und Rezeption: Festschrift für Peter Kurmann zum 65. Geburtstag,* ed. Stephan Gasser, Christian Freigang, and Bruno Boerner (Bern, 2006), 118 n. 76.

67. See Reinhardt, *La cathédrale,* 59–60, pl. 1.

68. I have previously suggested that Karolvs was moved to Bay 129 as part of the sixteenth-century repairs following the windstorm of 1580: Meredith Parsons Lillich, "Archbishops Named and Unnamed in the Stained Glass of Reims," in *The Four Modes of Seeing: Approaches to Medieval Imagery in Honor of Madeline Harrison Caviness,* ed. Evelyn Staudinger Lane, Elizabeth Carson Pastan, and Ellen M. Shortell (Burlington, Vt., 2009), 303. In that scenario he would have been moved several times, from his original twelfth-century location to the Gothic cathedral somewhere—possibly in the south transept, area of greatest damage in 1580—and moved again following the windstorm.

69. See my figs. 188 and 200 (top row). War damage destroyed the archbishops of Bay 127; the lower row is now replaced by figures salvaged from nave bays that were not remade (see below, at notes 96–97).

70. Robertson, *Guillaume de Machaut,* 29, 344 n. 96. Three kings named Charles were crowned at Reims in the fourteenth century: Charles IV (1322), Charles V (1364), and Charles VI (1380). Charlemagne had been declared a saint in 1165 by the antipope Pascal III at the request of Frederick Barbarossa: *Butler's Lives of the Saints,* ed. Herbert Thurston and Donald Attwater (New York, 1963), 1:188–89.

71. Desportes, *Reims et les rémois,* 48 and n. 8. Twice that number feature Laon, a suffragan diocese of Reims, as Charlemagne's capital.

72. Flodoard, *Historia,* bk. 3, chap. 5, ed. Stratmann, 199; Demaison, "Les cathédrales de Reims antérieures au XIIIe siècle" (as in note 22 above), 87.

73. Hinkle, *The Portal of the Saints,* 24; Richard A. Jackson, "Manuscripts, Texts, and Enigmas of Medieval French Coronation Ordines," *Viator* 23 (1992): 39–40; idem, "Who Wrote Hincmar's Ordines?" *Viator* 25 (1994): 33.

74. For the theme of avarice in the chevet program, see Hincmar's *De cavendis* (see chapter 2, at note 163). For the nave, see his oration at Sainte-Macre de Fismes, his coronation liturgies, and even his obscure *carmen figuratum* on Solomon's bed (see chapter 5). And for the west rose's unusual Assumption of the Virgin, see his luxurious manuscript containing his own Marian poem and the Pseudo-Jerome epistle (discussed in chapter 7, at notes 69–71).

75. Hinkle, *The Portal of the Saints,* 28–30, 36, based on Percy Ernst Schramm, *Der König von Frankreich* (Weimar, 1939), 1:132–33.

76. *Le trésor de Saint-Denis* (as in note 38 above), 47.

77. *Abbot Suger on the Abbey Church,* 62–63 (*De administratione* XXXIII), 190; *Le trésor de Saint-Denis,* 46, 54 n. 42, 92–98.

78. Elizabeth A. R. Brown, "Saint-Denis and the Turpin Legend," in *The "Codex Calixtinus" and the Shrine of St. James,* ed. John Williams and Alison Stones, Jakobus-Studien, 3 (Tübingen, 1992), 51–88 passim (51 quoted here).

79. Ibid., 71.

80. Lindy Grant, *Abbot Suger of St.-Denis: Church and State in Early Twelfth-Century France* (London, 1998), 119–20.

81. Elizabeth A. R. Brown and Michael Cothren, "The Twelfth-Century Crusading Window of the Abbey of Saint-Denis: *Praeteritorum enim recordatio futurorum est exhibitio,*" *Journal of the Warburg and Courtauld Institutes* 49 (1986): 1–40, pls. 1–12. See also Grant, *Abbot Suger of St.-Denis,* 158 and n. 14, where she points out that Brown and Cothren (pp. 33–37) admit that the window's style conforms to that of the 1140s.

82. *Abbot Suger on the Abbey Church,* 71, 129–31, 194, 197 (tomb); 61, 184–86 (golden altar frontal); 129–31, 198 (monthly anniversary). See also *Le trésor de Saint-Denis,* 51, 69

(tomb, which received a bronze gisant ca. 1220); 43, 123–24 (golden altar); Grant, *Abbot Suger of St.-Denis,* 199 (monthly anniversary).

83. *Abbot Suger on the Abbey Church,* 68–71 (*De administratione* XXXIII); 129–33 passim, 196–97.

84. This paragraph summarizes discussions and arguments in chapter 5.

85. For arguments for the 1285 dating, see chapter 7, at notes 15–20.

86. Various authors have identified this gesture with highborn figures. The most thorough investigation is by Roger Adams; see note 48 above.

87. See chapter 5, at note 7.

88. See chapter 3, at note 81. At present the archbishops in Bay 121 hold croziers, but both Guilhermy and Cerf (who worked independently) record that these bishops had cross-staffs: Guilhermy, "Notes," fol. 398v; Cerf, *Histoire,* 2:293. Westlake's drawing, quite inaccurate in numerous details, shows a crozier: Westlake, *A History of Design,* pl. XLVIIa. Can we trust Westlake sufficiently to assume a change in the glazing between 1861 and 1881?

89. Michael W. Cothren, *Picturing the Celestial City: The Medieval Stained Glass of Beauvais Cathedral* (Princeton, 2006), 235 n. 107.

90. See figs. 75, 81, 91, and 94.

91. See Robertson, *Guillaume de Machaut,* 24–25, 44, 219–20, 271, 403 n. 60, for the closure to the canons' choir before construction of the permanent *jubé* and for processions emanating from its central door. The altar of Saint Paul was later known as the altar of Mary, and after 1343 (when it received a statue) as the altar of the Belle Image.

92. This paragraph draws on Hinkle, *The Portal of the Saints,* 20–21.

93. Citations to the extensive scholarly literature on the famous lost church of Saint-Nicaise de Reims may be found in my article on its important stained glass: Meredith Parsons Lillich, "Heraldry and Patronage in the Lost Windows of Saint-Nicaise de Reims," in *L'art et les révolutions: XXVIIe Congrès international d'histoire de l'art* (Strasbourg, 1992), 8:71–102, reprinted in *Studies,* 434–66.

94. Isabelle Pallot-Frossard, "Le Palais du Tau à Reims," *Les dossiers d'archéologie* 186 (October 1993): 44–45; Desportes, *Reims et les rémois,* 531. The bronze stag survived until the seventeenth-century rebuilding of the Palais du Tau. The stag's original symbolism may have derived from the bestiary, where the stag, as the enemy of serpents, is a symbol of Christ, enemy of the devil; the stag is also a symbol of the good Christian. See chapter 4, at note 78.

95. The Rothier photo was published in Arthur J. de Havilland Bushnell, *Storied Windows* (Edinburgh, 1914), opp. p. 293, and in Louis Demaison, *La cathédrale de Reims* (Paris, 1913), 113.

96. The Deneux autochrome photo is published by Balcon, "Documents du fonds Deneux," 52 fig. 7, and Balcon-Berry, "Les vitraux," 213 fig. 14, stating that he is lost. He is not lost, thank God. The tracing is published in Simon, "Notes sur les vitraux," opp. p. 294, right image.

97. Guilhermy, "Notes," fol. 398v, states that the archbishops in Bay 130 have haloes and croziers. No archbishop west of Bay 130 (on the south) has a halo, while the haloed archbishop of the north (Bay 131) is bearded and holds a book.

98. Tourneur, *Histoire,* 35; Guilhermy's notes concur.

99. Cerf, *Histoire,* 2:293.

100. Guilhermy, "Notes," fol. 398v. Foldstools do not appear in the nave otherwise, except in the suspect Bays 122, 124, and 126. A remarkable foldstool supports the figure of St. Remi now in Bay 118; see my fig. 147.

101. On foldstools, see chapter 4, at notes 153–59.

102. Cerf, *Histoire,* 2:293; Guilhermy, "Notes," fol. 398v.

103. Recensement IV:390.

104. Louis Grodecki and Catherine Brisac, *Gothic Stained Glass, 1200–1300* (Ithaca, 1984), 118.

105. Nearly all the surviving nave rosaces include lobes with a red circular ring set into the ground, a design convention found in the north rose and before that in Bays 102 and 108. The borders of Bay 121 resemble those of 102 (right lancet) and 105; those of Bays 123 and 125 are similar to those of Bay 103, while the right border of Bay 127 is a type found in the right lancets of 102, 109, and 110. The ground of Bay 123 can be compared with that of 105, and the same type appears in Bay 121, with fleurs-de-lis substituted for the generic accents. The ground of the right lancet of Bay 128 copies that of 107, while the left lancet has a network grid occurring in a number of earlier designs.

106. Le Mans bays 209 and 211: see Meredith Parsons Lillich, *The Armor of Light: Stained Glass in Western France, 1250–1325* (Berkeley and Los Angeles, 1994), 38, fig. II.11A, also pl. 6B. A lozenge ground similar to the one in Bays 121 and 123 appears at Le Mans (figs. II.3 and II.11B) and elsewhere.

107. Cf. the Beauvais hemicycle (ca. 1255–65), where crockets are not the exception, as in the eastern nave bays of Reims, but the rule: Cothren, *Picturing the Celestial City,* chap. 2 illustrations passim. At Reims the crocketed canopies in the western nave can be compared with some at Sées cathedral (ca. 1270–85): Lillich, *The Armor,* 201. Crockets are rare on canopies before the midcentury, but when they occur—as in a few cases at Bourges—they stand straight up and look like some kind of fungal growth. Cf. Le

Mans bay 100 (ca. 1240, right lancet): Lillich, *The Armor,* 18; illustrated in Catherine Brisac and Didier Alliou, *Un vitrail,* Regarder et comprendre (Le Mans, 1985), 66–67.

108. The facade dating is argued in chapter 7.

109. See chapter 7, at notes 36, 37.

110. See the discussion in chapter 7, at notes 16–19.

111. See chapter 5, notes 6 and 62.

112. See also the Simon tracings of heads in Balcon-Berry, "Moyen Âge": 238 fig. 23 (Bay 136, bishop); 247, fig. 36 (Bay 137, king). For the nave rosaces, see fig. 161.

113. Cf. a miter in the Queen Mary Psalter (Brit. Lib., Royal 2 B.VII, ca. 1315–25), fol. 259v, illustrated in Herbert Norris, *Church Vestments: Their Origin and Development* (New York, 1950; reprint, Mineola, N.Y., 2002), pl. VIII (opp. p. 104). On the development of the miter shape, see Joseph Braun, "Mitre," in *The Catholic Encyclopedia,* vol. 10 (New York, 1911), 404–5. See also the following note.

114. This judgment first appeared in Lillich, *The Armor,* 232, based on evidence of the monuments studied in that volume. The "frayed-cabbage" crocket type appeared in Bay 134 (fig. 217), another indication that that bay, so different from the others, dated somewhat later.

115. The gesture of an open hand indicates acceptance: François Garnier, *Le langage de l'image au Moyen Âge: Signification et symbolique* (Paris, 1982), 174, 176–77.

CHAPTER 7

1. A sensitive appraisal of the verso design appears in Donna Sadler-Davis, "The Sculptural Program of the Verso of the West Facade of Reims Cathedral" (Ph.D. diss., Indiana University, 1984), 410–19.

2. Prosper Tarbé, *Notre-Dame de Reims,* 2nd ed. (Reims, 1852), 79; Étienne Povillon-Piérard, *Description historique de l'église métropolitaine de Notre-Dame de Rheims* (Reims, 1823), 135–36; Charles Cerf, *Histoire et description de Notre-Dame de Reims* (Reims, 1861), 2:298; Étienne Moreau-Nélaton, *La cathédrale de Reims* (Paris, 1915), pl. 19 (Rothier photo). François de Guilhermy, "Notes sur diverses localités de la France," Paris, BnF, nouv. acq. fr. 6106, fol. 402r, also noted a thirteenth-century angel and six sixteenth-century heads, one of them mitered.

3. Victor Tourneur, *Histoire et description des vitraux et des statues de l'intérieur de la cathédrale de Reims* (Reims, 1857), 59–61.

4. On Bays 139 and 140, see figs. 230, 238, and note 26 below. These grisailles, like those of the transept clerestories, were oil-painted with colored circles and stars for the coronation of Charles X in 1825: Tourneur, *Histoire,* 31–32. On the grisailles removed from some aisle windows in the eighteenth century, see fig. 229 and note 23 below.

5. Tourneur, *Histoire,* 14–15, 54, 57. The glazier was François Simon; on the Simon family of glaziers during that period, see Cerf, *Histoire,* 2:313.

6. See Peter Kurmann, *La façade de la cathédrale de Reims: Architecture et sculpture des portails, étude archéologique et stylistique* (Lausanne, 1987), vol. 2, pl. 531; Moreau-Nélaton, *La cathédrale,* pl. 16 (Rothier photo). Red medieval fragments were also used. Guilhermy, "Notes," fol. 401v, noted the cold painting.

7. For the Laon north rose (ca. 1190–1200), see Painton Cowen, *The Rose Window: Splendour and Symbol* (London, 2005), 70, 227. For Auxerre (ca. 1240s): ibid., 226 (bay 101); Recensement III:121.

8. Recensement I:31; Jean Lafond in Marcel Aubert et al., *Les vitraux de Notre-Dame et de la Sainte-Chapelle de Paris,* Corpus Vitrearum Medii Aevi, France, 1 (Paris, 1959), 19–26, 28–34. The Paris rose is divided into twelve sections, not eight; at Reims the months plus the seasons might have filled the sixteen quatrefoils of the small rose.

9. Peter Kurmann, "Le Couronnement de la Vierge du grand portail de Reims: Clef du système iconographique de la cathédrale des sacres," in *De l'art comme mystagogie: Iconographie du Jugement dernier et des fins dernières à l'époque gothique,* edited by Yves Christe, Civilisation médiévale, 3 (Poitiers, 1996).

10. Tourneur, *Histoire,* 19–20, 57.

11. Ibid., 16–19; Cerf, *Histoire,* 2:301–2.

12. William H. Hinkle points out that the Holy Ampulla is still present, atop his crown: Hinkle, *The Portal of the Saints of Reims Cathedral: A Study in Mediaeval Iconography* (New York, 1965), 25, fig. 35. For the baptism of Clovis, see ibid., figs. 52–56; also Jean-Claude Bonne, "Images du sacre," in *Le sacre royal à l'époque de saint Louis d'après le manuscrit latin 1246 de la BNF,* ed. Jacques Le Goff et al. (Paris, 2001), 122–23, 126. One of the jamb statues of the Calixtus Portal, in the north transept of Reims, is sometimes identified as Clovis. The figure is haloed, wears a mantle, and once had a crown and held an unknown object: Hinkle, *The Portal of the Saints,* fig. 42 (identified as Samuel); Patrick Demouy, "Le baptême de Clovis dans les monuments rémois (XIIIe–XVIe siècles)," in *Clovis: Histoire et mémoire,* vol. 2, *Le baptême de Clovis, son écho à travers l'histoire,* edited by Michel Rouche (Paris, 1997), esp. 809–11.

13. Tarbé, *Notre-Dame,* 80. Jean de Brienne was no longer king of Jerusalem in 1226, since in 1225 his daughter (heir to that throne) had married Frederick II, who assumed the title. See Hervé Pinoteau, *L'héraldique de saint Louis et de ses compagnons,* Les cahiers nobles, 27 (Paris, 1966), 30. Jean de Brienne was at the time of the 1226 *sacre* married to his third wife, Berengaria, who was a niece of Blanche de Castille and thus Louis IX's cousin.

14. Jean-Pierre Ravaux, "Les campagnes de construction de la cathédrale de Reims au XIIIe siècle," *Bulletin monumental* 137 (1979): 54, 57; Kurmann, *La façade,* 1:159. A good illustration of the labyrinth appears in Robert Branner, "Jean d'Orbais and the Cathedral of Reims," *Art Bulletin* 43 (1961): after p. 132.

15. Patrick Demouy, "Les *pueri chori* de Notre-Dame de Reims: Contribution à l'histoire des clergeons au Moyen Âge," in *Le clerc séculier au Moyen Âge: XXIIe Congrès des médiévistes de l'enseignement supérieur, Amiens, 1991* (Paris, 1993), 139, 141, 143.

16. Pinoteau, *L'héraldique de saint Louis,* 8. On the Chartres north rose, see idem, "Autour de la bulle 'Dei filius,'" in *Vingt-cinq ans d'études dynastiques* (Paris, 1982), 295–324, esp. 302–3.

17. Pinoteau, *L'héraldique de saint Louis,* 8.

18. Charles-Victor Langlois, *Le règne de Philippe III le Hardi* (Paris, 1887; reprint, Geneva, 1979), 104–7.

19. Joseph Strayer, *The Reign of Philip the Fair* (Princeton, 1980), 9–12, 371–72.

20. Philippe IV's quick reversal of Spanish policy seems to reflect personal affection for the family of his deceased mother, Isabelle of Aragon (d. 1271), his father's first queen, coupled with antagonism toward causes espoused by his hated stepmother, Queen Marie de Brabant, whom his father married in 1274. See Elizabeth A. R. Brown, "The Prince Is Father of the King: The Character and Childhood of Philip the Fair of France," *Mediaeval Studies* 49 (1987): esp. 300, 323, 331.

21. See my previous statements in Meredith Parsons Lillich, *Rainbow Like an Emerald: Stained Glass in Lorraine in the Thirteenth and Early Fourteenth Centuries* (University Park, 1991), 88, and earlier in eadem, "Stained Glass from Western France (1250–1325) in American Collections," *Journal of Glass Studies* 25 (1983): 126 n. 25.

22. Louis Grodecki in Aubert et al., *Les vitraux de Notre-Dame,* 243 pl. VI (bay D) and 79 pl. II (bay M).

23. On the location of the *coupure Tourneur,* see figs. 3 and 160 and chapter 6, at note 84. The lower windows of Reims are not as broad as the clerestories, and their borders are somewhat narrower. Grisailles were among the aisle glazing removed in the eighteenth century: Cerf, *Histoire,* 2:316. The grisaille panel under discussion here (fig. 229) is known only from a drawing published by Olivier Merson, *Les vitraux* (Paris, 1895), 80, fig. 42, reproduced in Marcel Aubert et al., *Le vitrail français* (Paris, 1958), 30 fig. 11. The elements of this grisaille suggesting a date in the 1260s are the (partial) central stem, crosshatched ground, naturalistic foliage, and repetitious *panneau* design with a small central accent. Compare grisailles at Saint-Germer-de-Fly (before 1266); Saint-Gengoult, Toul (ca. 1265–70); Saint-Urbain, Troyes (ca. 1267–70); the Châlons cathedral nave (ca. 1260–70); the Saint-Père de Chartres chevet (ca. 1260–70); etc.

24. Guilhermy, "Notes," fols. 398r–399r; Cerf, *Histoire,* 2:289, mentions them in passing.

25. Louis Ottin, *Le vitrail: Son histoire, ses manifestations à travers les âges et les peuples* (Paris, 1896), 151, fig. 149.

26. For the Bay 140 grisailles, see Simon's tracing in Sylvie Balcon-Berry, "Les vitraux du Moyen Âge," in *La grâce d'une cathédrale: Reims,* ed. Thierry Jordan et al. (Strasbourg, 2010), 236, fig. 22. For the Castille borders, see Tourneur, *Histoire,* 31–32; Cerf, *Histoire,* 2:287. Guilhermy, "Notes," fols. 398r (Bay 139), 398v (Bay 140).

27. Guilhermy, "Notes," fol. 400v, describes the various spolia that are still found in the Bay 39 rosace, but he saw "small lozenge borders" in the lancets below; he does not mention the wide Castille borders or grisaille fragments now located there. The most likely period for the addition of the grisailles and castle borders to these lancets would be World War I, when fragments could have been salvaged from the wreckage of Bay 139 or 140.

28. Aubert et al., *Les vitraux de Notre-Dame,* 79, pl. II.

29. The Vulgate; the Douay-Rheims Bible gives "violet" as a translation. Hervé Pinoteau, "La tenue de sacre de saint Louis IX roi de France, son arrière-plan symbolique et la 'renovatio regni Juda,'" in *Vingt-cinq ans,* 473. For the thirteenth-century ordines, see Richard A. Jackson, ed., *Ordines coronationis Franciae: Texts and Ordines for the Coronation of Frankish and French Kings and Queens in the Middle Ages* (Philadelphia, 2000), 2:300 (Ordo of Reims, ca. 1230), 326 (French translation of the Ordo of Reims, ca. 1300–20), 352 (Ordo of 1250, ca. 1240), and 384 (Last Capetian Ordo, ca. 1250–70).

30. On this preferred earlier dating of Paris, lat. 1246, see chapter 5, at notes 42–51. The illuminations are reproduced in color in fifteen plates at the front of *Le sacre royal.* On the color of the king's robes, see in that volume Bonne, "Images du sacre" (as in note 12 above), 166.

31. Jean de Joinville describes him at that event wearing a blue tunic and bright red surcoat, both satin, under a mantle lined in ermine, and a cotton cap: *Joinville and Villehardouin, Chronicles of the Crusades,* trans. M. R. B. Shaw (Baltimore, 1963), 187 (pt. 2, chap. 1); see also 171, 177, and 331 for references to the king's sober dress.

32. Jean-Michael Leniaud and Françoise Perrot, *La Sainte Chapelle* (Paris, 1991), 181, 189.

33. Gabrielle M. Spiegel, *The Chronicle Tradition of Saint-Denis: A Survey* (Brookline, Mass., 1978), 31–32.

34. The Coronation Book of Jeanne d'Evreux (Univer-

sity of Illinois at Urbana-Champaign) contains the Last Capetian Ordo (ca. 1250–70), which was used for the coronations of Philippe III and succeeding monarchs up to Charles V: Richard A. Jackson, *Vive le roi! A History of the French Coronation from Charles V to Charles X* (Chapel Hill, 1984), 26–27. The king's dark blue robe appears in color fig. 1 of Harry Bober, "The Coronation Book of Charles IV and Jeanne d'Evreux," in *Rare Books: Notes on the History of Old Books and Manuscripts Published for the Friends and Clients of H. P. Kraus*, vol. 8, no. 3 (November 1958): 1–12 (the rest of the twelve illuminations appear in black and white). Many thanks to Professor Eric Ramirez-Weaver for his real help in obtaining this material. On the manuscript, see Anne D. Hedeman, "The Commemoration of Jeanne d'Evreux's Coronation in the *Ordo ad Consecrandum* at the University of Illinois," *Essays in Medieval Studies* 7 (1990): 13–28; Bonne, "Images du sacre," esp. 211–12. The manuscript is attributed to Philippe VI de Valois and his second wife, Blanche de Navarre, married 1350, by Carra Ferguson O'Meara, *Monarchy and Consent: The Coronation Book of Charles V of France* (London, 2001), 100–102; this attribution is rejected in the review by Anne Hedeman in *Speculum* 78 (2003): 1359. See O'Meara also for the Coronation Book of Charles V (London, Brit. Lib., Cotton Tiberius B.VIII), the literature on which is abundant and the illustrations of which have been widely published. The regalia are dark blue in its illuminations, though described in the text as hyacinth: Jackson, *Ordines coronationis Franciae*, 2:476. Yet another example of a blue robe *semé* with fleurs-de-lis is the Mainneville statue of St. Louis, dated 1305–10: *L'art au temps des rois maudits: Philippe le Bel et ses fils, 1285–1328, Paris, Galeries nationales du Grand Palais*, exh. cat. (Paris, 1998), 102, no. 51 (color ill.).

35. Robert Fawtier, *The Capetian Kings of France: Monarchy and Nation (987–1328)*, trans. Lional Butler and R. J. Adam (London, 1960), 34.

36. *Joinville and Villehardouin*, 346 (pt. 2, chap. 19).

37. Compare data published by Fawtier, *The Capetian Kings*, 8: Philip Augustus reigned forty-two years; Louis VII, forty-three years; Louis VI, thirty-nine years; Philippe I, forty-eight years; etc.

38. *Joinville and Villehardouin*, 168 (pt. 1, chap. 1). For a discussion of the date(s) of composition, see M. Cecilia Gaposchkin, *The Making of Saint Louis: Kingship, Sanctity, and Crusade in the Later Middle Ages* (Ithaca, 2008), 183, 189. Louis IX's simple clothing was mentioned in Pope Boniface VIII's first sermon (August 6, 1297) upon canonization, and also in the liturgical office for St. Louis's feast day at the Sainte-Chapelle: ibid., 53, 106.

39. The full passage: "Haa doulce Vierge Marie, par ta grant humilité tu voulsise que nom royal feust en toy oblié du très grant & puissant roy Salemon, duquel lignaige tu estois estraite; & j'ai voulu tout mon lignaige surmonter, & les poures petit prisier, les fleurs de lys de France en mes parements peindre & démonstrer. Haa, Madame, en quel lieu list-on qu'en vos paremens vous meissiés les armes & signes du roy Sálemon, de David, ne des autres roys mondains. Et je, qui suis si miserable par dehors, estoie si royamment aournée, & par dedans estoie charoigne puante de si riches aournements & atours enveloppée." See "De felici obitu Johannae comitissae Alenconii et Blesensis, Ex ms. Praemonstratensi," in *Veterum scriptorum et monumentorum historicorum, dogmaticorum, moralium, amplissima collectio*, ed. Edmond Martène and Ursin Durand, vol. 6 (Paris, 1729; reprint, New York, 1968), cols. 1219–38 (here 1223). On Jeanne de Châtillon, see Meredith Parsons Lillich, "The Choir Clerestory Windows of La Trinité at Vendôme: Dating and Patronage," *Journal of the Society of Architectural Historians* 34 (1976): 245–50 passim; eadem, *The Armor of Light: Stained Glass in Western France, 1250–1325* (Berkeley and Los Angeles, 1994), 230, 233–34.

40. Frederick Maurice Powicke, *The Thirteenth Century, 1216–1307*, 2nd ed. (Oxford, 1962), 647. On Marie de Brabant, see Meredith Parsons Lillich, "Heraldry and Patronage in the Lost Windows of Saint-Nicaise de Reims," in *L'art et les révolutions: XXVIIe Congrès international d'histoire de l'art* (Strasbourg, 1992), 8:75, 80–86, reprinted in *Studies in Medieval Stained Glass and Monasticism* (London, 2001), 441, 444–55; eadem, "European Stained Glass Around 1300: The Introduction of Silver Stain," in *Europäische Kunst um 1300*, Akten des XXV. Internationalen Kongresses für Kunstgeschichte, vol. 6 (Vienna, 1986), 47–52 passim, reprinted in *Studies*, 41, 48–59 passim, 61 (addendum on the heraldry). Marie de Brabant's establishment of the Mantes chapel is now dated 1312: Philippe Plagnieux, "Une fondation de la reine Marie de Brabant: La Chapelle Saint-Paul Saint-Louis," in *Mantes médiévale: La collégiale au coeur de la ville* (Paris, 2000), 110–16.

41. Lillich, "European Stained Glass Around 1300," fig. 3; a color lithograph is in Paul Lacroix (Bibliophile Jacob), *Sciences & letters au Moyen Âge et à l'époque de la Renaissance* (Paris, 1877), opp. p. 440.

42. Queen Jeanne de Navarre's window dates ca. 1289–93, and Philippe IV's ca. 1300: Lillich, "Heraldry and Patronage," 75, 84–85, reprinted in *Studies*, 441, 449–50. Of course, heraldic robes appear at Chartres, most obviously in the gallery beneath the south rose window, as well as other places during Louis IX's reign. There is, however, no image of Louis IX so garbed until long after his death (see the end of note 34 above), and none that I know of depicting

Philippe III. It is a matter of degree, since on the battlefield, for example, such identification would have been necessary and in use much earlier.

43. Bonne, "Images du sacre" (as in note 12 above), 168–69 and 178–79, discusses the differences between the text of the Ordo of 1250 (Paris, BnF, lat. 1246) and its illuminations of the bare sword (fols. 17r, 26v). The ritual of the sword appears in three miniatures of the Coronation Book of Charles V: O'Meara, *Monarchy and Consent*, pls. 10 (fol. 49r, the king places the bare sword on the altar), 11 (fol. 49v, the archbishop returns the sword to the king), and 12 (fol. 50r, the king gives the sword to the seneschal).

44. For Karolvs see chapter 6, at notes 34–35, 70–71, figs. 188, 190. The gesture of the central king in the gallery is also peculiar: elbow flexed, hand raised, and fingers widespread as though he were holding something. If so, the object has been lost. While the hand most resembles the familiar gesture of a king pulling on his mantle straps, the hand is placed too high and too far forward, and the robe has no straps.

45. Anne D. Hedeman, *The Royal Image: Illustrations of the Grandes Chroniques de France, 1274–1422* (Berkeley and Los Angeles, 1991), 281 n. 46; Langlois, *Le règne de Philippe III*, 55. On the sword Joyeuse, see *Le trésor de Saint-Denis: Musée du Louvre, Paris, 12 mars–17 juin 1991*, exh. cat. (Paris, 1991), 204–9; Blaise de Montesquiou-Fezensac et Danielle Gaborit-Chopin, *Le trésor de Saint-Denis: Inventaire de 1634*, vol. 2 (Paris, 1973), 225, pls. 66–67A; William Martin Conway, "The Abbey of Saint-Denis and Its Ancient Treasures," *Archaeologia, or, Miscellaneous Tracts Relating to Antiquity* 66, 2nd ser., no. 16 (1915): 132 and fig. 1 of pl. V.

46. The possibility that the figures have been moved around, suggested by the 1845 lithograph (fig. 222), must be discarded. All mid-nineteenth-century witnesses describe the figures in their present order: Tourneur, *Histoire*, 16; Guilhermy, "Notes," fol. 401v; Cerf, *Histoire*, 2:301. The gallery was restored in 1833–34 but not again until after World War I.

47. This figure and the one to the far right are now truncated, their lights having been half-blinded vertically. This was done before 1911, since a Rothier photo published in that year in Paul Simon, *La grande rose de la cathédrale de Reims* (Reims, 1911), opp. p. 6, shows the truncation. The 1845 lithograph (fig. 222) shows them full-size (unblinded), and no mid-nineteenth-century witness mentions the truncation. It was most likely done following the 1886 hailstorm.

48. Strayer, *Philip the Fair*, 12–13.

49. See note 42 above.

50. Strayer, *Philip the Fair*, 242–45, 247, 253. For the epithet "Vicar of God, etc.," see ibid., 3, quoting Fawtier. In October 1290 the chapter, in dispute with the archbishop, ordered services suspended, and papal legates (one of them elected Boniface VIII four years later) came to settle the matter. They did so on December 4, ordering two silver statues of themselves to be made for the altar. See Agostino Paravicini Bagliani, "Boniface VIII and His Self-Representation: Images and Gestures," in *The Four Modes of Seeing: Approaches to Medieval Imagery in Honor of Madeline Harrison Caviness*, ed. Evelyn Staudinger Lane, Elizabeth Carson Pastan, and Ellen M. Shortell (Burlington, Vt., 2009), 404–5. Philippe IV's position in this conflict is unclear.

51. Lucien Magne, "Le vitrail," *Gazette des beaux-arts* 31 (1885): 158; Simon, *La grande rose*, 30. Simon's remark is based on the tracings his father and he had made before the 1886 hailstorm (see below). The rose's poor condition and illegibility are abundantly clear in the mid-nineteenth-century descriptions of Guilhermy, "Notes," fols. 401v–402r; Tourneur, *Histoire*, 29–30; and Cerf, *Histoire*, 2:304–12. Olivier Merson's drawing (my fig. 235), while published after the hailstorm, shows a prophet in 7A and unintelligible debris in 8A (see the chart in fig. 236); Simon (*La grande rose*, 77) replaced both with new glass and different subjects.

52. Recensement IV:386, 391, states that one-quarter of the rose and less than half of the gallery glazing are now original. Simon (*La grande rose*, 78–79) estimated in 1911 that one-half of the rose's ornament and about one-third of the figural medallions survived; since then the facade glazing "splintered" in the 1914 bombing.

53. Paul Simon's numbering of the rose lights differs from that suggested in the guidelines of the international Corpus Vitrearum. As yet no Corpus numbering for the lights of the Reims rose has been published.

54. Simon, *La grande rose*, 16.

55. Desportes et al., *Fasti*, 167. Several thirteenth-century archbishops included the Virgin and Child *en buste* on their counterseals: *Fasti*, 163 (Juhel de Mathefelon, 1248), 165 (Thomas de Beaumetz, 1252). No seals resemble Pierre Barbel's, however.

56. Ibid., 167.

57. Patrik Reutersward, *The Forgotten Symbols of God*, Stockholm Studies in History of Art, 35 (Uppsala, 1986): for circular patterns, see essays 1–4 passim; for foliage, essay 5. On pp. 102–3 he refers to circular motifs in a late-ninth-century pavement in the cathedral of Reims, illustrated in Henri Stein, *Recueil général des mosaïques de la Gaule*, vol. 1, pt. 1 (Paris, 1957), pl. 44.

58. For this reason it is less likely that the smaller tympanum rose below originally contained a Jesse Tree. Cerf saw among Paul Simon's tracings of the north rose, made before Oudinot's drastic 1873 restoration, a stopgap

medallion containing debris of two kings from a Jesse Tree, which he said were like the kings in the west rose: Charles Cerf, "La rose nord de la cathédrale de Reims," *Travaux de l'Académie nationale de Reims* 89 (1890): 274, 279. For an illustration and discussion of this tracing, Balcon-Berry, "Moyen Âge," 234–35, fig. 10. She suggests that the two figures were the Virgin and a king with a viol, and that their original location was in a Tree of Jesse located in the initial glazing of the eastern chapels of the chevet, possibly the axial bay, around 1210 to 1220. The axial chapel was opened to the cult in 1221.

59. Simon, *La grande rose,* 78; Charles Givelet, "La grande rose du portail occidental de Notre-Dame de Reims," in *Rapport fait au nom de la Commission d'archéologie, séance du 24 avril 1891, Académie nationale de Reims* (Reims, 1891), 5.

60. See chapter 3, at notes 102–5; Madeline H. Caviness, *Sumptuous Arts at the Royal Abbeys in Reims and Braine: Ornatus elegantiae, varietate stupendes* (Princeton, 1990), 110–11.

61. Both types were in use in grisailles of the 1280s. See, e.g., Sées cathedral (Lillich, *The Armor,* 298–90); Saint-Urbain de Troyes (Jane Hayward, "The Church of Saint-Urbain at Troyes and Its Glazing Program," ed. Meredith Parsons Lillich, *Gesta* 37 [1998]: 172–73).

62. Simon, *La grande rose,* 72: "Ce médaillon avait été déposé depuis bien des années, légèrement consolidé, et était conservé à l'agence des travaux de la cathédrale: un document ancien indiquait le dessin de la tête absente. Cette tête couverte d'un voile qui est une pièce de verre neuf est donc conforme à ce qu'elle était à l'origine." On p. 71 he says that fragments of the pillow survived. The tracings made between 1875 and 1886 (ibid., 19) indicate that neither of the Virgin's raised hands was old. For an illustration of the Coronation of the Virgin in the exterior sculpted gable of the facade, see Hans Reinhardt, *La cathédrale de Reims: Son histoire, son architecture, sa sculpture, ses vitraux* (Paris, 1963), pl. 41.

63. Simon (*La grande rose,* 29, 77) gave the child-soul a cruciferous halo because he followed Tourneur (*Histoire,* 26) in mistaking the figures for God the Father holding the Christ-child, a scene totally unknown in medieval art. The 1853 tracing by Pierre Simon (*La grande rose,* 17; my fig. 241) shows that the leading of the child-soul's halo was not then cruciferous. Givelet, "La grande rose," 5–6, reports that both haloes were solid blue.

64. Simon, *La grande rose,* 72–73, states that only one apostle (3D) was completely lost and that seven heads of apostles survived.

65. The Byzantine feast of the Koimesis was established in the sixth century. The scene appears on at least twenty Byzantine ivories found from the tenth century on in Germany and France. See Philippe Verdier, *Le couronnement de la Vierge: Les origines et les premiers développements d'un thème iconographique* (Montreal, 1980), 61; Joseph Duhr, "La 'Dormition' de Marie dans l'art chrétien," *Nouvelle revue théologique* (Tournai) 72 (1960): 134, 143; Jacques Vanuxem, "Autour de quelques objets des musées de Cologne: La 'Koimesis' en France et en Allemagne du XIe au XVe siècle," in *Mémorial d'un voyage d'études de la Société nationale des Antiquaires de France en Rhenanie: Juillet 1951* (Paris, 1953), 240.

66. Duhr, "La 'Dormition,'" 144, 147; Vanuxem, "Autour de quelques objets," 251–55 passim. For Angers, see Recensement II:294, color pl. XVI. For Chartres bay 42: Colette Manhès-Deremble, *Les vitraux narratifs de la cathédrale de Chartres: Étude iconographique,* Corpus Vitrearum, France, Études, II (Paris, 1993), 360. For the Chartres and Strasbourg tympana: Willibald Sauerländer, *Gothic Sculpture in France, 1140–1270,* trans. Janet Sondheimer (New York, 1972), pls. 78, 131.

67. The theme of Mary's bodily Assumption was mentioned briefly by Gregory of Tours (d. 593), *In gloria martyrum,* chap. 4: *Glory of the Martyrs/Gregory of Tours,* trans. Raymond Van Dam (Liverpool, 1988), 22. The Pseudo-Melito text is translated in James Keith Elliott, *The Apocryphal New Testament* (Oxford, 1993), 708–14. See Stephen J. Shoemaker, *Ancient Traditions of the Virgin Mary's Dormition and Assumption* (Oxford, 2002), 3, 143, 282; Marie-Louise Thérel, *À l'origine du décor du portail occidental de Notre-Dame de Senlis: Le triomphe de la Vierge-Église, sources historiques, littéraires et iconographiques* (Paris, 1984), 19, 21.

68. See chapter 2 (Hincmar's *De cavendis*) and chapter 5 (Hincmar's speech at the Synod at Fismes and his *In ferculum Salomonis*).

69. Flodoard (d. 966) is the source for this information (*Historia,* bk. 3, chap. 5): Flodoard of Reims, *Historia Remensis ecclesiae,* ed. Martina Stratmann, Monumenta Germaniae Historica, Scriptores, 36 (Hanover, 1998), 198. See Jean Devisse, *Hincmar, archevêque de Reims, 845–882* (Geneva, 1975–76), 1:58, n. 135; 2:916.

70. *Patrologia Latina* (online) 30, cols. 122–42. Modern scholarship has established that Pseudo-Jerome's letter IX was almost certainly composed by Paschasius Radbertus, abbot of Corbie in 844. One of his own monks, Ratramne, denounced his forgery; one of Hincmar's suffragans, Odon of Beauvais, alerted the archbishop to this denunciation, to which Hincmar responded with a letter hotly defending Jerome's authorship. See Cyrille Lambot, "L'homélie du Pseudo-Jérôme sur l'Assomption & l'Évangile de la nativité de Marie d'après une lettre inédite d'Hincmar," *Revue bénédictine* 46 (1934): 265–82; T. A. Agius, "On Pseudo-Jerome, Epistle IX," *Journal of Theological Studies* 24 (1922–23):

176–83; Germain Morin, "Du sermon pour l'Assomption attribué à saint Jérôme," *Revue bénédictine* 5 (1888): 347–51.

71. Ludwig Traube, ed., *Poetae Latini Aevi Carolini,* Monumenta Germaniae Historica, Poetae Latini Medii Aevi, 3 (Berlin, 1881; reprint, Munich, 1978), 410–12. Like Hincmar's poem *In ferculum Salomonis* (see chapter 5, at notes 31–35), his poem to the Virgin was a lead-footed, precious work of "arithmétique mystique." See Devisse, *Hincmar,* 1:58, 135; Lambot, "L'homélie du Pseudo-Jérôme," 266 n. 1.

72. Saint-Gall codex 53 is an evangelistary; the Tuotilo ivory, one of two plaques originally made as writing tablets, includes an inscription, "ASCENSIO SCE MARIE." Verdier notes that the Pseudo-Jerome letter, which also employs *ascensio,* appears in Saint-Gall codex 152, dated 872–83. See Verdier, *Le couronnement,* 66–67, nn. 37, 39, and pl. 84 (the Tuotilo ivory); he discusses later examples of the *Virgo orans* on 68–74 passim (pls. 64, 66, 67).

73. Ibid., 51 n. 6, also p. 94.

74. *Patrologia Latina* (online) 30, col. 129. The six kings in the lower half of the rose are generic types in varying postures; the four prophets above hold phylacteries. Completely new in 1909 were two of the kings (2A, 10A) as well as two of the prophets (8A, 4A, the latter having retained only the red ground providing the figure's silhouette). Although the prophets in the Simon reconstruction were named for the four major prophets, there is no evidence that any originally had an inscription. Above the prophets, Simon put two angels each holding two crowns (6A, 7A); 7A was modern, and (since the rose contains no groups of saints) 6A may have been a stopgap. Simon, *La grande rose,* 66, 71, 76–77.

75. Recensement II:39–40; Cowen, *The Rose Window,* 33, 84.

76. The words are from the Coronation Book of Charles V, and the scene is there depicted on fol. 44v: O'Meara, *Monarchy and Consent,* pl. 3. See the discussion in chapter 5, at notes 38–40. Le Goff has made a strong argument that the ceremony was already in place in the Ordo of 1250: see Jacques Le Goff, "A Coronation Program for the Age of Saint Louis: The Ordo of 1250," in *Coronations: Medieval and Early Modern Monarchic Ritual,* ed. Janos M. Bak (Berkeley and Los Angeles, 1990), 51.

77. Jacobus de Voragine, *The Golden Legend: Readings on the Saints,* trans. William Granger Ryan (Princeton, 1993), 2:119; Reinhold Hammerstein, *Die Musik der Engel: Untersuchungen zur Musikanschauung des Mittelalters* (Bern, 1962), 94, 223. I have been unable to identify the St. Gerard, bishop and martyr, to whom Voragine ascribes this homily. On the probable date of the Golden Legend, see Sherry L. Reames, *The "Legenda aurea": A Reexamination of Its Paradoxical History* (Madison, Wis., 1985), 193, 245 n. 1. According to Emanuel Winternitz, instrument-playing angels were first introduced into art, particularly in the Assumption and Coronation of the Virgin, by the popularity of the Golden Legend: Winternitz, *Musical Instruments and Their Symbolism in Western Art: Studies in Musical Iconology* (New Haven, 1979), 30, 136, 229.

78. Stephan Beissel, *Geschichte der Verehrung Marias in Deutschland während des Mittelalters* (Freiburg im Breisgau, 1909; reprint, Darmstadt, 1972), 583, 645; *Bruder Philipps des Carthäusers Marienleben,* ed. Heinrich Rückert, Bibliothek der deutschen National-Literatur, 34 (Quedlinburg, 1853), 266. In a later passage (line 9846, p. 267) the Saints and Blessed play "herpfen, gîgen unde lîren." Verdier, *Le couronnement,* 140, n. 106, dates the poem to the late thirteenth century. It is a free reworking of the *Vita Beatae Mariae virginis et salvatoris,* known in a thirteenth-century manuscript (Munich, Clm 12518), which, however, does not refer to contemporary musical instruments: Hammerstein, *Die Musik der Engel,* 95–96, 266 n. 89.

79. Paul Deschamps and Marc Thibout, *La peinture murale en France au début de l'époque gothique, de Philippe-Auguste à la fin du règne de Charles V (1180–1380)* (Paris, 1963), 134–36, fig. 50. For the instruments, see David Munrow, *Instruments of the Middle Ages and Renaissance* (Oxford, 1976), 8 (shawm), 27 (rebec and fiddle), 35 (cymbals). For the cittern, Winternitz, *Musical Instruments,* 62 and pl. 15c–d (Parma baptistery interior tympanum, early thirteenth century, and Strasbourg central west portal, ca. 1290); Monrow, *Instruments,* 26–27, identifies this instrument as a citole, ancestor of the cittern.

80. The Beauvais rosace, now installed in bay sVII, comes from bay nIV: Michael W. Cothren, *Picturing the Celestial City: The Medieval Stained Glass of Beauvais Cathedral* (Princeton, 2006), 175, 177 pl. 190. For Santa Maria Novella, see Giuseppe Marchini, *Italian Stained Glass Windows* (New York, 1956), 40, 245 n. 58, fig. 29.

81. Louis Demaison, "Maison des musiciens," *Congrès archéologique* 78, pt. 1 (1911): 127–33; Pierre Desportes, *Reims et les rémois aux XIIIe et XIVe siècles* (Paris, 1979), 469–70; Aymar Verdier and François Cattois, *Architecture civile et domestique,* vol. 1 (Paris, 1855; reprint, Farnborough, Hampshire, 1972), 17–26. Extremely eroded statues of musicians located between the gables of the cathedral facade have been associated with those of the rue de Tambour: Bruno Decrock, "Douze années de restauration de la cathédrale de Reims (1992–2004)," in *Nouveaux regards sur la cathédrale de Reims,* ed. Bruno Decrock and Patrick Demouy (Langres, 2008), 95–96, 104, figs. 16 and 18 (nineteenth-century photos). Bréhier, *La cathédrale* (as in note 62 above), 227–28,

connects the musician sculptures of the House of the Musicians with the archivolts of the cathedral's central portal, citing Guillaume de Machaut (cf. at notes 94–95 below) but without mentioning the musical angels of the west rose (which he describes on p. 253). I have been unable to identify his Machaut quote.

82. See Monrow, *Instruments,* 9–10 (bagpipe), 13 (pipe and tabor), 22 (harp); illustrations of medieval fiddles are on pp. 7 and 29.

83. Kurmann, *La façade,* 1:243; see his pls. 770, 772, 780, 782, 803, and 806. Pl. 806 is identified as King Solomon seated on a lion throne and playing a dulcimer; see also the Doucet photo in *Congrès archéologique* 78, pt. l (1911): opp. p. 34. Verdier, *La couronnement,* 109, cites the Ramsey Psalter (end of the thirteenth century) where David plays his harp while Solomon plucks a cithara. For the instruments in the cathedral sculpture, cf. Monrow, *Instruments,* 7 and 23 (psaltery); 9 and 13 (double-reed pipe); 24 (dulcimer); 26 (plucked gittern); 27 (bowed rebec). The music-making kings of Reims are all assumed to be Elders of the Apocalypse by Laurence Brugger-Christe, "Des Vieillards dans les voussures," in *Architektur und Monumentalskulptur des 12.–14. Jahrhunderts, Produktion und Rezeption: Festschrift für Peter Kurmann zum 65. Geburtstag,* ed. Stephan Gasser, Christian Freigang, and Bruno Boerner (Bern, 2006), 465–66.

84. Kurmann, *La façade,* vol. 2, pl. 267; Hammerstein, *Die Musik der Engel,* 222, 275 n. 13. For Honorius of Autun, "De forma sive figura psalterii," see *Patrologia Latina* (online) 172, cols. 271D–272A.

85. Besides the eighteen musical angels, there were three seraphim (3B, 7B, and 11C), two angels with censers and incense boats (2C, 10C), and an angel with instruments of the Passion (7C), another reference to the Last Judgment, traditional subject of a west facade. Simon, *La grande rose,* 73–75.

86. See Monrow, *Instruments,* 7–8 (shawms), 12–13 (double-reed pipes), 14 (gemshorns), and 20 (curved hunting horn). The pipe and tabor (fife and drum) played by 10B has a long musical history: ibid., 13; Winternitz, *Musical Instruments,* 135. Angel 9C (with shawm and bells) was Simon's modern design based on a medallion, not medieval but an old repair, showing those instruments; see that combination in Winternitz, *Musical Instruments,* 135 and fig. 63f (New York, The Cloisters, Book of Hours of Jeanne d'Evreux, ca. 1325).

87. See Monrow, *Instruments,* 7, 23 (psalteries); 7, 29 (fiddle and bow); and 26 (gittern).

88. Instrument-playing angels are frequent in the upper traceries of windows from the fifteenth century on, and somewhat later in rose windows, not always accompanying a Triumph of the Virgin. See, e.g., Sens cathedral, north rose, ca. 1517–19 (Recensement III, pl. IX, opp. p. 180); Saint-Jean-Baptiste in Villiers-sur-Tholon, rosace of bay 0, ca. 1530 (Recensement III:201, fig. 180); Saint-Sulpice in Nogent-le-Roi, south rose (Recensement II:77; Cowen, *The Rose Window,* 217).

89. Winternitz, *Musical Instruments,* 32. See also 145: "The simultaneous playing of both groups would make little sense." On p. 42 he lists among suggested topics for research the study of the "irruption of large and varied angel concerts into painting and sculpture with the rising popularity of Marian subjects . . . , and a systematic investigation of the extent to which their instrumental ensembles are symptomatic of the contemporary evolution of polyphony."

90. Monrow, *Instruments,* 5.

91. Edmund Bowles, "Haut and Bas: The Grouping of Musical Instruments in the Middle Ages," *Musica disciplina* 8 (1954): 129.

92. Ibid., 119–29 passim. On p. 128 he cites, for the poem about King Arthur as well as the Feast of Westminster, Francis Galpin, *Old English Instruments of Music: Their History and Character* (1910); see the 4th rev. ed. (London, 1965), 45. Galpin nowhere identifies the King Arthur poem further but does provide more references to the Westminster Feast on pp. 32, 59, 167, 179, 183, 193.

93. André van Hasselt, ed., *Li roumans de Cléomadès, par Adenès li rois, publié pour la première fois, d'après un manuscrit de la bibliothèque de l'Arsenal, à Paris,* vol. 2 (Brussels, 1865), 251 (lines 17273–83). Another passage listing instruments at a feast is at lines 2879–92 vol. 1:91), referred to by Bowles, "Haut and Bas," 119, 123. For the poet and circumstances of the poem's creation and dating, see Margaret Munroe Boland, *Cleomadés: A Study in Architectonic Patterns,* Romance Monographs, no. 11 (University, Miss., 1974), chap. 2.

94. Guillaume de Machaut, *Le jugement du roy de Behaigne and Remede de fortune,* ed. James Wimsatt and William Kibler (Athens, Ga., 1988), 3, 33–36. She died in 1349, the year before her husband became king. The *Remede de fortune* is dated before 1342: Anne Walters Robertson, *Guillaume de Machaut and Reims: Context and Meaning in His Musical Works* (Cambridge, 2002), 18.

95. Machaut, *Remede de fortune,* ed. Wimsatt and Kibler, 386, 390–91; translation of lines 3892–96, 3963, 3978–88.

96. Bowles, "Haut and Bas," 118.

Coda

1. Claudine Lautier, "Les vitraux de la cathédrale de Chartres: Reliques et images," *Bulletin monumental* 161 (2003); see especially the clerestories indicated in the plans

on pp. 9 fig. 7 and 20 fig. 16. The iconography of the chevet and transept clerestories is discussed in Brigitte Kurmann-Schartz and Peter Kurmann, *Chartres: La cathédrale* (La Pierre-qui-vire, 2001), 150–54. An overview of French clerestory glazing of the period appears in Madeline H. Caviness, *Sumptuous Arts at the Royal Abbeys in Reims and Braine: Ornatus elegantiae, varietate stupendes* (Princeton, 1990), 16–18.

2. Laurence Brugger and Yves Christe, *Bourges: La cathédrale* (La Pierre-qui-vire, 2000), 344–47; Recensement II:175–76, 178–80.

3. For Auxerre, see Recensement III:113, 121–23. For Troyes: Elizabeth C. Pastan and Sylvie Balcon, *Les vitraux de choeur de la cathédrale de Troyes (XIIIe siècle),* Corpus Vitrearum, France, II (Paris, 2006), 197–262, 373, 404–5, 481–82.

4. On the named archbishops in Bays 122, 124, and 126, which I believe to be late-sixteenth-century restorations, see chapter 6. Only Archbishop Henri de Braine (Bay 100), unquestionably a donor, has a name inscription otherwise (chapter 3). The recycled archbishop image now in Bay 118 has a halo and is proposed in chapter 4 to be St. Remi; the archbishop in the rosace of Bay 123 has a halo (chapter 5); the archbishops originally in Bay 127, one of whom survives now in Bay 129, were also saints, though unnamed (chapter 6).

5. This omission was made up for in the lavish sculpted verso of the west facade, also a unique program in Gothic art.

6. For Karolvs, in Bay 128, see below.

7. For the Ascension, see chapter 1, at note 41. On the Tree of Jesse fragments, now lost but recorded in tracings as stopgaps removed from the north rose in 1873: Sylvie Balcon-Berry, "Les vitraux du Moyen Âge," in *La grâce d'une cathédrale: Reims,* ed. Thierry Jordan et al. (Strasbourg, 2010), 234–35, fig. 10. She has suggested a few other subjects: Balcon-Berry, "Les vitraux de la cathédrale de Reims à la lumière de recherches récentes," in *Nouveaux regards sur la cathédrale de Reims,* ed. Bruno Decrock and Patrick Demouy (Langres, 2008), 155–56; Balcon, "Les vitraux," in Reims: *La cathédrale,* ed. Patrick Demouy (La Pierre-qui-vire, 2001), 336–41. However, the subjects noted by nineteenth-century witnesses in 1825 in the side tympana of the west facade were not thirteenth-century; see chapter 7, at note 2.

8. See chapter 6, at notes 51–52.

9. See Meredith Parsons Lillich, "Heraldry and Patronage in the Lost Windows of Saint-Nicaise de Reims," in *L'art et les révolutions: XXVIIe Congrès international d'histoire de l'art* (Strasbourg, 1992), 8:71–102, passim, reprinted in *Studies in Medieval Stained Glass and Monasticism* (London, 2001), 434–66.

10. Louis Grodecki, *Les vitraux de Saint-Denis: Étude sur le vitrail au XIIe siècle,* vol. 1, Corpus Vitrearum, France, Études 1 (Paris, 1976), 30 (report of Lenoir, 1842); see p. 27 for a review of hypotheses concerning lost glazing of Suger's Saint-Denis.

11. See Robert Neiss and Walter Berry, "La cathédrale du XIIe siècle," in *Reims: La cathédrale,* 57–59.

12. Caviness, *Sumptuous Arts,* 55–64; for the makeup of the choir clerestories, 142–44. See also Patrick Demouy, "L'image des archevêques dans l'abbatiale Saint-Remi de Reims au XIIe siècle," in *Architektur und Monumentalskulptur des 12.–14. Jahrhunderts, Produktion und Rezeption: Festschrift für Peter Kurmann zum 65. Geburtstag,* ed. Stephan Gasser, Christian Freigang, and Bruno Boerner (Bern, 2006), 627–39.

13. Fridtjof Zschokke, *Die romanischen Glasgemälde des Strassburger Münsters* (Basel, 1942), 127; references adopting the proposal are provided in Caviness, *Sumptuous Arts,* 17 nn. 128–30. For Zschokke's reconstruction, see now Victor Beyer, Christiane Wild-Block, and Fridtjof Zschokke, *Les vitraux de la cathédrale Notre-Dame de Strasbourg,* Corpus Vitrearum, France, IX-1 (Paris, 1986), 28–29 figs. 10–11.

14. Jean Bony, *French Gothic Architecture of the Twelfth and Thirteenth Centuries* (Berkeley and Los Angeles, 1983), 95 fig. 87 and 101 fig. 96; see also the four-story elevations preceding Saint-Remi.

15. For Troyes, see note 3 above. For Châlons: Meredith Parsons Lillich, "St. Memmie, Apostle of Châlons, and Other Bishop Saints in the Gothic Windows of Châlons Cathedral," *Studies in Iconography* 19 (1998): 75–103, reprinted in *Studies,* 168–201. On the introduction of grisaille and the band window: eadem, *The Armor of Light: Stained Glass in Western France, 1250–1325* (Berkeley and Los Angeles, 1994), 6–8, 68–69, 196–98.

16. Recent scholarship has labeled Reims the "sanctuaire national," and the coronation connection the "religion de Reims," recognizing Reims's preeminence in sociological (but never institutional) terms. See, e.g., Isabelle Pallot-Frossard, "La cathédrale de Reims otage de la guerre de 1914–1918," in *Architektur und Monumentalskulptur,* 741–54, esp. 750; Michael Bur, "Aux origines de la 'religion de Reims': Les sacres carolingiens; Un réexamen du dossier (751–1131)," in *Clovis, histoire et mémoire,* vol. 2, *Le baptême de Clovis, son écho à travers l'histoire* (Paris, 1997), 45–72.

Appendix 1

1. Yves Dossat, "L'hérésie en Champagne aux XIIe et XIIIe siècles," *Mémoires de la Société d'agriculture, commerce, sciences et arts du département de la Marne* 84 (1969): 58; Malcolm Barber, "Northern Catharism," in *Heresy and the Persecuting Society in the Middle Ages: Essays on the Work of R. I. Moore,* ed. Michael Frassetto (Leiden, 2006), 124; Patrick Demouy, *Genèse d'une cathédrale: Les archevêques de Reims et leur église aux XIe et XIIe siècles* (Langres, 2005), 467.

2. The clergy of Liège reported this in a letter to the pope: Dossat, "L'hérésie," 58–59.

3. Ibid., 59–60, 63; Patrick Demouy, "Synodes diocésains et conciles provinciaux à Reims et en Belgique seconde aux XIe–XIIIe siècles," in *La Champagne et ses administrations à travers le temps: Actes du colloque d'histoire régionale Reims/Châlons-sur-Marne, 1987* (Paris, 1990), 100; Barber, "Northern Catharism," 116–17.

4. On weavers, see note 17 below.

5. Dossat, "L'hérésie," 63–64; Barber, "Northern Catharism," 117, 127, 133–34. On Guillaume aux Blanches-Mains, highborn, a cardinal, papal legate, and a peacemaker, see Pierre Desportes et al., *Fasti ecclesiae Gallicanae: Répertoire prosopographique des évêques, dignitaires et chanoines de France de 1200 à 1500*, vol. 3, *Diocèse de Reims* (Turnhout, 1998), 151–54; Demouy, *Genèse*, 631–35.

6. Bernard Delmaire, "Un sermon arrageois inédit sur les 'Bougres' du nord de la France (vers 1200)," *Heresis: Revue d'histoire des dissidences européennes* 17 (1991): 5; Dossat, "L'hérésie," 65; Barber, "Northern Catharism," 117–18.

7. Madeline H. Caviness, *Sumptuous Arts at the Royal Abbeys in Reims and Braine: Ornatus elegantiae, varietate stupendes* (Princeton, 1990), 70 and n. 56; Dossat, "L'hérésie," 65; Barber, "Northern Catharism," 118, 136. On Gui Paré, cardinal, abbot of Cîteaux, and venerated by the Cistercians as *bienheureux*, see Desportes et al., *Fasti*, 154–56; Demouy, *Genèse*, 635–37.

8. Barber, "Northern Catharism," 129–30; Desportes et al., *Fasti*, 156–58. Aubry de Humbert in 1217 left on the Fifth Crusade to the Holy Land and died in Italy during his return. Simon de Montfort's southern campaigns of 1209–10 are discussed in Mark Gregory Pegg, *The Corruption of Angels: The Great Inquisition of 1245–1246* (Princeton, 2001), 5–8; Joseph R. Strayer, *The Albigensian Crusades* (New York, 1971; reprint, Ann Arbor, 1992), chap. 4.

9. Hercule Géraud, "Le comte-évêque," *Bibliothèque de l'École des chartes* 5 (1843–44): 28–29, 33. On the 1215 campaign of Prince Louis, see Pegg, *Corruption*, 12; Strayer, *Albigensian*, 101–2. The term "Cathars" is used here for convenience; it was not used in the Middle Ages (Pegg, *Corruption*, 15–19).

10. William Mendel Newman, *Les seigneurs de Nesle en Picardie (XIIe–XIIIe siècle): Leurs chartes et leur histoire* (Paris, 1971), 1:227, 242.

11. Desportes et al., *Fasti*, 158–60. On Louis VIII's 1226 crusade and death, and the Peace of Paris of 1229, see Pegg, *Corruption*, 13–14; Strayer, *Albigensian*, 129–35.

12. Barber, "Northern Catharism," 130.

13. Charles Homer Haskins, *Studies in Mediaeval Culture* (Oxford, 1929; reprint, New York, 1965), chap. 11, 245–55. This Reims council is known only from references in sermons delivered most likely in May 1231 at Laon and Bruyères by Philippe, chancellor of the University of Paris from 1218 to 1236. The Waldensians, of limited education, were lay preachers who used vernacular Bibles, took an extremely literal view of biblical prohibitions against oaths and the taking of human life, practiced lay confession, and rejected priestly absolution (ibid., 252).

14. Georges Despy, "Hérétiques ou anticléricaux? Les 'cathares' dans nos régions avant 1300," in *Aspects de l'anticléricalism du Moyen Âge à nos jours: Hommage à Robert Joly* (Brussels, 1988), 23–33. On the anticlericalism of the *Ménestrel de Reims*, see Pierre Desportes, *Reims et les rémois aux XIIIe et XIVe siècles* (Paris, 1979), 156, 177; Desportes et al., *Fasti*, 159.

15. For La Charité-sur-Loire, see Delmaire, "Un sermon arrageois" (as in note 6 above), 1–15. For the Reims trial (eyewitness Gervais de Tilbury): Barber, "Northern Catharism," 127.

16. Barber, "Northern Catharism," 126–27.

17. Haskins, *Studies*, 199, 202; Dossat, "L'hérésie," 60, 63. On the textiles produced in Reims, see Desportes, *Reims et les rémois*, esp. 93–103.

18. For Philippe, chancellor 1218–36, see Peter Biller, "Northern Cathars and Higher Learning," in *The Medieval Church: Universities, Heresy, and the Religious Life; Essays in Honour of Gordon Leff*, ed. Peter Biller and Barrie Dobson (Woodbridge, Suffolk, 1999), 47; Robert E. Lerner, *The Heresy of the Free Spirit in the Later Middle Ages* (Berkeley and Los Angeles, 1972), 22–23. For Jacques de Vitry: Desportes, *Reims et les rémois*, 161–62. See also the anonymous Parisian sermons discussed in Delmaire, "Un sermon arrageois," 4–5.

19. Emile Chénon, "L'hérésie à La Charité-sur-Loire et les débuts de l'inquisition monastique dans la France du nord au XIIIe siècle," *Nouvelle revue historique de droit français et étranger*, 3rd ser., 40 (1917): 304, 321.

20. Haskins, *Studies*, 217 n. 1. For the term "Bulgars" for dualist heretics, see Barber, "Northern Catharism," 129.

21. Desportes, *Reims et les rémois*, 161. At this council Archbishop Henri de Braine established the seating arrangement for his suffragans that appears in the windows of the cathedral chevet: Patrick Demouy, "Synodes diocésains et conciles provinciaux à Reims et en Belgique seconde aux XIe–XIIIe siècles," in *La Champagne et ses administrations à travers le temps: Actes du colloque d'histoire régionale Reims/Châlons-sur-Marne, 1987* (Paris, 1990), 104.

22. On the career of Robert le Bougre, see Haskins, *Studies*, 210–43 passim; for the quoted epithet, Charles Victor Langlois in Ernest Lavisse, *Histoire de France depuis les origines jusqu'à la Révolution*, vol. 3, pt. 2 (Paris, 1900–1911; reprint, New York, 1969), 73 (quoted and inverted by

Haskins, 224 n. 2). See also the bibliography provided in Barber, "Northern Catharism," 131 n. 43; Desportes, *Reims et les rémois,* 161–62 n. 38; Dossat, "L'hérésie," 68.

23. Brian S. Rosner, *Greed as Idolatry: The Origin and Meaning of a Pauline Metaphor* (Grand Rapids, Mich., 2007); Richard Newhauser, *The Early History of Greed: The Sin of Avarice in Early Medieval Thought and Literature* (Cambridge, 2000), 2–3, 18–19, 29–34, 77–78, 111, 127.

24. Jean Devisse, *Hincmar, archevêque de Reims, 845–882* (Geneva, 1975–76), 1:526–28; 2:680–86; Newhauser, *The Early History,* 199 n. 74. A sort of "mirror of princes" treating virtues and vices, Hincmar's treatise borrows heavily from the *Moralia in Job* of Gregory the Great (ca. 540–604).

25. Haskins, *Studies,* 235–39.

26. See above, at note 2.

27. The fortress of Mont-Aimé is described in some detail in Dossat, "L'hérésie," 69–71. It had a moat, six towers in its surrounding walls, a massive *donjon,* and so forth.

28. Haskins, *Studies,* 226–29. On the other hand, 1245–46 saw "the single largest investigation" into heresy, the great inquisition at Saint-Sernin, Toulouse, by the Dominicans Bernart de Caux and Jean de Saint-Pierre: see Pegg, *Corruption,* 3 and passim.

Appendix 3

1. The roundel is now modern and replaces Thomas's palace built in heaven, illustrated in Charles Cahier and Arthur Marie Martin, *Monographie de la cathédrale de Bourges* (Paris, 1844), vol. 2, Études XVIII, A (my fig. 8). See chapter 2, at notes 103–7.

2. Illustrated in Hervé Benoît, *Les grands vitraux du déambulatoire de Bourges* (Paris, 1995), color pl. U, after p. 28; chart on p. 36, medallion 22. See also the Stuttgart Passional (Stuttgart, Landesbibliothek, Cod. Bibl. 2° 57, ca. 1120–35), fol. 17v: Albert Boeckler, *Das Stuttgarter Passionale* (Augsburg, 1923), Abb. 55.

3. Colette Manhès-Deremble, *Les vitraux narratifs de la cathédrale de Chartres: Étude iconographique,* Corpus Vitrearum, France, Études, II (Paris, 1993), 334–35, medallion 22. Jacobus de Voragine, *The Golden Legend: Readings on the Saints,* trans. William Granger Ryan (Princeton, 1993), 1:35. Bay 213 of Tours cathedral, ca. 1270, shows Thomas kneeling, a short-skirted executioner holding his head and wielding a sword, as in the Reims ogive medallion: Henri Boissonnot, *Les verrières de la cathédrale de Tours* (Paris, 1932), pl. 1 (drawing).

4. See chapter 2, at notes 25–32.

5. Moreover, the medallion is too large for the light and overlaps the outer fillet of the ogive's latticework ground.

6. For example, several kings of a Tree of Jesse, patched into the north rose, were replaced in Oudinot's 1873 restoration; see chapter 7, note 58.

7. For the breakdown of the chevet program, see chapter 3, at note 51.

Appendix 4

1. On Philippe de Dreux, see Hercule Géraud, "Le comte-évêque," *Bibliothèque de l'École des chartes* 5 (1843–44), 8–36. For the Santiago pilgrimage, ibid., 10–11; see also Léon-Honoré Labande, *Histoire de Beauvais et de ses institutions communales jusqu'au commencement du XVe siècle* (Paris, 1892; reprint, Geneva, 1978), 204, 276. Philippe was elected bishop in 1175 but only consecrated in 1180.

2. Bishop Philippe's testament is given in Latin and in French translation in Pierre Louvet, *Histoire et antiqvitez dv diocese de Beavvais,* vol. 2 (Beauvais, 1635), 344–60, according to Henri Omont and Hervé Pinoteau. See Omont, "Recherches sur la bibliothèque de l'église cathédrale de Beauvais," *Mémoires de l'Institut national de France, Académie des inscriptions et belles-lettres* 40 (1916): 3–4 (Latin text from Louvet, *Histoire,* 349); Pinoteau, "La date de la cassette de saint Louis: Été 1236?" *Cahiers d'héraldiques* 4 (1983): 119 n. 84 (Louvet's translation). Géraud, "Le comte-évêque," 34, mentions the bishop's library, citing *Gallia christiana* 9, col. 739. On Henri de Braine at Beauvais, see William Mendel Newman, *Les seigneurs de Nesle en Picardie (XIIe–XIIIe siècle): Leurs chartes et leur histoire,* vol. 1 (Paris, 1971), 227, 242; Pierre Desportes et al., *Fasti ecclesiae Gallicanae: Répertoire prosopographique des évêques, dignitaires et chanoines de France de 1200 à 1500,* vol. 3, *Diocèse de Reims* (Turnhout, 1998), 161, 320–21.

3. Max L. Berkey Jr., "The *Liber Sancti Jacobi:* The French Adaptation by Pierre de Beauvais," *Romania* 86 (1965): 82.

4. Bernard F. Reilly, "The *Historia Compostelana:* The Genesis and Composition of a Twelfth-Century Spanish *Gesta,*" *Speculum* 44 (1969): 78–85 (on Girardus, 81). The work is edited by Emma Falque Rey, *Historia Compostellana,* Corpus Christianorum, Continuatio Mediaevalis, 70 (Turnhout, 1988); on Girardus, xv–xvi. The oldest surviving manuscript is Salamanca, Bibl. univ. 2658, ca. 1240–50 (pp. xxxiii–xxxv).

5. Reilly, *Historia,* 83 and n. 31.

6. Ibid., 81.

7. An accessible summary description of this work, about which the literature is vast, appears in Annie Shaver-Crandell, Paula Gerson, and Alison Stones, *The Pilgrim's Guide to Santiago de Compostela: A Gazetteer* (London, 1995), 24–25, with notes to the companion publication, a critical edition of the *Guide* in 2 vols. See also the introduction in *The "Codex Calixtinus" and the Shrine of St. James,* ed. John Williams and Alison Stones, Jakobus-Studien, 3 (Tübingen, 1992), ix–xiv. .

8. Elizabeth A. R. Brown, "Saint-Denis and the Turpin Legend," in *The "Codex Calixtinus,"* ed. Williams and Stones, 51.

9. Max L. Berkey Jr., "Pierre de Beauvais: An Introduction to His Works," *Romance Philology* 18 (1964–65): 387–98. On the *Mappemonde,* 394; see also Paul Meyer, "Notice sur deux anciens manuscrits français ayant appartenu au marquis de La Clayette (Bibliothèque nationale, Moreau 1715–19)," *Notices et extraits des manuscrits de la Bibliothèque nationale et autres bibliothèques* 33, pt. 1 (1890): 35–37.

10. Berkey, "Pierre," 389–91.

11. Berkey, "The *Liber*" (as in note 3 above), 77–103; the text is printed on 87–101, chiefly from the La Clayette manuscript (Paris, BnF, nouv. acq. fr. 13521). While the Latin original contains twenty-two miracles, Pierre's version has only eight.

12. Ibid., 82–83. Another contender has been Yolande, countess of Saint-Pol, who in 1195 inherited from her brother Baudoin of Flanders a copy of the Latin text and before 1205 had her clerk Nicolas de Senlis make a translation of the Pseudo-Turpin; the Turpin, however, is a version different from the one adapted by Pierre de Beauvais (see below).

13. Ronald N. Walpole, "Charlemagne's Journey to the East: The French Translation of the Legend by Pierre de Beauvais," in *Semitic and Oriental Studies: A Volume Presented to William Popper,* ed. Walter Joseph Fischel (Berkeley and Los Angeles, 1951), 433–56; critical edition of the text, 445–54. Walpole lists two nineteenth-century editions of the Latin *Descriptio* (434 n. 3).

14. Ibid., 437; for Pierre's text, 440. Pierre found it at Saint-Denis in "livres qui parolent des roys de France," which suggests that the *Descriptio* had already been incorporated into Latin histories at the abbey by the late twelfth century (ibid., 437–38).

15. Ronald N. Walpole, ed., *The Old French Johannes Translation of the Pseudo-Turpin Chronicle: A Critical Edition* (Berkeley and Los Angeles, 1976), xvii–xx, 9–11, 19, 89–95. The manuscripts containing Pierre's *Voyage* (his translation of the *Descriptio*) and his adaptation of the Johannes translation of the Pseudo-Turpin make up Walpole's Group II (pp. 2–3). On Saint-Denis as the source, see 93–94; also Brown, "Saint-Denis" (as in note 8 above), 57 n. 17.

16. In 1206 it was reworked by other authors. See Walpole's Group III: Walpole, *The Old French Johannes,* 58, 60. On the French translations of the Pseudo-Turpin, see Ronald N. Walpole, ed., *An Anonymous Old French Translation of the Pseudo-Turpin Chronicle: A Critical Edition* (Cambridge, Mass., 1979), 5, 28; Gabrielle M. Spiegel, *Romancing the Past* (Berkeley and Los Angeles, 1993), 71–72. The only translation predating the Johannes version used by Pierre was made by Nicolas de Senlis for Countess Yolande de Saint-Pol ca. 1200–1202 (see note 12 above). See Berkey, "Pierre," (as in note 9 above), 394–95.

17. Walpole, *Anonymous Old French,* 3.

18. Desportes et al., *Fasti,* 154; Géraud, "Le comte-évêque" (as in note 1 above), 25–27.

19. Humbert Jacomet, "L'énigmatique odyssée de saint Jacques," *Archeologia* 318 (1995): 64–65. For *Veneranda Dies,* see Walter Muir Whitehill, *Liber Sancti Jacobi, Codex Calixtinus* (Santiago de Compostela, 1944), 1:142.

20. The scene has been identified more often in stained glass than in other media, Chartres being the only example predating Reims. See chapter 2.

21. Natalis de Wailly, *Récits d'un ménestrel de Reims au treizième siècle* (Paris, 1876), 33, 59, 137, 142, 153, 157.

Appendix 5

1. Florence McCulloch, *Mediaeval Latin and French Bestiaries* (Chapel Hill, 1960), 62–68; Max L. Berkey Jr., "Pierre de Beauvais: An Introduction to His Works," *Romance Philology* 18 (1964–65): 394.

2. On the four exemplars of Pierre de Beauvais's "short-version" bestiary, see the recent, useful summary account in Baudouin Van den Abeele, "Deux manuscrits inconnus du *Bestiaire* attribué à Pierre de Beauvais," in *Bestiaires médiévaux: Nouvelles perspectives sur les manuscrits et les traditions textuelles,* ed. Baudouin Van den Abeele (Louvain-la-Neuve, 2006), 184–86, with citations to the basic literature. Also useful are the references provided in Claudia Rebuffi, "Studi sulla tradizione del bestiaire di Pierre de Beauvais," *Medioevo romanzo* 3 (1976): 169, nn. 22, 24–26.

3. Van den Abeele, "Deux manuscrits," 186–99. In addition to the five listed here, Van den Abeele has identified two parchment sheets found reused in a binding (Freiburg im Breisgau, Universitätsbibliothek 979), which he dates to the end of the thirteenth century.

4. This manuscript was purchased from Sotheby's in 1969 by the London dealer Bernard Quaritch: Sotheby and Co., *Catalogue of Manuscripts on Papyrus, Vellum, and Paper of the 13th Century* B.C. *to the 18th Century* A.D. *. . . Which Will Be Sold by Auction . . . by Sotheby & Co. [on] Tuesday, 25 November 1969,* Bibliotheca Philippica, Medieval Manuscripts, new ser., 5 (London, 1969), lot 454, pp. 38–41; McCulloch, *Mediaeval Latin,* 62–63, 66 n. 64; eadem, "L'éale et la centicore: Deux bêtes fabuleuses," in *Mélanges offerts à René Crozet,* ed. Pierre Gallais and Yves-Jean Riou (Poitiers, 1965), 2:1167–72; Van den Abeele, "Deux manuscrits," 189–90.

5. Paris, BnF, fr. 944 (beginning of the fifteenth century)

was in the library of Diane de Poitiers (formerly Bibl. du roi 7284): Bibliothèque nationale, Département des manuscrits, *Catalogue des manuscrits français: Ancien fonds,* vol. 1 (Paris, 1868), 161–62; Paulin Paris, *Les manuscrits françois de la Bibliothèque du roi,* vol. 7 (Paris, 1845), 299–302.

6. McCulloch, *Mediaeval Latin,* 65–66, provides Paul Meyer's transcription of the dedication to Philippe; see also Van den Abeele, "Deux manuscrits," fig. 59, illustrating it in Brussels, Bibl. Roy., II 6978, fol. 22.

7. The Louvain manuscript, formerly in Mechelen, is the base text of the translation by Guy R. Mermier, *A Medieval Book of Beasts: Pierre de Beauvais' Bestiary* (Lewiston, N.Y., 1992). The dedication to Count Robert is on p. 231. Since 1972 the manuscript has been in Louvain. On this manuscript, see Carlo de Clercq, *Catalogue général des manuscrits des bibliothèques de Belgique,* vol. 4, *Catalogue des manuscrits du Grand séminaire de Malines* (Gembloux, 1937), 85.

8. See appendix 4, note 2.

9. Craig Baker, "De la paternité de la Version longue du *Bestiaire,* attribuée à Pierre de Beauvais," in *Bestiaires médiévaux,* 1–29. Professor Baker's critical edition of the "long version," published too late for consideration in the present volume, is *Le Bestiaire: Version longue attribuée à Pierre de Beauvais,* Classiques français du Moyen Âge, no. 163 (Paris, 2010). My hypothesis concerning the bestiary owned by Henri de Braine, as I formulated it in "The Genesis Rose Window of Reims Cathedral," *Arte medievale,* n.s., 2, no. 2 (2003): 56–58 (before the publication of Professor Baker's study of the "long version"), must now be nuanced. The archbishop's hypothetical manuscript would have been a "short version," whereas the Genesis scenes resembling those in the Reims north rose appear in a "long version" (Arsenal 3516). Hopefully my observations will be of use to scholars of French texts in pursuing the connection between the two versions.

10. Paris, BnF, nouv. acq. fr. 13521 was the base manuscript for the edition by Guy R. Mermier, ed., *Le bestiaire de Pierre de Beauvais (version courte): Édition critique avec notes et glossaire* (Paris, 1977); he cites the manuscript incorrectly (as 13251) on p. 26. It is the so-called La Clayette manuscript, which was lost when Meyer discussed it on the basis of an eighteenth-century copy: Paul Meyer, "Notice sur deux anciens manuscrits français ayant appartenu du marquis de La Clayette (Bibliothèque nationale, Moreau 1715–19)," *Notices et extraits des manuscrits de la Bibliothèque nationale et autres bibliothèques* 33, pt. 1 (1890): 1–90 (on the bestiary, 22–23); more accessible is his summary of its contents in *Romania* 19 (1890): 305–7. The manuscript was purchased by the Bibliothèque nationale in 1952: Suzanne Solente, "Le grand recueil La Clayette à la Bibliothèque nationale," *Scriptorium* 7 (1953): 226–34; Albi Rosenthal, "Le manuscrit de La Clayette retrouvé," *Annales musicologiques* 1 (1953): 105–30. The motets it contains date no later than ca. 1250: Leo Schrade, "Unknown Motets in a Recovered Thirteenth-Century Manuscript," *Speculum* 30 (1955): 395–96; Gordon A. Anderson, ed., *Motets of the Manuscript La Clayette: Paris, Bibliothèque nationale, nouv. acq. f. fr. 13521* (N.p.: American Institute of Musicology, 1975), xi.

11. The bestiary in Paris, BnF, nouv acq. fr. 13521 contains thirty-seven miniatures: Solente, "Le grand recueil," 232. On the illumination of French bestiaries, see McCulloch, *Mediaeval Latin,* 69, 75.

12. The date derives from a table of dominical letters from 1268–1367 on a bifolio independent from the rest of the manuscript. Arsenal 3516 was the base manuscript for the edition of the "long-version" bestiary published by Charles Cahier and Arthur Martin, *Mélanges d'archéologie, d'histoire et de littérature* (Paris, 1851–56), 2:106–232, 3:203–88, and 4:55–87. On the manuscript Arsenal 3516, see Claudia Guggenbühl, *Recherches sur la composition et la structure du ms. Arsenal 3516* (Basel, 1998); Maria Careri et al., *Album de manuscrits français du XIIIe siècle: Mise en page et mise en texte* (Rome, 2001), 139–41; Charles Samaran and Robert Marichal, *Catalogue des manuscrits en écriture latine, portant des indications de date, de lieu ou de copiste,* vol. 1 (Paris, 1959), 439; Henry Martin, *Catalogue des manuscrits de la bibliothèque de l'Arsenal,* vol. 3 (Paris, 1887), 395–405. The manuscript is attributed to Artois since several bishop-saints of Thérouanne appear in the calendar.

13. This text is truncated at the beginning in Arsenal 3516; it corresponds to verses 349–858 of the *Bible anonyme:* Julia C. Szirmai, *La Bible anonyme du Ms. Paris B. N. f. fr. 763, édition critique* (Amsterdam, 1985), 13–14, 44–46, 54–57; Guggenbühl, *Recherches,* 144–45. On the author and dating of the *Bible anonyme,* see Szirmai, *La Bible anonyme,* 16, 22.

14. Szirmai, *La Bible anonyme,* 14–15, 44–45, 54–57; Guggenbühl, *Recherches,* 144; Samaran and Marichal, *Catalogue,* 6:319; Henri Omont, *Catalogue général des manuscrits des bibliothèques publiques des départements,* vol. 1 (Paris, 1849), 457–58. Montpellier H437 contains three texts, all found in Arsenal 3516. In addition to the "long-version" *bestiaire* (dated by Baker 1246–68) and Gossouin de Metz's *Image du monde* (dated 1246), both manuscripts originally commenced with the same poem on creation, including the *Histoire d'Adam* (late twelfth century).

15. Meyer, "Notice" (as in note 10 above), 9, 11, 32.

16. Ron Baxter, *Bestiaries and Their Users in the Middle Ages* (London, 1998), 209 (see also 194).

17. Cahier and Martin, *Mélanges,* 2:129 n. 5 and pl. XIX(F).

18. McCulloch, *Mediaeval Latin,* 100 n. 39.

Appendix 6

1. It should not be confused with "historical" Solomon narratives in which God appears to the sleeping Solomon: 3 Kings 3:5, 9:2–9, 11:9–10. Such scenes, sometimes known as the Dreams of Solomon, while also not common, appear in Romanesque art in eleventh-century Catalonia as well as in the Sainte-Chapelle in Paris in the 1240s (in the traceries of bay B). They are unrelated to the text and image discussed here. For Catalan examples, see Wilhelm Neuss, *Die katalanische Bibelillustration um die Wende des ersten Jahrtausends und die altspanische Buchmalerei* (Bonn, 1922), 78, fig. 81 (Roda Bible, Paris, BnF, lat. 6, vol. 2, fol. 75r). On the Sainte-Chapelle, see Alyce A. Jordan, *Visualizing Kingship in the Windows of the Sainte-Chapelle* (Turnhout, 2002), 25, 121, and fig. 49.

2. The bed (*lectulus*) of verse 7 is sometimes conflated with the litter (*ferculum*) of verse 9; see appendix 7. I know of only one art object connected with the *ferculum:* the so-called Bamberg Rational (Bamberger Domschatz, ca. 1050), a purple silk vestment worked in gold that includes among its numerous inscriptions several references to Song of Songs 3:9–10. See Karin Lerchner, *Lectulus floridus: Zur Bedeutung des Bettes in Literatur und Handschriftenillustration des Mittelalters,* Pictura et Poesis, 6 (Cologne, 1993), 245–48, Abb. 62. The interpretation of the *ferculum* as Ecclesia is that of Gregory the Great and Bede. The Bamberg Rational, however, does not contain an image of Solomon in Bed and cannot be considered an illustration of the scene under discussion here.

3. Herrad of Hohenbourg, *Hortus Deliciarum,* ed. Rosalie Green (London, 1979), 1:25. Michael Evans (in ibid., 1) dates it "before 1176–c. 1196," the last year Herrad is mentioned as abbess. I have retained her name in its familiar form, although she is no longer believed to have been a member of the Landsberg family. See Christine Bischoff in ibid., 10, 12 n. 30. On Solomon in Bed in the Herrad manuscript, see also Lerchner, *Lectulus,* 248–62, Abb. 63–66.

4. Translation by Aristide Caratzas in Caratzas, ed., *Herrad of Landsberg, Hortus Deliciarum,* commentary by Alexandre Straub and Gustave Keller (New Rochelle, N.Y., 1977), 186. The Latin text of *Hortus Deliciarum,* fol. 205r, is given in *Hortus Deliciarum,* ed. Green, 2:337, no. 711. For the text of Rupert of Deutz, see Ruperti Tuitiensis, *Commentaria in Canticum canticorum,* ed. Hrabanus Haacke, Corpus Christianorum, Continuatio Mediaevalis, 26 (Turnhout, 1974), 61–62. On Rupert of Deutz, see Bischoff in *Hortus Deliciarum,* ed. Green, 1:51–52 (it is noted that no manuscript of Alsatian origin is known); also Gérard Cames, *Allégories et symboles dans l'Hortus deliciarum* (Leiden, 1971), 74.

5. E. Ann Matter, *The Voice of My Beloved: The Song of Songs in Western Medieval Christianity* (Philadelphia, 1990), 4. This paragraph relies on Matter's book and on Ann Astell, *The Song of Songs in the Middle Ages* (Ithaca, 1990). The textual interpretations in the *Hortus Deliciarum* do not reflect the most current twelfth-century commentaries on the Song of Songs at the time of its compilation, that is, the mystical treatments by the Cistercians and the Victorines, in which the love of Christ and the Sponsa becomes a personal contemplative exercise.

6. Marvin H. Pope, ed. and trans., *Song of Songs: A New Translation with Introduction and Commentary,* Anchor Bible 7C (Garden City, N.Y., 1977), 119–20.

7. Jeffrey C. Anderson, "The Illustrated Sermons of James the Monk: Their Dates, Order, and Place in the History of Byzantine Art," *Viator* 22 (1991): 69–120, esp. 85; Lerchner, *Lectulus,* 254–55. On BnF, gr. 1208, see Henri Omont, *Miniatures des homélies sur la Vierge du moine Jacques (MS grec 1208 de Paris),* Société française de reproductions de manuscrits à peintures 11 (Paris, 1927). For a facsimile of Vat. gr. 1162: *Marien-homilien: Codex Vaticanus Graecus 1162,* ed. Paul Canart and Irmgard Hutter (Zurich, 1991). The image of the bed of Solomon in the Vatican manuscript (fol. 82v), very similar to the one in BnF, gr. 1208, is illustrated in Cosimo Stornajolo, *Miniature delle omilie di Giacomo monaco (Cod. Vatic. gr. 1162) e dell'evangeliario greco Urbinate (Cod. Vatic. Urbin. gr. 2)* (Rome, 1910), pl. 32; also *Hortus Deliciarum,* ed. Green, vol. 1, fig. 280; Andreas Xynagopoulos, "Au sujet d'une fresque de l'église Saint-Clément à Ochrid," in *Mélanges Georges Ostrogorsky,* ed. Franjo Barišić, Recueil de travaux de l'Institut d'études byzantines, 8, vol. 1 (Belgrade, 1963), fig. 3; and Lerchner, *Lectulus,* Abb. 64. On the possible patroness, the Sebastokratorissa Irene, see references in Cecily J. Hilsdale, "Constructing a Byzantine *Augusta:* A Greek Book for a French Bride," *Art Bulletin* 87 (2005): 476 and nn. 93–96.

8. This discussion relies on Sirarpie Der Nersessian, "Le lit de Salomon," in *Mélanges Georges Ostrogorsky,* 78–80, and Xynagopoulos, "Au sujet," 302–3.

9. Pope, *Song of Songs,* 118, 125.

10. See *Hortus Deliciarum,* ed. Green, 1:33–34, 197.

11. Anderson, "The Illustrated Sermons," 69.

12. Cames, *Allégories,* 1, 130–41.

13. Der Nersessian, "Le lit," 77, 80–82, fig. 1; Xynagopoulos, "Au sujet," 301–6, figs. 1–2; Dimitar Cornakov, *Les fresques de l'église de Saint-Clément à Ochrid* (Belgrade, 1961), fig. 54; Lerchner, *Lectulus,* 262–63, Abb. 67.

14. Xynagopoulos, "Au sujet," 303–4. For an icon depicting Solomon holding a bed (Florence, fifteenth or

sixteenth century), see Lerchner, *Lectulus,* 263–64, Abb. 68.

15. A brief overview of the history of anointing in medieval Europe is provided by Richard A. Jackson, *Vive le roi! A History of the French Coronation from Charles V to Charles X* (Chapel Hill, 1984), 4–5, 225–26 nn. 4–5.

16. The Judgment of Solomon, a type of the Last Judgment, was also a model for earthly justice. See particularly, in the voluminous literature on the south transept of Strasbourg, Louis Grodecki and Roland Recht, "Le bras sud du transept de la cathédrale: Architecture et sculpture," *Bulletin monumental* 129 (1971): esp. 21–25; Otto Von Simson, "Le programme sculptural du transept méridional de la cathédrale de Strasbourg," *Bulletin de la Société des amis de la cathédrale de Strasbourg* 10 (1972): 35–39; Bernd Nicolai, "Orders in Stone: Social Reality and Artistic Approach; The Case of the Strasbourg South Portal," *Gesta* 41 (2002): 111–28.

17. On the Throne of Solomon, see Daniel H. Weiss, *Art and Crusade in the Age of Saint Louis* (Cambridge, 1998), 22–24, 58–70 passim; idem, "Architectural Symbolism and the Decoration of the Ste.-Chapelle," *Art Bulletin* 77 (1995): 308–20; Francis Wormald, "The Throne of Solomon and St. Edward's Chair," in *De Artibus Opuscula* XL: *Essays in Honor of Erwin Panofsky,* ed. Millard Meiss (New York, 1961), 1:537–39, reprinted in idem, *Collected Writings,* ed. J. J. G. Alexander et al., vol. 2, *Studies in English and Continental Art of the Later Middle Ages* (London, 1988), 66–69; William Tronzo, *The Cultures of His Kingdom: Roger II and the Cappella Palatina in Palermo* (Princeton, 1997), 110 (tenth-century Byzantium), 130 (twelfth-century Norman Sicily).

18. Suzanne Lewis, *Reading Images: Narrative Discourse and Reception in the Thirteenth-Century Illuminated Apocalypse* (Cambridge, 1995), 203; she states that she will present her argument in *Picturing Visions* (to appear). John Lowden, *The Making of the "Bibles Moralisées"* (University Park, 2000), 2 vols.; my quote comes from the review by Mary Rouse in *Speculum* 77 (2002): 588.

19. The first two Moralized Bibles (Vienna, ÖNB 2554 and ÖNB 1179) do not include the scene.

20. The last eight folios (including the dedication page), separated from the Toledo Bible by the fourteenth century, are now MS 240 in the Pierpont Morgan Library, New York: Lowden, *The Making,* 1:4–5, 87, 132–35; 2:201–2. A facsimile of the Toledo Moralized Bible has been published by M. Moleiro: *The Bible of St. Louis* (Barcelona, 1999).

21. Lowden, *The Making,* 1:183–86; 2:201–2. Daniel H. Weiss, "The Three Solomon Portraits in the Arsenal Old Testament and the Construction of Meaning in Crusader Painting," *Arte medievale* 6, no. 2 (1992): 26–27; idem, *Art and Crusade,* 147–49.

22. In addition to Weiss's studies, see James Heinlen, "The Ideology of Reform in the French Moralized Bible" (Ph.D. diss., Northwestern University, 1991), particularly chap. 5; Véronique Germanier, "L'Ecclesia comme Sponsa Christi dans les Bibles moralisées de la première moitié du XIIIème siècle," *Arte cristiana* 84, no. 775 (July–August 1996): 247–48; Katherine Tachau, "God's Compass and *Vana Curiositas:* Scientific Study in the Old French *Bible Moralisée,*" *Art Bulletin* 80 (1998): 8.

23. Lerchner, *Lectulus,* 333, Abb. 85. Unavailable to me was the discussion of the Song of Songs in Tanya Alfillé, "The Psalms in the Thirteenth-Century 'Bible Moralisée': A Study in Text and Image" (Ph.D. diss., University of London, Courtauld Institute, 1992) (see Lowden, *The Making,* 1:6).

24. Lowden, *The Making,* vol. 1, chaps. 6–8. Cf. the pages in Alexandre de Laborde, *La Bible moralisée: Conservée à Oxford, Paris et Londres,* vol. 5, *Étude sur la bible moralisée illustrée* (Paris, 1927), 76, 97, 104. I am grateful to Professor Christina Waugh and to Dr. Patricia Stirnemann for photocopies of these manuscripts.

25. Tancred Borenius, "The Cycle of Images in the Palaces and Castles of Henry III," *Journal of the Warburg and Courtauld Institutes* 6 (1943): 40.

26. Ibid., 42, 49 (= tablet beside the king's bed). See also Paul Binski, *The Painted Chamber of Westminster* (London, 1986), 40, 44.

27. Binski has made a convincing case that the name Painted Chamber, which first appears ca. 1307–8, at the end of the reign of Edward I, derived from the great series of immense Old Testament scenes, largely military feats of the Maccabees, and that these paintings were not Henry III's but Edward I's commissions. They do not concern us here. My discussion is based on Binski (*Painted Chamber,* chaps. 1, 11 passim) unless otherwise noted. More recently the Painted Chamber has figured in two London exhibitions: "Age of Chivalry: Art in Plantagenet England, 1200–1400," Royal Academy of Arts, November 6, 1987–March 6, 1988, and "Westminster Kings and the Medieval Palace of Westminster," British Museum, November 1, 1995–January 14, 1996. See Jonathan Alexander and Paul Binski, eds., *Age of Chivalry: Art in Plantagenet England, 1200–1400* (London, 1987), 127–28, 341–44; John Cherry and Neil Stratford, *Westminster Kings and the Medieval Palace of Westminster,* British Museum Occasional Paper 115 (London, 1995), 11–27. See also Pamela Tudor-Craig, "The Painted Chamber at Westminster," *Archaeological Journal* 114 (1957): 92–105.

28. Borenius, "The Cycle," 45; Binski, *Painted Chamber,* 16–17, 40 (*lectulus noster floridus*).

29. Binski, *Painted Chamber,* 40. On St. Edward's life, legend, and iconography in art, see *Butler's Lives of the Saints,* ed. Herbert Thurston and Donald Attwater (New York, 1963), 4:100–103; Louis Réau, *Iconographie de l'art chrétien,* vol. 3, *Iconographie des saints,* pt. 1 (Paris, 1958), 411–13.

30. The style of these paintings, which Binski discussed on the evidence of antiquarian copies, can now be judged on the basis of the 1993 discovery in Bristol of two of the ceiling panels from this redecoration campaign. Now in the British Museum (MLA 1995, 4-1, 1 and 2, oil medium on oak planks with areas of stamped decoration), they depict a seraph and a prophet. Good illustrations may be found in Cherry and Stratford, *Westminster,* 18–20.

31. Binski (*Painted Chamber,* esp. 39–40, 43–44) is careful to maintain the caveat that some (or all) of these subjects may have been present in the Painted Chamber before the 1263 fire. However, the themes known, from documents, to have been ordered for the room's decoration before 1263 have the same casual, heterogeneous character as those mentioned above at Winchester; see Borenius, "The Cycle," 49, and Binski, *Painted Chamber,* 16–17, 22–23. They include the four Evangelists (one on each wall), a Tree of Jesse (on the fireplace), two large lions (in the gable of the west wall), a *mappa mundi,* an unspecified *magna historia,* and scenes from the bestiary. The most remarkable bestiary selection, ordered in 1256 for "the wardrobe where the King is wont to wash his head," depicted the story, based on Solinus, given for the dog in English "second-family" bestiaries: the rescue, by his dogs, of the king of the Garamantes from his enemies. It was identified by D. J. A. Ross, "A Lost Painting in Henry III's Palace at Westminster," *Journal of the Warburg and Courtauld Institutes* 16 (1965): 160, pl. 22; Binski, *Painted Chamber,* 16, 44–45.

32. Borenius, "The Cycle," 47–50. Most, but not all, were in chapels.

33. Translation from Henry Luard, ed., *Lives of Edward the Confessor,* Rolls Series 3 (London, 1858), 204 (original text on p. 50). See also v. 1373 (original text, p. 64; trans., p. 218). On the Cambridge manuscript, see *Age of Chivalry,* 216–17, no. 39, with bibliography. An earlier Anglo-Norman poem dated 1163–70 has a similar passage: *La vie d'Édouard le Confesseur, poème anglo-normand du XIIe siècle,* ed. Östen Södergård (Uppsala, 1948), 135, lines 837–38.

34. This literary tradition is outlined by Frank Barlow, ed. and trans., in *The Life of King Edward Who Rests at Westminster, Attributed to a Monk of Saint-Bertin,* 2nd ed. (Oxford, 1992), xxxvii–xl. The text of Ailred of Rievaulx, *Vita S. Edwardi regis et confessoris,* is in *Patrologia Latina* (online) 195, cols. 737–90.

35. Barlow, *Life of King Edward,* 6–7; see also 18–19. On the *Vita Aedwardi Regis,* see now Monika Otter, "1066: The Moment of Transition in Two Narratives of the Norman Conquest," *Speculum* 74 (1999): 579–85.

36. Wormald, "Throne of Solomon" (as in note 17 above), 537–39. See also the list of references to Solomon in Binski, *Painted Chamber,* 43.

37. Leopold G. Wickham Legg, *English Coronation Records* (Westminster, 1901), xxxviii, 5, 17, 92, 258. Percy Ernst Schramm, *A History of the English Coronation,* trans. Leopold G. Wickham Legg (Oxford, 1937), 108, believed that this antiphon was reinstated in 1308, having been omitted from the previous, so-called Anselm ordo. However, H. G. Richardson, "The Coronation in Medieval England," *Traditio* 16 (1960), established that the third recension ("Anselm") did not reflect actual English coronation practice: see pp. 116, 121, 137, 175–76.

38. Wormald, "Throne of Solomon," 539. Grossteste's letter is published and translated in Legg, *English Coronation,* 66–68. Schramm, *A History,* 128–29, notes that the king had asked Grosseteste "in what respect he took precedence of kings that had not been anointed"; the year was 1245.

39. The arguments of chapter 5 are summarized here.

40. See appendix 7.

41. Todor Petev, "Typology and Format in the Netherlandish Blockbook *Canticum canticorum,* ca. 1465," *Visual Resources* 13, nos. 3–4 (1998): 331. My thanks to Dr. Marilyn Lavin for this reference. Facsimiles, listed by Petev (356–57), include *Canticum canticorum: Facsimile druk van het 15e eeuwse zuidnederlandse blokboek,* ed. Adrien Jean Joseph Delen and M. Meertens (Antwerp, 1949). On the blockbook, see also Lerchner, *Lectulus,* 264–69, Abb. 69–73.

42. Folio 83r is illustrated in *Regensburger Buchmalerei: Von frühkarolingischer Zeit bis zum Ausgang des Mittelalters,* exh. cat. (Munich, 1987), Taf. 172 (no. 104, pp. 119–20).

43. Petev, "Typology," 360 n. 26; on the Moralized Bibles, 334, 348.

44. Ibid., 351.

45. Judith Glatzer Wechsler, "A Change in the Iconography of the Song of Songs in 12th and 13th Century Latin Bibles," in *Texts and Responses: Studies Presented to Nahum N. Glatzer,* ed. Michael Fishbane and Paul Flohr (Leiden, 1975), 73, 82–93 passim; Petev, "Typology," 331.

Appendix 7

1. See chapter 5, at notes 31–35.

2. This is the position taken by Roland E. Murphy in *The Song of Songs: A Commentary on the Book of Canticles or the Song of Songs* (Minneapolis, 1990), 149–50.

3. Marvin H. Pope, ed. and trans., *Song of Songs: A New Translation with Introduction and Commentary,* Anchor Bible 7C (Garden City, N.Y., 1977), 431.

4. Ariel Bloch and Chana Bloch, *The Song of Songs: A New Translation with an Introduction and Commentary* (New York, 1995), 160–65.

5. See Levi ben Gershom (Gersonides), *Commentary on Song of Songs,* trans. Menachem Kellner, Yale Judaica Series, 28 (New Haven, 1998), 53–54, and Leon Feldman, *R. Abraham ben Isaac ha-Levi TaMaKH: Commentary on the Song of Songs,* Studia Semitica Neerlandica, 9 (Assen, 1970), 101–3.

6. See Pope, *Song of Songs,* 441, and Karin Lerchner, *Lectulus floridus: Zur Bedeutung des Bettes in Literatur und Handschriftenillustration des Mittelalters,* Pictura et Poesis, 6 (Cologne, 1993), 192.

7. *Patrologia Latina* (online) 24, col. 108C. I am immensely grateful to Professor Mary Sommar for the graceful Latin translations in this appendix.

8. The Venerable Bede, *In Tobiam; In Proverbia; In Cantica Canticorum; In Habacuc,* ed. David Hurst, Corpus Christianorum, Series Latina 119B (Turnhout, 1983), 237, lines 269–73; Lerchner, *Lectulus,* 192.

9. Jean Devisse, *Hincmar, archevêque de Reims, 845–882* (Geneva, 1975–76), 3:1487; Frederick Carey, "The Scriptorium of Reims During the Archbishopric of Hincmar (845–882 A.D.)," in *Classical and Mediaeval Studies in Honor of Edward Kennard Rand,* ed. Leslie Webber Jones (New York, 1938; reprint, Freeport, N.Y., 1968), 56.

10. *Patrologia Latina* (online) 117, cols. 312D–313A; Lerchner, *Lectulus,* 212. A thumbnail sketch of Haimo is provided in Beryl Smalley, *The Study of the Bible in the Middle Ages,* 2nd ed. (New York, 1952; reprint, Notre Dame, 1964), 39–40.

11. Pope, *Song of Songs,* 442; cf. *The Glossa Ordinaria on the Song of Songs,* trans. Mary Dove (Kalamazoo, Mich., 2004), 70–73. Many thanks to Professor David Bell for his references and advice on these matters.

12. Pope, *Song of Songs,* 441, 447; Richard Frederick Littledale, *A Commentary on the Song of Songs from Ancient and Mediaeval Sources* (London, 1869), 137. The Moralized Bibles depict the *ferculum* of verse 9 as a throne, probably stationary; see Lerchner, *Lectulus,* fig. 85.

13. *Patrologia Latina* (online) 172, cols. 505A–B. I am grateful to David Bell for this reference. It is now believed that Honorius, after an early career in England, moved to Germany or Austria; his commentary on the Song of Songs is a late product, dated tentatively ca. 1132–33. See Valerie I. J. Flint, "The Career of Honorius Augustodunensis: Some Fresh Evidence," *Revue bénédictine* 82 (1972): 63–86, and eadem, "The Chronology of the Works of Honorius Augustodunensis," *Revue bénédictine* 82 (1972): 215–42, esp. 234, 236, and 241.

14. Honorius Augustodunensis, *Expositio in Cantica Canticorum,* in *Patrologia Latina* (online) 172, cols. 408B–C. See also cols. 404B–C.

15. Alain de Lille, *Distinctiones dictionum theologicalium,* in *Patrologia Latina* (online) 210, col. 788C.

16. *Patrologia Latina* (online) 16, cols. 226B–C. Lerchner, *Lectulus,* 201 n. 690.

17. Antonius Van Burink, ed., *Excerpta de libris beati Ambrosii super Cantica Canticorum,* in *Guillelmi a Sancto Theodorico, Opera omnia,* pt. 2, *Expositio super Cantico Canticorum; Brevis commentatio; Excerpta de libris beati Ambrosii et Gregorii super Cantica Canticorum,* ed. Paul Verdeyen, Stanislaw Ceglar, and Antonius Van Burink, Corpus Christianorum, Continuatio Mediaevalis, 87 (Turnhout, 1997), 207–384. The passage on Song of Songs 3:9 is on p. 283. On the date and purpose of Guillaume's compilation, see Mark DelCogliano, "The Composition of William of St. Thierry's Excerpts from the Books of Blessed Gregory on the Song of Songs," *Cîteaux: Commentarii cistercienses* 58 (2007): 58–59. Guillaume de Saint-Thierry was born in Liège, studied at Laon, and entered the Benedictine abbey of Saint-Nicaise in Reims. In 1118, while a monk of Saint-Nicaise, he met St. Bernard and wanted to join Clairvaux, but he was elected abbot of Saint-Thierry in Reims and served there until his retirement in 1135, when he became a Cistercian monk at Signy.

18. Jean-Marie Déchanet, OSB, *William of St Thierry: The Man and His Work,* trans. Richard Strachan, Cistercian Studies Series, 10 (Spencer, Mass., 1972), 35. See also Déchanet's introduction to *The Works of William of St Thierry,* vol. 2, *Exposition on the Song of Songs,* trans. Columba Hart, Cistercian Fathers Series, 6 (Shannon, County Clare, 1970), viii, n. 8.

19. On Reims, Bibl. mun. 142, see Van Burink, *Excerpta,* 199–200.

Appendix 8

1. Virginia Raguin and Helen Zakin, *Stained Glass Before 1700 in the Collections of the Midwest States,* Corpus Vitrearum, United States of America, VIII (London, 2001), 1:13; 2:13, 15–18 (Acc. 1979/1.161). The panel was published previously in the American CV checklist: *Stained Glass Before 1700 in American Collections: Corpus Vitrearum Checklist,* III, *Midwestern and Western States,* Studies in the History of Art, 28 (Washington D.C., 1989), 150.

2. Michael Michael, *Images in Light: Stained Glass, 1200–1550,* Sam Fogg, catalogue 26 (London, 2002), 14–15, 112 (Inv. 5714-2). It is now Acc. 2003.28 in the J. Paul Getty Museum, Los Angeles, Calif. According to Jeffrey Weaver, associate curator of sculpture and decorative arts, the provenance provided by Fogg is the pre–World War II Parisian art dealer Bacri Frères.

3. Michigan panel: 36.5 cm × 65.7 cm; Getty panel: 35 × 69 cm. The measurements given in Raguin and Zakin, *Midwest States,* for the Michigan panel are incorrect. I am grateful to Carole McNamara and to Gabrielle Ganther on her staff at the Michigan museum for checking measurements and information in the files for me.

4. Paul Simon, *La grande rose de la cathédrale de Reims* (Reims, 1911), 73–75.

5. Ibid., 32 (7B after hailstorm); 46 (11C before hailstorm). On these tracings, see 45 n. 1.

6. See illustrations in Painton Cowen, *The Rose Window: Splendour and Symbol* (London, 2005), 10, 33. Raguin and Zakin, *Midwest States,* 2:17, suggest that the fronds on the Michigan panel are stopgaps. This seems less likely now that the Getty panel, which also has such fronds, is known, and since the seraphim of the Chartres north rose also have them.

7. Michael, *Images in Light,* 15. For the dating of the Michigan panel, see Raguin and Zakin, *Midwest States,* 2:15–16, 18.

8. Raguin and Zakin, *Midwest States,* 2:18.

9. "Chimie—Contribution à l'étude chimique des vitraux du Moyen Âge: Note de M. G. Chesneau, présentée par M. H. Le Chatelier," *Comptes rendus des séances de l'Académie des sciences* (Paris) 160, no. 19 (May 10, 1915): 622.

10. This improvement in technology has scarcely been investigated as yet. See the brief remarks in Meredith Parsons Lillich, "Gothic Glaziers: Monks, Jews, Taxpayers, Bretons, Women," *Journal of Glass Studies* 27 (1985): 88–89, reprinted in *Studies in Medieval Stained Glass and Monasticism* (London, 2001), 29–31.

Selected Bibliography

Abou-El-Haj, Barbara. "Program and Power in the Glass of Reims." In *Radical Art History, Internationale Anthologie, Subject: O. K. Werckmeister,* edited by Wolfgang Kersten, 23–33, 226–33 (illus.). Zurich, 1997.

———. "The Urban Setting for Late Medieval Church Building: Reims and Its Cathedral Between 1210 and 1240." *Art History* 11 (1988): 17–41.

Architektur und Monumentalskulptur des 12.–14. Jahrhunderts, Produktion und Rezeption: Festschrift für Peter Kurmann zum 65. Geburtstag; Architecture et sculpture monumentale du 12e au 14e siècle, production et réception: Mélanges offerts à Peter Kurmann à l'occasion de son soixante-cinquième anniversaire. Edited by Stephan Gasser, Christian Freigang, and Bruno Boerner. Bern, 2006.

Aubert, Marcel, et al. *Les vitraux de Notre-Dame et de la Sainte-Chapelle de Paris.* Corpus Vitrearum Medii Aevi, France, I. Paris, 1959.

Balcon, Sylvie. "Nouvelles appréciations sur les vitraux de la cathédrale de Reims comportant des représentations architecturales à partir de documents d'archives." In *Représentations architecturales dans les vitraux: Acts du XXIe colloque du Corpus Vitrearum,* Dossier de la Commission royale des monuments, sites et fouilles, 9:67–73. Liege, 2002.

———. "Les vitraux." In *Reims: La cathédrale,* edited by Patrick Demouy, 333–83. La Pierre-qui-vire, 2001.

———. "Les vitraux de la cathédrale d'après les documents du fonds Deneux conservés à la Bibliothèque municipale de Reims." In *Mythes et réalités de la cathédrale de Reims de 1825 à 1975,* 47–55. Paris, 2001.

Balcon-Berry, Sylvie. "Les vitraux de la cathédrale de Reims à la lumière de recherches récentes." In *Nouveaux regards* (see below), 151–73, 212–15.

———. "Les vitraux du Moyen Âge." In *La grâce d'une cathédrale: Reims,* edited by Thierry Jordan et al., 230–53. Strasbourg, 2010.

Barnes, Carl, F., Jr. *The Portfolio of Villard de Honnecourt (Paris, Bibliothèque nationale de France, MS Fr 19093): A New Critical Edition and Color Facsimile.* Burlington, Vt., 2009.

Beyer, Victor, Christiane Wild-Block, and Fridtjof Zschokke. *Les vitraux de la cathédrale Notre-Dame de Strasbourg.* Corpus Vitrearum, France, IX-1. Paris, 1986.

Bony, Jean. *French Gothic Architecture of the Twelfth and Thirteenth Centuries.* Berkeley and Los Angeles, 1983.

Branner, Robert. "Historical Aspects of the Reconstruction of Reims Cathedral, 1210–1241." *Speculum* 36 (1961): 23–37.

———. *Manuscript Painting in Paris During the Reign of Saint Louis.* Berkeley and Los Angeles, 1977.

———. "The North Transept and the First West Facades of Reims Cathedral." *Zeitschrift für Kunstgeschichte* 24 (1961): 220–41.

Cahier, Charles, and Arthur Marie Martin. *Monographie de la cathédrale de Bourges.* Text vol. and plates vol. Paris, 1841–44.

Caviness, Madeline H. "Modular Assemblages: Reconstructing the Choir Clerestory Glazing of Soissons Cathedral." *Journal of the Walters Art Gallery* 48 (1990): 57–68.

———. *Sumptuous Arts at the Royal Abbeys in Reims and Braine: Ornatus elegantiae, varietate stupendes.* Princeton, 1990.

Cerf, Charles. *Histoire et description de Notre-Dame de Reims.* 2 vols. Reims, 1861.

———. "La rose nord de la cathédrale de Reims." *Travaux de l'Académie nationale de Reims* 89 (1890): 273–81.

Christe, Yves. "The Apocalypse in the Monumental Art of the Eleventh Through Thirteenth Centuries." In *The Apocalypse in the Middle Ages,* edited by Richard Emmerson and Bernard McGinn, 234–58. Ithaca, 1992.

Clark, William W. "Jean d'Orbais: Window and Wall at Reims." In *Architektur und Monumentalskulptur* (see above), 87–96.

———. *Medieval Cathedrals.* Westport, Conn., 2006.

———. "Reading Reims, I: The Sculptures on the Chapel Buttresses." *Gesta* 39 (2000): 135–45.

———. "Reims Cathedral in the Portfolio of Villard de Honnecourt." In *Villard's Legacy: Studies in Medieval Technology, Science, and Art in Memory of Jean Gimpel,*

edited by Marie-Thérèse Zenner, 23–51. Aldershot, Hampshire, 2004.
Clark, William W., and Richard King. *Laon Cathedral: Architecture.* Vol. 1. Courtauld Companion Text, 1. London, 1983.
Cothren, Michael W. *Picturing the Celestial City: The Medieval Stained Glass of Beauvais Cathedral.* Princeton, 2006.
Cowen, Painton. *The Rose Window: Splendour and Symbol.* London, 2005.
Demouy, Patrick. "Le baptême de Clovis dans les monuments rémois (XIIIe–XVIe siècles)." In *Clovis: Histoire et mémoire,* vol. 2, *Le baptême de Clovis, son écho à travers l'histoire,* edited by Michel Rouche, 805–19. Paris, 1997.
———. "Synodes diocésains et conciles provinciaux à Reims et en Belgique seconde aux XIe–XIIIe siècles." In *La Champagne et ses administrations à travers le temps: Actes du colloque d'histoire régionale Reims/Châlons-sur-Marne, 1987,* 93–112. Paris, 1990.
Deneux, Henri. "Des modifications apportées à la cathédrale de Reims, au cours de sa construction, du XIIIe au XIVe siècle." *Bulletin monumental* 106 (1948): 121–40.
Desportes, Pierre. *Reims et les rémois aux XIIIe et XIVe siècles.* Paris, 1979.
Desportes, Pierre, et al. *Fasti ecclesiae Gallicanae: Répertoire prosopographique des évêques, dignitaires et chanoines de France de 1200 à 1500.* Vol. 3, *Diocèse de Reims.* Turnhout, 1998.
Devisse, Jean. *Hincmar, archevêque de Reims, 845–882.* 3 vols. Geneva, 1975–76.
Duchesne, Louis. *Fastes épiscopaux de l'ancienne Gaule.* Vol. 3. Paris, 1915.
Elliott, James Keith. *The Apocryphal New Testament.* Oxford, 1993.
Erlande-Brandenburg, Alain. *La cathédrale de Reims: Chef-d'oeuvre du gothique.* Arles, 2007.
Flodoard, of Reims. *Historia Remensis ecclesiae: Die Geschichte der Reimser Kirche/Flodoard von Reims.* Edited by Martina Stratmann. Monumenta Germaniae Historica, Scriptores, 36. Hanover, 1998.
Frachon, Nathalie. "La rose nord du transept de la cathédrale de Reims." Mémoire de maîtrise, Université de Paris IV–Sorbonne, 1982.
Frodl-Kraft, Eva. "Zu den Kirchenschaubildern in den Hochchorfenstern von Reims: Abbildung und Abstraktion." *Wiener Jahrbuch für Kunstgeschichte* 25 (1972): 53–86.
Gailhabaud, Jules. *L'architecture du Ve au XVIIe siècle et les arts qui en dépendent.* Vol. 1. Paris, 1858.
Geruzez, Jean-Baptiste-François. *Description historique et statistique de la ville de Reims.* 2 vols. Reims, 1817.
Gilbert, Antoine. *Description historique de l'église métropolitaine de Notre-Dame de Reims.* Reims, 1825.
Grodecki, Louis. *Le vitrail roman.* Fribourg, 1977.
Grodecki, Louis, and Catherine Brisac. *Gothic Stained Glass, 1200–1300.* Ithaca, 1984.
Guilhermy, François de. "Notes sur diverses localités de la France." Paris, BnF, nouv. acq. fr. 6106, fols. 398r–403r (1828–64).
Hinkle, William M. *The Portal of the Saints of Reims Cathedral: A Study in Mediaeval Iconography.* New York, 1965.
Jackson, Richard A. "Manuscripts, Texts, and Enigmas of Medieval French Coronation Ordines." *Viator* 23 (1992): 35–71.
———, ed. *Ordines coronationis Franciae: Texts and Ordines for the Coronation of Frankish and French Kings and Queens in the Middle Ages.* 2 vols. Philadelphia, 2000.
———. "Le pouvoir monarchique dans la cérémonie du sacre et couronnement des rois de France." In *Représentation, pouvoir et royauté à la fin du Moyen Âge,* edited by Joël Blanchard, 237–51. Paris, 1995.
———. *Vive le roi! A History of the French Coronation from Charles V to Charles X.* Chapel Hill, 1984.
———. "Who Wrote Hincmar's Ordines?" *Viator* 25 (1994): 31–52.
Jacobus de Voragine. *The Golden Legend: Readings on the Saints.* Translated by William Granger Ryan. 2 vols. Princeton, 1993.
Junod, Eric, and Jean-Daniel Kaestli. *Acta Iohannis.* Corpus Christianorum, Series Apocryphorum, 1–2. 2 vols. Turnhout, 1983.
———. *L'histoire des actes apocryphes des apôtres du IIIe au IXe siècle: Le cas des actes de Jean.* Cahiers de la Revue de théologie et de philosophie, 7. Geneva, 1982.
Kimpel, Dieter, and Robert Suckale. *L'architecture gothique en France 1130–1270.* Paris, 1990.
Kurmann, Peter. "L'archevêque Henri de Braine: Son rôle à la cathédrale de Reims." In *Mémoire de Champagne,* vol. 1, *Actes du 2e Mois médiéval,* 119–36. Langres, 2000.
———. "Architecture, vitrail et orfèvrerie: À propos des premiers dessins d'édifices gothiques." In *Représentations architecturales dans les vitraux: Actes du XXIe colloque du Corpus Vitrearum,* Dossier de la Commission royal des monuments, sites et fouilles, 9:33–41. Liege, 2002.
———. "Le Couronnement de la Vierge du grand portail de Reims: Clef du système iconographique de la cathédrale des sacres." In *De l'art comme mystagogie: Iconographie du Jugement dernier et des fins dernières à l'époque gothique,* edited by Yves Christe, Civilisation médiévale, 3:95–104. Poitiers, 1996.
———. *La façade de la cathédrale de Reims: Architecture et sculpture*

des portails, étude archéologique et stylistique. Text vol. and plates vol. Lausanne, 1987.

———. “Mobilité des artistes ou mobilité des modèles? À propos de l’atelier des sculpteurs rémois au XIIIe siècle.” *Revue de l’art* 120/2 (1998): 23–34.

———. “Le portail apocalyptique de la cathédrale de Reims: À propos de son iconographie.” In *L’Apocalypse de Jean: Traditions exégétiques et iconographiques, IIIe–XIIIe siècles,* edited by Yves Christe, 245–317. Geneva, 1979.

Kurmann, Peter, and Brigitte Kurmann-Schwarz. “Französische Bischöfe als Auftraggeber und Stifter von Glasmalereien: Das Kunstwerk als Geschichtsquelle.” *Zeitschrift für Kunstgeschichte* 60 (1997): 429–50.

Kurmann-Schwarz, Brigitte, and Patrick Demouy. “Les vitraux du chevet de la cathédrale de Reims: Une donation de l’archevêque Henri de Braine.” In Desportes et al., *Fasti* (see above), 45–52.

Lafond, Jean. *Les vitraux de l’église Saint-Ouen de Rouen.* Corpus Vitrearum Medii Aevi, France, IV-2, 1. Paris, 1970.

Lasteyrie, Ferdinand de. *Histoire de la peinture sur verre d’après ses monuments en France.* Text vol. and plates vol. Paris, 1853–57.

Le Goff, Jacques. “A Coronation Program for the Age of Saint Louis: The Ordo of 1250.” In *Coronations: Medieval and Early Modern Monarchic Ritual,* edited by Janos M. Bak, 46–57. Berkeley and Los Angeles, 1990.

Le sacre royal à l’époque de saint Louis d’après le manuscrit latin 1246 de la BNF. Edited by Jacques Le Goff et al. Paris, 2001.

Lillich, Meredith Parsons. “Archbishops Named and Unnamed in the Stained Glass of Reims.” In *The Four Modes of Seeing: Approaches to Medieval Imagery in Honor of Madeline Harrison Caviness,* edited by Evelyn Staudinger Lane, Elizabeth Carson Pastan, and Ellen M. Shortell, 291–309. Burlington, Vt., 2009.

———. *The Armor of Light: Stained Glass in Western France, 1250–1325.* Berkeley and Los Angeles, 1994.

———. “The Genesis Rose Window of Reims Cathedral.” *Arte medievale,* n.s., 2, no. 2 (2003): 41–63.

———. “Gothic Glaziers: Monks, Jews, Taxpayers, Bretons, Women.” *Journal of Glass Studies* 27 (1985): 72–92.

———. “Heraldry and Patronage in the Lost Windows of Saint-Nicaise de Reims.” In *L’art et les révolutions: XXVIIe Congrès international d’histoire de l’art,* 8:71–102. Strasbourg, 1992.

———. “King Solomon in Bed, Archbishop Hincmar, the *Ordo* of 1250, and the Stained-Glass Program of the Nave of Reims Cathedral.” *Speculum* 80 (2005): 765–801.

———. “Monastic Stained Glass: Patronage and Style.” In *Monasticism and the Arts,* edited by Timothy Verdon, 207–54. Syracuse, 1984.

———. “More Stained Glass Spolia at Châlons Cathedral.” *Cahiers archéologiques* 45 (1997): 119–40.

———. “Observations on the Gothic Rose Window with Centripetal Tracery.” In *Arte d’Occidente: Temi e metodi; Studi in onore di Angiola Maria Romanini,* edited by Antonio Cadei et al., 1:197–204. Rome, 1999.

———. *Rainbow Like an Emerald: Stained Glass in Lorraine in the Thirteenth and Early Fourteenth Centuries.* University Park, 1991.

———. “A Redating of the Thirteenth-Century Grisaille Windows of Chartres Cathedral.” *Gesta* 11/1 (1972): 11–18.

———. “Remembrance of Things Past: Stained Glass Spolia at Châlons Cathedral.” *Zeitschrift für Kunstgeschichte* 59 (1996): 461–97.

———. “La ‘rose verte’ de la cathédrale de Châlons.” *Cahiers archéologiques* 49 (2001): 117–42.

———. *The Stained Glass of Saint-Père de Chartres.* Middletown, 1978.

———. “The Stained-Glass Spolia in the South Transept of Reims Cathedral and Rémois Ecclesiastical Seals.” *Gesta* 46 (2007): 1–18.

———. “St. Memmie, Apostle of Châlons, and Other Bishop Saints in the Gothic Windows of Châlons Cathedral.” *Studies in Iconography* 19 (1998): 75–103.

———. *Studies in Medieval Stained Glass and Monasticism.* London, 2001.

Mâle, Émile. *Religious Art in France: The Thirteenth Century.* Translated by Marthiel Mathews from the 9th ed., 1958. Princeton, 1984.

Manhès-Deremble, Colette. *Les vitraux narratifs de la cathédrale de Chartres: Étude iconographique.* Corpus Vitrearum, France, Études, II. Paris, 1993.

Marchini, Giuseppe. *Le vetrate dell’Umbria.* Corpus Vitrearum Medii Aevi, Italia, 1. Rome, 1973.

Marlot, Dom Guillaume. *Histoire de la ville, cité et université de Reims.* 4 vols. Reims, 1843–46.

McCulloch, Florence. *Mediaeval Latin and French Bestiaries.* Chapel Hill, 1960.

Migne, Jacques Paul. *Dictionnaire des apocryphes.* Vol. 2. Paris, 1856. Reprint, Turnhout, 1989.

Murray, Stephen. *Beauvais Cathedral: Architecture of Transcendence.* Princeton, 1989.

———. *Notre-Dame, Cathedral of Amiens: The Power of Change in Gothic.* Cambridge, 1996.

Norris, Herbert. *Church Vestments: Their Origin and Development.* New York, 1950. Reprint, Mineola, N.Y., 2002.

Nouveaux regards sur la cathédrale de Reims. Edited by Bruno Decrock and Patrick Demouy. Langres, 2008.
O'Meara, Carra Ferguson. *Monarchy and Consent: The Coronation Book of Charles V of France.* London, 2001.
Painter, Sidney. *Scourge of the Clergy: Peter of Dreux, Duke of Brittany.* Baltimore, 1937.
Pastan, Elizabeth C., and Sylvie Balcon. *Les vitraux de choeur de la cathédrale de Troyes (XIIIe siècle).* Corpus Vitrearum, France, II. Paris, 2006.
Pinoteau, Hervé. *L'héraldique de saint Louis et de ses compagnons.* Les cahiers nobles, 27. Paris, 1966.
———. *Vingt-cinq ans d'études dynastiques.* Paris, 1982.
Povillon-Piérard, Étienne. *Description historique de l'église métropolitaine de Notre-Dame de Rheims.* Reims, 1823.
Prache, Anne. *Saint-Remi de Reims: L'oeuvre de Pierre de Celle et sa place dans l'architecture gothique.* Geneva, 1973.
Raguin, Virginia Chieffo. *Stained Glass in Thirteenth-Century Burgundy.* Princeton, 1982.
Ravaux, Jean-Pierre. "Les campagnes de construction de la cathédrale de Reims au XIIIe siècle." *Bulletin monumental* 137 (1979): 7–66.
Recensement I = *Les vitraux de Paris, de la région parisienne, de la Picardie et du Nord-Pas-de-Calais.* Corpus Vitrearum Medii Aevi, France: Recensement des vitraux anciens de la France, I. Paris, 1978.
Recensement II = *Les vitraux du Centre et des pays de la Loire.* Corpus Vitrearum, France: Recensement des vitraux anciens de la France, II. Paris, 1981.
Recensement III = *Les vitraux de Bourgogne, Franche-Comté et Rhône-Alpes.* Corpus Vitrearum, France: Recensement des vitraux anciens de la France, III. Paris, 1986.
Recensement IV = *Les vitraux de Champagne-Ardenne.* Corpus Vitrearum, France: Recensement des vitraux anciens de la France, IV. Paris, 1992.
Recensement V = Hérold, Michel, and Françoise Gatouillat. *Les vitraux de Lorraine et d'Alsace.* Corpus Vitrearum, France: Recensement des vitraux anciens de la France, V. Paris, 1994.
Recensement VI = Bey, Martine Callias, et al. *Les vitraux de Haute-Normandie.* Corpus Vitrearum, France: Recensement des vitraux anciens de la France, VI. Paris, 2001.
Reims: La cathédrale. Edited by Patrick Demouy. La Pierre-qui-vire, 2001.
Reinhardt, Hans. *La cathédrale de Reims: Son histoire, son architecture, sa sculpture, ses vitraux.* Paris, 1963.
Robertson, Anne Walters. *Guillaume de Machaut and Reims: Context and Meaning in His Musical Works.* Cambridge, 2002.
Sadler, Donna. "Lessons Fit for a King: The Sculptural Program of the Verso of the West Facade of Reims Cathedral." *Arte medievale,* 2nd ser., 9, no. 1 (1995): 49–65.
Sadler-Davis, Donna. "The Sculptural Program of the Verso of the West Facade of Reims Cathedral." Ph.D. diss., Indiana University, 1984.
Saint-Thierry: Une abbaye du VIe au XXe siècle; Actes du colloque international d'histoire monastique, 1976. Edited by Michel Bur. Saint-Thierry, 1979.
Sandron, Dany. "La cathédrale et l'architecte: À propos de la façade occidentale de Laon." In *Pierre, lumière, couleur: Études d'histoire de l'art du Moyen Âge en l'honneur d'Anne Prache,* edited by Fabienne Joubert and Dany Sandron, 133–50. Paris, 1999.
Sauerländer, Willibald. *Gothic Sculpture in France, 1140–1270.* Translated by Janet Sondheimer. New York, 1972.
Sceaux et usages de sceaux: Images de la Champagne médiévale. Edited by Jean-Luc Chassel. Paris, 2003.
Schneemelcher, Wilhelm, ed. *New Testament Apocrypha.* Translated and edited by Robert McLachlan Wilson. Vol. 2. Louisville, Ky., 2003.
Simon, Paul. *La grande rose de la cathédrale de Reims.* Reims, 1911.
———. "Notes sur les vitraux de la cathédrale de Reims." *Congrès archéologique* 78, pt. 2 (1911): 288–304.
Tarbé, Prosper. *Notre-Dame de Reims.* 2nd ed. Reims, 1852.
Tourneur, Victor. *Histoire et description des vitraux et des statues de l'intérieur de la cathédrale de Reims.* Reims, 1857. (First published in *Travaux de l'Académie nationale de Reims* 24 [1855–56]: 123–95.)
Trésors de la Bibliothèque municipale de Reims. Exh. cat. Reims, 1978.
Villes, Alain. *La cathédrale Notre-Dame de Reims: Chronologie et campagnes de travaux.* Joué-lès-Tours, 2009.
Westlake, Nat Hubert John. *A History of Design in Painted Glass.* Vol. 1. London, 1881.
Wirth, Jean. *La datation de la sculpture médiévale.* Geneva, 2004.

Index

Illustration numbers are in *italics*. Manuscripts are listed under library and number.

Abel, 113–22 passim, 128, 133, *figs. 119, 123, 126, 139, 140*
Acts (Biblical book), 20, 50
  individual apostles in, 27, 30, 38, 52–54, 56
Acts of the apostles, apocryphal, 24, 27, 32, 39, 273 n. 78, 276 n. 116
  Acts of Peter, 24, 272 n. 64, 277 n. 138
Adam, 116, 119–20, 122, 131–32, *figs. 122, 138*
  and Eve, 111–13, 131–32, 290 n. 26, *figs. 115, 136–38*
Adenès li rois, *Cléomadès*, 219, 235
Agnus Dei, 146, 149, 298 n. 161, *fig. 157*
Ailred of Rievaulx, *Vita S. Edwardi regis*, 255
aisle and chapel glazing, xviii, 13–15, 86, 217, 245, 314 n. 58, 317 n. 7, *fig. 229*. *See also* Bay 39; heads from lost windows
Alain de Lille, 261
Albigensian crusade, 8, 43, 63, 241–42, 247
Ambrose, St., 130, 131, 164, 252, 261–62, 268 n. 6
Amiens, Bibl. mun., lat. 108 (Pamplona Bible), 33, 273 n. 74, 274 n. 89, 276 n. 126
Amiens, cathedral and diocese, 29, 71, 237, 278 n. 5, 287 n. 167, 288 n. 170
  in Reims Bay 105, 69, 71, 74, 90, *fig. 90*
Ampulla, Holy, 146, 153, 167, 179, 298 n. 158. *See also* Clovis; Remi, St.
Andrew, St., 22, 52, 68, 69, 273 n. 80, *fig. 37*. *See also* Acts of the apostles, apocryphal
  in Reims Bay 102, 28, 30–33, 75, 79–81, *figs. 33, 34, 36, 79, 82*
angel musicians, 225, 231–34, *figs. 243, 244, 249, 250*
angels. *See* Apocalypse; coronation, liturgy of; Last Judgment
Angers, cathedral, 32, 230, 272 n. 69
Ann Arbor, University of Michigan museum, stained glass seraph, 263–64
Apocalypse (Biblical book), 73–74, 136, 164, 283 n. 87. *See also* John the Evangelist
apostles. *See also* disciples; *individual names*
  attributes of, 46, 54, 68, 69, 248, 281 n. 45
  in chevet, 17–18, 47, 51, 62–63.
  lives of, 17, 20–25 passim, 27, 29, 273 n. 80
  on south rose, 111, 134–35
  in west rose, 225, 230, *figs. 243, 249*
apostolic succession, 18, 25, 33, 42, 44, 68–69
  source of, 34, 48, 50
archbishops. *See* vestments and regalia; *individual names*
architect, image of, 14, 86, 215, 285 n. 121, *figs. 21, 22, 88*
architectural drawings, medieval, 71–72, 138, 239, 283 n. 75
Arras, Bibl. mun., MS 779 (Gospel), 50
Arras, cathedral and diocese, 69, 99, 241, 243, 281 n. 49
artes mechanicae, 113, 128, *fig. 117*
Arthur, King, coronation banquet of, 234
Ascension of Christ, 14, 125, 155–56, 170, 237, *fig. 20*
Assisi, Bibl. del Sac. Con., MS 695 (Reims troper), 174
Assisi, San Francesco, Upper Church, 46, 50, 274 n. 84, 275 n. 99, 277 n. 135
Aubry de Humbert, archbishop, 7, 8, 149, 241–42, 318 n. 8
Augsburg University, Cod. I.3.2° IV (Old Testament), 258
Augustine, St., 39–41, 105, 122, 182, 268 n. 6, 290 n. 24
autochrome photographs of Henri Deneux, xviii–xix, 2
  chevet, 81, 100–101, 279 n. 7, 284 n. 107, 285 n. 114, 287 n. 151, *figs. 74, 80, 101*
  nave lancets, 217, 284 n. 99, 309 n. 96, *figs. 182, 190, 196, 201, 212, 214, 215, 217, 219*
  nave rosaces, 304 n. 53, *figs. 159, 162, 164*
  transept, *figs. 7, 149, 150*
Auxerre, cathedral, 74, 289 n. 7
  aisle bays, 32, 119, 271 n. 46, 272 n. 69, 274 n. 90, 287 n. 167
  clerestory, 66, 212, 237, 287 n. 167, 288 n. 169
avarice. *See* usury

Bamberg, Domschatz, Bamberg Rational, 322 n. 2
baptism and baptismal font, 125, 146–48 passim, 299 n. 170
Barnabas, archbishop, 180, 185, *figs. 184, 185*
Barnabas, St., 22, 68, 281 nn. 45, 46
  in Reims Bay 107, 52, 54–58, 94, 98, *figs. 63–67, 95*
Bartholomew, St., 22, 44–46, 69, 92, 286 n. 142, *figs. 52–54*
Baruc, archbishop, 178–79, 185, *figs. 181, 182*
Barucius, archbishop, 178, 180, *figs. 181, 183*
Bay 39, 14, 86, 155, 217–18, 237, 311 n. 27, *figs. 20–22, 230*
Bay 100, 10, 18, 25, 82, 245, 279 n. 7, *figs. 13, 24*
  lancets, 62–66 passim, 72–75 passim, 81, 280 n. 23, 295 n. 117, *figs. 69–72*
  rosace, 19–20, 47–48, 54, 74, *figs. 24, 25*
Bay 101, 68, 82, 92, 245–46, 247, 279 n. 7, *fig. 28*
  lancets, 63, 75–79, 84, 284 n. 107, *figs. 73–78*
  rosace, 22, 25–30, 47–48, 74, 248, 303 n. 41, *figs. 29–31*
Bay 102, 25, 56, 75, 245–46, 279 nn. 7, 11

lancets, 62, 68, 74, 78–82, 92, 283 n. 87, *figs. 79–83*
rosace, 22, 30–34, 96, *figs. 33, 34, 36*
Bay 103, 25, 69, 82–88 passim, 245–46, 269 n. 22, 303 n. 50
lancets, 63, 73, 75, 96, 99–100, 287 n. 151, *figs. 84, 85*
rosace, 22, 34, 39–44, 47, 48, 54, *figs. 48–51*
Bay 104, 25, 82, 88, 245–46, 279 n. 7
lancets, 63, 72–75 passim, 79, 84–87, 96, 99, *figs. 86, 87*
rosace, 22, 24, 34–39, 44, 47–48, 54, *figs. 38–40, 42, 43, 45–47*
Bay 105, 25, 62, 74, 92, 279 n. 7, 283 n. 85
lancets, 69, 73, 90, 280 n. 23, 281 n. 42, 287 n. 156, *figs. 90–92*
rosace, 22, 44, 47–52, 56, 286 n. 149, *figs. 56–60*
Bay 106, 25, 74, 90, 98, 286 n. 145
lancets, 46, 48, 69, 78, 92–94, 283 n. 85, *figs. 93, 94*
rosace, 22, 44–48, 52, 56, 286 n. 149, *figs. 52–55*
Bay 107, 25, 52, 62, 98–99, 287 n. 153
lancets, 69, 73, 94–96, 283 n. 86, *figs. 95, 96*
rosace, 22, 54–58, 68, 74, 246, *figs. 63–67*
Bay 108, 25, 68, 94, 96–99, 279 n. 7
lancets, 69, 73, 74, 246, 284 n. 94, *figs. 97, 98*
rosace, 22, 30, 52–54, 74, 286 n. 149, *figs. 61, 62*
Bay 109, 62, 284 n. 94, *fig. 99*. *See also* Bay 110
Bay 110, 25, 99–103, 143, 148, 279 n. 7, *figs. 100, 101*
figures, 63, 68, 94, 287 n. 165
grisaille, 58, 74, 105–6
Bay 111 through Bay 117, 106, 143, *figs. 7, 104, 105, 107–9*
Bay 118, 7, 62–65, 86–87, 138–43 passim, 147–48, 288 n. 4, *figs. 145–51*. *See also* Reinhardt, "first atelier"
"facade" of Reims, 72, 284 nn. 103, 106, *figs. 148, 150*
John the Baptist, St., 62–65, 146, 147, *figs. 147, 151*
Remi, St., 65, 138–39, 144–49, *figs. 147, 149*
Virgin and Child, 62, 65, 138–39, 143–44, 149, *fig. 148*
Bay 119 and Bay 120, 106, *figs. 104, 106, 110*
Bay 121, 200–201
lancets, 183, 191–92, 202, 217, 309 nn. 88, 105, 106, *figs. 192, 193, 197*
rosace, 160–63 passim, 168–70, 237, 257–59, *figs. 159, 161*
Bay 122
lancets, 169, 175–76, 182–84 passim, 307 n. 60, *figs. 11, 178–80, 186*
rosace, 156–58, 168–69, 304 n. 59, *figs. 161, 162, 173*
Bay 123, 200–201, *fig. 177*
lancets, 183, 191–92, 309 nn. 105, 106, *figs. 194, 195, 198*
rosace, 156–58, 168–69, 317 n. 4, *figs. 161, 163, 172*
Bay 124
lancets, 178, 180–84 passim, 306 n. 30, *figs. 181–83, 187*
rosace, 160, 168–70, 237, *figs. 161, 164*
Bay 125, 200–201, 300 n. 5, *fig. 177*
lancets, 183, 191–92, 217, 309 n. 105, *figs. 176, 196*
rosace, 156–58, 169, *figs. 161, 165*
Bay 126, 300 n. 5
lancets, 180–84 passim, 306 nn. 30, 31, *figs. 184, 185*
rosace, 156, 160, 168–69, 304 n. 59, *figs. 161, 166, 174*
Bay 127, 12, 206
lancets, 175, 188–89, 195–200 passim, 308 n. 68, 309 n. 105, 317 n. 4, *frontispiece*, *figs. 200–205*
rosace, 168–69, *figs. 16, 161, 167, 175*
Bay 128
lancets, 182, 185 89, 195–97, 206, 309 n. 105, *figs. 188–90*. *See also* Karolvs
rosace, 156, 300 n. 5, *figs. 161, 168*
Bay 129, 190, 194
lancets, 12, 175, 182, 195–200, 206, *frontispiece*, *figs. 200, 202–4*
rosace, 156, *fig. 161*
Bay 130, 190, 194
lancets, 12, 195–200, 206, 309 n. 97, *figs. 200, 205*
rosace, 156, *fig. 161*
Bay 131, 190, *fig. 211*
lancets, 206–9, 217, 305 n. 65, 309 n. 97
rosace, 156, *fig. 161*
Bay 132, 190
lancets, 206–7, 217, 305 n. 65, *figs. 212, 213*
rosace, *fig. 161*
Bay 133
lancets, 206–7, *fig. 214, 215*
rosace, *fig. 161*
Bay 134
lancets, 206–7, 310 n. 114, *figs. 216–18*
rosace, 156, *fig. 161*
Bay 135
lancets, 207, 217, 305 n. 65, *figs. 219, 220*
rosace, *fig. 161*
Bay 136
lancets, 207–9, 310 n. 112
rosace, 156, 304 n. 59, *fig. 161*
Bay 137
lancets, 207, 310 n. 112, *fig. 221*
rosace, 267 n. 41, *fig. 161*
Bay 138
lancets, 207, *fig. 221*
rosace, 156, 304 n. 59, *fig. 161*
Bay 139 and Bay 140, 171, 191, 206–9, 217–18, 221, 311 n. 26, *figs. 230, 238*
Beauvais, cathedral and diocese, 58, 88, 158, 165. *See also* Philippe de Dreux; Pierre de Beauvais
architecture, 71, 72, 282 n. 74
chapel glazing, 75, 232
clerestory glazing, 66, 78, 278 n. 5, 281 nn. 40, 46, 285 n. 115, 309 n. 107
Henri de Braine at, 29, 38, 63, 87, 242
in Reims Bay 104, 38, 71–73 passim, 84, 88, *figs. 86, 87*
Bede, 54–56 passim, 137, 243, 270 n. 32, 277 n. 152, 322 n. 2
Hincmar's use of, 261–62, 302 n. 33
belles verrières, 7, 138, 266 n. 14. *See also* Bay 118
Bennadius, archbishop, 180, 185, *fig. 184*
Bernard de Clairvaux, St., 130, 151, 242, 325 n. 17
Bernard de Soissons, architect, 215
bestiaries, 123–33 passim
Biblical books, 261–62. *See also* Acts; Apocalypse; Genesis; Kings; Song of Songs
Epistles, 122, 243, 278 n. 163, 292 n. 51.

Gospels, 18, 56–57, 84, 121–22, 279 n. 13, 300 n. 9
Old Testament, 125, 128, 158, 164, 218, 257
bishops, in chevet. *See* apostolic succession; preaching; suffragan bishops; *individual dioceses*
bishops, in nave rosaces, 156, 158, 165–70 passim, 304 n. 59, *figs. 161–63, 165, 172, 173. See also* peers of France
blockbook *Canticum canticorum*, 258, *fig. 259*
Bonaventure, St., 301 n. 25
borders, 15, 106, 221
in chevet, 54, 65–66, 79, 82, 92–94, 101, *figs. 76, 92, 96*
in nave, 13, 169, 206–7, 217, 305 n. 65, 309 n. 105, *figs. 213, 218, 221, 229*
Boston, Gardner Museum, 14–15, *fig. 23*
Bourges, cathedral, 18, 68, 237, 279 n. 10, 281 n. 45, 309 n. 107
ambulatory bays, north, 19, 66, 107, 271 n. 43, 272 nn. 67, 69
ambulatory bays, south, 19, 39–41, 66, 245, 271 n. 46, 274 nn. 86, 90, 275 n. 105
Braine, 8, 63, 241
Saint-Yved, 10, 65, 88, 101
Breviarium Apostolorum, 29, 43, 46, 52
Brunetto Latini, *Li livres dou tresor*, 124
Brussels, Bibl. Roy.
MS 10074 (*Physiologus*), 293 n. 59
MS 11 6978 (Pierre de Beauvais, bestiary), 249
Brussels, Musée du Cinquantenaire, Stavelot altar, 38, 43, 275 n. 96
Burgos, cathedral, 134

Cain, 113–16, 121–22, 128, 130, 132–33, 290 n. 25, *figs. 119, 124, 125, 139, 140*
caladrius, 123–24, 250, *figs. 127, 128, 130, 135*
Cambrai, cathedral and diocese, 69, 99, 242–43, 281 n. 49
Cambridge, Univ. Lib.
MS Ee.3.59 (*Seint Aedward le Rei*), 255
MS II.4.26 (bestiary), 125–26, 128, 292 n. 56
MS KK.4.25 (bestiary), 292 n. 56
MS Mm.v.31 (Apocalypse commentary), 124
Canon of the Mass, 18, 22, 52, 56, 79, 90
canons, 9, 34, 72, 94, 243, 313 n. 50. *See also* glazing programs
civic strife and exile in 1230s, 9–10, 25, 48, 52, 75, 88–89
canons' choir, 99, 129, 156, 170, 190–91
canopies. *See* crockets
Carolus. *See* Karolvs
carré cadrilobé medallions, 168–69
carrying the cross, Christ, 19, 268 n. 7
cartoons, 99, 103, 191, 207, 287 n. 160, 288 n. 170
Cassiodorus, 73
castles, heraldic, 13, 191, 206, 215–17, 221, 304 n. 64, *figs. 226, 227, 230*
Cathars, 43, 47, 242, 293 n. 74. *See also* Albigensian crusade
Cellier, Jacques, 147, 194, *figs. 88, 199*
chaire de saint Remy, 65, 150, 281 n. 44
Châlons-en-Champagne (formerly Châlons-sur-Marne), cathedral and diocese, 63, 158, 167, 241, 303 n. 51
architecture, 68, 71, 134, 282 n. 65
glazing, choir clerestory, 63, 66, 105, 237–38, 279 n. 10
glazing, donated by Henri de Braine, 10, 65, 88, 146, 167
glazing, Matthias in, 54, 277 n. 148, 281 n. 48
glazing, north rose, 54, 135–36, 277 n. 148, 281 n. 48, 289 n. 18, *figs. 143–44*
glazing, Romanesque, 66
grisaille, nave, 311 n. 23
in Reims Bay 103, 71, 73, 82–84, 88, *figs. 84, 85*
Châlons-en-Champagne (formerly Châlons-sur-Marne)
heresy at, 9, 89, 129, 241, 243
saints of, in Ordo of 1250, 12, 167
chapter. *See* canons
Charlemagne, 165, 174, 189, 219, 247–48, 308 nn. 70, 71. *See also* Pseudo-Turpin
Charles Borromeo, St., 184–85
Charles the Bald, 59, 147, 156–58, 164, 189–90, 243
Chartres, Bibl. mun., MS 500 (cathedral lectionary, lost), 37, 274 n. 92
Chartres, cathedral, 71, 86, 296 n. 132
sculpture, 46, 122, 144–46, 230, 276 n. 131, 301 n. 20
Chartres, cathedral, stained glass, 22, 105, 121, 144, 307 n. 48
ambulatory, north, 28, 39, 41–42, 47, 245, 271 n. 46
ambulatory, south, 27, 32, 215, 272 n. 69
Belle Verrière, 143, 266 n. 14
clerestory, 18, 28, 78, 121, 237, 285 nn. 115, 124
grisaille, 289 n. 7, 304 n. 64
nave aisles, 19, 107, 230, 268 n. 7, 269 n. 23, 274 n. 90
rose, north, 107, 216, 231, 263, 279 n. 19, 326 n. 6
rose, south, 63, 312 n. 42
Chartres, Saint-Père, 269 n. 12, 278 n. 4, 281 n. 46, 289 n. 7, 311 n. 23
scenes of apostles, 32, 271 n. 43, 272 n. 69, 276 n. 126
Chenu (Sarthe), glass at Rivenhall (Essex), 121
choir screen, 156, 193–94, *figs. 160, 161. See also* canons' choir
Christ, as Creator, 113, 121–22, 134–35, 245, *figs. 24, 28, 121. See also* Virgin and Child; *individual scenes*
establishing the Church, 155, 170, *figs. 167, 175*
giving James Major a baton, 28, 248, *figs. 30, 32*
holding the Virgin's soul, 230, *fig. 241*
types and symbols of, 120, 122–25, 128, 309 n. 94
Cividale, Museo arch. naz., Codici sacri 7 (Saint Elisabeth Psalter), 276 n. 126
Clermont-Ferrand, cathedral, 32
Clovis, 146–51, 158, 214–15, 296 n. 130
Cluny, Notre-Dame (parish church), 72, 129, 277 n. 150
Codex Calixtinus, 28–29, 79, 247–48
color and palette, 293 n. 62. *See also* yellow
Bay 118, 65, 138
chevet, 54, 245–46, 286 n. 128, 287 n. 165
facade glazing, 214, 218–21 passim
hemicycle bays, 20, 25, 28–33 passim, 39, 65, 81–84 passim, 87
nave lancets, 175, 186, 201, 206, 302 n. 35
north rose, 115, 120, 124, *fig. 120*
straight-choir bays, 48, 50, 56–57, 90–92, 98
Corbie, abbey, 231, 314 n. 70

coronation, 105, 142–43, 195, 209, 218, 295 n. 113. *See also* Last Capetian Ordo; Ordo of Reims; Ordo of 1250
liturgy of, 153–62 passim, 165–66, 174, 219, 253, 257
removal of glass for, 1, 145, 185, 296 n. 132, *figs. 7, 146*
ritual of sleeping king, 165–66, 231, 302 n. 39
coronations, 174, 214, 235, 255, 302 n. 39, 312 n. 34
of Capetians, 6–7, 63, 139–42, 195, 206, 215–20 passim
of Edward the Confessor, St., 255–57
of 14th–16th centuries, 165–66, 179, 300 n. 11, 307 n. 55, 308 n. 70, *fig. 171*
by Hincmar, 156–58, 162
of 17th–19th centuries, 1, 145, 179, 185, 207, 305 n. 65, *figs. 5–7, 238*
Counter-Reformation, 184–85
coupure Tourneur, 170, 190, 206, 304 n. 58, *figs. 3, 160, 161*
crane, 124, 125, *figs. 131, 135*
Creation cycle, 111–23, 131–33, 137, 250, *fig. 117*. *See also* individual scenes
crockets, 201–7 passim, 309 n. 107, 310 n. 114
Crown of thorns, 155, 248, 268 n. 7, *figs. 16, 167*
Crucifixion of Christ, 19, 63, 65–66, 211, *figs. 26, 69*
crusade. *See* Albigensian crusade; Louis VIII; Louis IX

Dante, *Purgatorio*, 123, 292 n. 57
dating of glazing campaigns, xxii, 10–13
Belles verrières, 149
chevet lancets, 66, 72–75 passim, 87–89, 96–99
chevet rosaces, 20–23 passim, 25, 34, 48, 52, 58
facade, 215–21 passim
nave, 156, 167–71, 191, 196–97, 200–209 passim, 217
transept, 106, 129–30
dendrochronological evidence, 1
Deneux, Henri, 14, 61–62, 99, 147, 275 n. 103, 296 nn. 124, 134. *See also* autochrome photographs
watercolors of, 220, *figs. 226, 248*
Dérodé, Nicolas, glazier, 134, 135, 184, *fig. 141*
Dijon, Notre-Dame, 32, 273 n. 80
disciples of Christ, 68, 94
Discolius, 305 n. 12
dog, 125–28, 325 n. 31, *fig. 134*
Donatianus, St., 175–77, 185, 303 n. 49, *figs. 178, 179*
drapery painting, 15, 87
antiquizing ("wet"), 34, 48, 82, 139. *See also* Reinhardt, "first atelier"
broken-fold ("*dur*"), 65
in hemicycle, 25, 30, 34, 81, 82, 279 n. 11
in straight-choir lancets, 92, 98, 100, 287 n. 151
in straight-choir rosaces, 48, 54–57, 96
Dreux family. *See* Henri de Braine; Philippe de Dreux; Pierre Mauclerc

Ecclesia and Synagoga, 111, 135, 151, 160, 294 n. 104
Edward the Confessor, St., 254–57
eel, 125, *figs. 127, 132*
Elders of the Apocalypse, 232, 316 n. 83
Epernay, Bibl. mun., MS 1 (Ebbo Gospels), 84
Eusebius, Church History, 38, 43
Evangelists. *See* individual saints
Eve, 111–21 passim, 125, 128, 131–33, 290 n. 24, *figs. 115, 125, 126, 136–39*
Evron, Notre-Dame de l'Epine, 275 n. 107
eyes, 84, 92, 99, 245–46, 287 n. 165
leaded as "eyeglasses," 78, 79, 92

"facades," glass images of, 68–74 passim, 78, 151, 239, 282 n. 74, *fig. 71*
Bay 104 rosace, 38, 88, *fig. 45*
Bay 118, 138, 144, 149, *fig. 148, 150*
Ferentillo, San Pietro in Valle, frescoes, 292 n. 57
Ferrara, cathedral, 120
"first choir program." *See* Reinhardt, Hans
fish, 125, *figs. 127, 132*
Flagellation of Christ, 19, *figs. 24, 25*
fleurs-de-lis, 13, 218–19, 221, 292 n. 44, 312 n. 34
in facade gallery, 214, 218, *fig. 227*
of Henri de Braine, 65–66, 75, *fig. 70*
of Louis IX, 48, 92–94, 216–17
in nave, 171, 201, 206–7, 217, 305 n. 65, *figs. 213, 229*
Flodoard, *Historia Remensis ecclesiae*, 174–76, 178, 180, 189, 302 n. 33, 314 n. 69
Florence, Bibl. Laurenziana, cod. Plut. I, 56 (Rabbula Gospel), 277 n. 145
Florence, campanile (Giotto's Tower), 113
Santa Maria Novella, occhio, 232
foldstool, 148–49, 182, 199
Freiburg im Breisgau, Universitätsbibliothek 979 (fragments in binding), 320 n. 3

Genesis (Biblical book), 113, 115–16, 118–19, 122–23, 125, 289 n. 18. *See also* Creation cycle
Gersonides, 261
Gervais, archbishop, 195
Gervais de Tilbury, 241, 318 n. 15
gestures, hand, 56, 74, 84–86, 231, 285 n. 127, 313 n. 44, *figs. 167, 207*
holding mantle strap ("royal gesture"), 191, 197, *figs. 190, 204*
waving (acclamation), 206–9 passim, *figs. 210, 212, 214, 219*
glass making, changes in, 13, 170, 264, 275 n. 107
glazing methods, 89, 90, 245–46, 278 n. 5. *See also* cartoons; trial pieces
glazing programs and themes, xix, 15, 237–39, 243
chevet, lancets, 68–69, 73–75, 90, 103, 283 n. 85, *fig. 27*
chevet, rosaces, 17–18, 22–25, 46–47, 58–59, *fig. 27*
facade, Gothic, 214–15, 220–21, 224–25, 230–31, 235, 317 n. 7
facade, Romanesque, 144, 150–51
nave lancets, 173–74, 190–91, 193–97, 206, 209
nave, rosaces, 153–56, 162, 167–71, *fig. 161*
transepts, 107, 128–38 passim
Glossa Ordinaria, 73, 74

goat, 125–28, *figs. 134, 135*
Golden Legend, 20, 24, 232, 315 n. 77
 individual apostles in, 43–46, 50, 52–54, 245, 275 n. 100, 277 n 152
Gossouin de Metz, *Image du monde*, 321 n. 14
"Gothic order" (or protocol), 22, 47, 68
Gregory IX, 242–43
Gregory of Nyssa, St., 252
Gregory of Tours, 24, 146, 273 n. 72, 314 n. 67
Gregory the Great, 52, 56, 302 n. 33, 319 n. 24, 322 n. 2
griffin, 123, *figs. 129, 135*
grisaille, 89–90, 238, 286 n. 141, 304 nn. 58, 64, 311 n. 23, 314 n. 61
 Bays 109 and 110, 58, 74, 99, 101, 105–6
 Bays 139 and 140, 171, 191, 206–7, 217, *fig. 230*
 nave aisles and tympana (lost), 13–14, 211, 217, 267 n. 39, *figs. 223, 224, 229*
 painted in 1825, 1, 207, 305 n. 65, *figs. 7, 238*
 transepts, 105–9, *figs. 103–10*
Guillaume de Champagne (aux Blanches-Mains), archbishop, 8, 149, 241
Guillaume de Joinville, archbishop, 8, 63, 149, 242
Guillaume de Machaut, 235, 316 n. 81
Guillaume de Saint-Thierry, 262, 325 n. 17
Gui Paré, archbishop, 8, 241

Haimo of Auxerre, 261
haloes
 in chevet, 65, 81–84 passim, 92–98 passim, 100, 245, 286 n. 149
 in nave, 178, 180–82, 197–200, *fig. 210*
heads from lost windows, 14–15, *fig. 23*
Hegesippus, 275 n. 94
Henri de Braine, archbishop, 8–10, 58, 63–66, 87–89 passim, 167, 241–44. *See also* Philippe de Dreux; Pierre Mauclerc; Robert II de Dreux
 chevet program of, 68–69, 90, 94, 96, 99, 103
 glass donations, 29–30, 63–66, 87–88, 146, 167, 297 n. 135
 image in Bay 100, 18, 20, 63–65, 75, 146, 148, *figs. 69, 70*
 library of, 29–30, 79, 123, 130–31, 247–48, 249
Henri de France, archbishop, 8, 63, 148, 241, 244, 248
Henry III, English king, 163, 254–57
heraldry, on garments, 218–19, 312 n. 42, *fig. 227*. *See also* castles, heraldic; fleurs-de-lis
heresy and heretics, 8–10, 120–22, 130, 241–43, 292 n. 51. *See also* Albigensian crusade; Cathars; Manichaean heresy
 as theme in chevet, 25, 43–46, 58, 89
 as theme in north rose, 123, 129–31
heron, 123–24
Hildesheim, doors, 120
Hincmar, archbishop, 50, 146, 153, 175, 189, 314 n. 70
 books of, surviving, 48–50, 261–62, 274 n. 87
 De cavendis vitiis et virtutibus exercendis, 58–59, 243
 In ferculum Salomonis, 163–64, 260–61, *fig. 170*
 Libellum de ortu sanctae Mariae, 230–31, 315 n. 71
 Life of St. Remi, 297 n. 138
 Ordo of Charles the Bald, 156–58, 189, 301 n. 13
 Ordo of Louis the Stammerer, 158, 162
 Synod of Sainte-Macre de Fismes, 154–58 passim, 170–71, 174
Histoire d'Adam, 131–33, 250, *figs. 136–40*
Historia Compostellana, 29, 79, 247–48
Holy Ghost, 121–22, 245–46
Holy Women at the Tomb. *See* Marys at the Tomb
Homer, *Odyssey*, 273 n. 78
Honorius Augustodunensis, 123–24, 232, 261
Hortus Deliciarum, 54, 163, 251–53, 255, 301 n. 21, *fig. 255*
Hugh of Saint-Victor, 151
Hugues de Bourgogne, grand archdeacon, 149, *fig. 157*
Hugues de Fouilloy, *De avibus*, 293 nn. 59, 63

ibis, 125, 293 n. 69
idols and idolatry, 25, 43–47, 51, 58–59, *figs. 53, 55–57*
Incarnation of Christ, 136–37, 232, 300 n. 9
 theme in nave rosaces, 154–56, 170–71
Innocent III, 32, 148, 241–42
inscriptions, 50, 149, 298 n. 160
 in Bay 118, 138, 144
 in chevet lancets, 68–69, 94, 185, 287 n. 156
 in chevet rosaces, 27, 78, 281 n. 50
 in nave bays, 160, 164, 173, 175, 308 n. 64
ironwork, 106, 211, 224
 in rosaces, 44, 47–48, 74, 168
Isidore of Seville, 43, 44, 46, 123, 131

Jacques de Vitry, 8, 242
James Major, St., 22, 79, 271 n. 56, 279 n. 13, 284 n. 109
 in Reims Bay 101, 25–30, 63, 68, 75, 86, *figs. 29, 30, 73, 77*
 and Santiago cult, 28–29, 79, 131, 247–48, *fig. 32*
James the Less, St., 22, 284 n. 109
 in Reims Bay 104, 37–39, 42, 84, 88, 269 n. 22, 273 n. 81, *figs. 38, 39, 45–47*
Jean Beleth, Summa, 33
Jean de Brienne, 215
Jean de Courtenay, archbishop, 12
Jean de Joinville, 218–19, 311 n. 31
Jean d'Orbais, architect, 86, *fig. 88*
Jeanne de Châtillon, princess, 219
Jeanne de Navarre, queen, 13, 219, 221, 312 n. 42
Jerome, St., 54, 182, 261–62, 270 n. 32
John the Baptist, St., 144–47 passim, 150, 297 nn. 137–38. *See also* Agnus Dei; Bay 118
John the Evangelist, St., 22, 38, 79, 182, 274 nn. 82–86, 279 n. 13, *figs. 41, 44*
 evangelist portrait of, 34, 36, 48, 68, 84, *fig. 40*
 on Patmos, 34, 48, 274 n. 86, 285 n. 118
 in Reims Bay 104, 24, 34–37, 62–63, 75, 84–86, *figs. 38–40, 42, 43, 86*
John of Damascus, St., 252
Josephus, "Jewish Wars," 272 n. 64
Joyeuse, sword, 189, 219
jubé. *See* choir screen

Judas Iscariot, 52, 68, 120–21
Jude, St., 22, 23, 47, 276 n. 128
in Reims Bay 105, 48, 51–52, 94, 98, 281 n. 42, *figs. 56, 57, 60*
Juhel de Mathefelon, archbishop, 11, 103, 107, 130, 167, 313 n. 55

Karolvs, 182, 185–90 passim, 219, 238, 284 n. 99, *figs. 188–90*
Kings (Biblical books), 160, 253, 257, 261, 322 n. 1
Koimesis, 230, 314 n. 65
Kokkinobaphos, Jacopus of, 252, *fig. 256*

labyrinth, 86, 215, 285 n. 121, *fig. 88*
La Charité-sur-Loire, 242
La Clayette manuscript. *See* Paris, Bibl. nat. France, nouv. acq. fr. 13521
Lactantius, *De Ave Phoenice*, 124
Laon, cathedral and diocese, 71–73, 129, 237, 280 nn. 24, 33, 296 n. 127, 308 n. 71
bishop, 158, 165
in Reims Bay 101, 71, 73, 75, 78
rose windows, 18, 96, 129, 212, 271 n. 59
Last Capetian Ordo, 218, 312 n. 34
Last Judgment, 126, 136–37, 234, 294 n. 104
in nave rosaces, 155, 160, 169–70, 304 n 59, *figs. 162, 166, 174*
Last Supper, 211
laudes regiae, 174
lectionaries. *See* martyrdoms
Le Mans, cathedral, 28, 36, 201, 272 n. 69, 273 n. 80, 309 nn. 106, 107, *figs. 32, 41*
Liège, Saint-Laurent, relief of nursing Virgin, 121
London, Brit. Lib.
Add. 10546 (Grandval Bible), 290 n. 24, 291 n. 38
Add. 18719 (Moralized Bible), 254
Cotton Tiberius B.VIII (Coronation Book of Charles V), 165, 218, 312 n. 34, 313 n. 43, 315 n. 76, *fig. 171*
Harley 4751 (bestiary), 293 n. 61
Royal 2 B.VII (Queen Mary Psalter), 310 n. 113
Los Angeles, J. Paul Getty Museum, stained glass seraph, 263–64
Louis VIII, 7–8, 63, 139, 149–50, 216, 242
Louis IX, 182, 206, 215–19 passim, 242, 253, 300 n. 3
and Henri de Braine, 8–9, 25, 36, 58, 63, 87–88
heraldry of, 48, 92, 217, 279 n. 19
as New Solomon, 162, 257
and Ordo of 1250, 11–12, 166–67, 303 n. 45
Louis Hutin, 221
Louvain, Bibl. der Godgeleerdheid, Fonds Groot-seminarie Mechelen 32 (Pierre de Beauvais, bestiary), 249
Luke, St., 22, 68, 94, 274 n. 87, 278 n. 159
Lyon, Bibl. mun., MS 539 (Jully Psalter), 14
Lyon, cathedral, 274 n. 84
chevet, lower bays, 32, 33, 123, 272 n. 67, *fig. 37*
south rose, 19, 111

Mainneville, Saint-Pierre, statue of St. Louis, 312 n. 34
Manichaean heresy, 24, 41, 47, 241
Mantes, Notre-Dame, 312 n. 40
Marie de Brabant, queen, 219, 235, 311 n. 20
Mark, St., 68, 94, 269 n. 20, 274 n. 87, 278 n. 159
Marlot, Dom Guillaume, 1, 184–85, 237–38, 280 n. 26, 297 n. 135
Marq, Benoît, studio, 14, 111, 169, 177, 183, 289 n. 14. *See also* Simon family
Mars Gate, castle, 8–9, 58, 243, *fig. 17*
martyrdoms, of saints, 22, 24, 27, 43–47 passim, 90, 275 n. 97. *See also* individual saints
Marys at the tomb, 19–20, 28, 66, 280 n. 33
masons, 72, 86, 89, 275 n. 105
Matthew, St., 22, 56–57
evangelist portrait of, 36, 48, 50, 274 n. 87, 276 n. 131
in Reims Bay 105, 47–51, 92, 94, *figs. 56–59*
Matthew Paris, 9, 242–43
Matthias, St., 22, 52–54, 68, 94, 96, 281 n. 45, *figs. 61, 62*
Ménestrel de Reims, 242, 248
Ménillot (Meurthe-et-Moselle), 20, 280 n. 32
Moissac, cloister capital, 272 n. 64
Mont-Aimé, 9, 241, 243
Montpellier, Bibl. interuniv., Sect. méd., H 437 (Pierre de Beauvais, bestiary), 249–50
Moralized Bibles, 125, 137, 163, 253, 258, 289 n. 18, 325 n. 12
Paris, BnF, lat. 11560, 43, 253–54, *fig. 257*
Toledo, Tesoro del Cabildo de la catedral, MSS 1–3, 253
Vienna, ÖNB, cod. 2554, 120, 323 n. 19
Morinie. *See* Thérouanne
Munich, Staatsbibliothek
CLM 12518 (*Vita Beatae Mariae*), 315 n. 78
CLM 13074 (Regensburg Martyrology), 38, 43, 50, 56, 269 n. 20, 276 n. 128
Xylograph 32 (*Canticum canticorum*), 258, *fig. 259*
musical instruments, *bas* and *haut*, 232, 234–35

name-saints, 86, 87, 285 n. 124
Nazareth, Museum of the Church of the Annunciation, capitals, 50, 269 n. 18
New York, Pierpont Morgan Library, M 92 (Soissons Psalter/hours), 56
New York, The Cloisters, Book of Hours of Jeanne d'Evreux, 316 n. 86
Nicaise, St., 177, 194–95
Niederhaslach, Saint-Florent, 286 n. 149
Nogent-le-Roi, Saint-Sulpice, rose, 316 n. 88
Noli me tangere, 19, *fig. 24*
Noyon, cathedral and diocese, 71, 158, 243, 283 n. 74
in Reims Bay 106, 71, 72, 90, 96, 283 n. 74, *fig. 93*

ogives, glazed
over hemicycle bays, 18, 25, 245–46, 275 n. 97, *figs. 13, 24, 28, 34*
over north rose, 120–22, 128, *fig. 126*
over west rose, 121, 224, 230, 314 n. 63, *fig. 241*
Ohrid (Macedonia), St. Clement, fresco, 253
Old Testament heroes. *See* prophets; Solomon; Tree of Jesse

Ordo of Reims, 146, 158, 165, 179, 218
Ordo of 1250, 12, 153–54, 165–67, 306 n. 34, 313 n. 43. *See also* Paris, Bibl. nat. France, lat. 1246
Origen, 252
Osnabrück, Diözesanarchiv, Inv. no. Ma 101 (Gisela von Kerssenbrock Gradual), 273 n. 75
Oudinot, Eugène-Stanislas, restorer, 113, 120, 122, 289 n. 17, 290 nn. 26, 27, 292 n. 58
ox and ass, 125, 128, *fig. 133*
Oxford, Bodleian Library
MS Auct. D.4.8 (East Anglican Bible), 274 n. 85
MS Bodley 764 (bestiary), 128, 292 n. 56, 293 n. 61

palette. *See* color
Pannonhalma, abbey church, 294 n. 86
Paris, Bibl. Arsenal
MS 1169 (Autun Troper), 33
MS 1186 (Psalter of Saint Louis and Blanche de Castille), 14
MS 3516 (Pierre de Beauvais bestiary, etc.), 120, 131–33, 249–50, *figs. 128, 135–40*
Paris, Bibl. nat. France
fr. 166 (Moralized Bible), 254
fr. 167 (Moralized Bible), 254
fr. 834 (Pierre de Beauvais, bestiary), 249
fr. 944 (Pierre de Beauvais, bestiary), 249, 320 n. 5
fr. 19093 (Villard de Honnecourt), 61, 71–73, 86, 285 n. 127, *fig. 89*
gr. 1208 (Jacobus of Kokkinobaphos), 252, *fig. 256*
lat. 2 (Roda Bible), 322 n. 1
lat. 1023 (Breviary of Philippe le Bel), 281 n. 45
lat. 1246 (Ordo of 1250), 12, 158, 166–67, 179, 218, 303 n. 45, *fig. 169*
lat. 5563 (Pseudo-Abdias from Saint-Thierry), 24, 46, 270 n. 34, 274 n. 82
lat. 7193 (*Breviarium Apostolorum*), 52, 271 n. 53
lat. 8846 (copy of Utrecht psalter), 120
lat. 9376 (Annals of Saint-Nicaise), 287 n. 157
lat. 9428 (Drogo Sacramentary), 273 n. 78
lat. 10525 (Psalter of Saint Louis), 290 n. 25
lat. 11560 (Moralized Bible), 43, 253–54, *fig. 257*
nouv. acq. fr. 13521 (La Clayette ms.), 249–50, 320 n. 11, 321 nn. 10, 11
Paris, Cabinet des Médailles, Dagobert's throne, from Saint-Denis, 148, 182
Paris, cathedral Notre-Dame, 50, 68, 277 n. 135, 284 n. 92
rose windows, 105, 107, 212–14
Paris, Musée du Louvre, St. Matthew writing his Gospel, from Chartres *jubé*, 276 n. 131
sword Joyeuse, from Saint-Denis, 189, 219
Paris, Musée nat. du Moyen Âge, St. James Major, glass from Château de Rouen, 29
Paris, Sainte-Chapelle, 19, 216–18, 279 n. 19, 312 n. 38
Solomon at, 163, 302 n. 30, 322 n. 1
Paris, Saint-Germain-des-Prés, Lady Chapel, 105
Parisian style in glazing, 10, 65, 87, 101
Parma, baptistery, tympanum, 315 n. 79
Paschasius Radbertus, St., 314 n. 70
Passion of Christ, 19–20, 144, *fig. 24*. *See also* individual scenes
instruments of, 316 n. 85, *figs. 161, 166, 253*
patternbooks. *See* cartoons
Paul, St., 22, 27, 56, 69, 273 n. 80, 281 n. 46
in Reims Bay 101, 25–29 passim, 68, 75–79, 284 n. 107, *figs. 29–31, 72–74, 78*
peers of France, 158, 165, 179, *fig. 169*
Pentecost, 33, 50–51, 281 n. 40
Pepin le Bref, 238
Peter, St., 20, 23, 54, 69, 269 n. 23, 285 n. 113. *See also* Acts of the apostles (*Acts of Peter*); Simon Magus legend
crucifixion of, 22, 30–33 passim, 273 n. 80, 279 n. 10, 286 n. 142, *fig. 35*
in Reims Bay 102, 30–33, 62, 68, 75, 79–81, 279 n. 11, *figs. 33, 34, 79, 80*
in Reims Bay 127, 155, *fig. 167*
Peter Comestor, 120
Peter Damian, 243
Peter Lombard, 268 n. 6
Peter the Chanter, 74, 283 n. 88
Petit-Quevilly, fresco, 291 n. 42
Philip, St., 22, 39, 42–44, 52, 82–84, 269 n. 23, *figs. 48, 49, 84, 85*
Philippe III le Hardi, 12, 191, 206, 216–20, 225
Philippe IV le Bel, 13, 215–21 passim, 225, 312 n. 37
Philippe de Dreux, bishop of Beauvais, 8, 63, 130–31, 242, 244
library of, 29, 79, 247–48, 249
and Reims Bays 103 and 104, 38, 87
Philippe de Thaon, bestiary, 293 n. 63
Philipp the Carthusian, Brother, *Marienleben*, 232
Phillipps, Sir Thomas, Ex-Phillipps 6739 (Pierre de Beauvais, bestiary), 249
phoenix, 124–25, *figs. 127, 130, 135*
Physiologus, 123–25 passim, 131, 249–50, 293 nn. 59
Pierre Barbet, archbishop, 224–25
Pierre de Beauvais, 29–30, 79, 130–33, 247–48, 249–50, *figs. 128, 135*
Pierre Mauclerc, 10, 58, 63, 66, 244, 308 n. 64
pilgrimage. *See* Santiago de Compostela
Pliny the Elder, *Historia naturalis*, 131
Poitiers, cathedral, 42
glass, 20, 27, 32, 66, 272 n. 69, 279 n. 10, *fig. 26*
Pontigné (Maine-et-Loire), fresco, 121
Porte du Cerf, 12, 190, 194–95, 200, 206
preaching, theme in chevet, 24–25, 38, 44, 47, 51, 74. *See also* individual apostles
Presentation in the Temple, 211
prophets and Old Testament heroes, 62–63, 111, 135, 143–44, 160–62, 237. *See also* rose window, west; Solomon; Tree of Jesse
Prudentius, *Hamartigenia*, 130
Pseudo-Abdias, 23–24, 43, 52, 245, 270 n. 34, 273 n. 82. *See also* individual apostles
Pseudo-Dionysius the Areopagite, 54, 105

Pseudo-Hegesippus, 272 n. 64
Pseudo-Jerome, letter IX, 231, 314 n. 70
Pseudo-Linus, 27
Pseudo-Marcellus, 30, 272 n. 64
Pseudo-Marcus, 56–57
Pseudo-Melito, 24, 36, 230, 274 n. 82
Pseudo-Turpin, 29, 79, 189, 247–48
Psychomachia, 251, 255

Rabanus Maurus, 302 n. 33
rational, 175–77, 180–82, 197, 199, 306 n. 30, *figs. 190, 209*
in Bay 100, 65, 72
red circles in medallion grounds, 30, 54, 96, 168, 286 n. 149, 309 n. 105, *figs. 34, 62, 122, 129–32, 162–68*
Reims, Bibl. mun.
MS 7 (Saint-Thierry, Hincmar's Gospel), 48–50, 274 n. 87
MS 8 (Saint-Thierry, Sacramentary fragments), 52
MS 9 (Saint-Remi, Gospel), 274 n. 87
MS 13 (cathedral chapter, Gospel), 274 n. 87
MS 23 (Saint-Thierry, Bible), 187
MS 142 (Guillaume de Saint-Thierry, St. Ambrose on Song of Songs), 262, 270 n. 28
MS 221 (cathedral, Missal), 281 n. 41
MS 295 (cathedral chapter, Lectionary of Manasses de Châtillon), 33
MS 299 (Saint-Thierry, life of St. Bartholomew), 276 n. 122
MS 434 (Hincmar's Bede). 261–62
MS 1403 (cathedral chapter, legendarium), 43
MS 1407 (Saint-Thierry, life of St. Bartholomew), 46
MS 1609 (Cocquault, "Histoire de ... Reims"), 183–84
Reims, cathedral, architecture, xviii, 211. *See also* architectural drawings; *coupure Tourneur*
buttresses, 72–73
chapels, 79, 177, 271 n. 56
dating, 1, 12–13, 61, 215–16
measurements, 61, 96, 265 nn. 1, 2, 286 n. 150, 288 n. 5, 295 n. 123
plan, *figs. 4, 145, 160*
roses, transept, 54, 72, 280 n. 24
vaulting, 61–62, 170, 193, 278 n. 5, 296 n. 124, 304 n. 58
Reims, cathedral, liturgy and feasts, 34, 52, 174, 216, 269 n. 24, 272 n. 62
Reims, cathedral, Romanesque, 6–7, 63, 187–88, 238, 271 n. 56, 308 n. 66
facade, 143–44, 147, 296 n. 130, *figs. 145, 160–61*
glass, 20, 66, 75, 144, *fig. 153*. *See also* Bay 118; Karolvs
Reims, cathedral, sculpture, 34, 79, 82, 87, 160, 277 n. 150
chevet chapels, exterior, 74
facade, 148, 150–51, 176, 211, 214, 224
facade, archivolts, 232, 283 n. 87, *fig. 252*
facade, buttress reliefs, 27, 274 n. 83
façade, jambs, 87, 143–44, 146, 151
facade, verso, 150, 195, 299 n. 170, 301 n. 14, 317 n. 5
transept portals, north, 46, 143, 148, 175–77 passim, 297 nn. 137, 143, 310 n. 12
transept roses and gables, 111–15 passim, 120, 128–30, 134–35, 137, *fig. 117*
Reims, civic rebellion in, 8, 58
as theme in chevet, 25, 36, 39, 41, 43, 44
as theme in north rose, 129
Reims, Musée de Saint-Remi, sculptures from House of the Musicians, 232, 315 n. 81, *fig. 251*
Reims, Saint-Nicaise (lost), 63–65, 195, 306 n. 21
glass, 10, 13, 219, 221, 238, 297 n. 135
Reims, Saint-Remi, 6, 71, 143–44, 153, 167, 182–88 passim, *fig. 152*
clerestory glass, 63, 101, 175–76, 230, 238, 284 n. 102
Clovis (lost), 146
Crucifixion window, 66
grisaille, 288 n. 6
St. Remigius panel, 75, 187, *fig. 191*
Reims, Saint-Thierry. *See* Saint-Thierry
Reims Palimpsest, 71-72, 138
Reinhardt, Hans, xviii, 5, 15, 99, 160
"first atelier," 75, 86–87, 96, 99, 286 n. 128, 287 n. 165
"first choir program," 7, 62–63, 75, 99–101, 142, 279 n. 14
on chevet lancets, 73, 280 n. 23, 287 n. 152
on chevet rosaces, 17, 28
relics and reliquaries, 195, 269 n. 24
Remi (Remigius), St., 75, 144–51 passim, 158, 167, 177, 195, *figs. 147, 149, 154, 162, 191*. *See also* Bay 118; Clovis
restorations and alterations, xviii–xix, 42, 211, 313 n. 47. *See also* Oudinot; Simon family; rose window, west
in chevet rosaces, 29, 41, 43, 50, 271 n. 51, 273 n. 81
in hemicycle lancets, 88, 284 n. 107, 285 n. 114, 286 n. 134
in north rose, 111–24 passim, 128, 132, 293 n. 76, *fig. 113*
in straight-choir lancets, 48, 62, 92, 99, 287 n. 151
16th century, 7, 169, 177, 183–84, 214, 304 n. 59
17th and 18th centuries, 111, 120, 224, 289 n. 14, 292 n. 44
Resurrection of Christ, 19–20, 66, 156, 170. *See also* Marys at the Tomb
bestiary symbols of, 123–25 passim
Robert II de Dreux, 131, 241–42, 244, 247–49
Robert III de Dreux, 66, 244
Robert Grosseteste, 257
Robert le Bougre, inquisitor, 9, 129, 242–43
Robert of Saint-Victor, 74
Rome, Lateran Museum, Good Shepherd sarcophagus, 292 n. 57
Rome, Old Saint Peter's, Oratorio of John VII, mosaic, 272 n. 65
rosaces of chevet
design, diagonal (asterisk), 34, 39, 54, 82. *See also* ironwork
design, horizontal, 19, 25, 28, 30, 33, 79
design, spinning, 48, 54
rosaces of nave, design, 168–69
rose window, centripetal tracery in, 72–73, 134, 211, 280 n. 24
north, 11, 30, 107–33 passim, 137–38, 250, 283 n. 77, *figs. 111–14*
south (lost), xix, 11, 134–37, 183–84, 280 n. 24, *figs. 141, 142*

west, 13, 221–35 passim, 263–64, 315 n. 74, *figs. 10, 231–50, 253*
west rose gallery, 13, 214–21 passim, *figs. 226–28*
west tympanum-rose, 13, 211–14, 313 n. 58, *figs. 222, 223, 225*
Rothier, François, photographer, 197–99, 313 n. 47, *figs. 202, 240*
rouelle de Saint-Nicaise, 177, 190, 194–95, 206
Rouen, Bibl. mun., MS 3016 (Leber Psalter), 14
Rouen, cathedral, 27, 120, 122, 266 n. 14, 272 n. 69
Rouen, Saint-Ouen, 50, 277 n. 135
Rupert of Deutz, 73, 251–52, 259

Saint-Denis, abbey, 6–7, 142–43, 187–90 passim, 238, 303 n. 45
library and authors at, 131, 189–90, 248, 250, 320 n. 14
Saint-Gall, codex 53 (evangelistary), ivory covers by Tuotilo, 231, 315 n. 72
codex 152 (Pseudo-Jerome, letter IX, etc.), 315 n. 72
Saint-Germer-de-Fly, 311 n. 23
Saint-Julien-du-Sault, 19, 36, 37, 271 n. 43, 272 n. 69, 274 n.90, *fig. 44*
Saint-Quentin, collegiate church, 287 n. 166
Saint-Thierry, abbey library
Bible (12th c.), 187
Gospel of Hincmar, 48, 50, 274 n. 87
Guillaume de Saint-Thierry, St. Ambrose on Song of Songs, 258, 262, 270 n. 28
Life of St. Bartholomew, 46, 269 n. 21
Pseudo-Abdias, 24, 46, 58, 274 n. 82
Sacramentary fragments, 52
Salamanca, Bibl. Univ. 2658 (*Historia Compostelana*), 247, 319 n. 4
Samson de Mauvoisin, archbishop, 6, 8, 143, 187, 190, 241–42. *See also* Reims cathedral, Romanesque
Sankt Paul im Lavanttal, codex 58/1 (Ramsey Psalter), 316 n. 83
San Marino, Calif., Huntington Library, HM 3027 (Golden Legend), 56
Santiago de Compostela, 28, 29, 79, 247–48
scepter, in coronation, 153, 160–62
seals, 65–66, 148–51, 182, 224, 298 n. 161, 313 n. 55, *figs. 154–58*
sede vacante, 12, 129, 142, 149, 220, *fig. 158*
in 1218–1219, 7, 62, 142, 149
Sées, cathedral, 288 n. 170, 309 n. 107, 314 n. 61
sella curulis. *See* foldstool
Semur-en-Auxois, portal, 41–42
Senlis, cathedral and diocese, 99, 281 n. 49
in Reims Bay 105, 69, 90, 92, 283 n. 85, 287 n. 156
Sens, cathedral and diocese, 142, 238, 243, 308 n. 66
glass, 19, 36, 41, 107, 316 n. 88
grisaille, 105, 288 n. 2, 305 n. 64
seraphim, 15, 225, 231–32, 263–64, *figs. 245, 246, 253*
silver stain, 42
Simon, St., 22, 276 n. 128
in Reims Bay 106, 44–47, 51–52, 90, 286 n. 143, *figs. 52, 53, 55, 60*
Simon family, glaziers, xix, 2, 15, 183, 221–24, 263. *See also* tracings
François, 224, 310 nn. 5, 6
Jacques, 5, 42, 134
Paul, 7, 139, 175, 224–30 passim, 300 n. 6, 304 nn. 59, 63, *figs. 14, 203, 249, 250, 253*
Pierre, 111, 289 n. 17, 290 n. 24, 293 nn. 71, 77, 314 n. 63
Simon Magus legend, 30, 32, 272 n. 69
socle figures, 79, 92, 192, 201, 283 n. 85, 287 n. 156, *figs. 75, 91, 197, 198*
Soissons, cathedral and diocese, 63, 71, 88, 101, 220, 237
in Reims Bay 102, 71, 74, 79–81, 285 n. 114, *figs. 79–83*
Solomon, 160, 237, 251–54, 301 n. 21, 316 n. 83
in bed, 163–66, 251–59, 260–62, 301 n. 21, *figs. 159, 170*
Judgment of, 160, 169, 294 n. 104, 323 n. 16, *fig. 164*
Louis IX as, 162, 171, 257
Throne of, 253, 257, 261
Song of Songs (Biblical book), 162–64, 171, 251–59, 260–62, 322 nn. 2, 5
spolia, 6–7, 14, 266 n. 14, 275 n. 97. *See also* Bay 39; Bay 118; Karolvs
stag, 125–28, 195, 309 n. 94, *figs. 134, 135*
stalls. *See* canons' choir
sticklighting, 54, 98, 286 n. 149
stopgaps and debris, 211, 245–46, 310 n. 2, 313 n. 58, 315 n. 74, 317 n. 7, *figs. 162, 167*
in north rose, 111, 132, 237, 245, 290 n. 25, 291 n. 29, 313 n. 58
stork, 124
Strasbourg, cathedral, 46, 78, 286 n. 149, 301 n. 20
Romanesque glass, 75, 187–88, 238, 286 n. 149, *fig. 254*
sculpture, 230, 294 n. 104, 315 n. 79, 323 n. 16
Strasbourg, Dominican church, 46, 276 n. 126
Strasbourg, Musée de l'Oeuvre Notre-Dame, architectural drawings, 138
Stuttgart, Landesbibliothek
Cod. Bibl. 2° 23 (Stuttgart Psalter), 268 n. 8
Cod. Bibl. 2° 56–58 (Stuttgart Passional), 22, 43, 56, 275 n. 96, 319 n. 2
Cod. Hist. 2° 415 (Zweifaltern Martyrology), 54, 275 n. 96
suffragan bishops, 74
images in chevet, 18, 42, 68–69, 75, 90, 239
provincial councils of, 8–10, 48, 88, 280 n. 39
seating of, 20, 25, 66, 73, *fig. 18*
sword, held by king, 153, 182, 214, 219–20, 306 n. 34, 313 n. 43, *figs. 186, 190, 227*
of Charlemagne, 189, 219, 248

telamon. *See* socle figures
Tertullian, 30, 36, 270 n. 32
textores. *See* weavers and textiles
Thann, Saint-Thiébaut, 120
Theodore the Studite, St., 46
Thérouanne (Morinie), cathedral and diocese, 69, 96, 283 n. 86, 321 n. 12
Thomas, St., 22, 68, 69, 245. *See also* Acts of the apostles, apocryphal
in Reims Bay 103, 39–42, 69, 75, 82–83, *figs. 48–51, 84, 85*
Thomas de Beaumetz, archbishop, 12, 313 n. 55

throne, high-backed, 175–76, 178, 180–83, 191, *figs. 187, 208.* See also *chaire de saint Remy*; foldstool; Solomon, Throne of
Tilpinus (Turpin), archbishop, 150, 248
Toledo, Tesoro del Cabildo de la catedral, MSS 1–3, 253
tonsure, 34, 38, 274 n. 83
Toul, cathedral, 290 n. 25
Toul, Saint-Gengoult, 19–20, 280 n. 32, 311 n. 23
Tournai, cathedral and diocese, 71, 243, 281 n. 49, 282 n. 58
  in Reims Bay 108, 71, 73, 96
Tours, cathedral
  aisle bays, 19, 271 n. 46, 273 n. 80, 274 nn. 83, 90
  clerestory, hemicycle bays, 19, 272 n. 69
  clerestory, straight-choir bays, 28, 39, 120, 274 nn. 83, 90, 319 n. 3
tracings, xix, 2, 43, 305 n. 8, *figs. 13, 15, 16, 22,* 65. *See also* Simon family
  of chevet lancets, 62, 92, 99, *figs. 77, 78, 82, 83*
  of nave lancets, 175, 310 n. 112, *figs. 179, 193, 203, 220*
  of north rose, 111, 313 n. 58, *figs. 115, 127*
  of west rose, 224, *figs. 241–47, 249, 250*
Transfiguration of Christ, 156, 170, 300 n. 9
Tree of Jesse, 225, 230, 231, 237, 313 n. 58, 317 n. 7
trial pieces, 27, 78, 225, 230, *fig. 232*
Trier, cathedral treasury, Saint Andrew triptych, 273 nn. 73, 75
Trinity, 18, 20, 121–22, 245–46, 292 n. 57, 302 n. 33
Troyes, Bibl. mun.
  MS 177 (aviary), 293 nn. 59, 61
  MS 1951 (Reims cathedral missal), 281 n. 41
Troyes, cathedral, 28, 237–38, 285 n. 115
  aisle bays, 32, 272 n. 69
  hemicycle clerestory, 19, 32, 34, 66, 271 n. 42, 274 n. 90
Troyes, Saint-Urbain, 28, 311 n. 23, 314 n. 61

Urbana-Champaign, University of Illinois, Coronation Book of Jeanne d'Evreux, 218, 312 n. 34
usury and usurers, 8–10, 89–90, 241–43
  theme in chevet, 25, 42, 44, 46, 58
  theme in north rose, 122, 125, 129–30
Utrecht, Universiteits-bibliotheek, MS 32 (Utrecht Psalter), 268 n. 8

Vatican, Bibl. apost.
  gr. 1162 (Jacobus of Kokkinobaphos), 252
  Reg. lat. 466 (St. Theodore the Studite, life of St. Bartholomew), 46
  Reg. lat. 1323 (Pierre de Beauvais, bestiary), 249
Vatican, Museum of Saint Peter's Basilica, Junius Bassus sarcophagus, 27
Vendôme, La Trinité, 20, 275 n. 107
Veneranda Dies, 28, 247–48
Venice, San Marco, xix, 17, 22–24, 38, 43, 47, 50
Vercelli, MS CIX (Hincmar fragments), 164, 302 n. 32
Vernais (Cher), fresco, 232
Verona, San Zeno, 120
vestments and regalia, 32–33, 99, 146, 180, 207, 286 n. 134, *fig. 167. See also* rational
  of archbishops, 65, 73, 96, 191, 200, 220, *figs. 72, 98, 209*
  of James Major, 63, 79, 284 n. 109
Viacryl, 289 n. 14
vidimus of 1252, 12
Vienna, ÖNB
  cod. 2554 (Moralized Bible), 120, 323 n. 19
  lat. 1010 (*Physiologus*), 124
Villard de Honnecourt, 61, 71–73, 86, 285 n. 127, 295 n. 114, 296 n. 124, *fig. 89*
Villiers-sur-Tholon, Saint-Jean-Baptiste, rosace, 316 n. 88
Viollet-le-Duc, Eugène, 106, 291 n. 29, 296 n. 130
Virgin and Child, 13, 63, 118, 121, 212, *fig. 225. See also* Bay 118
  in Bay 100, 65, 280 n. 23, *fig. 69*
  in nave rosaces, 155–56, 170, *figs. 168, 211*
  on seals, 65, *figs. 155, 156*
Virgin Mary, 34, 62, 121, 137, 182, 271 n. 56, *fig. 241*
  Assumption of, 121, 137, 211, 224, 230–31, 315 n. 77, *fig. 240*
  Coronation of, 214, 224, 230–32
  Dormition of, 230, 235
  and Song of Songs, 163, 251–52, 258–59
Vita Adae et Evae, 120, 291 n. 34
Viventius, archbishop, 169, 176, 183, 185, *figs. 176, 180*
Voragine. *See* Golden Legend

Waldensians, 242
war damage, 42, 62, 99, 134, 154–55, *figs. 177, 189*
  in facade, 211, 224, 313 n. 52, *fig. 239*
  in nave lancets, 173–75, 183, 186, 195, 308 n. 69, 311 n. 27, *figs. 19, 201*
weavers and textiles, 8, 122, 129–30, 241–42
Westminster, Feast of, 234
  Painted Chamber, 163, 254–57, *fig. 258*
Winchester Castle, 163, 254
Wissembourg, Saint-Pierre-et-Saint-Paul, 286 n. 149

yellow, connotation of, 120–21
Yolande de Coucy, 29, 79, 131, 241, 244, 248
Yolande de Saint-Pol, 320 nn. 12, 16